DEEG PALACE

Its Romance and Wonder

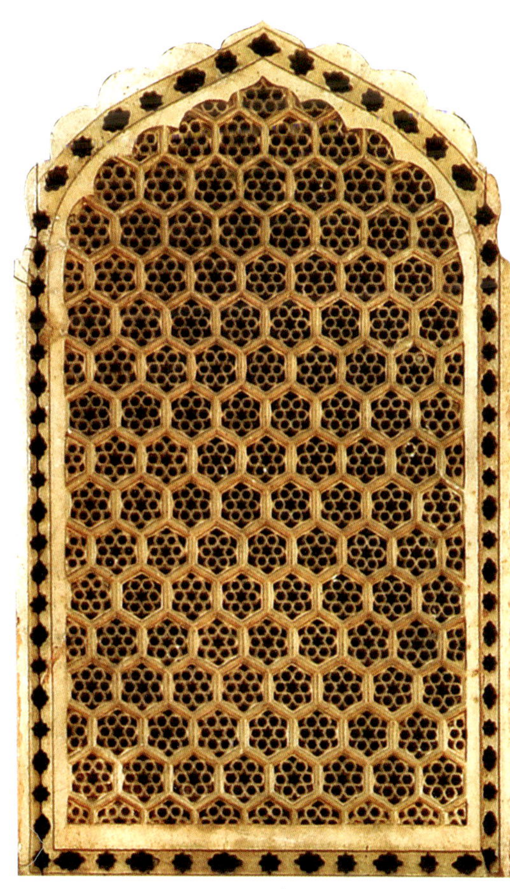

Deeg Palace

Its Romance and Wonder

Bharat Chugh
Shalini Chugh

NIYOGI
BOOKS

Published by
NIYOGI BOOKS
D-78, Okhla Industrial Area, Phase-I
New Delhi-110 020, INDIA
Tel: 91-11-26816301, 49327000
Fax: 91-11-26810483, 26813830
email: niyogibooks@gmail.com
website: www.niyogibooksindia.com

Editor: Shaurya Shaukat Sircar
Design: Shashi Bhushan Prasad
Cover design: Nabanita Das

ISBN: 978-93-83098-53-8
Publication: 2014

Printed at: Niyogi Offset Pvt. Ltd., New Delhi, India

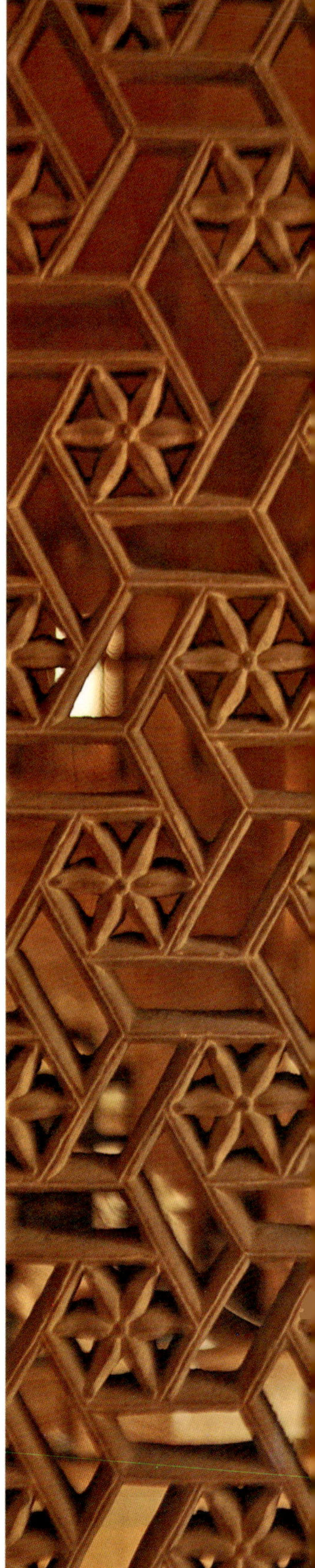

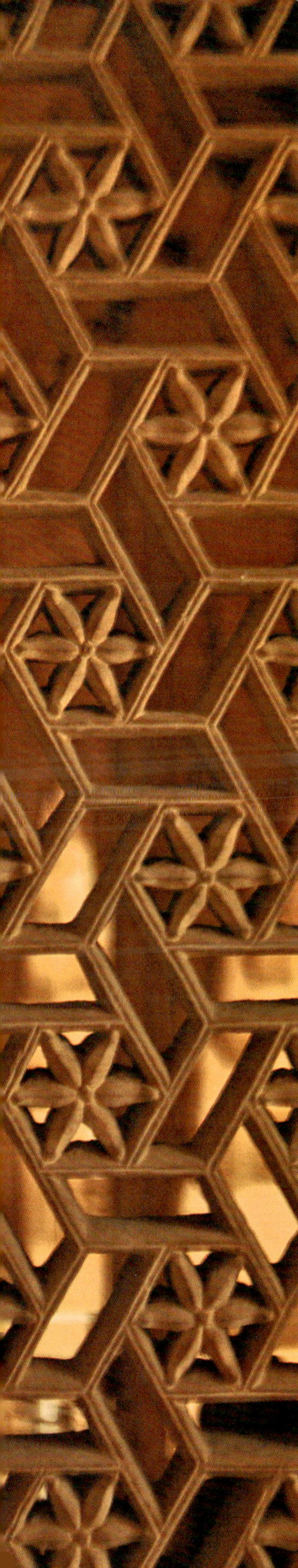

CONTENTS

Site Plan of Deeg Palace Complex

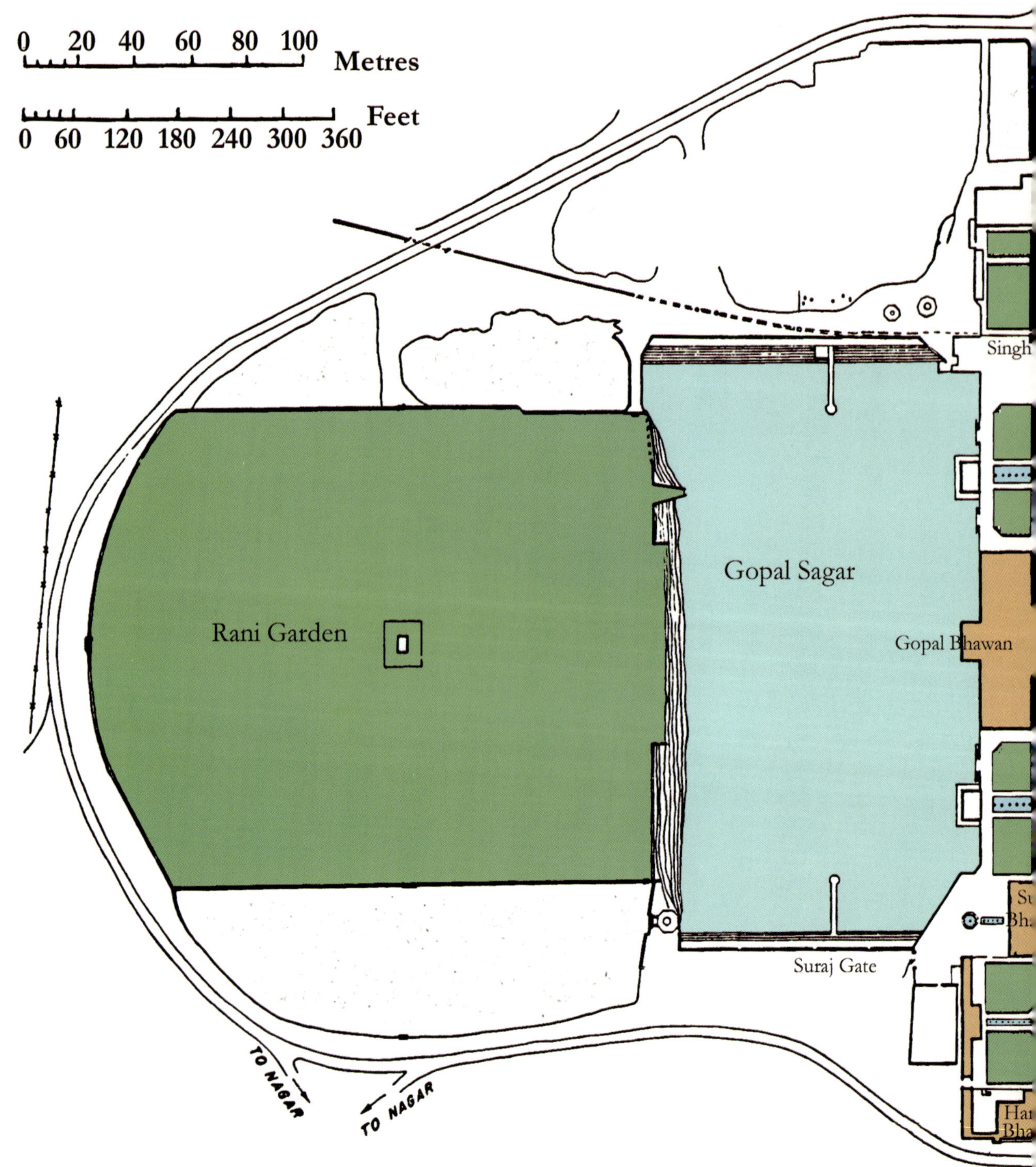

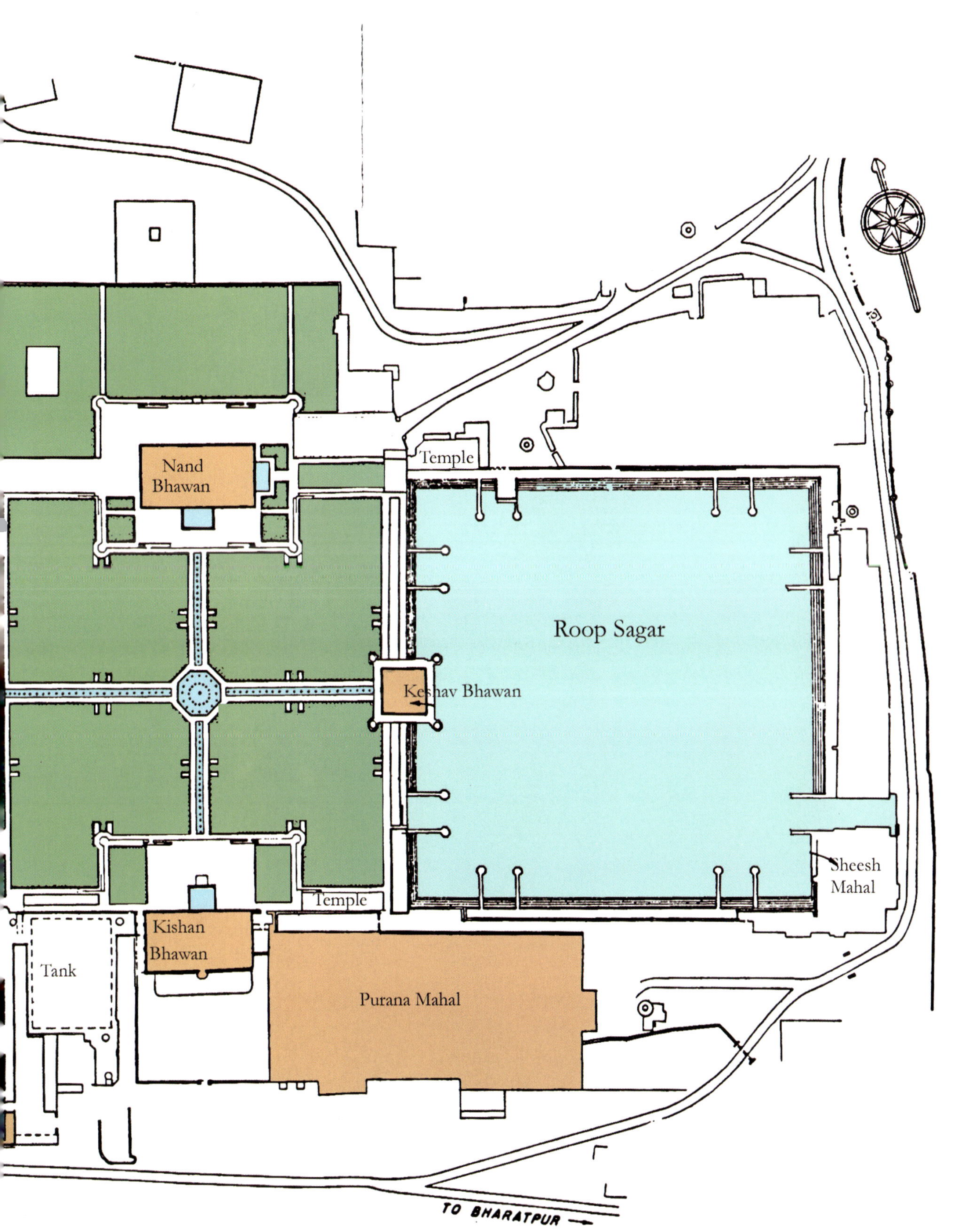
Nand
Bhawan
Temple
Roop Sagar
Keshav Bhawan
Temple
Sheesh
Mahal
Kishan
Bhawan
Tank
Purana Mahal
TO BHARATPUR

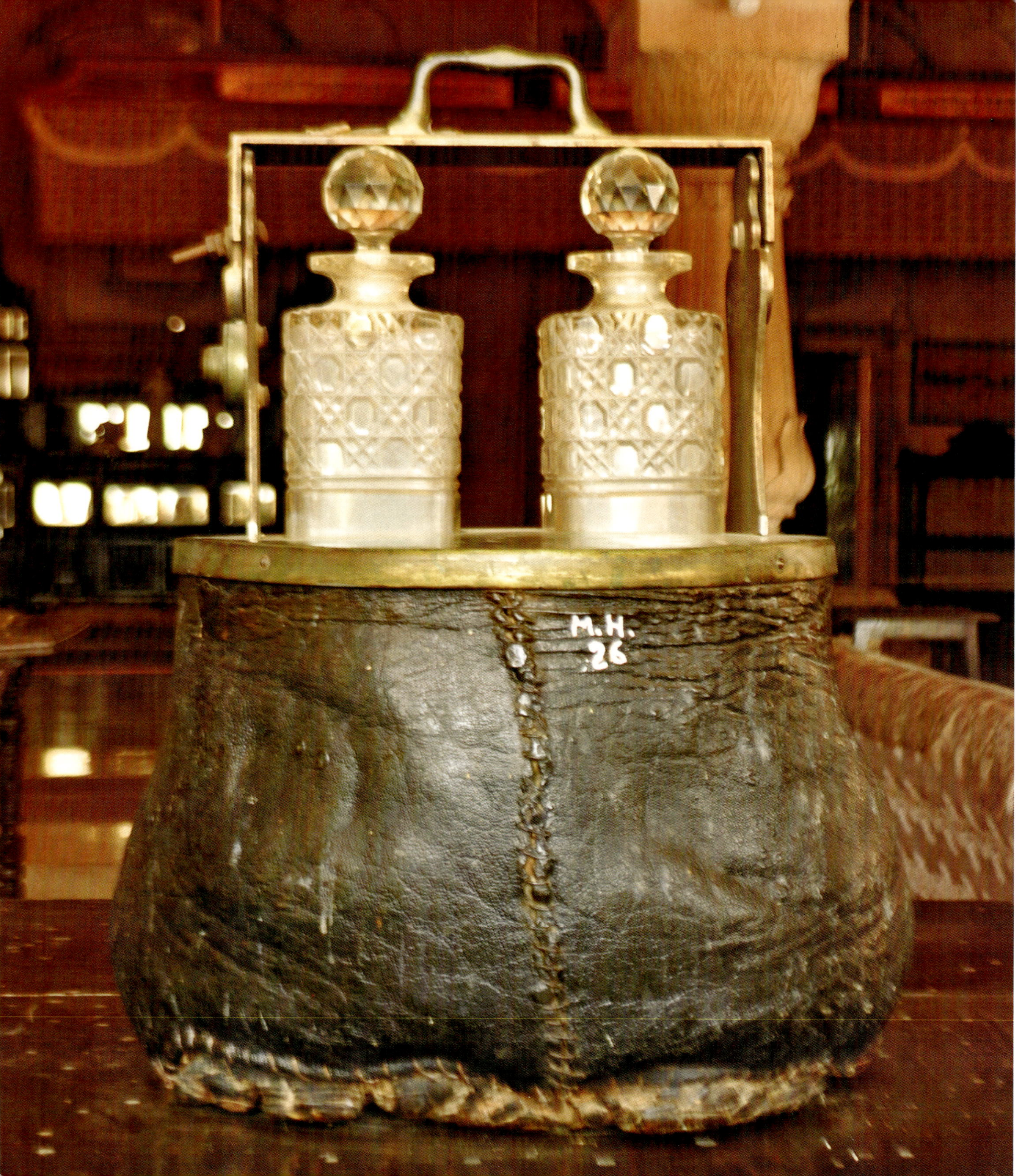
M.H.
26

PREFACE

Our first trip to Deeg was made way back in 1996, while sourcing stone and studying designs for stone architectural embellishments. The purpose behind the research was to refurbish the grand palatial mansion at Kensington Palace gardens, London for Favermead Ltd, restored by Professor Nasser David Khalili. Eventually, this mansion was bought by Shri Lakshmi Mittal. The enchanting designs left a permanent impression on our minds. Subsequent work and projects distracted us to marble and *pietra dura* for years. In 2010, our prestigious friends Mr and Mrs Sandhu commissioned us to do up their Haveli in Nuh, Haryana. The stone shortlisted was from Bansi Paharpur and the chosen style was the Mughal-Rajput. Yes, Deeg, the masterpiece encapsulating a rich legacy had to be revisited. Perhaps, this time, we went with a more experienced eye. The view and the walks were all the more magnificent. The camera we were carrying was a Nikon DSLR and we took around 1,000 photographs. Our clients appreciated the colour, texture and workmanship of the stone from Bansi Paharpur. The stone was eventually procured from Bayana and its surrounding areas and the project turned out to be yet another amazing experience. The idea for a book was always in our minds.

Meanwhile Facebook helped us to get connected to a school friend, Divay Gupta, Principal Director, Architectural Heritage, INTACH who instilled the final vigour and the idea took conclusive shape at a coffee table in a Defence Colony restaurant. A small summary of the concept along with the printouts of some photographs was prepared. This was sent to the publishing house, Niyogi Books, for review. Mr and Mrs Niyogi appreciated the idea and encouraged us to

Facing Page: *A scent case, made from the legs of the elephant that is said to have broken the Delhi gate, is housed in the Gopal Bhawan museum*

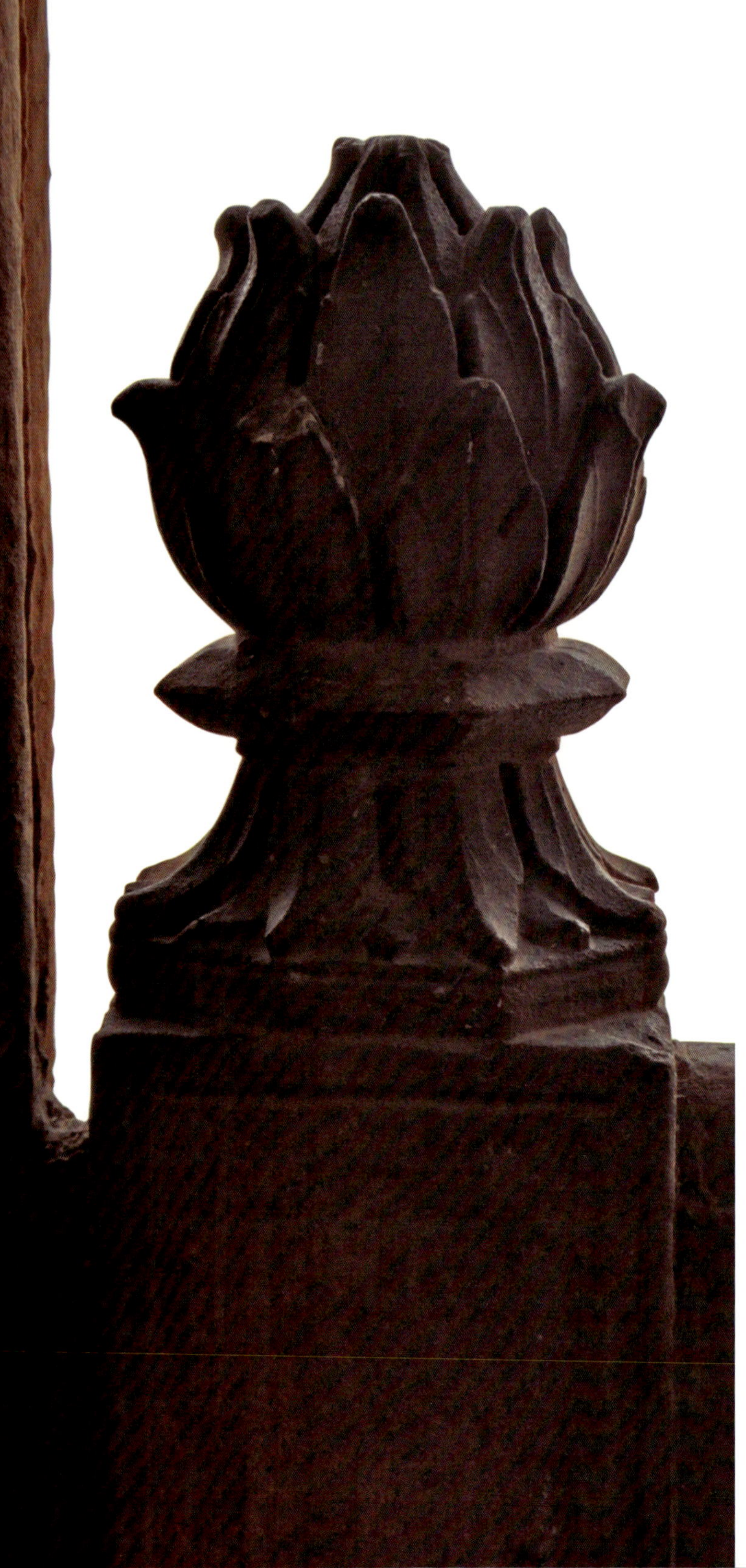

work on it with full sincerity. We thank them as our first patrons. Several trips to the Deeg Palace, National Museum, National Archives and Archaeological Survey of India (ASI), Delhi and Jaipur circles have inked this endeavour.

It may not be possible to name all, but inspirations were derived from writings of Kunwar Natwar Singh, Elizabeth B. Moynihan, M.C. Joshi, Ebba Koch, C.M. Villiers-Stuart and many unnamed scholars and authors to whom we are highly indebted. Udita Gupta, a budding architect helped us with the measured drawings and 3D visuals.

From a point of view that acknowledges the importance of tradition, precedent, style and ideology in architectural construction, in this book we discuss critical details from a contextual and technical standpoint; considering how they perform, how they add to or distract from the building as a whole and how some have been adopted in Deeg.

Left: *A carved lotus bud adorns the baluster of Gopal Bhawan overlooking Rani Bagh. The prototype* Mir-i-farsh *was used extensively in Mughal and Rajput architecture even for carpet weights and door stoppers*

Facing Page: *Decorative floral inset panels in a* jharokha

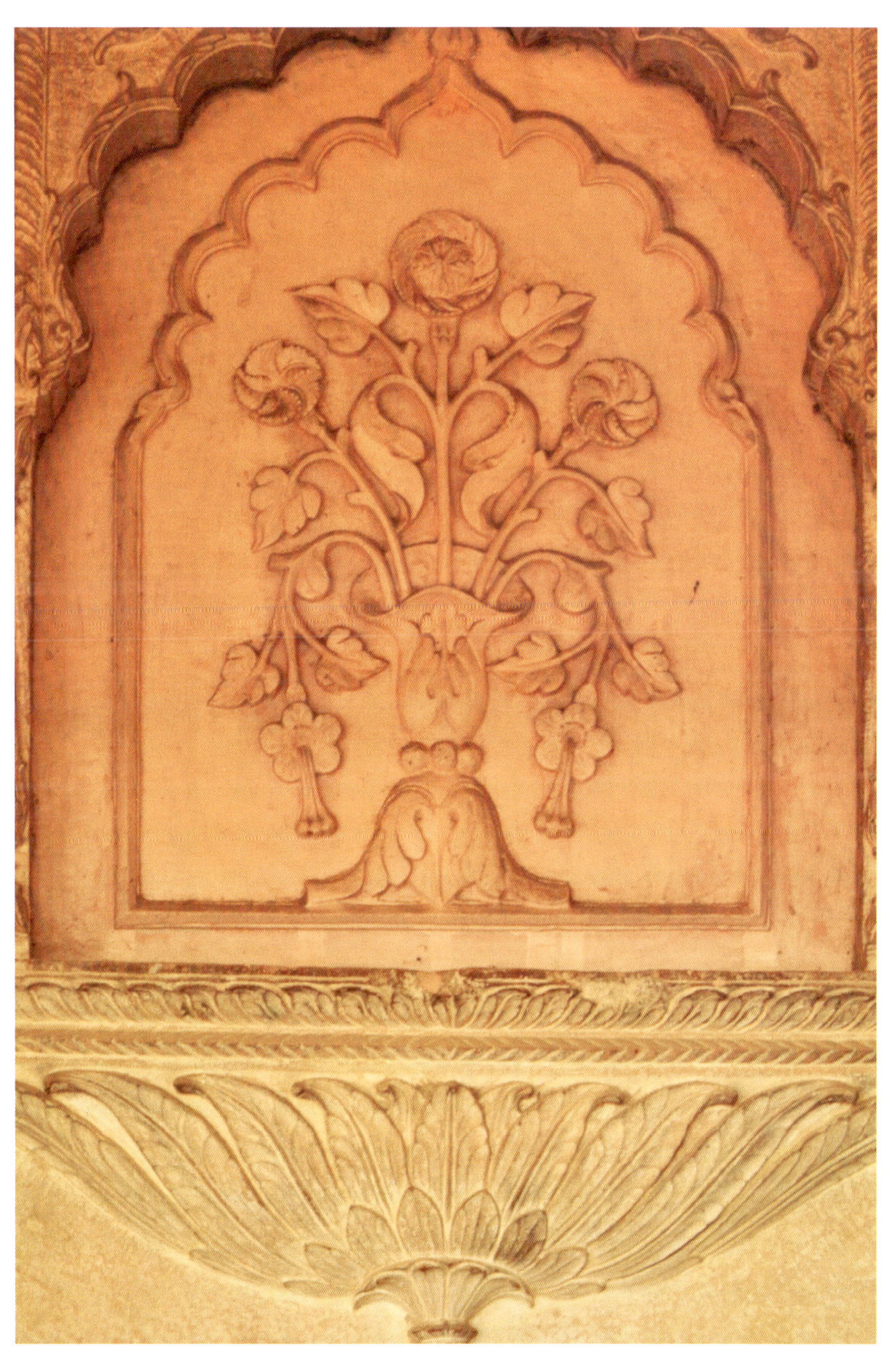

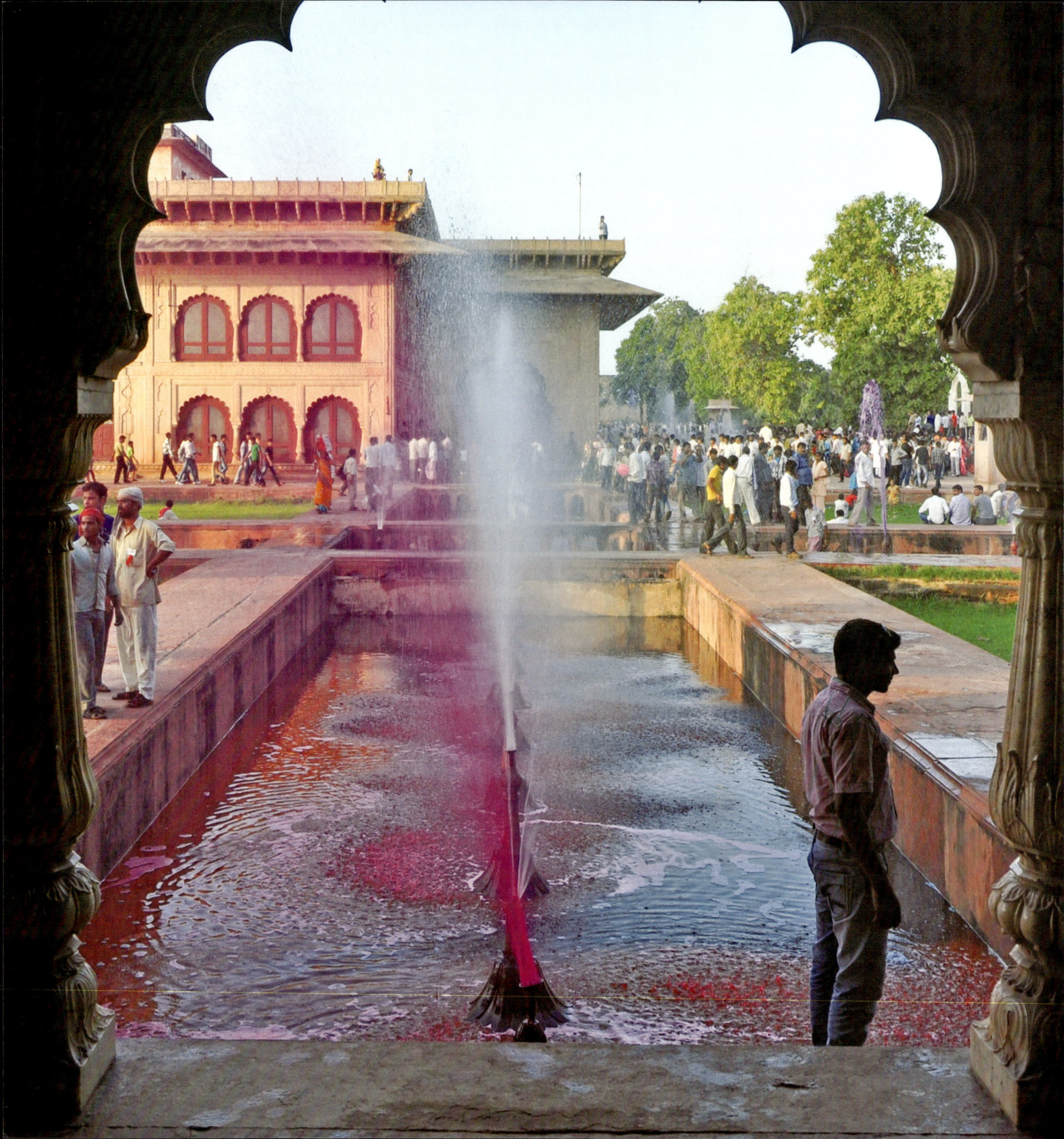

INTRODUCTION

This book *Deeg Palace* is a journey through the wondrous and alluring palaces of Deeg (also called Dig), created by the Jats on the enticing plains of Braj in the early 18th century, when they were on the verge of conquering Delhi at the behest of the falling Mughal Empire. Not much has been said of this fantasy palace, which was recreated to symbolise Radha and Krishna's *Raas Leela*, though it was much admired by the British.

The palace complex together with its water gardens was a summer retreat for the maharajas of Bharatpur. The layout comprises of several palaces called bhawans, interwoven with series of *char baghs* (four gardens) and water gardens. The speciality of the gardens is their remarkable water system that works even till date. Over 900 fountains were built to be fed by an overhead water tank through earthen pipes and many of them go through ostentatious water displays twice a year.

Deeg was chiselled in the times when the whole of north India was going through transitional episodes of several political, socio-economic, religious and demographic developments. It is not a solitary entity, rather a complex interplay of theological, social, cultural, economic, political and technical factors.

The book captures this spirit of Deeg by not only analysing the marvellous stonework and architecture, but also the modulations and metamorphosis of events which led to the shaping of Deeg. It sees Deeg as part of a larger fabric beyond just its magnificent superstructure and decorations as buildings are a mirror to the times they were constructed in.

Discussed in straightforward language, the book starts with the origin of the palace and outlines the continuous development through its various

Facing page: *Locals and tourists throng to see the charismatic display of fountains at the biannual celebrations at Deeg*

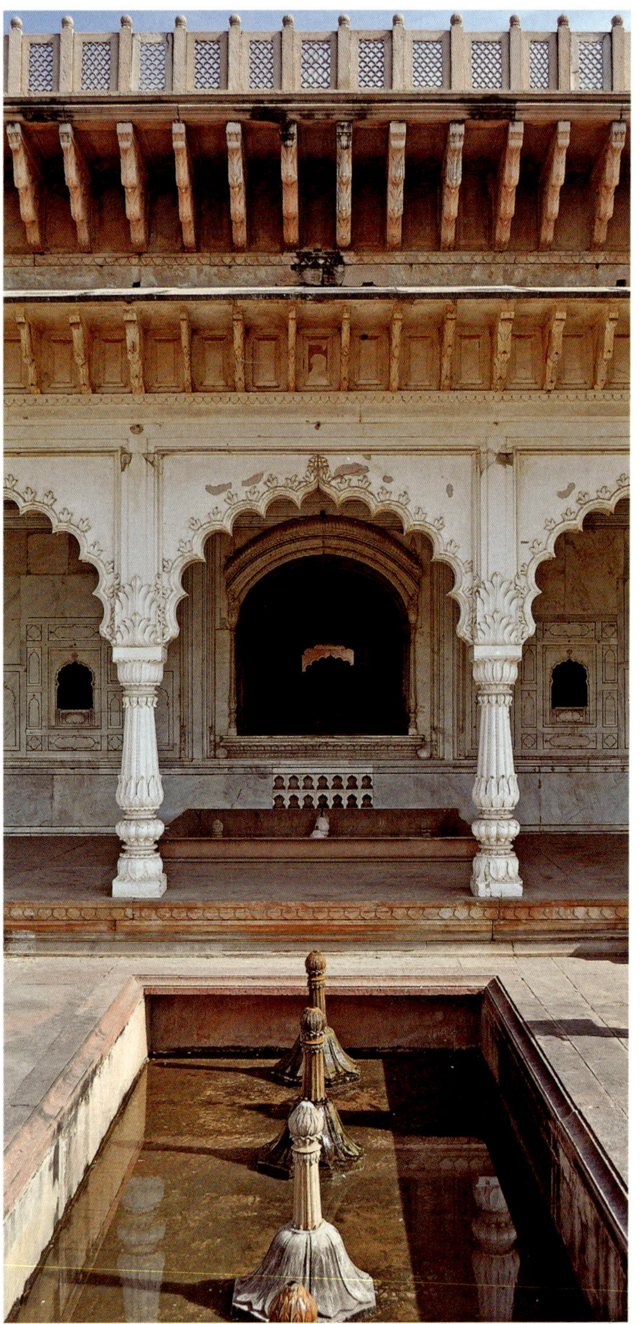

manifestations during the rule of the Jats. Subsequently, the layout and planning principles are highlighted. Enhancing its utility are the clearly drawn plans in 2D and 3D. The photographs celebrate the richness of classical architecture with elevations of its symmetry and details. Not inclined to theorise, we have tried to express our concepts mainly by way of photographs. The double-eaved *chhajja* with brackets, axial water channels and extensive use of Mughal baluster columns on Shahjahani cusp-engrailed arches mark the architectural style of the palace complex.

Every fort and palace has its own destiny in which glory and despair alternate, so too it is with Deeg which has been veiled in obscurity for many years. Through this book we have tried to bring to life imprints of time by looking at it with new perceptions, unravelling the mysteries of history to establish a sense of permanence, where the stones of palaces and bhawans speak to the living. Instead of its strategic importance as a military stronghold in the past, it now has significance in terms of tourism and as a centre for art.

This magical and spatial palace epitomises the Jat and Rajput composite culture, for here, science and art, principles of aesthetic and engineering, form and function, history and legend, blend together to give an unparalleled experience.

Left: *Double-eaved* chhajja *with brackets and axial water channels are characteristic of the architectural style at Deeg*

Facing page left: *Multi-cusped engrailed arches resting on colossal stone baluster columns*

Facing page right: *The grand entrance of Deeg Palace—the Singh Pol*

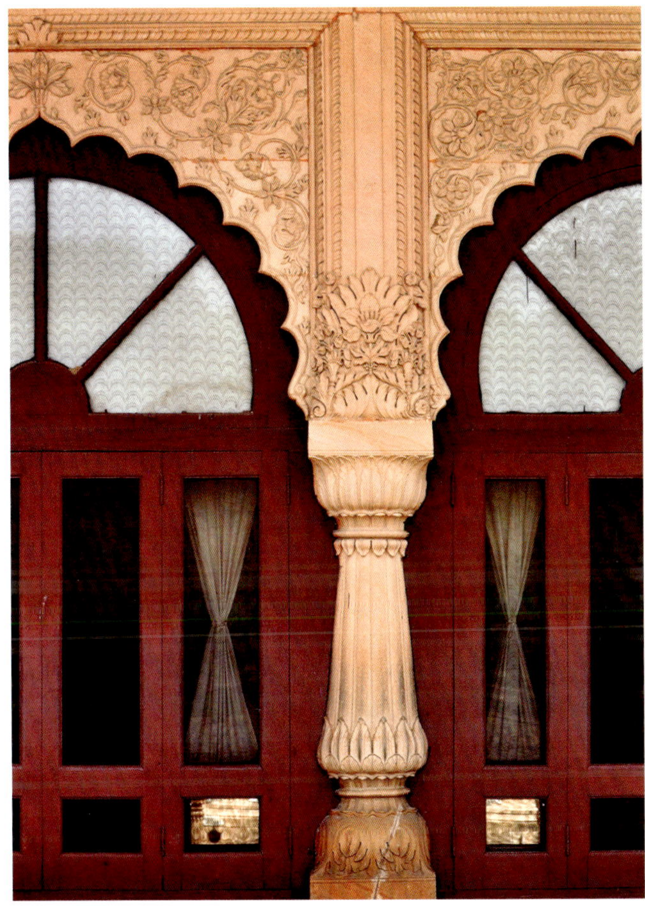

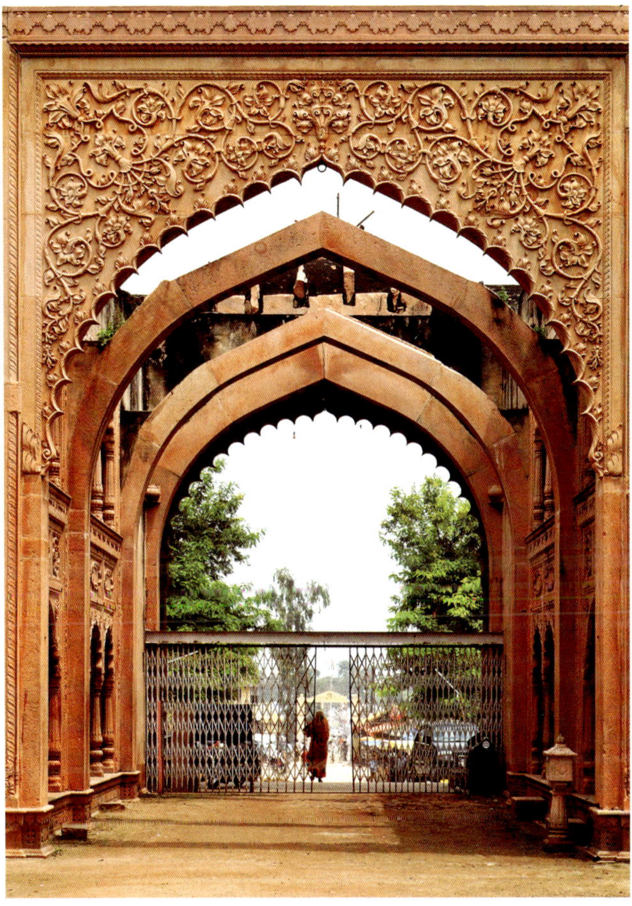

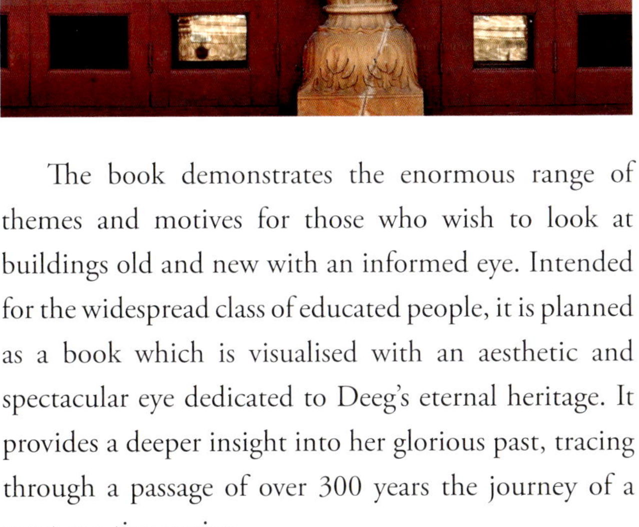

The book demonstrates the enormous range of themes and motives for those who wish to look at buildings old and new with an informed eye. Intended for the widespread class of educated people, it is planned as a book which is visualised with an aesthetic and spectacular eye dedicated to Deeg's eternal heritage. It provides a deeper insight into her glorious past, tracing through a passage of over 300 years the journey of a great creative genius.

Devised to serve a dual objective, the book on one hand is an academic endeavour elucidating epic building traditions, their various styles along with their historical, social, political, religious and cultural background so as to arrive at the intrinsic meaning and artistic merit of these monuments. On the other hand, the complex technical nuances of the architecture are easily explained by the book's strong pictorial and visual character. Its aesthetic and breathtaking aspects thus

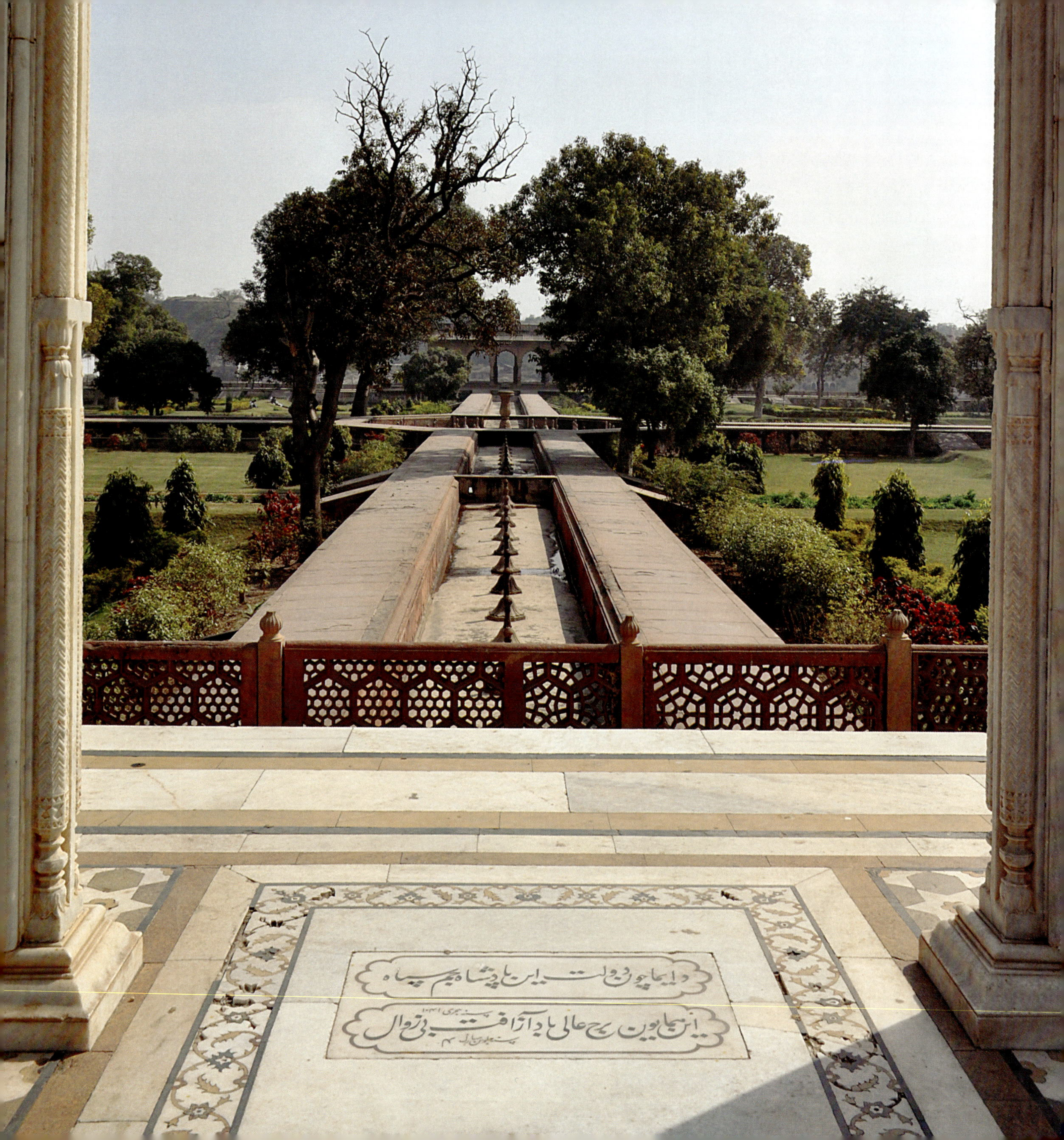
دایما چون دولت این پادشاه جم سپاه
این همایون برج عالی باد از آفت بی زوال

help a reader/visitor to seek his own interpretation of the magnificent monuments. The primary information provided is generally useful, serving as a manual for common art lovers, who would find a rich treasure of material in it. This book is not only meant for conservation and architecture professionals, rather a vivid and intellectual treat awaits every kind of reader.

Like all the Rajput palaces and mansions, the first area of interest in terms of its structure is the grand entrance of Deeg Palace: the Singh Pol or the Lion Gate. Here the journey begins into the historic past of the city palaces, their architectural grandeur and historical achievements, which is also the starting point in understanding, expressing and communicating the continuity of a vibrant cultural heritage rooted in the entire palace complex. Within this gateway, the quadrangles are piled with huge open paved areas, spacious courtyards, handsome sandstone bhawans and a paradise water garden.

Each one of these bhawans or palaces is discussed as individual chapters, the first one being Gopal Bhawan or the grand reception palace. Marked by a common rhythmical coherence, this palace is the hallmark of a comprehensive technical, historical and aesthetic analysis. The planning of this symmetrical palace mirrors the perpetuity in the cultural evolution of Deeg Palace. The other palaces discussed individually are Kishan Bhawan or Diwan-i-Khas, Nand Bhawan or wrestling palace, Keshav Bhawan, Suraj Bhawan and Hardev Bhawan. An entire chapter is devoted to the concept of the symmetrically arranged twin pavilions of Sawan and Bhadon. The buildings are often more fascinating than beautiful. The jewel in the crown of Deeg, the *hindola*, a lone example of a free-standing white marble arch, is another enigma where we try to demystify the entire Indian monumental architecture by excavating away the layers of the past to discover underlying facets of the universal truth. The penultimate chapter deals with the water gardens, its features and ongoing restoration work.

This book presents Deeg in the context of its past and present and poses an important question about its future the issue of conservation. The present-day usage of the complex, mainly due to population growth, has brought it on the verge of collapse. While the structure still exists even after so many centuries, its continued survival cannot be assumed without an active commitment to its maintenance.

Facing page: *Expansive view of the gardens framed in the free-standing marble arch or* hindola

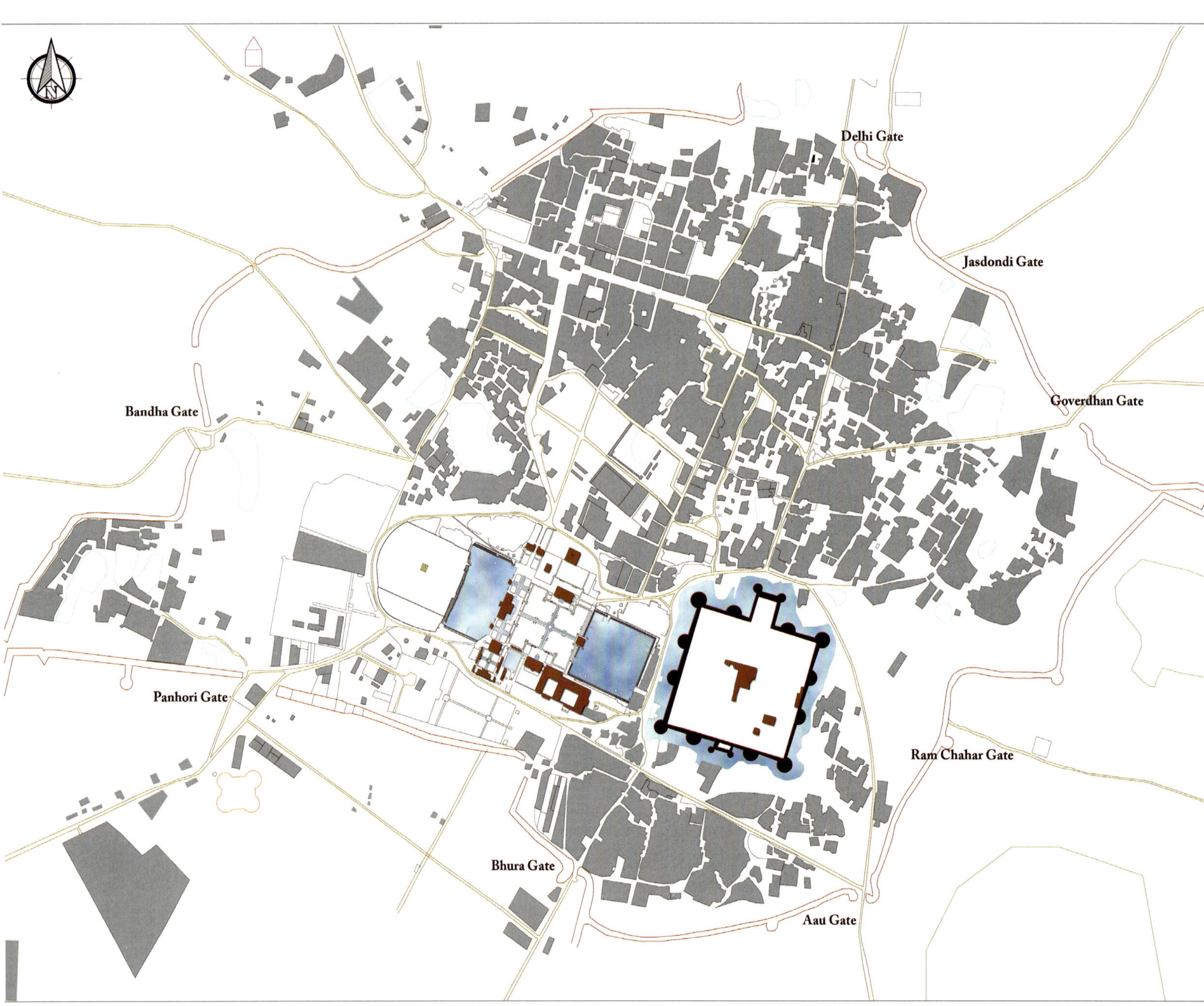
Delhi Gate
Jasdondi Gate
Goverdhan Gate
Bandha Gate
Panhori Gate
Ram Chahar Gate
Bhura Gate
Aau Gate

DEEG PALACE

A TOWN CALLED DEEG

Deeg is a little-known historical town in district Bharatpur, Rajasthan (27°25' North and 77°15' East). This is an 18th century stronghold of the Jat rulers. At a distance of 34 kilometres from Bharatpur, it is well connected by road with Alwar, Mathura and Delhi.[1] It is located very close to the Bharatpur Bird Sanctuary and popular tourist places like Mathura, Agra, Govardhan and Vrindavan.

It was known as Dirghapura in ancient times. This name occurs in the *Skanda Purana* and *Bhagwat Purana*. It came under the Jats in the beginning of the 18th century. Before that it was part of the numerous unknown villages of eastern Rajasthan forming a part of the Mughal Empire. Traditionally, it is part of the Brajbhumi—the land of Krishna and Yadhavs.[2] It also forms part of the 84-*kos* Braj Mandal Parikrama.

According to local belief, the Jat leader Badan Singh started looking for a suitable site for his new capital, after succeeding Churaman and consolidating his authority over several districts around Thun and Sinsini. He singled out Deeg on the advice of a holy man named Mahanta Makhan Das (Pritam Das) who was also invited to the foundation ceremony. When Pritam Das had dug out eleven spades full of earth, Badan Singh stopped him stating he must be tired now and that eleven was enough. Then, Pritam Das dropped the spade and put his hand on Badan Singh's shoulder saying, 'For eleven generations your family will rule'. His prophecy came true. In due course of time a new capital at Bharatpur was carved out, but Deeg remained an important summer retreat.

1 M.C. Joshi, *Dig*, Archaeological Survey of India (ASI), 2006. p. 1.

2 M.C. Joshi, *Dig*, ASI, 2006. p. 2.

Facing page: *The town plan together with the fort and adjoining garden palace complex*

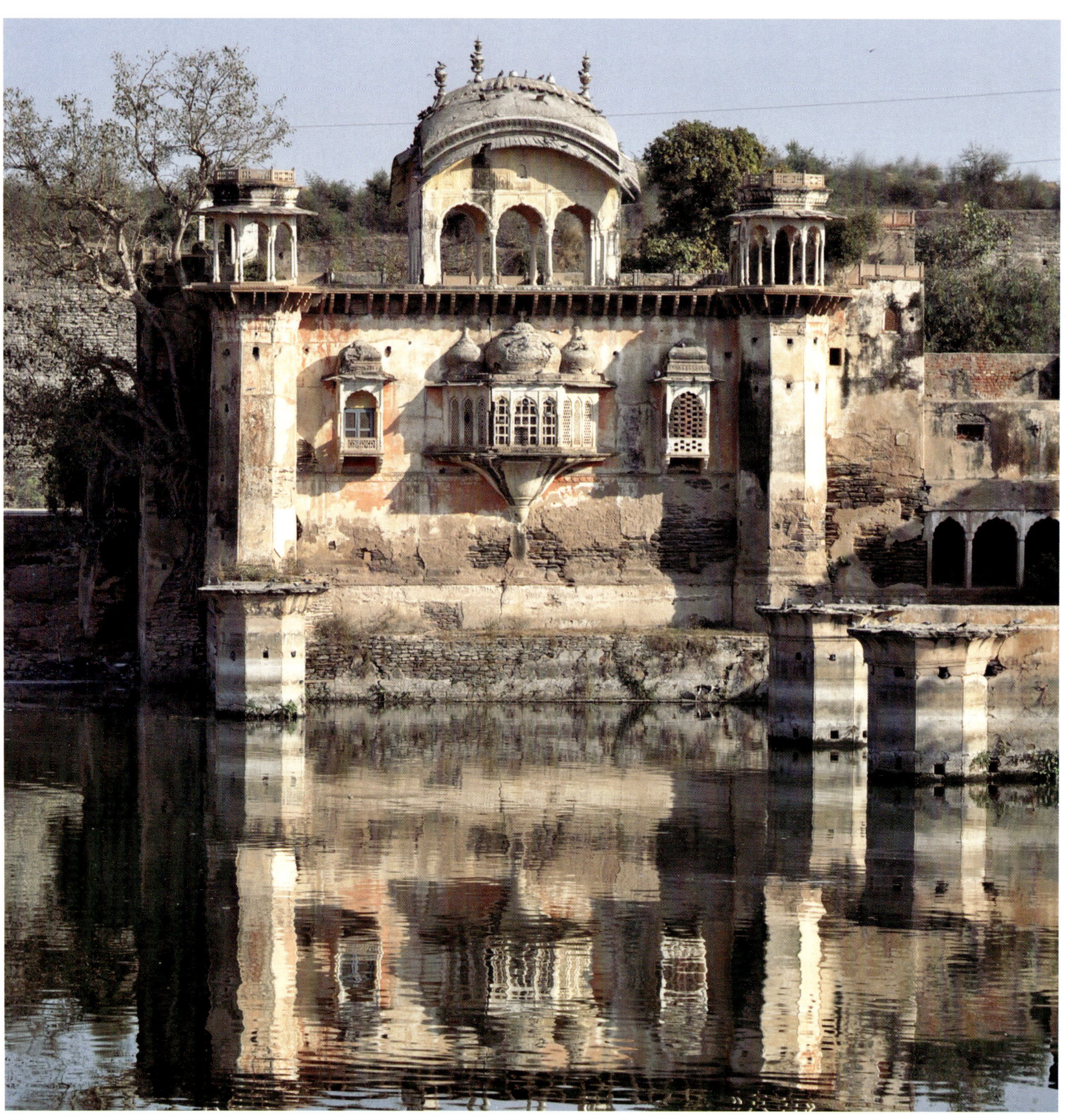

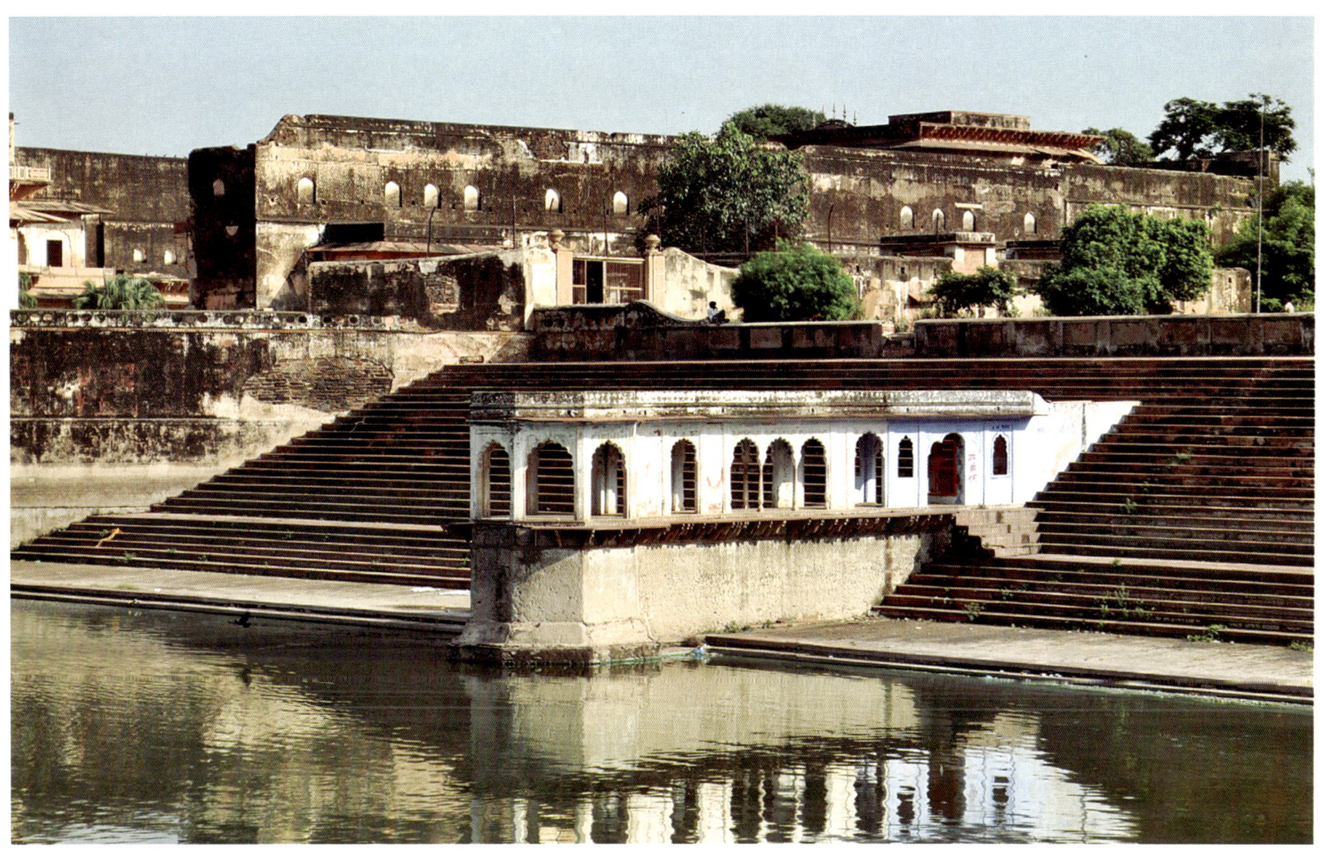

ABOVE: *The bathing ghats of Gopal Sagar*

FACING PAGE: *Purana Mahal across the Rup Sagar from the garden palace complex*

The credit of urbanising the city of Deeg thus goes to Badan Singh who was virtually the founder of this house of Jats. Though illiterate, he had an amazing aesthetic sense and along with his son Suraj Mal conceived the grand designs of the garden palaces of Deeg. In the era when there was chaos and disorder in Delhi, the credit of which to some extent goes to them and no craft flourished, the kingdom at Bharatpur provided some security of life and order. The master builders of Agra and Delhi sought work under the Jats who had newly acquired wealth to create works of art. The exposure to the grand palaces of the Mughals at Delhi and Agra may have instilled an ambition to create grandiose mansions.

As a consequence, Deeg was set on course to achieve its own political milestone, continuing the saga of the Mughals where the gardens were a royal symbol of territorial control and appropriation of land. Later on, this fusion of garden and palace became a dynastic abode of the Jat rulers for centuries.

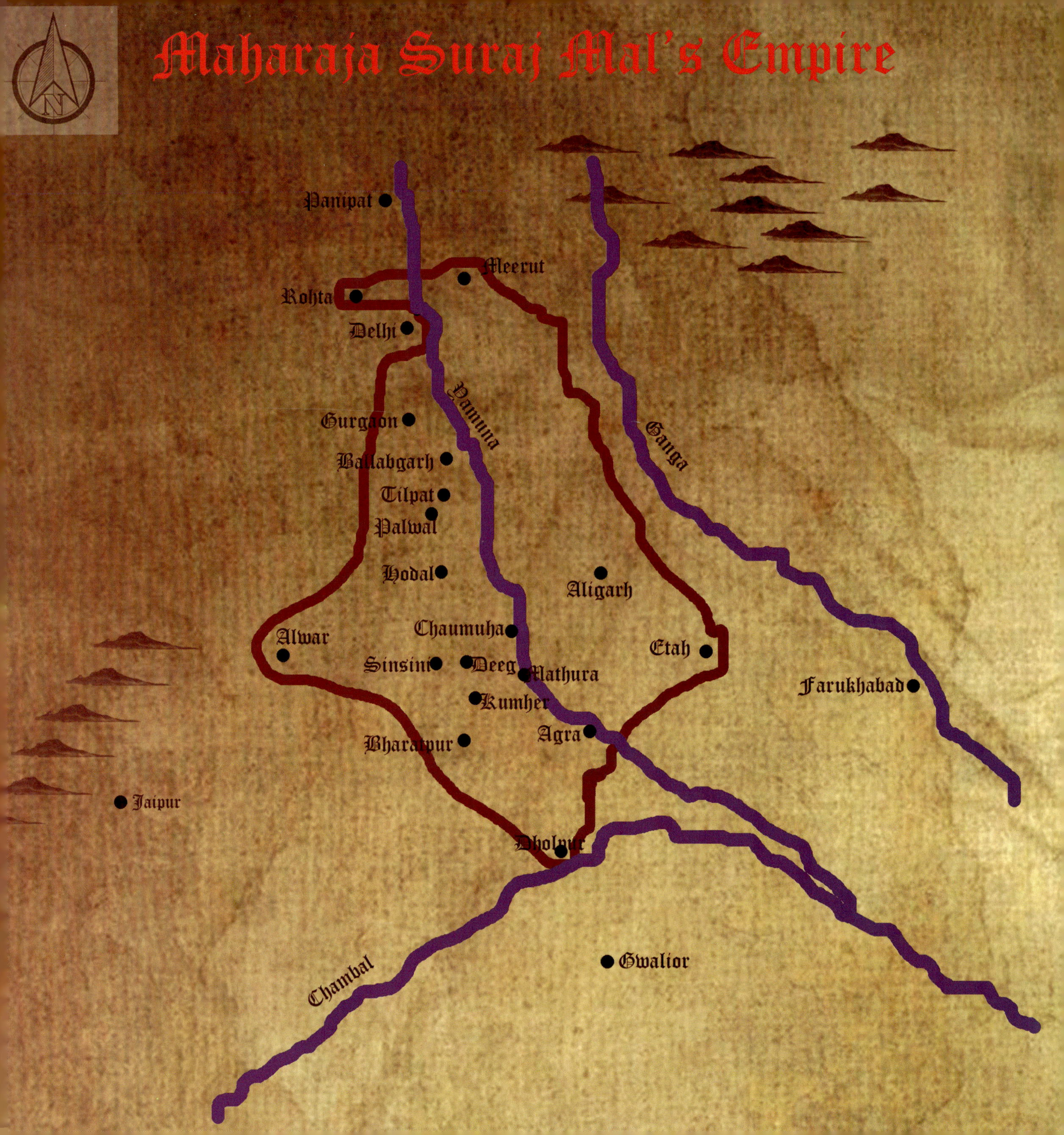

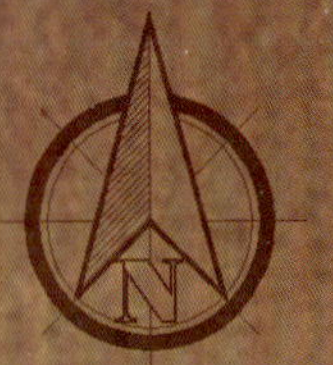

Maharaja Suraj Mal's Empire

Panipat
Meerut
Rohta
Delhi
Yamuna
Gurgaon
Ganga
Ballabgarh
Tilpat
Palwal
Hodal
Aligarh
Chaumuha
Alwar
Etah
Sinsini
Deeg
Mathura
Farukhabad
Kumher
Agra
Bharatpur
Jaipur
Dholpur
Gwalior
Chambal

RISE OF THE JATS

THE MAKING OF BADAN SINGH AND SURAJ MAL

The stories and myths surrounding the Jats have continued to baffle the minds of historians and archaeologists alike. This mystery is even more deepened due to several conflicting theories and limited historical data about them. However, two major claims view them as being between Indo-Aryan and Indo-Scythian descent.

According to historical anthropologist Susan Bayly, the Jat people are a community of traditionally non-elite tillers and herders from Northern India and Pakistan. They migrated into the Punjab region in late medieval times, and afterwards into the western Gangetic Plain in 17th and 18th centuries.

After the death of Mir Raja Jai Singh of Amber, when Aurangzeb took an about-turn from Akbar's policy of religious tolerance, this headstrong community of pastoralists who were known to have taken up arms several times to resist repression in the past, revolted again. The fanatic and aggressive policies of Aurangzeb in 1669 led to widespread destruction of temples especially the grand Keshava Dev temple of the holy city of Mathura, which was one of the chief objects of his iconoclasm. Subsequently, his insensitive decision to build a mosque on the temple's ruins and the reimposition of *jizya*, the Islamic tax on idol worshippers and non-Muslims, in 1679 provoked the Jat rebellion in the region.

Aurangzeb's incapability to control his subjects and those who ceased paying land revenue due to his long absence from Delhi gave fuel to this defiance, which further sowed the seeds for the glorious Bharatpur Empire. The leader of this uprising, a Jat named Gokul Ram or Gokula, fought several battles against the Mughals and is said to have been finally captured

Facing page: *At its peak, the empire of Suraj Mal included both the imperial capitals namely Agra and parts of Delhi*

and killed after the battle of Tilpat, in which as per K. Natwar Singh, 4,000 Mughals and 5,000 Jats perished. Following this, the activities of the Jats remained in check for some time.

In 1691, continued persecution of Hindus provoked another Jat leader Raja Ram to desecrate Akbar's grave, exhuming and burning his bones to avenge Gokula's execution. He was instrumental in uniting the Jat clans of Sinisiwars and Sogharias.

After Raja Ram, his nephew Churaman raised and strengthened the resources of the Jats. Aurangzeb's death and fratricidal war gave Churaman the opportunity to keep on accumulating Mughal wealth, gold, priceless jewellery, arms and so on. This fortune enabled him to build and fortify the Thun fort. Churaman cleverly kept on shifting his allegiance according to the rewards offered to him. At some point, he was also appointed in-charge of the royal highway from Delhi to Chambal by the Emperor himself. Thus he acquired the seal of imperial sanction to levy tax on traffic where he once looted the convoys.

The two nephews of Churaman, Badan Singh and Rup Singh, were raised by him after his brother's death. Badan Singh was made the noble of Sinsini while Churaman ruled Thun. Badan Singh's opinions differed from that of his uncle's and he was against Churaman's policies as he wanted to change the perception of Jats from being rebels to rulers. When Sawai Jai Singh of Amber was sent by Emperor Farrukh Siyar to suppress the Jat leaders, he met with no success until the two Jats fell out. Once on a feeble excuse, Churaman sensing rebellion against him, had his own nephews arrested and confined them to Thun. Historians call this the beginning of the decline of Churaman. The protests of the Jat sardars against Churaman and the unfair arrest he made led to the release of both Badan Singh and Rup Singh. Badan Singh allied himself with Sawai Jai Singh and together they caused the destruction of Thun. Churaman, who refused to be captured alive, committed suicide before the Amber army aided by Badan Singh reached Thun.

After taking over the Thun fort, Badan Singh was made the 'Samanta' of the Jaipur *durbar* and later honoured with the title of *Brijraj* (King of Brij) by Jai Singh around 1722. He was allowed to use the *pachrang* flag (five-coloured flag) sacred to Rajputs and was also bestowed with a symbol (*nishan*) and a kettledrum (*nagara*). He was given the *kotwali* of Agra and the *jagirs* of Mewat and Braj regions. He succeeded to the headship of the Jats. He was a good administrator and under his leadership the Jats of Bharatpur gained in power and stability. Badan Singh's clan, the Sinsini Jats, thus achieved respectability and a degree of security. They enhanced respectability by claiming kinship with the Rajputs and increased their security through territorial conquest.

While maintaining friendly terms with both Mughals and Rajputs, Badan Singh succeeded in winning over the confidence of his own Jat community. With the vision of preserving these relationships, he set

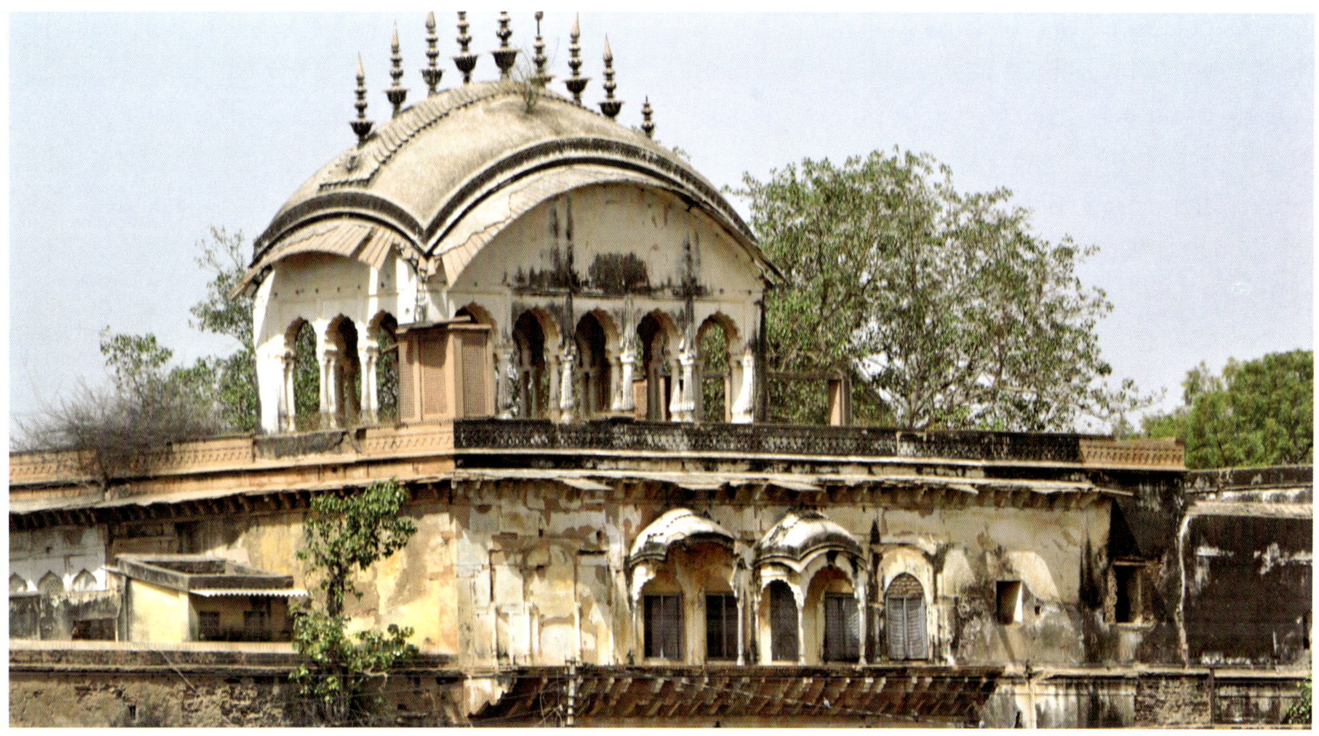

Above: *Purana Mahal, Deeg Palace complex*

out to search for a new capital as Thun held unpleasant memories and the village of Sinsini did not have adequate water. He zeroed down on Deeg where he established his capital and permanent residence.

In a bid to get as many powerful and influential zamindars and sardars to his side, he married into prominent families. Having twenty-five wives made him very powerful as he then became related to twenty-five dominant families. He was also successful in recruiting people not only from Jats and Rajputs but Brahmins too. He also won over the alliance and loyalty of people by giving titles like *Faujdar*, *Bakhshi* and *Sardar* to them.

Badan Singh can truly be called the founder of Bharatpur. He had a passion for architecture, art, poetry and craftsmanship and thus made great contributions to these fields. It was he who started the Deeg Palace, as only he alone could conceive such grand designs of the beautiful gardens. Badan Singh did not like wars and bloodshed. He expanded his kingdom through his vision and his apt political skills. He provided safety to his people and they in turn gave him their full loyalty.

Towards the end of Badan Singh's life, it was his son Suraj Mal who ruled Bharatpur. He was described as the 'Jat Odysseus' and 'The Plato of the Jat people' by writers and historians because of his unclouded vision, political shrewdness and enduring intuition. Suraj Mal was married to the daughter of the Chaudhary of Jatwara Ratiram by his father in his mission to make significant families his allies. Maharaja Suraj Mal possessed all the qualities of a good ruler and showed his capabilities by vastly increasing the royal treasure. He was an ambitious and a very powerful man. Gifted as he was, in terms of wisdom, he was able to carve out a large kingdom with minimum expense to Jat blood and treasure. Blessed with calculating far-sightedness and admirable prudence, Suraj Mal was a distinguished statesman. This Jat king had a vision and maturity to understand the inherent quality of Jat brotherhood and the deep-rooted democratic instinct. Therefore, he wisely abstained from an authoritarian system like that of the Mughals. That he was a secular ruler is borne out by the fact that he did not destroy any mosque and also employed Muslims at high posts. But he also followed the better aspects of Mughal governance through *diwans*, *nazims*, *munsifs*, *kotwals*, *lumberdars* and *patwaris*. He did not issue any new currency and Mughal coins were used all over his kingdom too. The Jat kingdom had grown to about 200 miles in length and 140 miles in breadth. Delhi and three-fourths of Agra came under this kingdom. This great ruler met his unfortunate end on 25 December 1763 during a war with Najib-ud-Daula. His heir and son, Maharaja Jawahar Singh, succeeded him.

Maharaja Suraj Mal, very much like his father, possessed a great love for the arts and literature. He was also very pious and lavishly spent on religious deeds and charity. Suraj Mal was a great builder and besides carrying invaluable pieces of Mughal grandeur from Agra and Delhi to adorn his palaces, he also patronised a vast team of architects and builders creating a new hub of art in Deeg and Bharatpur. Apart from forts, Suraj Mal also spent a fortune in beautifying Deeg, Bharatpur, Wair and Kumher with fascinating gardens, buildings and ponds. Some of the buildings were so outstanding that the kind of these could not be found anywhere. The impregnable Bharatpur fort with its 250 feet wide and 20 feet deep ditch and 30 feet wide and 25 feet high walls was built so strategically that the British could not conquer it even after laying a siege for four months in 1805.

At its peak, the empire of Suraj Mal included both the imperial capitals namely Agra and parts of Delhi—the grand cities which had the best of the monumental Mughal gardens, forts and palaces to be inspired from. His empire thus comprised of the gardens and forts at Dholpur (with the first Mughal garden of Babur), several riverfront gardens in Agra like the Itmad-ud-Daulah, Taj Mahal and Anguri Bagh, the Hayat Bakhsh gardens, Sawan Bhadon pavilions and Rang Mahal of Delhi fort. All this and his scholarly interactions with the Mughal architects and builders may have also exposed him to the metaphors of the beautiful gardens of Lahore and Kashmir.

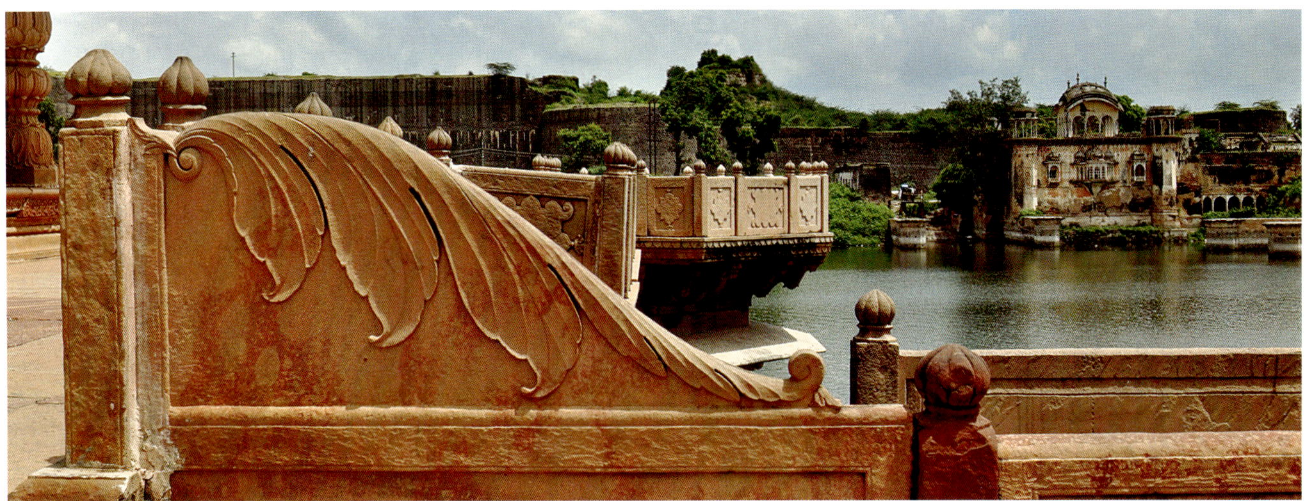

Above: *View of the Purana Mahal across the Rup Sagar*

These accomplishments paved way for the foundation of the palace which went on to become another gem—the architecturally sumptuous and superb water palace of Deeg. This had been planned and constructed by Suraj Mal on such an ostentatious scale that although the work on it started in 1725, it did not end by 1768. K. Natwar-Singh has given an account of the making of Deeg in his book *Maharaja Suraj Mal 1707–1763*:

> Badan Singh had at his command, men, money and material to supervise his great architectural undertaking. He appointed Jiwan Ram Banchari as his minister of works. For him he built a huge red sandstone house which today is occupied by the local medical authority. A poetic description of the fort gardens, lakes, palaces and temples is given in Sujan Vilas, written by Suraj Mal's lesser known court poet Somnath. One thousand bullock carts, two hundred horse carriages, 1500 camel carts and 500 mules were employed to carry marble from Bansi Paharpur and red stone from Baretha in Bayana to Deeg, Bharatpur, Kumher and Weir. 20,000 men and women worked around the clock for almost a quarter of a century to complete the building at these four places and minor works at Vrindavan, Govardhan and Bhallabhgarh.

The palace gardens of Deeg with the play of moving water and fountains in the setting of charming Mughal gardens surpassed in beauty and symmetry all the previous known Charbagh gardens except perhaps that of the magnificent Taj Mahal.

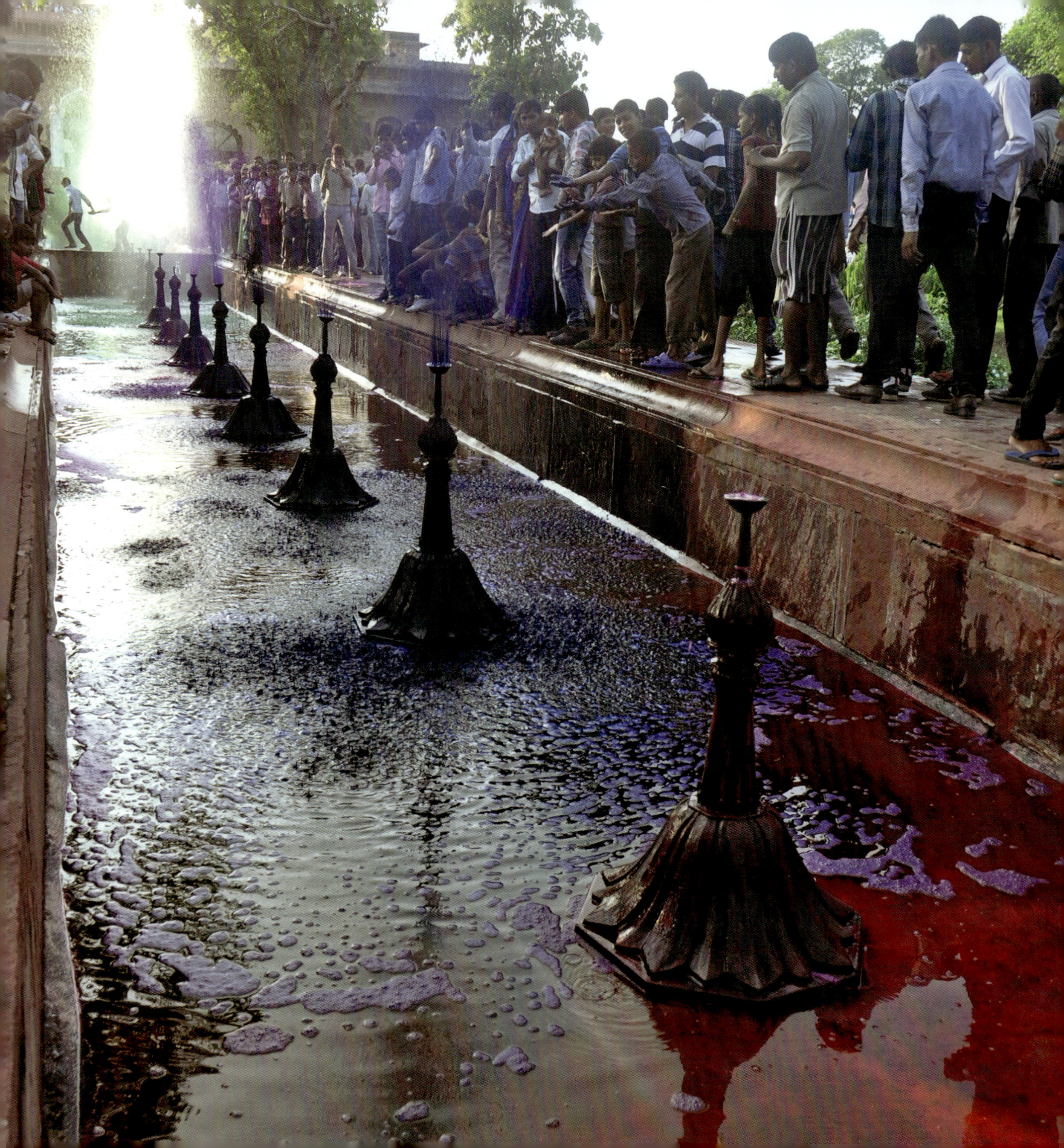

THE 'HINDU' MUGHAL GARDENS

Since the time when humans settled near water, it has been the controlling force in people's lives. In prehistoric times plants and trees along with water were believed to contain divine presence. The Upanishads of ancient India depicting the *kalpavriksha* tree as growing from heaven to earth and the Quran's accounts of the Tuba tree in paradise are prime examples amongst other mentions and depictions of trees in exalted positions universally throughout the world. Water is often shown symbolically and physically as the source of life. In the earliest ciphers, water channels symbolising the four rivers of life crossed in the centre of a garden dividing the area into four quarters. The cross formed by the intersecting of the water channels has been the symbol of the meeting of humanity and god in many religions.

Facing page and following pages: *The display of colourful water from the fountains at the Deeg Palace complex is enjoyed by several visitors*

The reverence for water, the mystical feeling for trees and the symbolic division of the earth into quarters by the four rivers of life became the basic essence of a garden, the meeting place of spiritual and material things, wedding the practical needs of irrigation and protection with religious symbolism. It is also the most ancient and enduring traditions of Persian gardens which bring out the paradise myth—the vision of paradise as a garden. In paradise, the crossing of the water courses represents the four rivers of life and Persian gardens which echoed this came to be known as Charbaghs. This division of the earth into four quarters is also echoed in the Hindu tradition of the four divine abodes, *Char Dhams*, one at each compass point.

Hindu mythology describes 'The Holy Land' with Mount Meru in the middle. It is believed that the waters of a secret spring flow in four directions from Mount Meru as great fertilising streams. On the central mound grows the 'Sacred Tree'—the tree of knowledge of good and evil with Naga, the holy water snake and the embodiment of spring, coiled about its roots. The tree of ages and fragrance, the 'tree of every perfect gift' is also supposed to grow on Mount Meru. Similarly in Islam, paradise or *jannah* is described as a garden surrounded by eight principal gates. The four cardinal directions are divided by the four rivers of paradise—water, milk, honey and wine—that feed pools where believers quench their thirst. Raised thrones or platforms ready for the rich with brocade carpets line the rivers where the righteous could recline, plucking the readily accessible fruits and their hearts refreshed by the clear flowing water. Even the Book of Genesis has a similar description: 'a river went out of Eden to water the garden; and from hence it was parted and became into four heads'.

These religious beliefs resonated in much of the Indian architecture and symbols that can be found in Deeg.

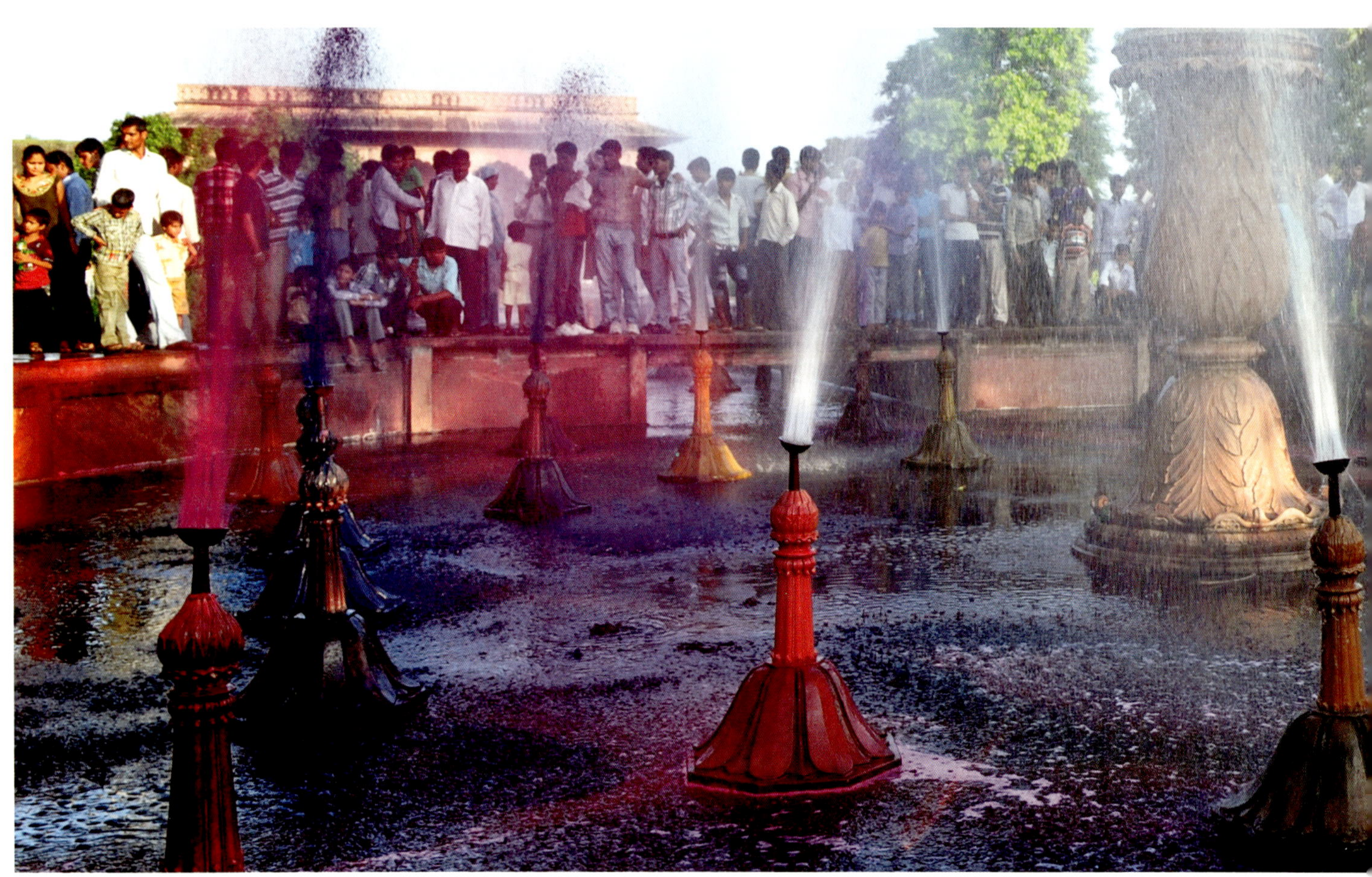

The basic geometry of the Persian gardens was defined by decorative carved stone water courses, trees and shrubs planted symmetrically in plots. The water courses were raised above the level of the surrounding ground for the purpose of irrigation. Each side of the canal was usually lined with trees and the quarters filled with flowers. This whole was enclosed by a wall to keep out the neighbouring desert with a purpose to give it privacy and perfection. Cyprus or evergreen trees were planted alternating with flowering/fruit trees (representing renewal of life) in Persian gardens bordering the water courses and dividing the gardens into plots. This was also seen as an association of the tree of immortality with water, the elixir of life.

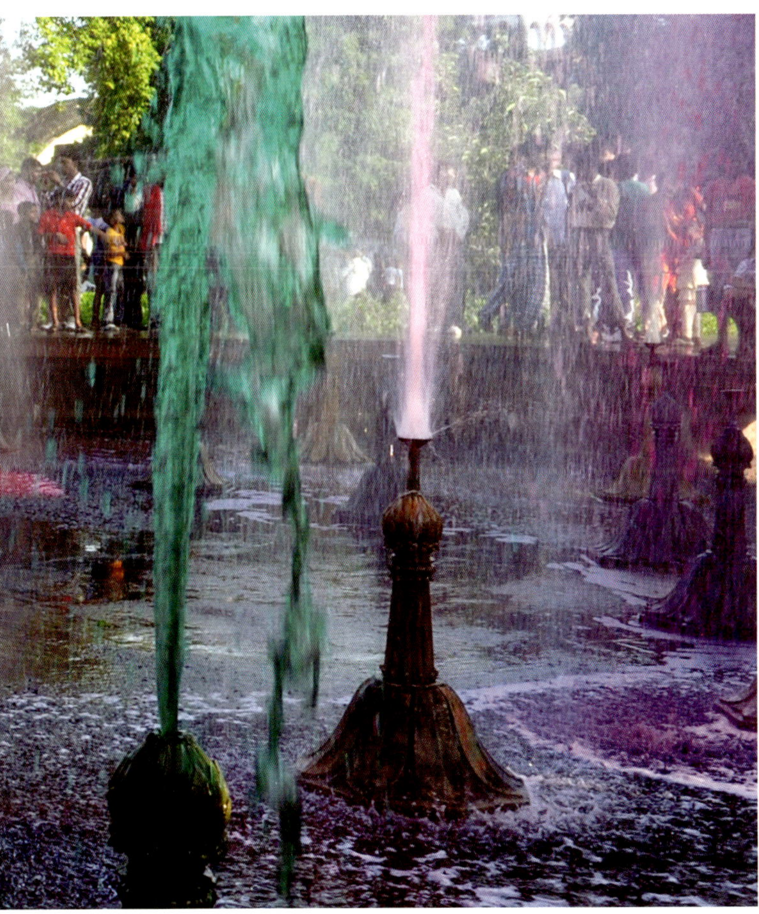

The six famous names—Babur, Humayun, Akbar, Jahangir, Shah Jahan and Aurungzeb—a marvellous line of emperors were men of genius in their own way and contributed to the tradition of Mughal or Persian gardens in India. When Aurangzeb abandoned the religious tolerance of his predecessors, especially Akbar the Great, and withdrew generous support given by his predecessors to the arts, the artists from his court withdrew. They were welcomed and employed by the local rulers who were influenced by the Mughal-Persian culture and court language. Among them the foremost was Suraj Mal, raja and builder of Bharatpur. He was wise enough to realise the virtues of the formal gardens of irrigation. At Deeg he laid out a garden epitomising the Charbagh tradition by adapting it for the hot lands.

So well attuned to the Indian climate and way of life was this garden that it may be said, in the words of C.M. Villiers-Stuart: 'the chapter of Indian garden history which Babur opened at Agra and culminated at Pinjore, reopened with the story of this Hindu palace builder'. The principle of Babur to create moving water in order to overcome the heat, dust and strong wind were so much liked by this young prince that he created his own environmental metamorphosis in the form of a summer retreat at Deeg. Around him blew the scented

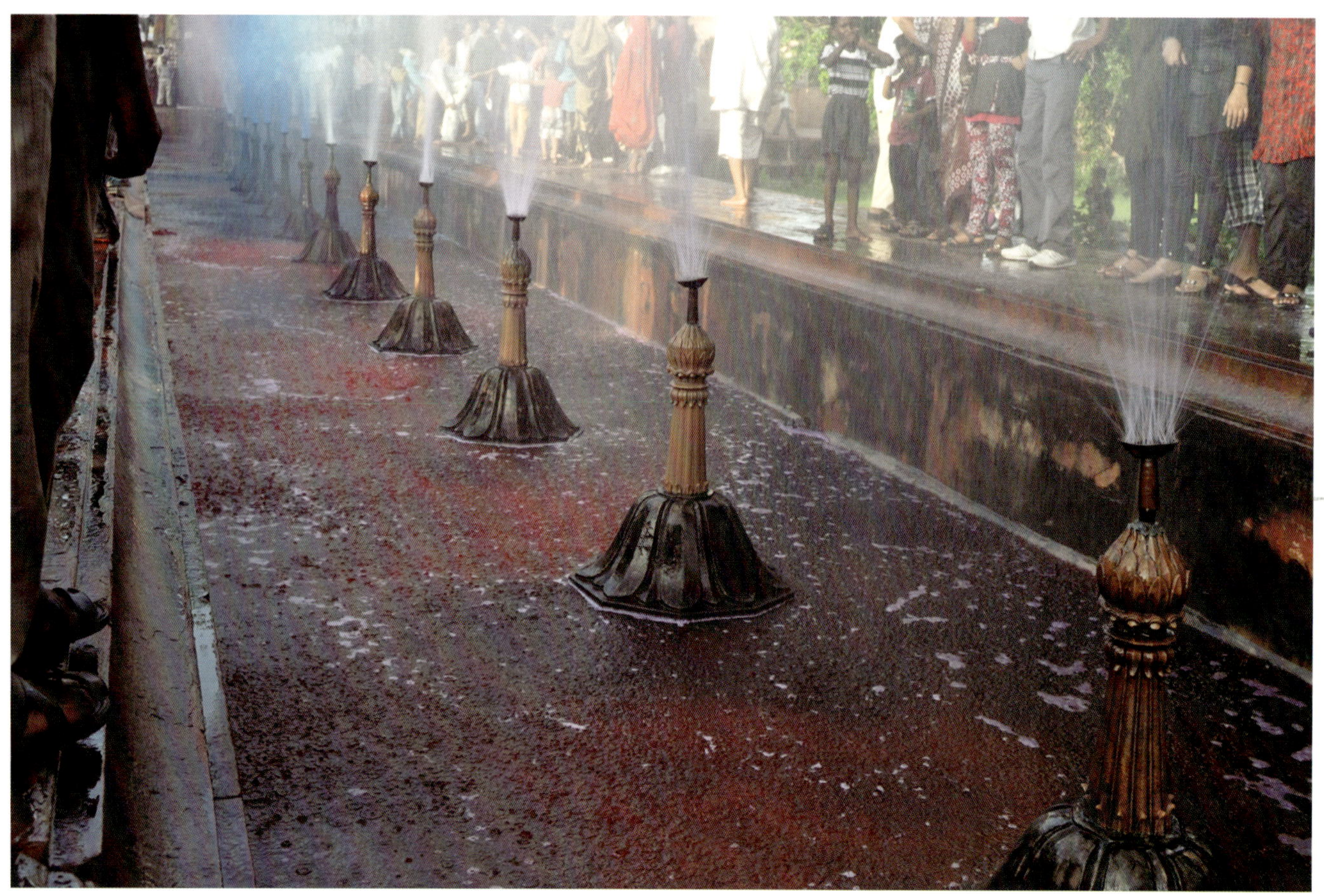

breeze from Rani Bagh cooled by the Gopal Sagar. He also built recreational underground chambers adjoining the water bodies. His gardens had ambrosial flowers and lush fruits. Thus even after the creativeness of the Mughal garden makers had ended, their influence continued and Deeg is an example of one such accomplishment.

In some ways Islamic art was the antithesis of Hindu art as Hindu adornment was individualistic, irregular and symbiotic, while Islamic decoration was mathematical, continuous and abstract.

But a common thread between the ancient Indian gardens and Persian gardens remains that of religion. Both Hindus and Muslims treated and enjoyed art and beauty not for its own sake but for the religious and traditional ideas and values. In fact, the idea of paradise or heaven as a garden is one of man's oldest ideals. It is a secure and everlasting garden, a place of perfect and eternal peace and plenty. The Hindus and Buddhists, with their wide sympathies and their simple, joyous love of nature, made much use of flowers in their

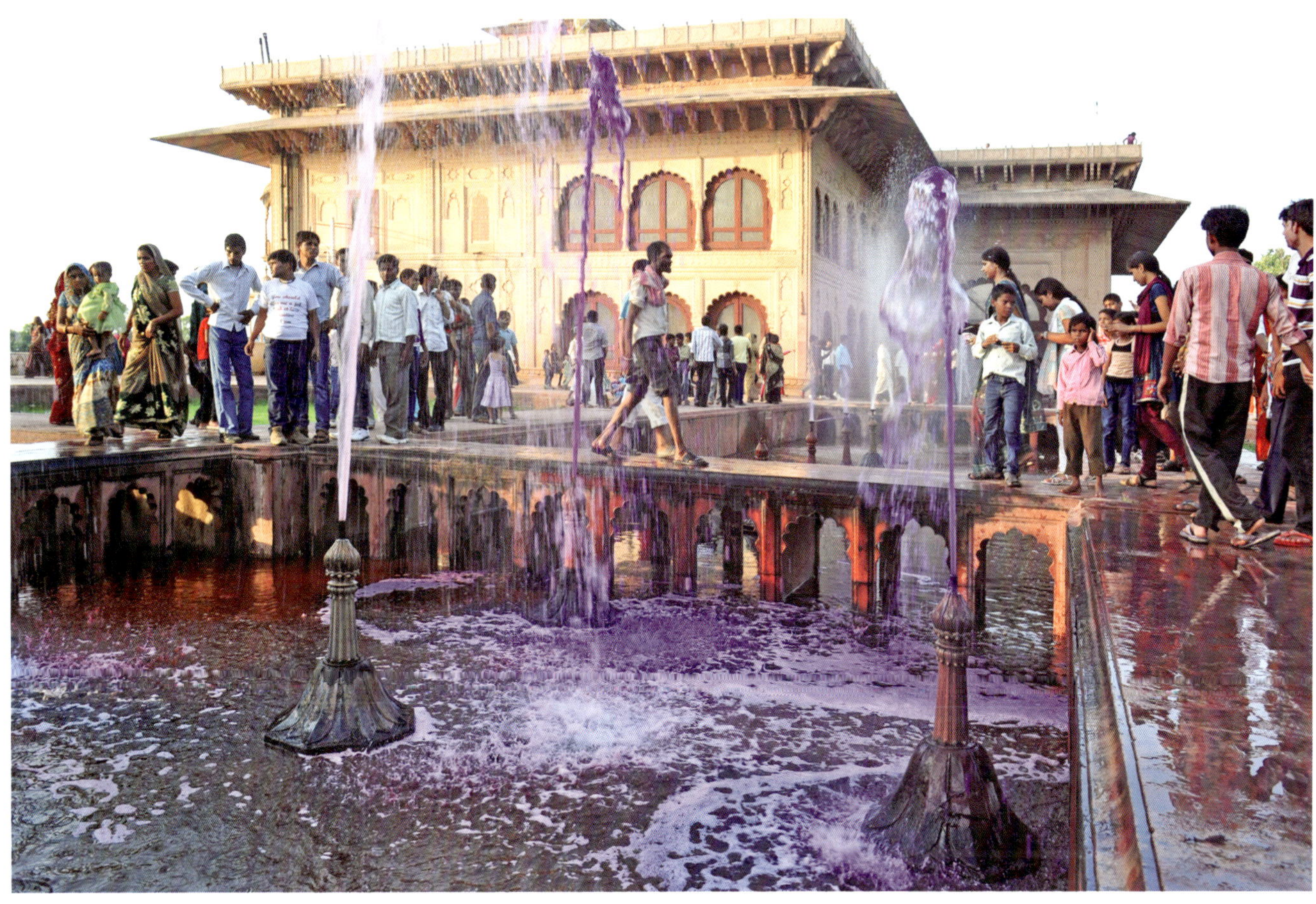

religious rituals. A lotus floating on the cosmic waters is the symbol of the creation of the world. The same lotus flower is represented in various forms in many of the gardens, not only in the Buddhist shrines or Hindu temples but even the Mughal gardens made a liberal use of the lotus symbol.

The Deeg garden was a revival thus inspired not only by the splendour of the Mughal gardens but also the upholding of an old, lapsed tradition of the ancient pre-Mughal gardens of India. A garden with waterways has always been a traditional component of early Hindu temples and palaces. Megasthenes' account of Asoka's palace in Patliputra in 3rd century BC describes a palace garden and its artificial ponds of great beauty. Kalidasa and other poets also describe beautiful gardens with lakes, lotuses and flowering trees. Such gardens can also be taken as precedents for the palace garden at Deeg.

Above and facing page: *Although several centuries have passed, the fountains and waterworks are still very much operational at Deeg*

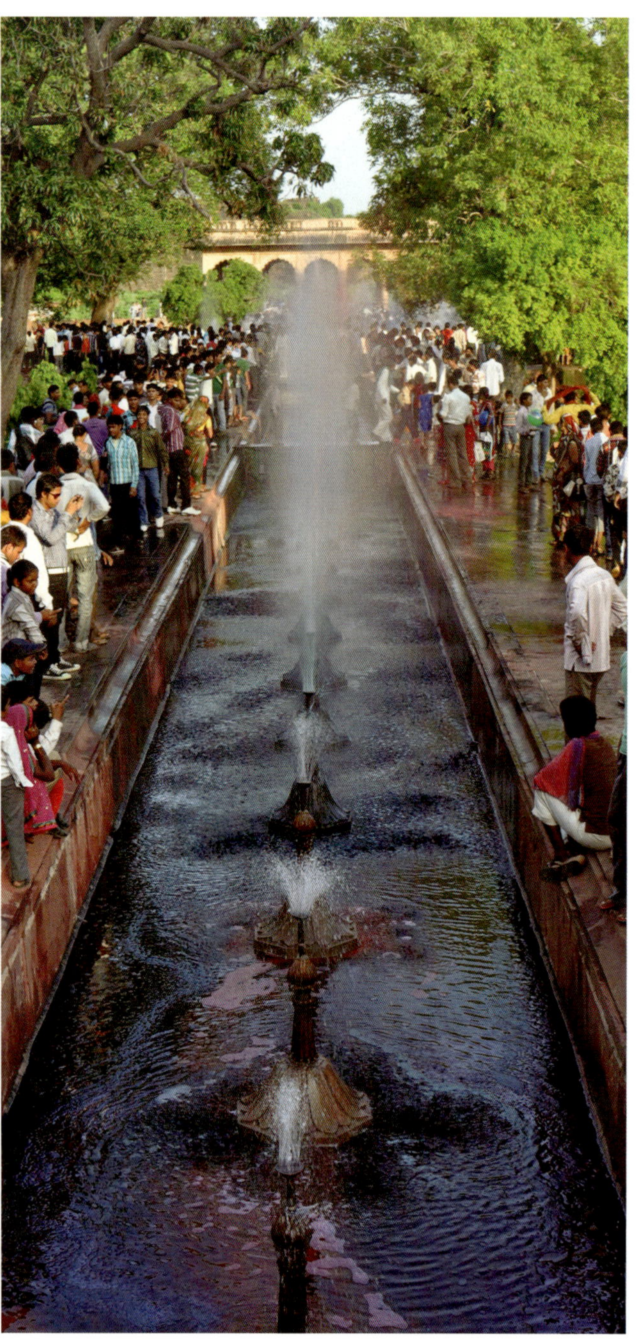

The Deeg Palace gardens also draw on the Hindu romantic tradition, both literarily and symbolically. Romance in Hindu tradition is associated with the monsoon or the *varsha ritu*. This is a recurrent theme in the gardens at Deeg. The romantic monsoon theme can be traced back to Valmiki's *Ramayana*. In the *Kishkinda Kanda*, the entire chapter and prose 28 is dedicated to a eulogy of the monsoon when Rama is unable to start his search of Sita and misses her. On one hand, Rama gives monsoon the prime status among all the seasons and calls it a heavenly elixir. Yet, on the other hand, he calls it a turbulence comparing it to the one in his heart.

The Hindu romantic tradition attached to the *varsha ritu* had some influence even on the Mughal gardens for the principal water pavilions of the Hayat Bakhsh garden in the Red Fort, Delhi and Shalimar Bagh, Lahore are named after the monsoon months *Sawan* and *Bhadon*. Likewise, the Rajput builders made the Sawan and Bhadon pavilions in their palaces at Udaipur. Therefore the concept of Jal-Mahal probably became a secular trend for those times. Hence they are very beautifully depicted at the Deeg Palace with the re-creation of an artificial rainy season as and when one wishes.

The same theme is taken up in the contemporary miniature paintings of those times particularly the Ragamala cycle based on the musical modes, for the cycle includes the Todi *ragini* represented by a lonely girl awaiting her lover who is delayed by the monsoon. Also the same theme is recurrent in Hindi folk and contemporary songs.

Miniature paintings also describe another important aspect of the Deeg Palace—the formal gardens. Charbaghs, water features, ponds, tanks, pavilions, boats, *shamianas* were often represented in paintings especially by artists rendered jobless by Aurangzeb who took up positions at various royal courts of the Rajputanas. These paintings depicted beautiful landscapes.

It is commonly known that the Mughal Charbagh were formal gardens but not so well known is the fact that the earlier Rajput palaces such as those at Amber and Jaipur were inspirations for some of these later Charbaghs. Rajputs even imitated a water palace at Chitoor and continued the same tradition at their Udaipur and Jaipur palaces which probably influenced the architecture at Deeg.

Another important and customary feature of every Hindu garden is a swing. This can again be seen in some Ragini Todi series of paintings where an impatient girl is shown on a swing against a stormy background. The accelerating action of swinging might be taken to symbolise her anticipated sexual pleasure just as the storm clouds symbolise the lover's tempestuous mood. Another parallel to the same can be drawn from the Rajasthani festival of Teej in which women play on the swings in the gardens during the monsoon months. This tradition was perhaps at the back of the mind of the Jats when they brought a marble framework from

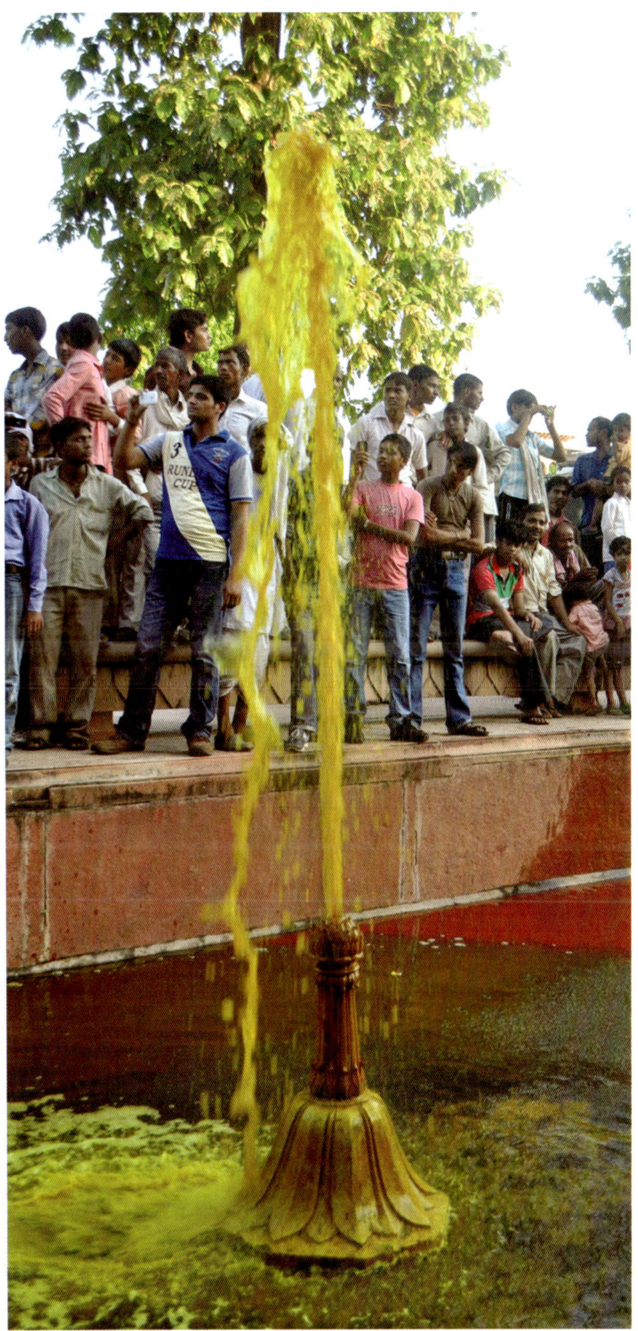

Right and facing page: *Locals and tourists flock to the Deeg Palace complex to see the magnificent water displays that occur twice a year*

the Mughals and installed it at the focus of the whole complex in the form of a swing with a beautiful view of the garden.

Krishna has had a perpetual influence on every aspect of the Braj region for ages. According to F.S. Growse, when Mahmud of Ghazni sacked and destroyed Mathura in AD 1017 during his ninth

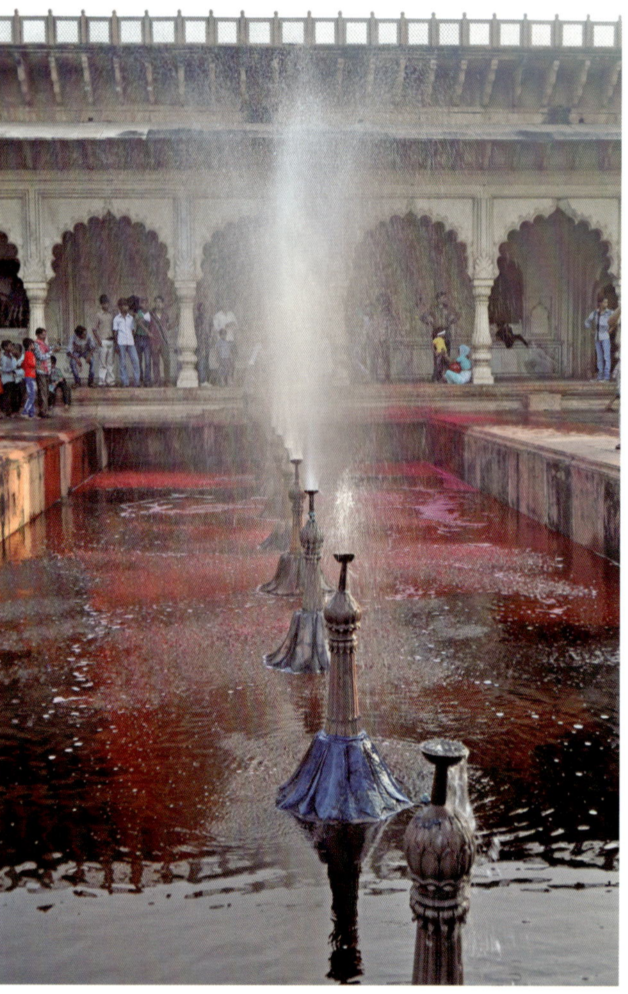

invasion of India, he is said to have acknowledged that the holy city was unparalleled in wealth and architecture to what he had ever seen before. This holy region of Brajbhumi has an ancient history for being a major seat of learning for number of religions including Buddhism, Jainism and Hinduism.

Krishna's *braj leela* is also synonymous with streams, rivulets and *upvans* (grove/orchard). The Braj Mandal Parikrama is an 84-*kos* (20 *yojanas* or 140 miles) *vana* (forest) *yatra*, stopping at every spot of Krishna Leela. Deeg is near Goverdhan, a spot where Krishna is said to have lifted the mountain to protect the natives from the celestial rains. The *parikrama* path passes through Deeg for Kam Vana: a forest which is perhaps the only leftover *upvan* of Krishna Leela. The rajas of Deeg are said to have forcibly stopped the *yatra* at Deeg to make it a spot for visitors. The palace was created to impress the pilgrims who formed an important part of the travellers from all over the country. What a great way to advertise the glory and grandeur of Deeg in the times when there was no media! Religion was the only core connection in the caste-based society for any individual to spread thoughts.

Krishna brought forward the cows and played on his flute through the forests of Vrindavan which were full of flowers, fruits, vegetables and pastures along with several bees. There were chirping birds and clear water lakes with waters that could relieve one of all fatigues. A sweet-flavoured breeze always blew, refreshing the mind and body.

So we see that the Deeg Palace garden owes as much as to the Persian Mughal garden tradition as to the Rajput or more generally Hindu traditions. Together these threads, the formal garden palace, water palace, monsoon romance and the Krishna culture form the crux of Deeg Palace gardens. The synthesis of these is the apotheosis of them all and is what gives the garden its distinct character and individual beauty. It also illustrates how two traditions existed alongside each other and contributed to and modified each other and yet for the most part remained distinct.

In addition to the paradise Charbagh symbolism, the Deeg gardens served various other symbolic, functional and aesthetic connotations. The political symbolism for the Deeg gardens stand out as being most prominent. These Charbagh gardens were used for royal picnics, to receive dignitaries, for rulers to conduct sessions with ministers and also as halting places for the army. A number of gates for the garden are testimony to this effect. Purana Mahal is still used a district court. The fact that huge terraces and platforms were used as base for tents is confirmed by the numerous ring hooks grouted on the terraces.

Environmentally the gardens were a relief from the torrid, dusty, disorderly landscape. Open pavilions and insulated high ceilings of the palaces can be seen as adaptation to the hot and humid climate and to maximise the circulation of breeze. The gardens were self-sustaining and even generated profit as a number of exotic fruits and vegetables could be grown in addition to the flowers for daily rituals, hence catering to the economic and social aspect.

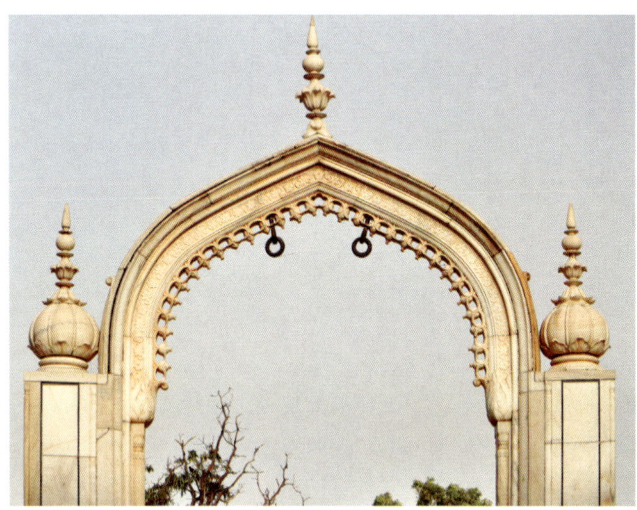

Above: Hindola *facade; it forms the main focus of the gardens*

Facing page: *The 'Hindu' Mughal gardens are enhanced by the colourful water from the fountains*

Aesthetically the gardens with picturesque waterfront landscapes, brilliant symmetry, balanced mass and form on a monumental scale were a treat to the eyes of any visitor. The placement of built forms with linear axis geometry and formal simplicity also explored various textures like carving and inlay to generate miraculous elevation sciography. Admirable configuration of spaces and voids on sprawling sandstone paving of terraces and walkways sustains a continuous interest and delight for excursions. Thus the Deeg complex became not just a place for experience but rather an object of art produced through a formal arrangement of architectural elements and spaces.

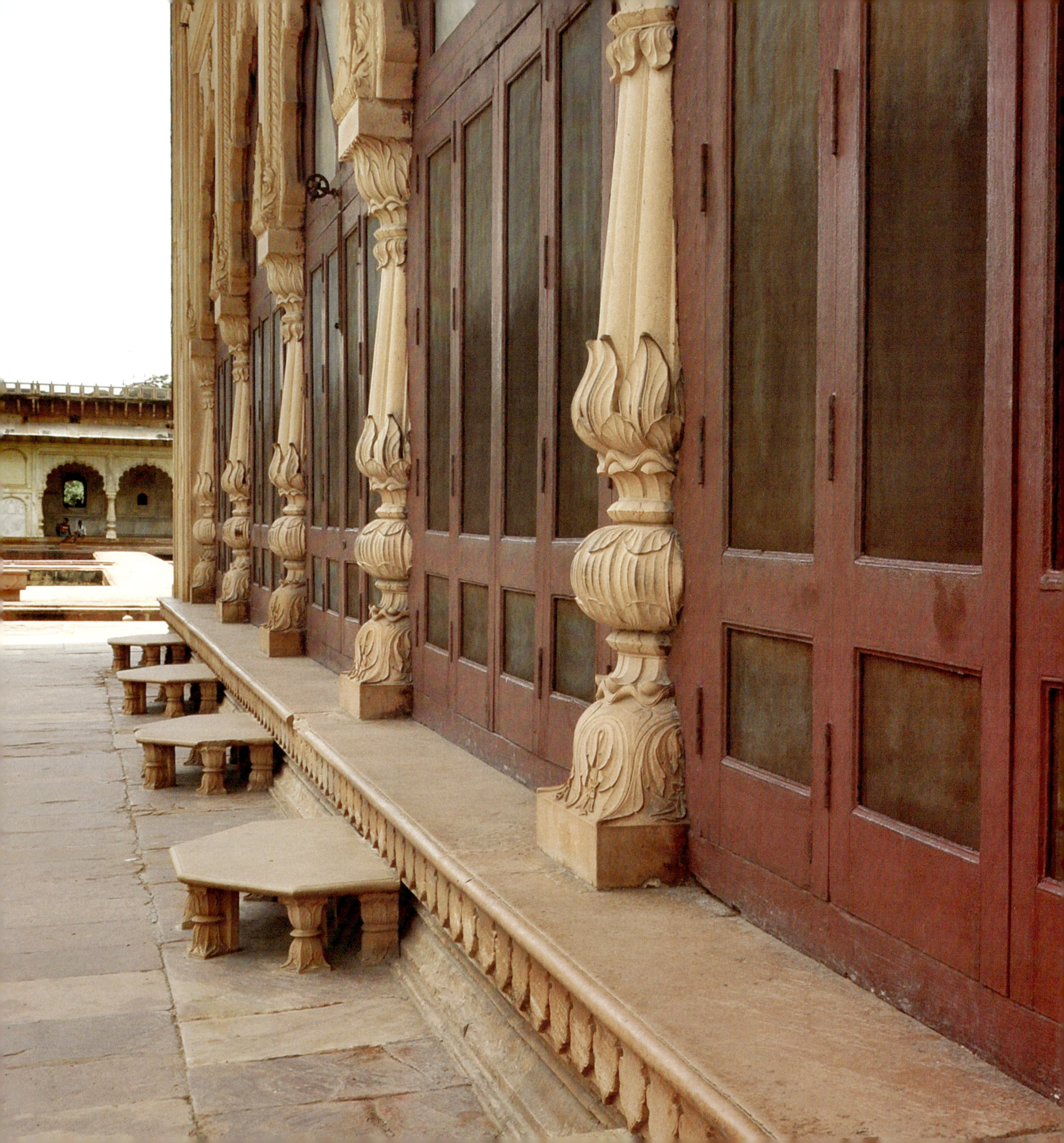

THE WEAVING OF POETRY

TALKING STONES

The work on the gardens and palaces of Deeg fort began in 1725 and continued till the end of the 18th century. The gardens at Deeg are the loveliest of the Mughal-style gardens built after Pinjore. Borrowing from the riverfront gardens of the Mughals in Agra, two huge tanks or water reservoirs were built on the western and eastern sides, namely the Gopal Sagar and Rup Sagar. They flanked the spacious palaces surrounding a Charbagh lined with tall shady trees and enriched by wide grassy platforms.

Though Badan Singh constructed Purana Mahal, the major work was done during the reign of Suraj Mal. Generations of scholars and travellers have responded to this palace complex, which is the centre of attraction and pulls the visitor warmly towards itself with its coherence, spatial arrangement and geometry. A courtly city, the uniform architecture and design of Deeg gives an impression of Suraj Mal's personality.

He made the large formal garden in the centre, the Nand Bhawan to the north, Kishan Bhawan to the south, the Keshav Bhawan to the east on the Rup Sagar and Gopal Bhawan to the west on Gopal Sagar. The charming tank Rup Sagar was built by Badan Singh's brother Rup Singh. Each subsequent ruler added a building or a pavilion, altered the garden or resized the tank.

Unlike most of the Rajput palaces, Deeg is built on a perfectly levelled site. Water and the surrounding flat country which was once a morass formed the principal defences of Deeg. It was more of a pleasure palace than a Garh palace. This was made possible by the change of political scenario in the early 18th century. Warfare techniques had advanced to such an extent that the once impenetrable Rajput palaces of Jodhpur and

Facing Page: *Ornamented individual steps resembling ceremonial* chowkis *grace the raised plinths of Deeg Palace*

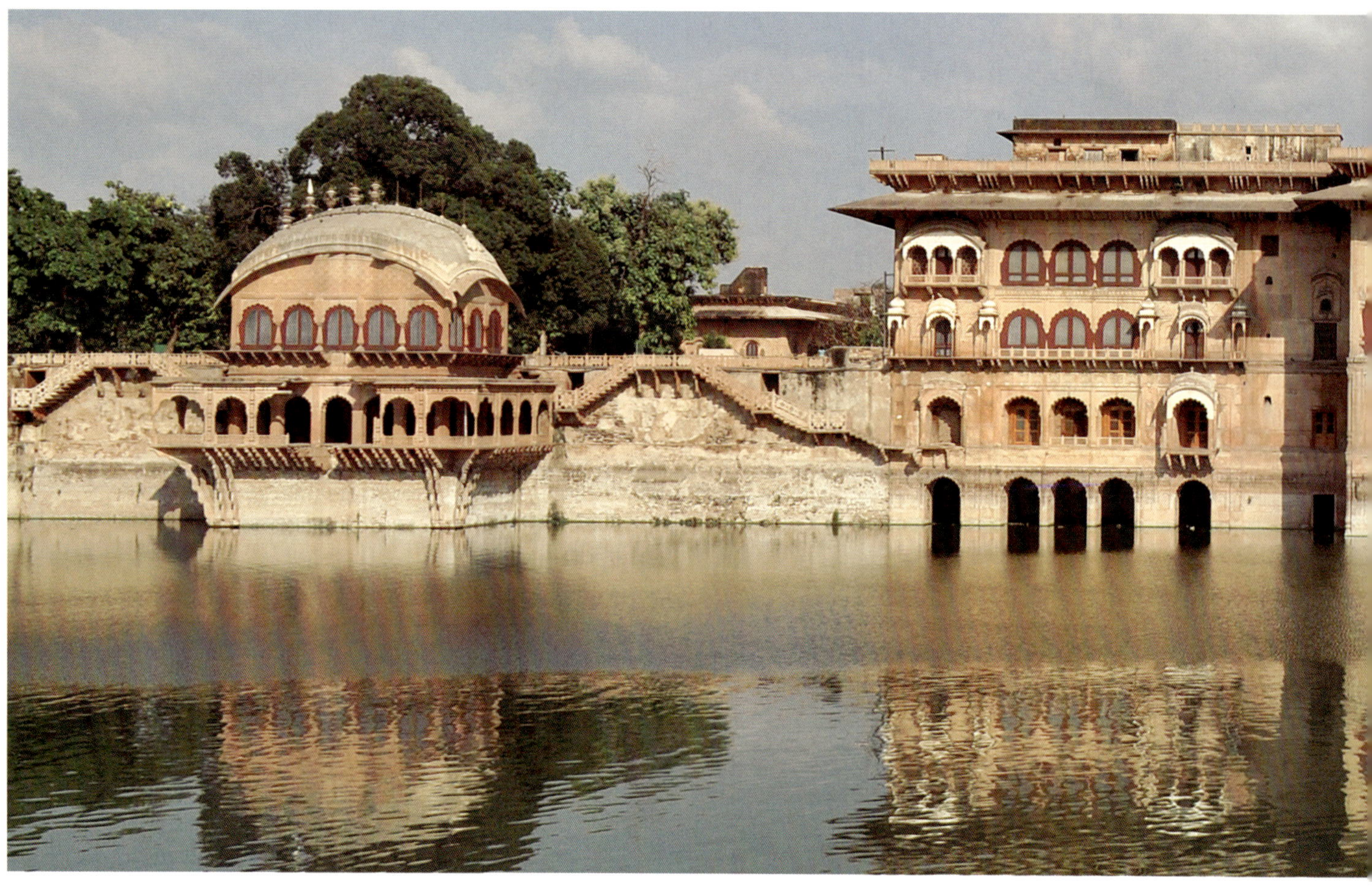

Udaipur could be easily won with modern artillery. Bitter struggles and hand-to-hand battles were reduced and their place was taken over by diplomatic channels. Deeg Palace, along with Jag Mandir and the Jag Nivas of Udaipur were built with basic fortification. Thus the palace became an example of a standard in the palaces of the ruling families of India.

The essential elements of the Deeg Palace were running water and a pool to reflect the beauty of the sky and gardens; trees of various sorts, some to provide shade, and others to produce fruits; flowers, colourful and sweet-smelling; grass, usually growing wild under the trees; birds to fill the garden with songs; the whole place cooled by a pleasant breeze. These extensive water gardens were supplied by four Persian wheels which raised the water to a massive tank at the level of the palace roof. The flow of water was controlled by plugging the big holes in the tank with wooden plugs.

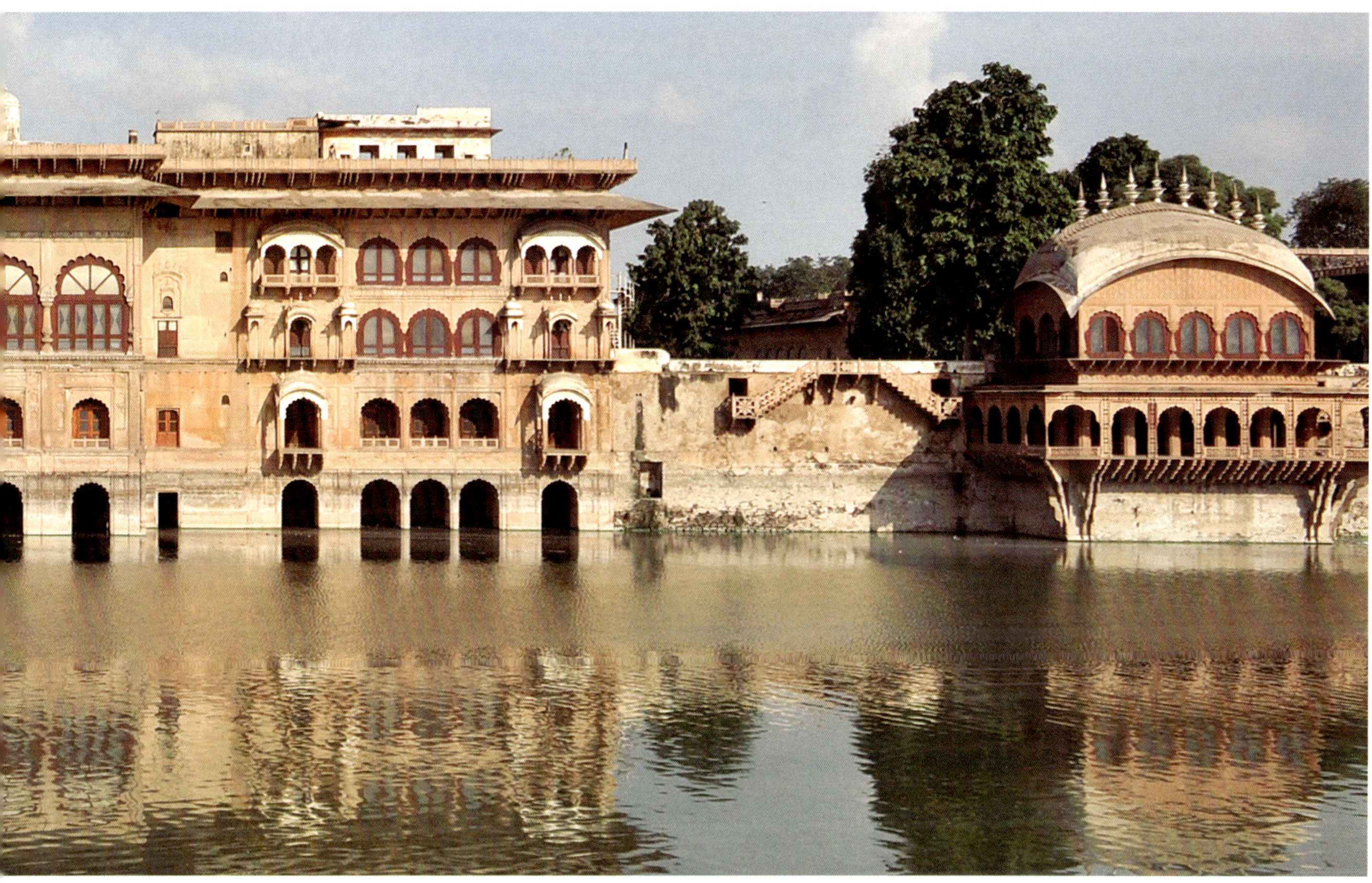

Above: *Panoramic view of the elevation of the Deeg Palace complex from Gopal Sagar. Gopal Bhawan is flanked by the symmetrically arranged Sawan and Bhadon pavilions*

The gardens at Deeg are based on the formality of Charbagh. Each plot is divided into four equal-sized parterres by means of a water channel with fountains in the middle. These parts were further subdivided with a walkway in the middle. The remains of these can still be seen. According to various writers, the floriculture planned was less of Mughal style in which the floral bed patterns were visible as they were planted thinly with flowers or low shrubs. In Deeg the plantation was thicker representing the Rajput miniature paintings. They perhaps wanted to create the effect of mysterious moonlit gardens frequented chiefly by women, again reminiscent of Ram's lonely wanderings in the Nilgiri forest after Sita's abduction. Still some plots like the one at Gopal Bhawan and at the corner of Kishan Bhawan (as seen in the old photographs at the British

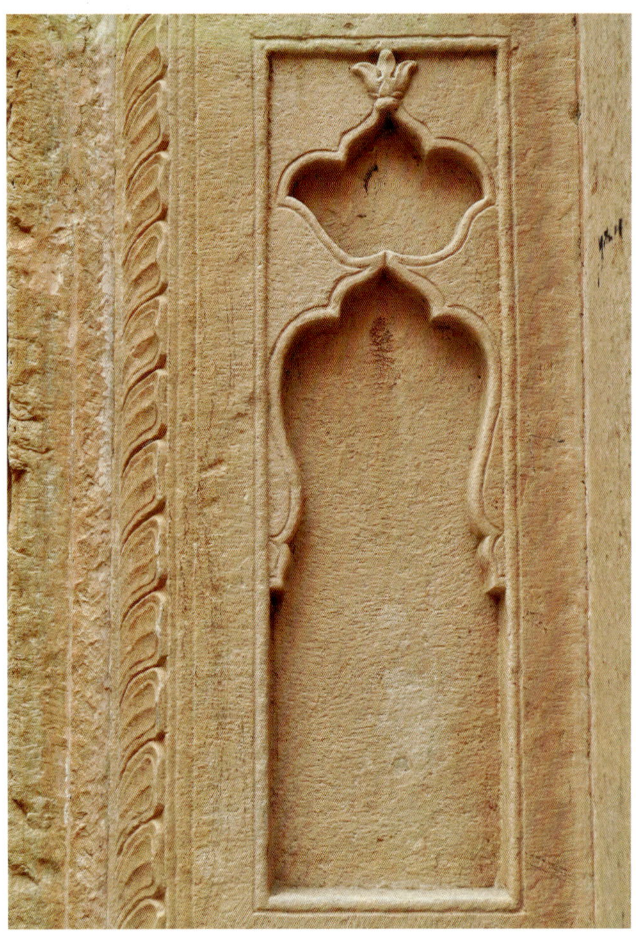

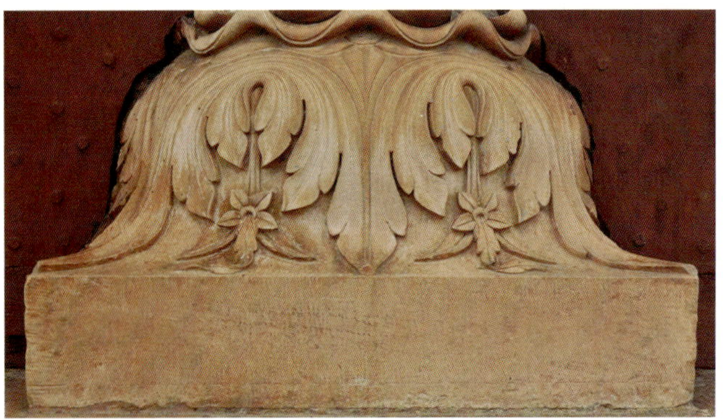

Library) show a very geometric division of planters for a landscape pattern resembling strongly the Anguri Bagh, Agra.

We see here that the borrowing of Mughal planning principles which were initiated in the courtyard additions of the Jaipur palace became central to the conception of Deeg Palace. The group of low, detached, open pavilions formally arranged on a level ground follow the formula of the Mughal palace. Deeg's sunken axial waterways which divide the garden into four parterres have open pavilions on terraces at the culmination of each central axis. The outer end of each water course has a low wall of niches or *chini khanas* from where the water falls in sheets. These niches had flowers in the morning and lamps at night to give it a romantic feel. This feature is definitely borrowed from the Mughal gardens.

The Deeg gardens and waterways are rich in sculptured fountains, tanks and other fine architectural ornaments which rival those of the Mughal palaces at Agra and Delhi. Some of these could well have been the same ones as the Jats had captured and looted both the palaces. The material used in the construction is stone, brick and mortar. Mostly pink sandstone, which is hard and good for sculptural work, from quarries of Bansi Paharpur is used though some buildings like Suraj Bhawan are made of marble.

The basic architectural style of the Deeg Palace is often called the Jat style and is of trabeated order. It comprises mainly of the Bhawans around a single garden complex and Purana Mahal. Though most of the elements were inspired, the treatment and presentation gave it an individuality of its own. While the buildings (Purana Mahal) built by Badan Singh are massive and simple, those built by Suraj Mal are systematic and ornate.

The general features of this style are engrailed arches resting on ornate pillars, hypostyle halls, flat terraces, balconies and pavilions. This choice of architectural forms used in the Deeg complex marked the culmination of the process which developed the Rajput style of the 18th century. One finds that many archaic Hindu forms were replaced by forms of Mughal architecture. For example, we do not find any temple-style columns in the palace. Instead, the Mughal baluster and fluted pillars with floral bases and tapering shafts surmounted by carved capitals are found everywhere. But surprisingly the trefoil arch used in many places is not a copy of the Tudor arch of the Mughals. Rather it resembles the early Buddhist sharply pointed and rounder arch. Also, the trefoil arches are similar to the ones that are present in the Sun Temple at Martand, which in turn were probably inspired from Shankaracharya's shrine in Kashmir. This leads us to the further conclusion that the Deeg complex was intended to be a symbol of universal fraternity—a fact that assumes a greater significance, as the symbol had arisen amongst the tillers of the soil.

Another great feature of the palace apart from its gardens is the fine roof terraces. Most of the bhawans here have double *chhajja* brackets which can be

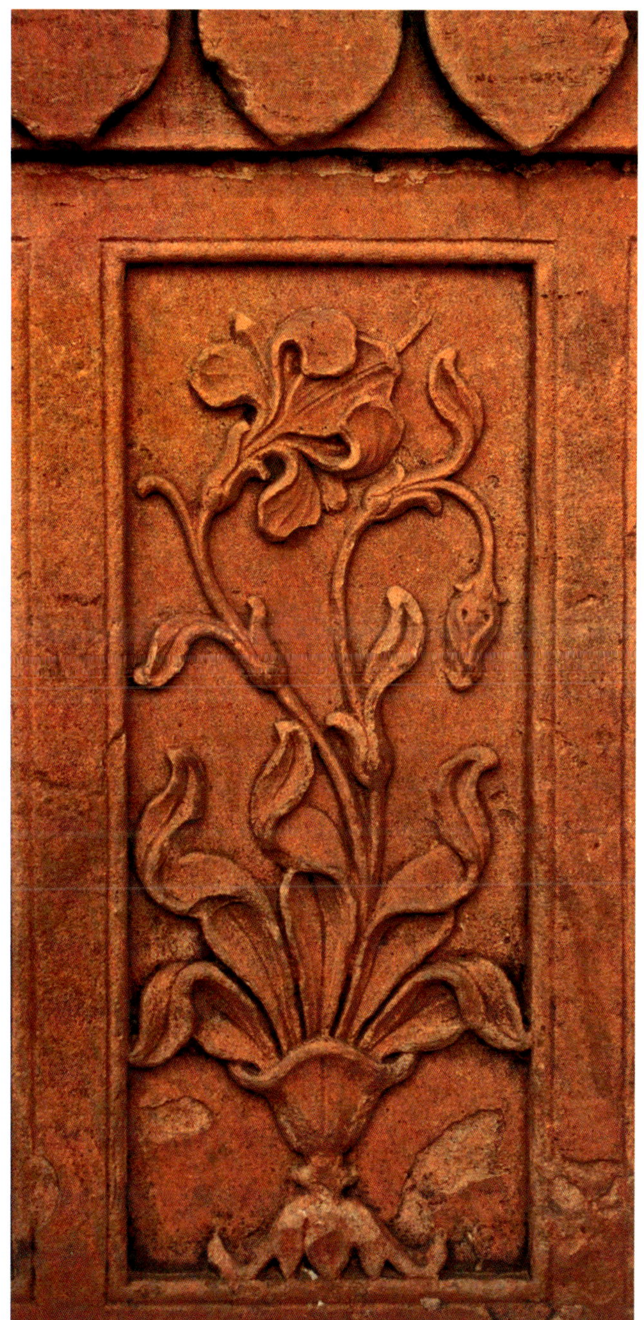

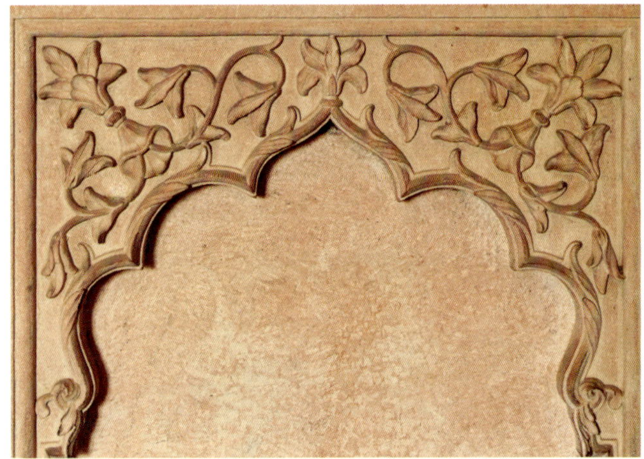

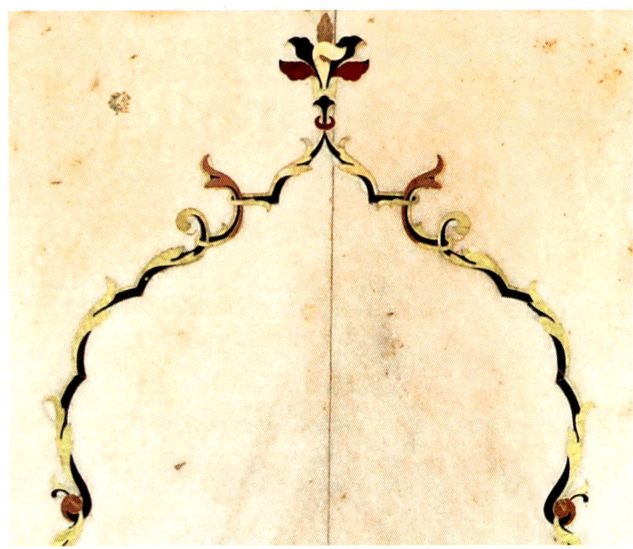

Previous pages, above and facing page: *Rich ornamental stonework adornments embellish the palace complex*

considered an innovation of the Jats, a feature which is absent from the older buildings of Purana Mahal. The upper *chhajjas* or eaves project horizontally from the facade extending on all four sides beyond the walls of the building with the help of a bracketed, pierced stone cornice forming extended balconies. The lower *chhajja* slopes in the customary way which is in turn again supported by a profusion of richly carved brackets. These brackets are not evenly spaced but arranged in groups. In some places like the central section of the Gopal Bhawan, the grouping on the upper *chhajja* differs from that of the lower. This system of counter-rhythms unexpectedly interrupts the unison on either side. There are pre-carved holes in the most stable area of the brackets to hang curtains or stretch *shamiana* tents. The unique combination of double roof *chhajjas* provide a very large roof space which was used for promenading in the cool of the evening as well as presented a rich effect of light and shade to the building in the sunshine. Thus it was not in vain that the flat Indian roof was known as 'the best roof of the garden'.

Another noteworthy element is the Bengal roof domes which are used quite a lot. In some places it is carved in shallow relief while in others it forms the *bangladar* pavilions. The Gopal Bhawan is flanked by two elegant pavilions—the Sawan Bhawan to the north and Bhadon Bhawan to the south. This vista comprising of the three bhawans has become symbolic of Deeg.

The Deeg complex was a collage of mostly open and semi-open spaces with minimal closed spaces. All the pavilions originally were open and drapes were hung in front of the arcades from metal rings. But now except the Keshav Bhawan, all the pavilions have been closed with the help of wooden shutters. At its centre is a well-laid garden with walkways, decorative flowerbeds, shrubs, trees and numerous fountains that cool the place considerably during summers. Deeg Palace was more of a summer retreat for the rulers and hence it was designed in such a way as to allow one to take maximum advantage to deal with the summer climate.

The Jats had risen from an agricultural background and were first generation rulers, so perhaps they were not in the habit of making distinctions based on *aam* or *khas*, a formality of the Mughals. Also, as it was not a formal administrative hub functionally, the buildings cannot be broadly classified. It seems they were more a statement of volume and grandeur than mere pieces of architecture and works of art. Except perhaps the Gopal Bhawan which seems to be self-contained as the palace has a separate reception hall, dining halls, bedrooms, private and recreational chambers. In the long run some functions were attributed to the various bhawans like the Nand Bhawan was treated as *durbar* hall and wrestling hall, maybe even a recreational private palace because of the attached swimming or plunge pool. The Kishan Bhawan also has a *durbar* hall and separate private or public audience areas with some attached antechambers and galleries connected to the side facing Hardev Bhawan and Suraj Bhawan. Thus these gardens also became centres for courtly, recreational and zenana (the part of a house for the seclusion of women) functions similar to those of the Mughal gardens.

Various types of experimentation were done in the waterways. An assortment of fountains like *chadar*, *chini khanas*, *kamal burjis*, nozzle jet sprays, needle-thread sprays, canals, octagonal and square tubs with delicate *cyma-recta* carved edges inspired by

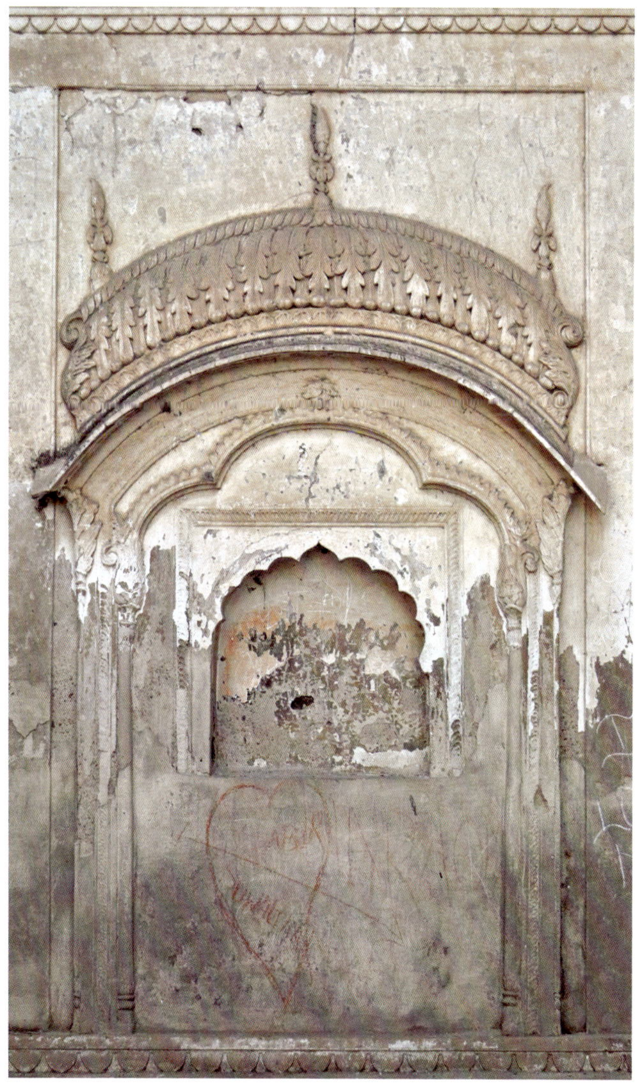

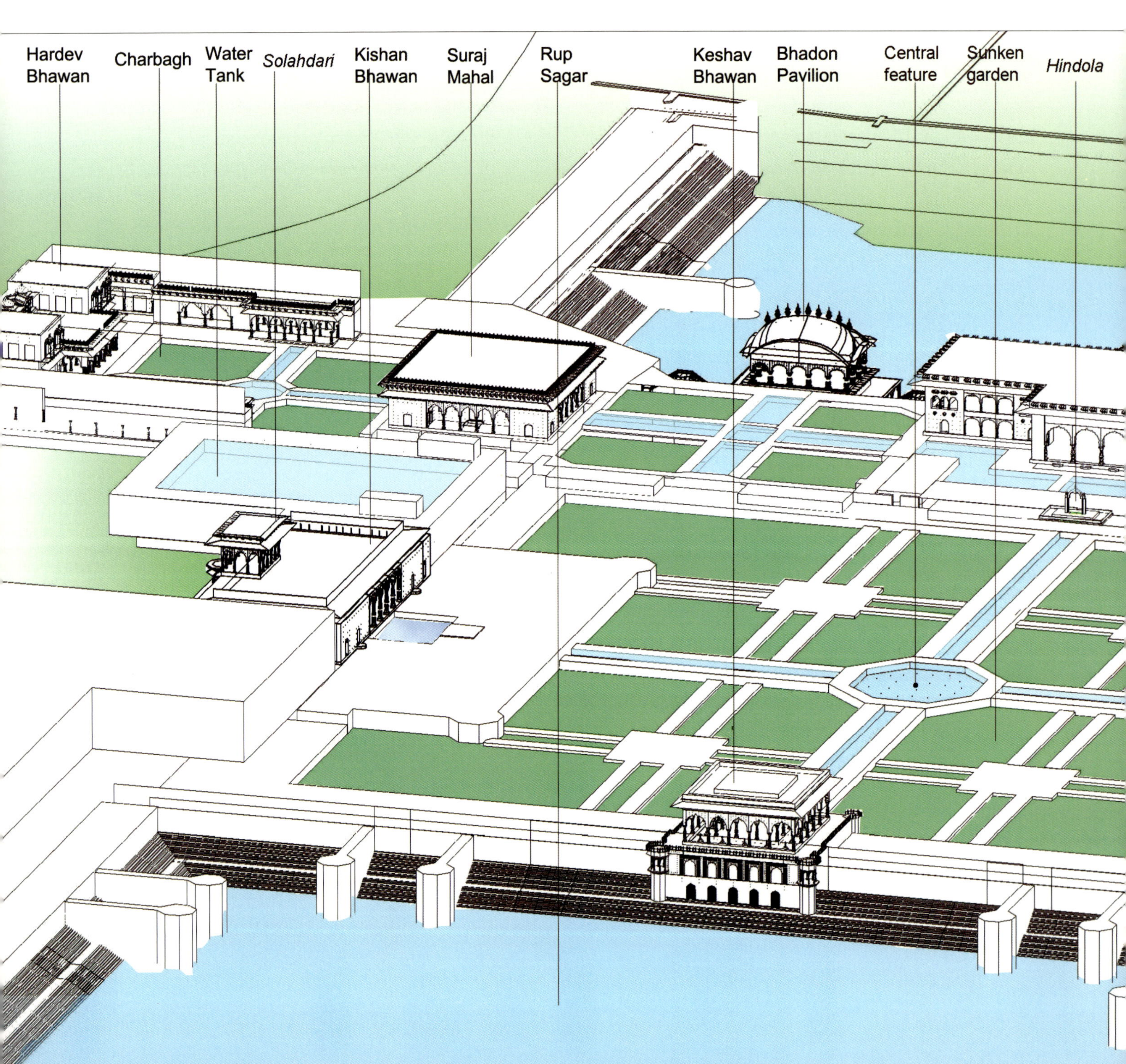
Hardev Bhawan
Charbagh
Water Tank
Solahdari
Kishan Bhawan
Suraj Mahal
Rup Sagar
Keshav Bhawan
Bhadon Pavilion
Central feature
Sunken garden
Hindola

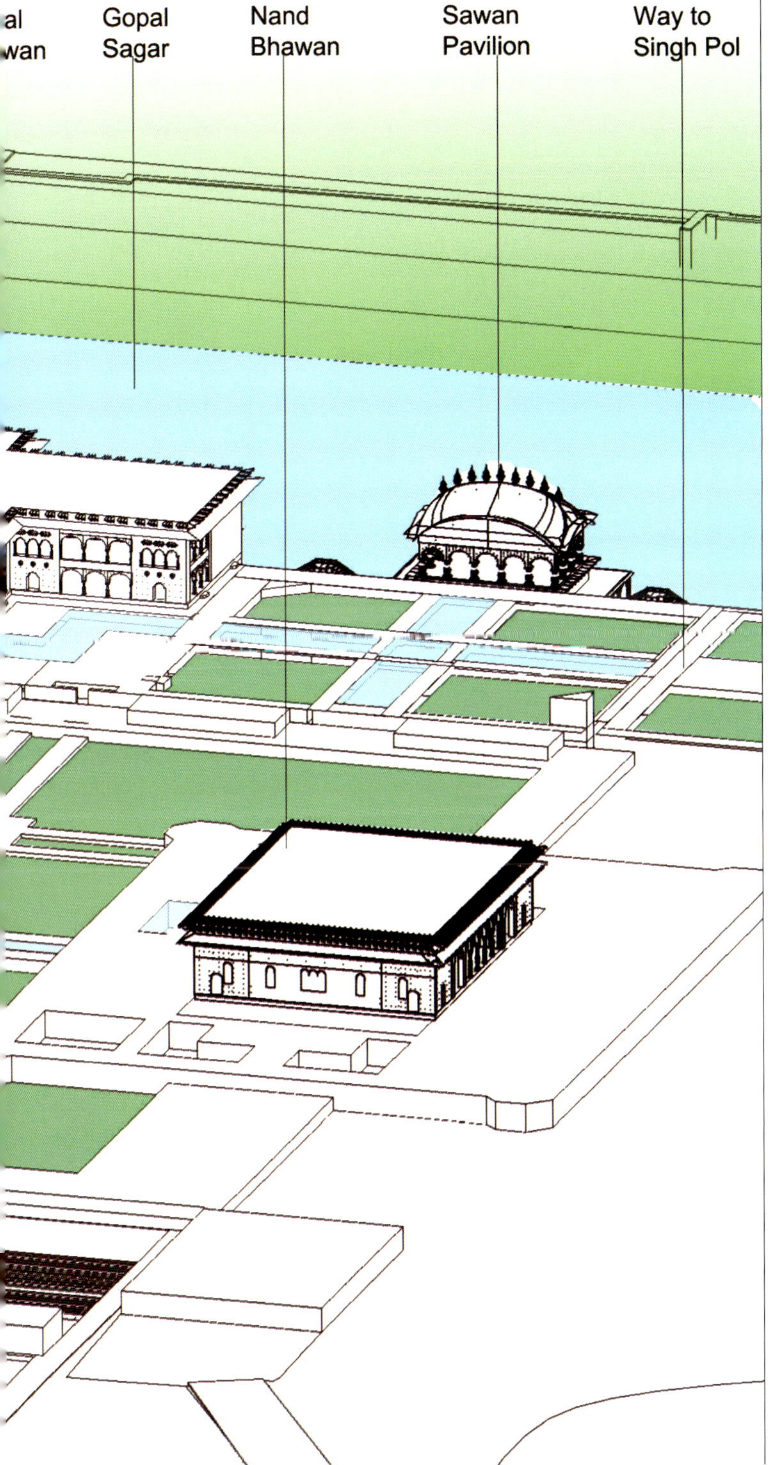

lotus petals, sunken tubs, waterfalls with recessed and carved lotus petals intrigue the visitor. A rhythm is created by the recurring patterns of beautiful nozzle jets all around the garden.

Another charming garden ornament is the marble swing placed on a platform under the trees in front of Gopal Bhawan where someone swinging vigorously could sway through the nearest fountain spray. Its ropes were said to be made of scented fibres and covered with wreaths of flowers.

Till date Deeg Palace serves as a glorious memorial to the celebrated hero of the Jat tribe, Suraj Mal, because of its artistic accomplishments. The royal family lived here until 1951 and inside the complex one can still see the royal furniture and *objets d' art*. It is said that a number of Britishers wanted to see the palace but were not allowed to enter the city by the Jats. In 1972, a movie by Conrad Rooks called *Siddhartha*, based on Herman Hesse's novel, was shot in Deeg and Bharatpur.

Left: *A 3D visual of the Deeg Palace and garden complex*

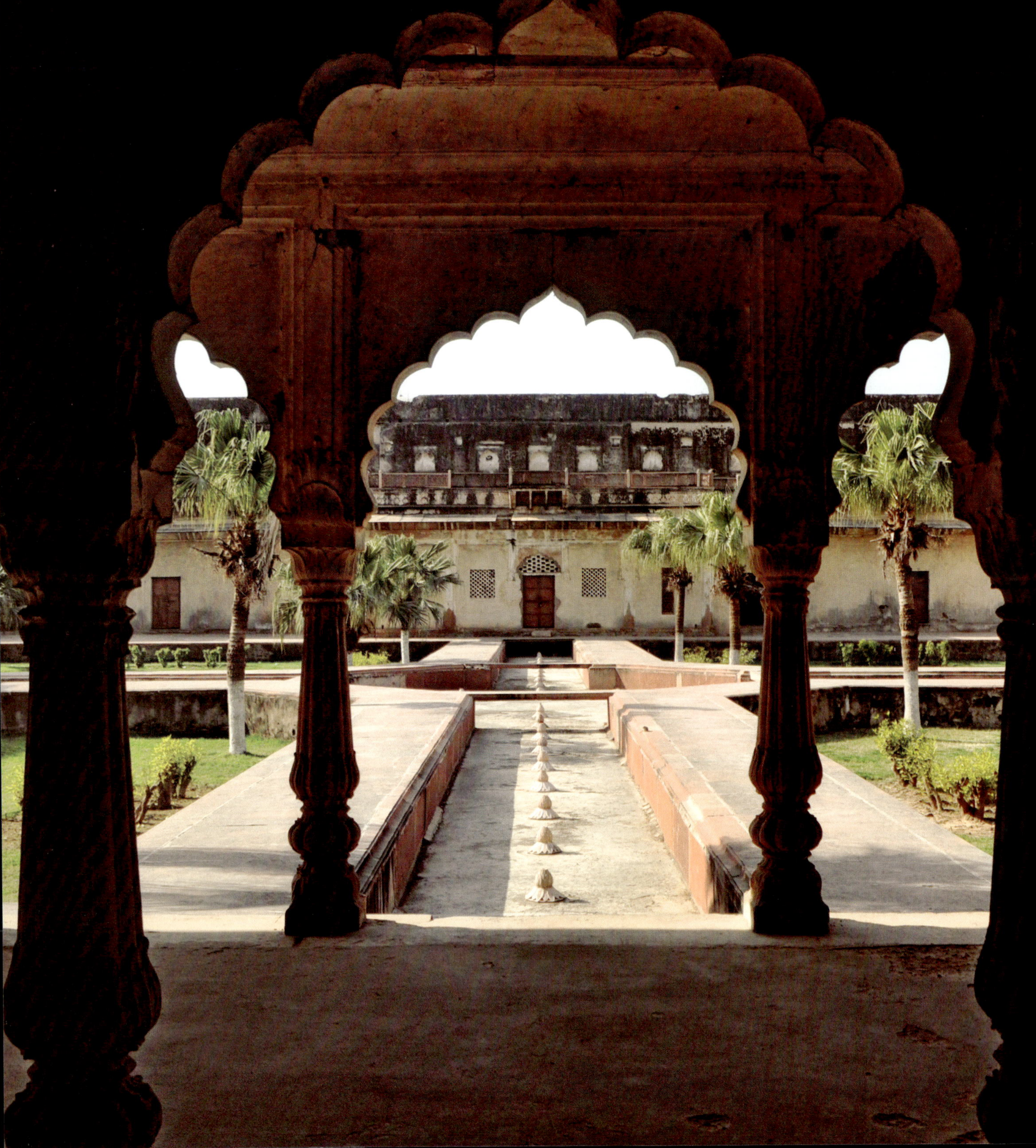

ARCHITECTURAL STYLE AND LAYOUT

CANONICAL PLAY OF THE AXES

Axial Geometry: The layout and positioning of the Deeg Palace complex unfolds some planning principles which are worth mentioning. The bhawans, built in beige-pink stone from Bansi Paharpur, overlooking a spacious garden divided according to the best Charbagh manner into four main squares by raised walkways are consciously defined by axial water channels with fountains. This cross-linear positioning is canonically followed for all the bhawans and Singh Pol. The plan is a cruciform articulation of various major and minor axes.

The major palaces of the Deeg Bhawan complex form a quadrangle. The principal building of the complex is the Gopal Bhawan, west side of which faces a bathing tank called Gopal Sagar. This main palace forms the major focus from which the central linear axis begins. Gopal Bhawan has two buildings—Sawan on the north side and Bhadon on the south side. These open pavilions together with the balconies of Gopal Bhawan form a beautiful waterfront in the Gopal Sagar. The central linear axis originating from Gopal Bhawan moves through the marble swing platform and culminates at Keshav Bhawan complex (*baradari* or pavilion with twelve doors). This *baradari* again overlooks another water tank—the Rup Sagar. A strong geometric blueprint formalises the relationship among the forms and spaces of the various structures within the two extents, i.e., the waterfront buildings of Gopal Sagar and Rup Sagar. Two equivalent superstructures namely the Kishan Bhawan and the Nand Bhawan are arranged symmetrically to balance the distribution of forms and spaces about this axis. Another strong axis is formed with these two buildings at its periphery diagonally cutting across the first axis.

FACING PAGE: *A majestic view of the rearside garden through the elegant arches of Hardev Bhawan*

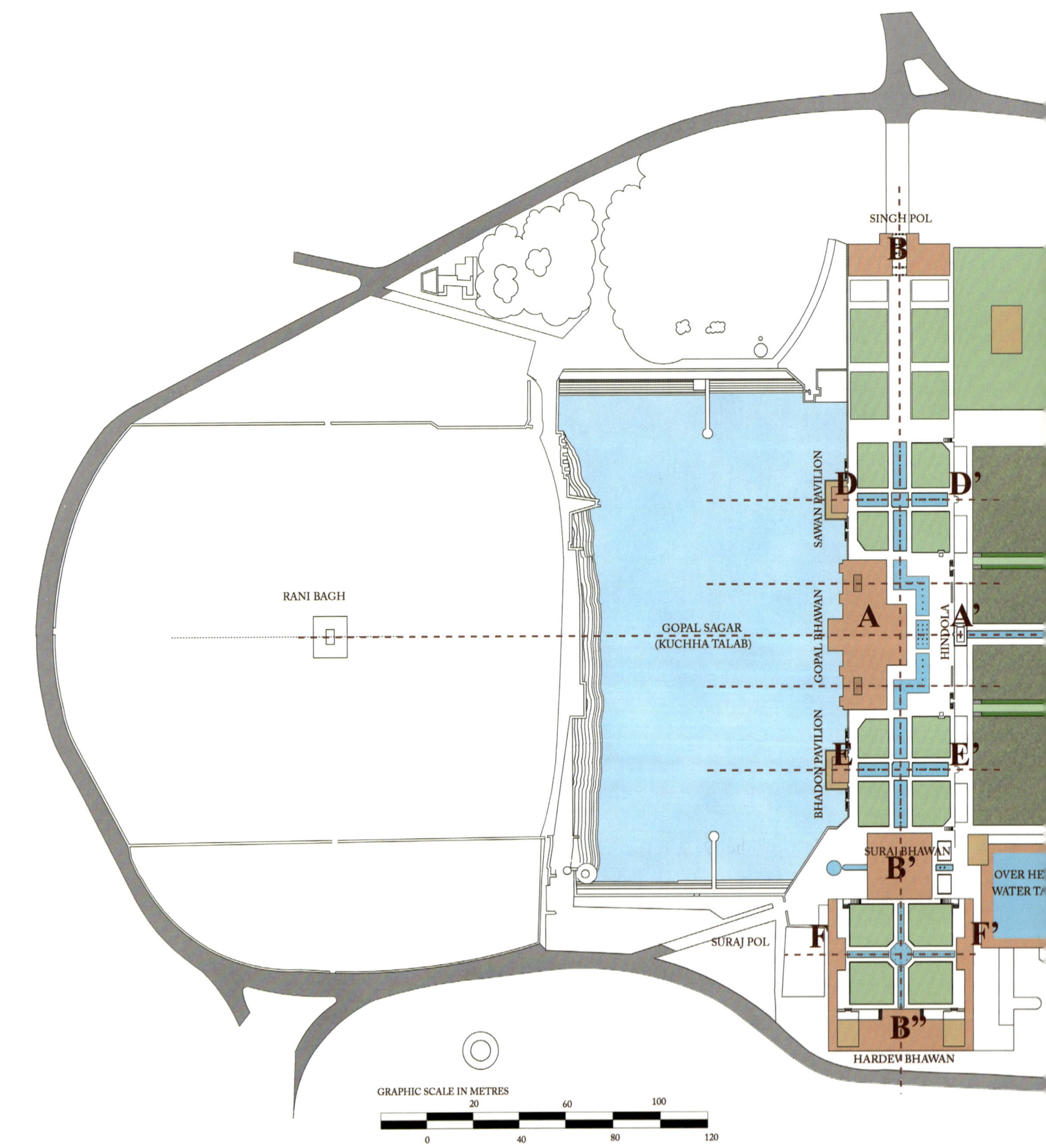
SINGH POL
B
D
D'
SAWAN PAVILION
RANI BAGH
GOPAL SAGAR
(KUCHHA TALAB)
GOPAL BHAWAN
A
A'
HINDOLA
E
E'
BHADON PAVILION
SURAJ BHAWAN
B'
OVER HE
WATER TA
F
F'
SURAJ POL
B''
HARDEV BHAWAN
GRAPHIC SCALE IN METRES
20
60
100
0
40
80
120

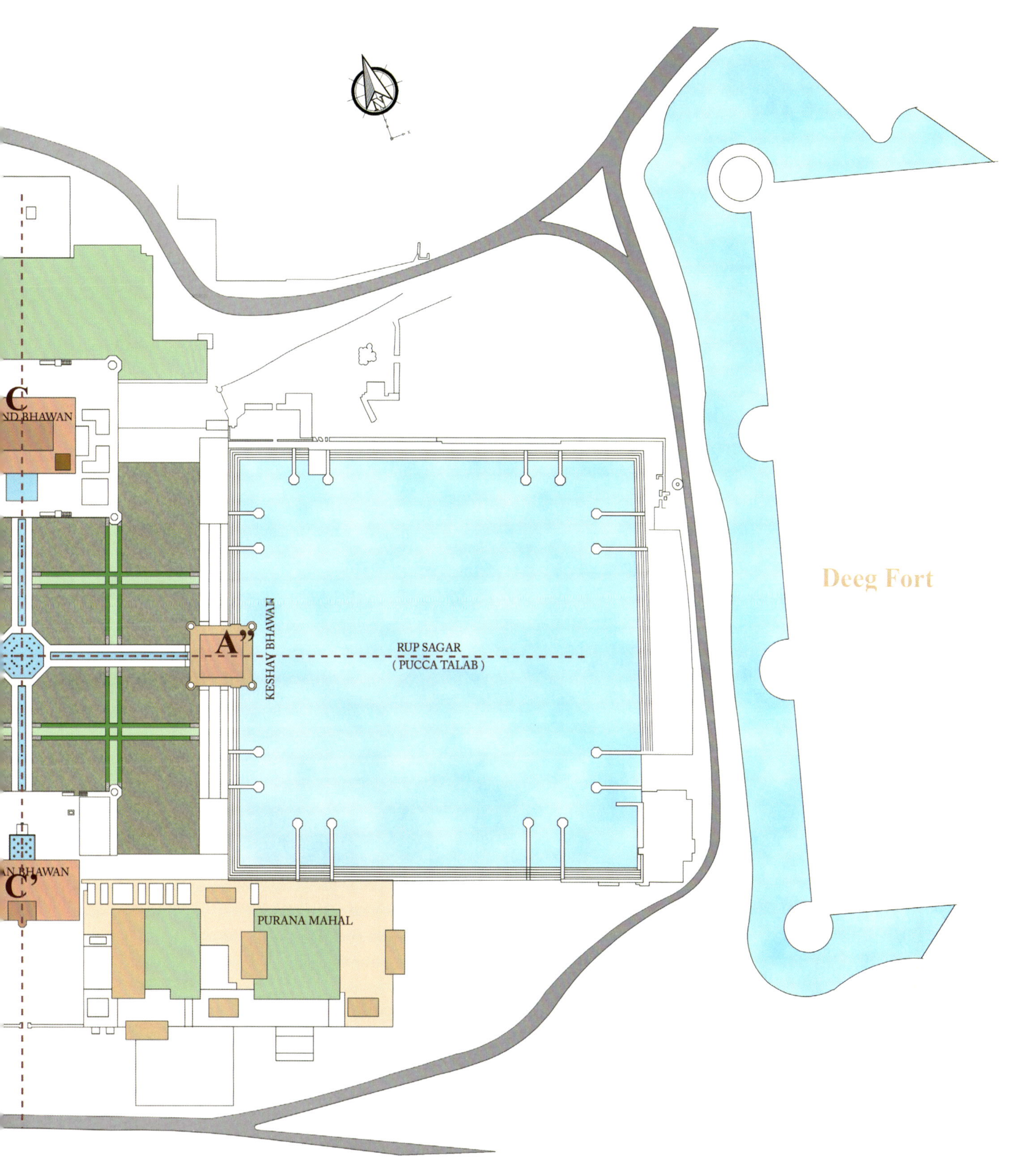

C
ND BHAWAN
A"
KESHAV BHAWAN
RUP SAGAR
(PUCCA TALAB)
Deeg Fort
AN BHAWAN
C'
PURANA MAHAL

At the back of the southern side of the quadrangle are two palaces facing north, namely the Hardev Bhawan and the Suraj Bhawan made of marble. The play of the axial arrangement continues to the placement of these two palaces as well. This is explained in the attached diagram with coordinates.

The node of the complex is a large octagonal pool of size 18m × 18m (62ft × 62ft) with a distinct tall lotus bud feature in the centre. This node is formed by the intersection of two major axis (A-A'-A") and (C-C'). The axis (A-A'-A") is the central linear axis from Gopal Bhawan to Keshav Bhawan or the axis connecting the two water bodies: Gopal Sagar and Rup Sagar. The *hindola* terrace or A' is strategically placed overlooking the sunken garden on the same axis. Towards the west this axis continues even across the Gopal Sagar to the pavilions of Rani Bagh. The perpendicular axis (C-C') connects the two most ornate pavilions: the Nand Bhawan and the Kishan Bhawan. Incidentally the terraces of all the four pavilions at point A, A", C, C' are approximately at same level commanding an all-pervading view of the sunken central greens. The four water channels originate with a spout and a *chini khana* from the base of these four coordinates converging at the central octagonal pool. Visitors are tempted to use the raised walkways created on either side of these water channels. The walk is made more interesting by the connecting bridges on the water channel which give shape to the central octagonal feature.

A third axis (B-B'-B") is formed by the water channel starting from the Singh Pol which negotiates a rectangular bend in front of the Gopal Bhawan to meet at its axial counterpart the Suraj Bhawan. Visually, the Suraj Bhawan is directly connected to the Singh Pol through the projected veranda of the Gopal Bhawan. The same axis B-B' continues on the other side of the Suraj Bhawan to Hardev Bhawan (B") where a beautiful Charbagh with an octagonal pool is revealed. A perpendicular axis F-F' from this pool focusses at the other two pavilions of the Hardev Bhawan complex. Similarly an axis connects the Suraj Bhawan to the water tank towards Suraj Pol and Suraj Bhawan Annexe on its opposite side.

Two more parallel axes originating from the Sawan and Bhadon pavilion diagonally intersects the axis B-B'. The axis D-D' originating from the Sawan pavilion to the *kamal burjis* (D') also points to the scalloped, melon-shaped corner projections of the Nand Bhawan terrace. Similarly, the axis E-E' originating from the Bhadon pavilion to its respective *kamal burjis* points to the corner projections of the Kishan Bhawan.

The strong axial hierarchy points to a very important fact that although the Deeg Palace construction continued for more than half a century, the planning of its founders based on the geometry of axial directions was not challenged but very ritualistically followed by the various successors.

Mandalas: One cannot fail noticing the occasional formation of strong Hindu mandalas in the architecture and planning. The makers of the palace were not very

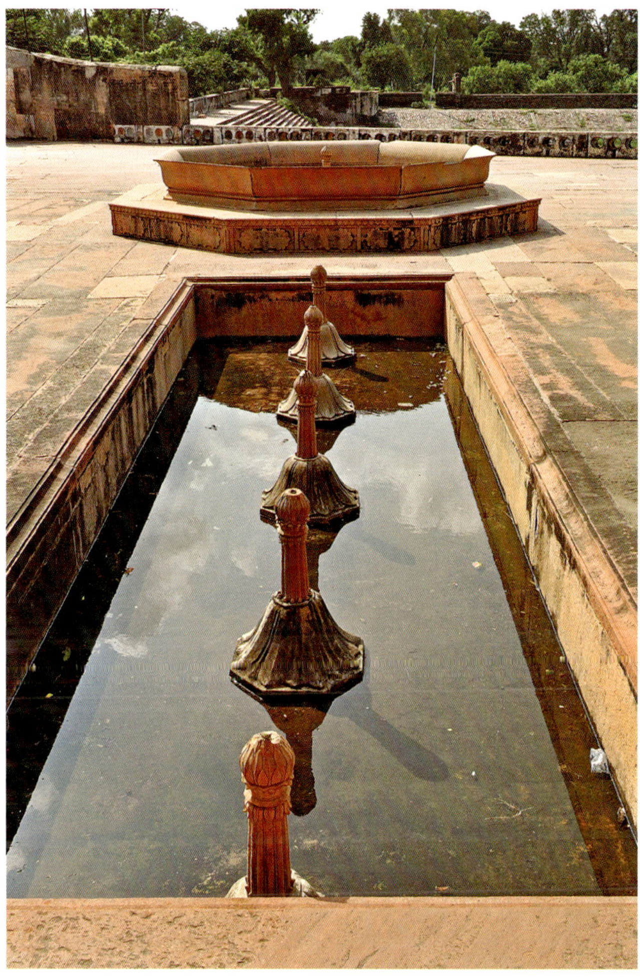

Above: *Micro level maintenance of axis*

Previous pages: *Layout plan of the Deeg Palace complex showing the play of the axes*

well educated and relied heavily on Brahmins and priests for interpretations. A week long puja was conducted before the making of the Bharatpur Palace. Thus it is obvious that the Hindu planning principles would have an impact on the design and architecture. This may have been deliberate or subconscious. According to the Indian texts on *Vastu Shilpa Shastra*, a *vastu purush* mandala is used to develop the architecture plans. A *purusha* is seated within a mandala symbolising the supreme *atman*. Various configurations are created within this enclosure by the subdivisions of the square in order to create the desired special configurations.

It is seen that an effort is being made to arrive at a square and also to make a plan based on division of the square. The two most obvious examples are the Suraj Bhawan and Keshav Bhawan. In case of the Keshav Bhawan, a series of circumambulations are achieved around a central square. The plan seems to be based on seven to nine divisions of a square. Similarly, the Suraj Bhawan when seen in plan shows nine divisions on each face, although not equal. In both these structures, the central area or the *brahmasthan* is given utmost importance. In the Suraj Bhawan, it is a dark chamber resembling the *garbhagriha* of a temple plan while in Keshav Bhawan, a pleasant platform traps cool air and heat inside it depending on the climate. In winter, it traps a warmer climate inside and in summer, it traps cool air inside. It is the most energy-efficient structure of the mandalas. Various other squares also emerge as seen in the proportions of the Hardev Bhawan together with its gardens.

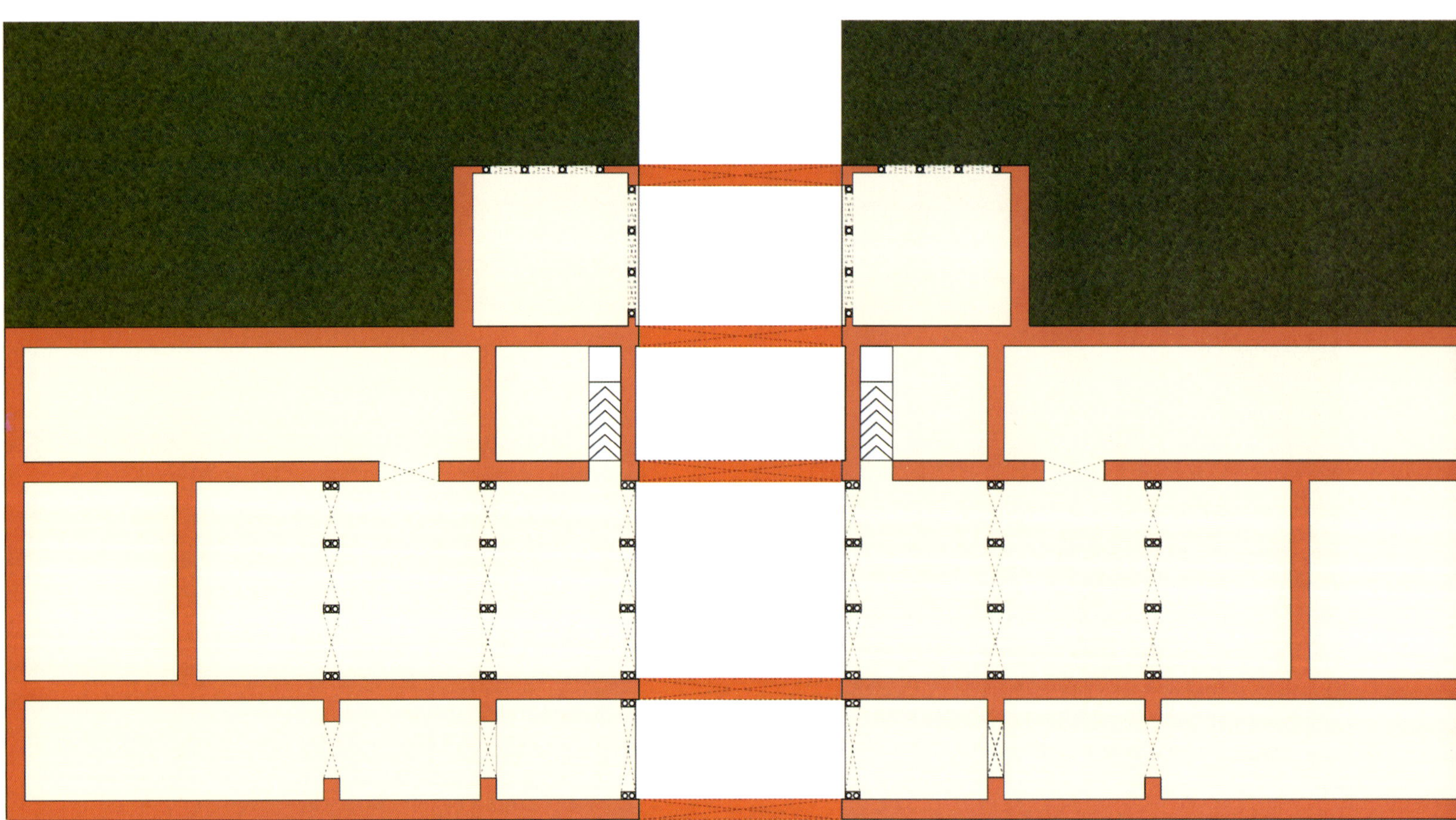
Entry from the road side
Inside of the palace complex

ROARING GATE
SINGH POL

Singh Pol is the magnificent entrance gate to the mystery of the Deeg Palace. Built in the tradition of the arched entrances of the Islamic Mughal tombs, it echoes the European tradition of building arches to commemorate certain occasions (Fig. 2). One of the inspirations could be the marble arch of London which was built as ceremonial entrance to the courtyard of the new Buckingham Palace in 1826 and traditionally only members of the Royal family and the King's Troop, Royal Horse Artillery, were allowed to pass through the arch in ceremonial processions. The theory of European influence is further strengthened by the fact that the gate was built in the early 20th century as opposed to the rest of the structure built in the 18th century. The Maharaja of Bharatpur was among the exhibitors in the Indian section of the Imperial Exhibition held as part of the Festival of Empire, in 1911 at the Crystal Palace in London to mark the coronation of King George V.

Another European feature is the presence of the coat of arms of Bharatpur state which was awarded by the Royal family of England. The Bharatpur coat of arms, a deviation from the usual Rajput designs featuring either the sun or the moon, had none of these. This coat of arms features a shield flanked by a lion and an elephant. A bull is engraved within the shield signifying piety, with two crossed daggers on either side. Crowning the shield is the monkey god Hanuman's flag. The emblem is held by the figures of two lions in relief with one of their forepaws raised. This occurs above the central arch of the main entrance facade. This is also called the *lion passant guardant* or the leopard and is a symbol of British Royalty. The lions give the name Singh Pol (Lion Gate) to the structure.

Facing page (Fig. 1): *Layout plan of the Singh Pol which is the main entrance to the Deeg Palace complex*

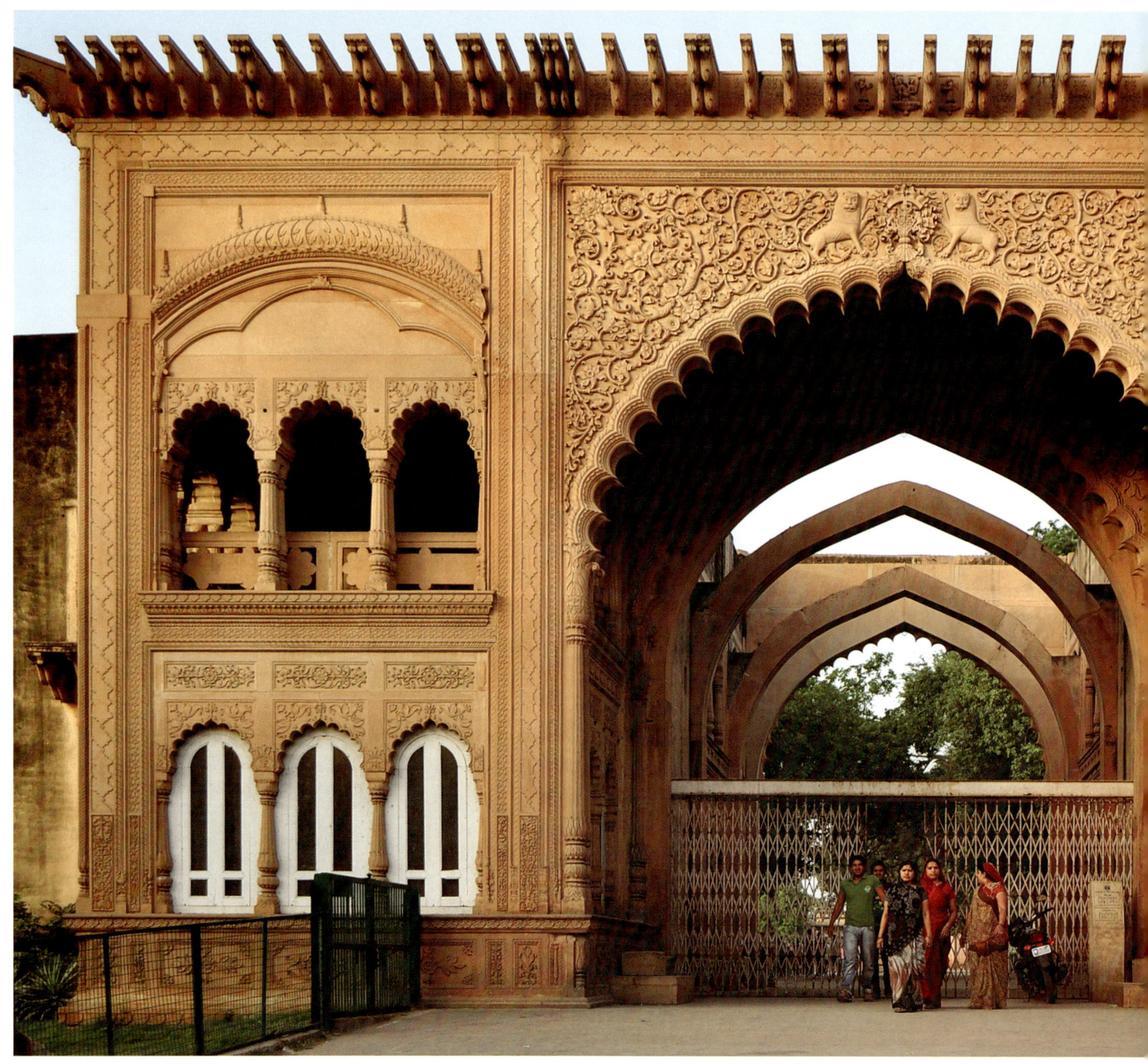

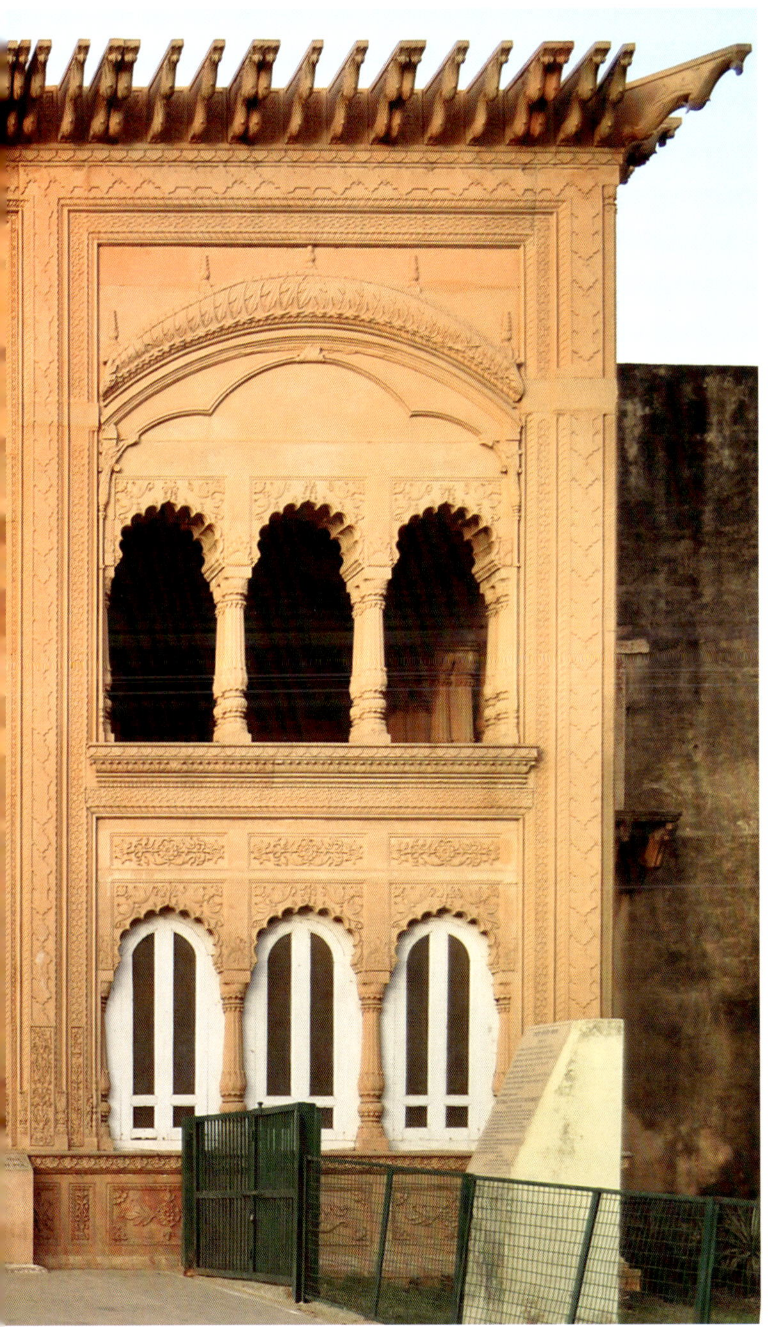

A significant coincidence is the occurrence of similarly carved lions with their forepaws raised at the entrance of its contemporary: the Shahji temple of Vrindavan built in 1866. Another noteworthy example is that of the elevation of the entrance gate for the Rangji temple at Vrindavan, which again echoes the same feeling as the facade of Singh Pol. In fact, the entire Braj region also went through several architectural metamorphoses linked to the political scenarios during the time.

All through the European influence the builder did not lose sight of his Indian connections. The central, double height carved arch of the facade is inspired by the Mughal arabesque. But it is predominantly a Hindu design because of the depiction of mythological figures. On both sides of the front arch there are mythological creatures—the *makar* that form a part of the radical cartouche carving. A *makar* has the head of a crocodile, the body of a reptile, a tail of foliage and is symbolic of the zodiac sign Capricorn, sometimes also depicted as the vehicle of the river goddess Ganga. The two *makars*, juxtaposed as depicted on the arch, are considered a symbol of fertility and good health. These *makars* are shown emitting intertwined vines forming branched floral patterns as well as a floral cartouche between them. (Fig. 3)

Presiding on the gate between the brackets is the carved image of the elephant-headed god Ganesha

Left (Fig. 2): *The Singh Pol hints at the splendid Indian stone art expressed on a Western framework*

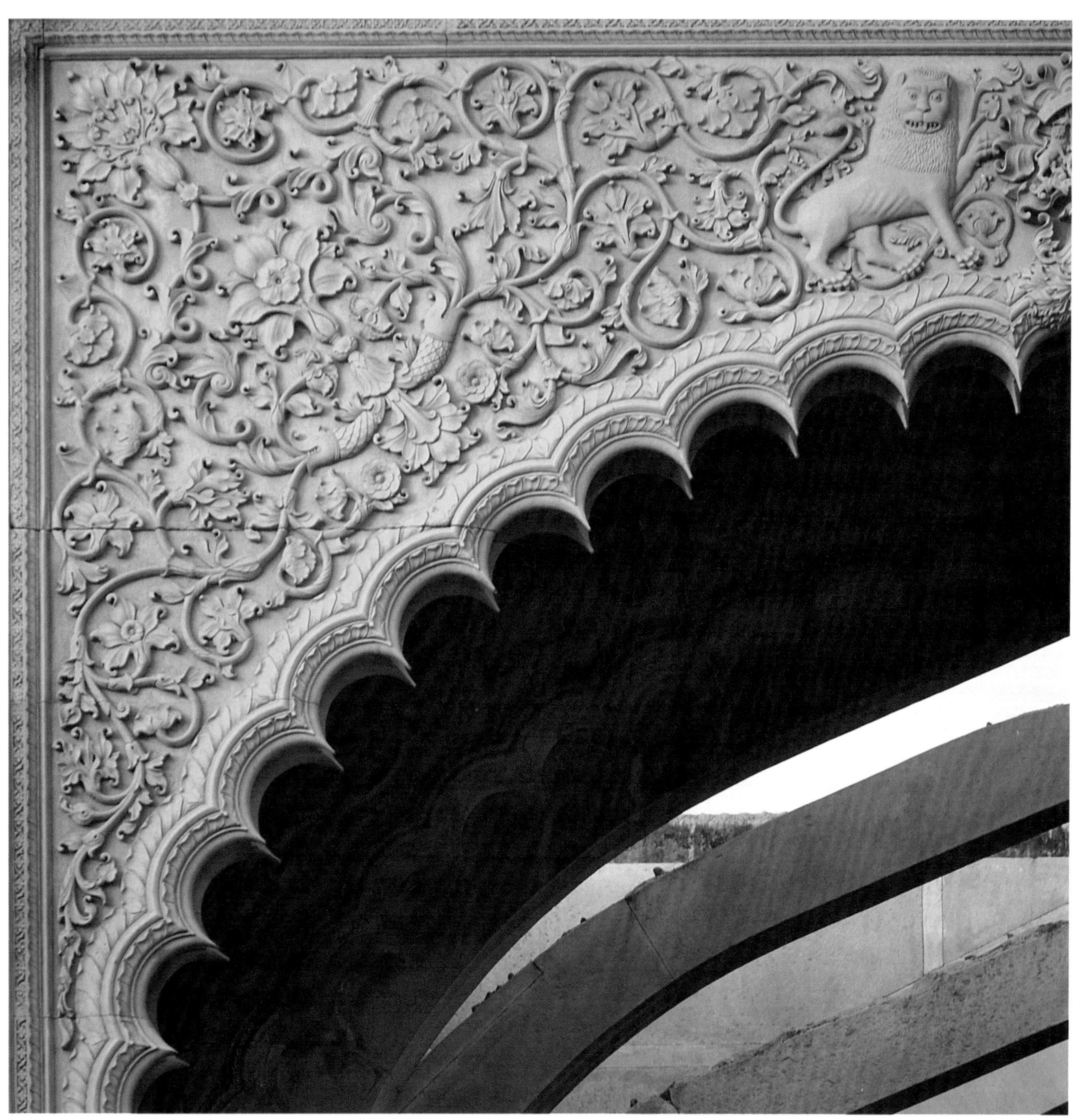

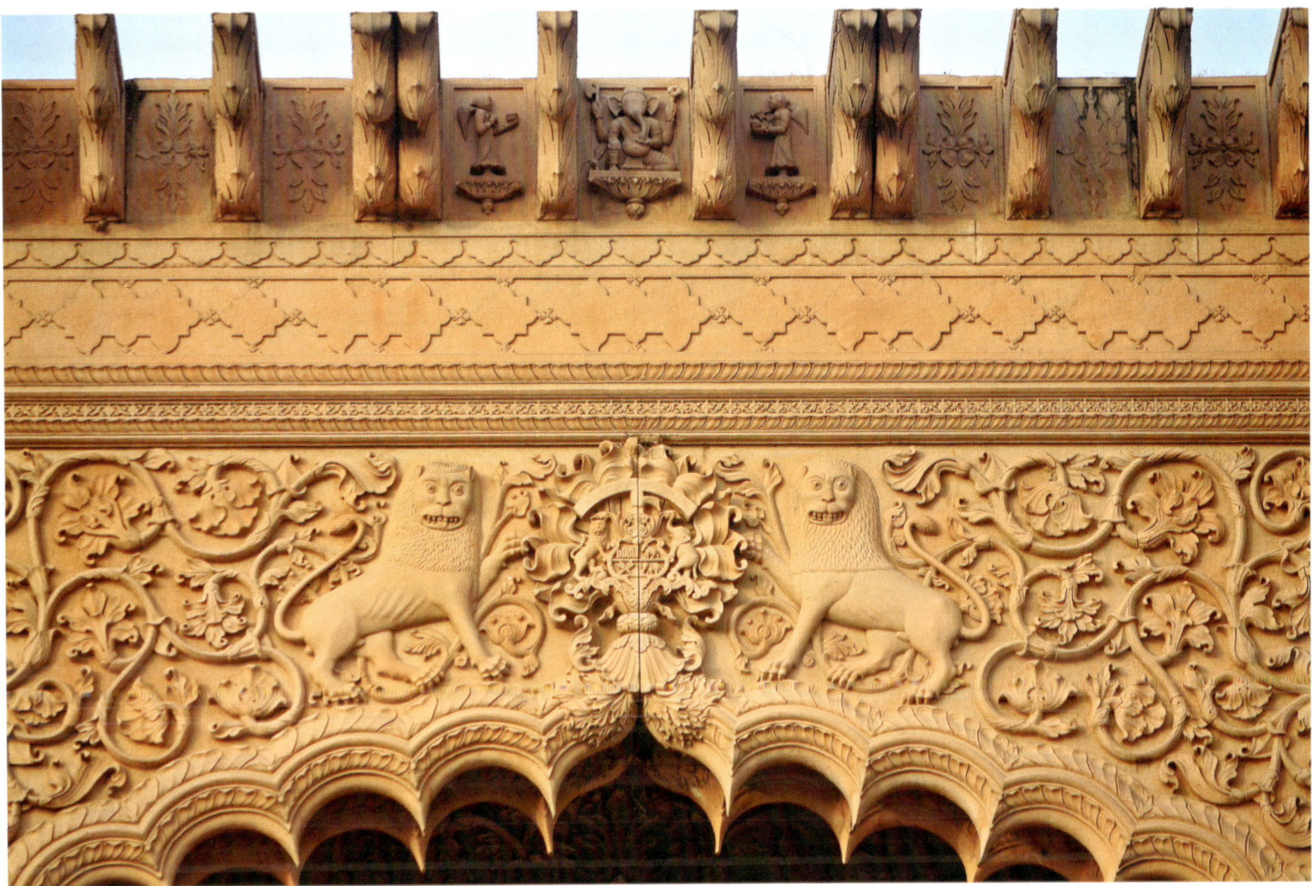

flanked by his consorts Riddhi and Siddhi. The four-handed Ganesha is depicted in sitting position with his *vahana* 'mushak', the rat, placed close to his feet. The symbolism of this is not lost on anyone as Lord Ganesha is always honoured at the beginning of rituals and ceremonies. He is widely revered as the 'Remover of Obstacles' and more generally as 'Lord of Beginnings'. Hence, he holds the prime position on the zenith of the entrance arch. His depiction along with Riddhi (goddess of wealth and prosperity) and

Above (Fig. 4): *Lord Ganesha, with his consorts Riddhi and Siddhi, presides on the incomplete* chhajja *eave. Two lions guard the Bharatpur coat of arms adorning the central arch of the main entrance*

Facing page (Fig. 3): *Mythological* makars *are interwoven in the arabesque of the radical cartouche carving at the spandrels*

Siddhi (goddess of intellectual and spiritual powers) has the additional significance of being bringer of success and wisdom. (Fig. 4)

The deity of the region, Lord Krishna, is depicted on either side of the inside secondary arch. The cowherd Krishna is depicted in a graceful tri-bent mudra playing

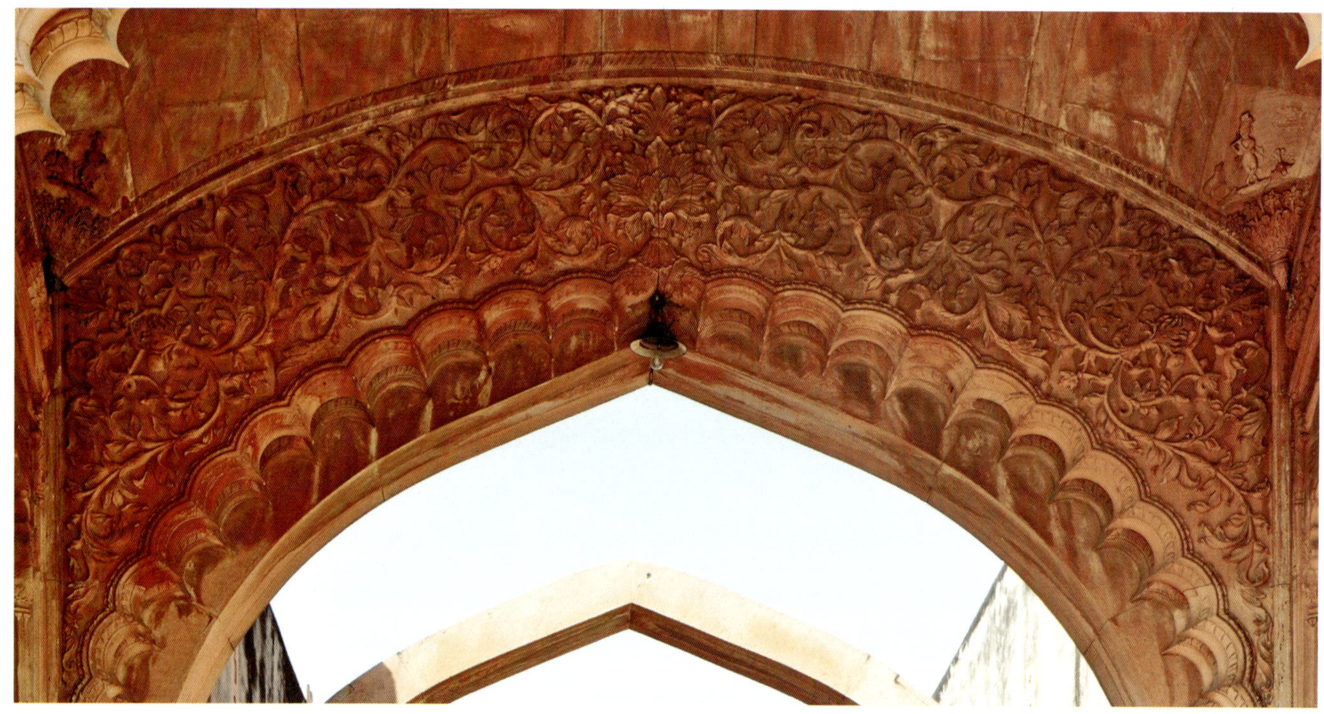

Above (Fig. 5): *The secondary, inner cusped arch, supported on pointed arches depicts Lord Krishna on either side*

Facing page (Fig. 6): *A* bangladar jharokha *crowns the triple-arched balcony on each side of the facade*

a flute, enchanting a cow and peacock. The cow here is manifested as the *kamadhuk* meaning *kamadhenu*, the wish-fulfilling cow. Cows are considered auspicious, sacred and as the bestowers of blessings. While the peacock is considered as a possessor of some of the most admired human characteristics of beauty and knowledge, it is also symbolic of glory, immortality, royalty and incorruptibility. (Fig. 5)

The main entrance facade of the Singh Pol is broadly divided into three vertical parts—the central cusped arch and a double-storeyed composition of layers of triple arches occurring on either side. The row of the triple arches on the upper floor forms an opening that resembles a balcony with a typical Bengal *jharokha* above, all in relief. The whole ensemble is carried around and repeated on either sides of the entrance bay, which becomes apparent as one enters the gateway. (Fig. 6) Even the balcony formed below the *chhatri* does not have a cantilever and is more like a relief feature on the facade. The rows of triple arches on the ground floor are now covered with wooden shutters, which is a recent addition.

On analysis, an interesting feature of the facade is revealed. It is in compliance to the proportions of 'phi'

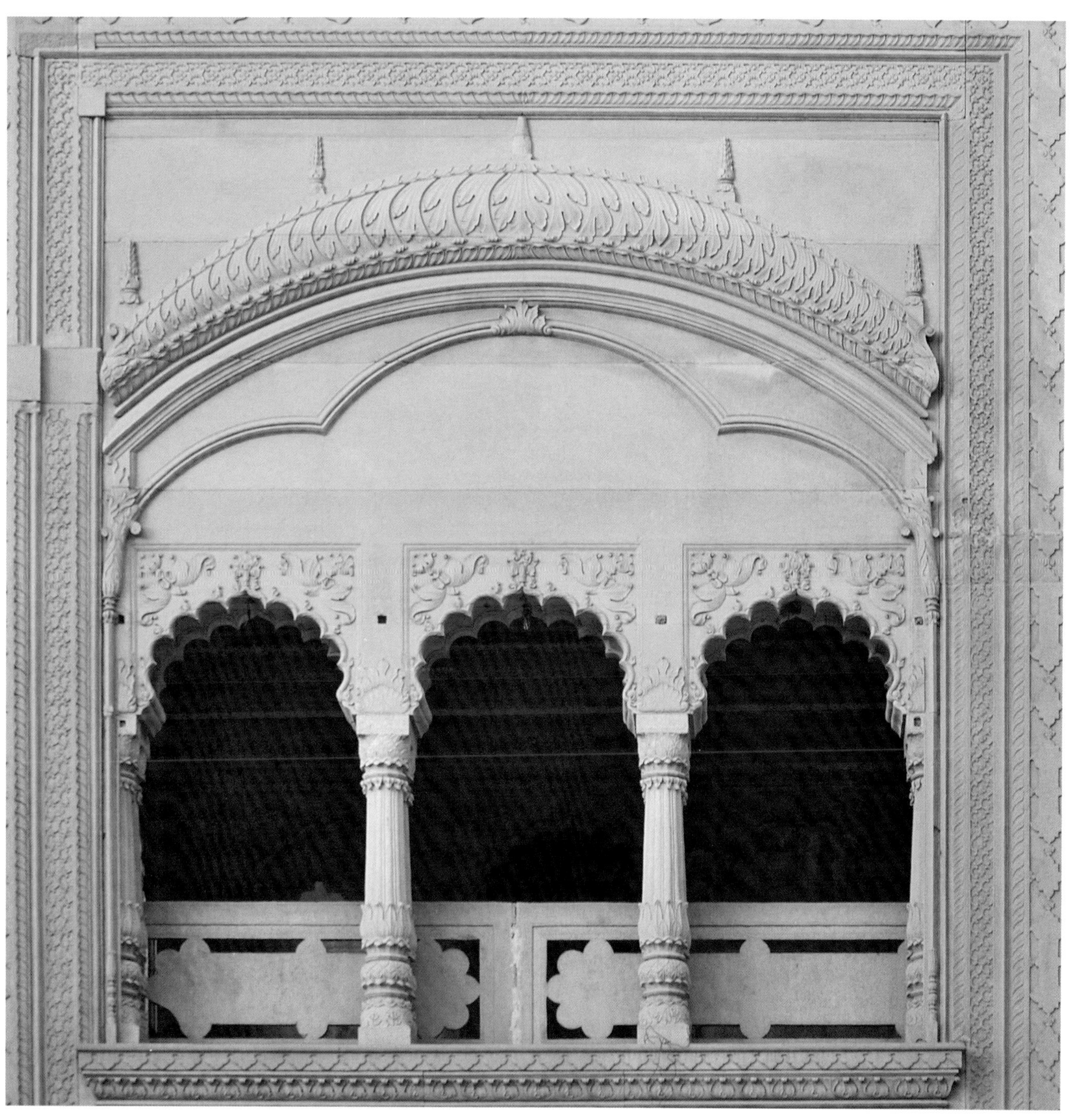

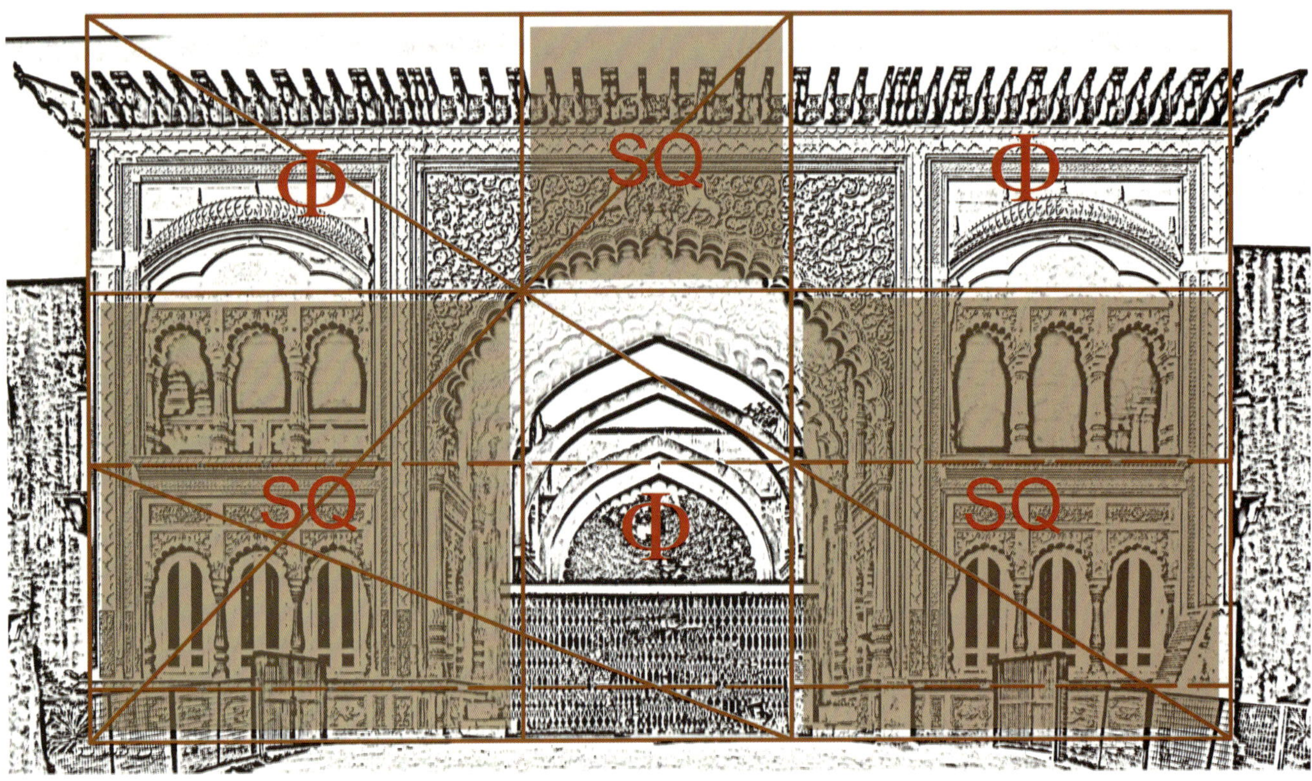

(Φ) described by Johannes Kepler as being one of the two treasures of geometry together with the Pythaogoras theorem. This 'golden rectangular rule' ('golden ratio') has been seen applied from ancient times by the Greeks in the Parthenon to the Taj Mahal in modern times. The graphical section illustrates and analyses the use of the golden ratio in the proportioning of the facade of the Singh Pol, which is very similar to the proportions of the Parthenon at Athens (447–432 BC). (Fig. 7)

The lower panels of the gate facade are intricately carved in marble and articulate around the baluster columns. Vertical vines comprising of a variety of floral leaves, tendrils and peacocks are carved. These panels continue vertically with the geometrically carved border. The frame of the arch is carved with an acanthus scroll along with the carved border. (Fig. 8)

Above the arch there are projecting brackets which may have supported *chhajja* eaves but were left incomplete due to certain reasons. The terrace of the building seems to never have gone beyond the fixing of these brackets. As one moves towards the palace from Singh Pol, the first block has ramps on either side going to underground chambers. These underground chambers were important for protection from heat as well as for storing goods.

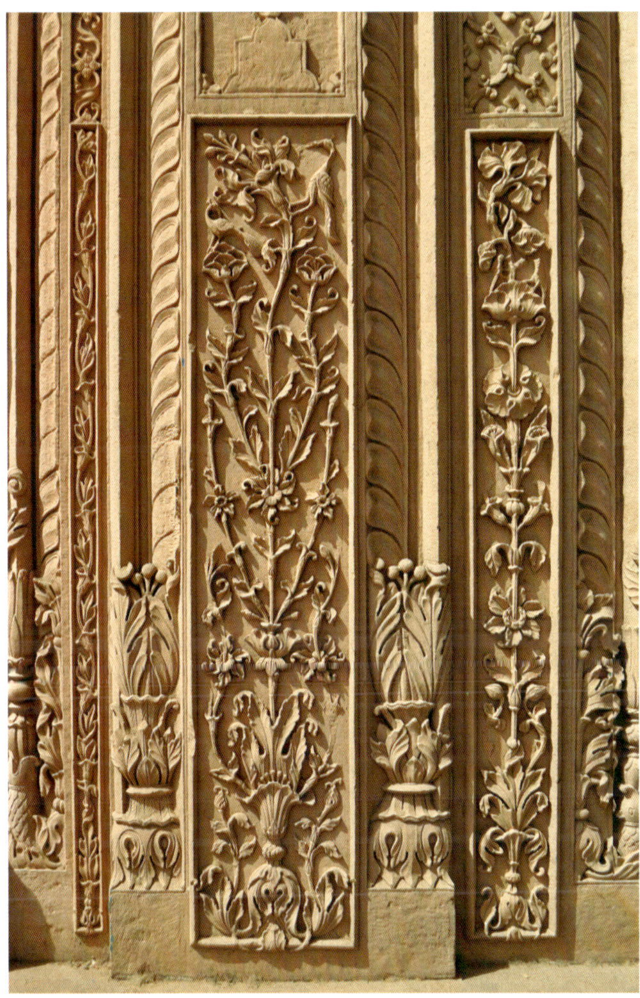

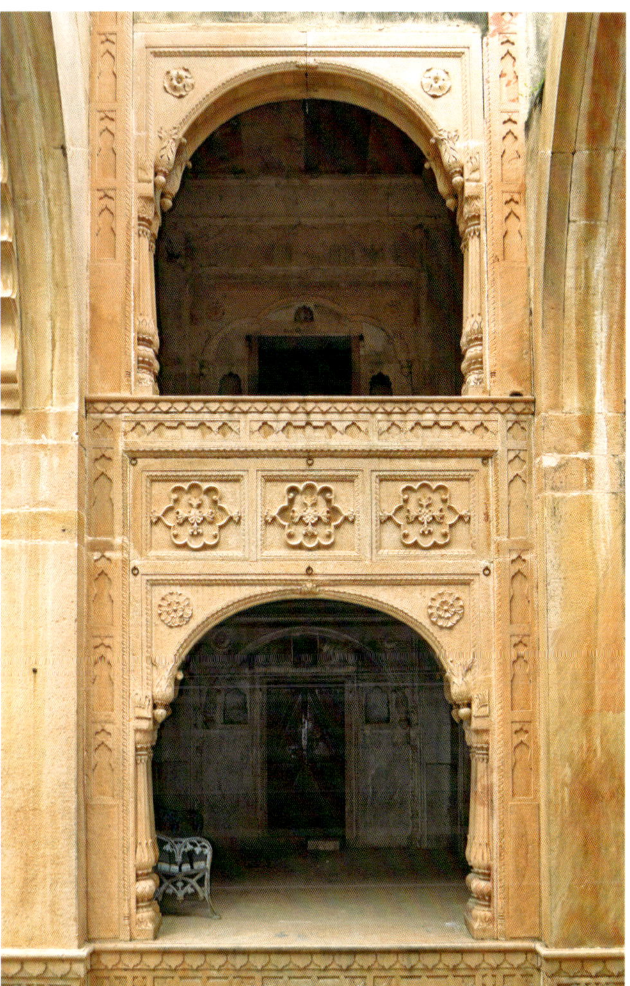

Above (Fig. 10): *Cartouches carved in counter-relief frame the decorative archways on the side of the vestibule bays*

Above left (Fig. 8): *Elaborate and intricately carved lower panels forming vertical lines comprising of flowers, vines and peacocks*

Facing page (Fig. 7): *The analogy of 'phi' and square in the proportioning of the facade of the Singh Pol is similar to the Parthenon in Athens*

On entering the gate it is seen that the rear superstructure of the entrance vestibule comprises of three more bays, the vestibule of which was never roofed. One can still see free-standing structural skeletons of pointed arches, without spandrels, made in stone. In fact the same skeleton framework has been used to mount the decorative arched panels in the front and back of the gateway. All the arches are made of stone using concealed joints. The entrance bay

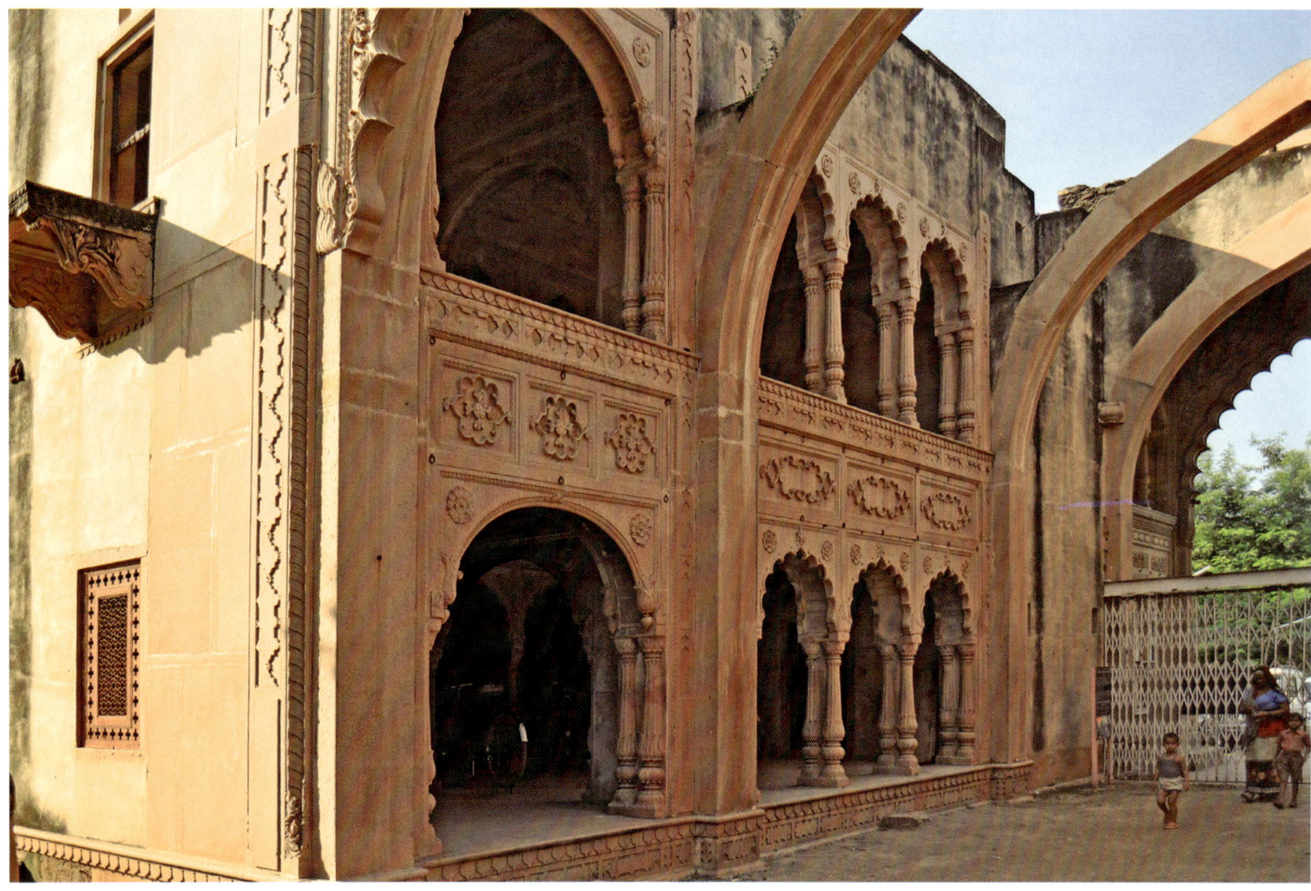

is about 6 metres wide. The arches are buttressed by a colonnaded arcade on either side. (Fig. 9)

The first bay after the entrance has blank walls flanking either side while the second bay has triple-arched forecourts on both the ground and the first floor. This is adorned with various elements of design such as carved double-shaft columns with high relief acanthus capitals, engrailed arches with lotus medallions carved on spandrels and carved Mughal cartouches with cusped patterns in mid-relief. The framing is done by similar cartouches carved in counter-relief as well as carved acanthus scrolls. (Fig. 10) A decorative frieze carved with inverted miniatures engrailed arched patterns with bull-nose moulding adds a distinctive feature to the raised platform.

The use of decorative step stones (*chowkis*) to climb on the plinth, which are commonly found all around the complex, begins here. These become elaborate inside and transform into proper *chowkis*. Iron rings are prefixed all over the facades to facilitate hanging of

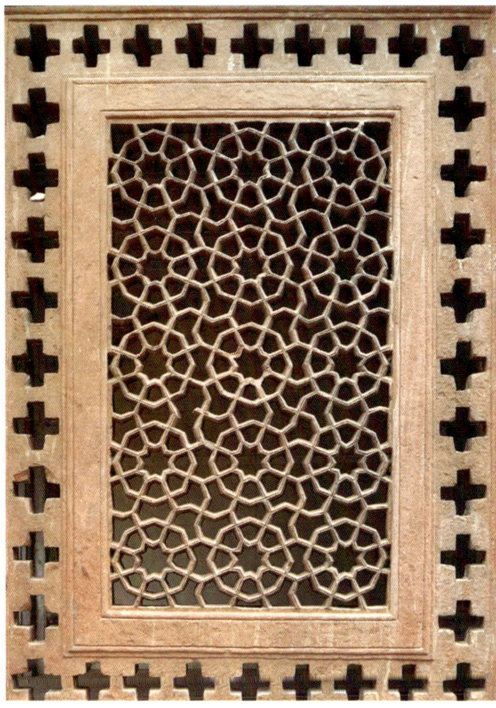

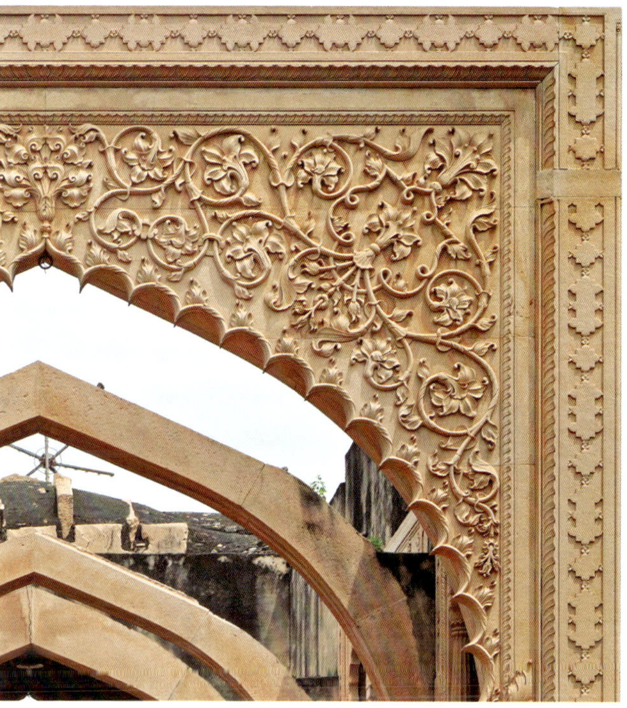

shamianas or possibly muslin curtains for womenfolk who would shower the kings with flower petals during processions and ceremonies. The character of the triple arch suddenly changes to a semicircular, single arch with carved buds in the last bay. Behind these on either side there are series of well-built antechambers. These are now being used as the offices of the Archaeological Survey of India (ASI). The decorative elements inside include bird-shaped brackets on either side of the opening to hang lamps. The plinth comprises of an inverted, cusped, arched border with a cartouche panel at the base. This projecting cartouche becomes a recessed cartouche in the ornamentation of the upper-storey crenulations.

Above **(Fig. 11):** *A majestic view of the details of the inside arch carving of Singh Pol from the gardens*

Left **(Fig. 12):** *One of the two* jalis *of red sandstone, with a design of octagons and eight-pointed stars, adorns the rear walls of the archway*

Facing page **(Fig. 9):** *Decorative side walls of the vestibule bays*

Turning back after crossing the complete vestibule, one can devour another majestic view of the meticulously carved archway with a series of pointed arcuate skeletons in the background. The carving on this arch is typical Mughal arabesque. Each cusp of the arch unfolds a carved rolling out leaf (Fig. 11). There are also two outstanding *jalis* finely carved out of red sandstone in a skilfully balanced design of octagons and eight-pointed stars embellished on the plain walls on either side of this archway. (Fig. 12)

Facade on Gopal Sagar

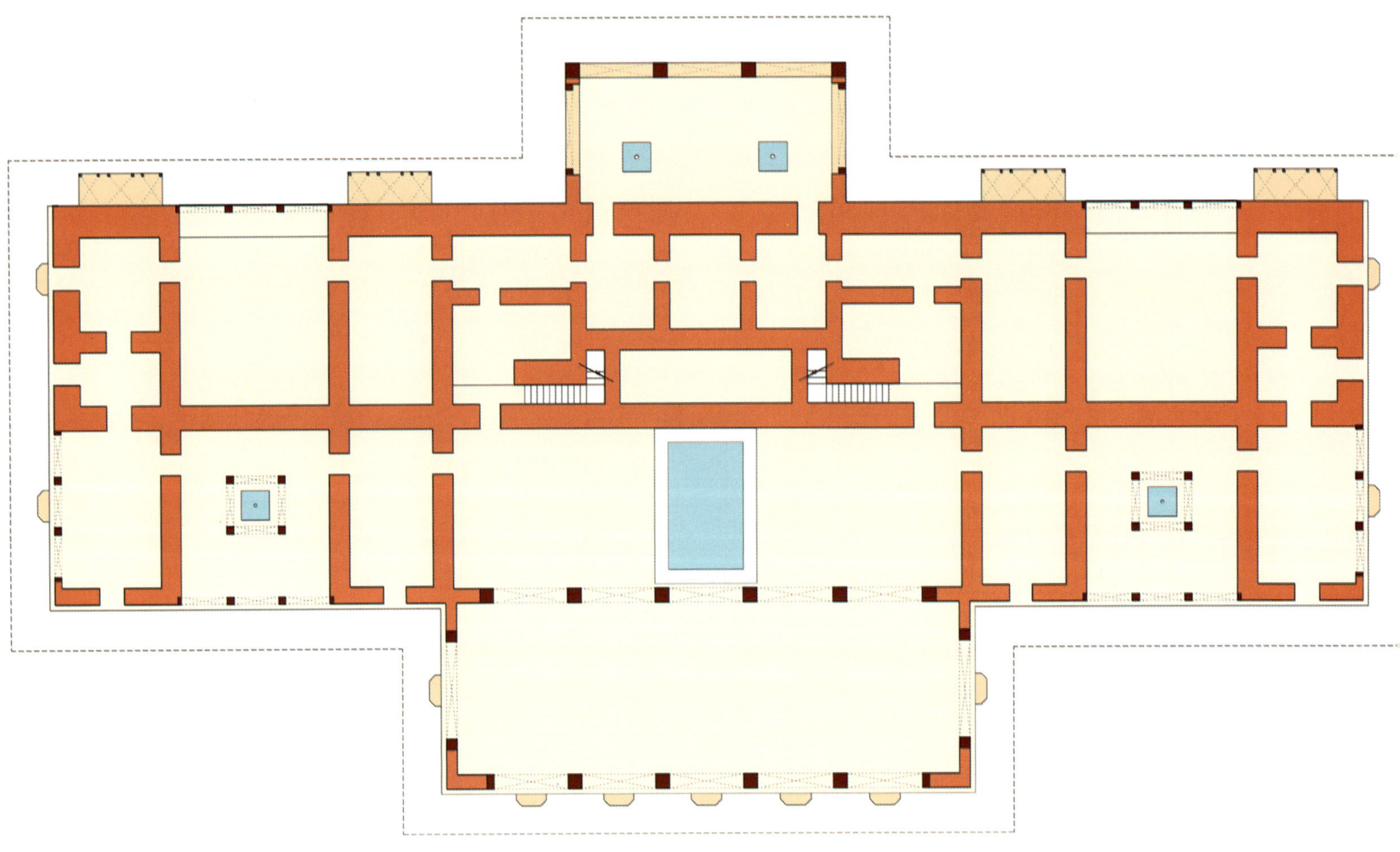

Entrance arcade facing the Hindola

GRAND RECEPTION
GOPAL BHAWAN

Gopal Bhawan, though named such, because of its connection with Brajbhumi, was in appearance and function more closely linked to the Diwan-i-Aam of the Mughal Emperor Shah Jahan.

Gopal Bhawan is the largest building of the Deeg complex. Its imposing dimensions not only make it a dominating feature, but also establish its primary functions as the 'Hall of Public Audience' and the palace of the maharaja. It was probably built with the aim of making it the principal palace of Suraj Mal in this otherwise summer retreat. It was a complete palace in terms of its having residential quarters as well as a reception hall.

It seems that Suraj Mal had the image of Shah Jahan's Agra Fort in mind as he went about building the structure. The layout of the Gopal Bhawan along with its flanking two pavilions is inspired by the waterfront elevation of Khas Mahal at Agra Fort. The Khas Mahal consists of three pavilions standing on a plinth overlooking the river Yamuna. The central pavilion being an airy edifice has three arches on each side, five in front and two turrets rising out of the roof. It was exclusively used by the emperor or his family as a sleeping chamber or *aramgah*. It is flanked by two pavilions with curved *bangladar* roofs and finials on either side. One of the two side buildings was Shah Burj which was used for *jharokha darshan*. This panoramic formation also overlooks a water pool and the Anguri Bagh, with a fountain on the opposite side.

Similarly, the Gopal Bhawan is placed on a raised terrace and is entered through a five-arched opening. It is the chief palace of the emperor and also has the private chambers of the king and queen. (Fig. 2) Gopal Bhawan has two pavilions—Sawan and Bhadon—

Facing page (Fig. 1): *Layout plan of the Gopal Bhawan*

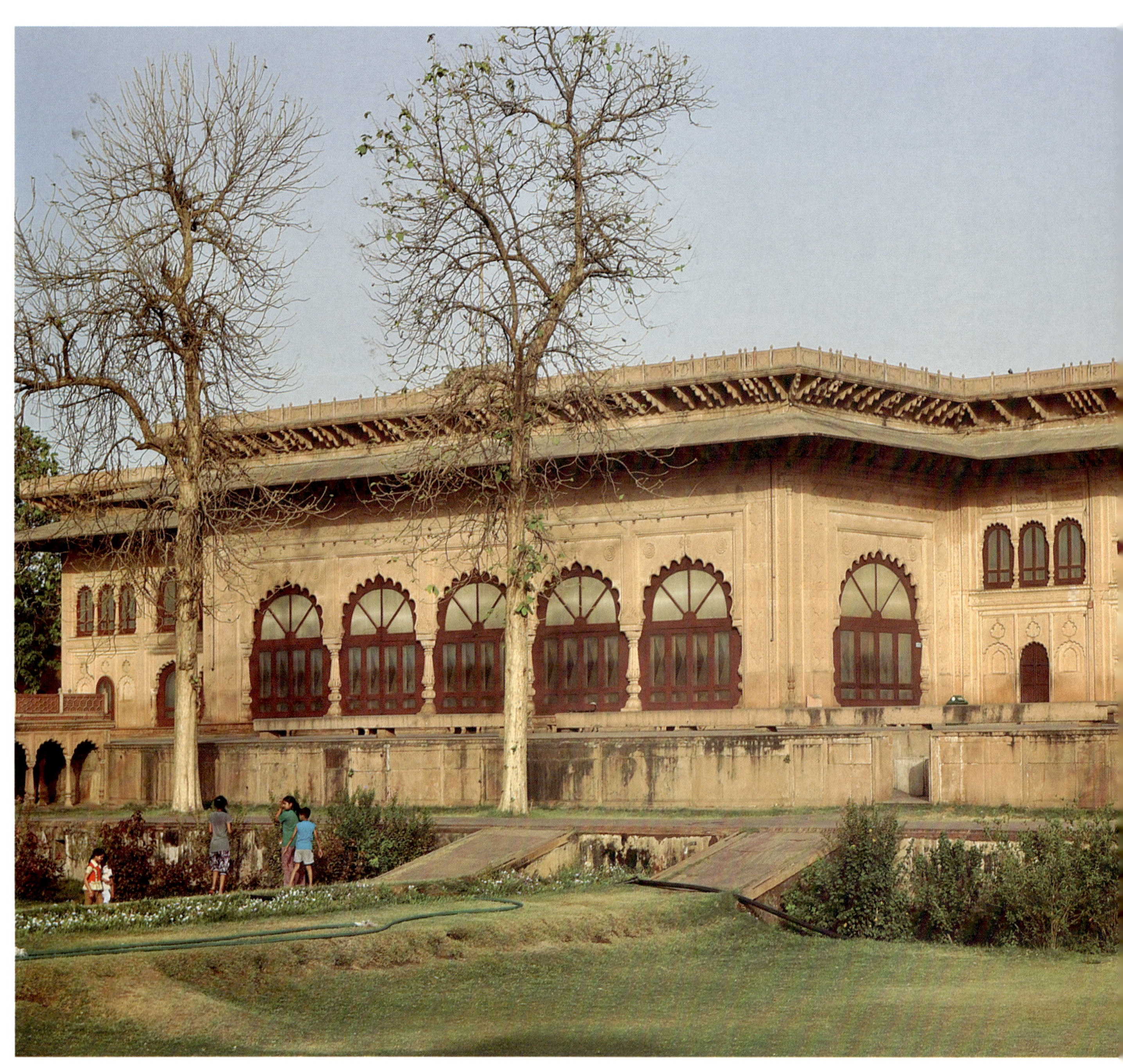

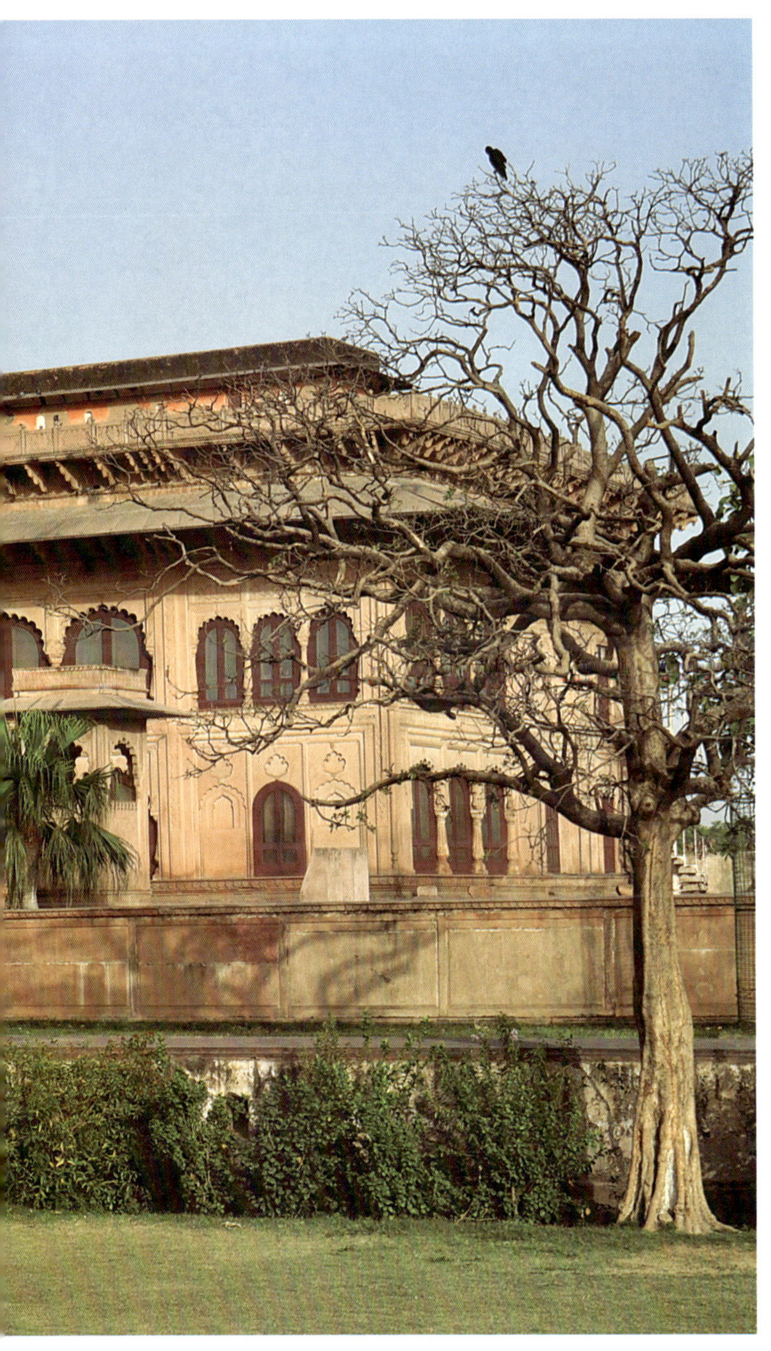

flanking it on both the sides. Just like the two buildings of Khas Mahal they have curved sloping *bangladar* roofs with finials. This whole vista overlooks the Charbagh with its central or main waterway and fountain. The western side overlooking the Gopal Sagar completes the Khas Mahal view of the Yamuna.

Architecturally in top view, two central projections mark the oblong plan on the eastern and western facade of the Gopal Bhawan. The prominent protrusion on the eastern side is the half portion of the five-arched double height reception hall, whereas the subtle projection on the western side is the double height dining hall. The rest of the palace has various rooms spread across two levels. This skilful duplex planning interweaves the levels in a tantalising play of spatial arrangements cleverly divided into private and public areas. The Gopal Bhawan when seen from the eastern side or the garden is a single-storeyed structure, resolving into a double-storeyed structure from the middle on either side. The same set of buildings when seen from the western side or across the Gopal Sagar come across as a four-storeyed structure having two more storeys below the ground level. (Fig. 3)

The rectangular projection of the reception hall has a massive pool with fountains in the front. It seems that the entrance was planned from the side arches. (Fig. 4) There are five large and prominent cusped arches on the entrance face of the 'Hall of Audience'.

Left (**Fig. 2**): *Picturesque view of the majestic Gopal Bhawan from the central sunken gardens*

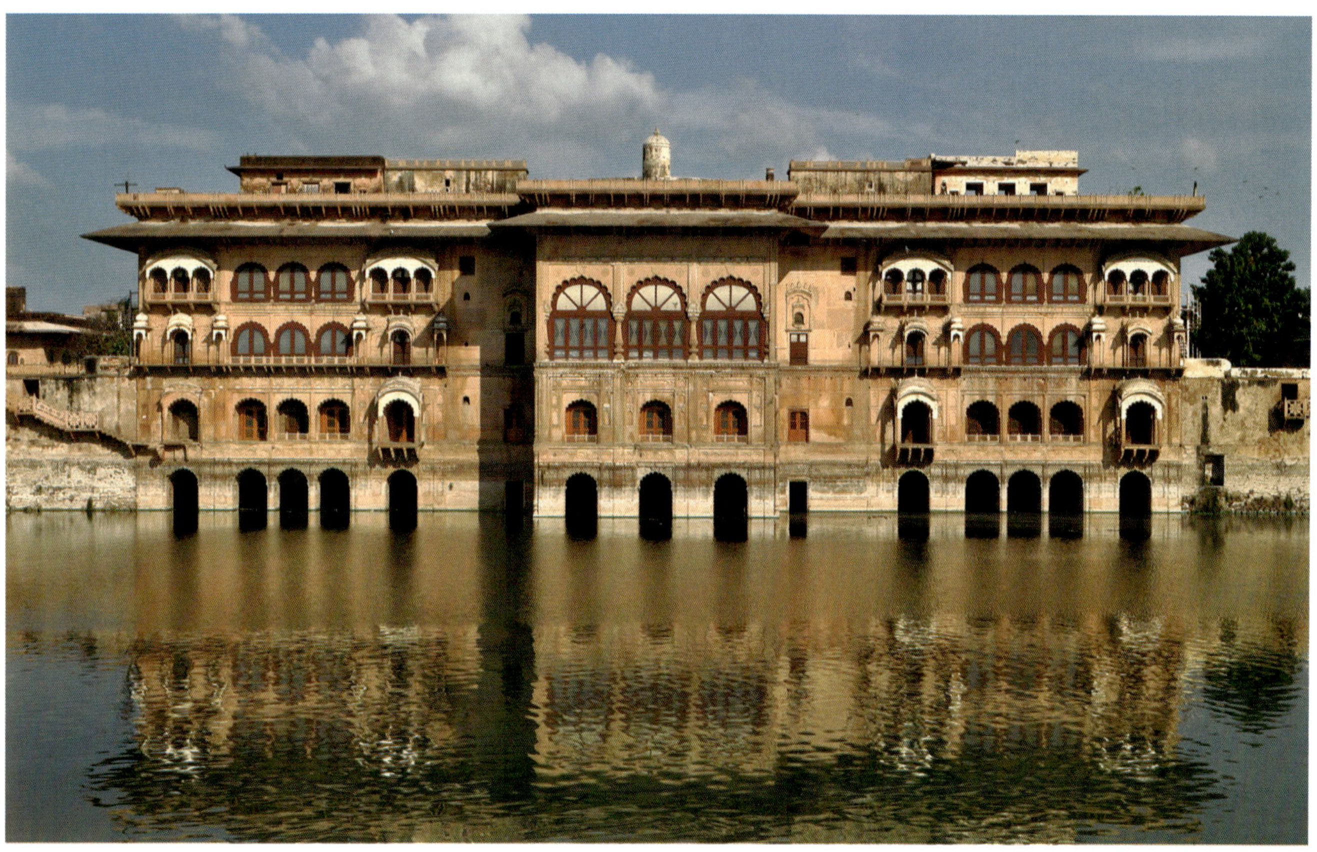

Above (Fig. 3): *The structure of the Gopal Bhawan as viewed from the western side or across the Gopal Sagar*

Facing page (Fig. 4): *The eastern face of Gopal Bhawan with the five-cusped entrance hall and a pool in the front framed within the* hindola *arch*

These engrailed arches have cartouche stone panels above and one medallion on either side of all arches. The columns below the arches show the Rajput-Mughal influence—similar to the Red Fort in Delhi and Amber Palace in Jaipur. The end column and starting column of the row of five arches are only half-expressed as they butt the wall. The most striking feature of this hall is the massiveness of the whole structure and not the carving details. It echoes an opulent, ceremonial aura comparable to the majestic grandeur of the Mughals.

Functionally the Gopal Bhawan is divided into three parts. The central block constitutes of the front and back sides of the double height rooms with a two-storeyed core in the middle. These were the public and semi-public areas comprising of the reception hall, Indian dining hall, Western dining hall and their respective service rooms. Two symmetrically arranged additional blocks on either side of this central block

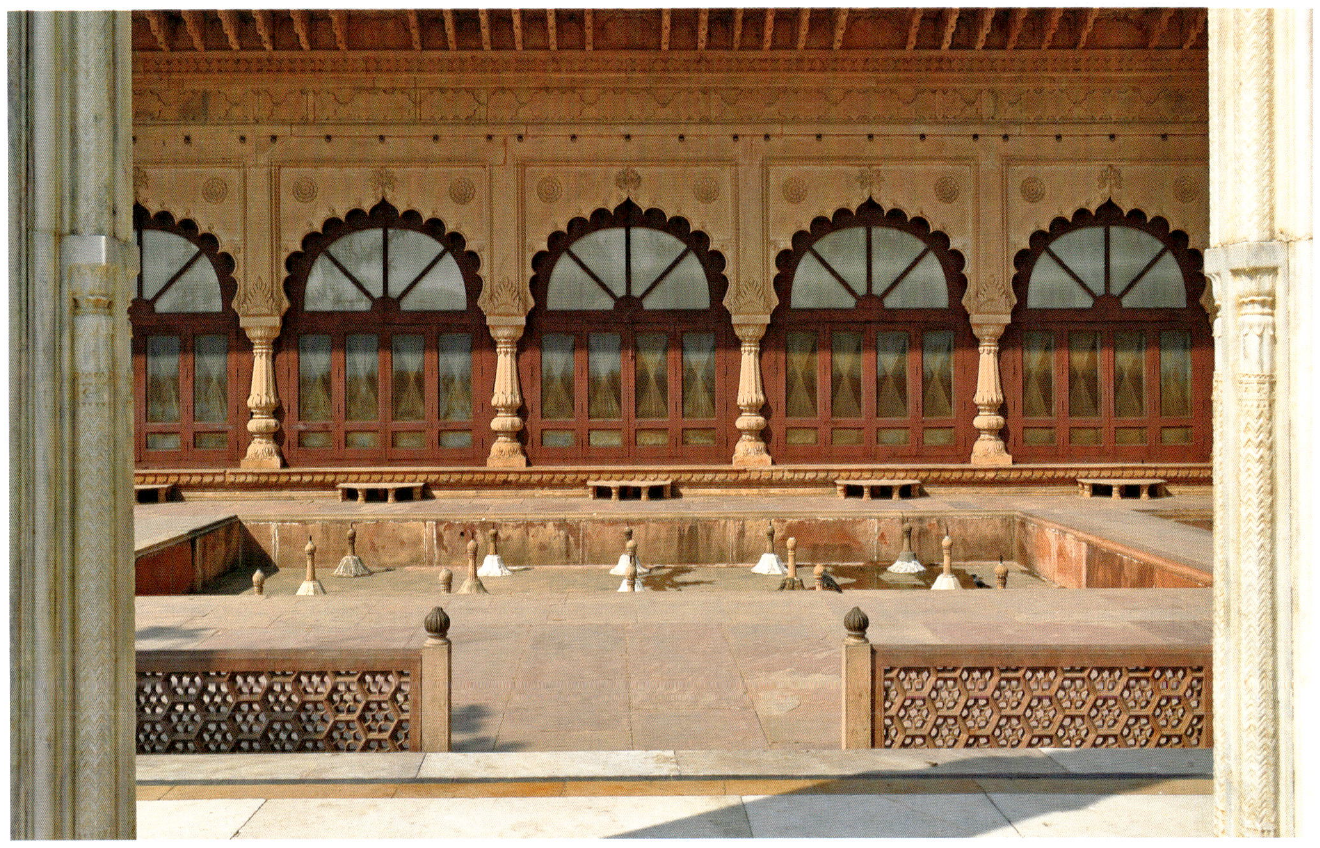

complete the building. These private palaces consist of living rooms, bedrooms, recreation rooms, toilets and guest rooms. Two small secretariats mark the buffer between the central block and the ancillary blocks on each side.

Five engrailed arches on bulbous columns similar to the entrance arches divide the main reception hall into two distinct spaces. (Fig. 5) Owing to the large span of arches, the two rectangular spaces flow into each other. (Fig. 6) However, in the second rectangular space after the five-cusped arches, there are five readily recognisable balconies called *jharokhas* that are visible on the first floor of the wall ahead. All the *jharokhas* have alcoves with stone *jali* panels, handrails and balusters, as seen from the main hall.

The main reception hall of the Gopal Bhawan seems to have been changed to a drawing room especially by the last rulers for entertaining guests. All the outer arches were enclosed by glass and wooden shutters during the British era. The high-quality colonial furniture, sculptures, stuffed skin artefacts in this hall reminds the visitors of the days of the Raj. This

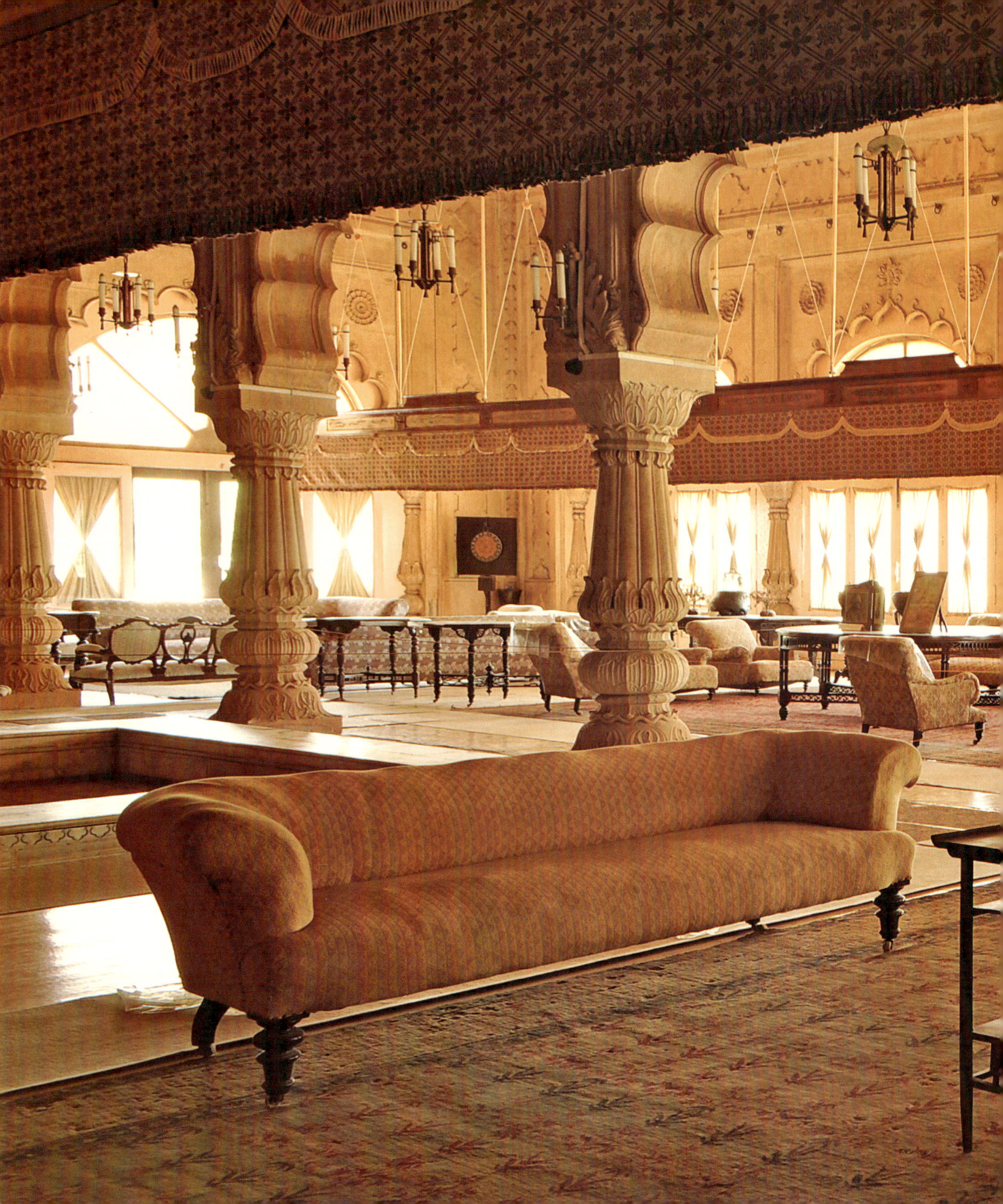

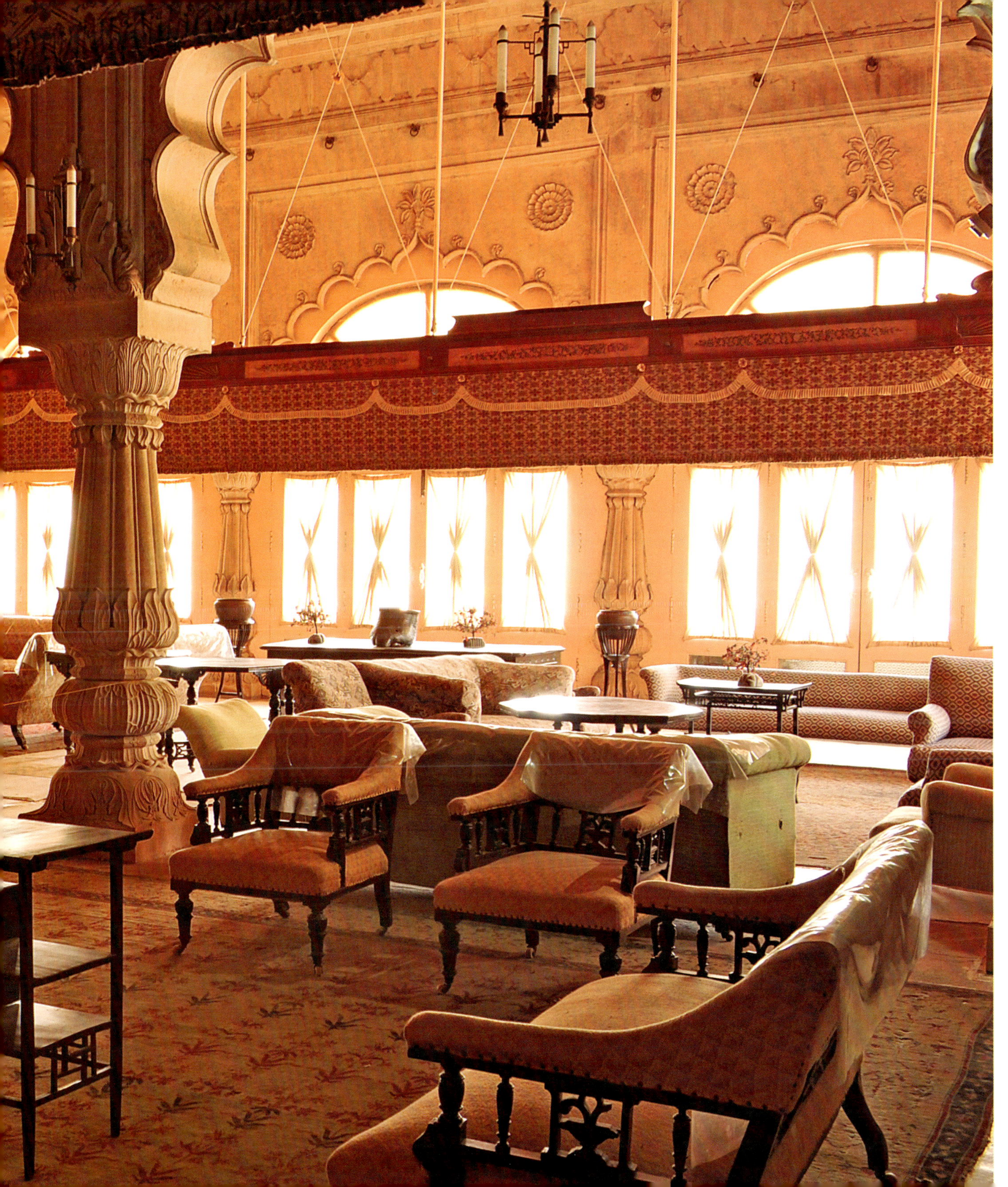

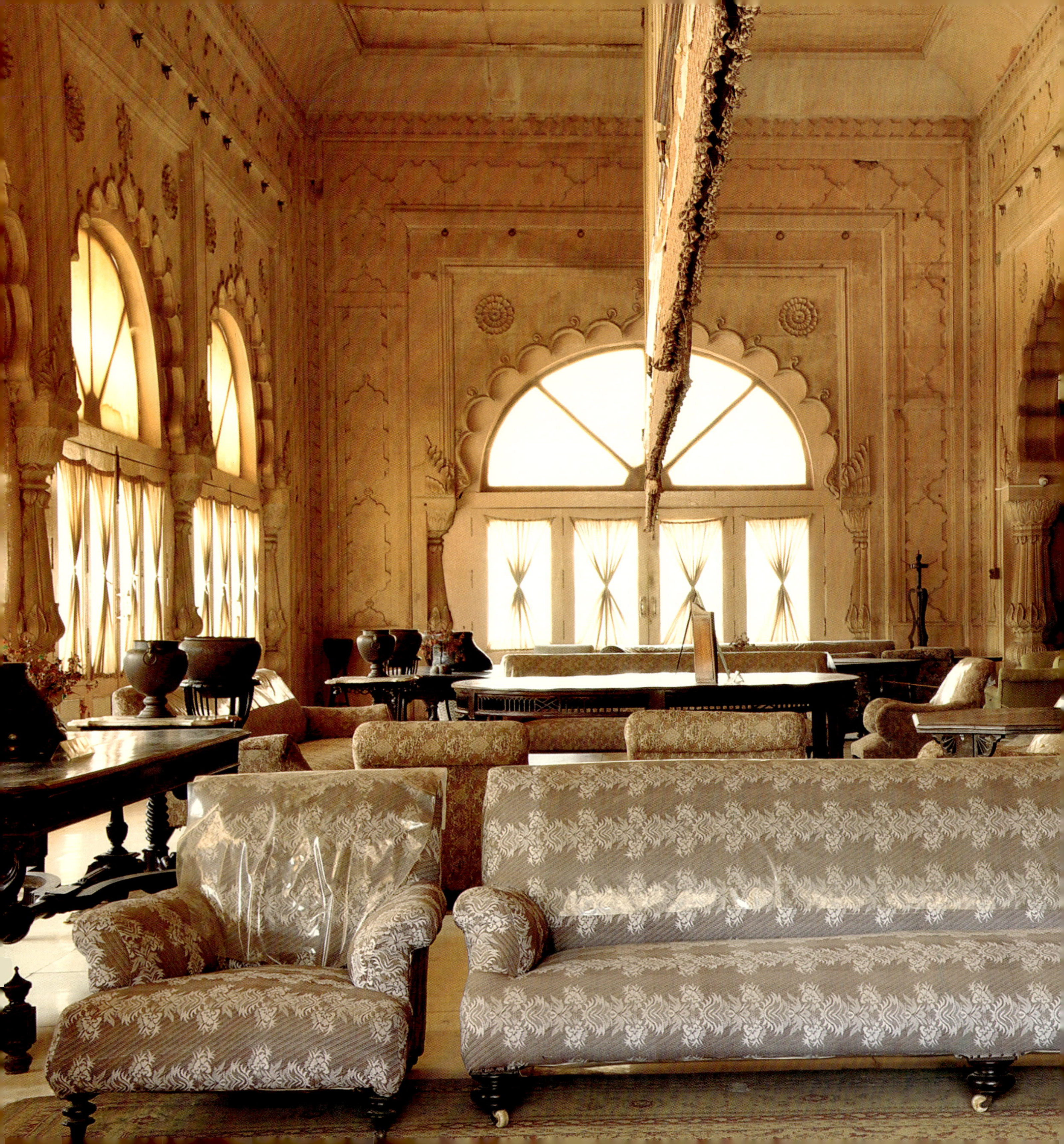

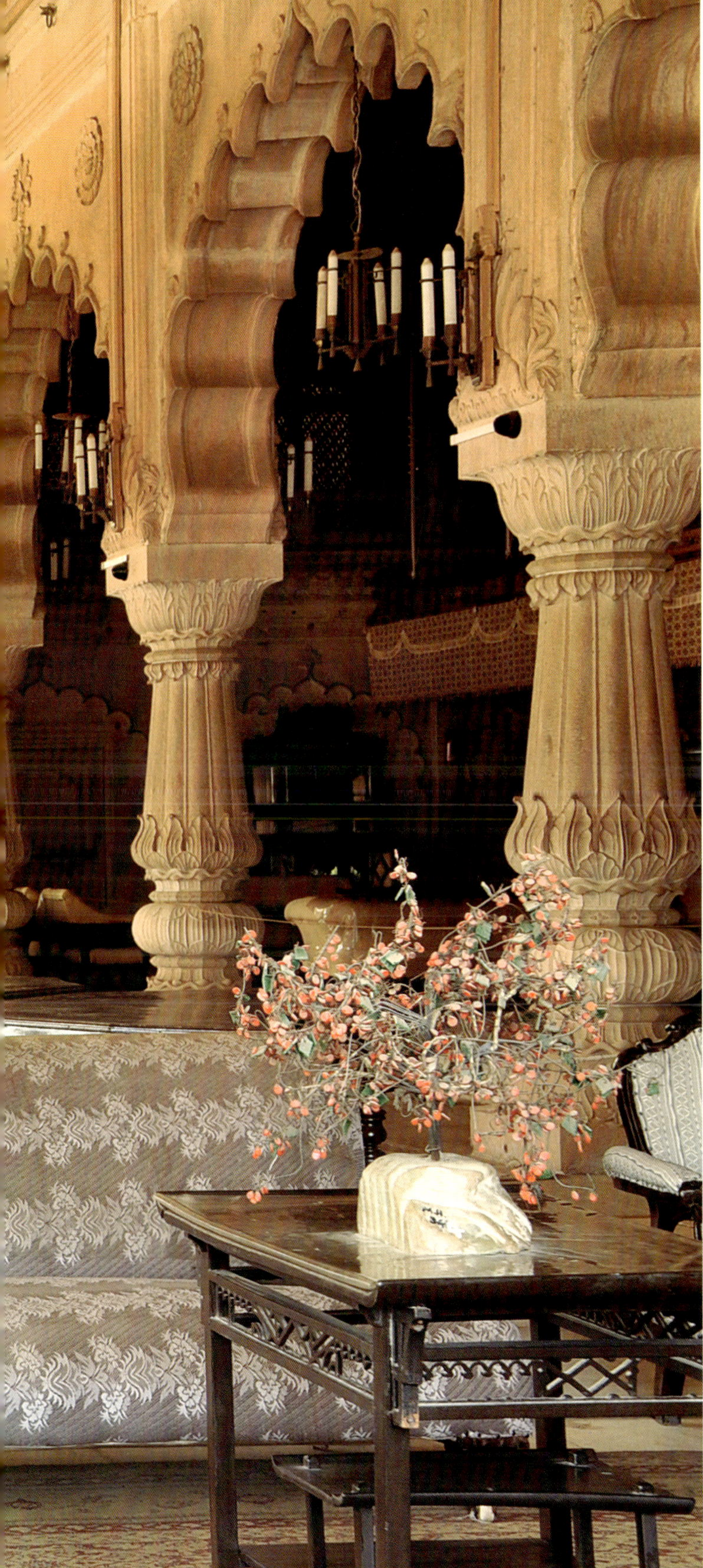

hall would have been used for ceremonial occasions like the reception of an ambassador, the granting of an award, dispensing of justice and was an assertion of the presence of royal power and control. At present the area is decked up with refurbished European furniture and Persian carpets. The wooden dressing tables are made of Kashmir walnut wood and Belgian glass. These are said to belong largely to the last rulers Maharaja Kishan Singh and Maharaja Brijendra Singh. (Fig. 7)

Of the five *jharokhas* on the front wall, the central *jharokha* being the largest was probably the balcony from where visitors got a *darshan* of the maharaja. The two smaller *jharokhas* on the sides were used by the queens in order of hierarchy. Even today one can see rings on the *jharokhas* from where veils or curtains would have been hanged. The *jharokha darshan* was a daily practice of public appearance (*darshan*) at the balcony (*jharokha*) introduced by the great Mughal ruler Akbar. He would appear before his subjects every morning before sunrise (the ritual also called *Surya Darshan*), so he could see and be seen by them from a small balcony in the Agra Fort. This tradition was continued by Jahangir, Akbar's son, who appeared before his subjects along with his wife Nur Jahan and also used it for his golden 'chain of justice' setup. Shah Jahan carried this tradition to his newly built Red Fort in Delhi. The practice was

Left (Fig. 5): *Five engrailed arches similar to the entrance arches divide the main reception hall into two distinct flowing spaces*

Previous page (Fig. 6): *The five huge archways ensure bright light in the opulent reception hall*

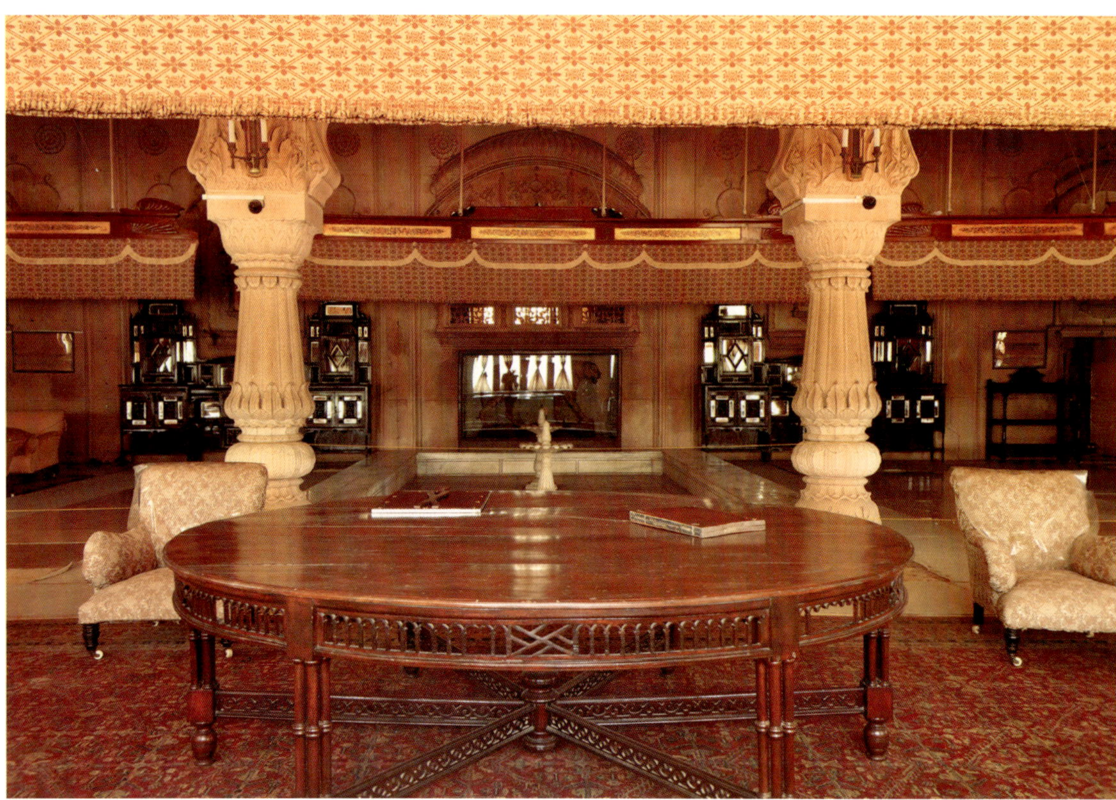

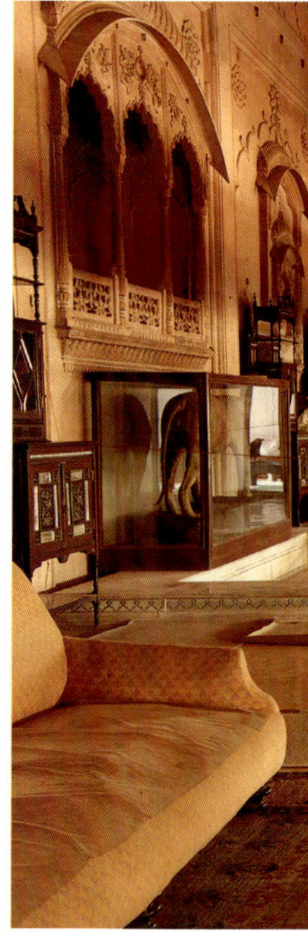

Above (Fig. 7): *Refurbished European and Kashmir walnut wood furniture on Persian carpets*

Above centre (Fig. 8): *An expansive view of the main reception hall showing the facing wall on the left with five* jharokhas. *Towards the end is the queen's chamber on the upper storey*

Facing page (Fig. 9): *Two free-standing marble fountains in a marble pool surround beneath the central* jharokha

discontinued by Aurangzeb around 1629 because he regarded it as a form of idolatry. Perhaps this was the image which the Jat rulers had in mind when they planned the structure. (Fig. 8)

In the foreground of the biggest *jharokha* in the main audience hall, there are two free-standing marble fountains. These are short, bulbous and ornate column-like pedestals holding a carved lotus plate, and a lotus bud. (Fig. 9) Around the pedestals is a simple rectangular marble pool surround almost a foot high. The floor is simply tiled with marble. The broad edge of the pool is made of white marble with a rectangular border inlay of black Belgian stone (a rock that is no longer quarried today) on the inside and a trefoil design on the outside. The rest of the flooring of the 'Hall of Audience' of Gopal Bhawan is made of a mixture of hand-ground lime, gum, shells and *belgiri*. It was used to achieve a polished or glistening effect like marble and the style

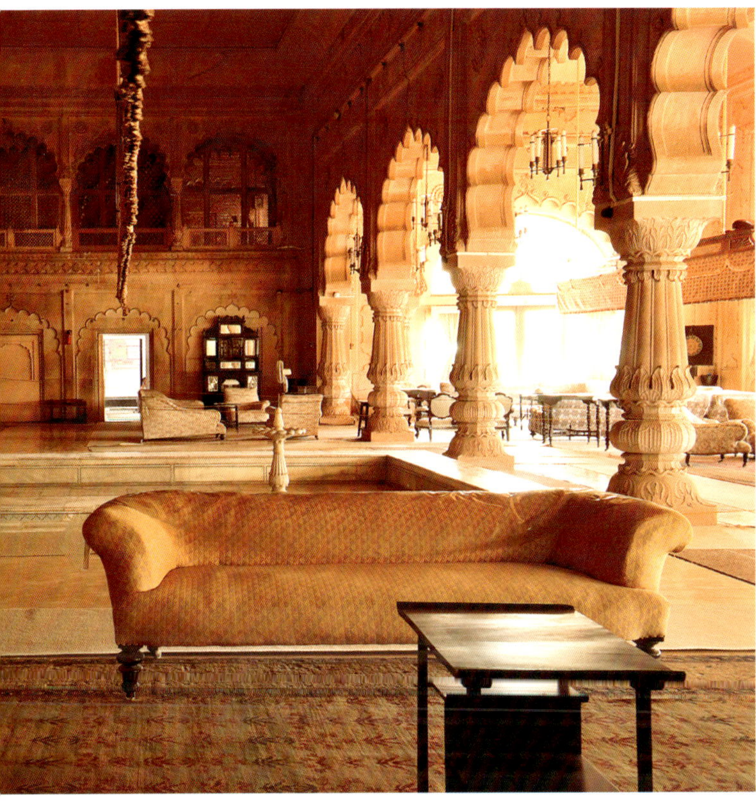

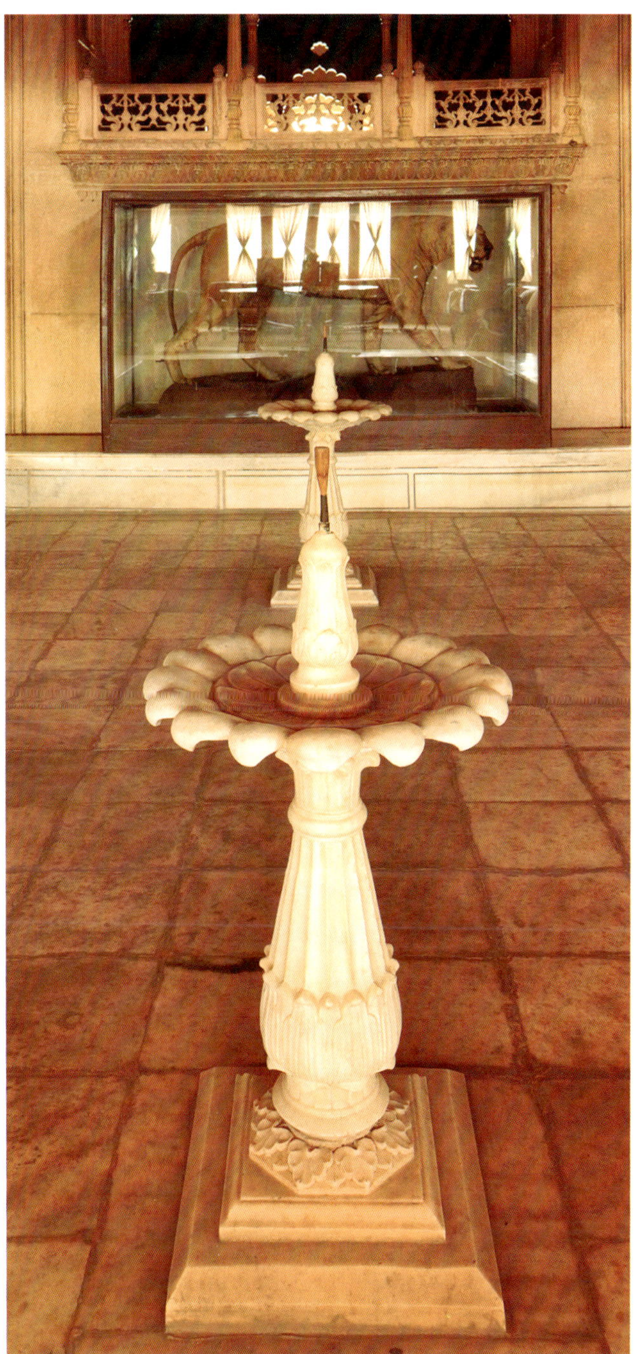

was referred to as 'araish'. The white marble surround was for a shallow pool of water that produced cooling in the hall when the fountains were operational. It seems that the pool was added later to the hall and may not have been planned originally because the construction material is marble against sandstone used all around.

The other devices for cooling the hall were the hand-drawn fans or *pankhas* that were a prominent feature of the hall. (Fig. 10) There are three big *pankhas* in each half of the hall suspended from the ceilings. These swinging fans were run manually by tugging at the rope connected to it. The ropes passed through

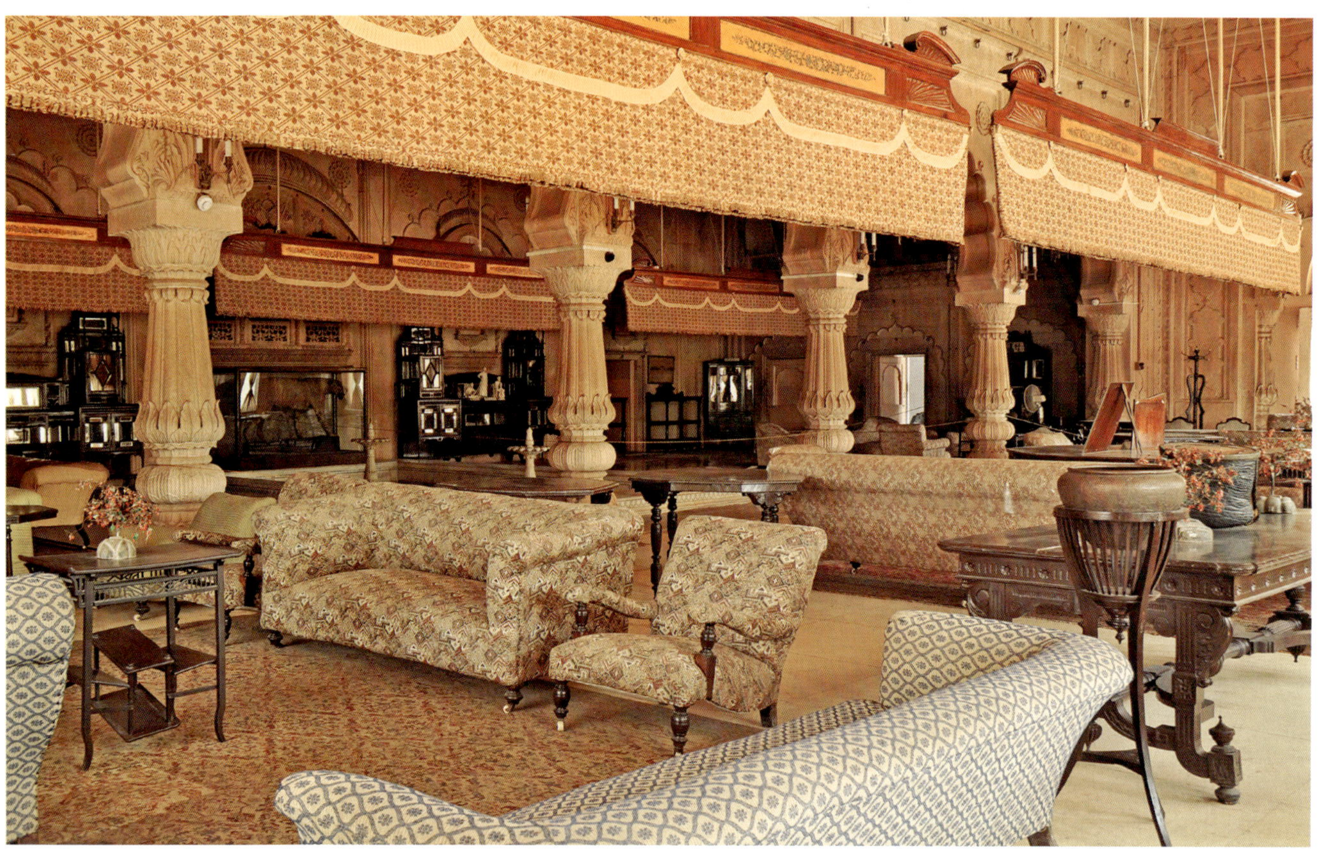

jharokha-like openings to reach the hand of the *pankha-wallah* or coolie on the hidden side. At the turning a tiny mechanism was fixed to run the rope on a pulley. These *jharokha*-like carved niches can be seen on the first floor on the same wall as that of the *jharokha darshan*. However, these niches are currently closed by carved inset panels. (Fig. 11)

This facing wall of the central hall consists of two levels, with the upper level being the Indian dining room. Two staircases lead to the Indian dining room from either side of the central *jharokhas*. Also continuing this symmetry there are two butting double-storeyed palaces on each side. Entrance to the rectangular Indian dining hall is from its shorter sides via the secretariats which abut the shorter sides of the Indian dining hall. (Fig. 12) The secretariats are identical, painted green, decorated with accentuated lime-plaster niche work and raised decorative platforms for sitting. They probably were the rooms for the private secretaries or accountants. The dining room connected the two secretariats thus forming a bridge between the ladies quarters' (zenana) and the king's living quarters. It

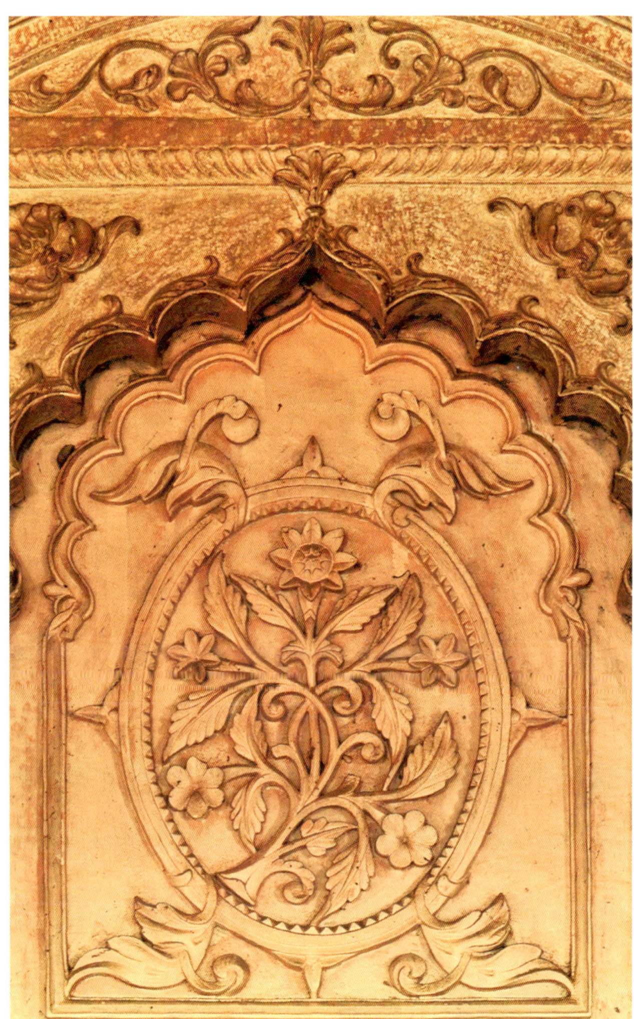

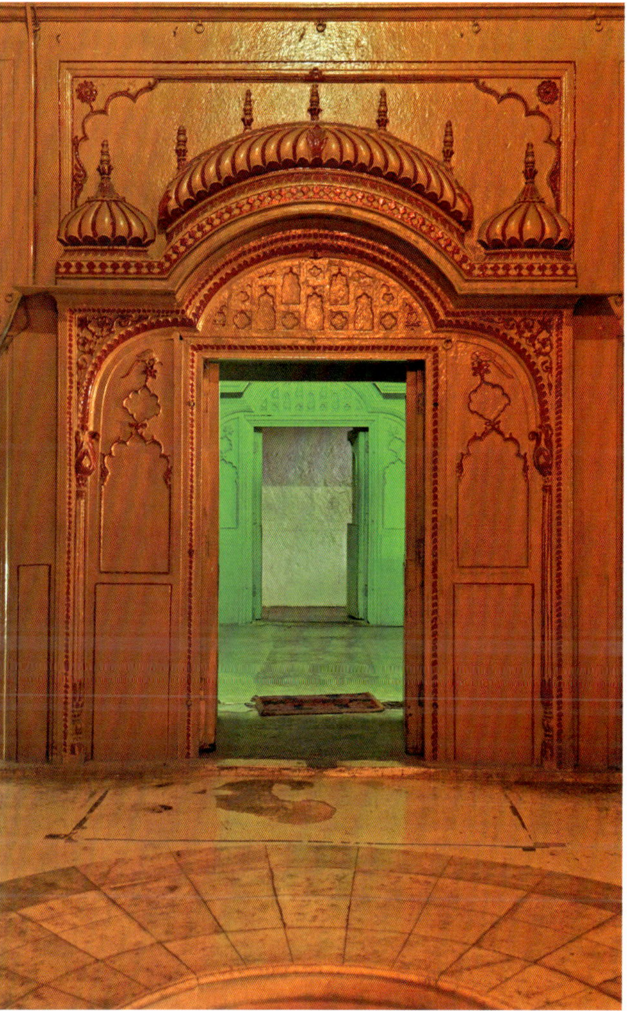

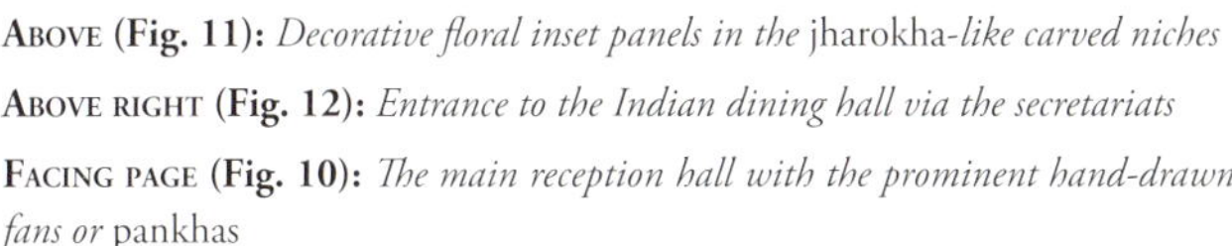

Above (Fig. 11): *Decorative floral inset panels in the* jharokha-*like carved niches*
Above right (Fig. 12): *Entrance to the Indian dining hall via the secretariats*
Facing page (Fig. 10): *The main reception hall with the prominent hand-drawn fans or* pankhas

was conventional for kings to have secretariats in their private palaces from the time of Akbar who used to spend up to six hours a day with his accountants and secretaries in the zenana. These rooms also served as a buffer between the private palaces and the Indian dining room. The dining hall has no external walls. The hall has a charismatic ambience of Mughal and Rajput Sheesh Mahals which were dimly lit and used highly reflective finishes. The room, though made of sandstone, is lime-plastered and painted with enamel paints emphasising its ostentatious display of highlighted carved niches, ornate *bangladar* ceilings and domes of the niches. The room has highly decorative relief carvings on all sides along with two framed entrances on the shorter side and three *jharokhas* on either of the longer sides that are lime-plastered and painted in bright yellow and red. (Fig 13) The *jharokhas* on both the longer sides are made of intricately carved parapet *jalis* and arches. The one overlooking the 'Hall of Audience' has a very fluidic *jali* design (Fig. 14) while the one overlooking the European dining room has a simple geometric hexagonal *jali*. A central chandelier marks the beauty of this little dining hall. On the floor occurs a U-shaped 9-inch raised dining platform, which is

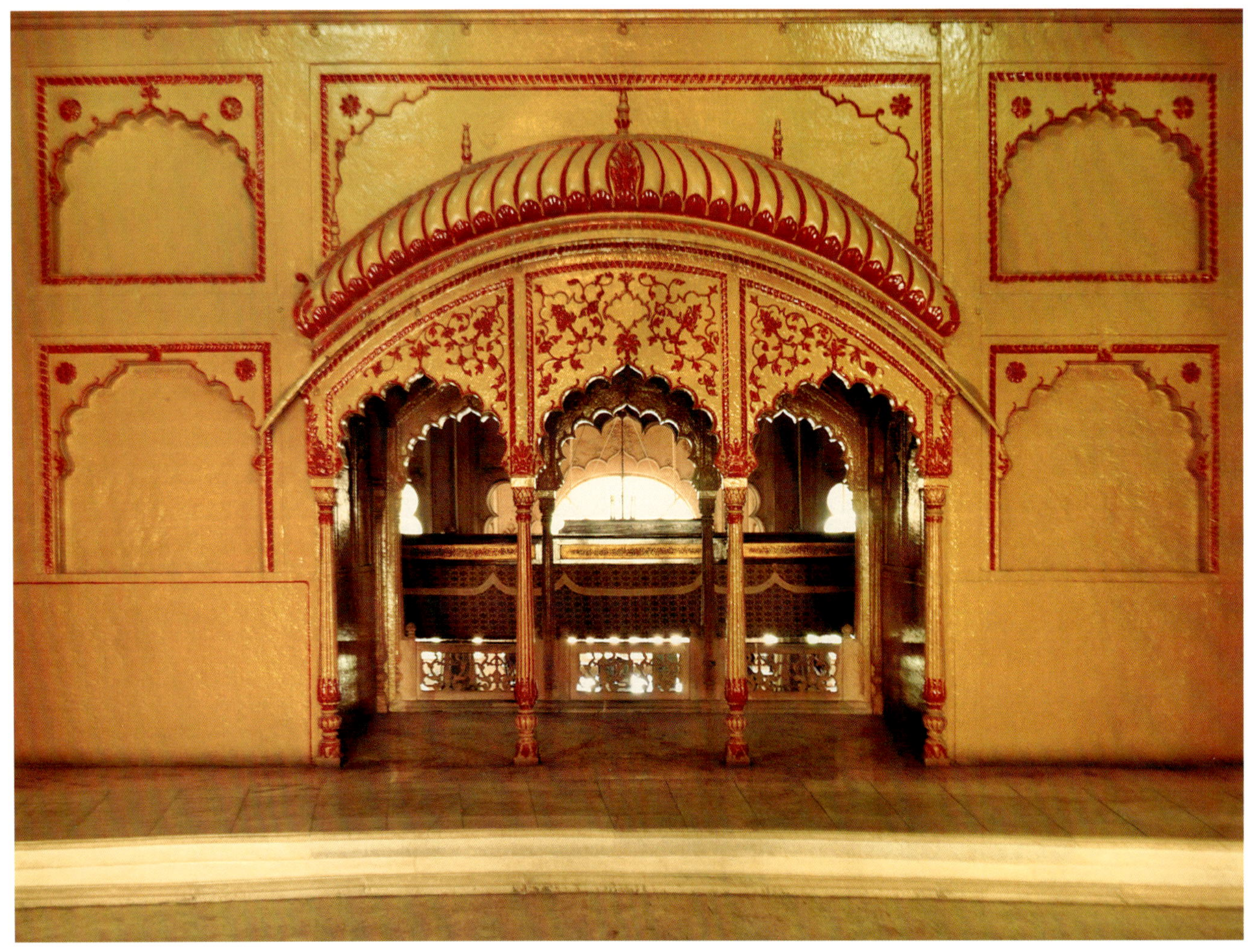

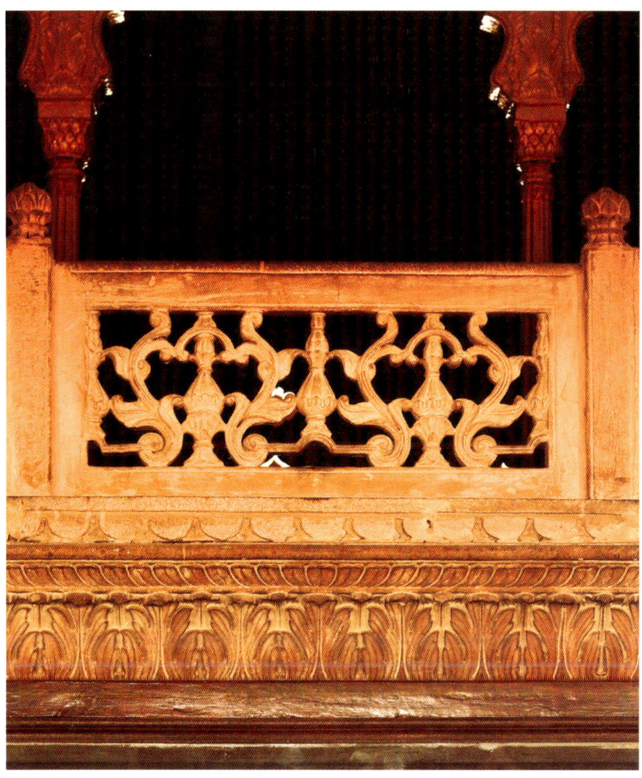

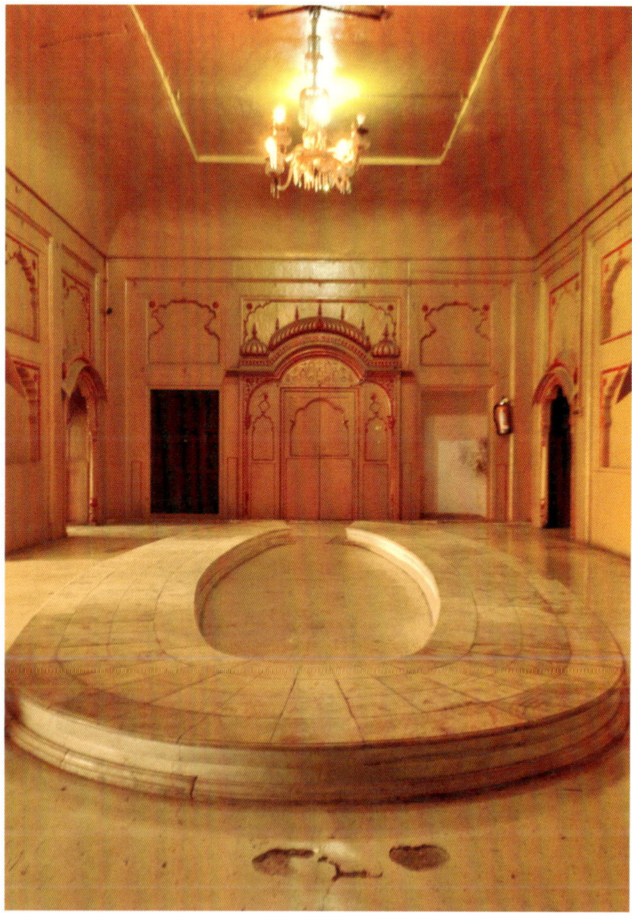

Above (Fig. 15): *A U-shaped 9-inch high dining platform made of marble layers with moulded edges*

Above left (Fig. 14): *Fluidic* jali *designs of the central* jharokha *parapet overlooking the central hall*

Facing page (Fig. 13): *A view of the lime-lastered walls with embossed painted patterns on the inside of the central* jharokha *from the Indian dining room*

made of marble layers with moulded edges. The marble slab served as a sit-down dining table with the diners sitting on the outer edge and the servers serving from the inside. (Fig. 15)

At the back of the central block and on the western side of Gopal Bhawan projecting into Gopal Sagar is a smaller oblong chamber. This double height hall now used as a European-style dining room (Fig. 16) provides a sumptuous view of the Gopal Sagar reservoir. One set of *jharokhas* on the longer side of the Indian dining hall also peeks into this space. This has two beautifully carved water basins with a water spout in the centre on either end of the room. (Fig. 17) The raised water basin is carved out of pink sandstone with lotus leaves. The standing spout is an elongated lotus bud. This room is enclosed with three arches on the

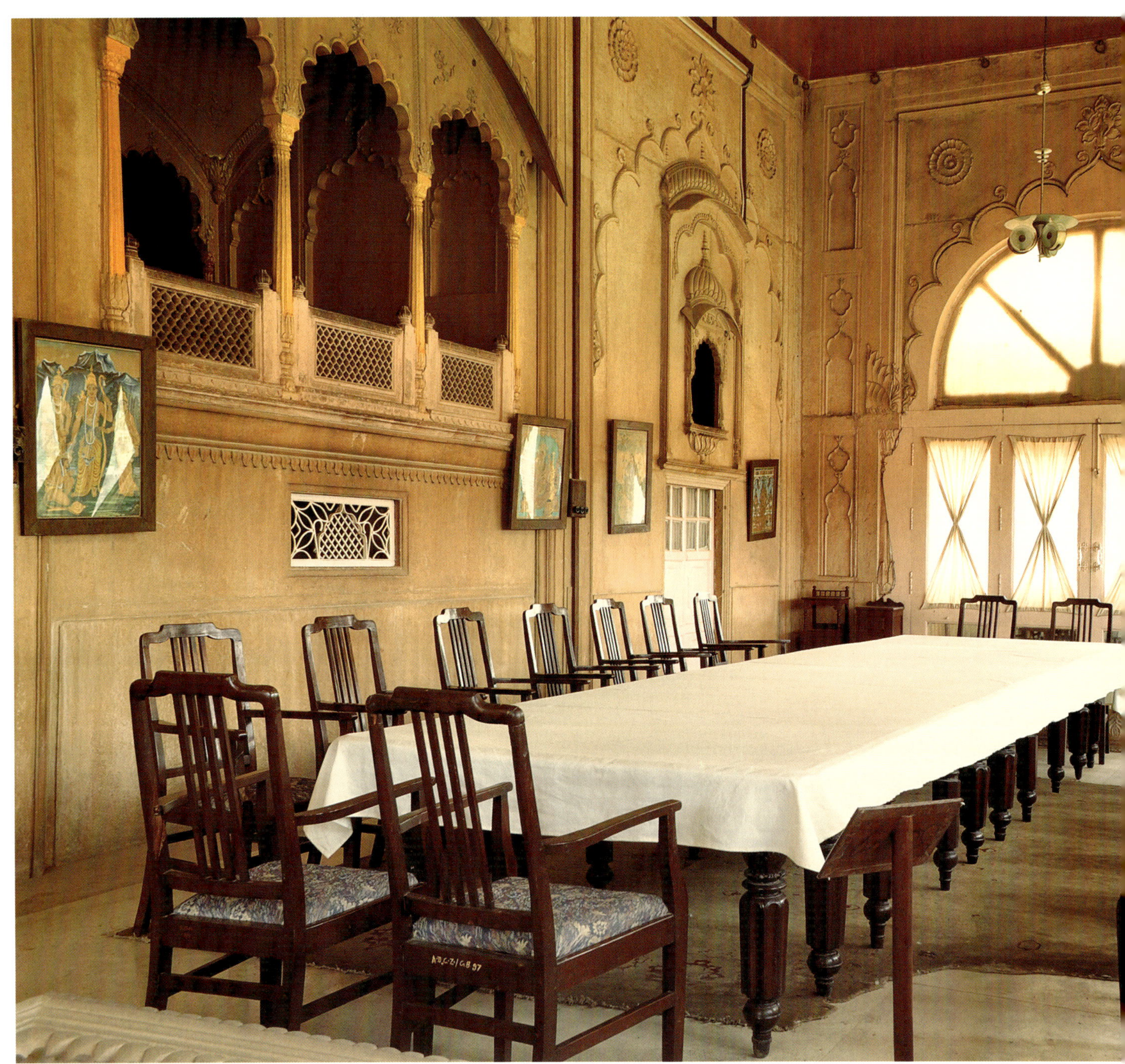

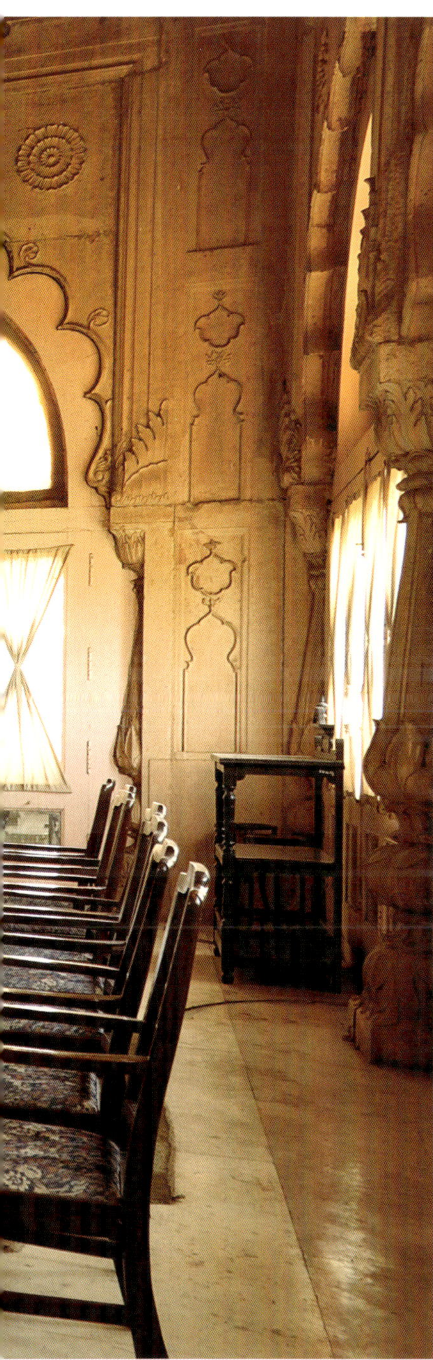

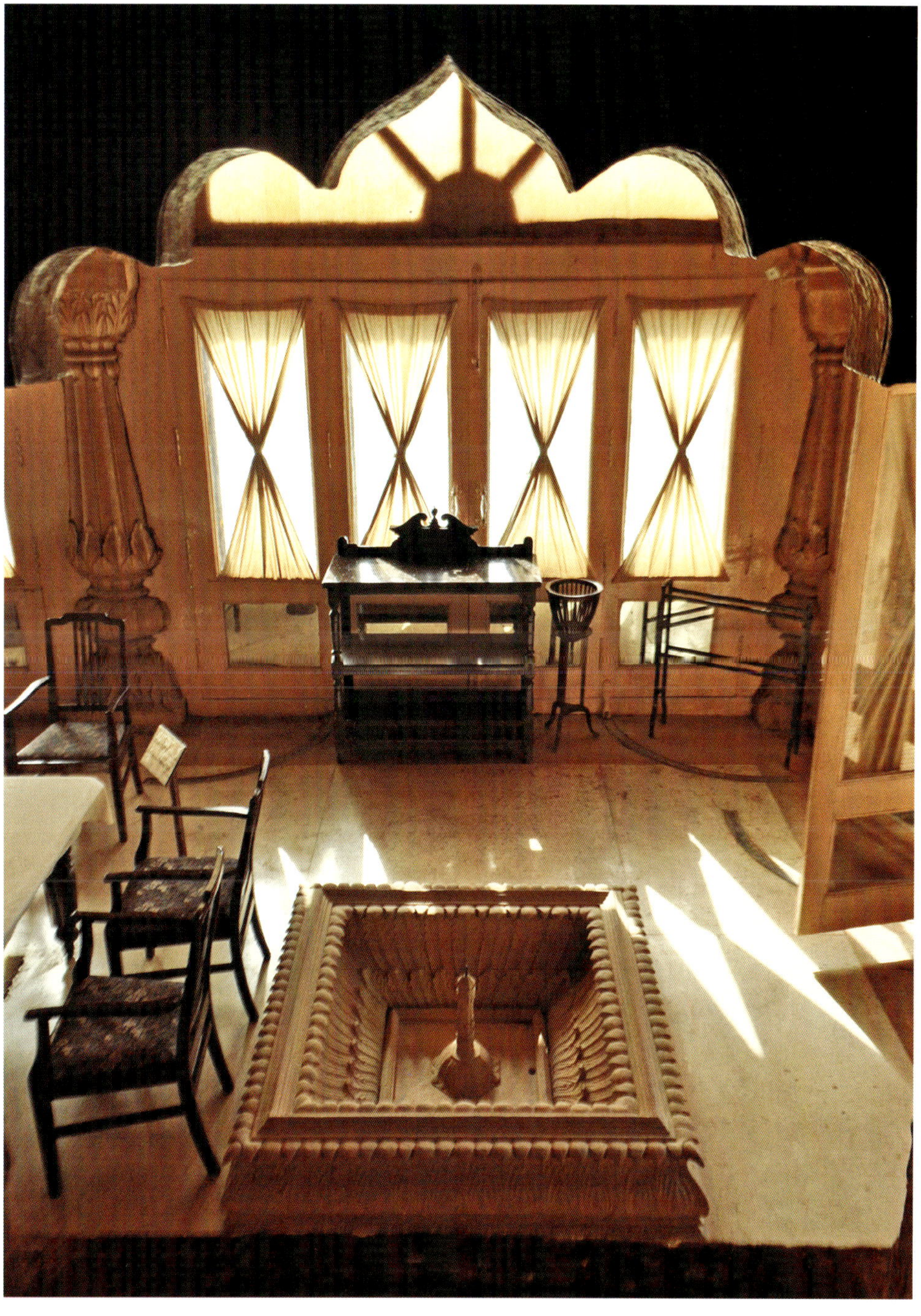

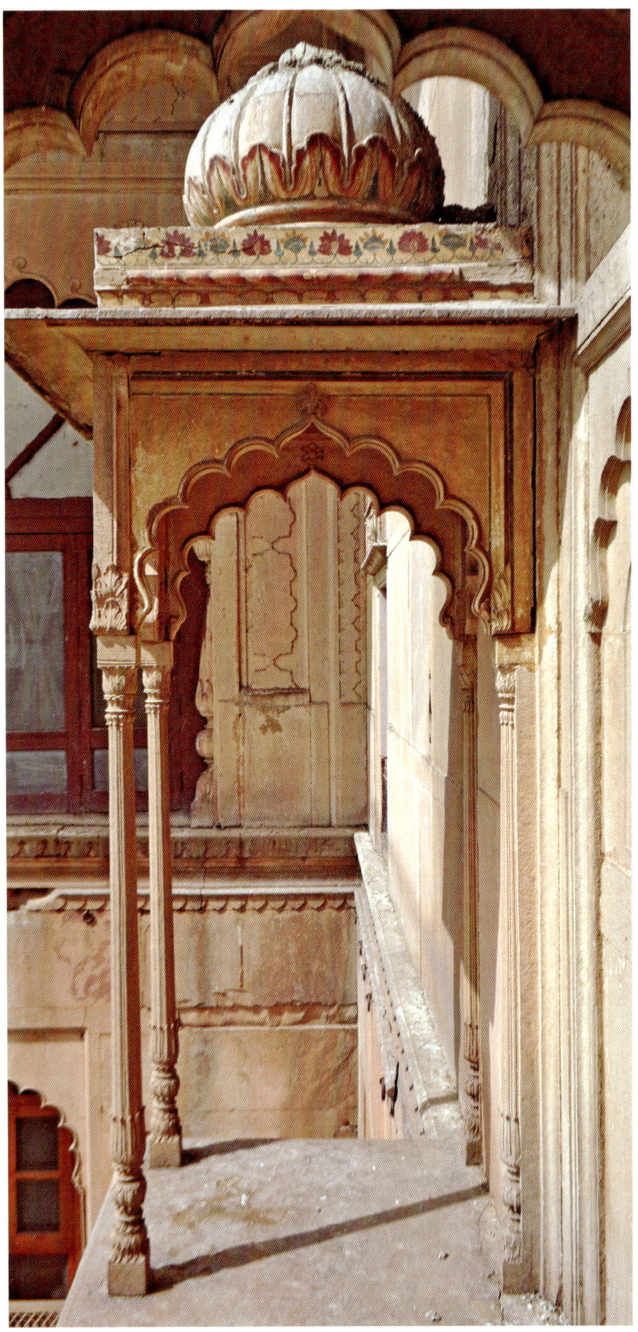

Gopal Sagar side and a single arch on either side. These three sides seem to stretch out into the Gopal Sagar. Thus it commands a beautiful view of the Gopal Sagar and the Rani Bagh (garden) beyond. The fourth side is decorated with carved niches, the upper level being one with the overlooking *jharokhas*. (Fig. 18) The last king used it as a European-style dining room. It currently has a long table with eighteen chairs placed between the fountains. This dining room has sandstone interiors and is painted with enamel paint. The westerly breeze blowing through the garden over the Gopal Sagar—opulent and sensuous—must have had a languid air in spite of the fruit trees, birds and music that surely would have brought coolness to this spacious place.

On either side and below the Indian dining room, at same level as the Diwan-i-Aam, are the other ancillary service rooms as necessary to fulfil the administrative role of the building. Below the European-style dining room is another two-storeyed complex. The first of which would have been used by the rulers for recreation and fishing during the summers. It has carved arches and columns and is at the same level as the Sawan and Bhadon pavilions' monsoon room. One could enjoy the artificially created rainy scene of the two pavilions

---

Left (Fig. 18): *Fresco ornamentation is retained on some of the projecting* jharokhas

Facing page (Fig. 20): *The king and queen's chambers have delicately carved* jali *screens for a one-side view of the ceremonial hall*

Previous page left (Fig. 16): *The double height hall used as a European dining room provides a magnificent view of the Gopal Sagar reservoir*

Previous page right (Fig. 17): *The European dining chamber with a raised water basin bracketing the dining table*

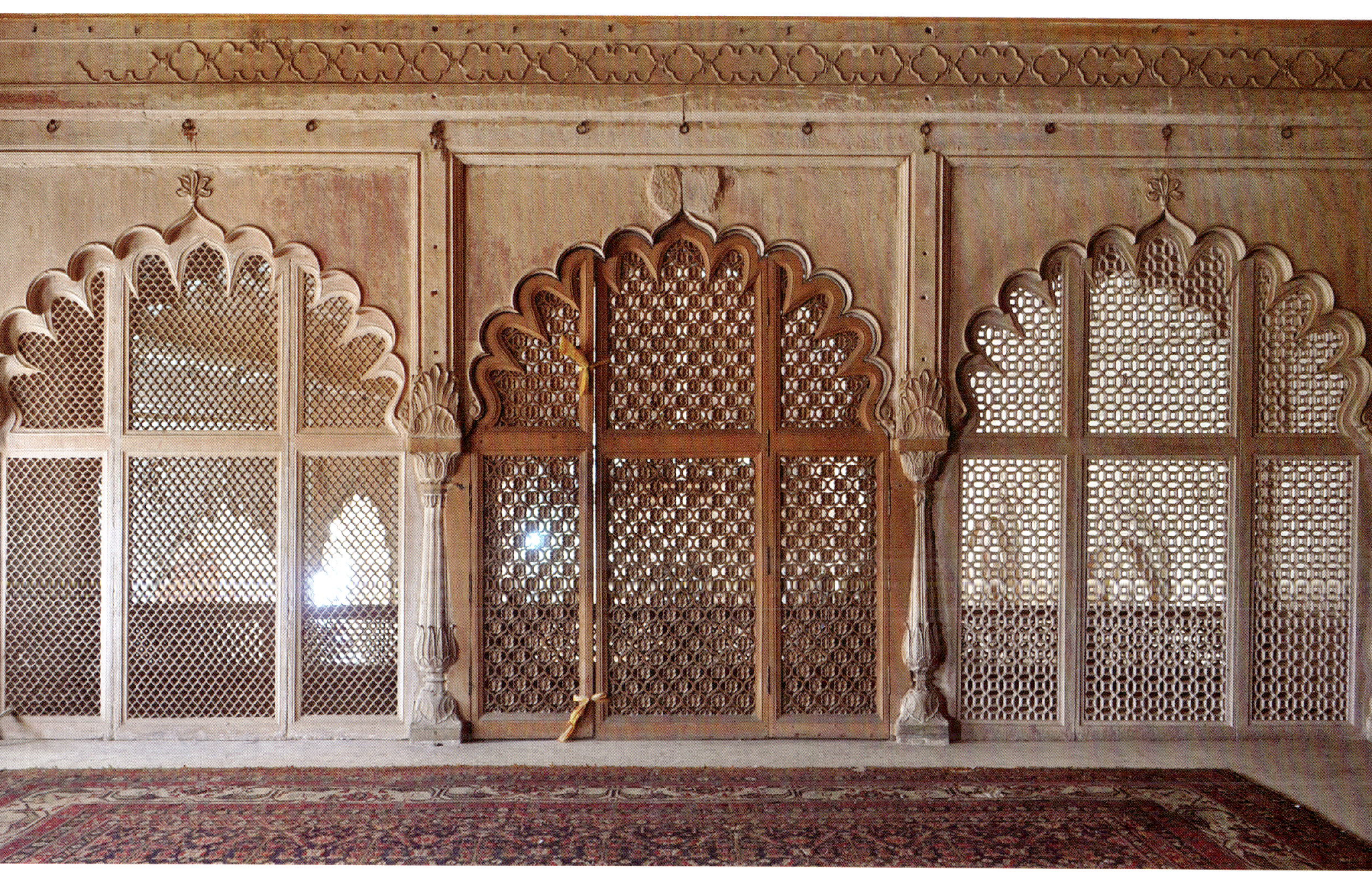

sitting right there. (Fig. 19) Another storey below this was filled with water most of the year to provide coolness to the entire structure.

Ancillary blocks or private palaces are also visually connected to the double height main reception hall through their overlooking arrangement of balconies and parapet *jalis*. On the balconies, there are delicately carved *jali* screens set in the engrailed arch openings beyond which lie the royal residences. (Fig. 20) Intricate stone and wooden *jali* screens are suitably used at these arched openings to provide required privacy. It was not easy to look beyond these screens from the reception hall but the balconies afforded a view of the hall below, from the royal residences.

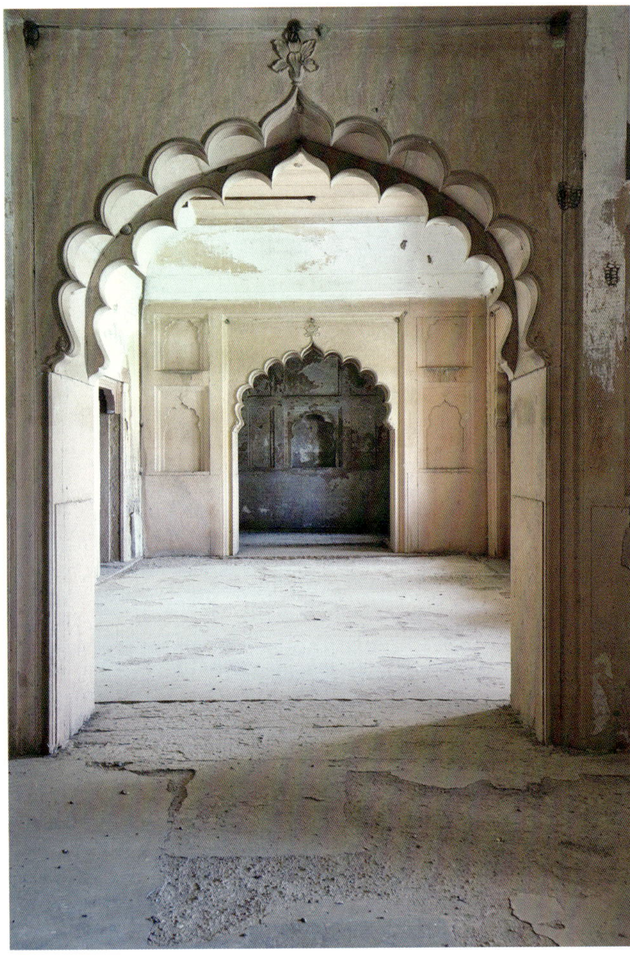

Above (Fig. 19): *Alleyway of the underground two storeys with ancillary chambers are articulated with the Gopal Sagar*

Right (Fig. 22): *The recreation room towards the queen's chamber depicted with effeminate interiors*

Following pages (Fig. 21): *The three-arched opening to the recreation or Chess room of the king's chamber*

These were symmetrical chambers belonging to the king and the queen, even up to the rule of the last king when it must have been renovated to suit their modern lifestyle.

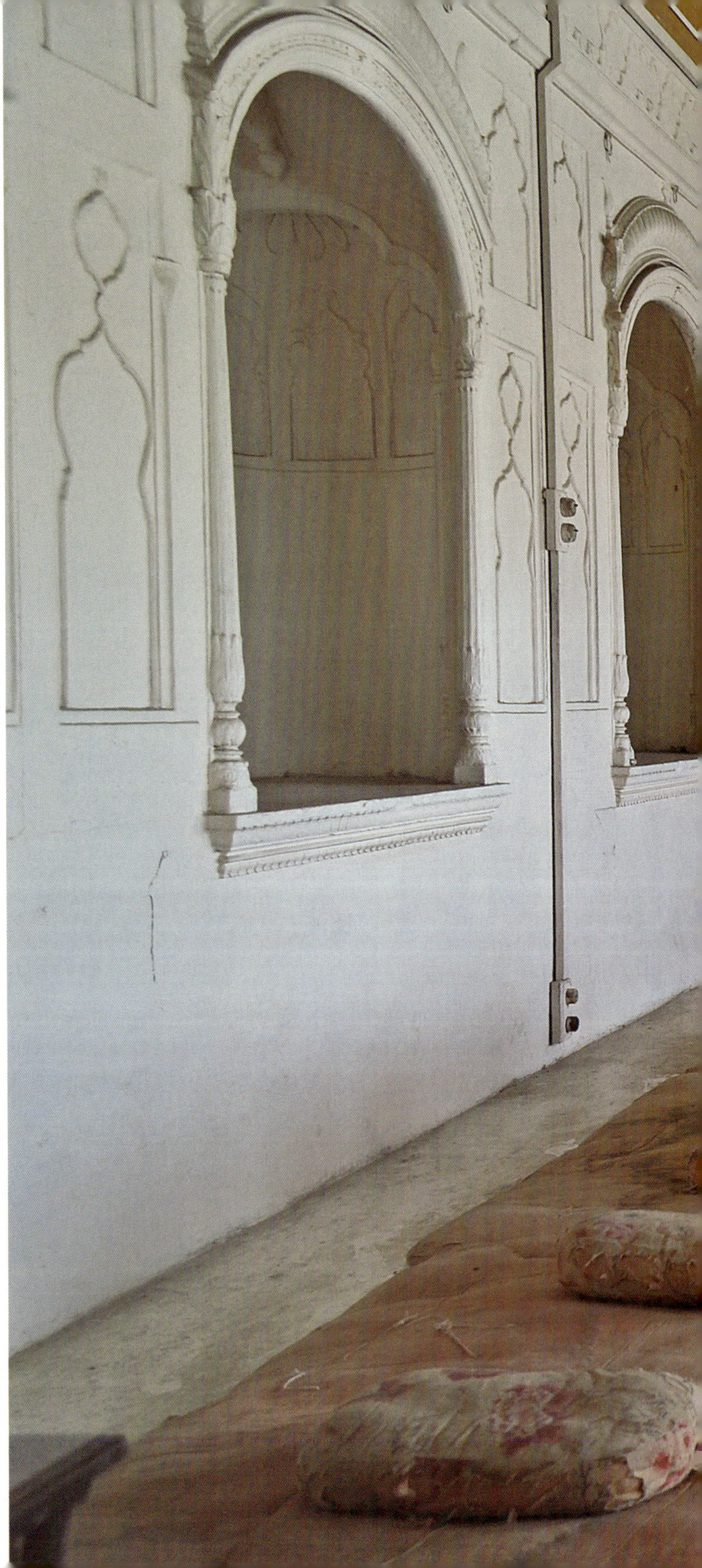

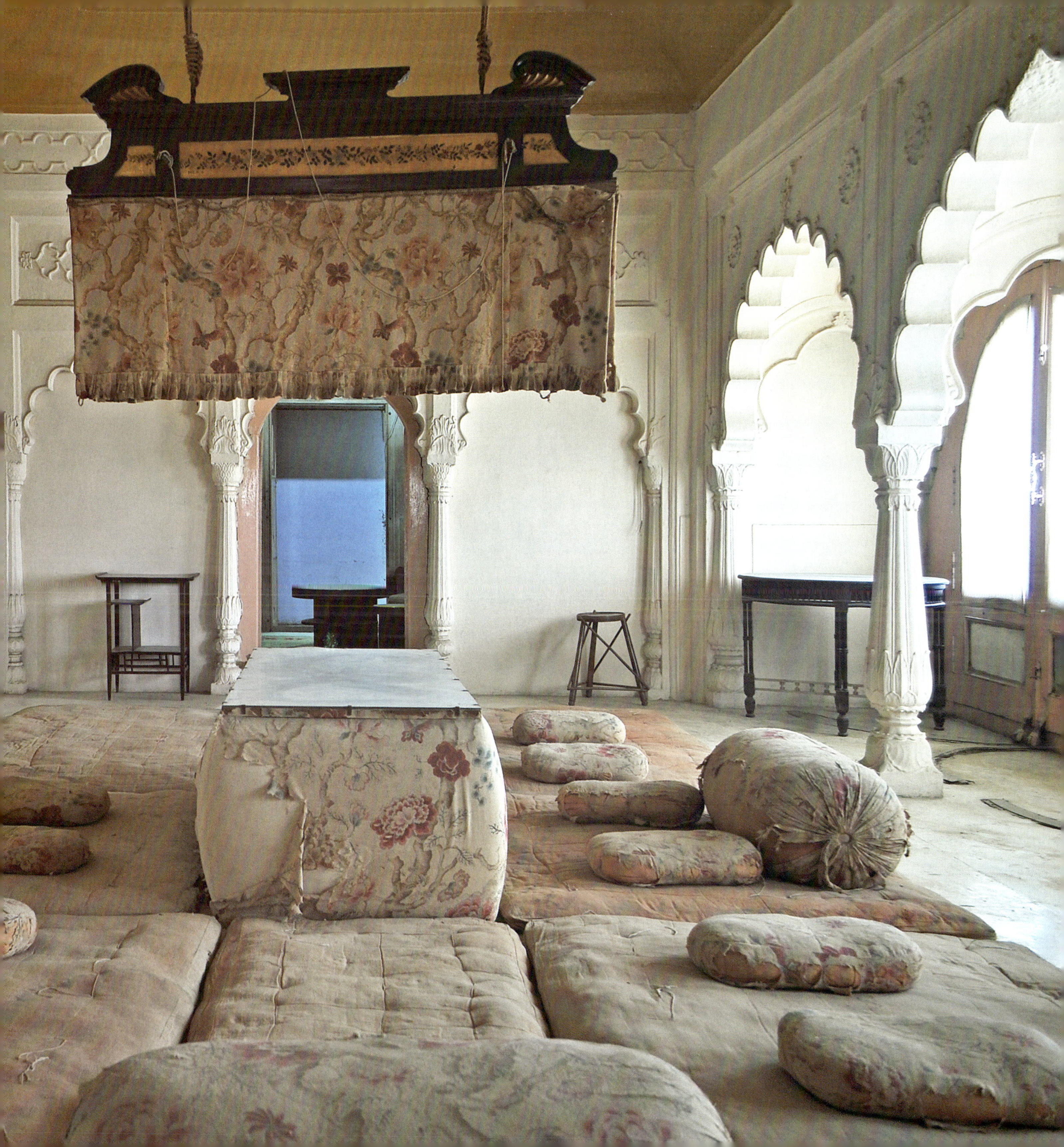

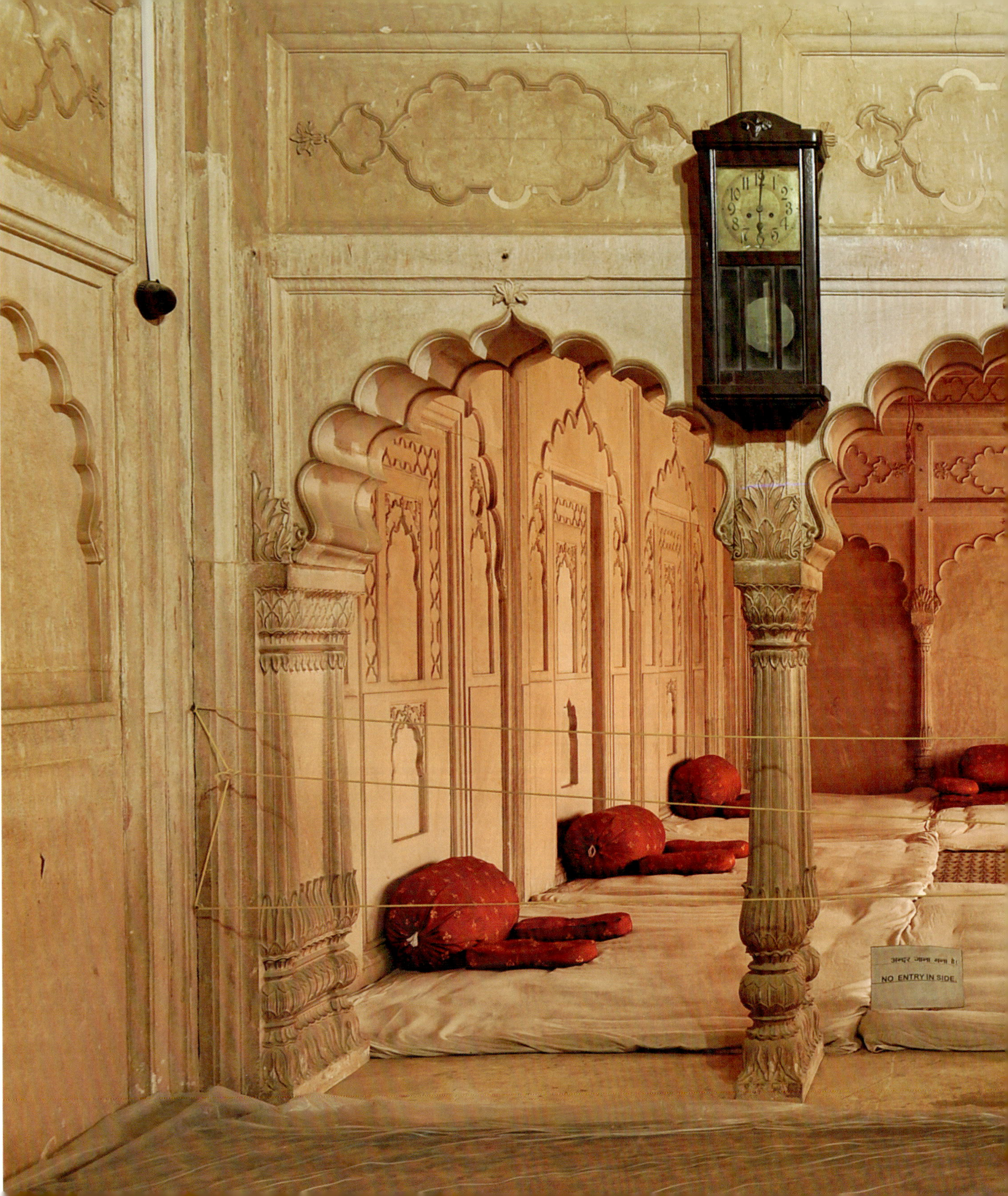
NO ENTRY IN SIDE.

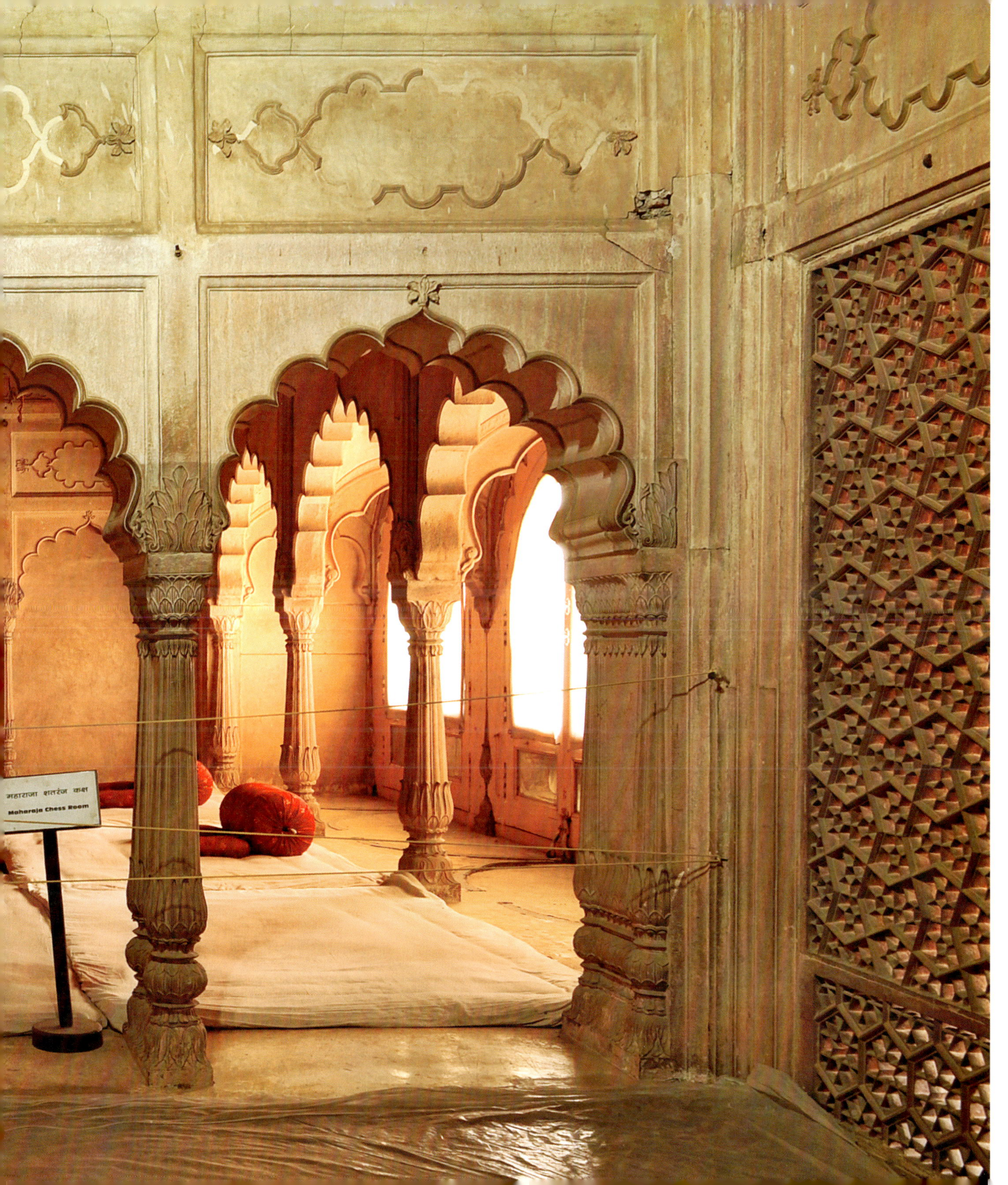
महाराजा शतरंज कक्ष
Maharaja Chess Room

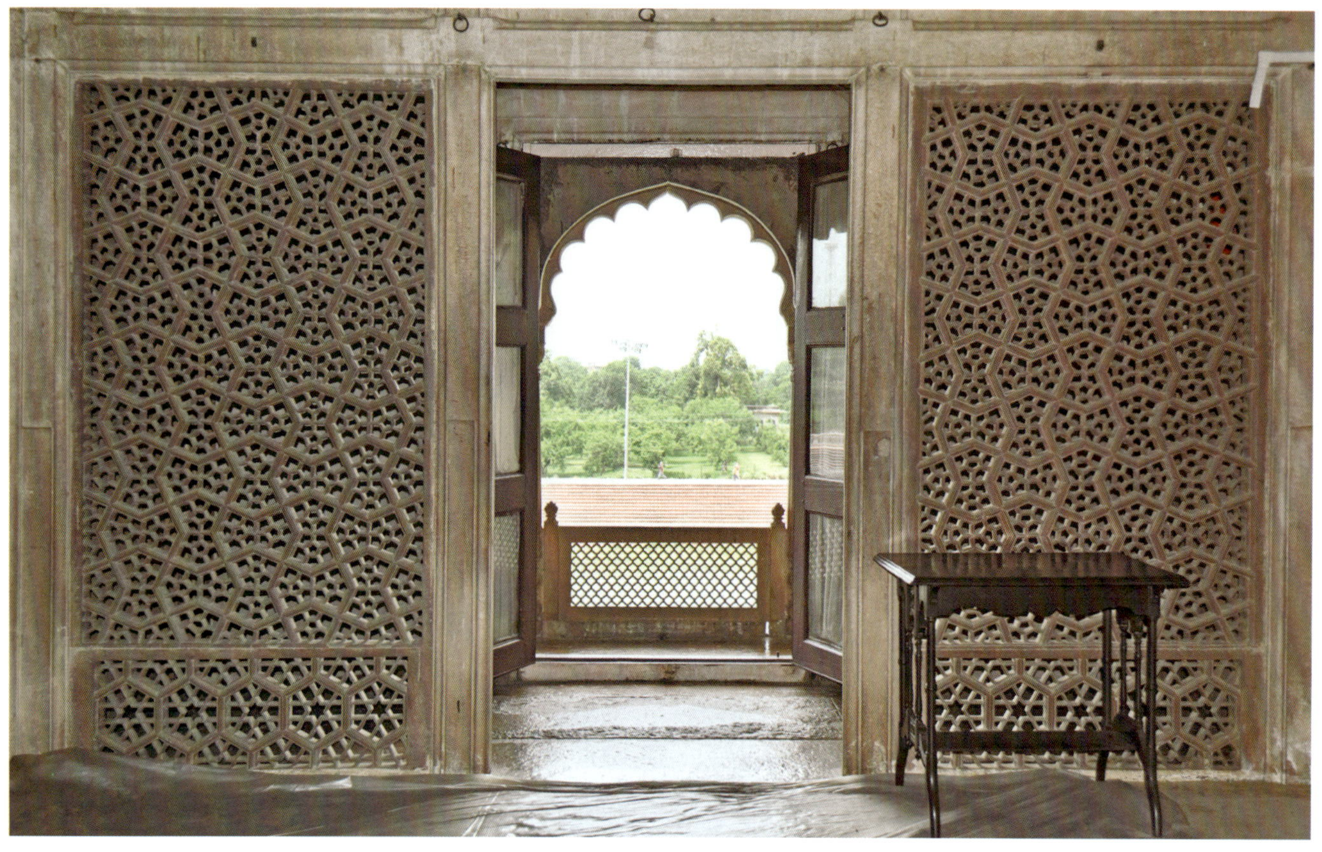

Above (Fig. 23): *The balcony overlooking the Gopal Sagar is studded with two big* jalis *on either side*

Facing page (Fig. 24): *In the central area, the extravagantly carved stone panel with four hooks is fixed in the ceiling right above the bed*

The same staircase which takes us to the Indian dining hall skilfully leads upwards to the respective private palaces. The entrance is marked by a square lobby with openings on each side. Immediately in the front is a triple-arched opening to the private sitting room towards the king's chamber, which served both as a recreation as well as a meeting room. It was also called the Chess room. (Fig. 21) (Fig. 22) This deep room overlooks into the Gopal Sagar on the west as well as leading to the bathrooms on the same axis.

On the western side is a balcony overlooking the Gopal Sagar. This is studded with two big *jalis* with an opening in-between. These *jalis* are of red sandstone and appear to have been brought from some other place as the rest of the decor is in pink sandstone. The *jalis* are similar to the ones in Fatehpur Sikri when comparing carving skills. (Fig. 23)

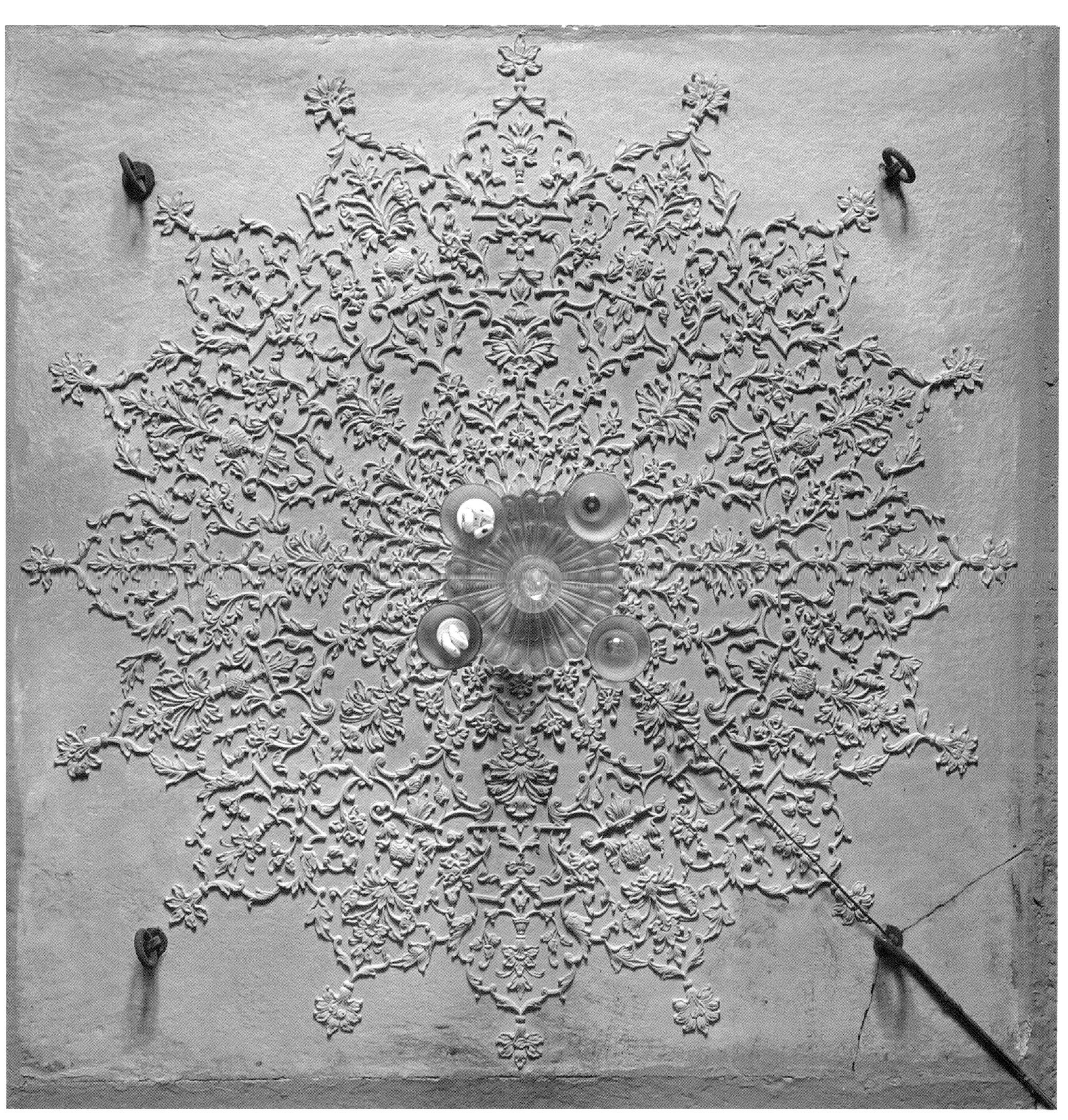

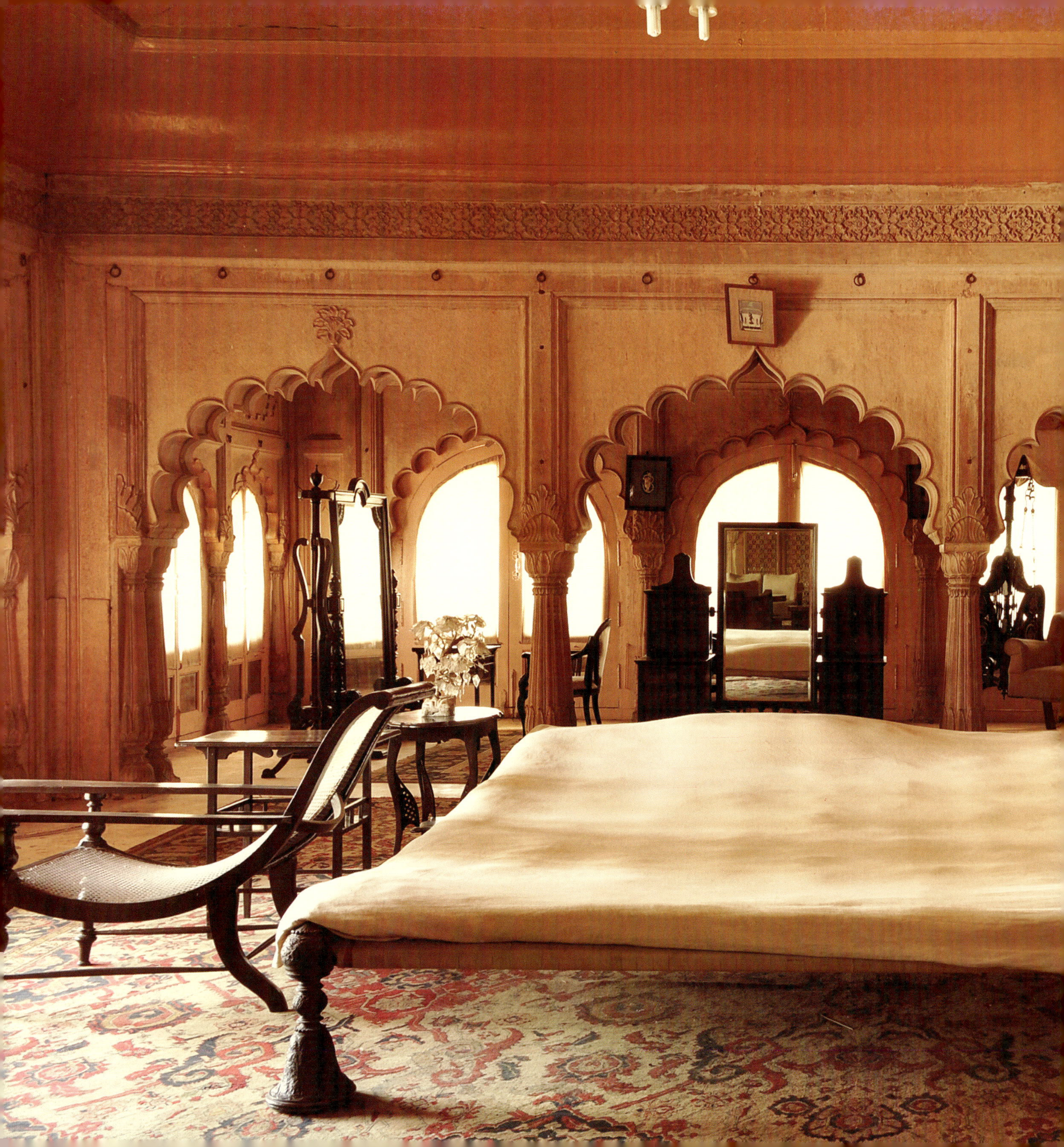

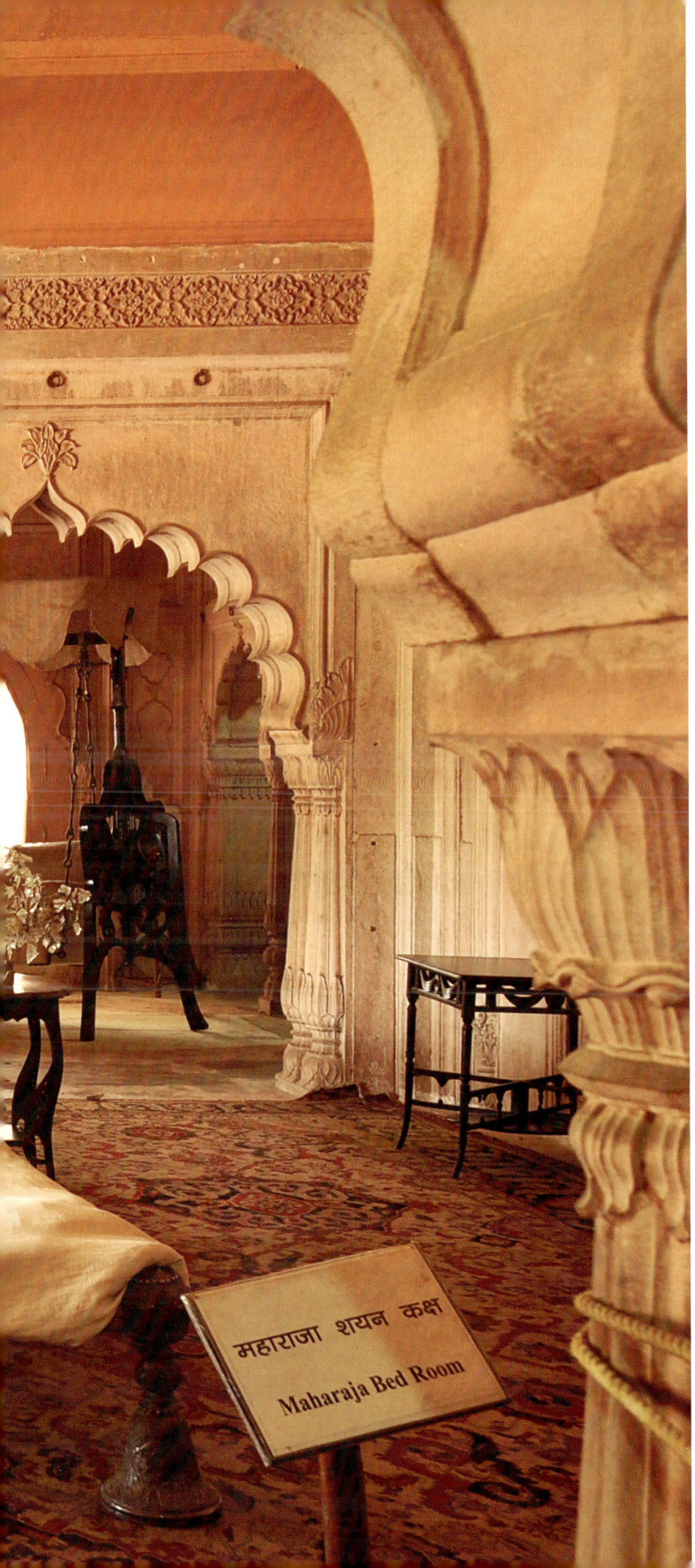

महाराजा शयन कक्ष
Maharaja Bed Room

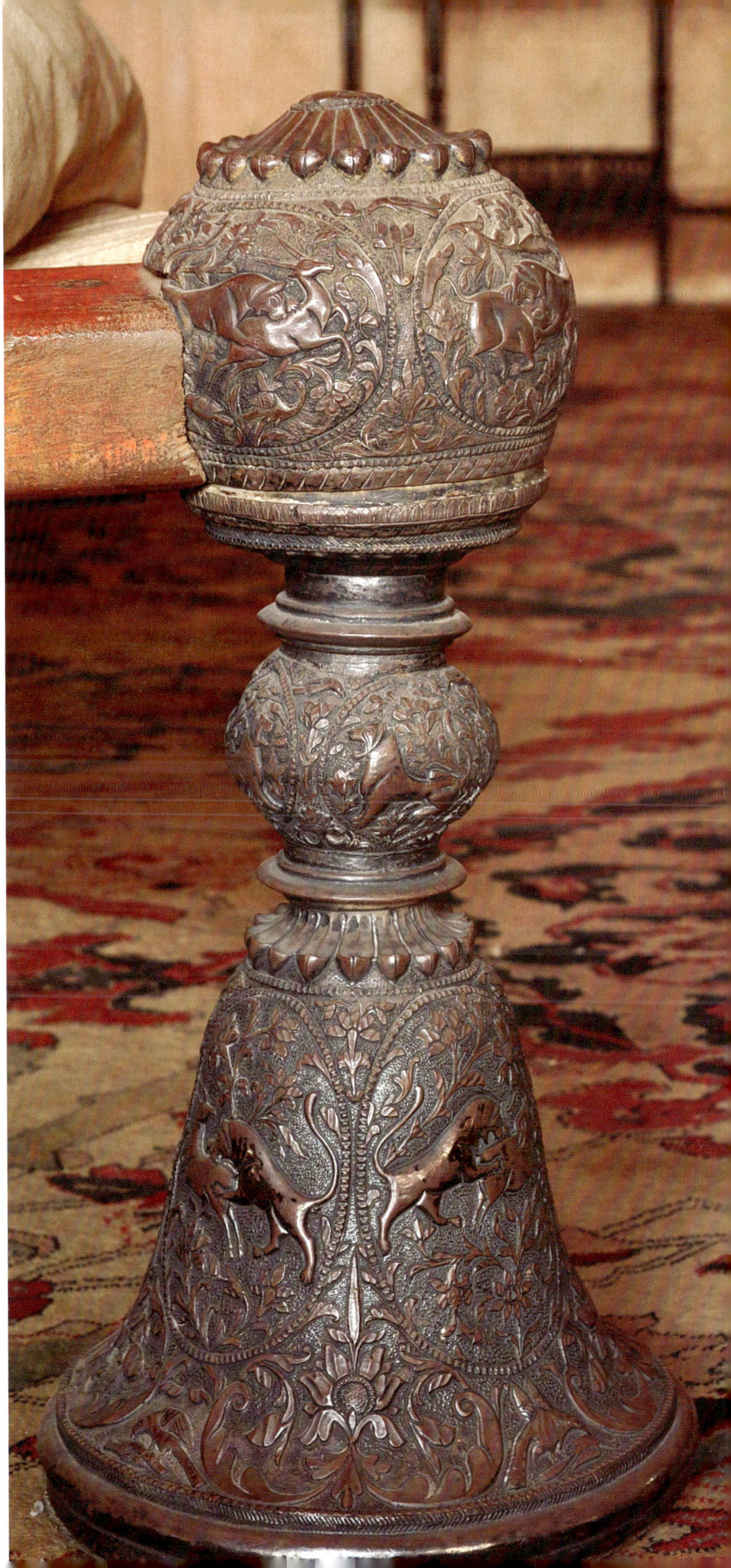

The lobby leads to the main bedroom on the east. The bedroom has three partitions with a square central area and two oblong vestibules on either side separated by columns and arcades. In the middle of the central area on the ceiling is a carved stone panel from which are suspended four hooks. (Fig. 24) This carved stone panel is the centre of attraction in the otherwise plain ceiling.

Previous page left (Fig. 25): *The square central area of the king's bedroom houses a huge royal bed in the middle*

Previous page right (Fig. 26): *A silver leg of the king's bed*

Facing page (Fig. 29): *The vestibule on one side of the bedroom functions as a sitting area and overlooks the reception room*

Below left (Fig. 27): *Partition wall of the bedroom is a carved niche ornamented with cartouche panels*

Below (Fig. 28): *Detail of the carved wooden screen in the middle of the king's chamber*

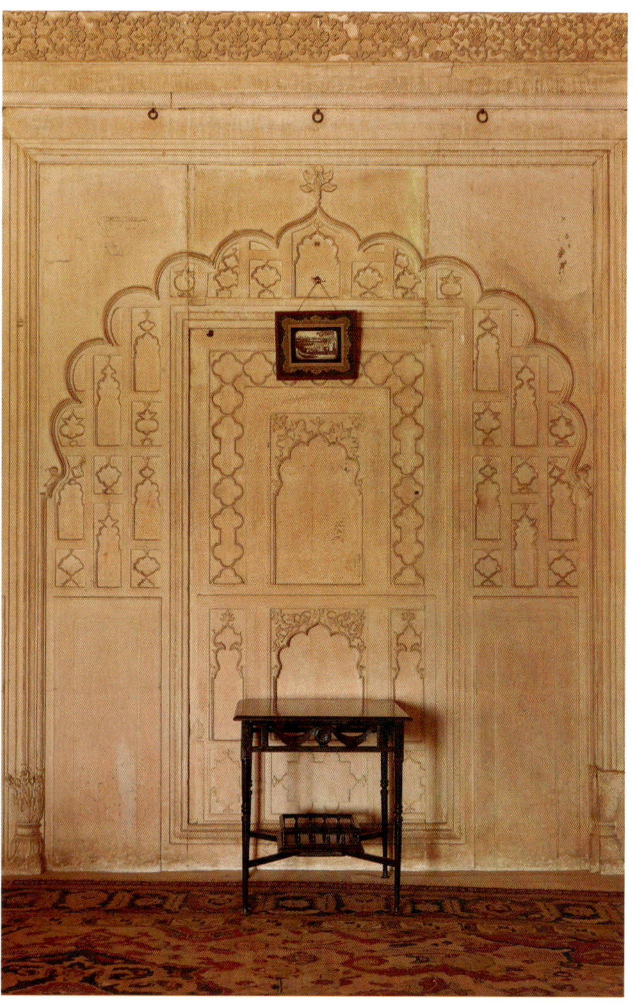

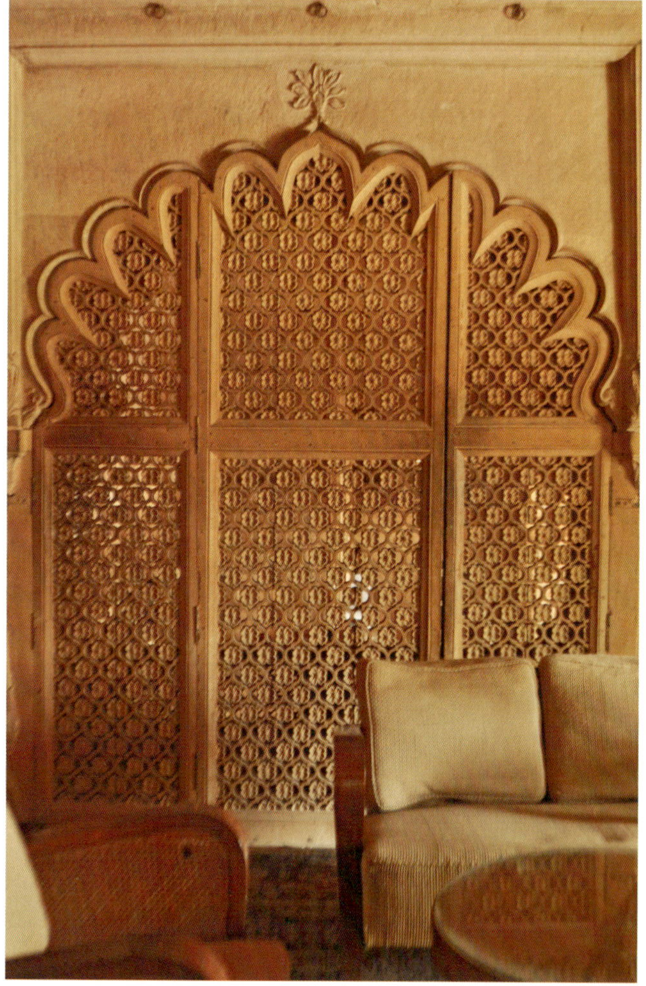

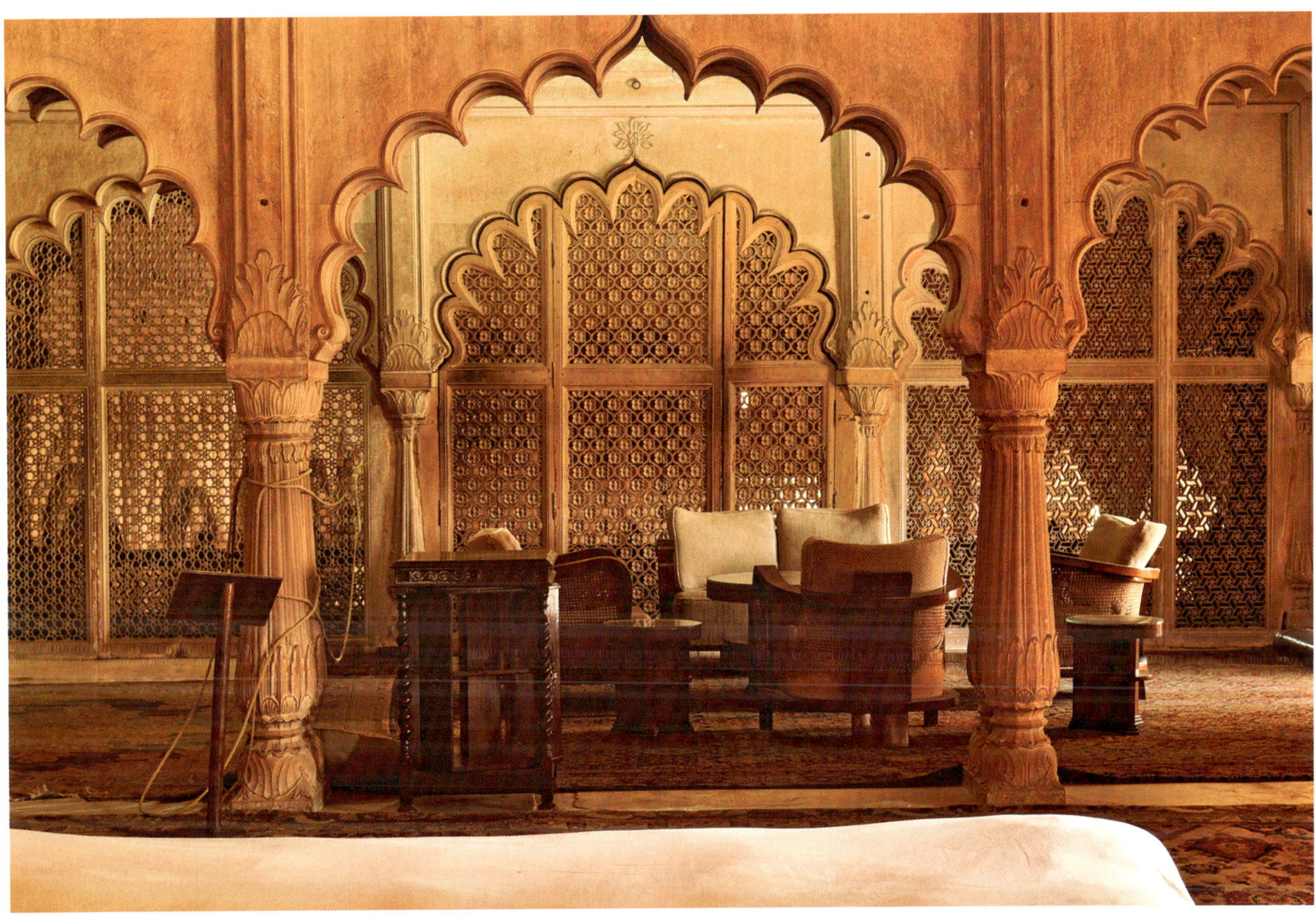

The centre of the room is occupied by a big 8ft × 11.5ft bed (Fig. 25) with four silver bell-shaped ornaments which serve as legs of the bed. Two of these were stolen and melted while the remaining two are intact displaying the intricately carved hunting scenes. (Fig. 26) Some claim that the four hooks exactly overhanging the centre of the bed from the ceiling were used to suspend the bed as a natural swing. This theory is further justified by the presence of a pulley on the windowsill exactly at the place where a rope from the four hooks on top would have gone through. This window is towards the front of the bedroom and has three arched openings overlooking the garden. On the opposite side of the room is a decorated wall with carved niches. (Fig. 27) Earlier, this connected the private recreation or meeting hall but is now closed with wooden partitions decorated in a similar way to the sandstone wall. All along the walls of the main bedroom are installed elaborately carved friezes.

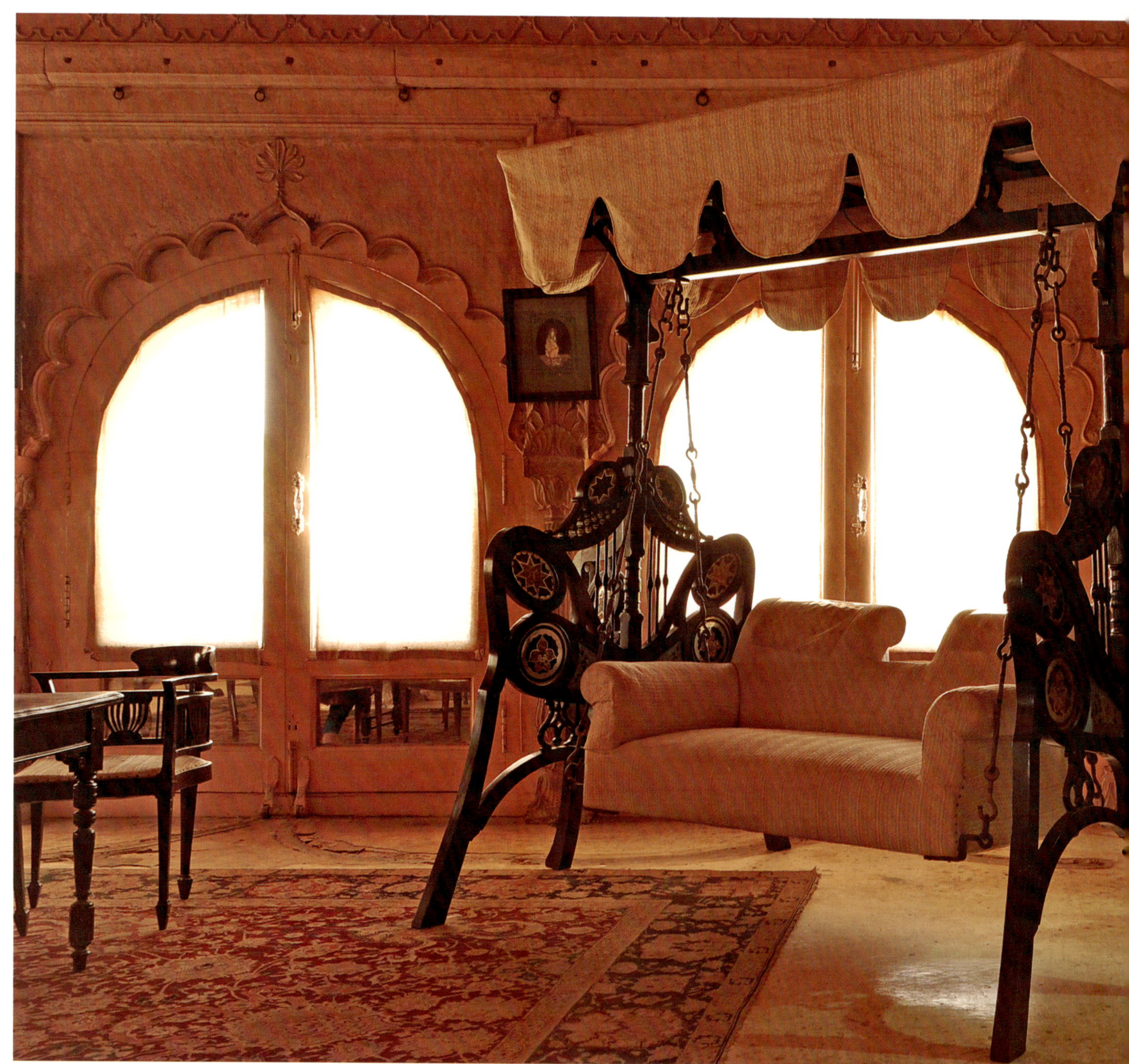

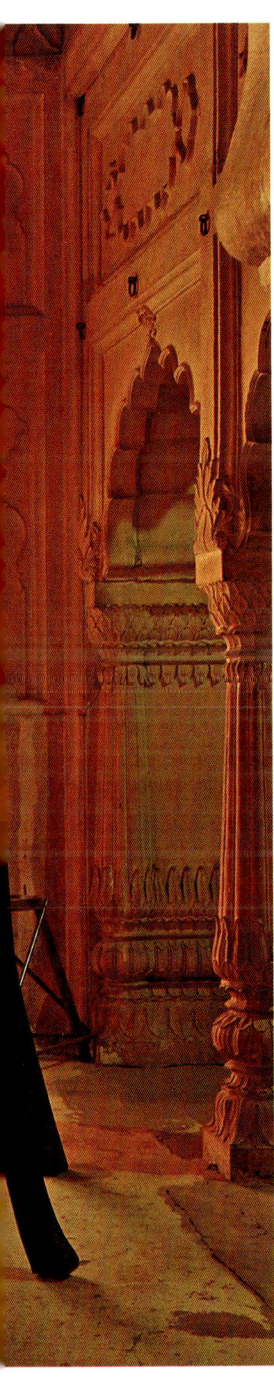

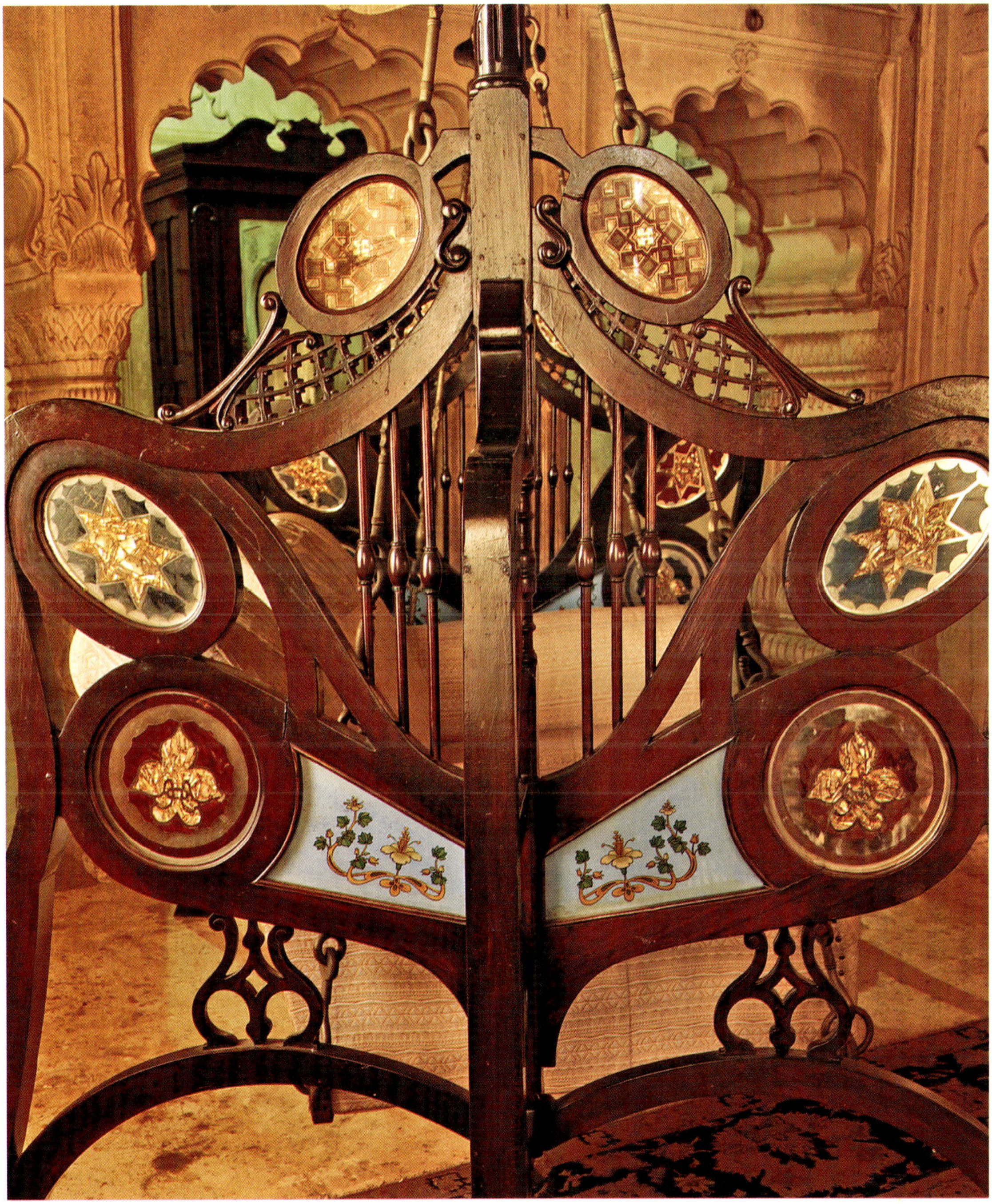

The vestibule on one side looks into the double height reception hall through the detailed carved lattice screens (*jalis*). (Fig. 28) The two side *jalis* are carved of sandstone and the middle one in wood. The design of the stone *jalis* is again similar to those found in Fatehpur Sikri and Agra. The vintage furniture is arranged in order to give it an appearance of a sitting area for observation of the commemorations in the reception room (Fig. 29). The vestibule on the other side overlooks the Sawan and Bhadon pavilions respectively. This area is again furnished by the last kings' possessions of which the most noteworthy one is a butterfly-shaped swing.

Previous page left (Fig. 30): *The vestibule on the opposite side of the bedroom contains a dressing table and the butterfly-shaped swing*

Previous page right (Fig. 31): *Detail of the butterfly-shaped swing made of rich enamel and lacquer*

Facing page (Fig. 33): *Wall of the bathroom featuring a free-standing basin and dressing table*

Below (Fig. 32): *The carved bathtub surround with equally stunning latticework in the backdrop*

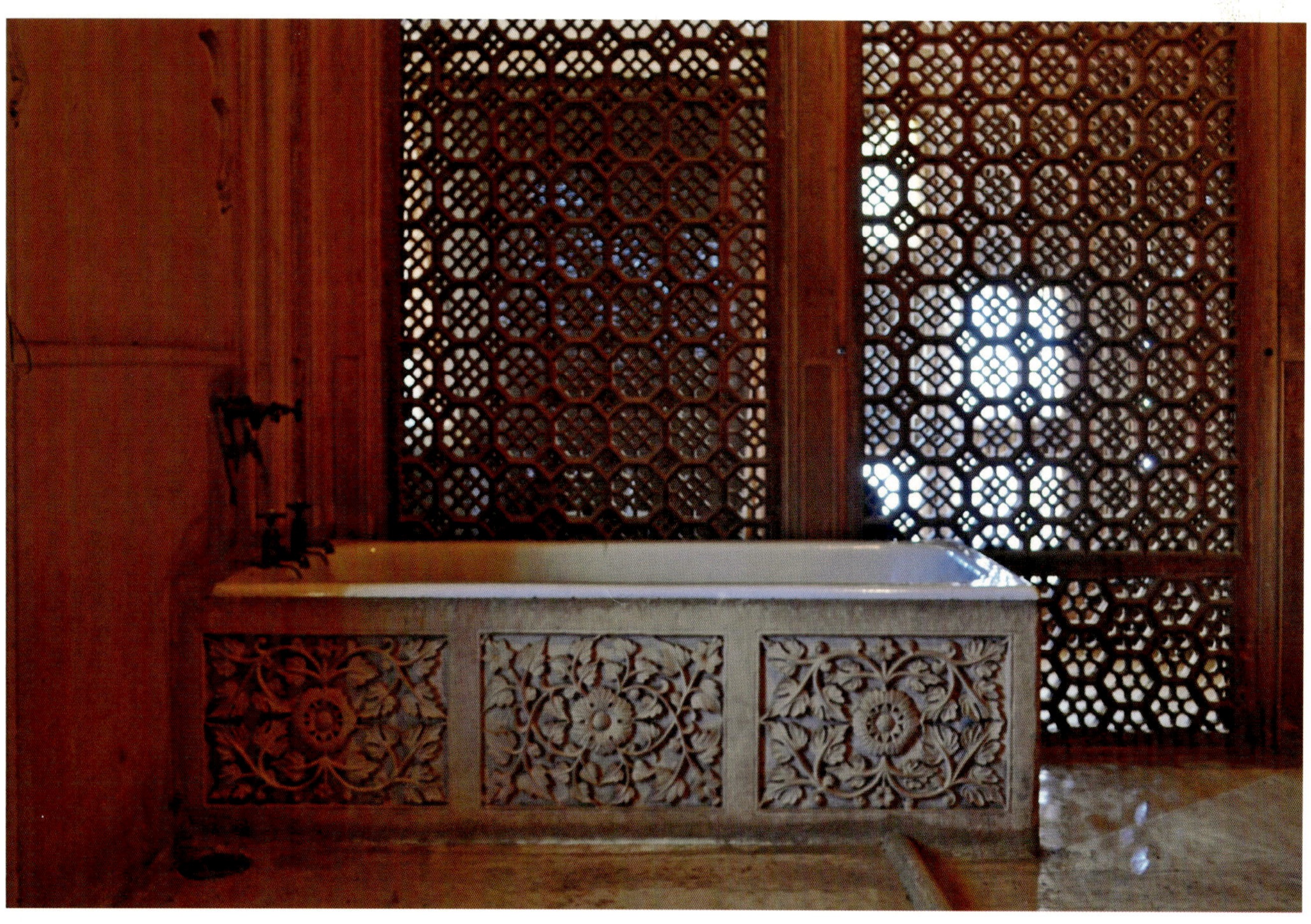

(Fig. 30) The butterfly swing is another classic example of the tastes of the rulers. This swing is made from Kashmir wood whose sides are inspired by the wings of a butterfly. It has embossed mirror work which depicts the various colours of a butterfly wing. The decoration is with rich, coloured enamel and lacquer work. (Fig. 31)

This vestibule further opens into a bathroom at the back, towards the west. A carved stone panel encases a modern bathtub as well as the surround of the shower area with a decorative hand carving of English flowers. (Fig. 32) The flowers in the shower tray are truly delightful. Though added later, the workmanship has not been compromised in any way. The finely carved wall panels add a unique charm to the area. Especially noticeable are the lattice screens in the backdrop of the bathtub. The wall of the bathroom features a free-standing basin and dressing table. (Fig. 33) A western-style water closet next to the Gopal Sagar balcony

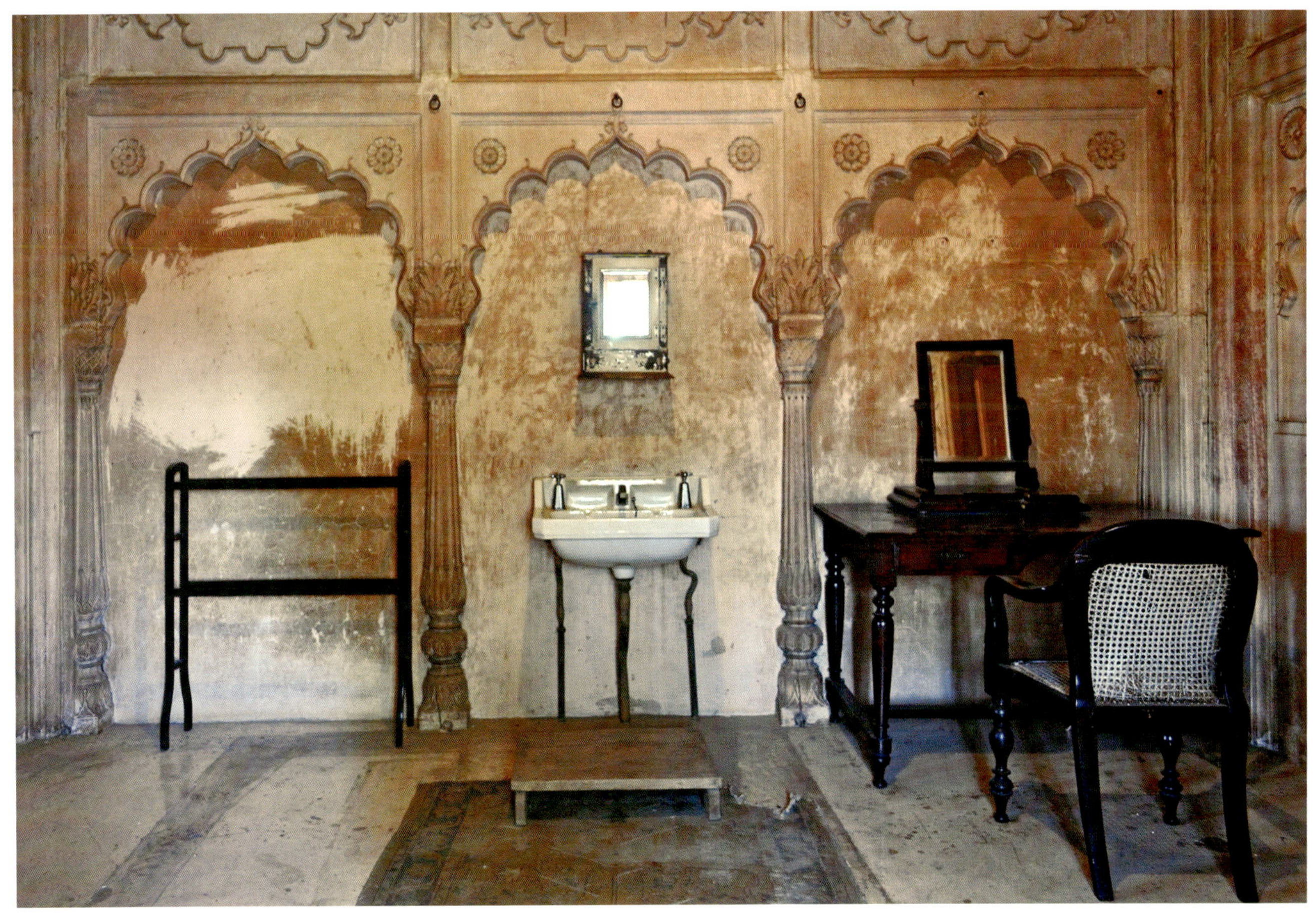

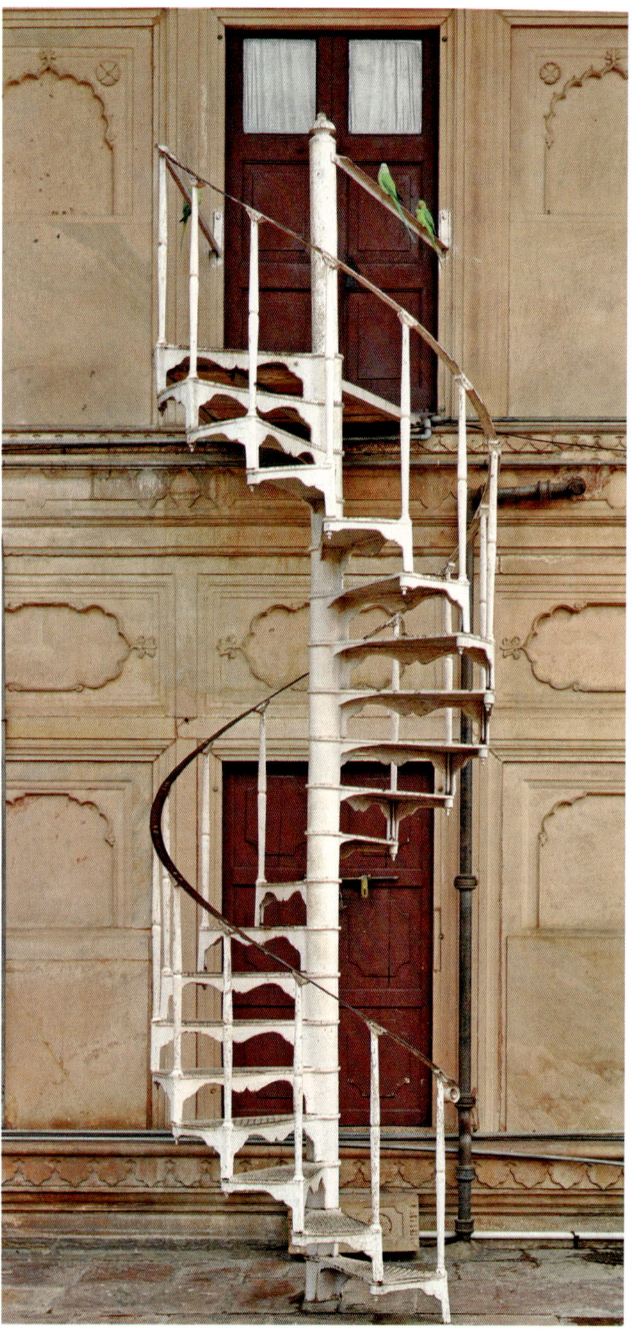

against the *jali* backdrop gives the impression of a modern-day spa. There is also a separate iron spiral staircase to this area which may have been used for servicing the bathrooms on the upper levels in the chambers of the king and queen. (Fig. 34)

One may notice several stone dado panels with peepholes around the walls of the palace. Some time there are even three cut-outs in one panel. According to the caretakers, while some of these holes were way for trash chute, others had an access to the other side of the building and were often used for communication. There are some more royal chambers on the northern and southern part of the Gopal Bhawan at the level of the central hall. These are physically segregated by *jali* screens on the arched wall of the ground floor reception hall, though there are *jharokhas* on the upper floor overlooking the hall.

Perhaps the most exhilarating space of the Gopal Bhawan is the little palace tucked beneath the bedroom on the same level as the reception hall with a throne and a fountain. The middle of the large room is characterised by a vivacious, sunken, carved square fountain with a canopy resting on four carved columns stretched to the ceiling forming an islet *chhatri*. (Fig. 35) This fountain is made of white marble and the square is 66in × 66in together with an 11-inch

Left (Fig. 34): *The spiral staircase on either side of the Gopal Bhawan was used to service the bathrooms on the upper level for the chambers of the king and queen*

Facing page (Fig. 35): *The sunken, carved, square marble fountain with a canopy resting on four carved columns stretched to the ceiling form an islet* chhatri

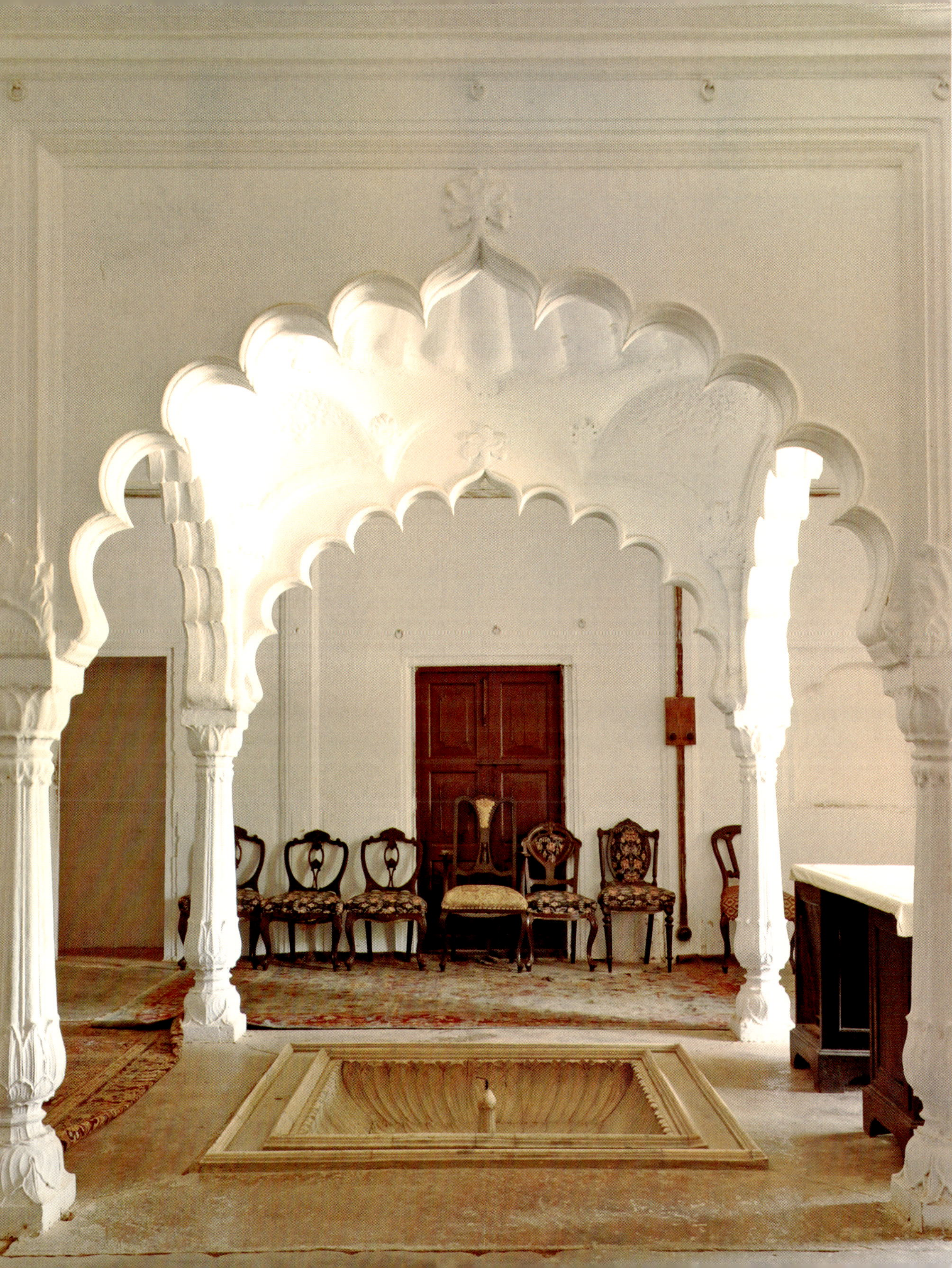

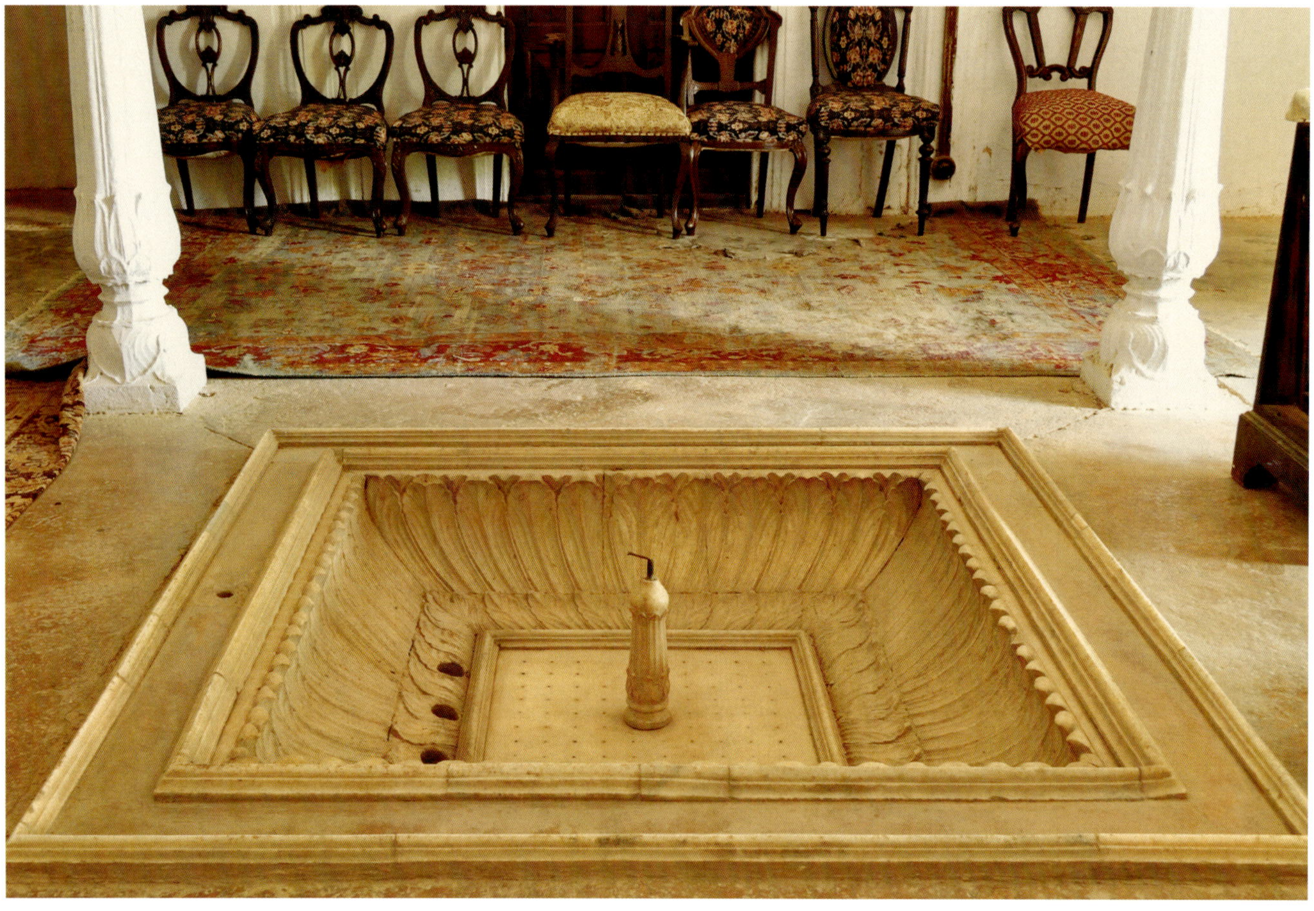

water channel framed by mouldings all around at the floor level. The middle basin is sunken inside the floor by approximately 11 inches with carved lotus leaves at a double level all around its edges. The fountain has a flat base slab of 22in × 22in with 100 needle-hole water sprinklers, ten in each direction, supporting an 11-inch tall central spout in the shape of a lotus bud. (Fig. 36) The four columns of the *chhatri* that arise around this fountain capture everyone's attention. This

ABOVE **(Fig. 36):** *The white marble fountain with 100 needle-hole water sprinklers at the base supports a tall, central lotus-shaped spout*

FACING PAGE **(Fig. 37):** *The gigantic, wooden, manually operated desert cooler that used to cool the Nand Bhawan is now housed in the ASI Museum at Gopal Bhawan*

contemplating, therapeutic, canopied fountain feature is like the *axis mundi* of this recreation room. A raised platform with a royal seat framed by a *bangladar* niche arch overlooking this *chhatri* with an axis continuing to the front terrace and Charbagh makes this a dream

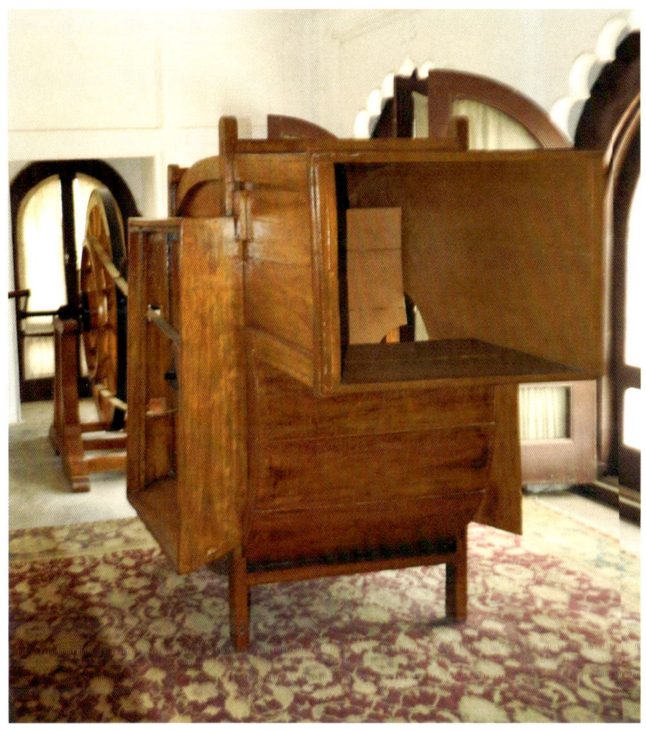

palace or a royal fantasy pavilion. It reminds us of the setting of Shah Jahan's throne in the Diwan-i-Aam of Red Fort, Delhi. The same spatial miracle has been achieved with lime-plastered sandstone as opposed to the intricately carved marble and *pietra dura* using semi-precious stones in the Delhi fort. Though at totally different scales, one was for the 'Emperor of the world' while the other was for a humble raja's personal fascination.

According to M.C. Joshi, 'a room on the northern wing contains a throne or throne-platform of black marble and another of the southern of white marble, and both these are believed to be the spoils of war removed by Jawahar Singh from the imperial palaces of Delhi'. The axial rule continues to be applied here. The line starting from the throne seat continues via the fountain features strongly abets a bend in the water channel running parallel to the Gopal Bhawan, forming a Z-turn and changing its directions towards Suraj Bhawan to the south and Singh Pol to the north, as shown before.

The Gopal Bhawan now houses a museum for the ASI. It includes pieces of historical as well as cultural significance for the Jat rulers. The museum tour starts with a jumbo-sized bathing bed for the dead, made of black granite, which is said to be carried by the Jats from the Mughals as they mistook it to be a king's bed. Several sculptures including a sandalwood sculpture of Lord Venugopal and an alabaster sculpture of a dancing girl greet the visitors. The main reception hall has a stuffed hunting trophy of a lioness whose two cubs are exhibited in the Kishan Bhawan. A cigarette and scent case made from the legs of the elephant that is said to have broken the Delhi gate is proudly displayed on the colonial wooden table. All along the different rooms of the Gopal Bhawan one can find Persian carpets, furniture and crockery. In one of the smaller rooms, even the seat of the marble *jhula* (swing) is displayed. But the most awe-inspiring object is the mammoth, wooden, hand-run desert water cooler, which was originally used to cool the gathering during the wrestling matches held at the Nand Bhawan. This cooler is still in running condition. (Fig. 37)

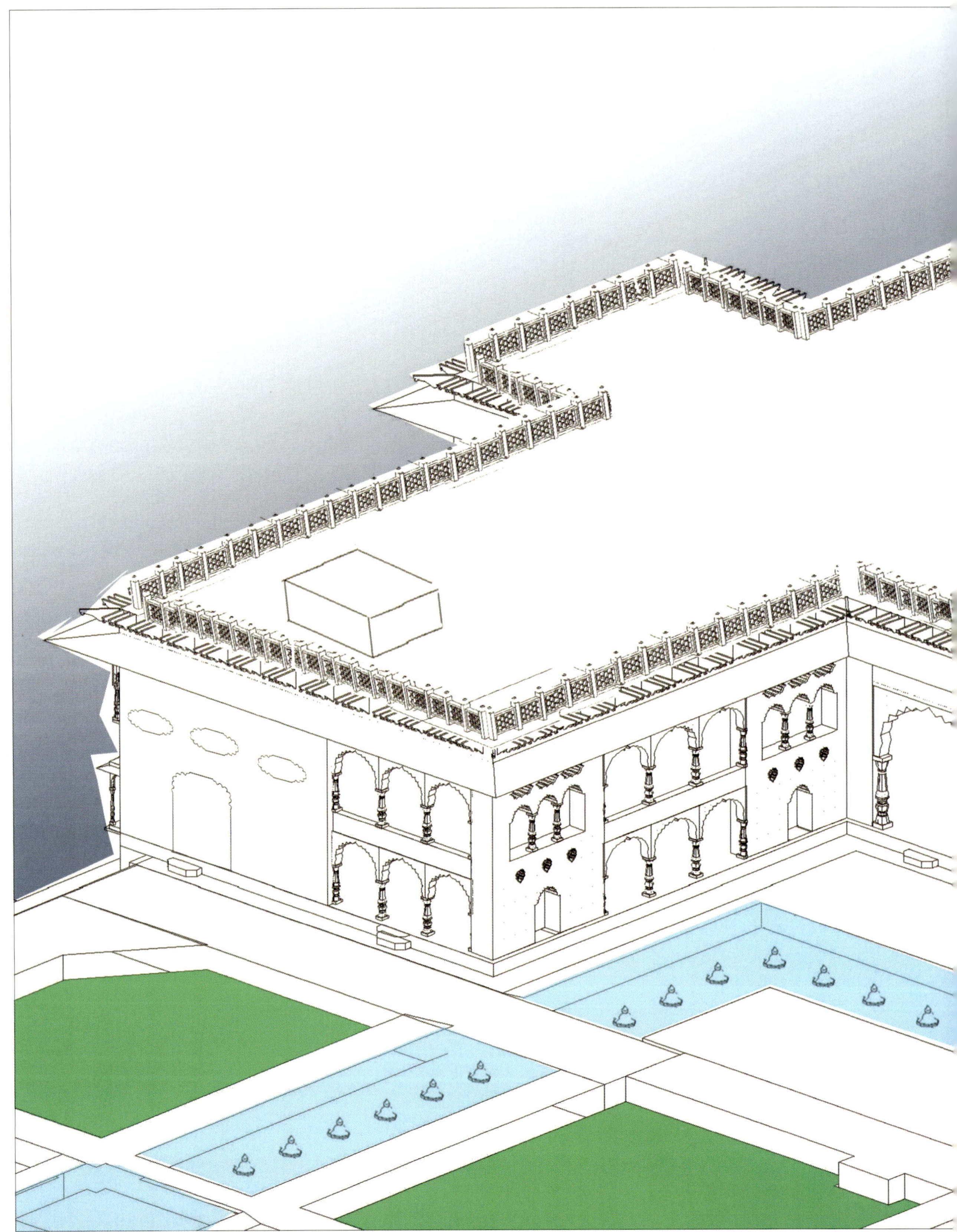

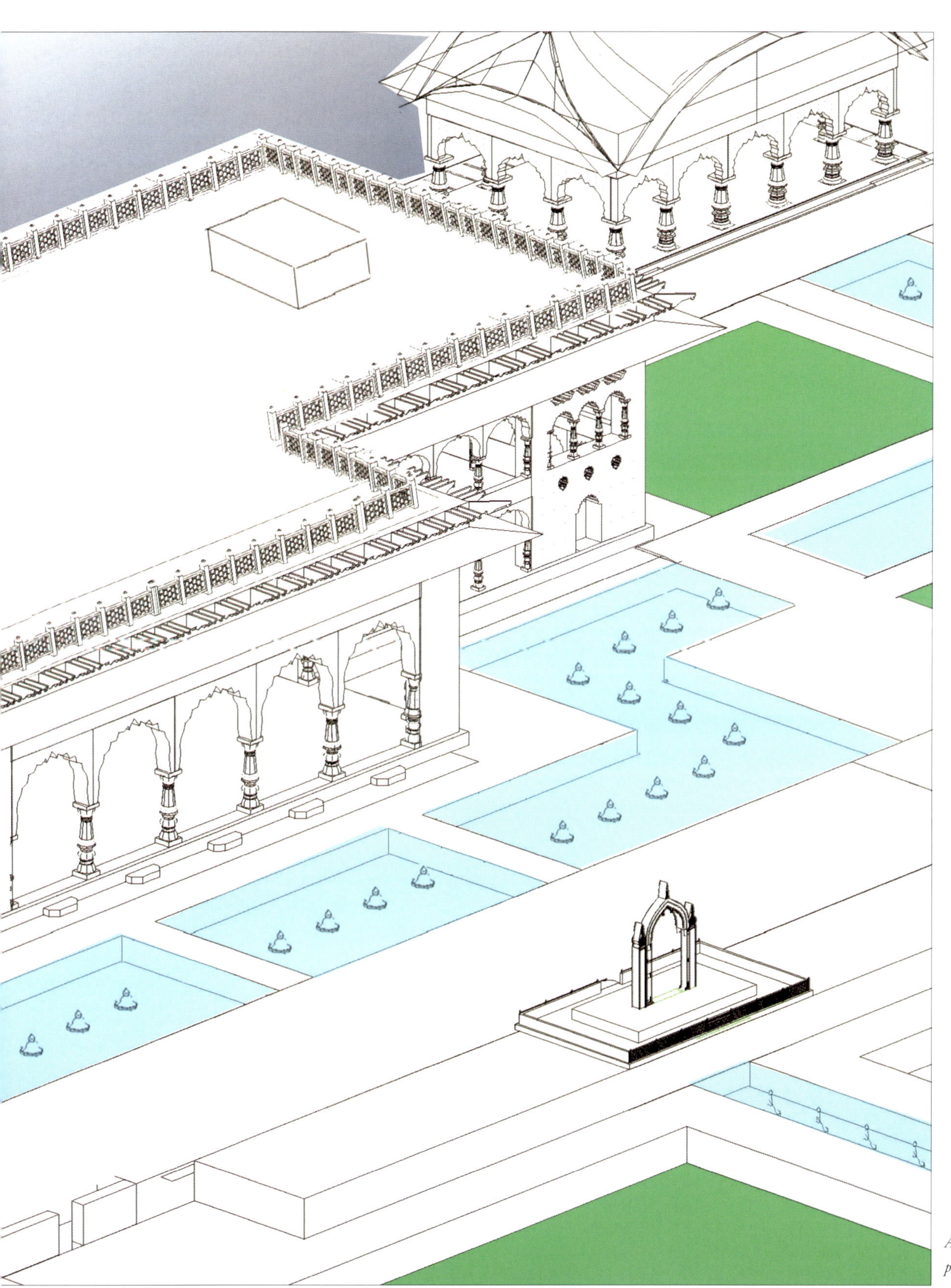

A 3D visual of the Gopal Bhawan positioned across the marble swing arch

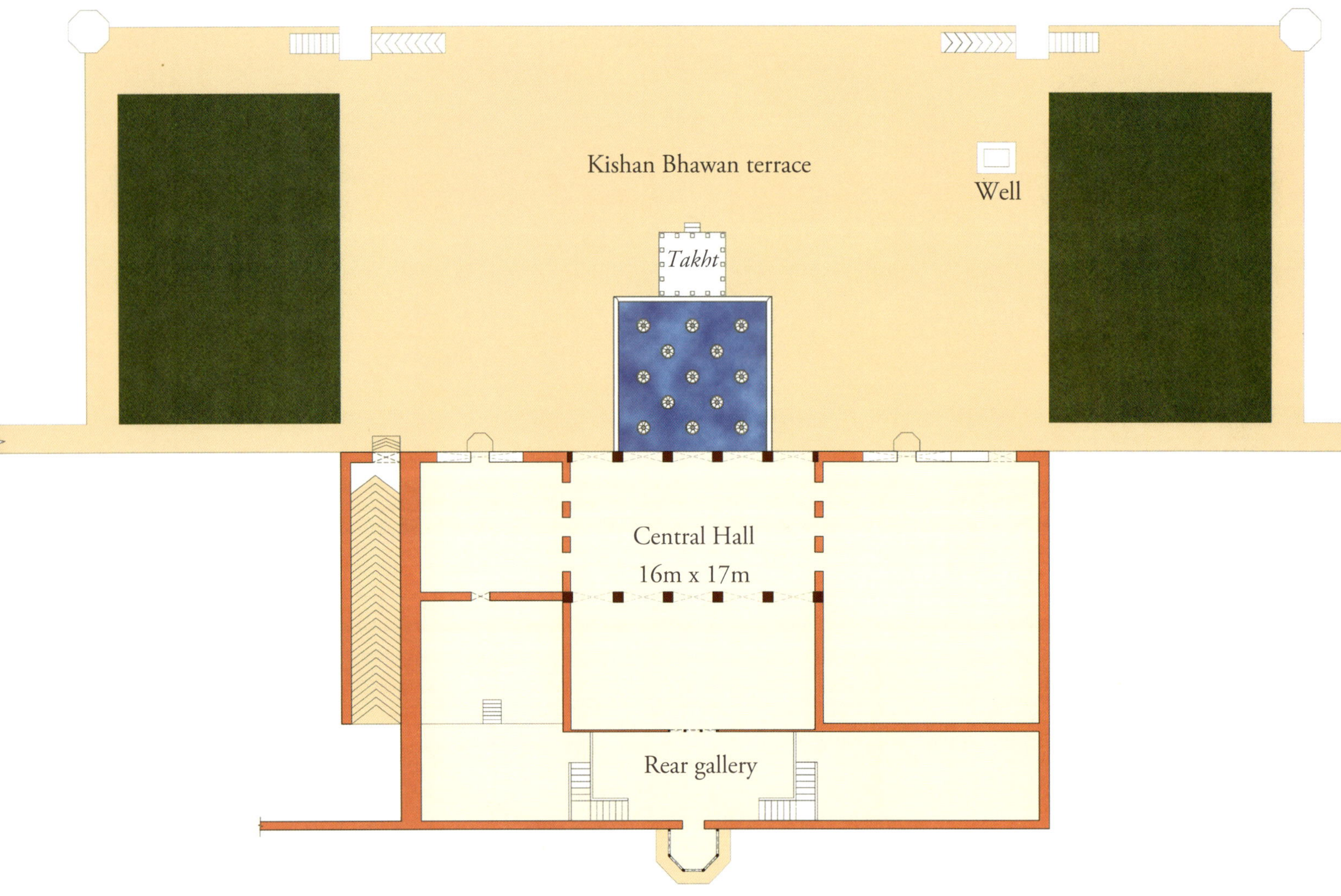
Sunken Charbagh
Kishan Bhawan terrace
Well
Takht
Central Hall
16m x 17m
Rear gallery

DIWAN-I-KHAS

KISHAN BHAWAN

The symmetry around the axis connecting the Gopal Bhawan and Keshav Bhawan is balanced by two equal structures on either side namely, the Kishan Bhawan to the south and the Nand Bhawan to the north. These incumbent buildings are single-storeyed with huge spans. When one walks towards the southern axis of the main Charbagh, the Kishan Bhawan is a flamboyant structure with panelled fabric on a raised plinth. (Fig. 2) This high raised plinth of 1.6 metres is characterised by two fluted, melon-shaped *burjis* of massive size profusely carved with intricate petals. (Fig. 3) All along the plinth, between the two *burjis*, there are carved panels depicting various designs of the cartouches.

Right (Fig. 3): *Fluted, melon-shaped* burjis *of massive size profusely carved with intricate petals*

Facing page (Fig. 1): *Layout plan of the Kishan Bhawan and its terrace, which shows its raised rear gallery overlooking the central hall*

Following pages (Fig. 2): *A panoramic view of the Kishan Bhawan displaying the fountains, cartouches on the raised plinth and the terrace*

The ramp and steps are well negotiated and cleverly cloaked within the plinth so as not to obstruct the decoration. This also mellows down the height of this enormous plinth. The extensive facade of the Kishan

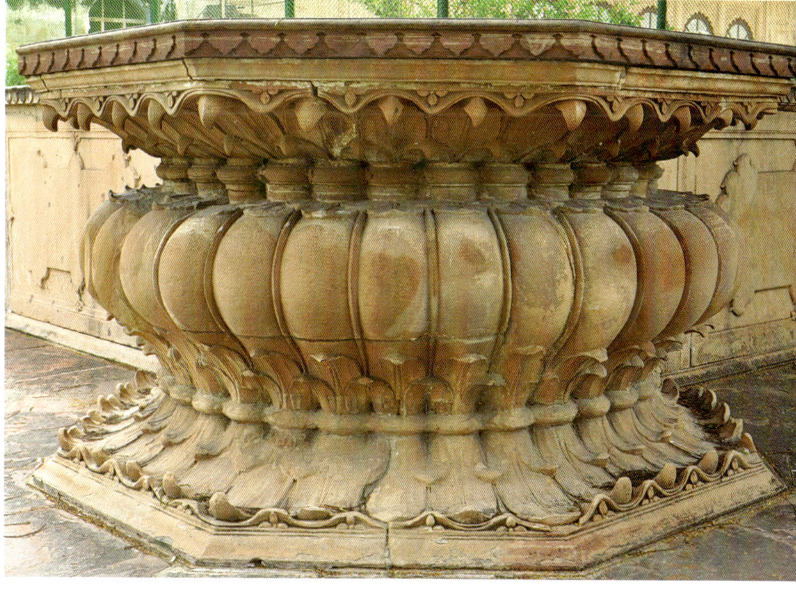

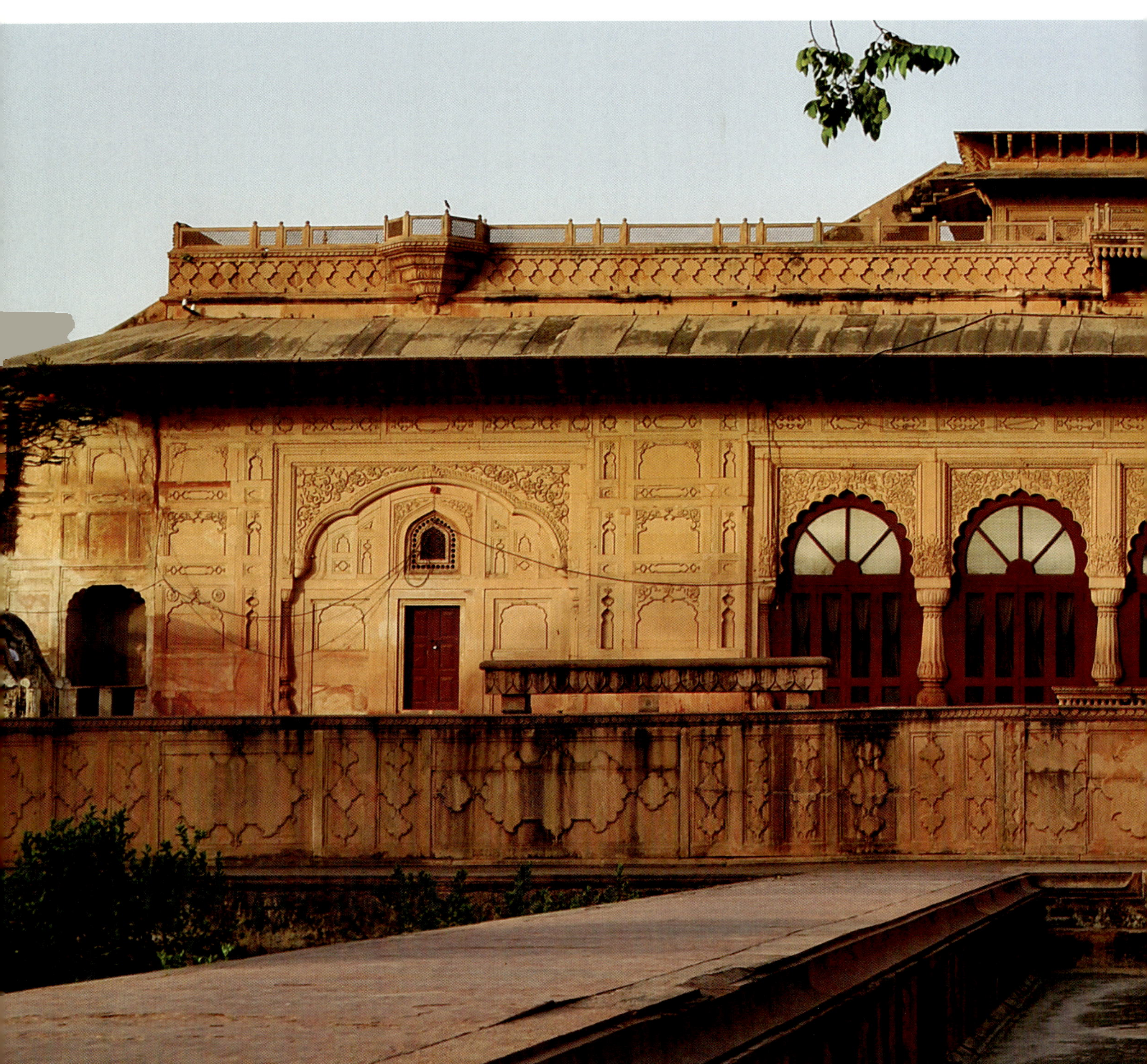

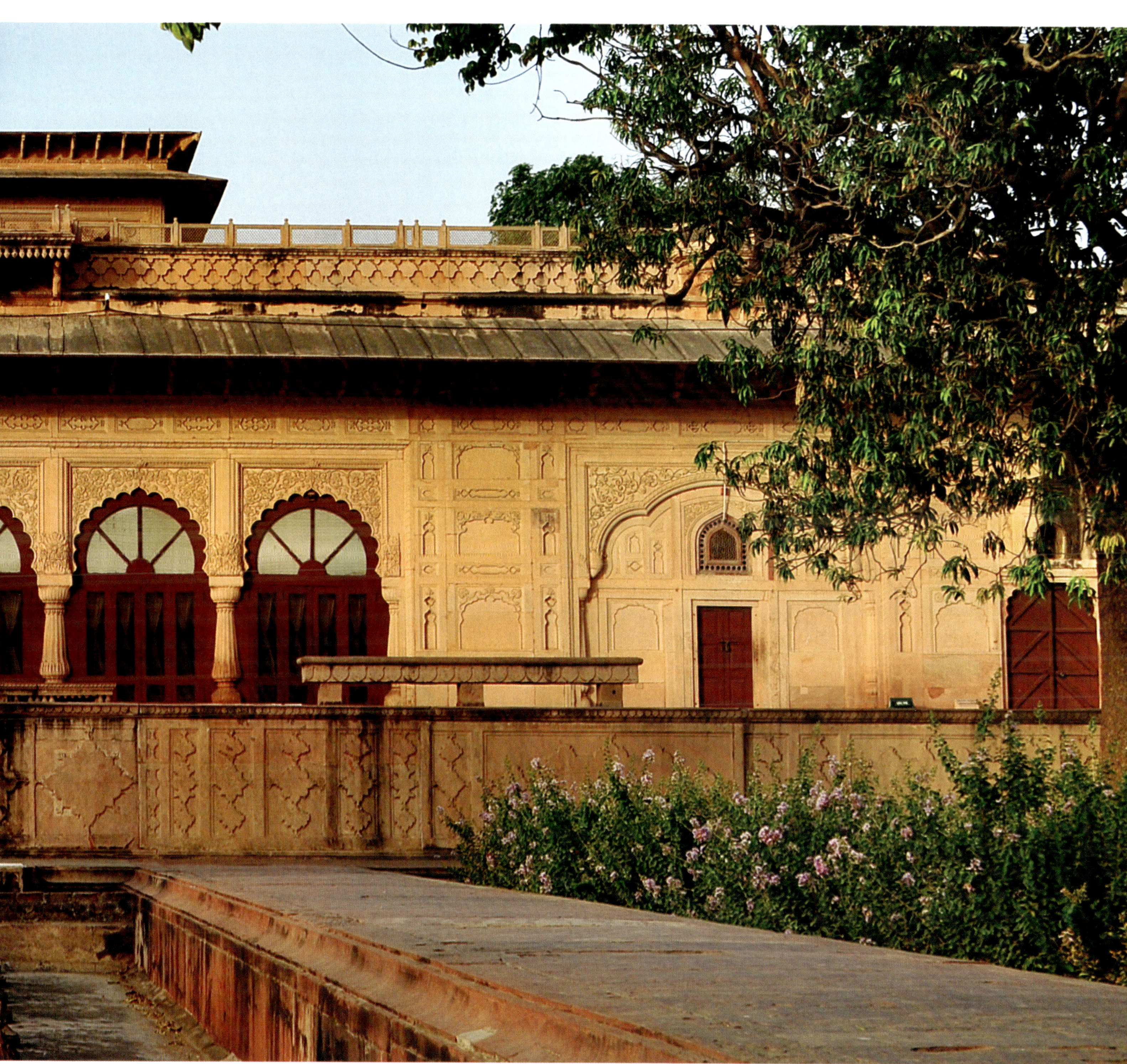

Bhawan rises by another 9.5 m above the plinth with a huge trough of 10m × 10m in its forecourt. This tank has thirteen raised fountain spouts. In front of this trough, facing the garden is a huge and graceful *takht* (sofa or long bench) of the size 4.4m × 4.4m. This is made of four equally thick stone slabs, joined together and supported by a beam. The edge of these stones is carved by a pan leaf-shaped moulding on top and a leaf on the bottom. The top portion of the beam is in geometrical design and from its lower half hangs a magnificent fringe (*jhalar*) of inverted lotus buds decorating it all along. (Fig. 4) These lotus buds are now fast disappearing and only a few are left. The main supports of this beam are twenty columns or piers. The outer posts are richly carved while the inner ones are made of plain stone. The old photographs of the 1900s show this *takht* being placed on the east of the terrace with a garden on the other side. Nowadays it is being heavily used by the general public who even use it as an exercise bench during early mornings and evenings. The terrace also has hooks on the corners which were used to put stretched canopies or *shamianas* during the general *durbars* held here. The last coronation was held on this terrace.

The symmetrical building has five-arched openings with a caboose on either side. The facades of the sides are heavily panelled and decorated with niches and arches. The panels are carved with birds and arabesque designs amongst others. There are also two red sandstone *jalis* symmetrically aligned on the facade. These may have been brought from outside. (Fig. 5)

The arches with carved spandrels (Fig. 6) lead inside to the massive *durbar* hall whose dimensions are approximately 16m × 17m. A similar five-arched row of carved arches and pillars is present in the middle of the room dividing it into half. These arches are elaborately

Facing page (Fig. 5): *The caboose on either side of the Kishan Bhawan with heavily panelled niches and arches have symmetrically aligned red sandstone* jalis *on the facade*

Below (Fig. 4): *The massive* takht *in the forecourt adorned by a magnificent fringe* (jhalar*) of inverted lotus buds*

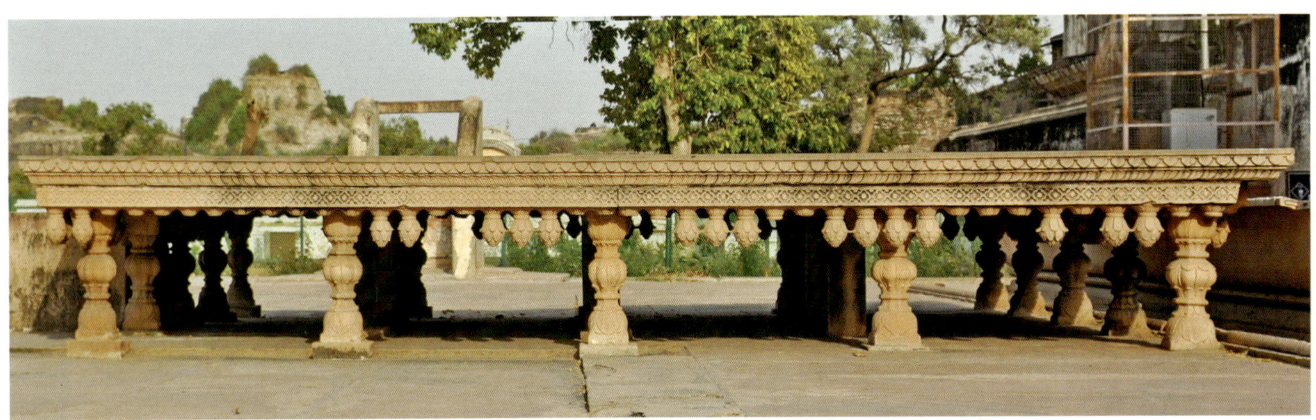

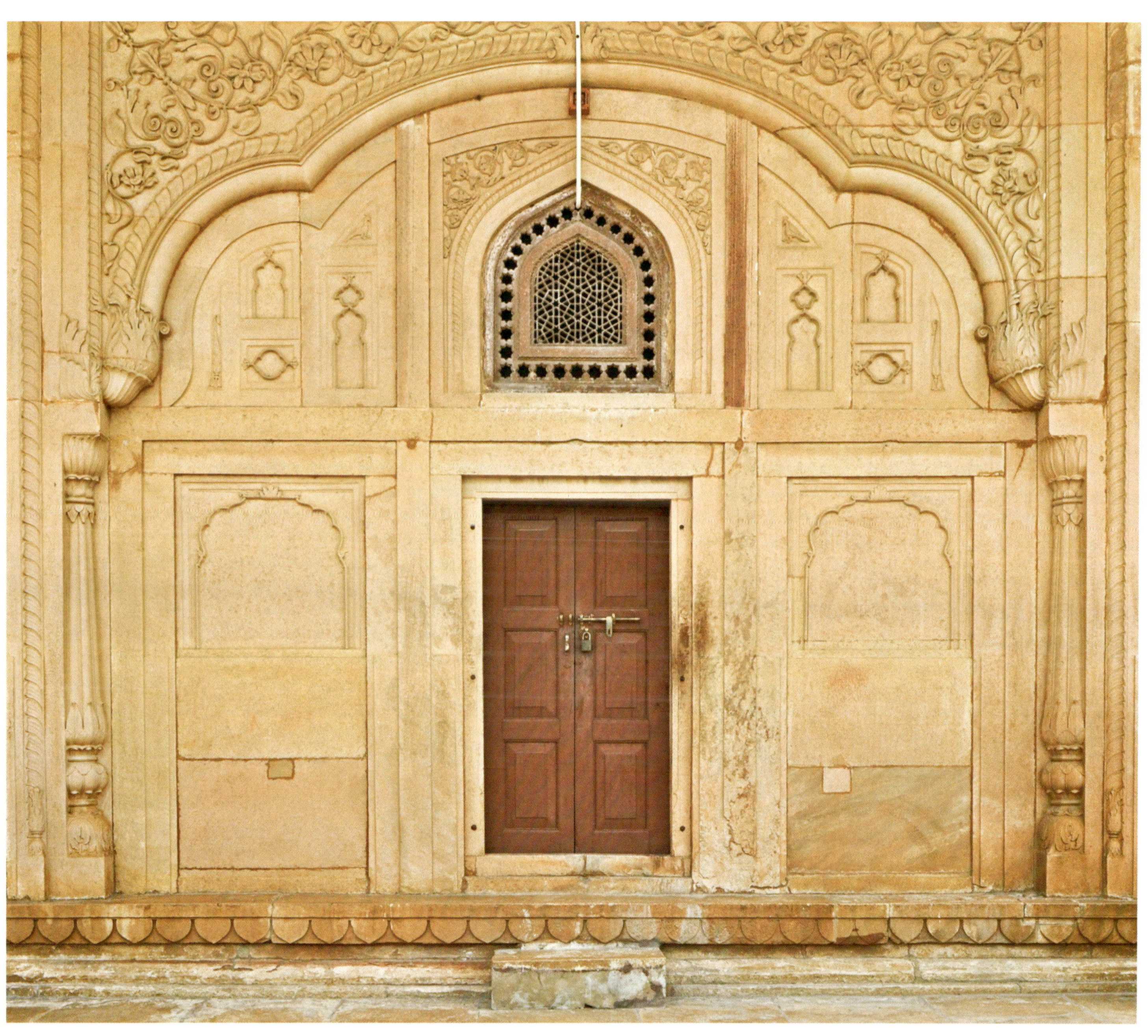

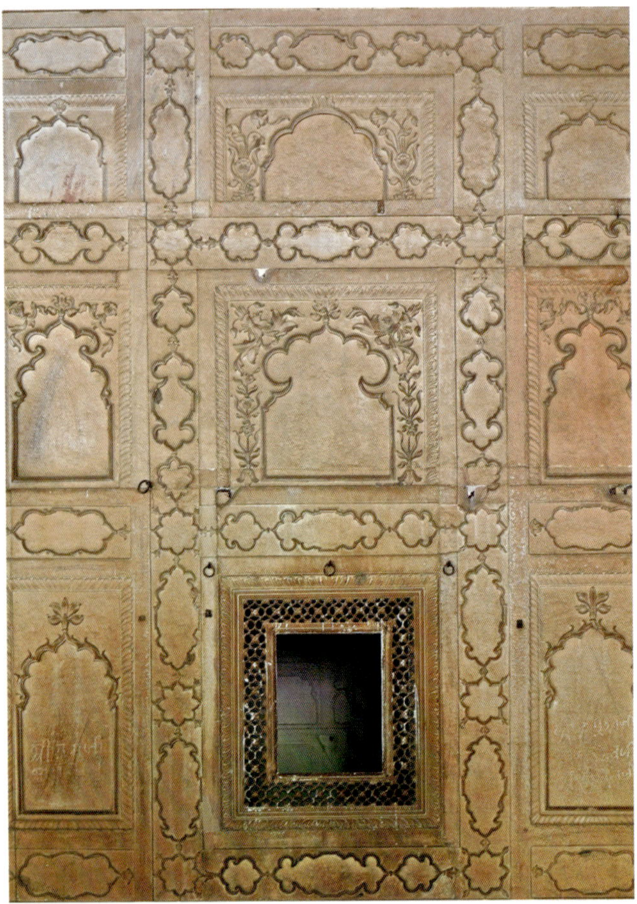

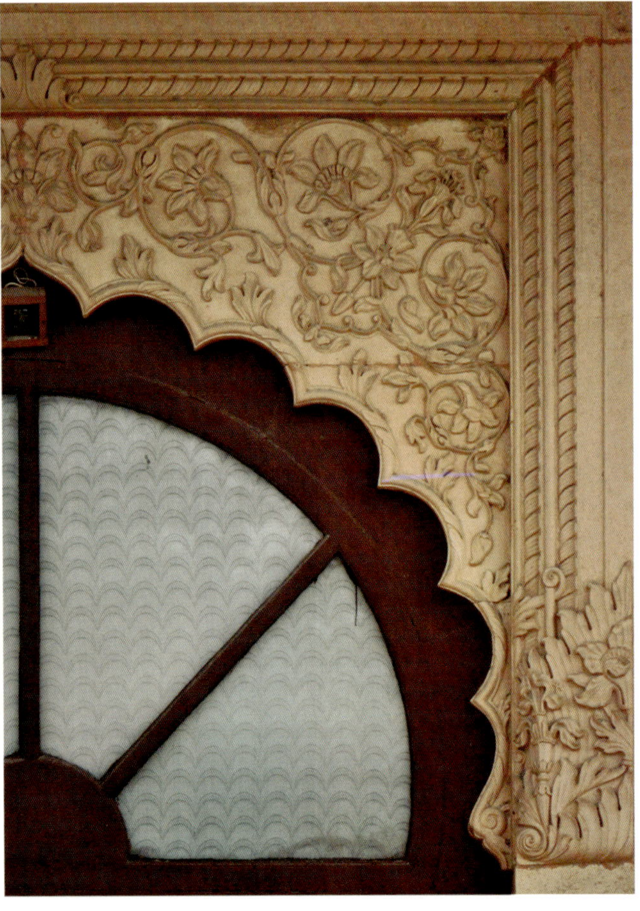

carved with different arabesque patterns on all the arch spandrels, but are plain with no carving on the inside face. The columns supporting these arches are massive and carved with floral capitals.

The back wall is the main facade of the *durbar* hall. It consists of a projecting central *bangladar* three-arched balcony. The decoration on the *bangladar jharokha* is noteworthy with carved floral leaves in scalloped patterns. It does not have any finials in the centre but is characterised by a carved *kalash* and *kalgi* on either side. (Fig. 7) The fascia of this *jharokha* has carved panels in floral vines with a peacock on each side. This balcony's designs are also replicated on the back to gives it a special background for the king to sit and give *darshan* or conduct the *durbar*. The main window is flanked on both sides by a niche window again framed in a decorative *jharokha* carved in relief. Further towards the end there are two larger square openings with a lattice border set in the geometry of the highly panelled wall. These window openings were said to be used by the queens in veil during ceremonies. (Fig. 8) There were hooks all around the openings and at the lintel level to hang muslin and fabric drapes. Behind these runs a gallery which connected to the private chambers on either side. The gallery widens to form a room because of the articulation of the central *bangladar* balcony.

The shorter sides of the hall are again decorated with similar carvings and panels with a red sandstone *jali* on the outer wall. (Fig. 9) It seems that the Jat designers were not tempted to explore anything new and relied heavily on the same magnificent patterns being repeated in the bhawan. As the hall is divided into halves, each part is identically decorated with trefoil arches framing the openings of the three doors. (Fig. 10) The extensive relief work consists of arabesque in the spandrels and cartouche arches in the fascia with occasional birds that add a charm to the carvings.

The flooring is of lime and 'araish' work whereby the lime was sieved and cured for at least a year. The fine lime was mixed with sea shells, egg shells and lentils to form an exceptionally fine paste for the flooring. Though most of the flooring is plain, it also has some beautiful stone ground painted borders and motifs in blue colour.

Huge domed mouldings rising from the walls bracket the ceiling comprising of flat stone slabs. It has a huge roof section for double insulation with the hollow section filled with earthen pots to keep the interiors

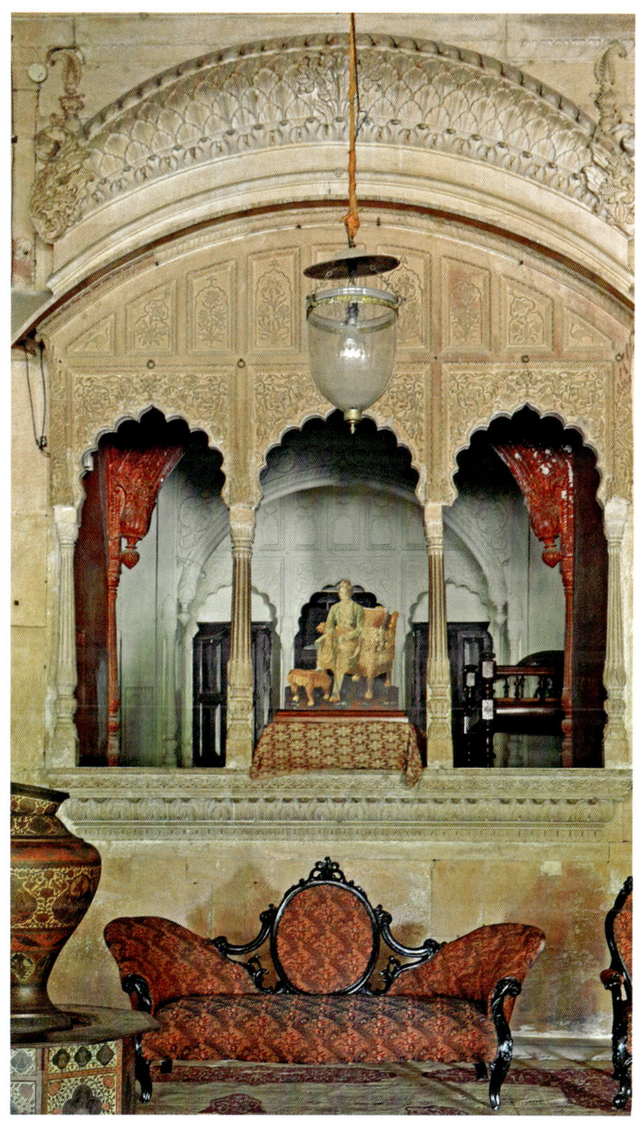

Above (Fig. 7): *Projecting central* bangladar *three-arched balcony decorated with a carved* kalash *and* kalgi *on either side*

Facing page left (Fig. 8): *Large square openings with a lattice border, used by the queens in veil during ceremonies, are set in the geometry of the highly panelled wall*

Facing page right (Fig. 6): *The arches with carved spandrels lead inside to the massive* durbar *hall*

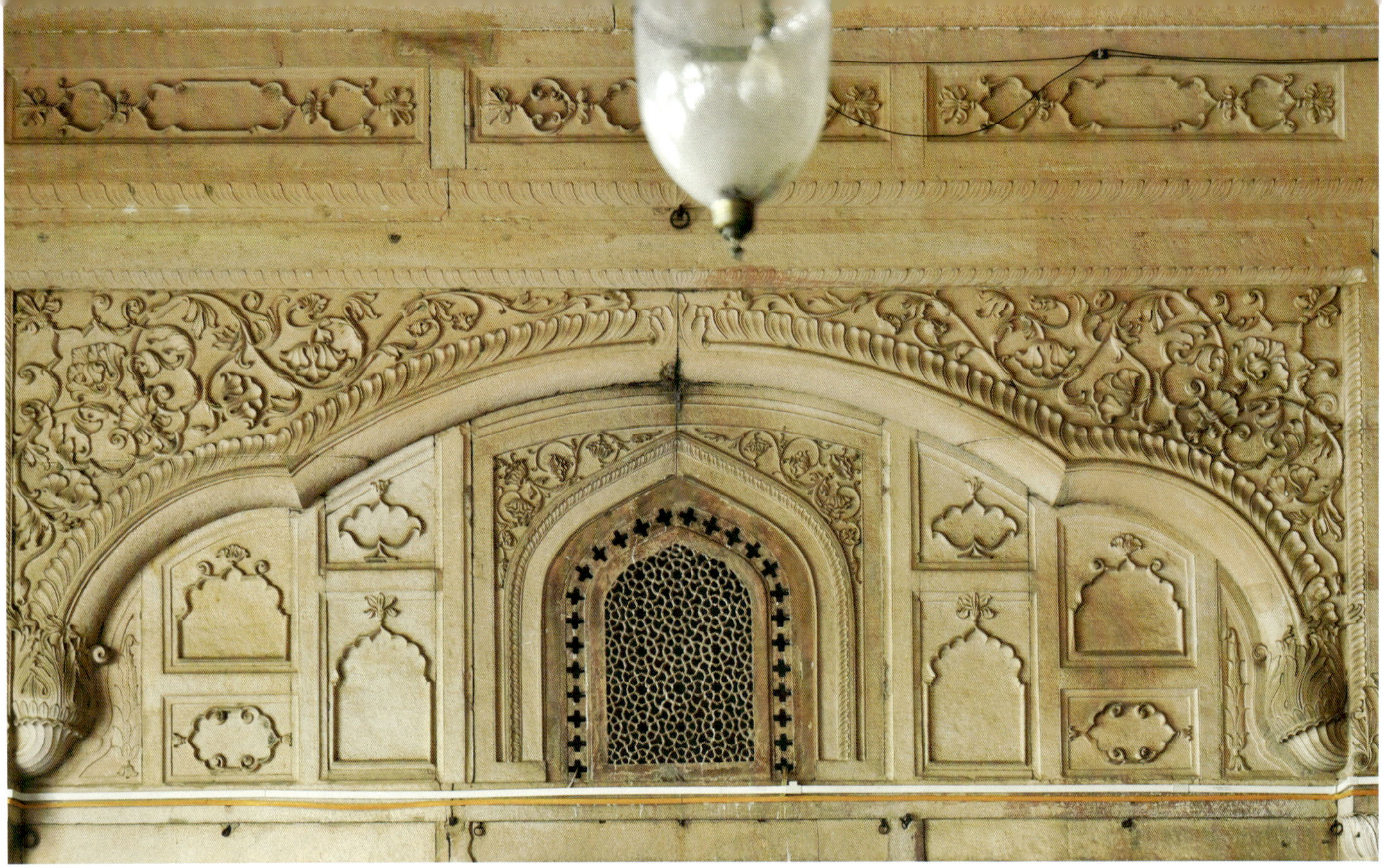

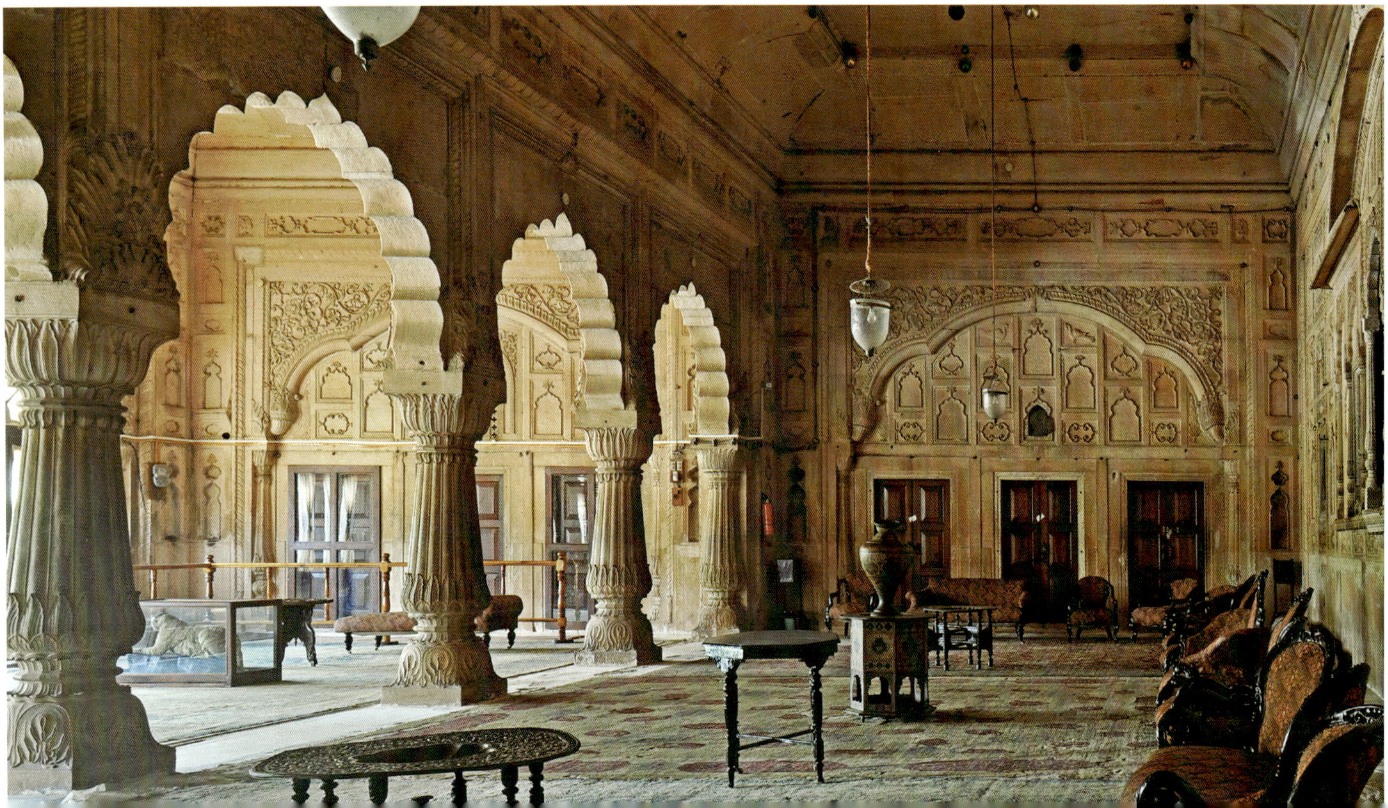

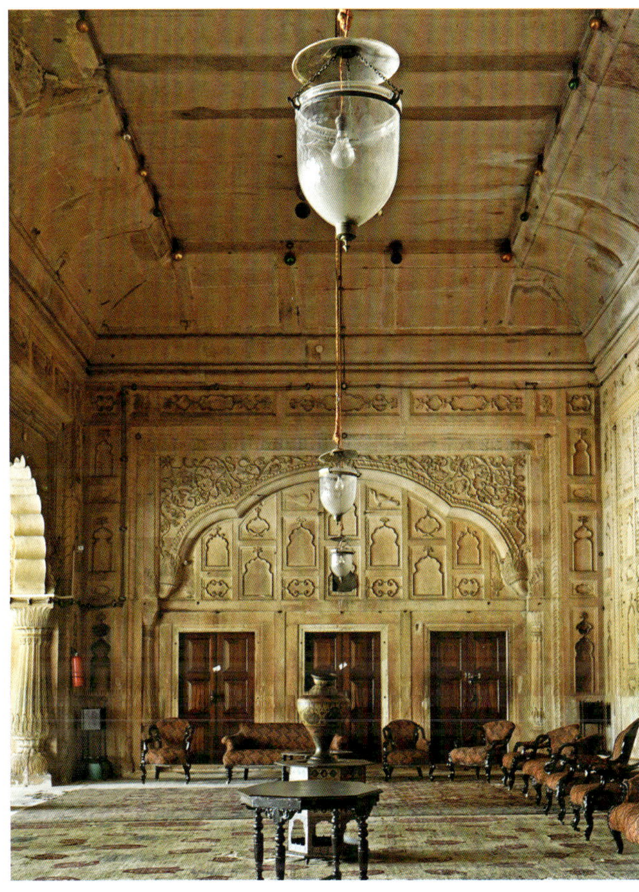

cool during the summers. (Fig. 11) This bhawan was used as the Diwan-i-Khas and also served as a private recreation chamber. It is furnished with Persian carpets and colonial wooden furniture. The artefacts consist of an enamelled metal plate depicting the scenes from the stopovers of the 84-*kos parikrama*. Also displayed are two cubs of the tigress which is exhibited in the Gopal Bhawan. (Fig. 12) The side room is now converted into a museum and displays photographs of the rulers of Bharatpur and Deeg.

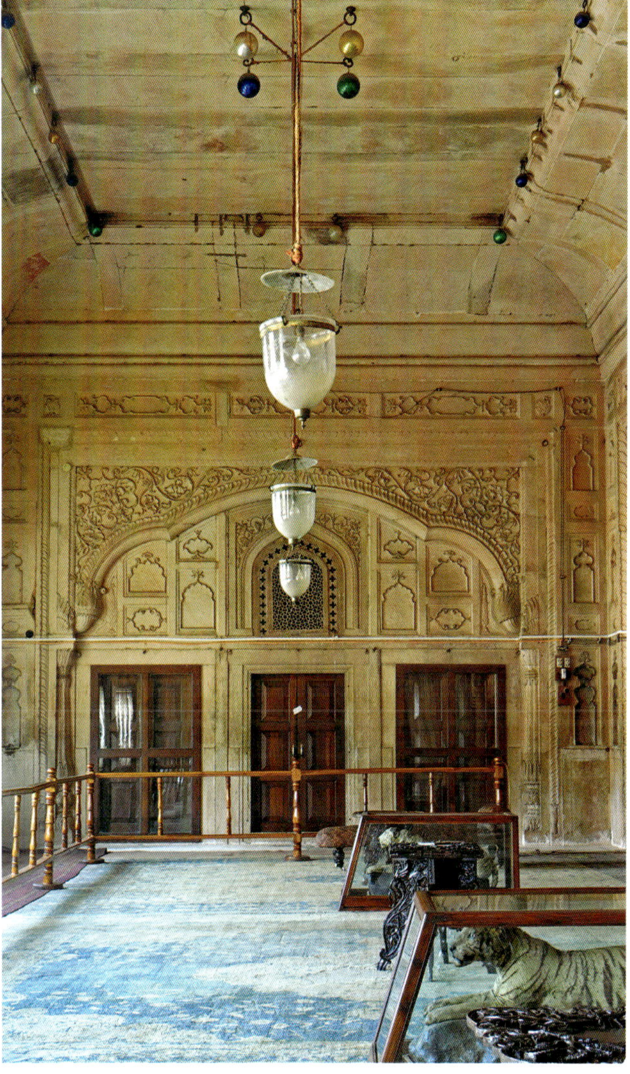

Above (Fig. 12): *The Diwan-i-Khas or the private recreation chamber is furnished with Persian carpets and two stuffed tiger cubs*

Above left (Fig. 11): *Huge domed mouldings rising from the walls bracket the ceiling comprising of flat stone slabs*

Facing page above (Fig. 9): *The shorter sides of the hall are decorated with carvings and panels and a red sandstone* jali *on the outer wall*

Facing page below (Fig. 10): *The main hall is divided into halves with each half being decorated with trefoil arches framing the openings of the three doors*

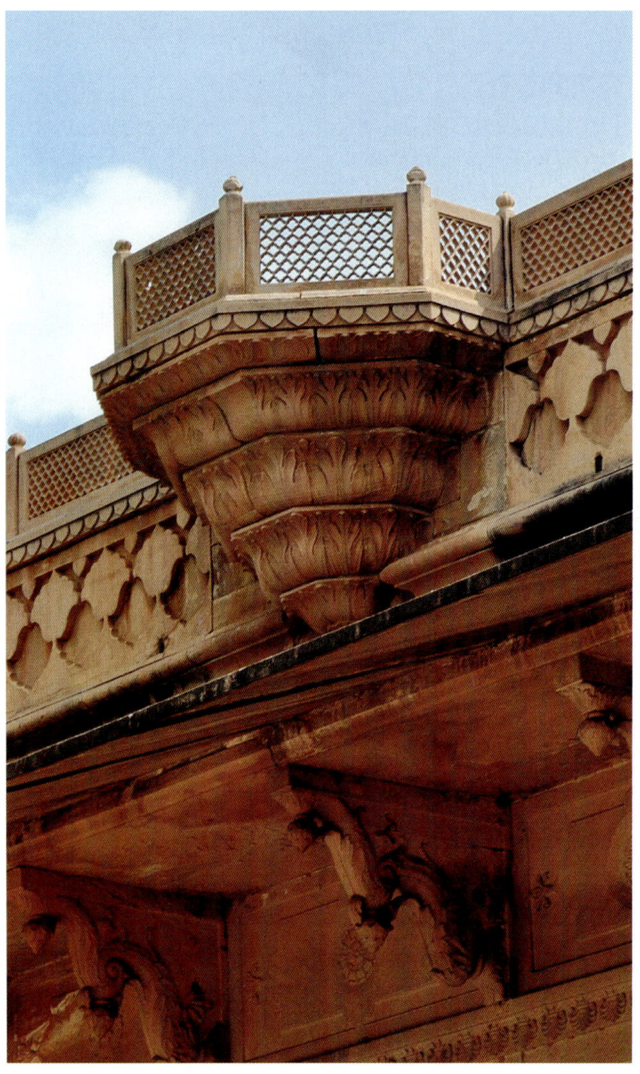

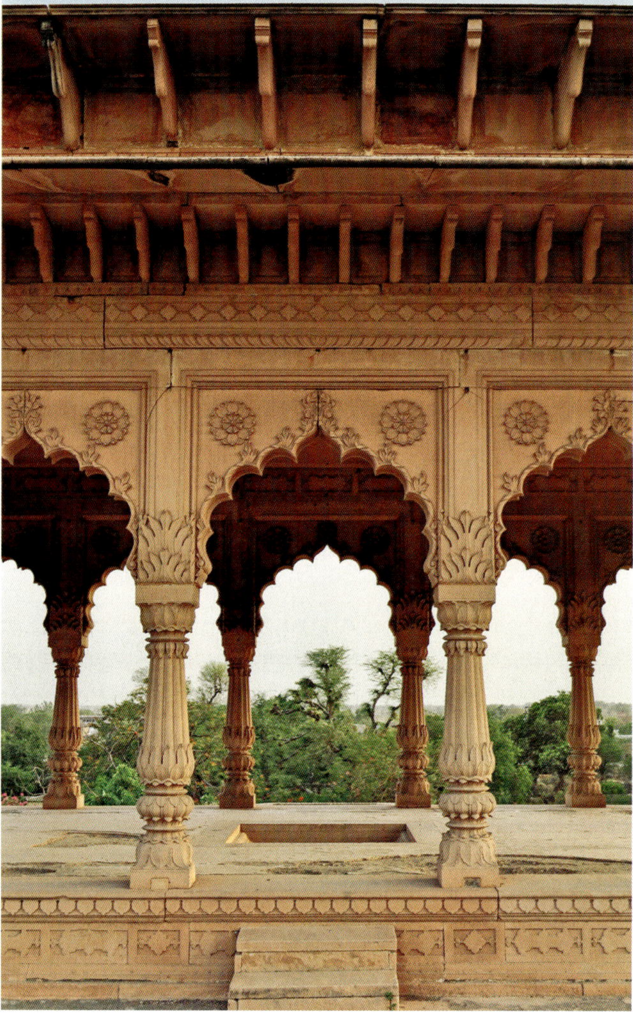

The terrace of the Kishan Bhawan is a huge flat platform with a parapet *jali* all around it. Three short, decorative balconies projecting from the front wall garnish the elevation. The central one is rectangular while the two at the sides are octagonal. The rectangular projection is supported by four brackets and has inverted lotus buds as a *jhalar* for decoration. The two half-octagonal balconies are made in Rajput style. (Fig. 13) The top of the terrace has another pavilion commonly called the *solahdari* (pavilion with sixteen doors). This pavilion has a total of sixteen openings in the form of five arches on its longer side and three arches

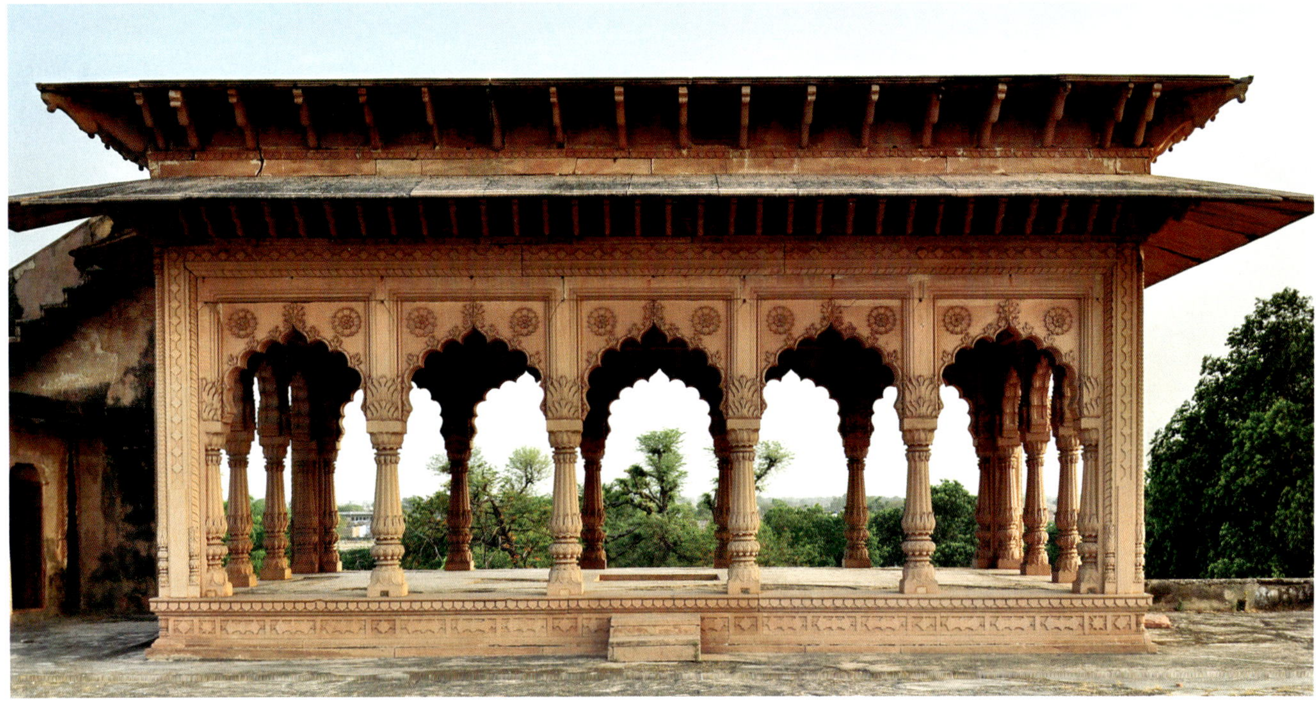

on the shorter side with a central fountain feature. It replicates the same double *chhajja* concept (Fig. 14) as found in the rest of the structures though it was built much later by Raja Balwant Singh of Bharatpur during his tenure. The lower eaves are stretched out more than its proportions, to possibly get extra shade. (Fig. 15) The design and engraving has been done at leisure. It is raised on a high plinth with counter-relief carvings. The corner load-bearing piers have attached shafts bearing chevron (V-shaped) patterns. The expanse in between is divided by four columns on the longer and two on the shorter side.

The arches are elegantly but delicately carved with very fine open lotus medallions on either side of the spandrels. The arch is constructed in bracket system, i.e., both spandrels are in separate pieces of stone with a stylised carved flower at the joint. There are five cusps on either spandrel of the arch. (Fig. 16) Each cusp is characterised by acanthus leaf carvings. Even the capitals are carved with acanthus flowers. The columns are again captivatingly etched (refer to Fig. 14). All along the archway the border is carved with cartouches. The upper ceiling consisting of a plain stone slab supported

Above (**Fig. 16**): *The arches of the* solahdari *are elegantly carved with very fine open lotus medallions on either side of the spandrels and a stylised carved flower at the joint*

Facing page right (**Fig. 14**): *The* solahdari *replicates the same double* chhajja *concept as found in most of the structures at Deeg*

Facing page left (**Fig. 13**): *Short, decorative, half-octagonal balconies projecting from the front wall garnish the elevation*

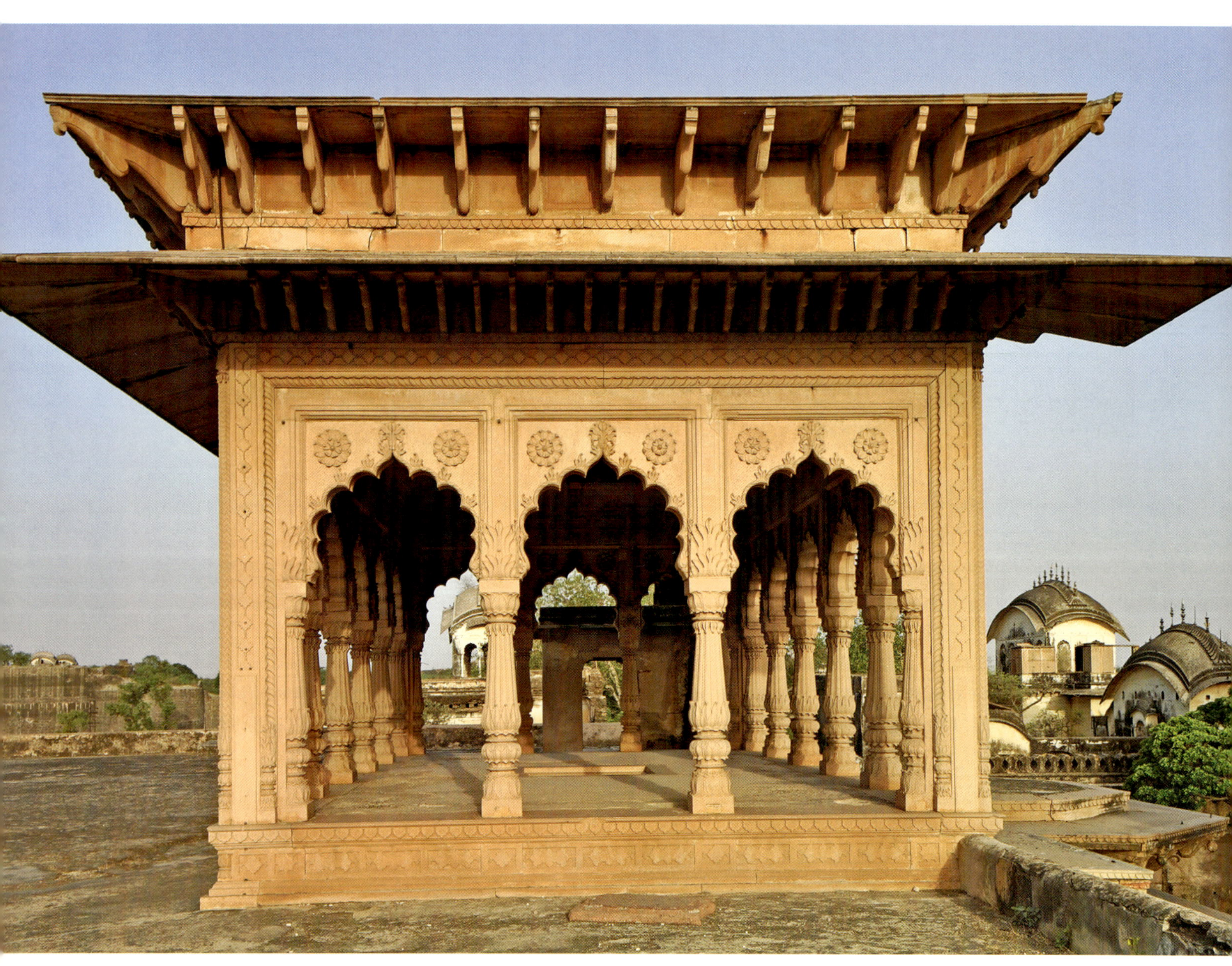

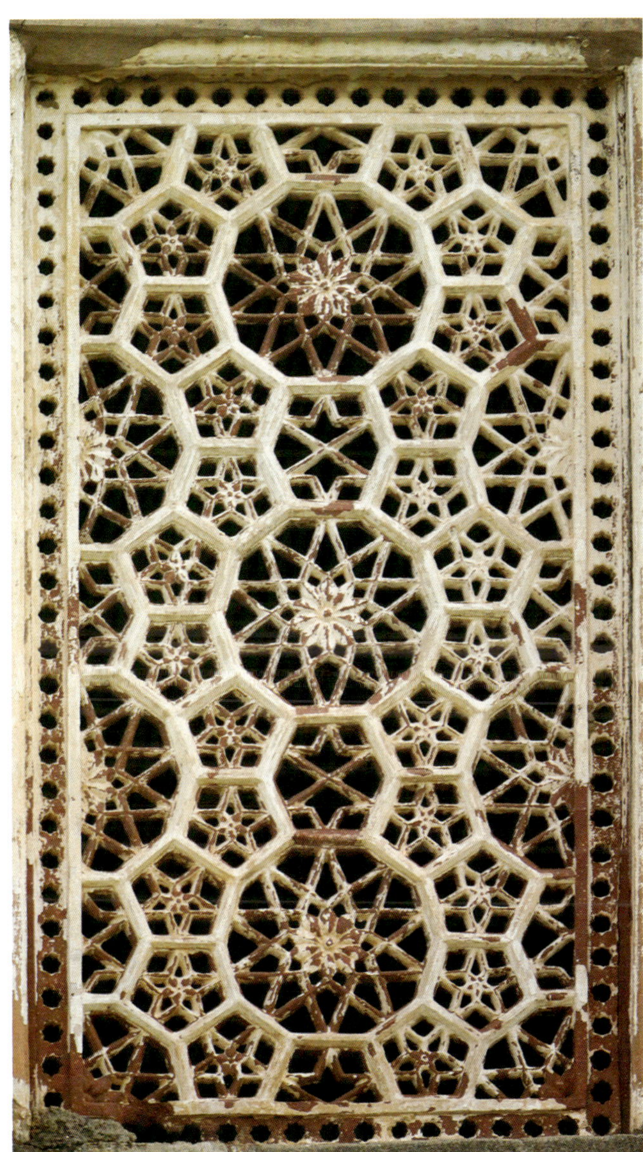

Above (Fig. 17): *An unusual star-shaped juxtaposition of five-pointed and ten-pointed stars regulated by Islamic geometry in a red sandstone* jali

Facing page (Fig. 15): *The lower eaves are more stretched out than its proportions to possibly get extra shade*

by iron girders is visible. The ceiling from the inside is either incomplete or has fallen down. The floor has a little sunken tank-shaped fountain. Upper level eaves and parapets seen in earlier photographs are no longer visible. There is an open staircase on one side to climb on the terrace of the pavilion to have a sweeping view of the complex. At the back of the pavilion there is an elaborate octagonal balcony in the centre, flanked by rectangles on either side, looking into the private gardens from the top.

On the ground floor, at the rear side of the Kishan Bhawan is a private garden which once bore fruits and flower trees and is a nursery now. Adhered on an obscure wall at the back of the Kishan Bhawan, one can get a glimpse of an unusual star-shaped geometric *jali.* The juxtaposition of five-pointed and ten-pointed stars regulated by Islamic geometry in this red sandstone *jali* could yet be another war trophy brought by Jawahar Singh, but escaped the discerning eye of the designers as it is in the backyard. (Fig. 17)

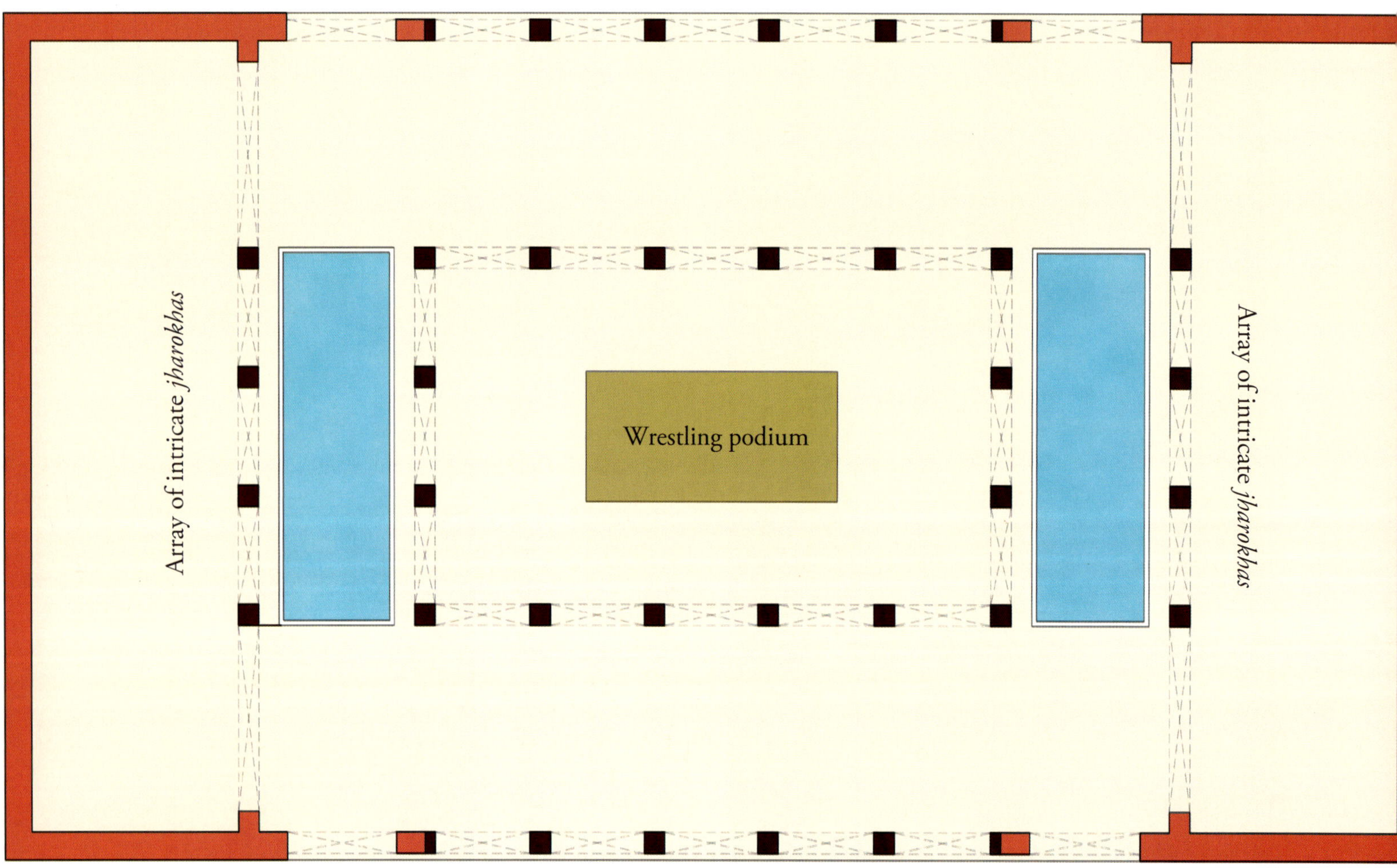
Entry facing rear gardens
Array of intricate *jharokhas*
Wrestling podium
Array of intricate *jharokhas*
Entry facing the Charbagh with a swimming pool in its forecourt

WRESTLING PALACE

NAND BHAWAN

A distinguished edifice, the Nand Bhawan stands raised on a terrace exactly opposite to the Kishan Bhawan towards the north of the Charbagh. The design of the plinth and terrace reciprocates the shape and size of the Kishan Bhawan, with two similar melon-shaped *burjis* also adorning the plinth corners.

The Nand Bhawan is 45m × 26m and comprises of a spacious, oblong hall resembling an auditorium. The north and south elevation comprises of seven-arched openings bracketed within two *jharokha* walls. The central five are engrailed arches while the two larger openings on the side are trefoil arches. The *jharokha* wall (Fig. 2) carries the same proportion and the cartouche framework as the trefoil arch openings. Lotus medallions grace the spandrels of the central five arches. (Fig. 3)

The shorter sides are an assemblage of five intricately carved vivid *jharokhas*. (Fig. 4) The *jharokha* in the middle is the largest one with a *bangladar* roof supported on a triple-arched opening. (Fig. 5) Just below the central *jharokha*, the spandrels and crenellations are intricately

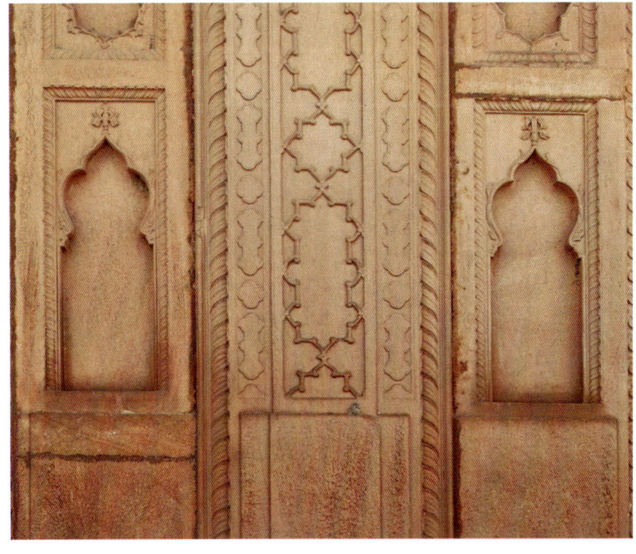

Right (Fig. 2): *Articulation of stonework integrated with carved scrolls on the walls of Nand Bhawan*

Facing page (Fig. 1): *Layout plan of the Nand Bhawan*

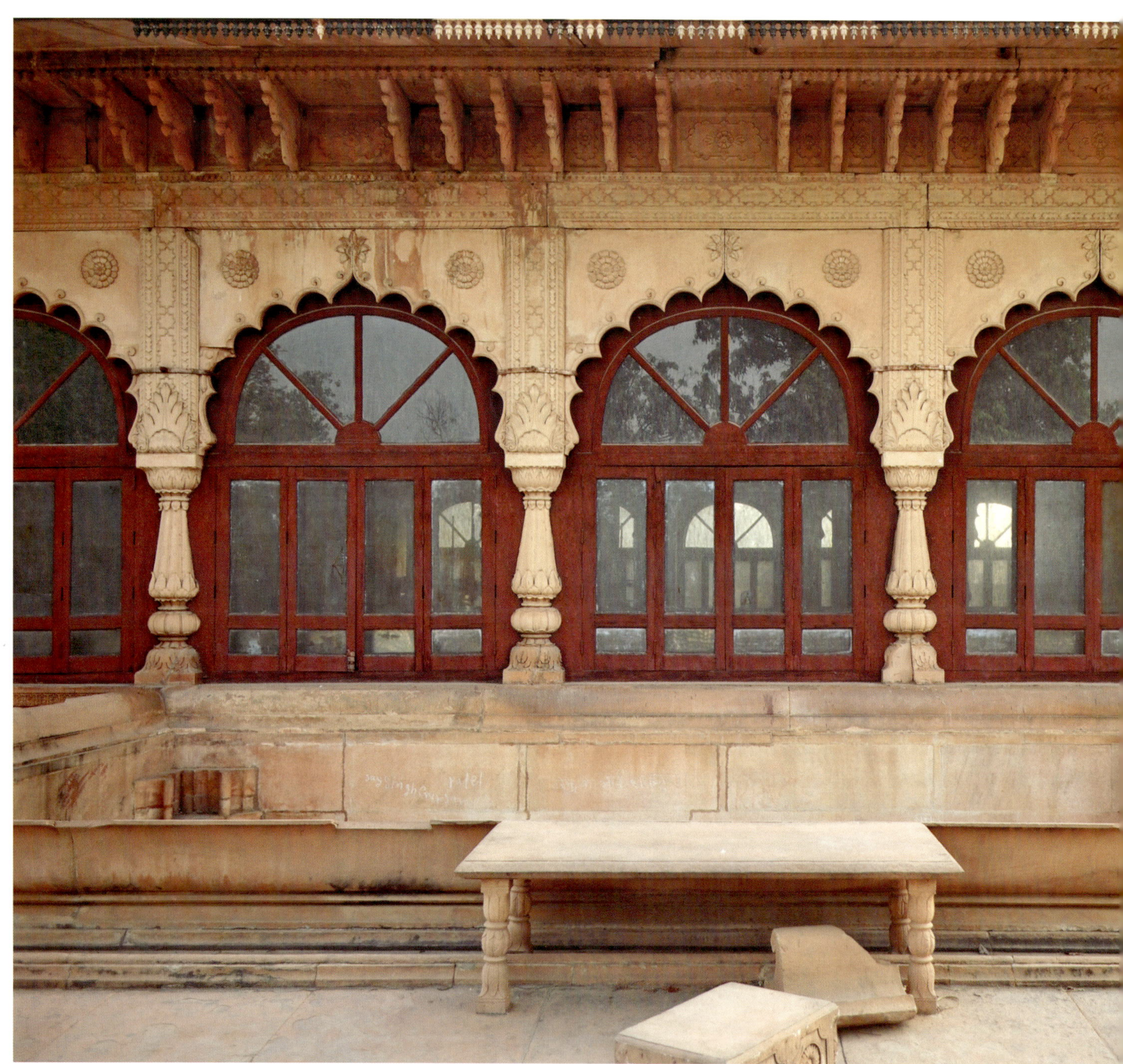

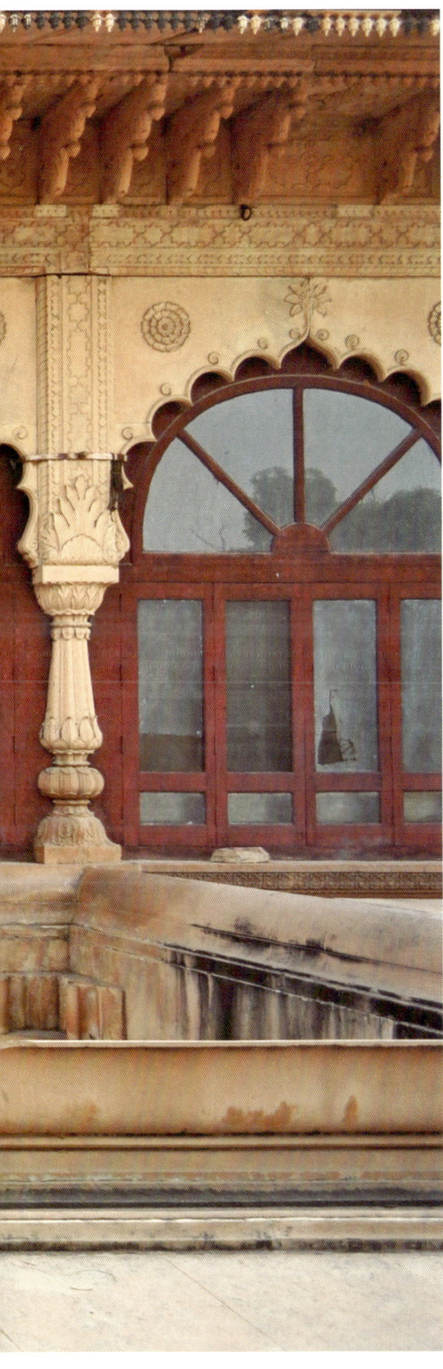

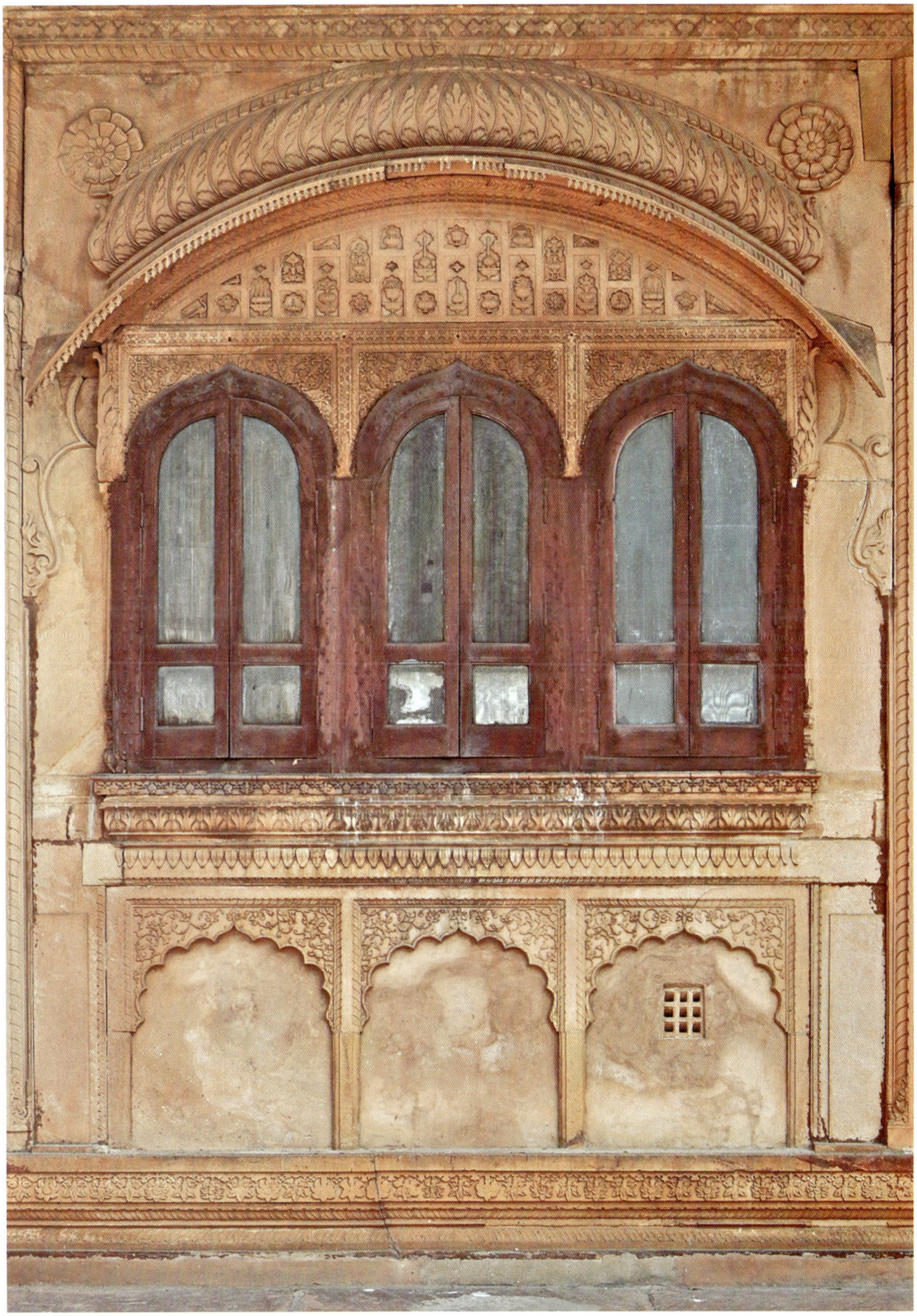

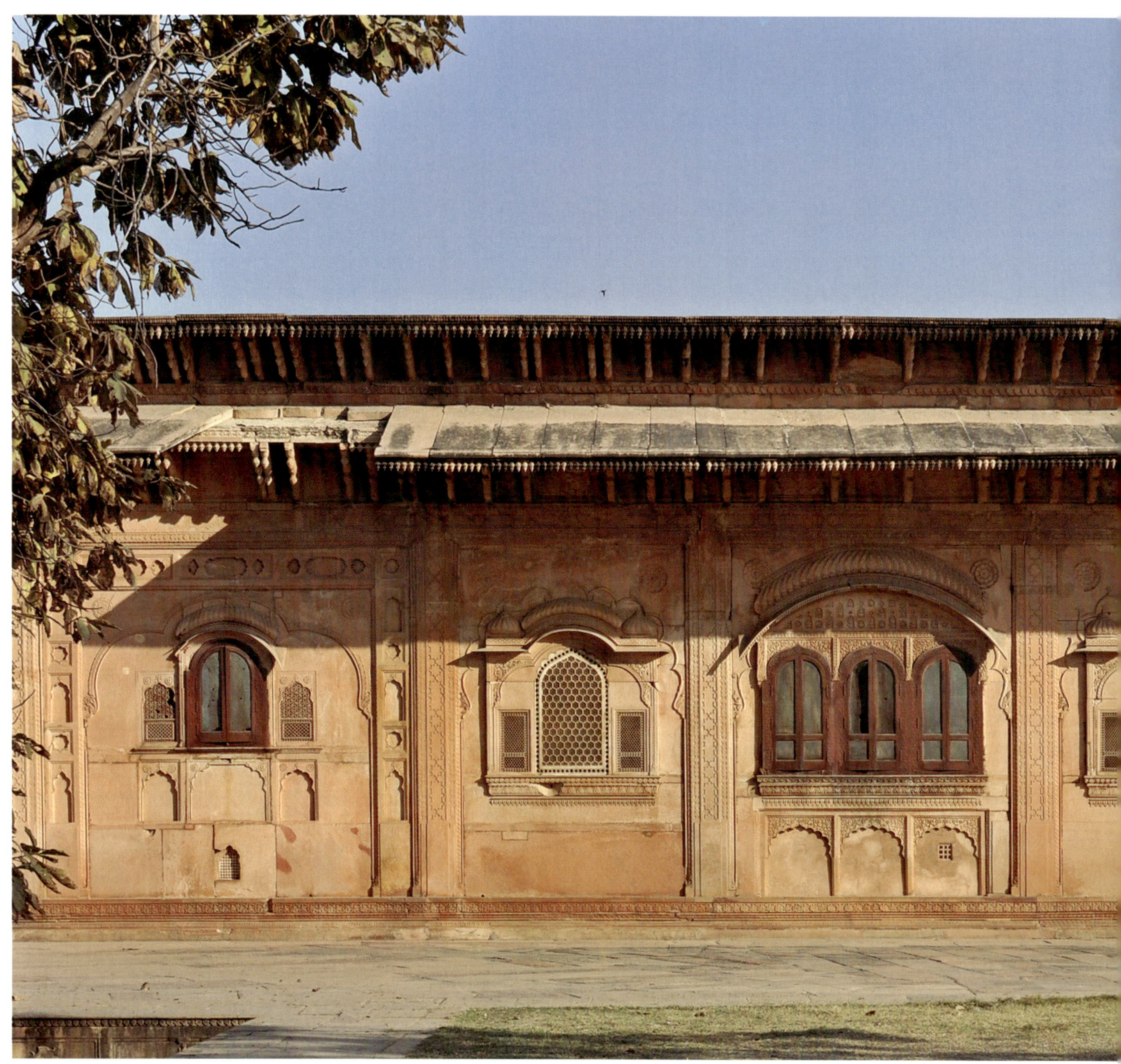

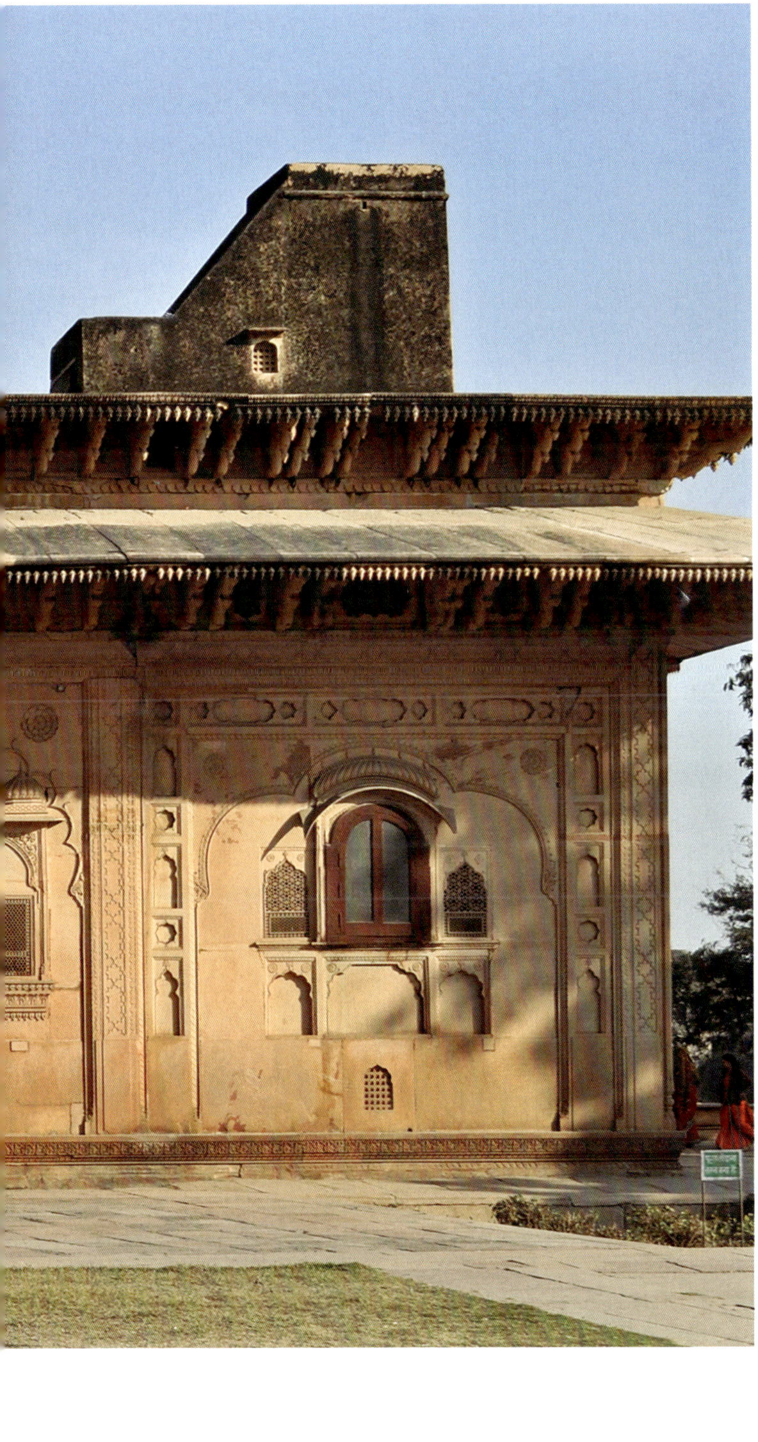

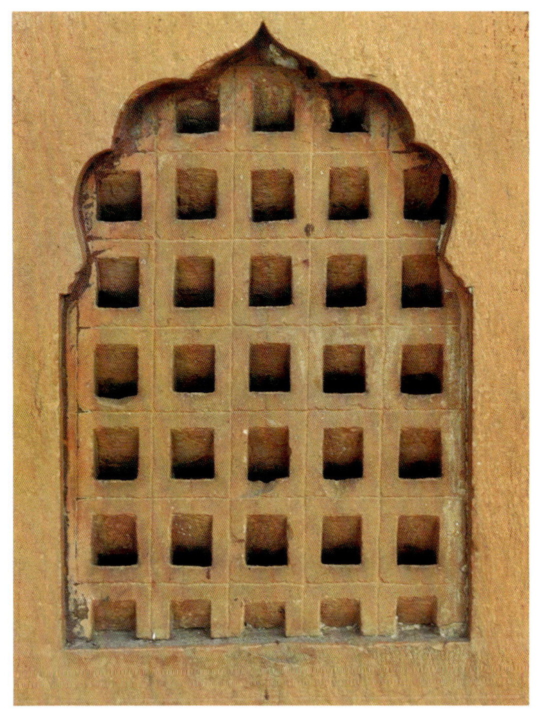

carved. This is immediately flanked on both sides by window *jharokhas* with marvellously carved latticework. (Fig. 6) The two extreme panels contain a relatively small *jharokha* window panelled in a trefoil decoration framed by cartouche designs. (Fig. 7) The eastern elevation also contains an assembly of *bangaldar jharokhas* and panels sporting double *chhajja* eaves. (Fig. 8)

Above (Fig. 7): *The two extreme panels contain a* jharokha *window with functionally carved louvered* jalis

Left (Fig. 4): *The western elevation shows an assemblage of* bangladar jharokhas *and panels*

Previous page right (Fig. 5): *The middle* jharokha *with a* bangladar *roof is supported on a triple-arched opening*

Previous page left (Fig. 3): *The southen facade has a five-arched entrance with a swimming pool in the forefront*

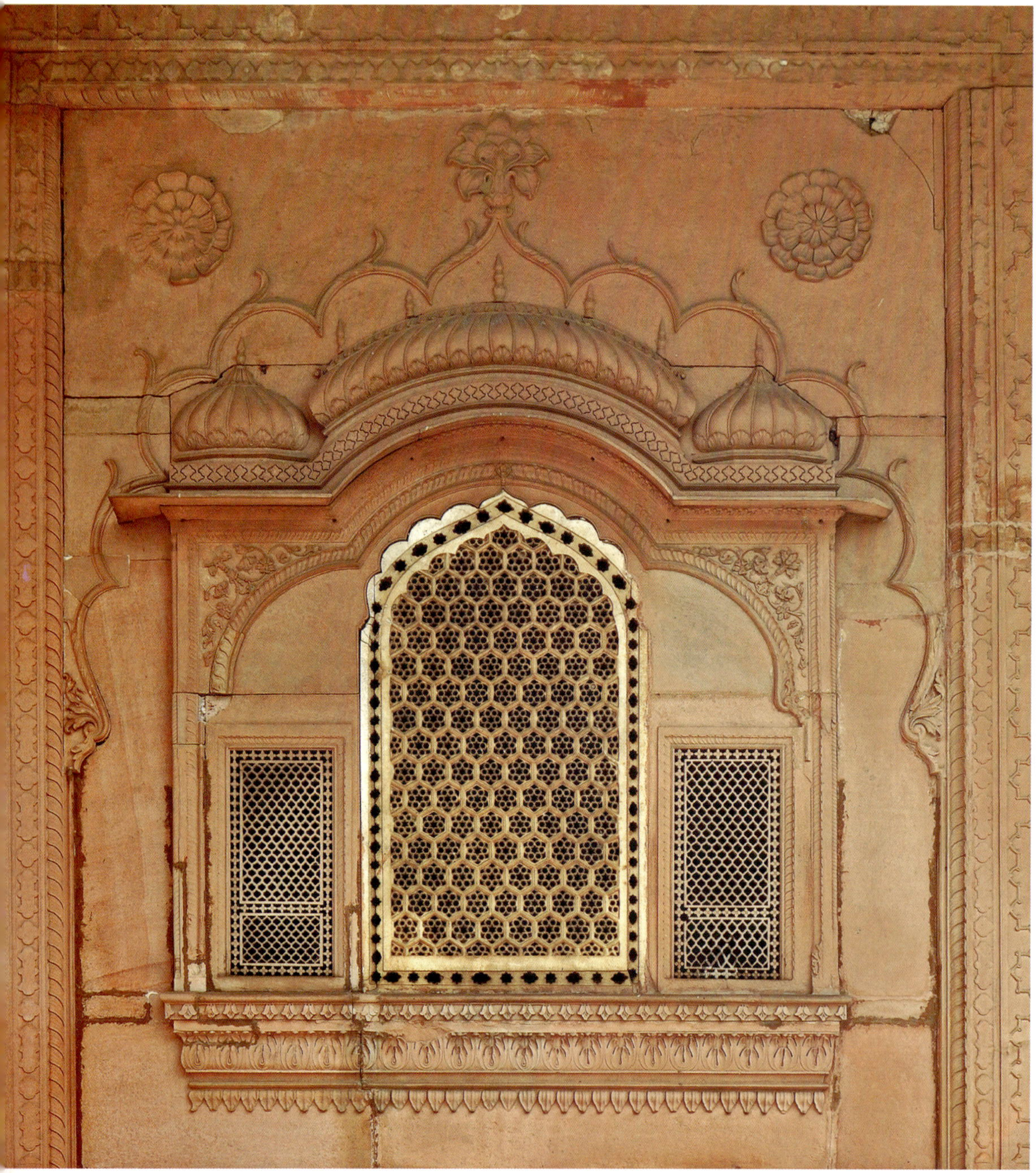

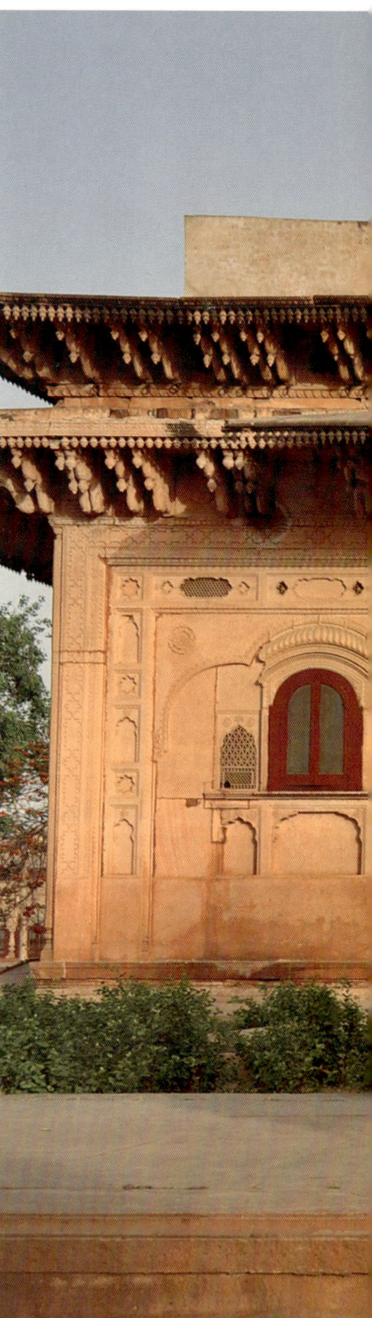

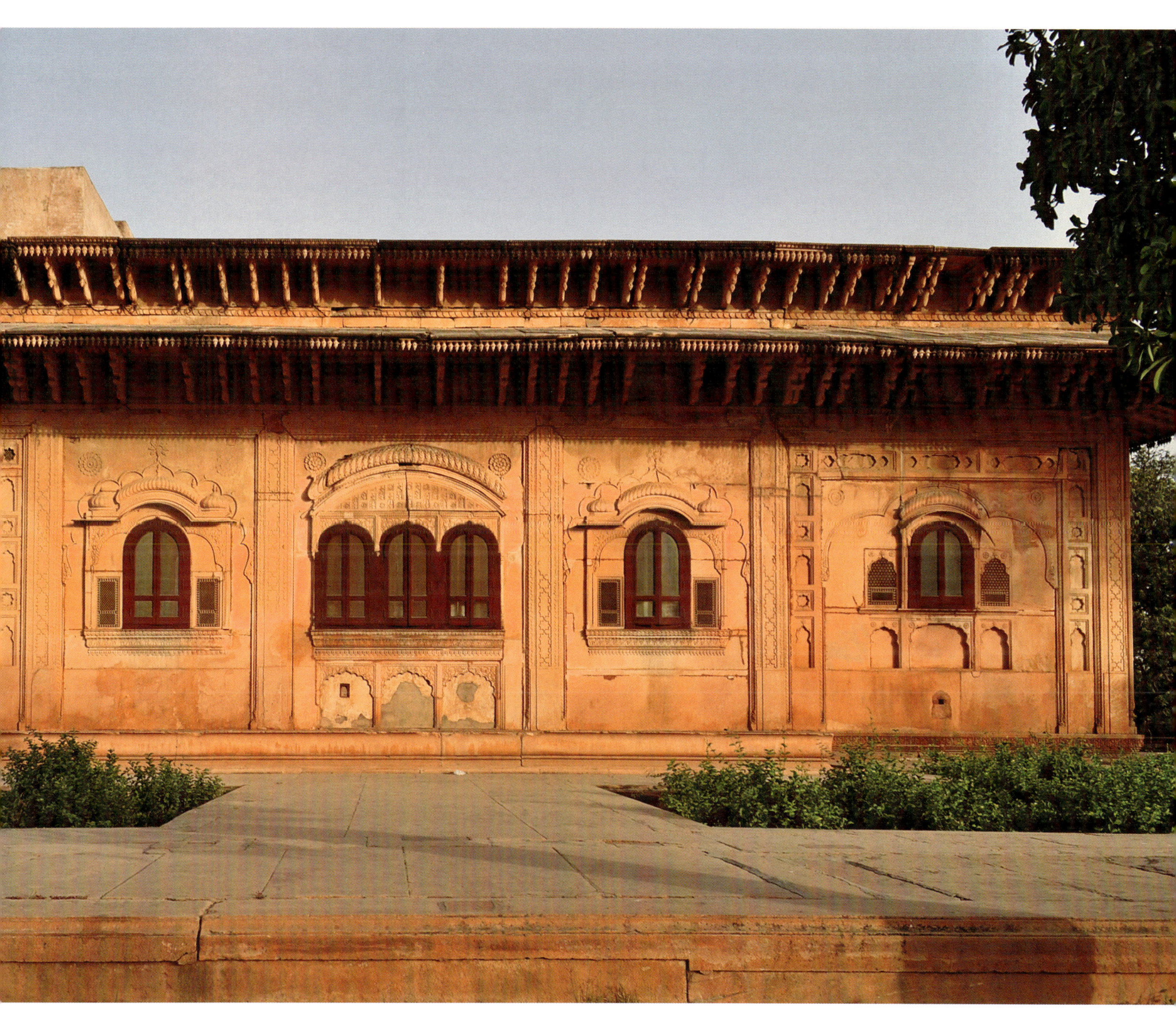

In the layout plan, the two shorter sides are the outer facade of a gallery with a raised floor. The width of this wing corresponds with the outermost *jharokha* of the longer side. These flanking wings are covered by intercommunicating compartments having walls decked with ornamental alcove balconies, three of which facing the hall are in marble inlaid with semi-precious stones. These were used to seat the royals to have a spectacular view of the ceremonies inside. Dividing the remaining hall into an inner and an outer sector, there is a central arcade of usual type arranged in a rectangular pattern. The central portion is divided into two parts by a row of columns all around forming five openings on the longer side and three on the shorter. There is a decorative, lotus-edged, shallow, sunken basin between the shorter side of the central arcade and the side wings. This marble basin enriched with *pietra dura* work along with the marble of the

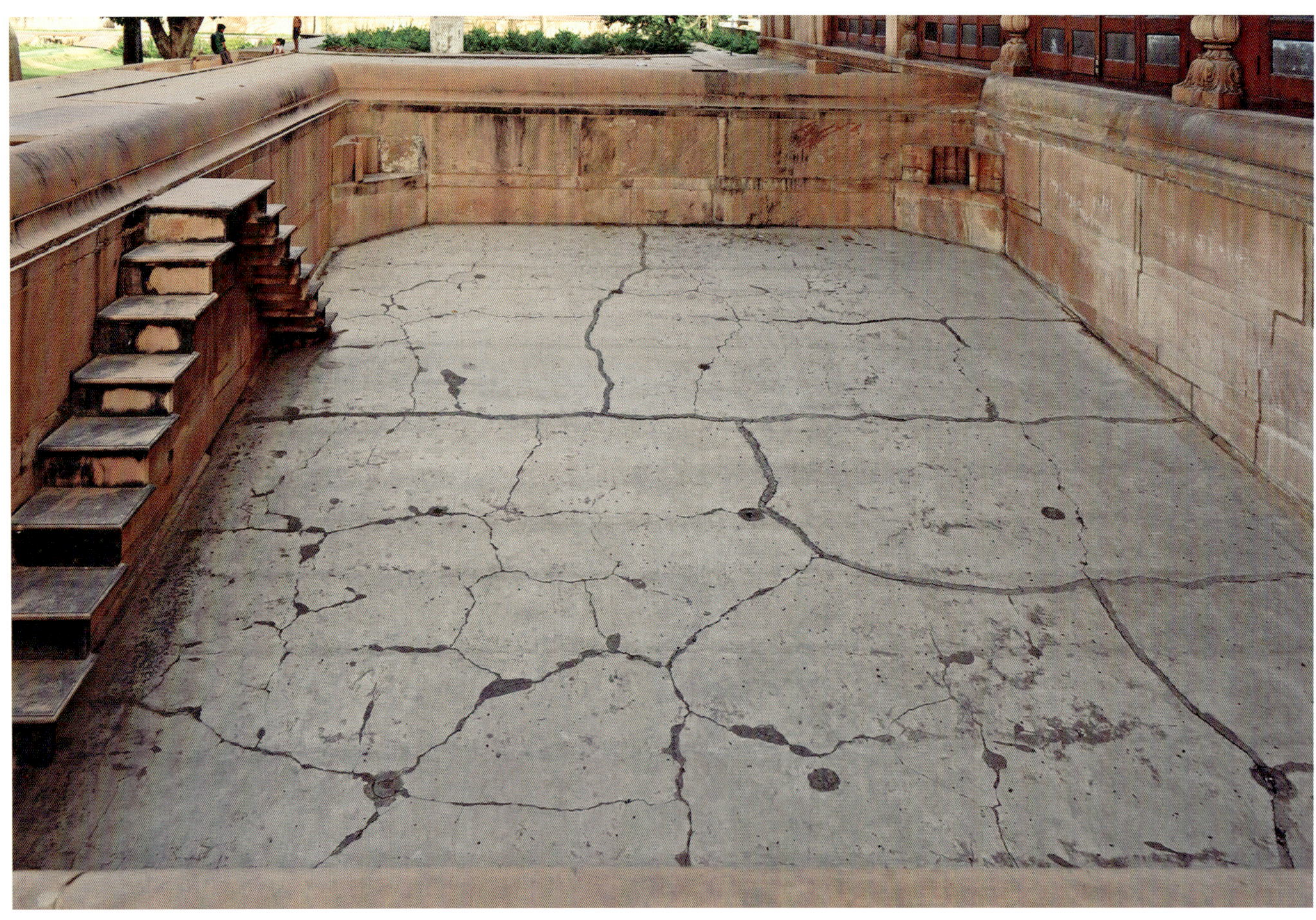

balconies is said to have come from Delhi as part of the king's booty.

The ceiling of the central portion of the hall in wood suggests that the designers wanted to embellish it on the lines of the ceiling of the Diwan-i-Khas in Delhi. The roof above this part also rested on timber beams; consequently it collapsed in 1867 but was restored by the use of iron girders. Perhaps the building needed more pillars to serve as support for its flat roof. So to prevent the roof from further dilapidation, massive piers have lately been raised in the hall. The piers at the corners bear crude paintings done mostly in a

Previous page left (Fig. 6): *Another interpretation of the* bangladar jharokhas

Previous page right (Fig. 8): *The eastern elevation with an assembly of* bangaldar jharokhas *and panels sporting double* chhajja *eaves*

Facing page (Fig. 9): *The transformation of the usual water trough to a deep swimming pool with sloping depth along with an equally dramatic cantilever stone stairway*

Below (Fig. 10): *The low height adorable pavilion would have served as a sitting platform to enjoy the panoramic northern gardens*

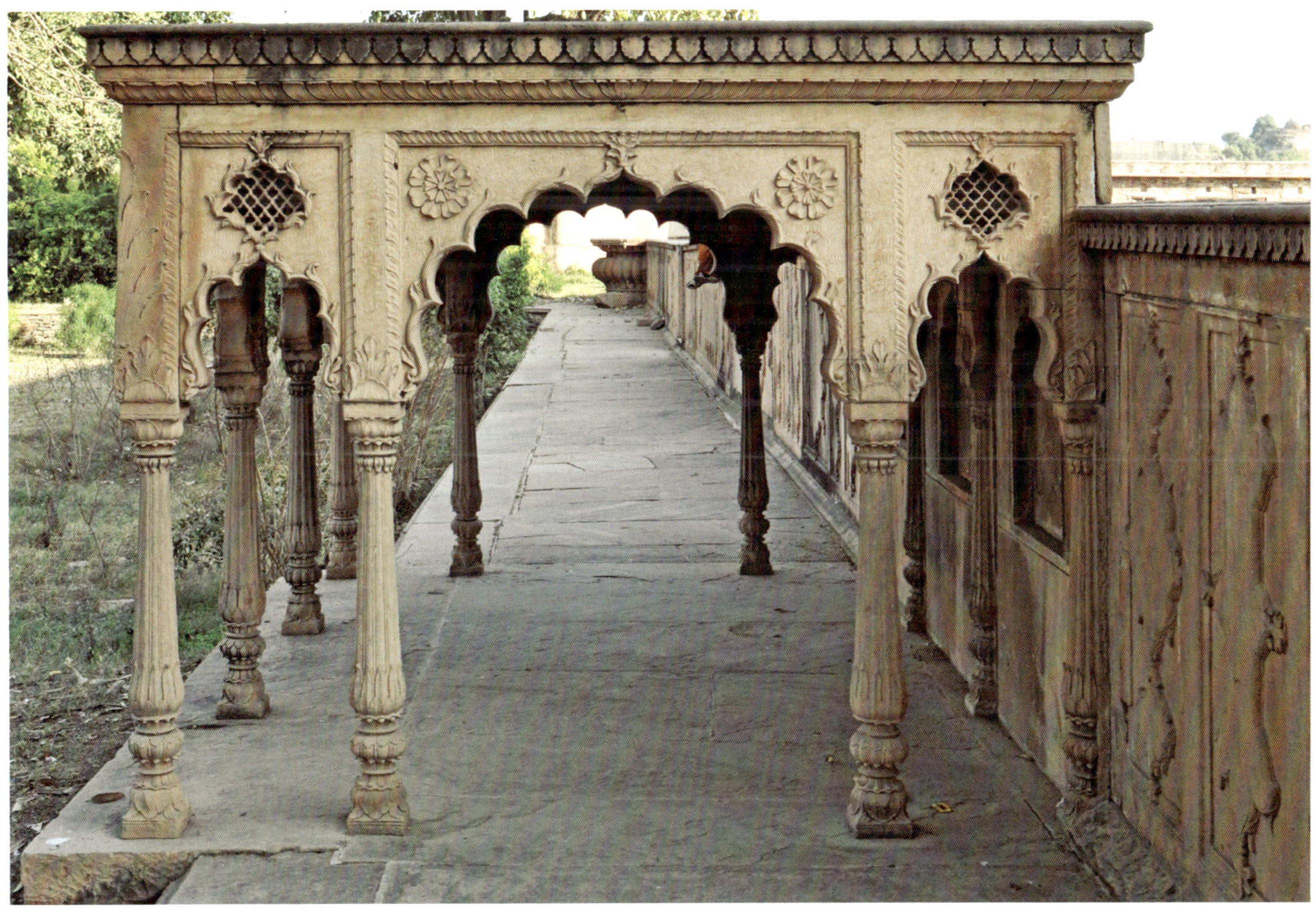

degenerated local style showing some Mughal influence and still a few of them are interesting.

The Nand Bhawan, initially designed as a Diwan-i-Khas, ultimately transformed into a recreation hall famous among the locals as the *akhara* or the wrestling arena. A raised platform in the middle of the hall with a sandpit was used to hold such events.

A pleasant surprise is the transformation of a usual water trough in the foreground of the southern terrace to a deep swimming pool with sloping depth. An equally dramatic cantilever stone stairway projects into the pool from the centre towards both directions. (Fig. 9) In north India, the direction to get the best sunlight is the south. In winters, since the sun tilts to the south, the southern facades get the sun almost throughout the day while the sun moves from east to west. In summers, when the same sun is at its highest point during the day, the southern facades escape its wrath.

The northern side which has the same facade as the southern side, together with melon-shaped *burjis*, has a spacious, sunken garden in the front. The distinguishing features of which are an adorable little pavilion and a raised platform with a decorative plinth. The artful pavilion is very similar in concept to the pavilion in front of the Gopal Bhawan below the *hindola* platform

Facing page (Fig. 12): *Water trough on the eastern face bracketed between gardens*

Below (Fig. 11): *The massive raised platform is said to have hosted royal ceremonies*

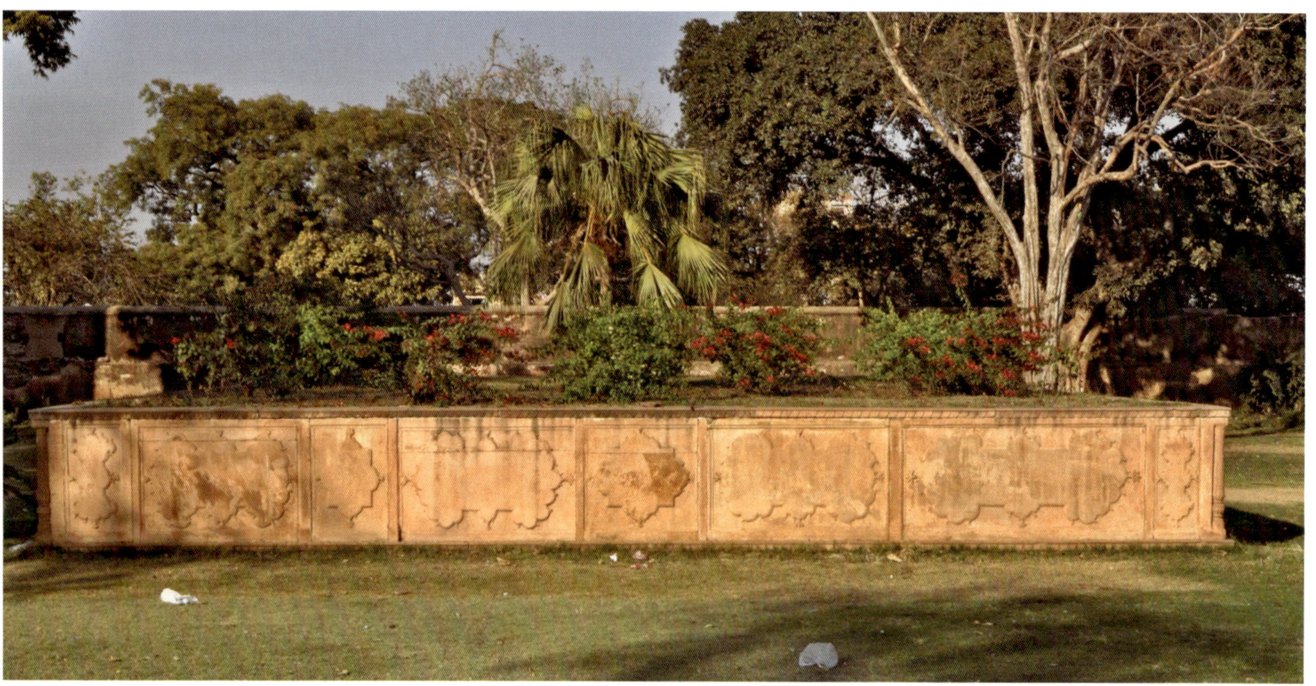

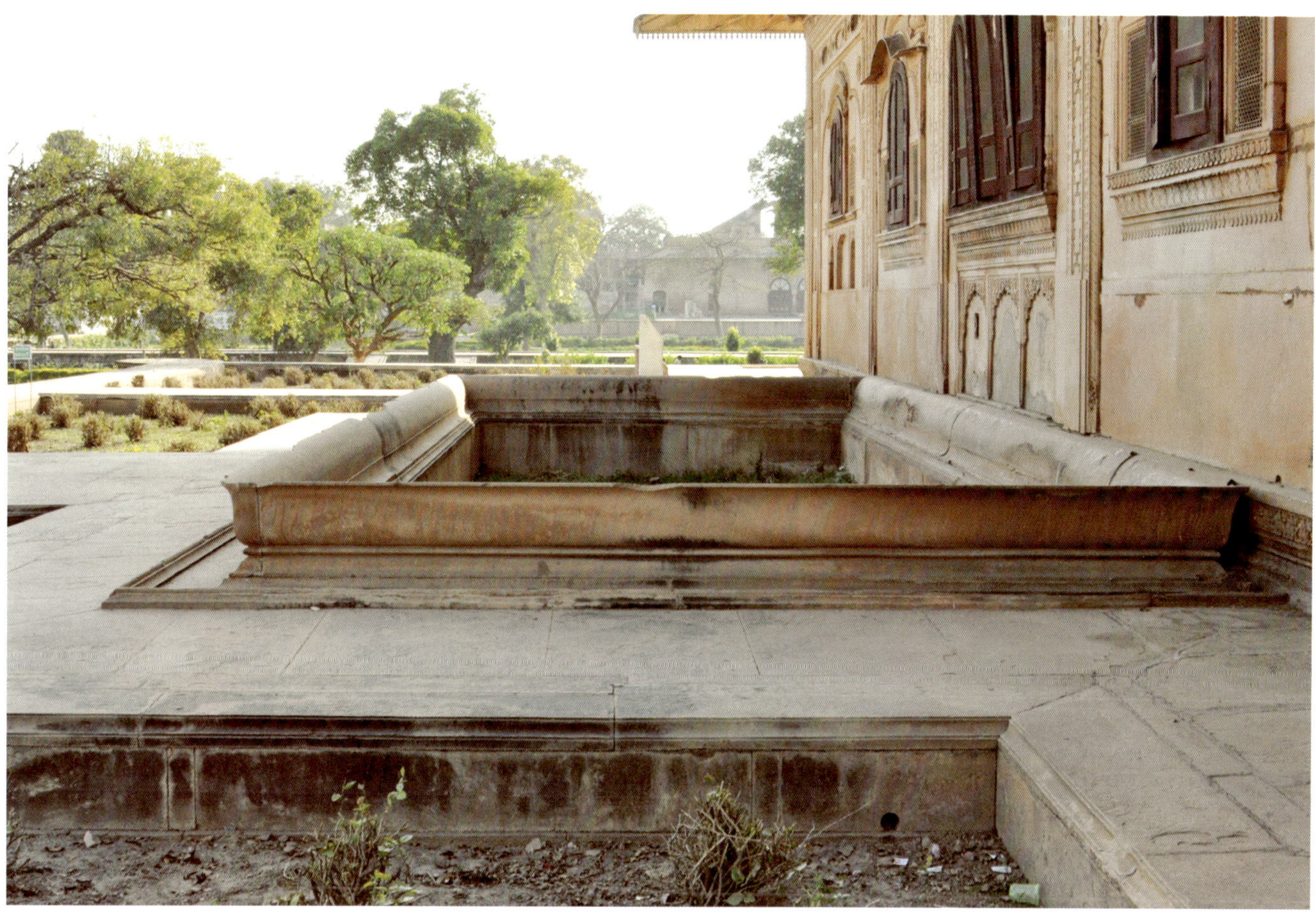

with a step-up roof from the Nand Bhawan terrace. The low-height pavilion would have served as a sitting platform to enjoy the panoramic northern gardens. (Fig. 10) Not far from this is a massive raised platform said to host royal ceremonies. (Fig. 11) The plinth of this platform has the same cartouche embellishment as the rest of terrace.

Plausibly the Nand Bhawan also had the provision for an upper storey which however could not be built due to some unknown reason. Like the other buildings it also has a tank in front of the eastern facade with fountainhead spouts. Symmetrical green plots have been cut within the terrace all round suggesting flower beds and nurseries. (Fig. 12)

Facing the Rup Sagar

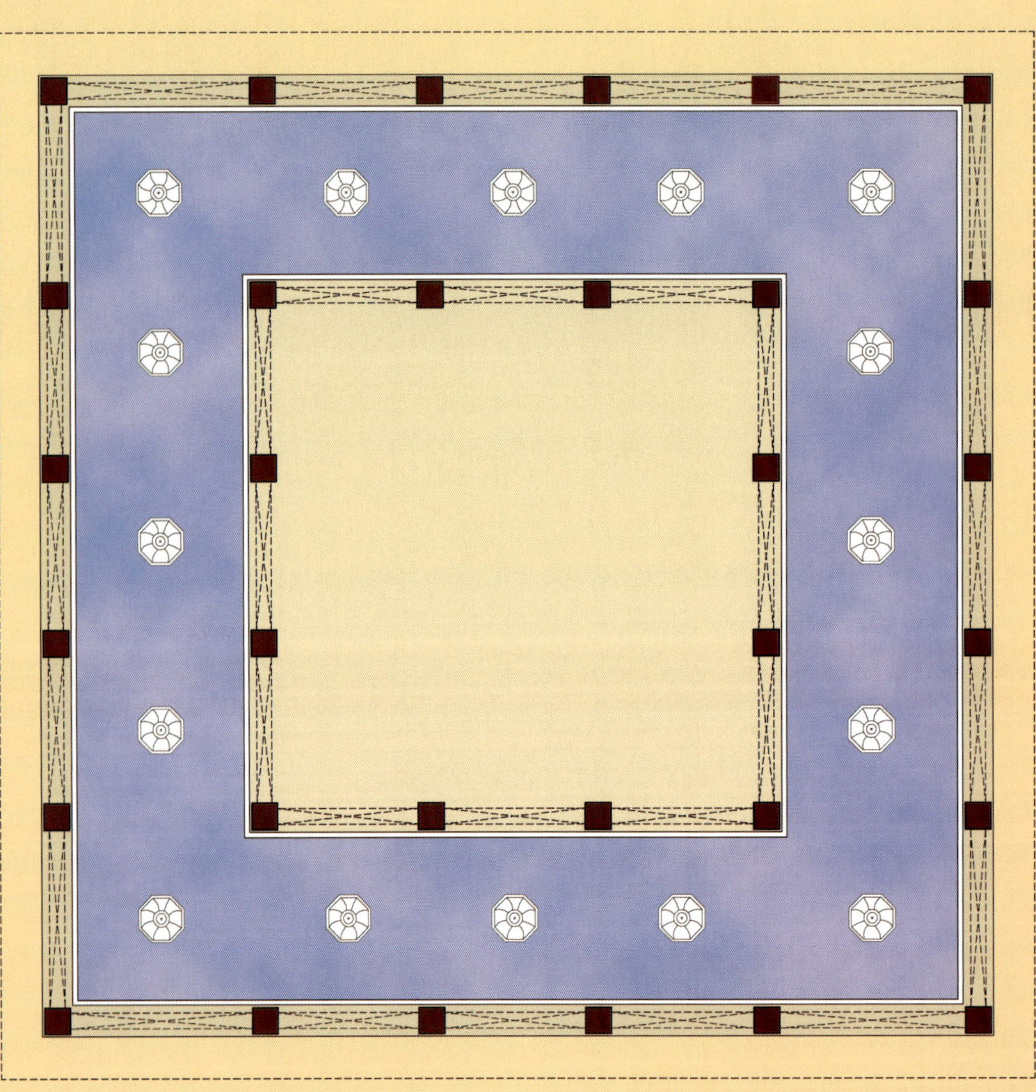

Facing the Charbagh

THE CLASP OF THUNDER

KESHAV BHAWAN

Water-spraying clouds for elephants in rut
Lightning for a banner and thunderbolts for drums:
The rains, longed for by lovers, have arrived in full splendour,
My darling, like a king in all glory.

—First verse of the second *sarga*, *Ritusamhara* by Kalidasa

Since ancient times 'Bharat Varsha' has been defined by the monsoons, a season which brings exuberant rains to the plains and mountains of the subcontinent. Though rain has been an inspiration to spirited and vivacious art forms all over the world, India has a unique heritage as all the epics from *Ramayana* to *Ritusamhara* and *Meghadutam* of Kalidasa, to modern folk songs, music and dance, all sing praise of the rains. The reason could be that it is only the Indian subcontinent which has the Himalayas to block the rain-bearing clouds, thus bringing the magical dance of rain every year. Millions anxiously wait for the monsoons to turn the parched land into soothing greens as they revitalise fields and forests. Monsoon is thus like the *prana*—the life-giving nectar of India. Even special ragas like the Megh Malhar were composed by legendary poets like Tansen to initiate rain showers for the scorched lands and to bless plenty. This music has inspired painters, dancers and writers for generations. No wonder then that India's agriculture, art, music, dance, literature and religious texts are replete with magical vignettes of rain to celebrate India's ornate culture.

The flamboyant surge of monsoons in the ghats and the respite brought by the glorious Indian monsoon after a parched summer is incomparable to anything else that might bring rest and nourishment to an aching

Facing page (Fig. 1): *Layout plan of the Keshav Bhawan or* baradari *from the terrace level*

earth and its longing souls. The intoxicating smell of sprouting leaves, crisp air, not to forget the dark ominous clouds rolling across the sky with thunder and lightning could mesmerise anyone.

The Jat rulers must have wanted to display their dominance over nature by capturing rain and thunder in an artificial system which could be executed at their pleasure. The Keshav Bhawan was probably a way to proclaim their supremacy by taming the natural forces.

The concept of rain was taken to an unprecedented level by the builders of Keshav Bhawan, an open pavilion which thundered like the clouds and produced rain with rainbows glittering, defying the scorching sun. This delightful pavilion is draped with water from three rows of jets and fountains and by water falling from the eaves, thereby creating the impression of a rainstorm, an event which gladdens all hearts. To this is added the thrill of thunder; water is forced up a hollow pillar, causing large stone balls to roll around in the ceiling.

Though there are several aspects of the Deeg Palace garden which market it as an evocation of the monsoon, the Keshav Bhawan is architecturally the most comparable.

On the eastern side of the main axis originating from the Gopal Bhawan and the *hindola* of the formal Charbagh garden of Deeg Palace is the Keshav Bhawan. Popularly known as the *baradari*, the Keshav Bhawan is a charming pavilion built on the edge of Rup Sagar—overlooking the garden on the other side. It has a square plan which terminates in an octagonal orientation at the corners as in the tradition of *Shilpa Shastra*, hence it can be said to be designed on the principles of *Paramasayika Mandala* (a mandala based on series of circumambulations). According to traditional Hindu architecture, temples are placed in the east along with the main entrance of a house. The east (*purva*) or the preceding direction is ruled by Lord Indra, the king of gods and Lord Aditya or Surya, the god of sun and energy. It is the personification of enlightenment, affluence and fulfilment. The rays of the sun in the morning are also known to be enriched with ultraviolet B-rays, some of which are highly beneficial for life.

As one approaches the bhawan from the walkway of the Charbagh, it is seen as a consciously aloof, yet a graceful thirty-two-pillared symmetrical pavilion, recalling perhaps, the ancient tradition of the hypostyle halls. (Fig. 2) The Anup Talab at Fatehpur Sikri which has similar attributes is worth a mention here. Situated in front of the Khwabgah, it is an open pavilion sitting within a water tank. The platform is connected to the sides of the tank via four causeways that are supported on stone pillars with bracketed capitals. The raised seat in the middle of this platform perhaps expressed Akbar's obsession of being at the centre of the world. The tank was connected to the waterworks system towards the north of the city to ensure the flow of fresh water into it and on to the Sukh Tal, outside the southern wall, to avoid overflowing of water.

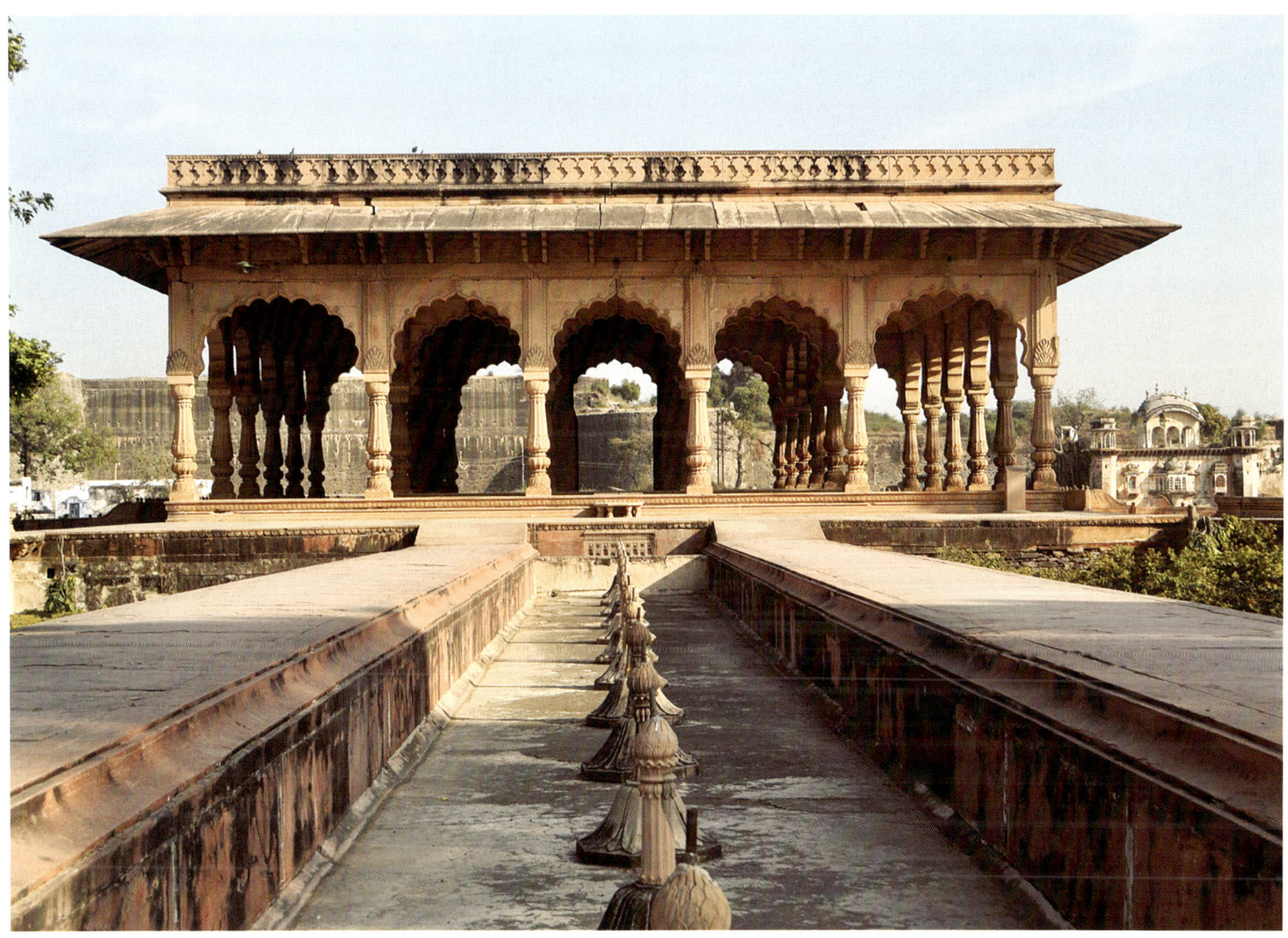

Above (Fig. 2): *Aloof, yet a graceful thirty-two-pillared symmetrical pavilion sitting at the end of the central waterway viewed from the* hindola

This unique feature may have paved the way for the development of the Keshav Bhawan. The central platform takes the shape of a covered *baradari* with twelve openings and columns. The ceiling is extended over the surrounding water channel to make it a part of a larger pavilion. Thus, an additional colonnade of five openings is created around the water channel, giving the impression of a pavilion within a pavilion. The approach to the central pavilion was via four bridges that were again supported by stone pillars. (Fig. 3)

On closer observation this pavilion turns out be a surreptitious masterpiece of the Deeg Palace. This pavilion sits on a square platform (about 55 feet square) about 4 feet high from the surrounding

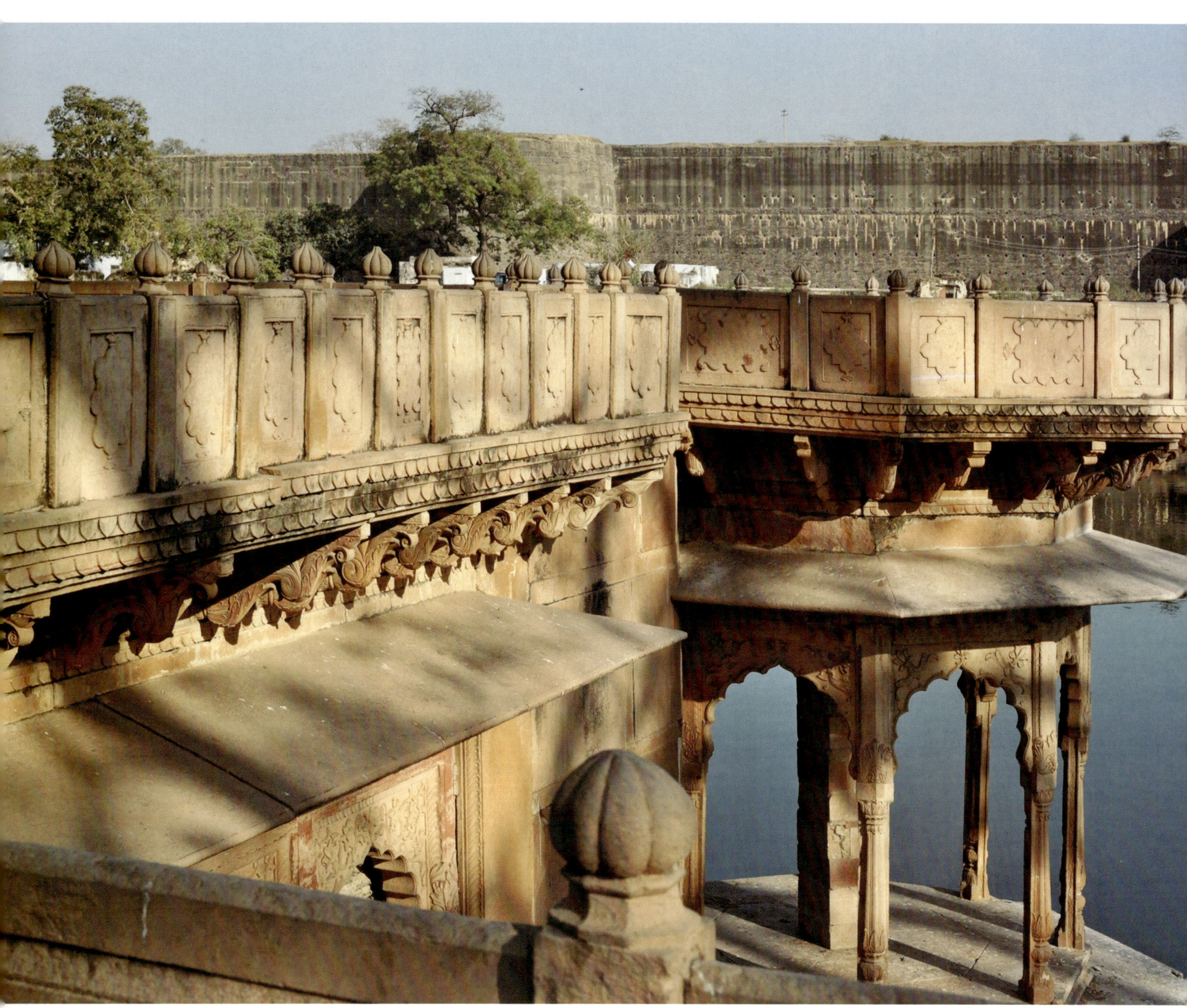

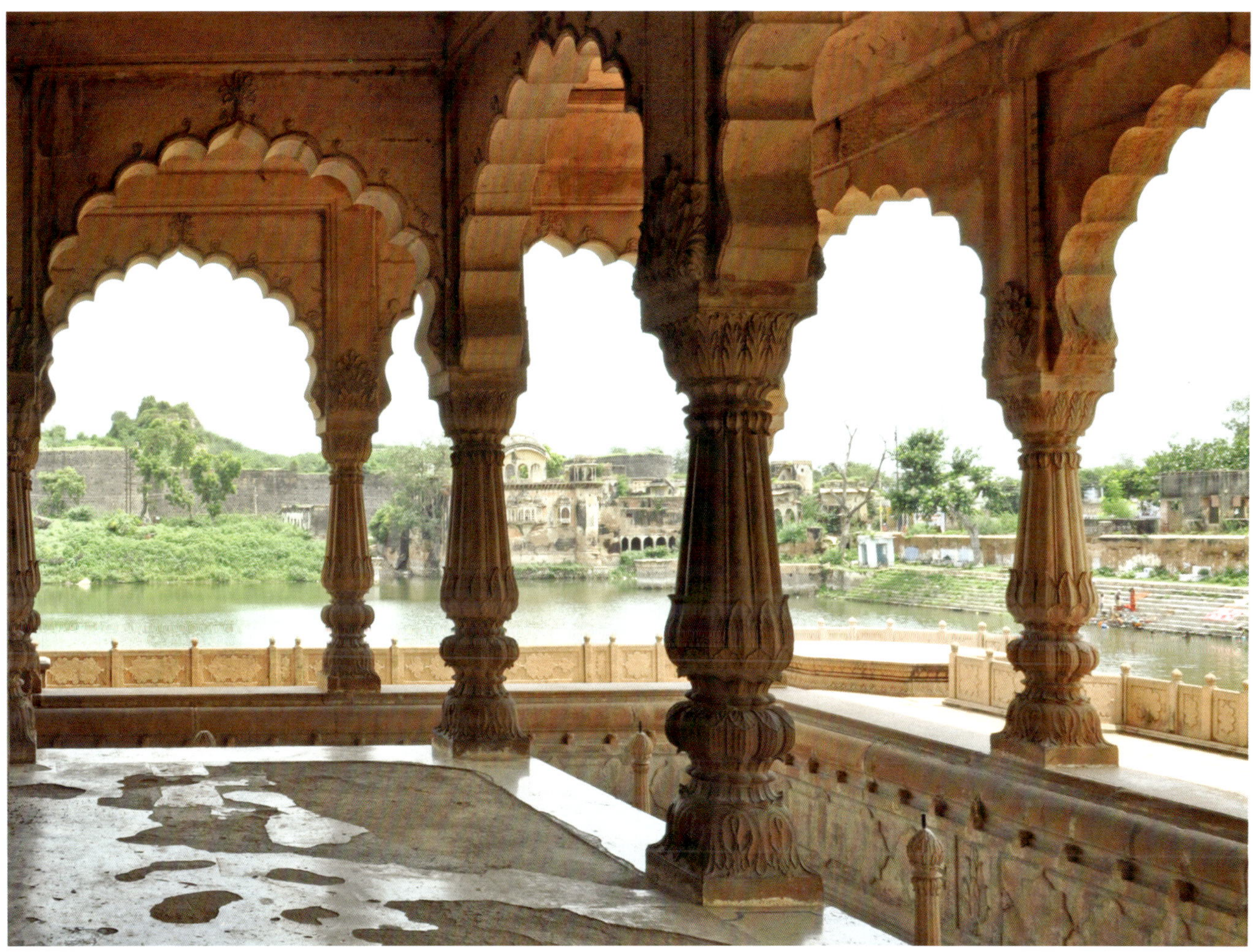

garden and just a foot higher than the Charbagh walkway. The pavilion has octagonal corner balconies underneath which occur abstruse, octagonal *chhatris* on the Rup Sagar side, reminiscent of Rajput water palaces. (Fig. 4) (Fig. 5)

The outer pavilion is supported majestically on six rows and six columns of bulbous pillars with the

Above (Fig. 3): *An inner island is created within the geometry of columns and water channels*

Facing page (Fig. 4): *The octagonal corner balconies underneath which occur abstruse, octagonal* chhatris *on the Rup Sagar side*

familiar *kalash* form at the base. The base of these baluster columns is 20 inches square. They are placed on a raised plinth 17 inches high and 24 inches wide.

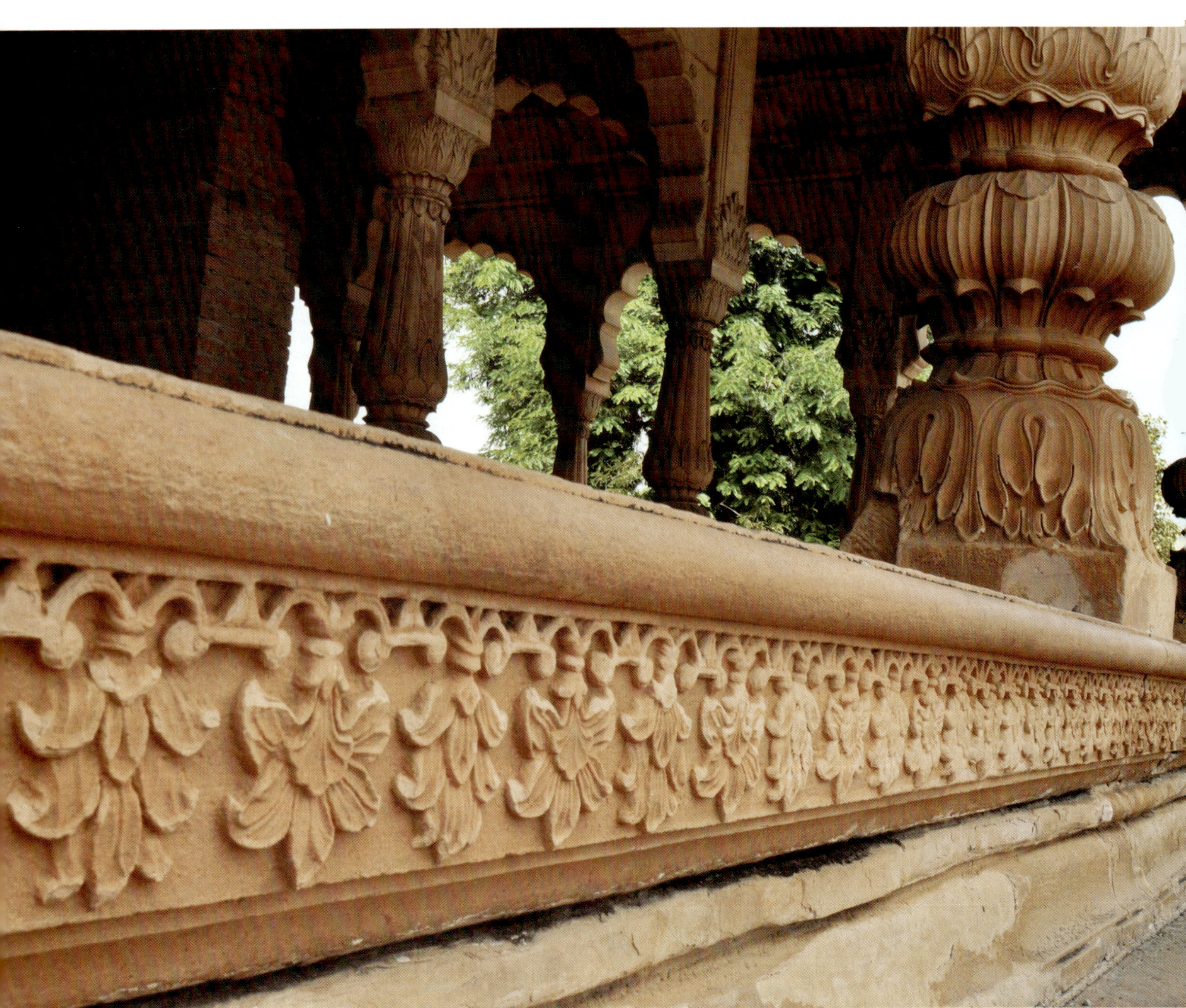

The plinth is decorated with a series of mouldings and a beautiful scroll of hanging flowers in full blossom on the outside. (Fig. 6) The same plinth recedes towards the inside by 17 inches in an intricate profile of curves, culminating with a row of finials placed as buds which are actually water spouts. From that level there is a further vertical drop of 34 inches to form a water channel. The lower joints are moulded and the walls are carved with cartouche panels and cypress trees in low relief. (Fig. 7) This is all made of sandstone. On the floor stand handsome bud spouts with octagonal bases and raised columns, typical of the Deeg style, totalling to fifteen in number all around. A similar carving on the other side of the channel continues to rise back to the same level as the plinth, though not identically. The crossing over was made possible by slabs of stone placed as causeways or bridges supported by carved pillars. (Fig. 8) The platform of the inner pavilion is 30 feet square or 10 metres square, a typical square *baradari* with twelve openings and decorative columns, again 20 inches square. A variety of cartouches decorate the parapets. (Fig. 9)

Facing page **(Fig. 6):** *Exquisitely carved* jhalar *at the base*

Below **(Fig. 5):** *Detail of the vivid carvings on the octagonal corner balconies*

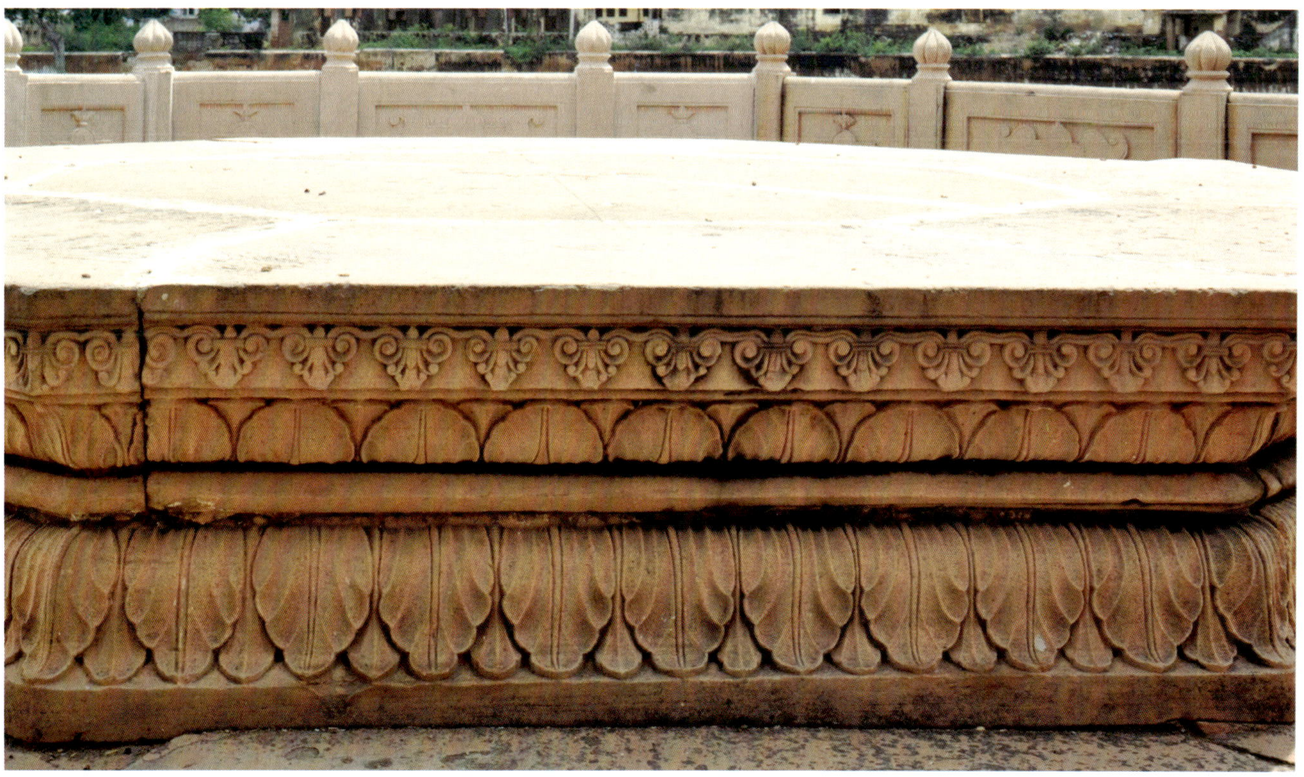

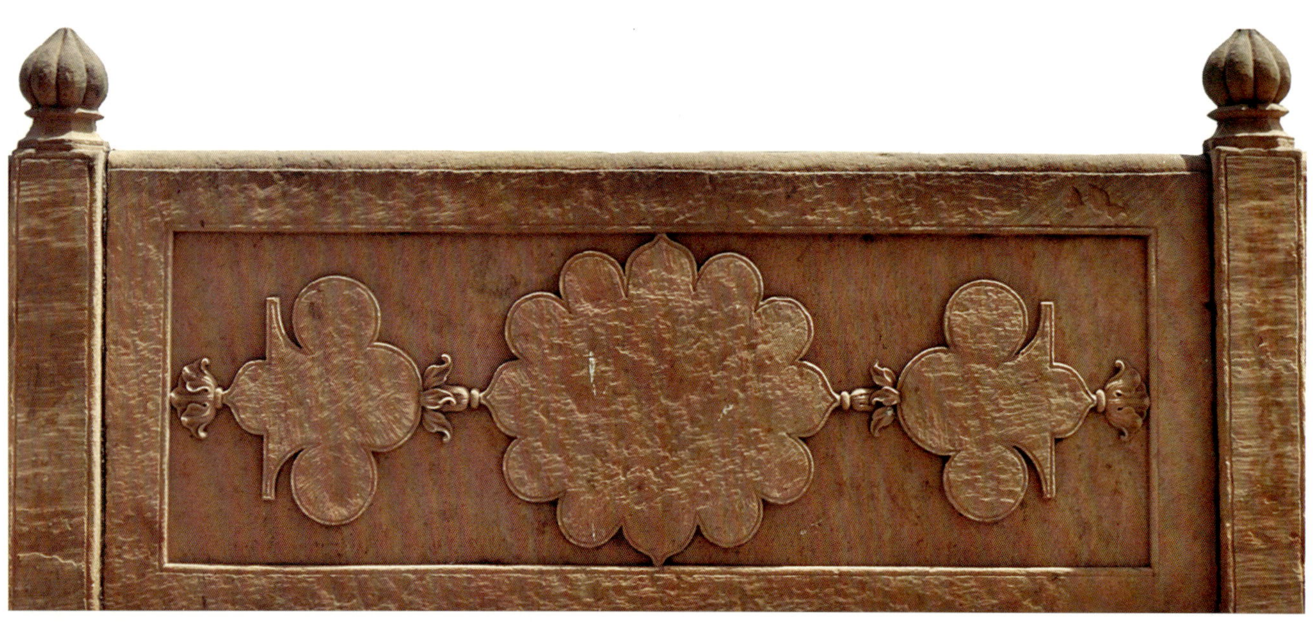

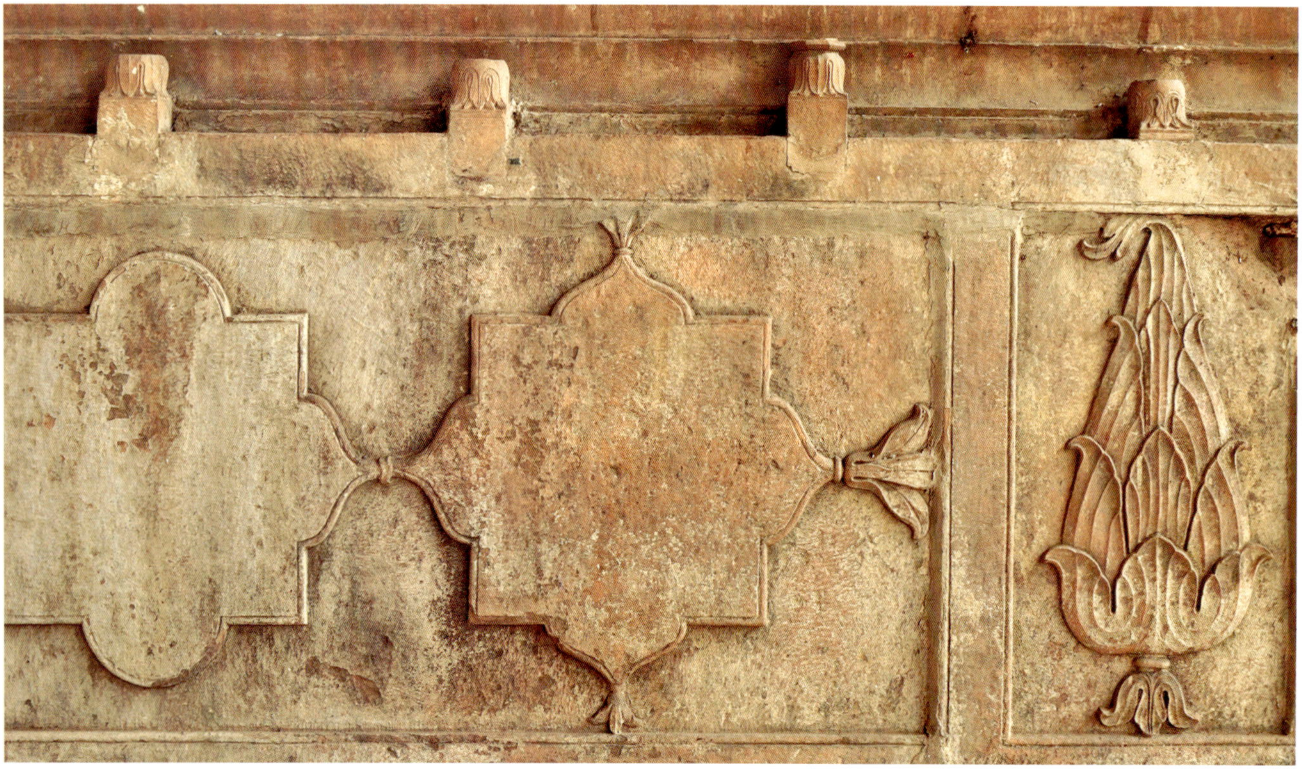

The elevation arches that connect the outer columns are engrailed and they surround an inner square pavilion with a periphery of similar arches and columns. Among the five outer arches the ones at the corner are wider than the three inner ones. The spandrels of these engrailed arches are the least decorated with just a framing of acanthus scrolls. Each of the cusps is highlighted with a turned petal leaf. These simple yet aristocratic arches are balanced by elaborate, carved, bulbous columns, the special feature of some being a highlighted flower panel carved on an acanthus capital.

Above the arches are brackets framing cartouche flat panels on either side, which support the lower part of the ceiling. The tapered *chhajja* eaves over these flat panels give an extra space above the ceiling. Thus, though it appears to be single-roofed, it has a concealed double roof just like the rest of the buildings. One can see copper outlets for water sprays projecting all around the outside and inside at the transition of the arches and carved flat panels. (Fig. 10)

The central pavilion thus is surrounded by a 3-metre wide water canal with two bridges to reach the inner pavilion, between the outside elevation arches and the arches of the inner square. The existence of this rectangular water channel converts the inner pillared

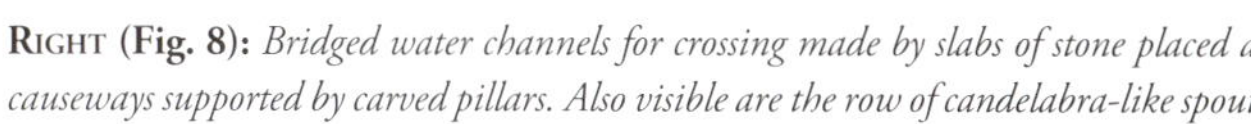

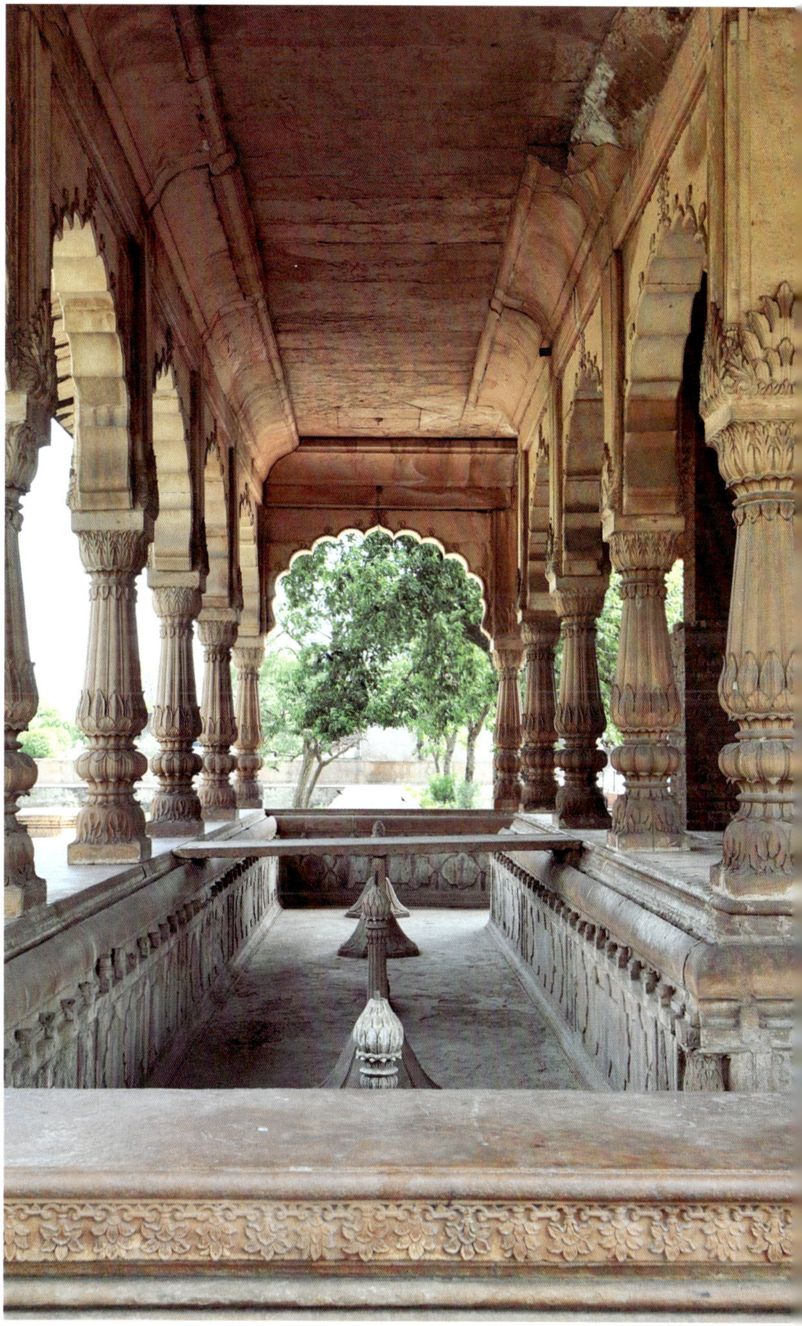

Right (Fig. 8): *Bridged water channels for crossing made by slabs of stone placed as causeways supported by carved pillars. Also visible are the row of candelabra-like spouts*

Facing page above (Fig. 9): *Cartouche detail of the parapet*

Facing page below (Fig. 7): *The inner facade of the water channel with geometric cartouche panels and cypress trees*

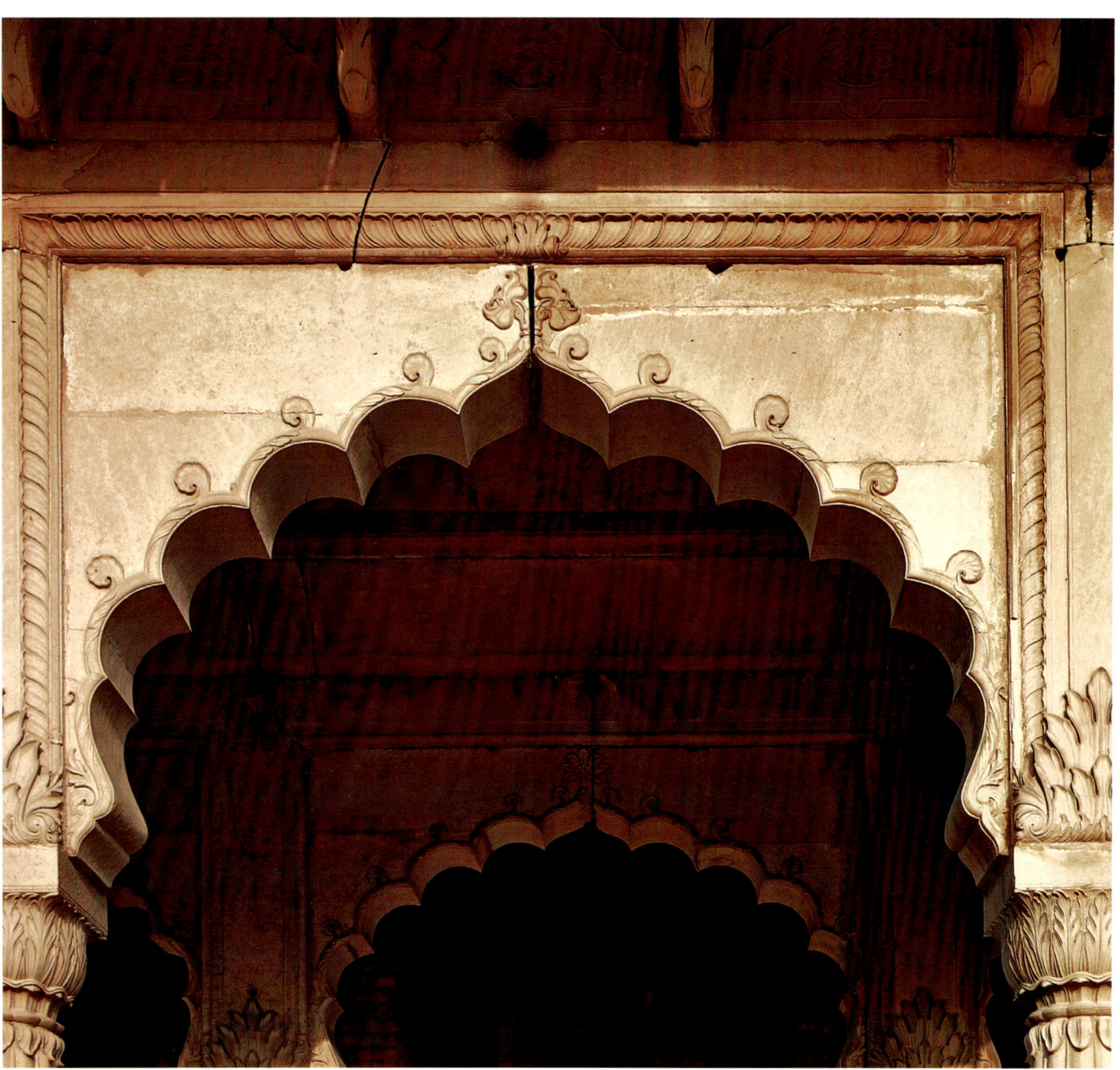

space into an island. This canal is lined by water jets on either side, just below the plinth level, to form a water spray into the canal. (Fig. 11) Inside the canal are also water spouts which sent the water straight up. Whenever the water was released, these water jets enclosed the inner pavilion in fountains. The actions of these water spouts, throwing jets of water on the inner spandrels of elevation arches, caused water to splash and form a falling curtain over the opening. Thus was created artificial rain, whenever the waters were discharged. The broad canal running around the edge of the pavilion increased the sense of being encased in water. The water body is deep enough to even swim and take baths. The water probably flowed from this *baradari* channel, decorated with carved cartouche panels, to the central octagonal pool of the Charbagh. (Fig. 12)

An interesting accompaniment to this artificial rain was the delicate sound of thunder, or *Megh-garjana* as mentioned in the *Gita Govinda*. This sound of thunder was effected by an innovative and, perhaps, unheard of detail in the subcontinent. The Keshav Bhawan originally included elaborate devices to reproduce the effects of thunder. The purpose of double roofs was to create this effect artificially which made the *baradari* unique. This so-called 'music' was achieved by the rolling of copper balls placed in the hollowed cavity of the roof above the pavilion.

According to M.C. Joshi, there are some hollow columns which take water up to the ceiling and contain

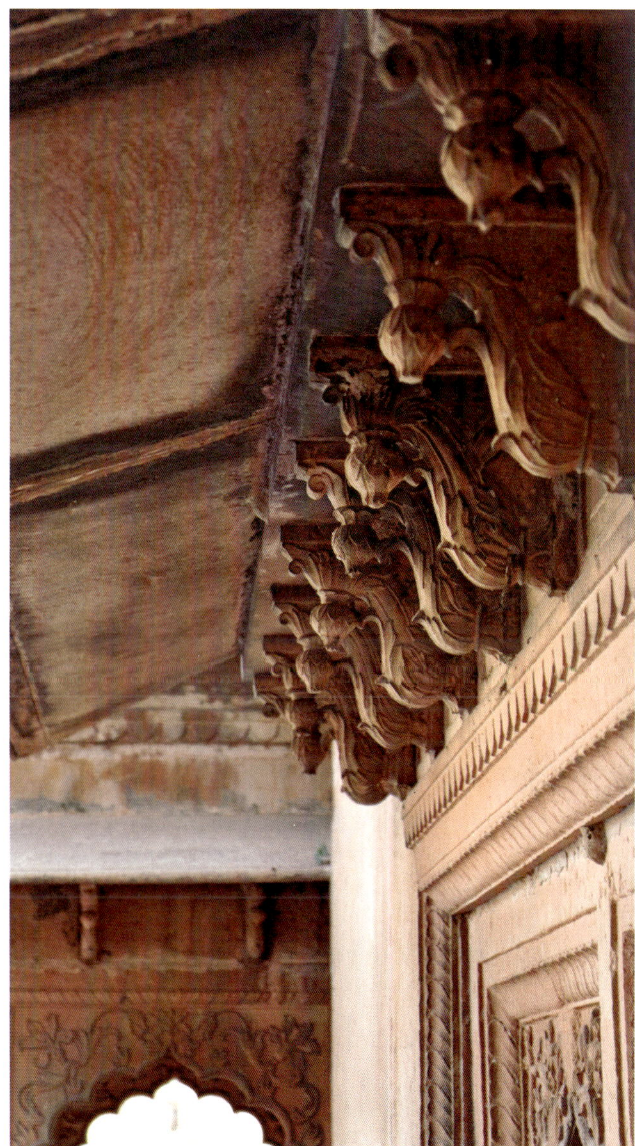

Above (Fig. 13): *Brackets form the integral structural system to carry the load of the* chhajja *eaves and projections to the base via columns*

Facing page (Fig. 10): *Water that tumbled the stone balls to create the sound of thunder in the ceiling was released through copper pipes placed above the arches around the elevations*

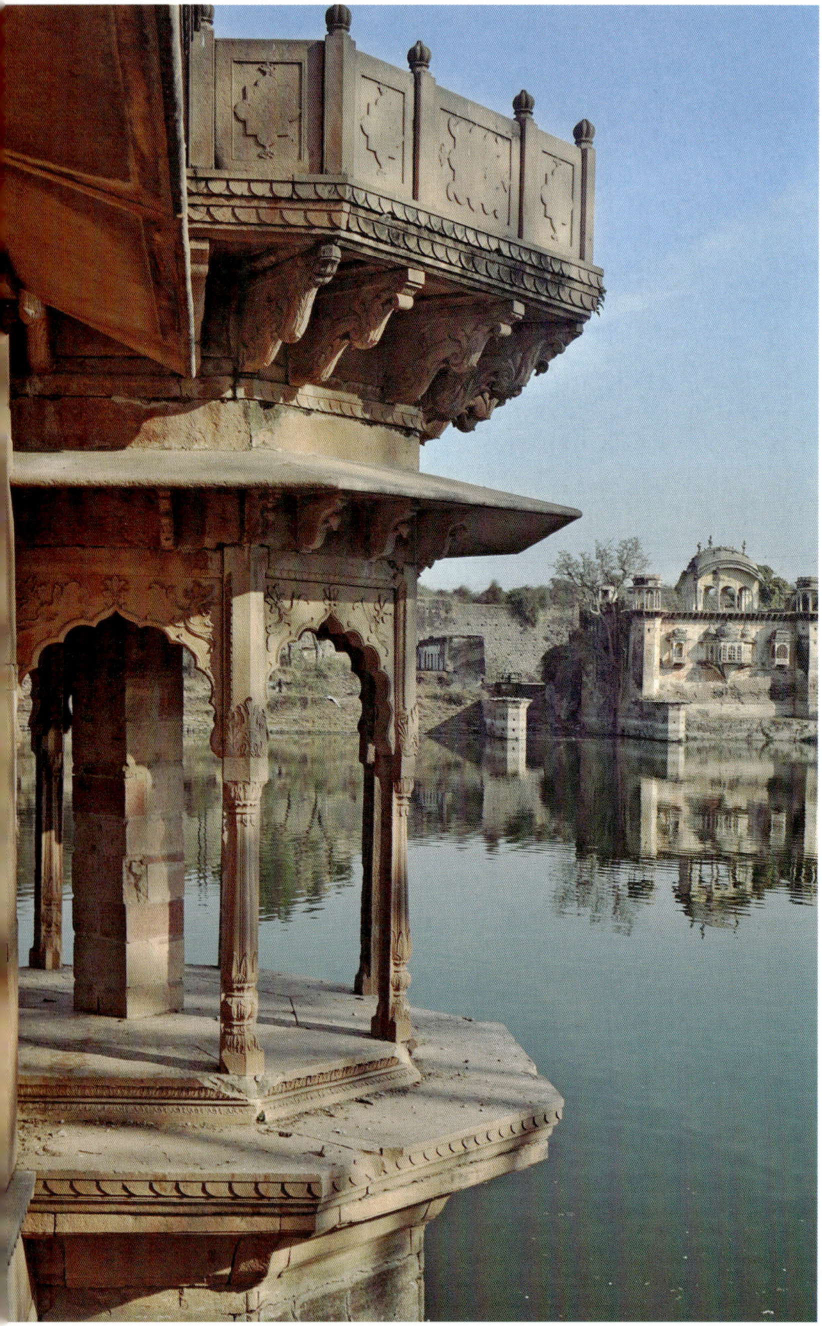

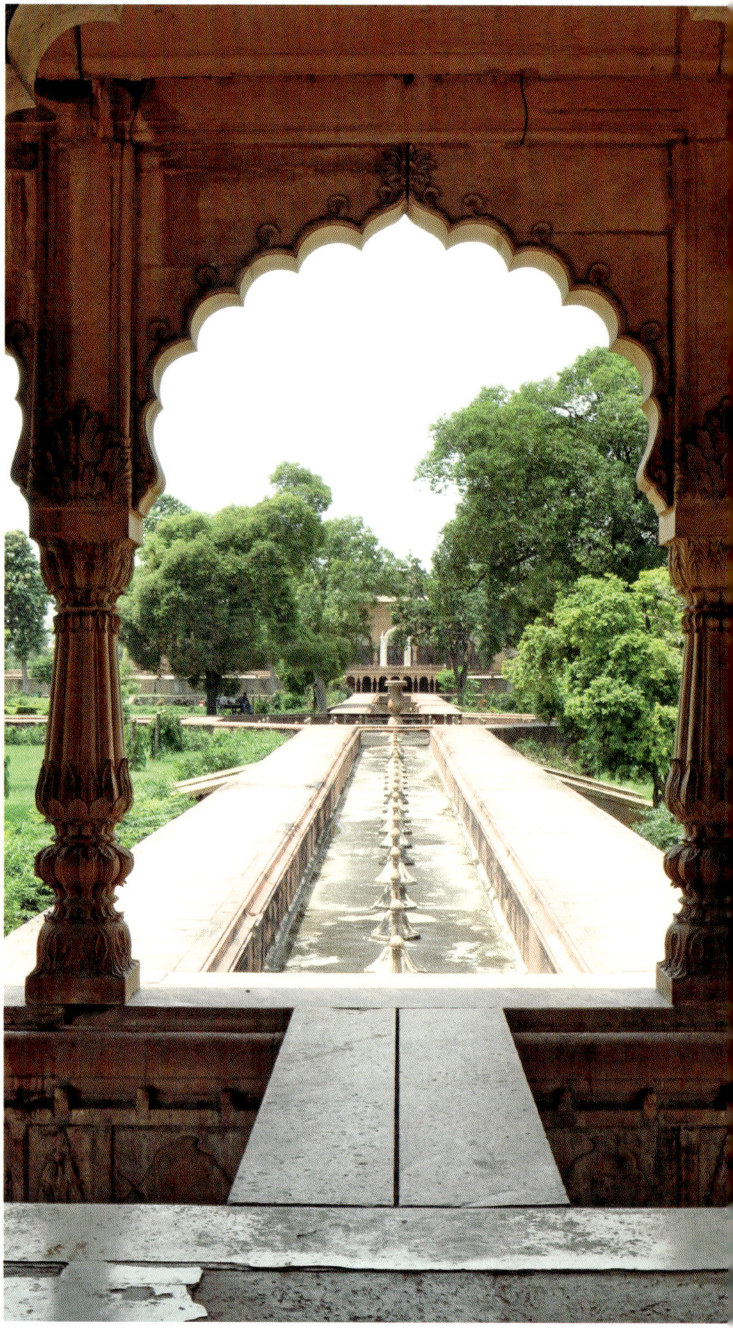

concealed lithic balls. The pressure of this water made the balls rotate and play with each other thus producing the sound of thunder. The second theory revolves around a tank as well on the roof of the Keshav Bhawan. This could also be true as the shape of the roof is inverted, caved in at the terrace level, and could have held water. Water from the tank could have been routed to the hollow cavity of the double roof which contains heavy stone balls. This release of running water could have led to the rolling/agitation of the heavy stone balls that recreated the sound of thunder and the water was set free through copper spouts positioned on top of the arches to fall as sheets of splashing rain around the open hall. The brackets are closely placed in order to give extra strength to the ceiling. (Fig. 13) *Chhajja* eave stone slabs approximately 3 inches thick and 36 inches wide overhang from the bracket's outer edge, being supported with closely placed brackets carved out of a 4-inch thick stone.

On the edges of the outer terrace of the Keshav Bhawan are four semi-quoins with octagonal platforms. These give the impression of the corner *minars* (towers) of Mughal structures, converting this modest-looking pavilion into the centre of attraction of the Deeg garden complex. (Fig. 14) The enigma of empty space beyond pulls one towards itself and on reaching there a new vista opens. This dormant pavilion emerges as a complete palace when viewed from the ghats of the Rup Sagar. Though not visible from the Charbagh side, there are two storeys under this pavilion which are equally notable features of this quaint structure. (Fig. 15)

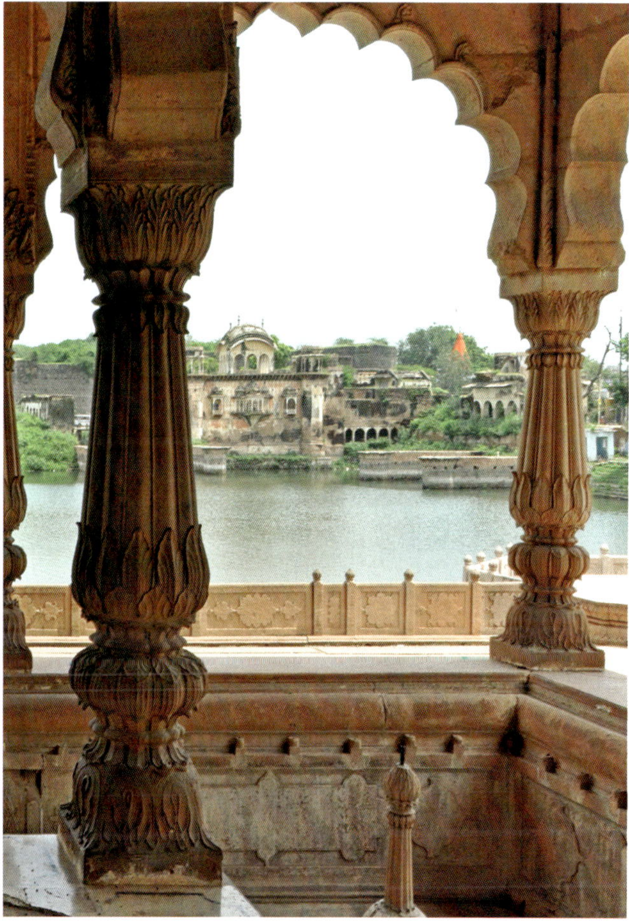

Above (Fig. 11): *A sublime view of the old palace and the fort across the Rup Sagar through the arches of the Keshav Bhawan also showing the water jets below the plinth*

Facing page left (Fig. 14): *The abstruse, octagonal* chhatris *below the octagonal corner balconies*

Facing page right (Fig. 12): *The* hindola *viewed backwards through the arches, water channels and fountains*

The *chhatris* on either side of the gallery underneath form a gorgeous setting of a palatial hallway adjoining the water body, which constitutes the first storey under the Keshav Bhawan. When seen from the elevation of the Rup Sagar the gallery consists of five bays corresponding to the five arches of the Keshav Bhawan and are in the same proportions. The two outer bays are formed by trefoil arches while the inner with Mughal engrailed arches. All the arches are framed by a fragile, carved stone lattice on three sides. (Fig. 16) This gallery is divided into different sections by carved panelled partitions and could have been used as a recreation or fishing area. (Fig. 17) The turret-like *chhatris* stand on either side of the arcade. These two are octagonal with arched openings. The lower level comprising of plain stone masonry gets submerged in the water and has trenches to connect to the water of the Gopal Sagar.

The seating of the pavilion on the Rup Sagar reservoir assured that the hot summer winds travelling into the pavilion were cooled by the mass of the water body of the Rup Sagar. The winds, even when calm, produced a pool of cool air around the pavilion, thereby bringing down the ambient temperature. The use of water fountains must have further brought about a lowering of temperature within the pavilion. The internal arrangement of the building to recreate the rainy season made it all the more remarkable. The wind when filtered through the water curtains probably cooled down the pavilion in a manner identical to the desert coolers that cool the metropolitan homes of today during summers.

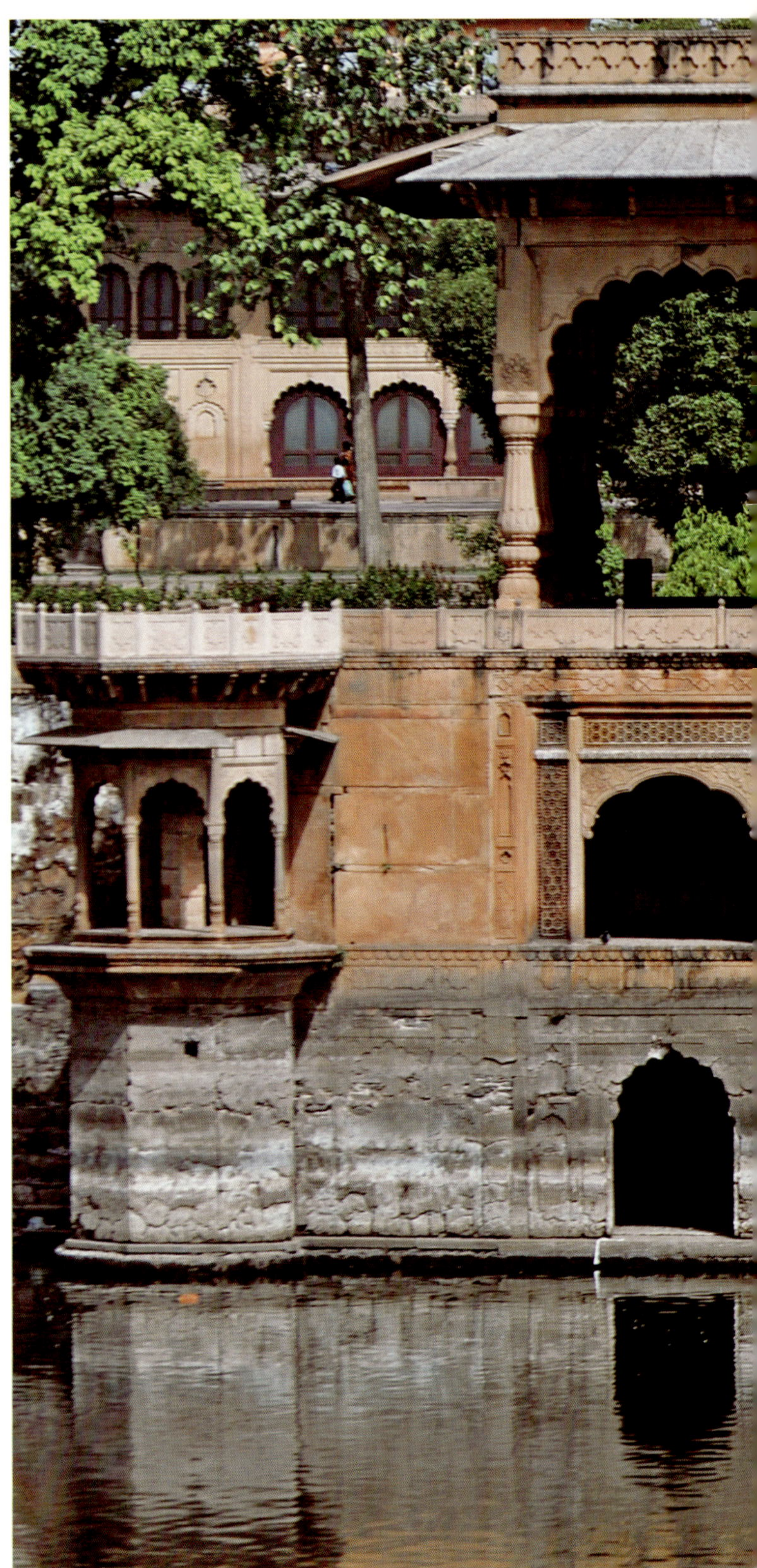

Right (Fig. 15): *The eastern elevation of the Keshav Bhawan facing the Rup Sagar*

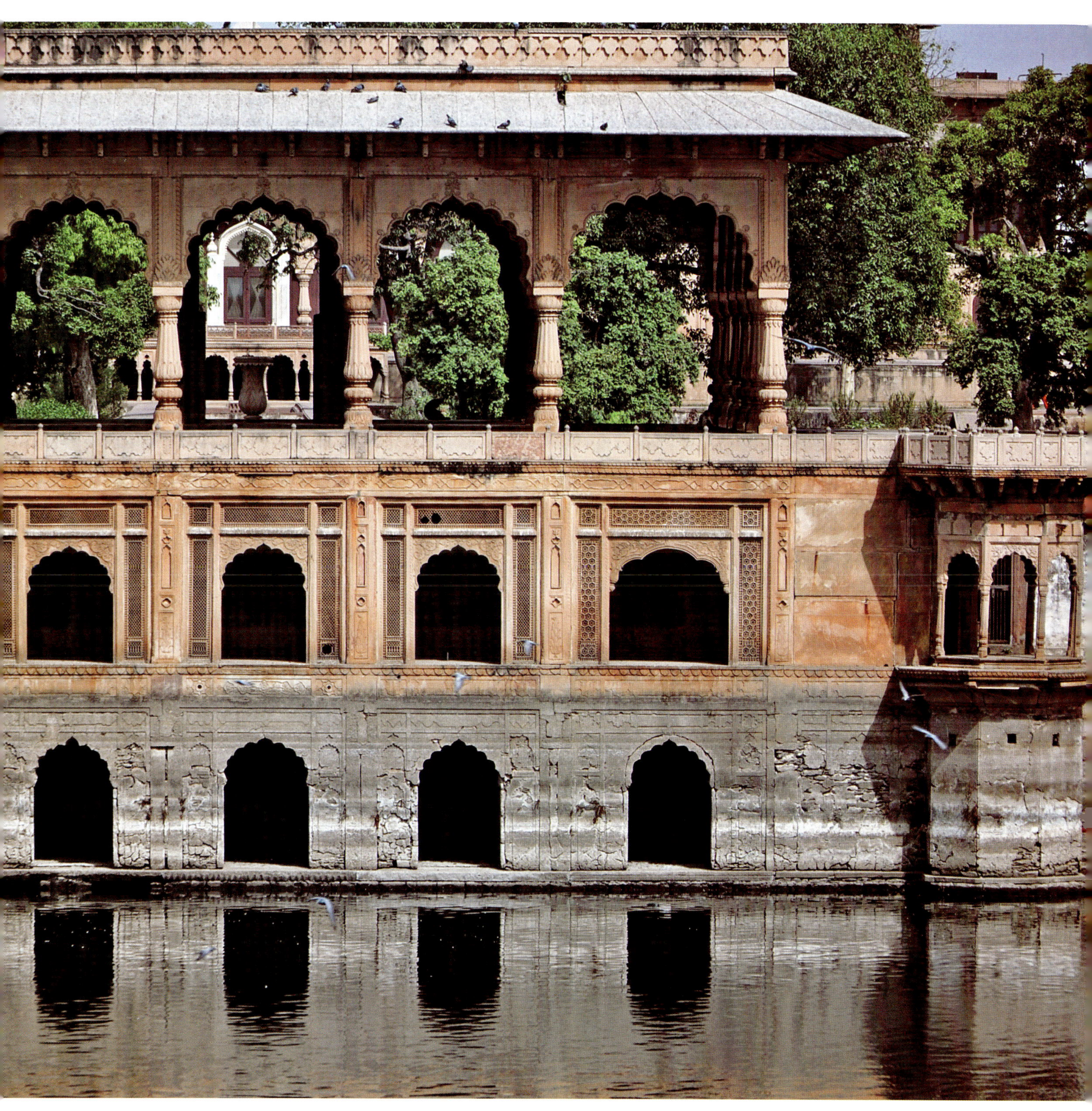

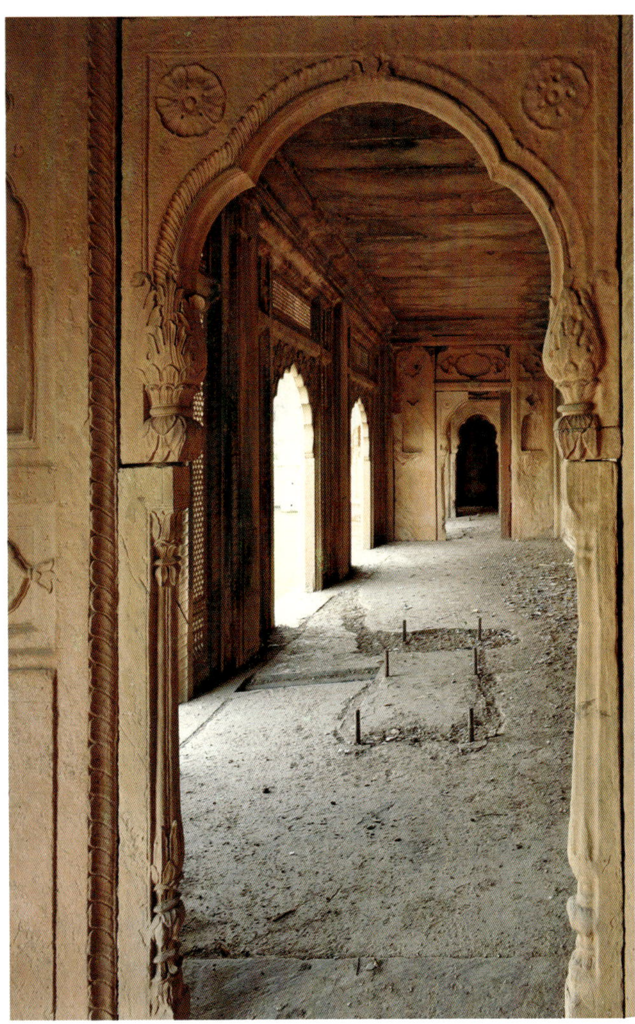

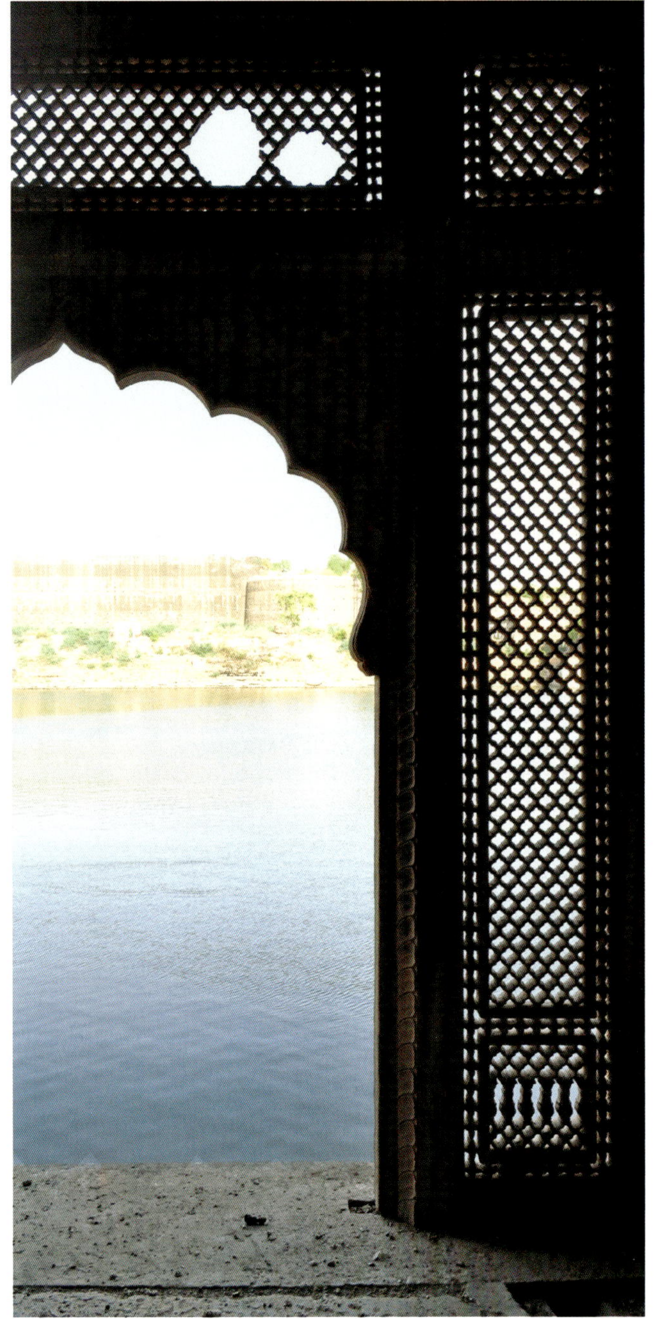

Above (Fig. 17): *Lower recreation gallery to enjoy water sports*

Right (Fig. 16): *View of the water forming ripples from the fine lattice screens of the lower gallery*

Facing page (Fig. 18): *A 3D visual of the Keshav Bhawan from the Rup Sagar side*

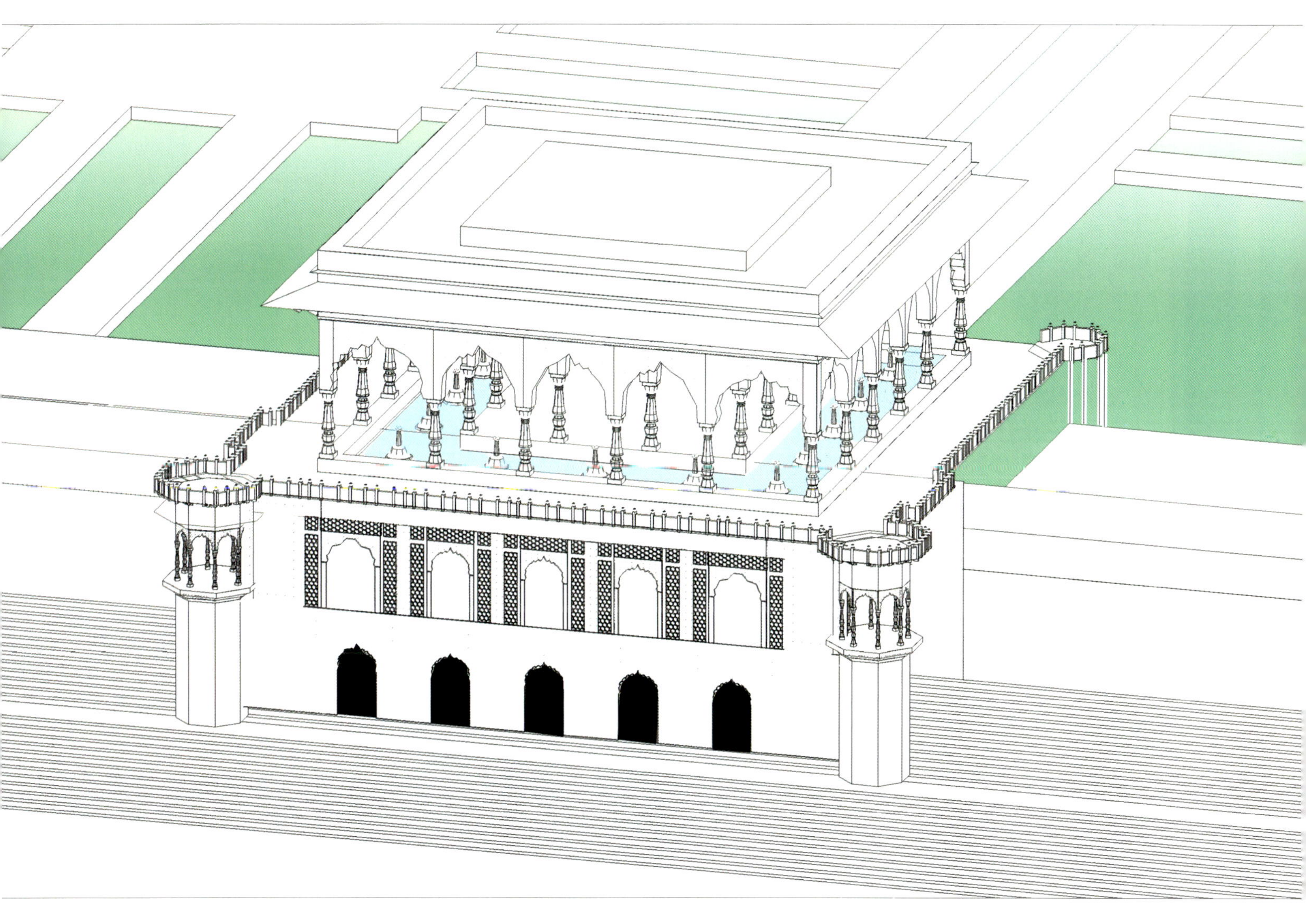

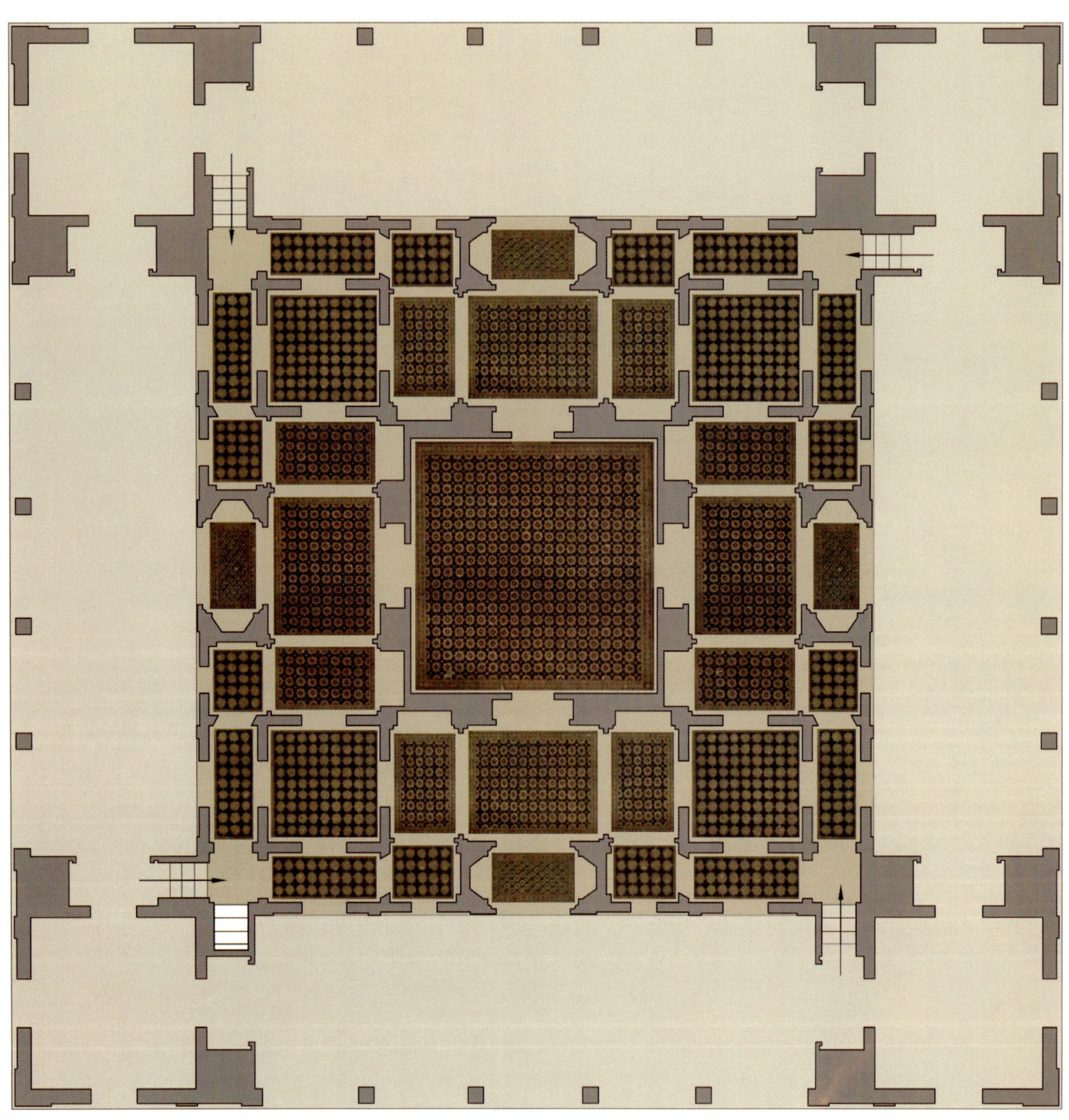
Facing Charbagh and Gopal Bhawan
Facing Suraj Pol
Facing Annexe and Kishan Bhawan
Facing Charbagh and Hardev Bhawan

SYMPHONY IN MARBLE

SURAJ BHAWAN

Suraj Mal envisaged the Deeg Palace as a grand garden retreat based on the Mughal ideal of an earthly paradise. He served as one of the able successors of the artistic legacy of Shah Jahan. Therefore, formality, balance and symmetry are the essential elements of his architecture. Several palaces were also developed based on the tradition of romance associated with the Indian monsoon. Aptly one of the most dazzling bhawans made of incandescent white marble at Deeg Palace derives its name from Raja Suraj Mal and is known as the Suraj Bhawan. It is the most charming and captivating of all the bhawans in the complex, exuding an aura of grandeur and opulence with its intricate carvings.

The architectural charisma of the Suraj Bhawan in Deeg Palace can be compared to the enigma of Salim Chishti's *dargah* in Fatehpur Sikri. The graceful white marble tomb sitting on a raised plinth with decorative lattice and mosaic work gives the complex of Fatehpur Sikri, otherwise built in red sandstone, an ethereal feel. A parallel can be drawn with the Suraj Bhawan built in white marble, elaborately carved, studded with semi-precious stones and sitting on a plinth in an otherwise pink-beige sandstone complex.

The bhawan is primarily Mughal in character with engrailed arches, Mughal-style columns, cartouches, *pietra dura* work and has the same symmetry as many Mughal buildings. (Fig. 2) But on closer inspection the plan of the building makes many revelations. It seems it was designed to create an ambience of mystery for the purpose of recreation, inspired by a mausoleum. Still another meticulous thought throws up the Hindu archetype of the bhawan which is based on *Paramasayika Mandala*—the perfect square

Facing page (Fig. 1): *The Suraj Bhawan is 28 metres square. The plan shows the articulated staircases along with the recreated mosaics of flooring patterns based on old images*

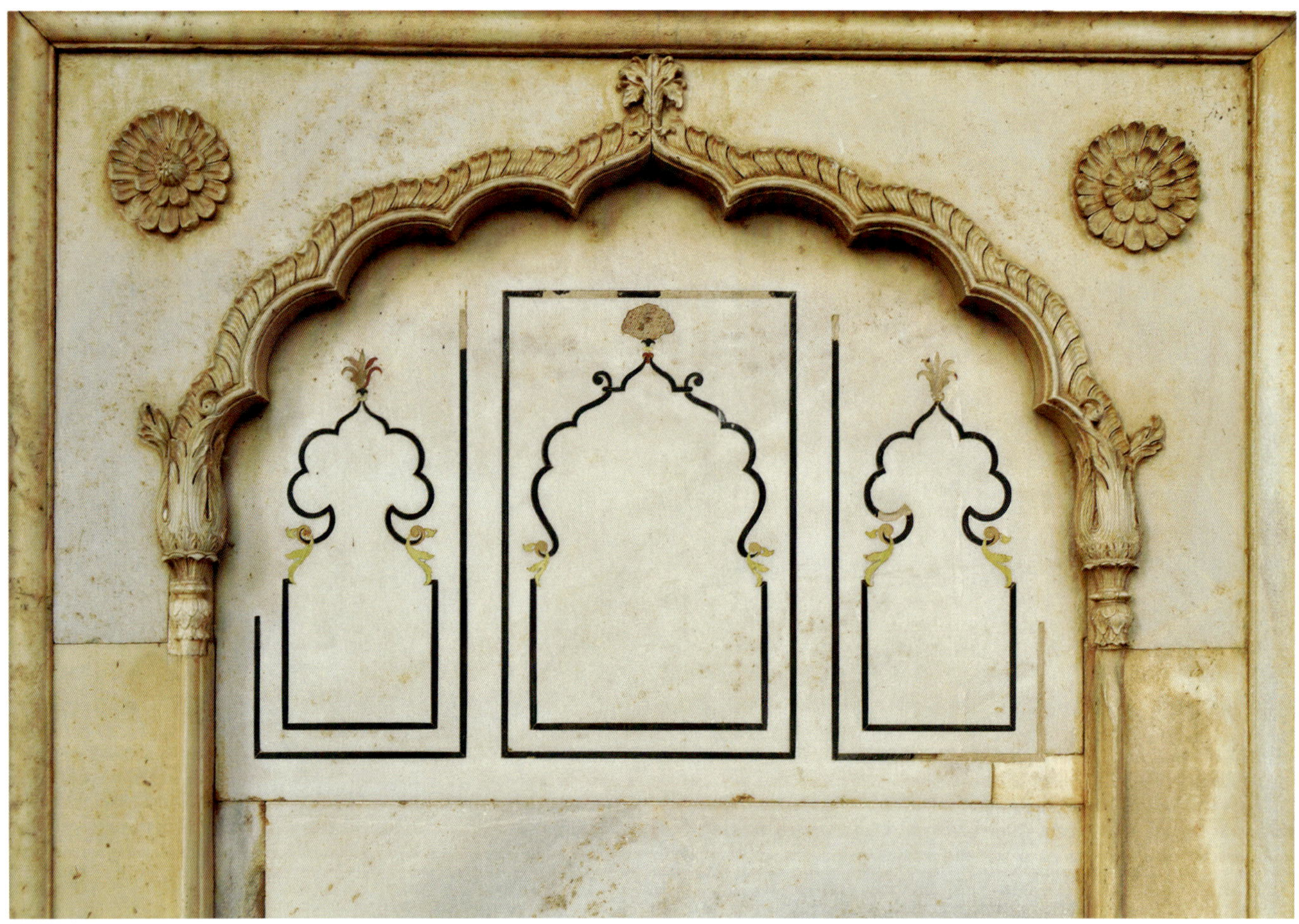

Above (Fig. 2): *The nine-cusped Shahjahani arch with baluster columns carved in relief grace the many niches and arches around Suraj Bhawan*

Facing page (Fig. 3): *A view of Suraj Bhawan across its own Charbagh gardens, the axis from the Singh Pol continuing through the Gopal Bhawan veranda culminating here*

plan with series of repetitive circumambulations and a central chamber—that reminds one of the Hindu cosmic arrangements. This theory is further strengthened by the circuitous formation of the four stairs on each of the vertices leading to the plinth. The stairs are arranged in four different directions forming the Hindu symbol of swastika, an ancient symbol of Vedic Aryans used as a charm to bring good fortune and generate positive energy. (Refer to Fig. 1)

The common theory about the structure says that it is an example of transplant architecture from a madrasa for the Royal Mughal princesses in the Red Fort, Delhi. But the presence of Hindu symbols and the fact that the overall architecture of the building echoes that of

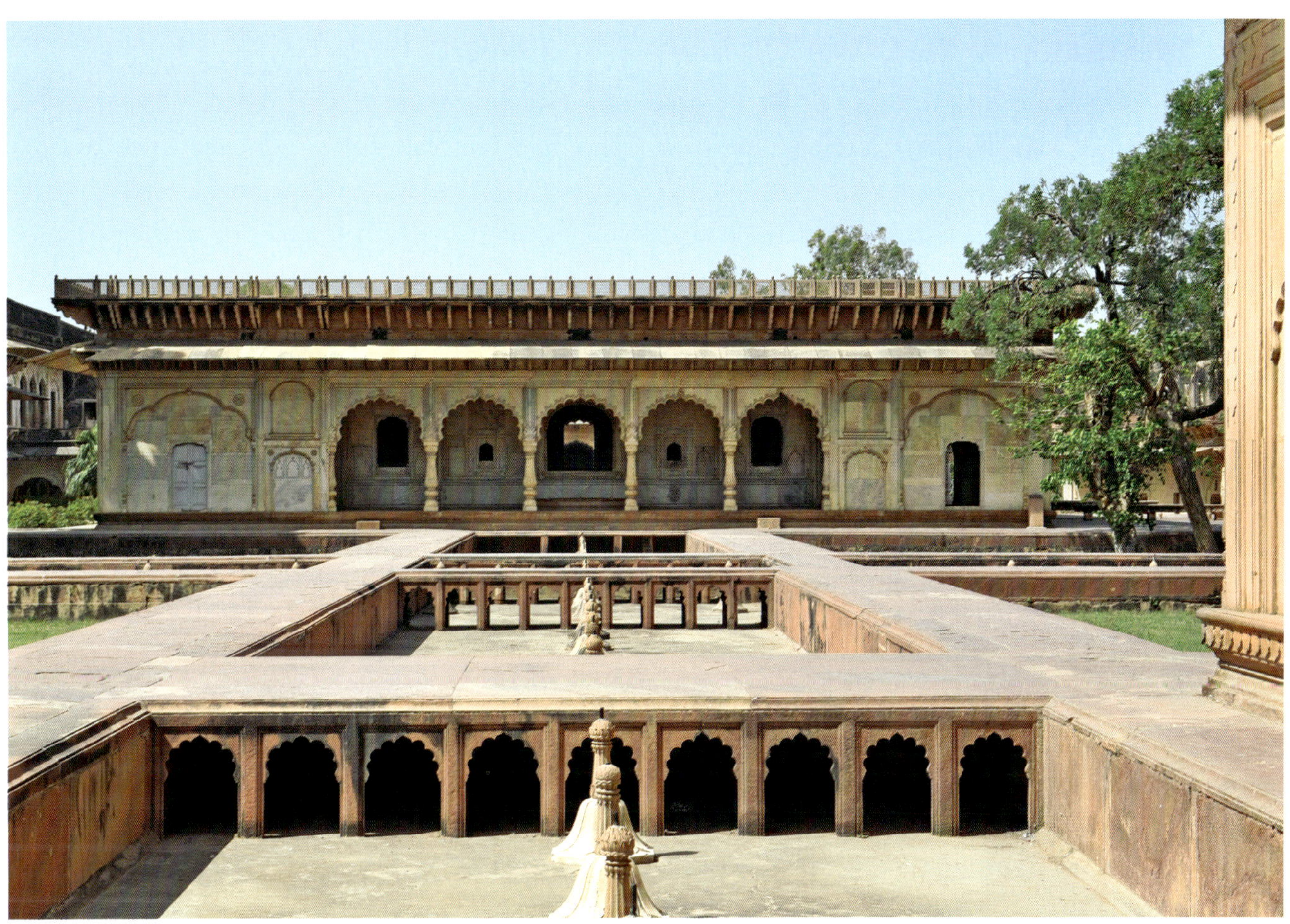

the Deeg complex makes it unlikely. Suraj Mal was highly impressed by Mughal architecture and the Jat rulers brought many trophies from Agra and Delhi. Thus the bhawan is an assimilation of those parts with the new corresponding elements being carved *in situ* in local marble procured from the nearby mines of Alwar.

The bhawan is a white luminous rectangular mass, punctuated by five large-arched openings, capped by horizontal bands of sandstone and parapet which appear to float over the assemblage. It sits at the interface of Gopal Bhawan and Hardev Bhawan with its own Charbagh garden on either side. (Fig. 3) One of the other entrances to the Deeg Palace complex, the Suraj Pol, is on the west of this bhawan.

At the basic level, the Suraj Bhawan was probably meant for the exclusive use of the ladies of the royal household. Its location as a connector between Hardev Bhawan and Gopal Bhawan probably meant that this was a space for rest and recreation of the women in the harem. Its internal arrangement is such that it is very easy to see what is going on outside, however from the outside, it is not possible to see inside (Fig. 4) giving credence to its function as a palace for meeting of the king with the ladies. This becomes possible because

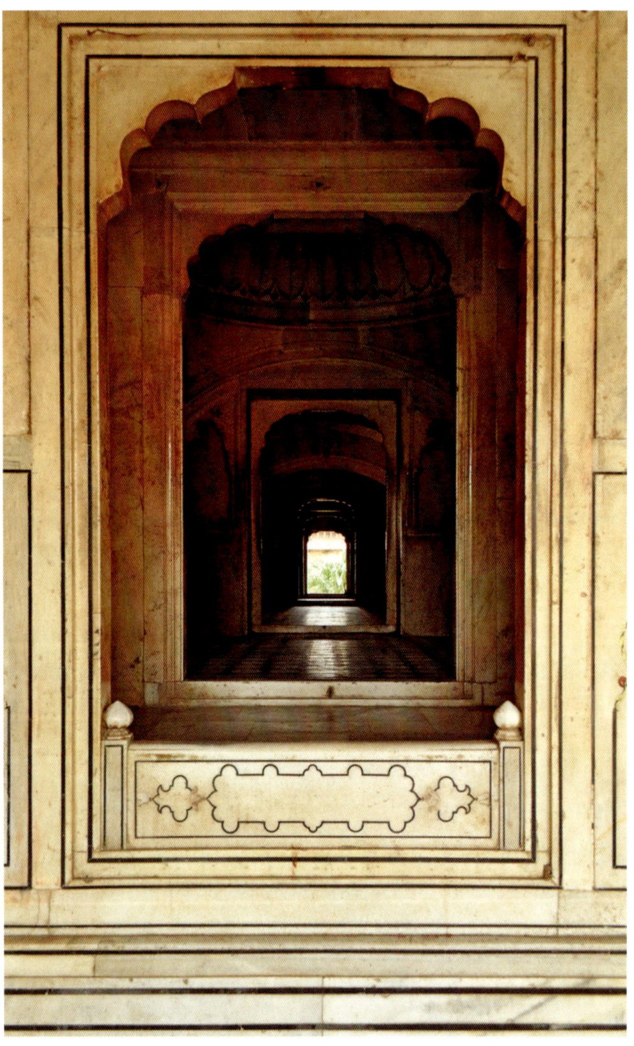

of small *jharokhas* present all around the inside from which one can get a peek of the outside world. But since the white marble appears brighter than the dimly illuminated interiors, no one can get a view of the inside from outside. The central hall of the pavilion is totally empty and dark, and might have been used as an *aramgah* or private sleeping place by the king.

With a parapet detail of a double row of brackets, the Suraj Bhawan, in spite of being single-storeyed, also recalls images of the Jahangiri Mahal at the Agra Fort, built during Akbar's time. The Jahangiri Mahal was the principal zenana, a palace for women belonging to the royal household. It is a double-storeyed building made of red sandstone with protruding balconies and comprises of a complex arrangement of rooms, halls, corridors, galleries and verandas around a square central courtyard. The five-arched openings with closed ends is the main feature of the facade with profuse carvings on stone, heavily fashioned brackets, piers and crossbeams. Skilfully carved brackets support the *chhajja*; a whispering gallery in the second storey and the latticework balustrade crown each facade.

Similarly, it is possible that the Suraj Bhawan was used as a zenana as its placement echoes the Mughal concept of placing the private palaces further off than the public palaces, in this case the Gopal Bhawan being the prominent public hall. Further it seems the arched facade of the Jahangiri Palace courtyard has been lifted and wrapped around the outside enclosing the rooms, halls and corridors in the Suraj Bhawan. The brackets

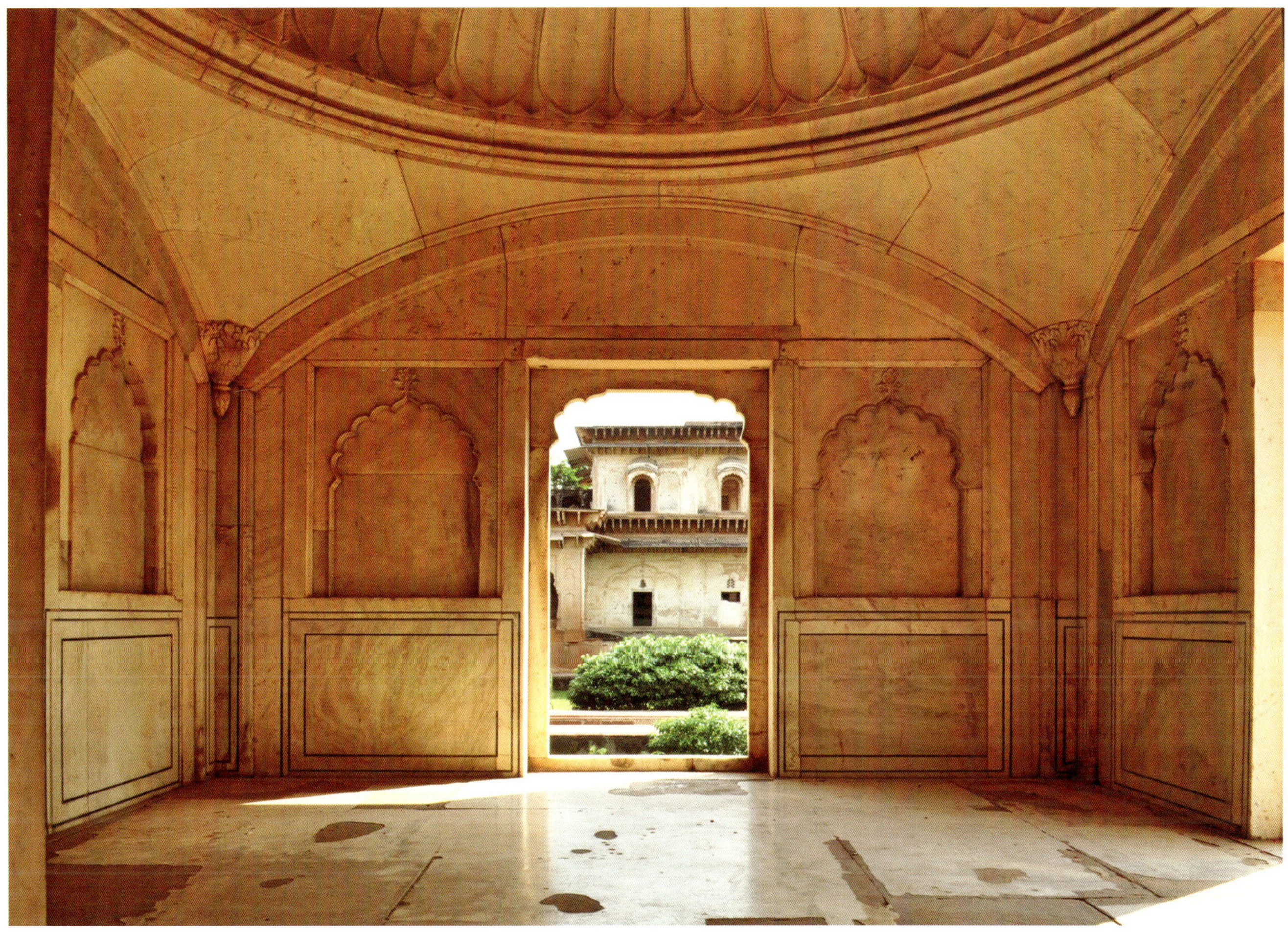

Above (Fig. 5): *The domical ceiling of the four chambers at the corner blocks of the external corridors*

Facing page (Fig. 4): *The internal arrangement is such that it is very easy to see what is going on outside, but not vice versa*

support the *chhajja* but the whispering gallery of the second storey gives way to the double roof structure for added insulation of the building. The same principle is followed in all the buildings of the Deeg Palace.

The single-storeyed symmetrical structure consists of a veranda all around a central pavilion, standing on a fairly high plinth approximately 4 feet and 6 inches above the surrounding ground. The outer corridor, which is 12 inches around the square plan, resolves itself into four separate parts by the introduction of four corner blocks. The four chambers at the corner blocks of the external corridors have a domical ceiling that is not expressed externally. (Fig. 5) Each such corridor is sufficiently secluded and independent so as to function completely without the intrusion of the other. (Fig. 6) The northern side facing the Gopal Bhawan aligns itself to the axis of the Singh Pol and continues to the water

Right (Fig. 7): *On the east elevation is a small herbal garden facing intricate private chambers in sandstone*

Below (Fig. 8): *The annexe on the east of Suraj Bhawan is an arched hallway with ancillary chambers on a raised plinth*

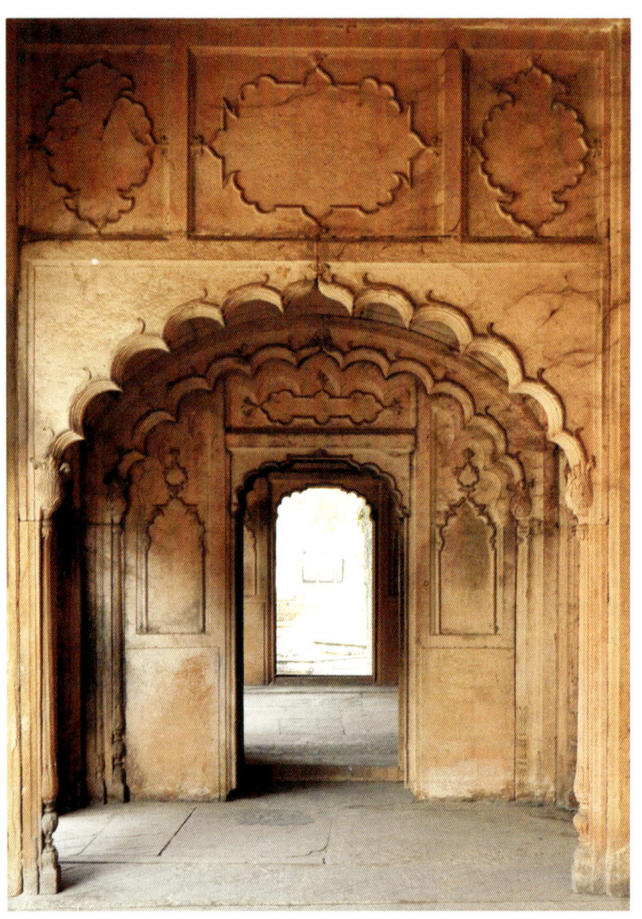

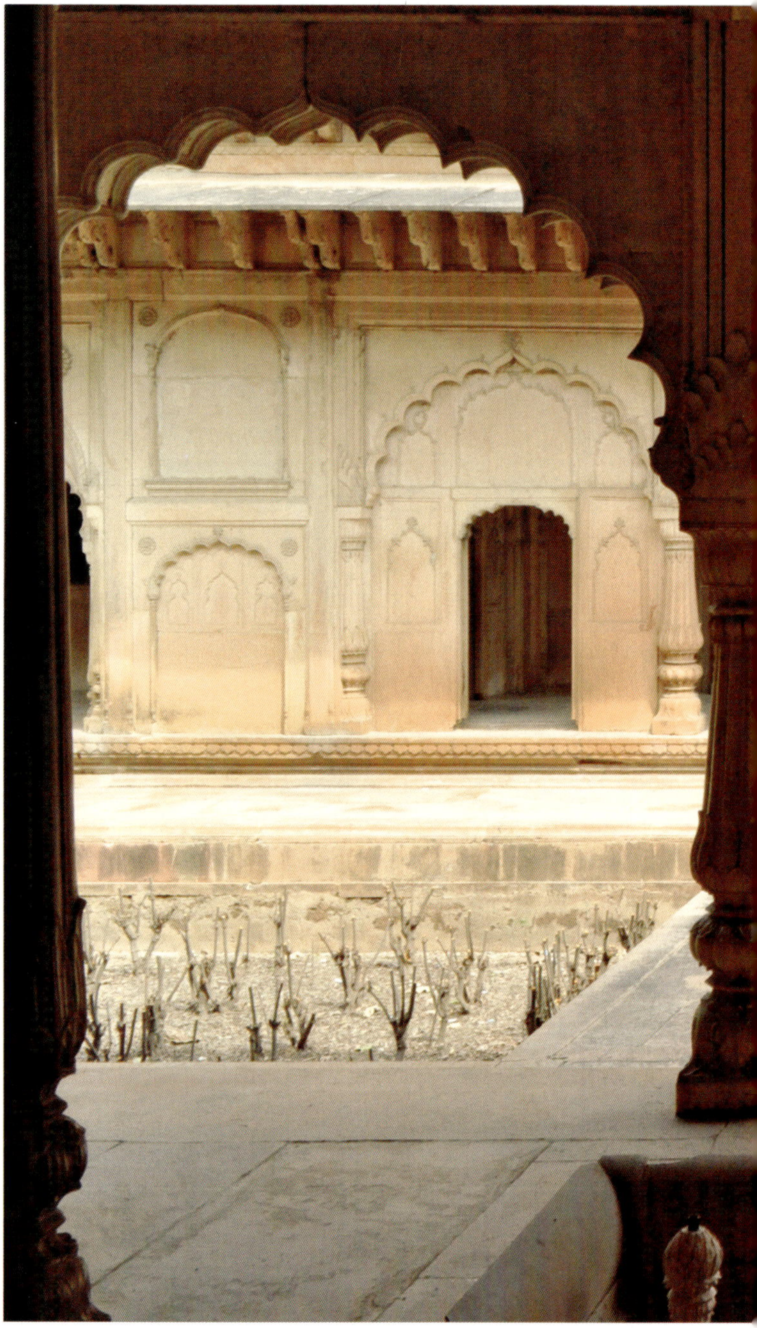

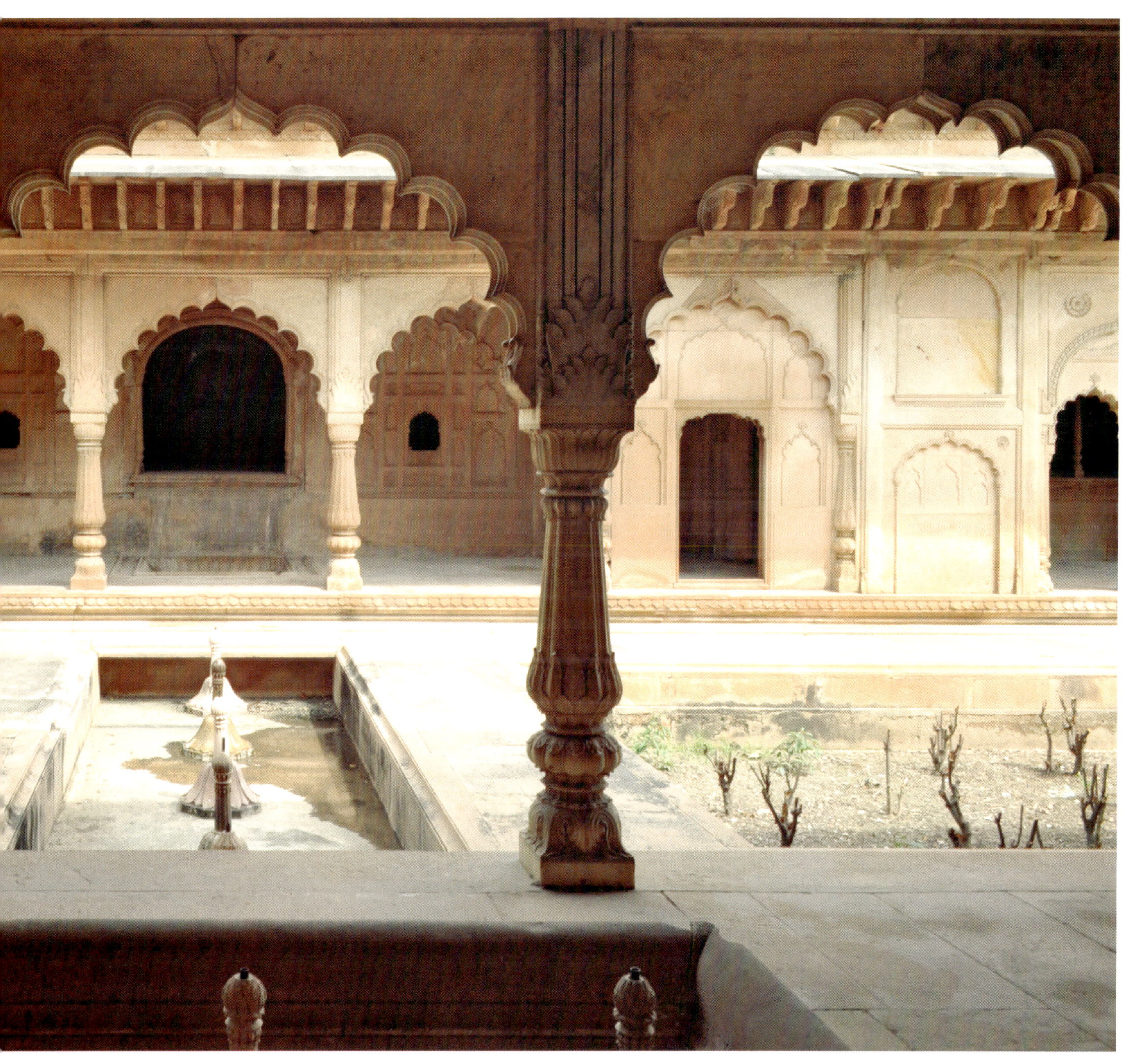

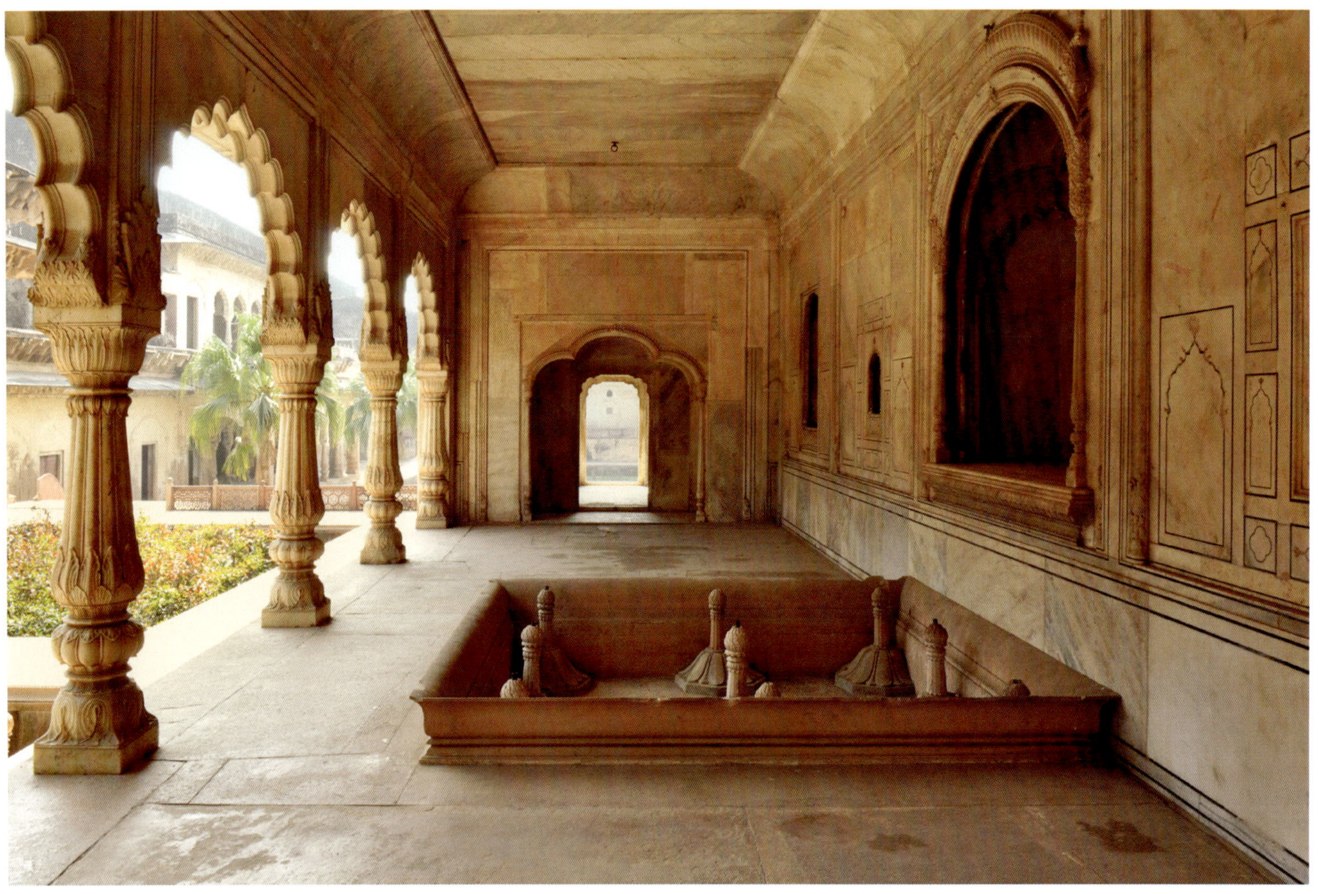

channel of the Hardev Bhawan water garden on the southern side. On the east elevation is a small herbal garden facing intricate private chambers in sandstone called the Suraj Bhawan annexe (Fig. 7) (Fig. 8), while the west facade faces the entrance from the Suraj Pol.

Each veranda has five engrailed arches on elegant baluster columns (Fig. 9) (Fig. 10), placed centrally on the elevation. (Fig. 11) On the ends of the elevation occur large, single trefoil arches in relief over a solid white mass, punctured with a small opening. (Fig. 12) Two smaller cusped arches linearly arranged between the trefoil arch and the columns complete the facade elevation. The history of trefoil arches can be traced back to the Sun Temple at Martand, as discussed before.

The length and breadth of this single-storey bhawan is approximately 92 feet (or 28 metres) each, and it displays a fusion of sandstone and white marble work on its elevations. This exotic medley and adventurous eclecticism suggests a daring approach in architecture. In more direct terms, the marble-clad exterior of the

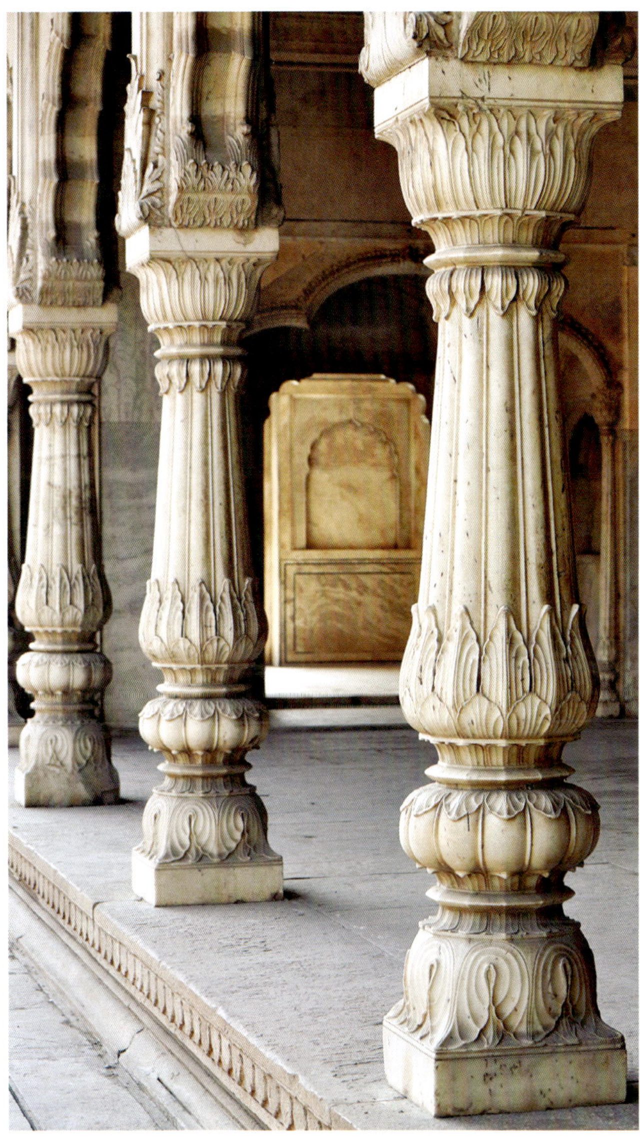

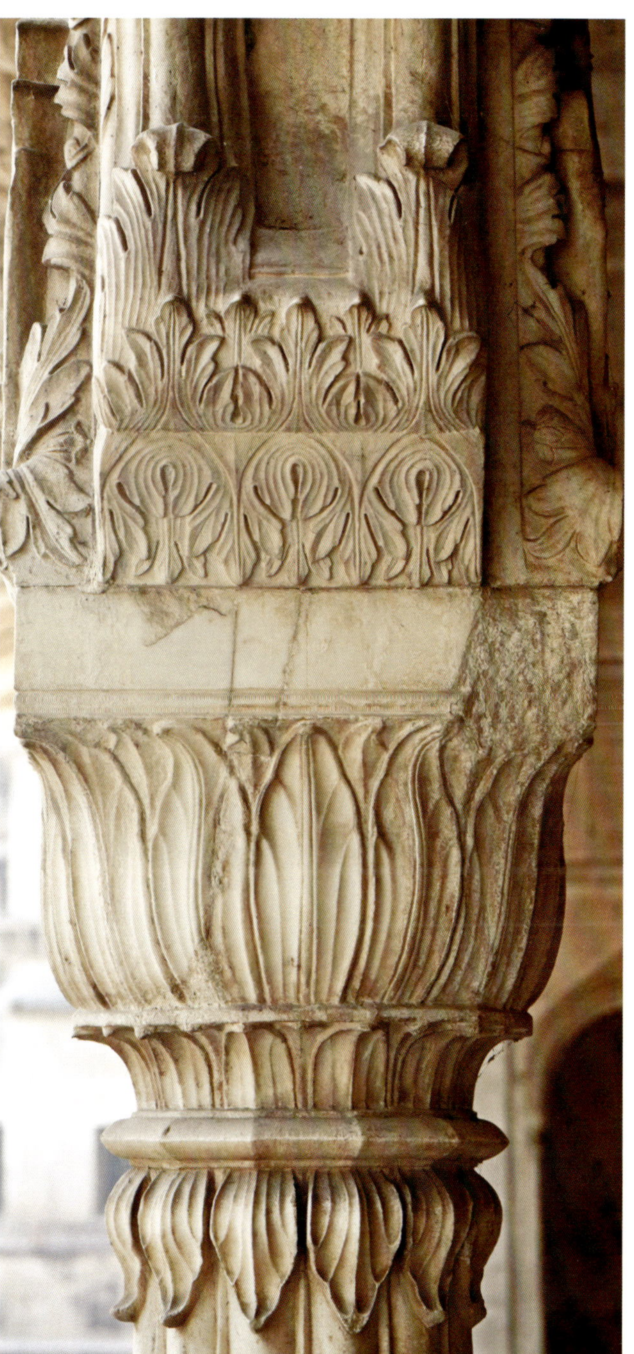

Above (Fig. 10): *A row of elegant and elaborately carved baluster columns support five eleven-cusped Mughal arches on each of the four facades*

Right (Fig. 9): *Detail of the capital of a baluster column with acanthus and lotus leaves*

Facing page (Fig. 6): *Each corridor is secluded and separate so as to function independently*

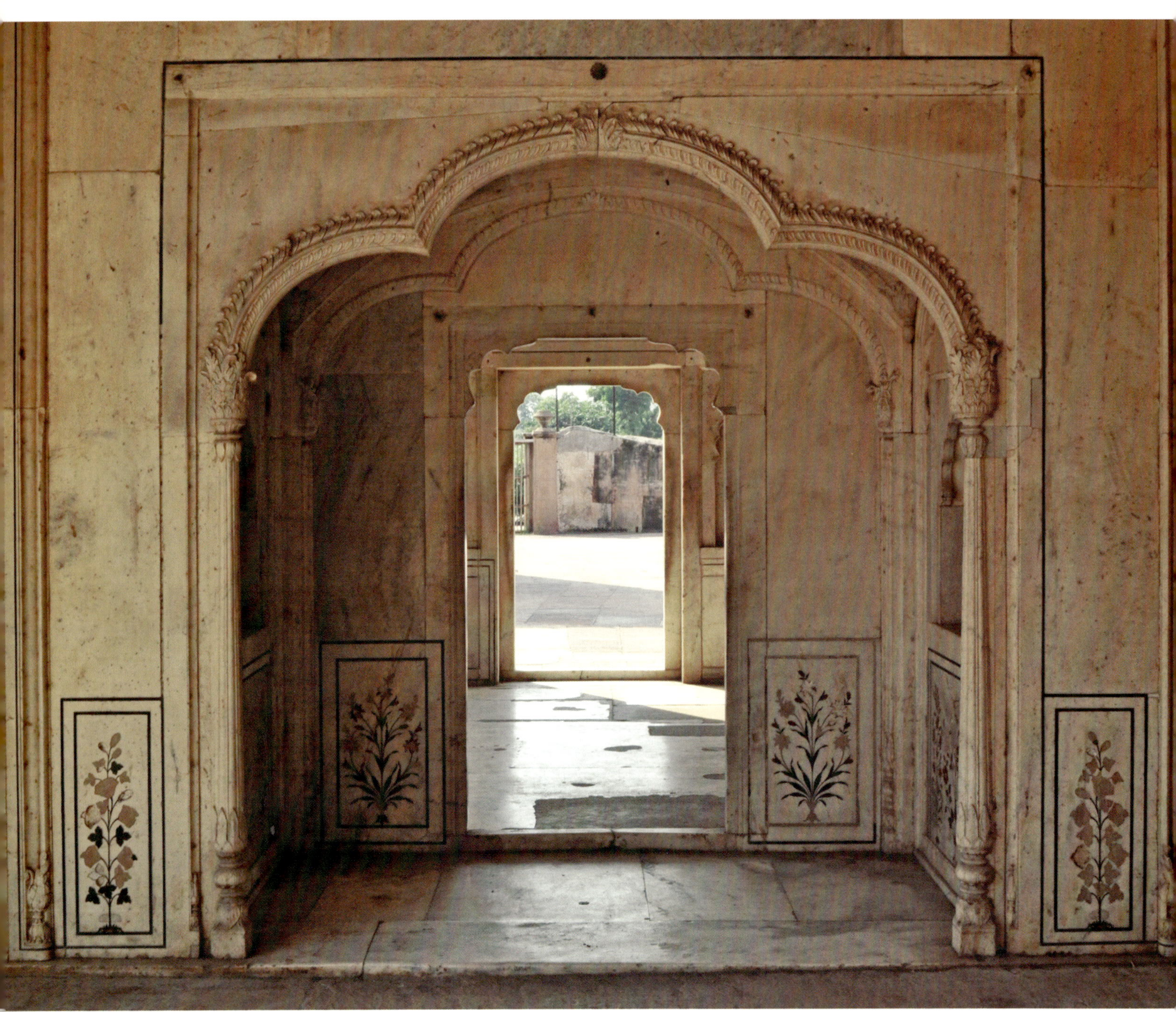

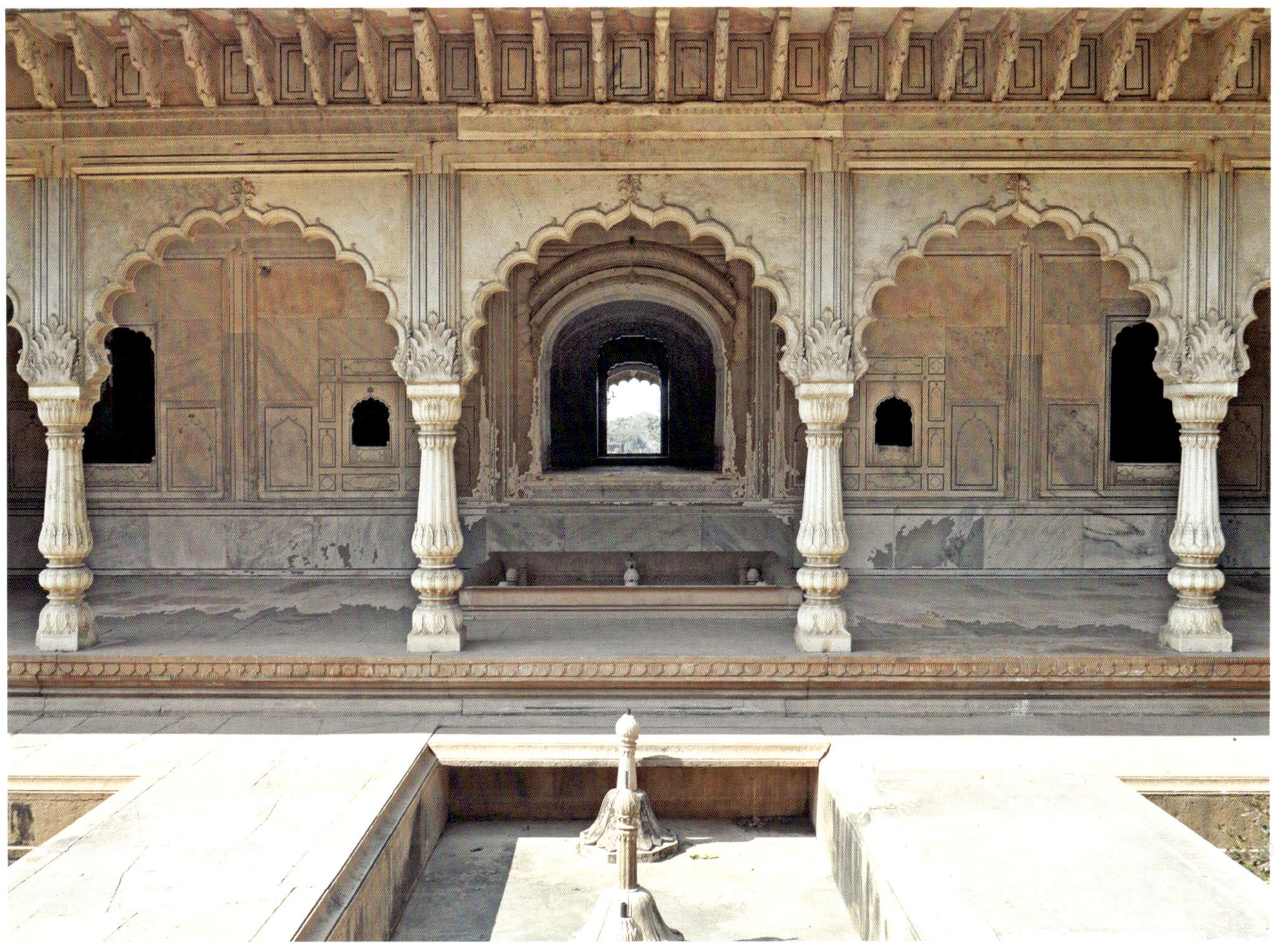

Above (Fig. 11): *Each veranda has engrailed arches on baluster columns, placed centrally on the elevation*

Facing page (Fig. 12): *The trefoil arched vestibule from the corridor to the corner block*

Following pages (Fig. 13): *The southern elevation with the Charbagh of the zenana*

Suraj Bhawan extends from the plinth to the *chhajja* level, while the *chhajja* and the brackets above are made of sandstone. The sloping sandstone *chhajja* (or brackets) encircles the bhawan, above the arches, while there is another set of brackets, supporting the extended roof parapet. The *jali* work in the roof parapet stands vertically while the structure of the parapet projects horizontally from the building face. This is contrary to the sandstone *chhajja*, which is at an angle. (Fig 13)

This pavilion encased by a colonnade veranda all around appears to be an enigma from a distance as there seems to be no path leading to the elevated pavilion. The

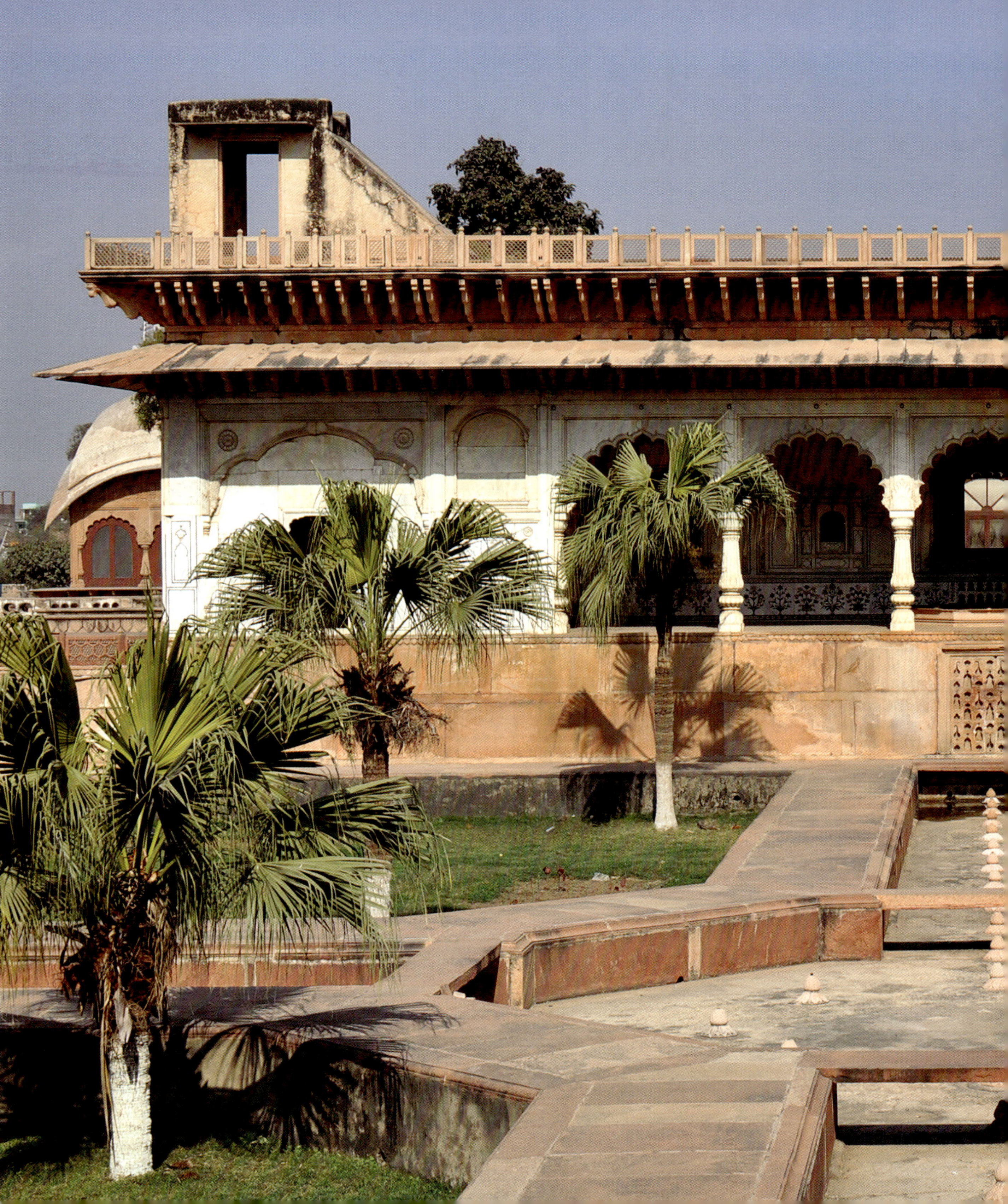

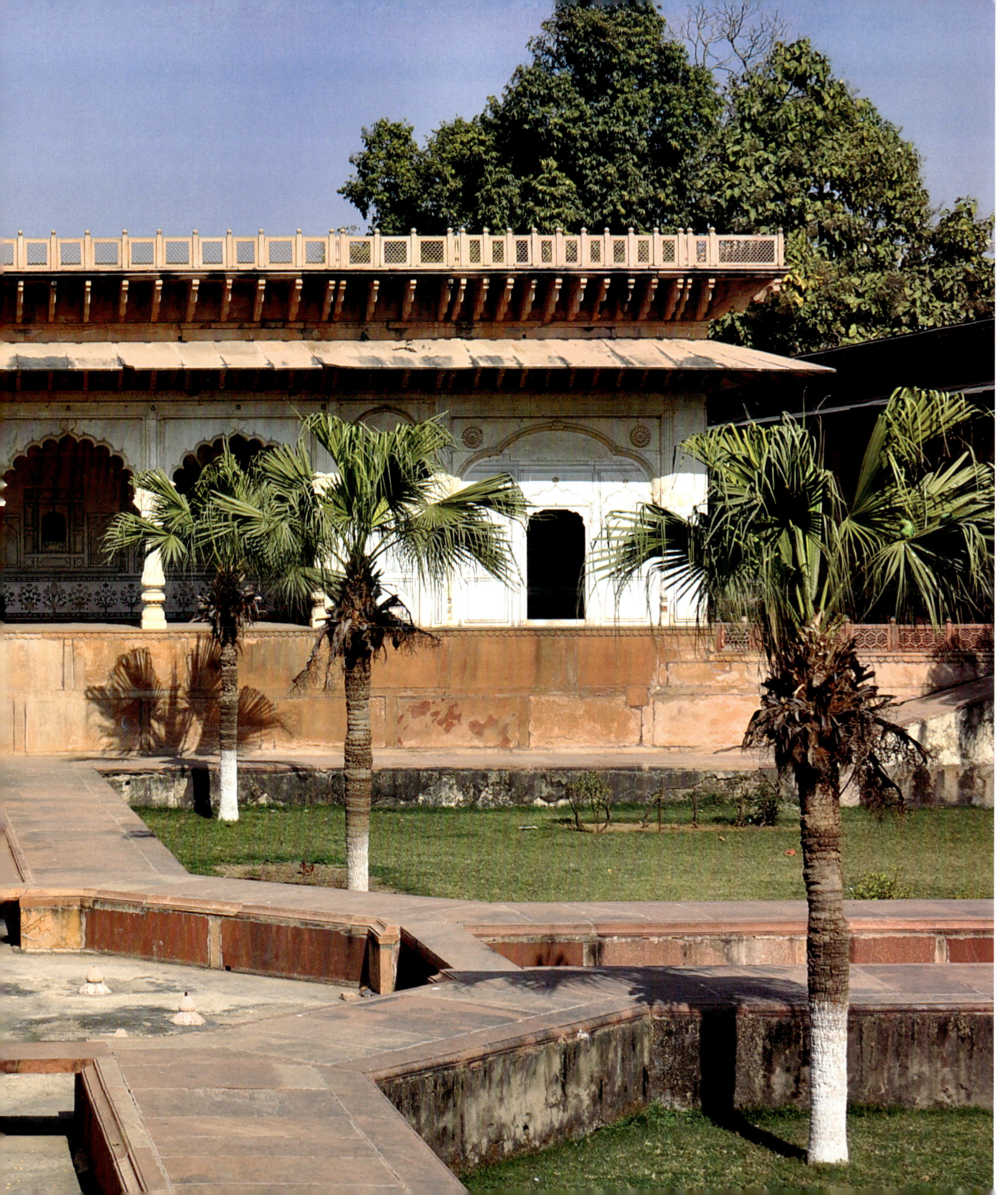

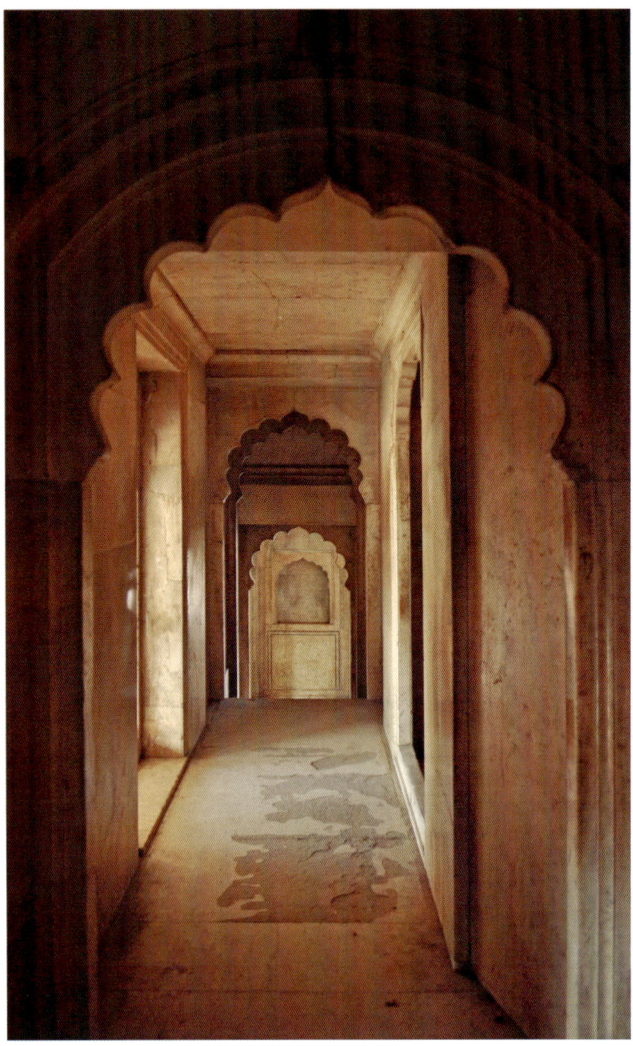

Above (Fig. 14): *The staggered openings of various shapes allow a subtle interplay of light and shade*

Facing page above (Fig. 17): *The whole corridor has beautiful inlaid flooring pattern with* abri, ajuba, *yellow jasper and black Belgian stone on white marble*

Facing page below left (Fig. 15): *Geometric pattern framed by a cusped cartouche border inlaid with* abri *and* ajuba *fossil stones*

Facing page below right (Fig. 16): *Inlaid cartouche panels surround and frame the cusped window opening in the marble wall*

path to the pavilion is not revealed at first glance. The mystery unfurls in the form of four staircases hidden in the four corner blocks of the veranda. To enter the central portion, one has to ascend a few steps at the vertices of this inner enclosure.

A hand-drawn plan of the Suraj Bhawan in the Gopal Bhawan Museum gives a clear indication of the internal plan of the Suraj Bhawan. From this, it appears that the progress of construction of this building must not have been smooth and as there is variation in the elevations and material used, as well as incomplete interiors, especially the flooring.

The internal layout consists of a square central hall (6.3m × 6.3m) which has bracketed arched openings on all four axis walls. These openings lead to niches which are part of a hallway running all around. On the other side of this hallway there is a beautiful interplay of alternating niches and alcove formations which runs along the periphery of the whole building as a gallery. The staggered openings of various shapes allow a subtle interplay of light and shade to the discerning visitor (Fig. 14).

The walls of the central hall are decorated with cartouche panels and arched niches, some in relief and some beautifully carved at different levels. There are three arches carved in relief on each wall. The central one framing the opening and the two side ones framing a niche and an inlaid wall with complex geometric designs made using *ajuba*, *abri*, yellow jasper, black Belgian stone (Fig. 15) while some are with plain black

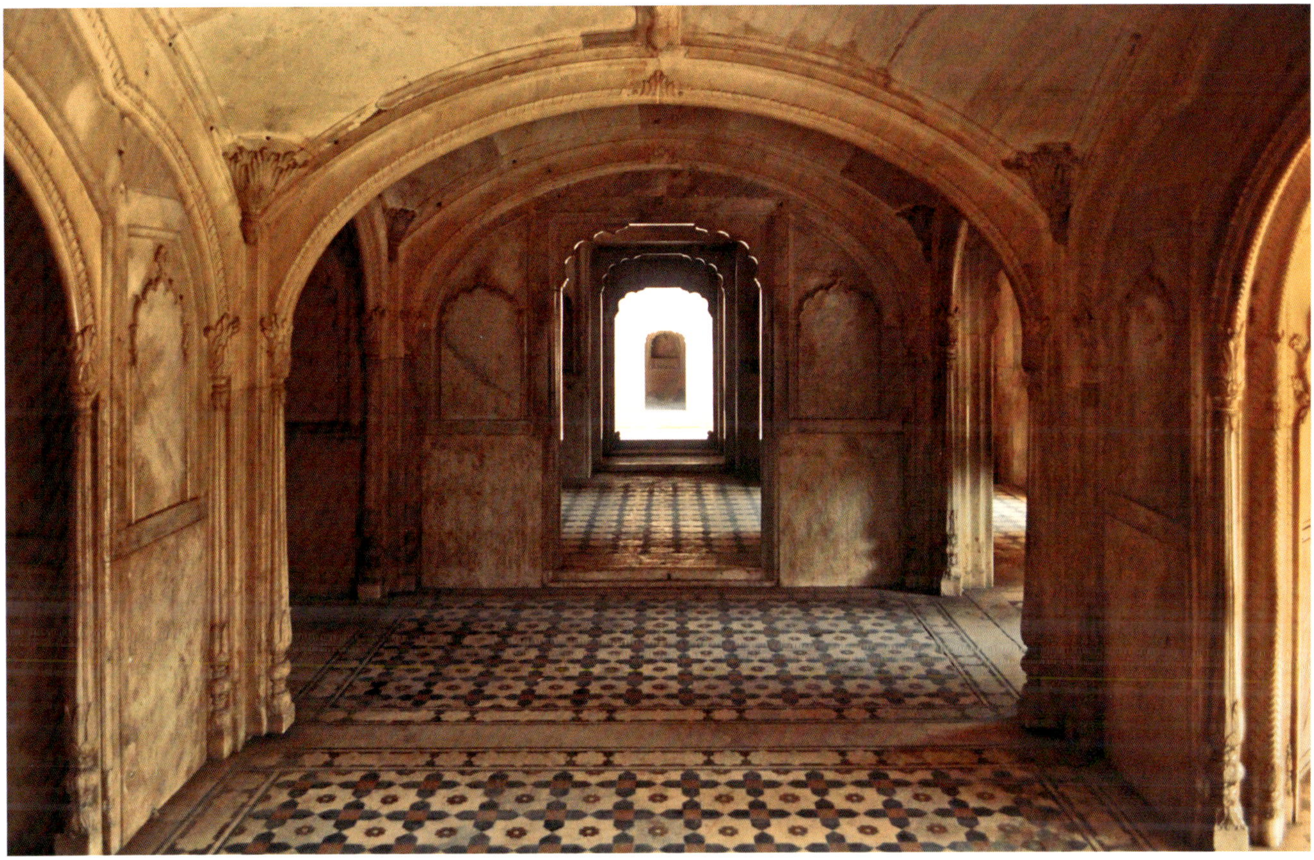

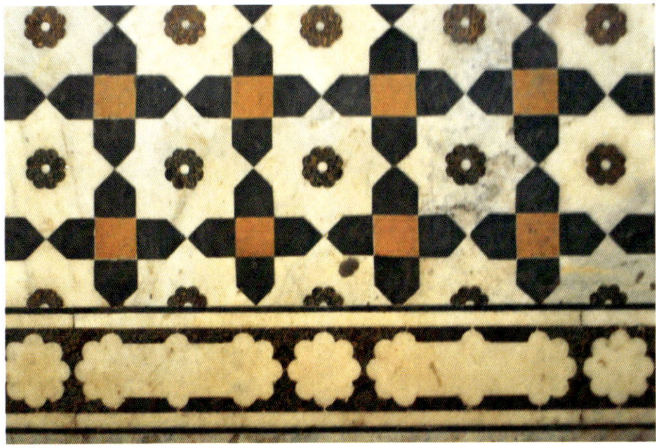

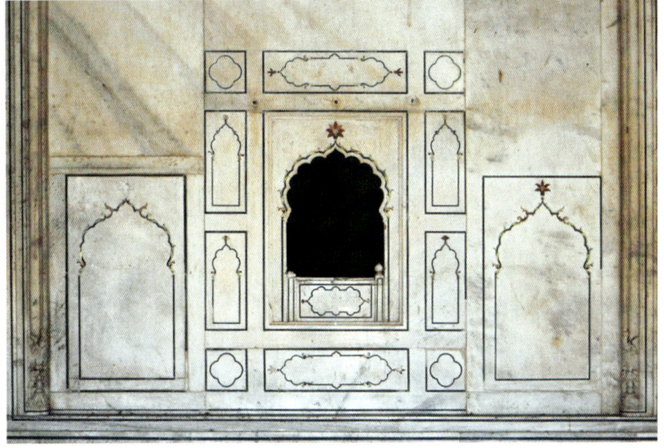

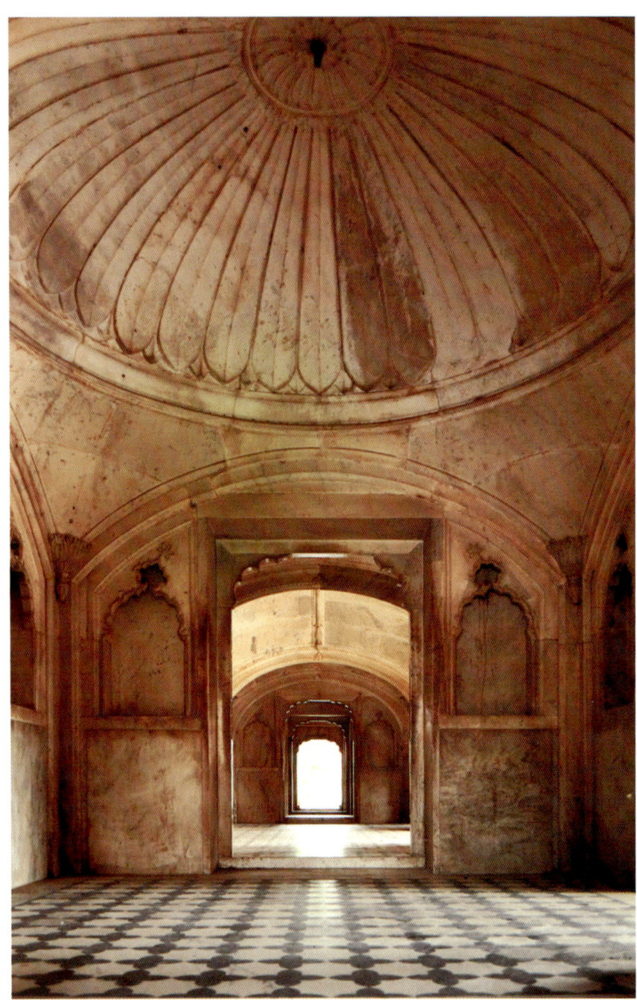

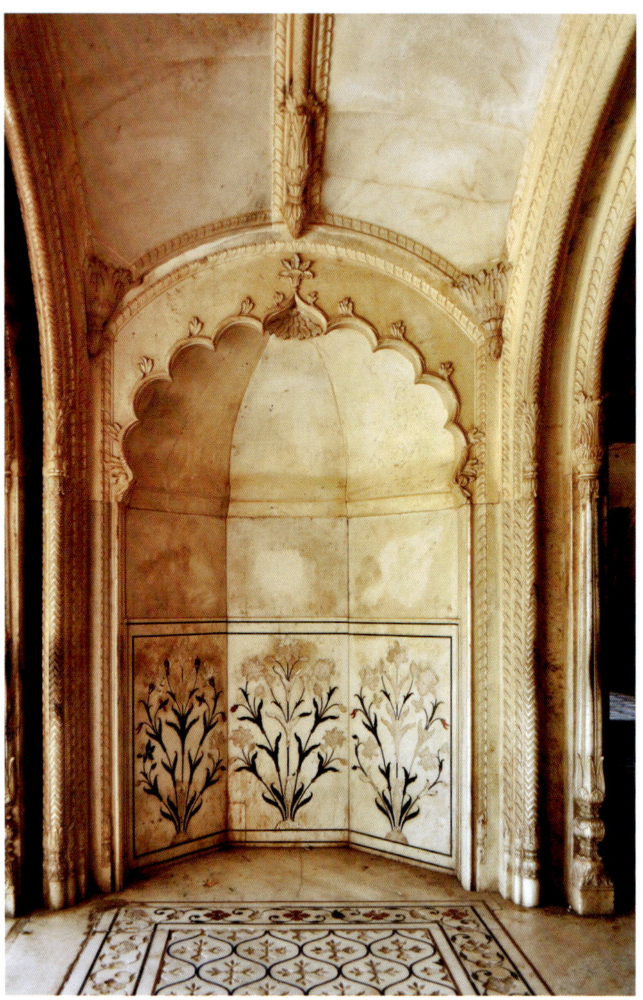

borders very similar to the panels on Itmad-ud-Daulah's tomb wall. The three arches are framed by carved cartouche panels on three sides. (Fig. 16) A miniature yet graceful arch fenestration (window) with multiple utility adorns the sides of the wall. It could have been a windcatcher or a vent at the junctions of the wall and may have provided some light to the hall, in addition to being used as veiled windows by the ladies. The floor of this hall is of plain lime plaster and 'araish' work but is broken now. The ceiling curves up from the sides to give a square vault appearance.

On the outside, this hallway or gallery is subdivided into small and interesting spaces. The whole corridor has beautiful inlaid flooring pattern with *abri* and *ajuba* fossil stones, yellow jasper, black Belgian stone on white marble. (Fig. 17) This is the same pattern of inlay which has been used below the *hindola* floor. Interestingly, similar patterns and stones are used at Itmad-ud-Daulah's tomb in Agra. There are a few openings in the floor leading to aqueducts.

The four corners of the hallway are inlaid with a geometric black-and-white design. They are accentuated with a domed roof carved like a lotus. (Fig. 18) These domes symbolise an inverted lotus in full bloom radiating from a hanging carved floret. The leaves radiate from the central bud to flow on the dome and turn upward at the junction of the lintel. The walls have interesting articulation of niches and carved arches along with the opening to the main corridor. The four corners of the inner enclosure also have similar domical ceilings, though of smaller size. But the most beautiful

Facing page left (Fig. 18): *The four corners of the hallway are inlaid with a geometric black-and-white design along with a lotus-shaped domed roof*

Facing page right (Fig. 19): *The four niche windows on the four axes are accentuated by two half-octagonal arches on either side*

Below (Fig. 20): *Inlaid carpet-like pattern of flooring studded with red jasper, lapis lazuli, carnelian and bloodstone*

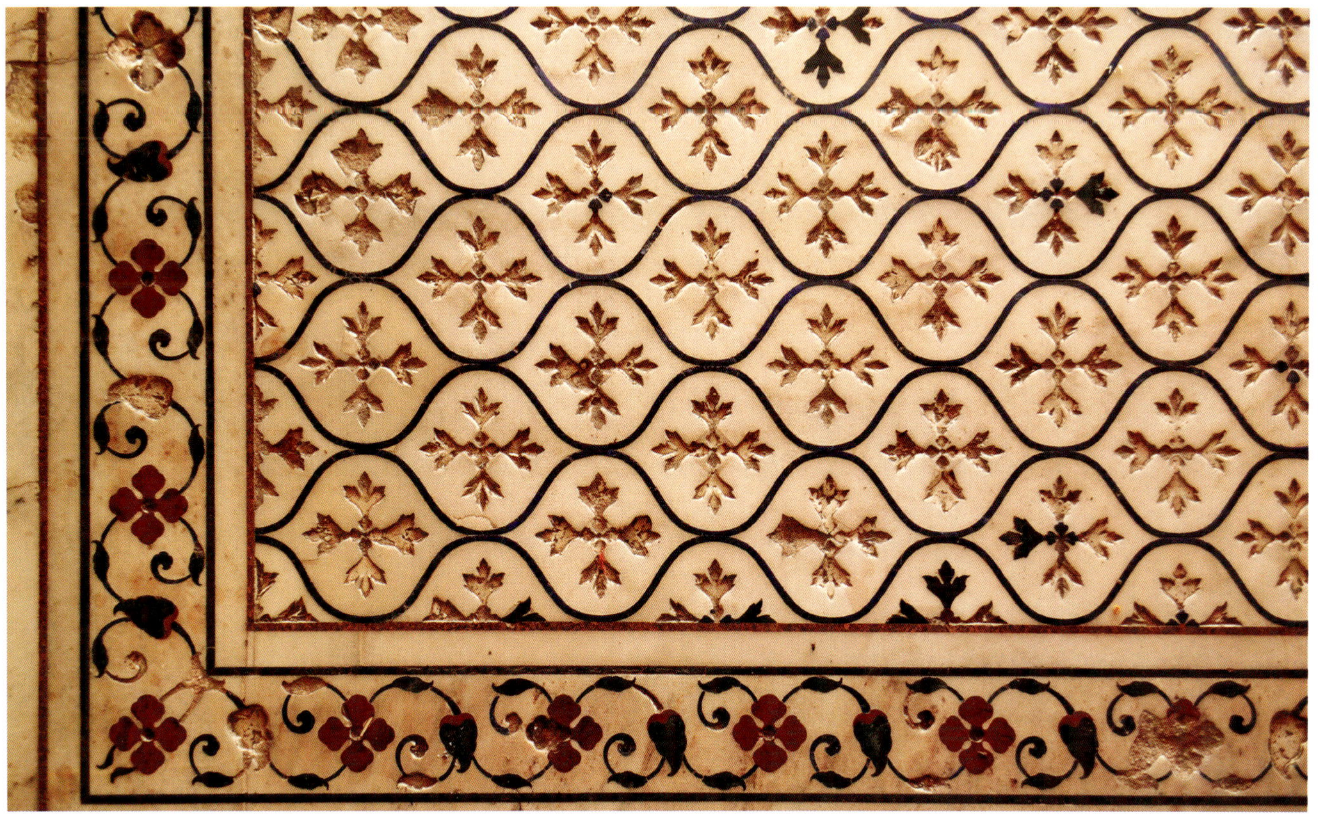

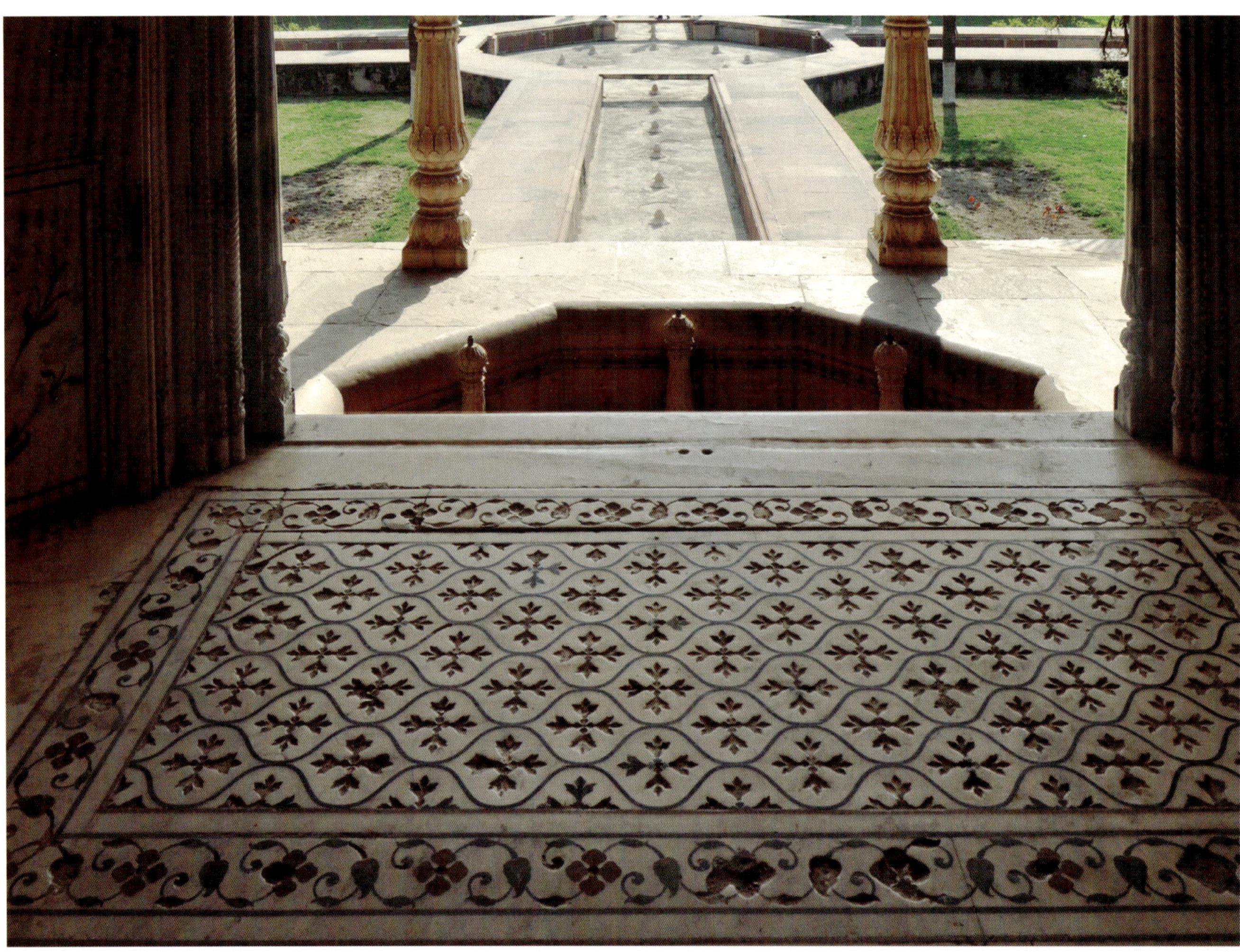

of the elements are the four niche windows on the four axes which are accentuated by two half-octagonal arches on either side. (Fig. 19) The niche facing the Hardev Bhawan had an elaborate inlaid carpet-like pattern of semi-precious stones which have now been dug out of the flooring. (Fig. 20) (Fig. 21) Even the walls here have floral inlaid patterns. The niches facing the east and west have a 'badron' pattern of lapis lazuli and a rosette. (Fig. 22) The niche which is facing the Gopal Bhawan has remnants of similar design, being traced for inlay but it was never completed.

Another important feature of these niches is a narrow slot in the marble wall. This was used to put sliding shutters as is emphasised by the slide and latch marks on the marble floor and is also confirmed from old photographs. This is the only structure in the whole of Deeg Palace which originally had this system of barricading, thus giving more reliability to the fact that this was the private hall of ladies or used by the kings for their private entertainment.

The roof of these niches is a single-arched *bangladar* top supported by thin decorative columns. (Fig. 23) The sill stone projects 4.5 inches out of the wall and has elaborately carved lotus leaves. There is a channel underneath this stone which at one time must have carried water that flowed like a sheet over the *chini khanas* (multi-lobed decorative niches) as well as kept the floor cool during summer. These *chini khanas*

Facing page (Fig. 21): *The niche facing the Hardev Bhawan had an elaborate inlaid carpet-like pattern of semi-precious stones which have now been dug out*

Below (Fig. 22): *The niches facing the east and west have a 'badron' pattern of lapis lazuli and a rosette*

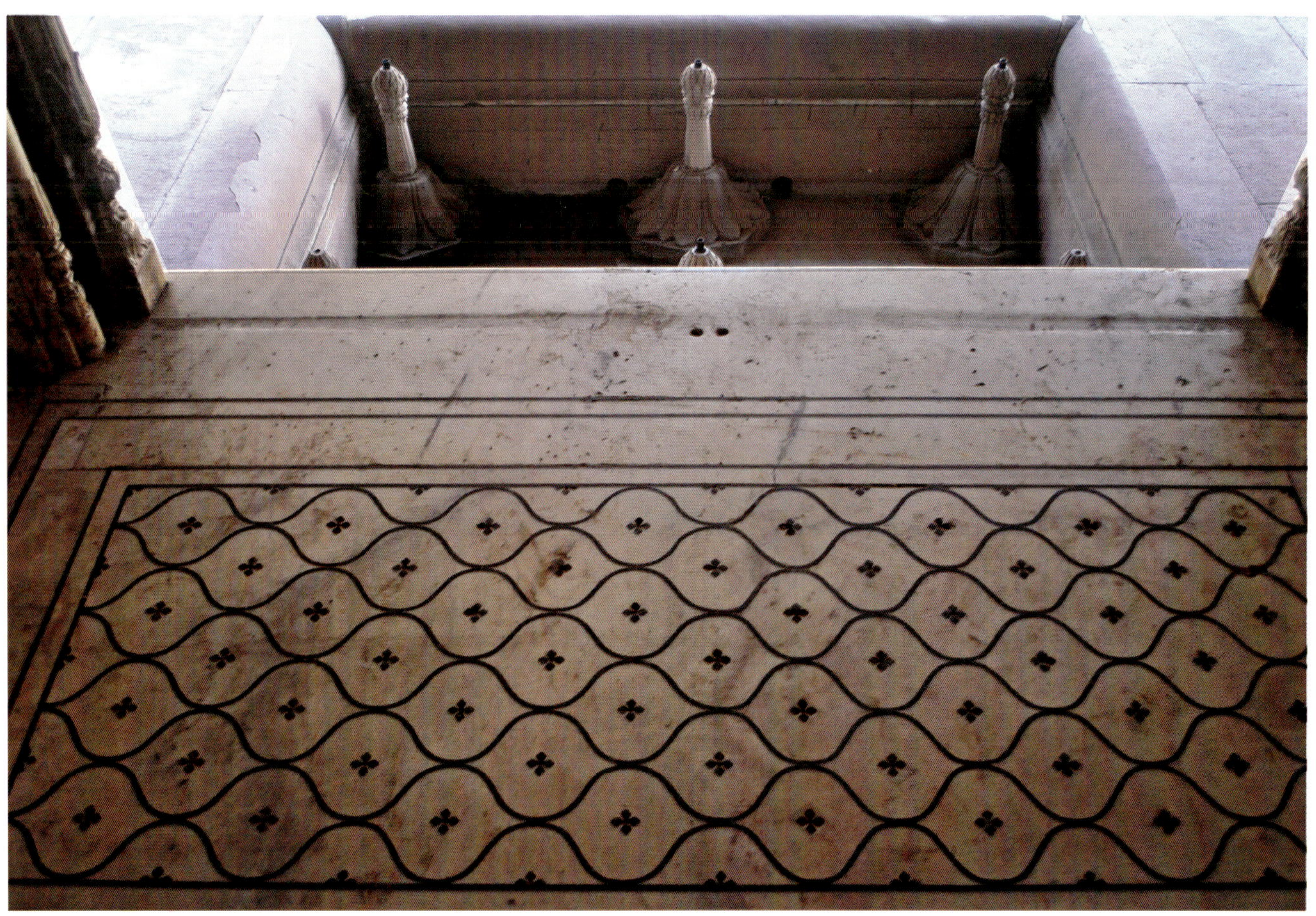

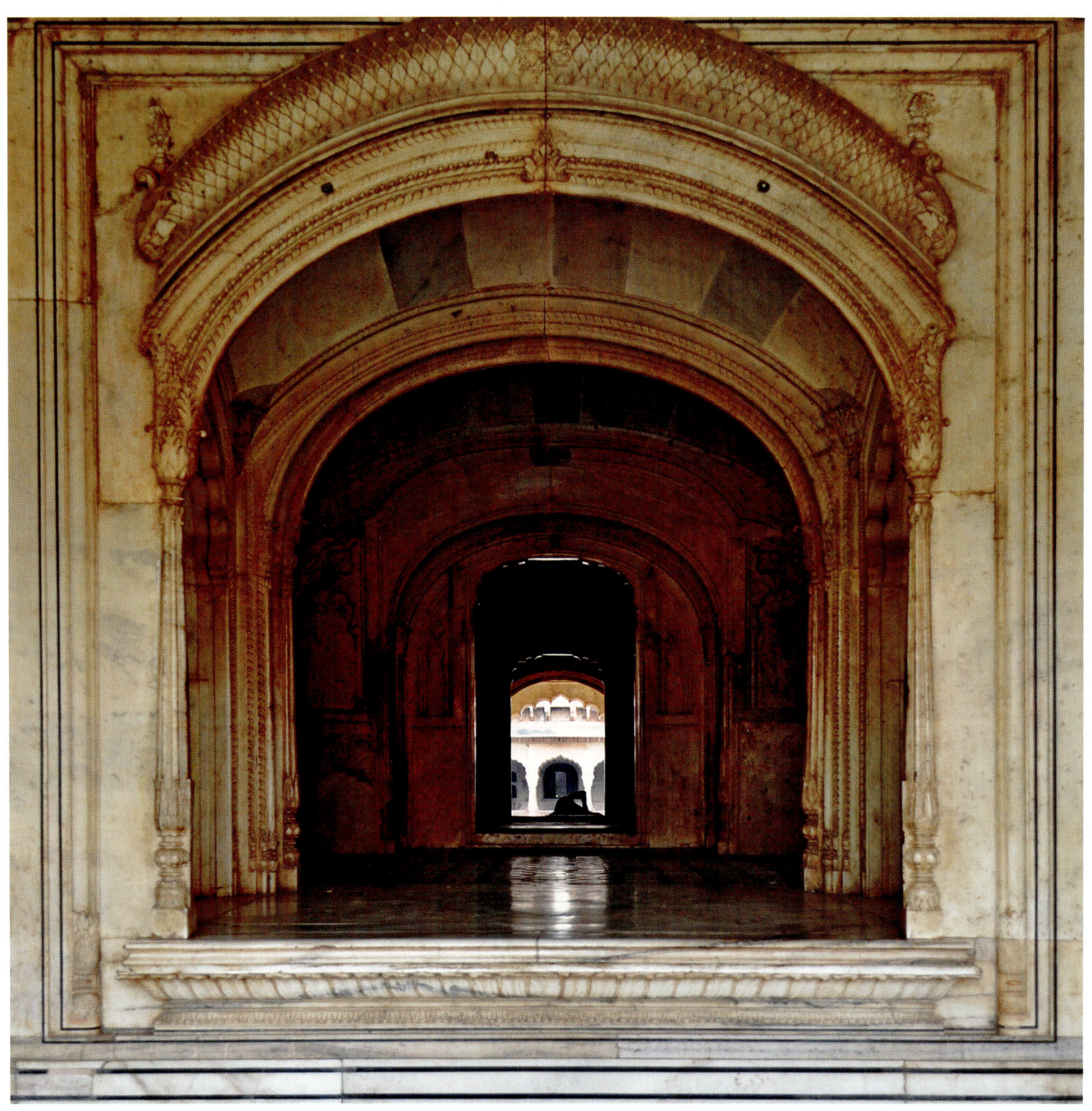

are another remarkable feature of the veranda. They embellish two sides of the pavilion, one facing the Hardev Bhawan and the other facing the Suraj Pol. The *chini khanas* were decorative niches introduced by Mughals in their Charbagh to enhance the play of falling water. Flowers in the morning and *diyas* or candles in the evenings were placed in these niches to create ripples in the falling water. The *chini khanas* are present all around the Deeg complex but the two present at the Suraj Bhawan are the only ones in marble. They have three rows of seven niches each though at present only two rows are visible, the third being obscured by the sandstone water tank. (Fig. 24) This tank seems to be a later addition, perhaps because the water system did not work properly and they are placed such that they rudely obstruct the lower row of *chini khanas*. These sandstone water tanks have been placed on all the four sides including the two sides where *chini khanas* were not present. The two on the north-south axis are octagonal while the other two are square. These water tanks contain spouts with fountains inside the tank as well as one in the centre. Adjoining the *chini khanas* facing the Hardev Bhawan are four inlaid panels of floating iris and lotus flowers with buds. (Fig. 25) These are exact copies of the iris and lotus in the crenellations around the tombs of Shah Jahan and Mumtaz Mahal in the Taj Mahal, that shows the architect's eye for detail.

A raised plinth forms a dado on all four sides of the pavilion. All along the dado and the corridor are wall panels decorated with fine *pietra dura* patterns.

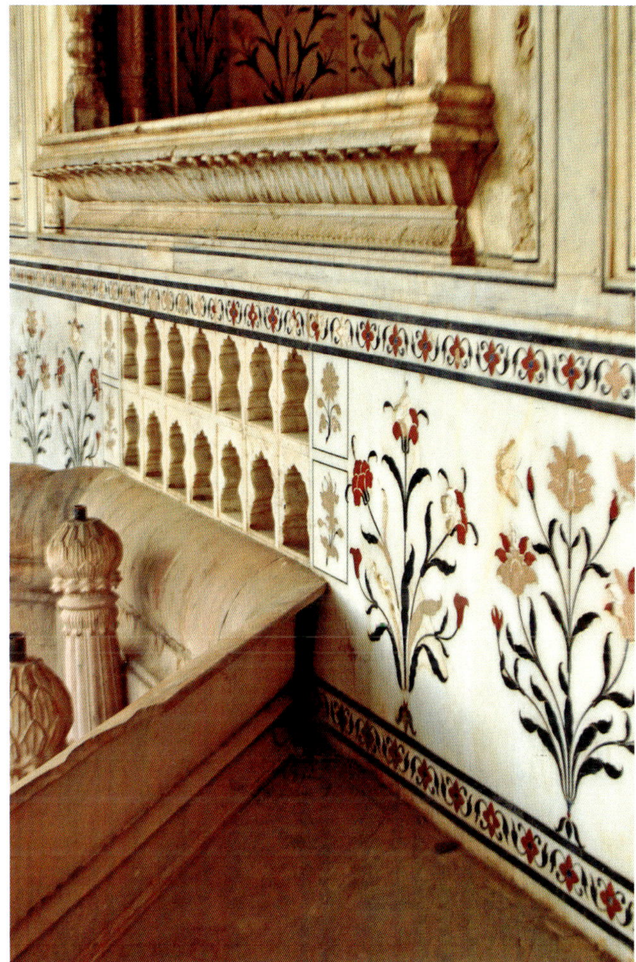

Above (Fig. 24): *At present only two of the three rows of* chini khanas *are visible, the third being obscured by the sandstone water tank*

Facing page (Fig. 23): *A single-arched* bangladar *top supported by thin decorative columns frames the central* jharokha *windows on all four sides of the raised pavilion inside the corridor*

(Fig. 26) *Pietra dura*, as is well known, means the delicate inlay work done on marble panels, often using precious or semi-precious stones. (Fig. 27) The Florentines popularised it and is found in many Mughal

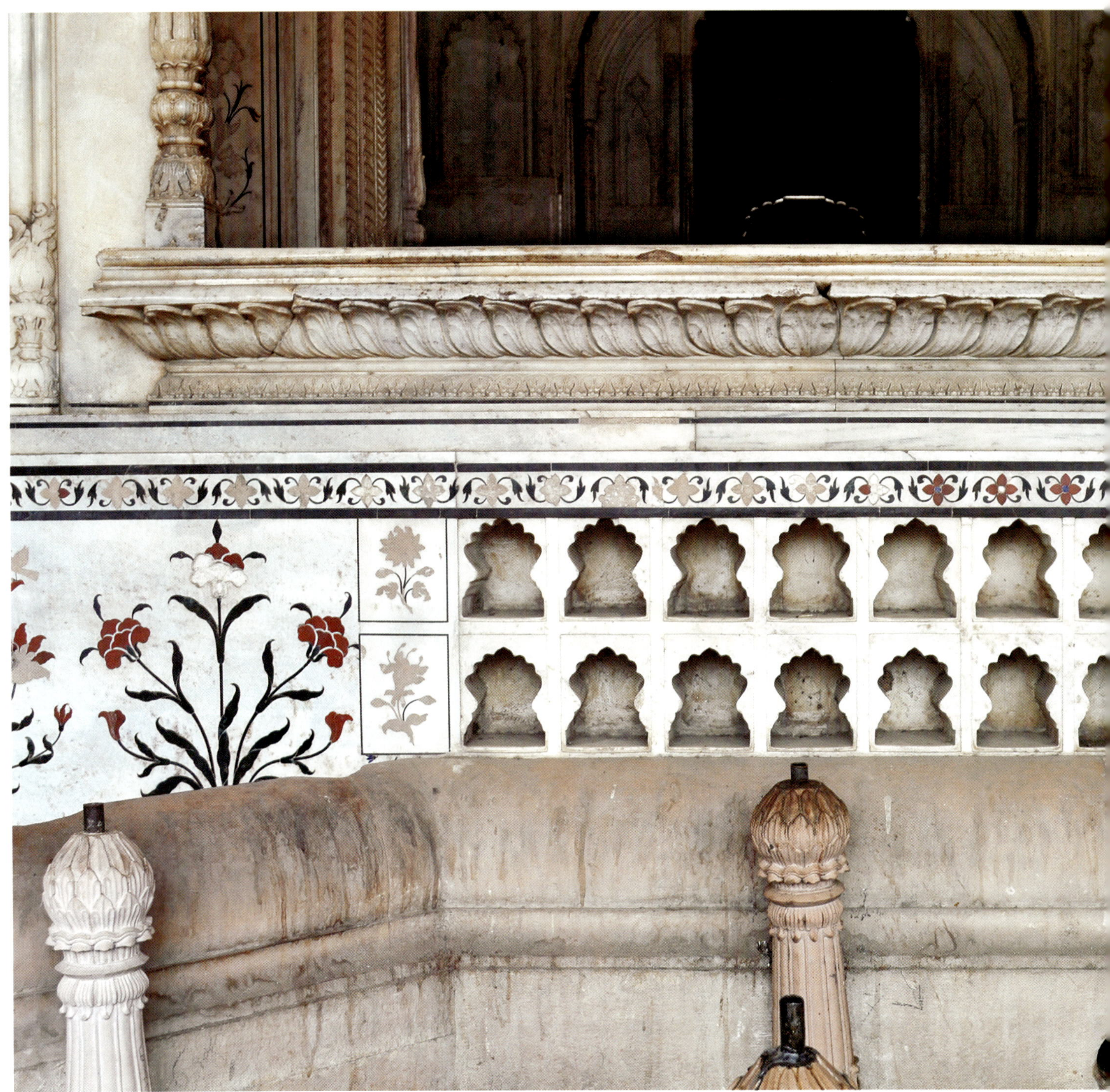

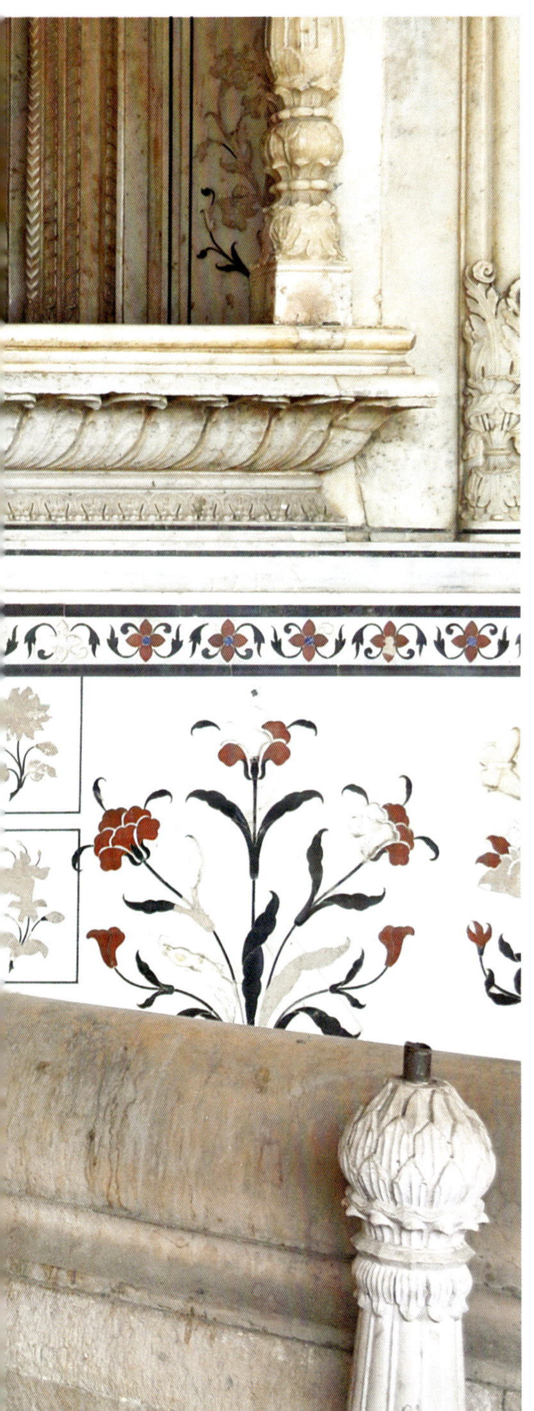

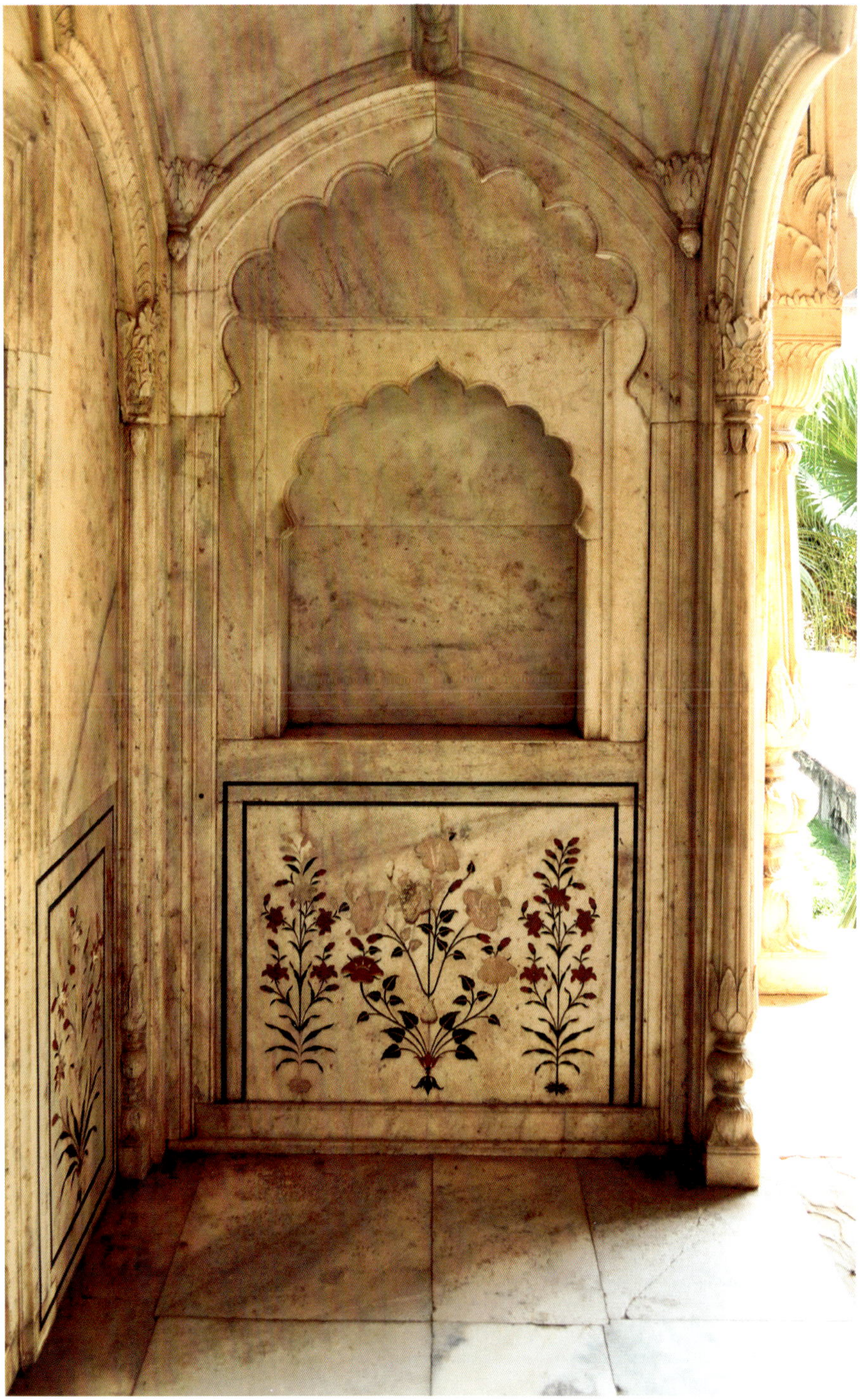

monuments, especially the ones constructed during the reigns of Jahangir and Shah Jahan.

The *pietra dura* patterns on the walls in the Suraj Bhawan are not true graphic descriptions of floral vegetation, but rather a play of different foliage patterns or flowers. The *pietra dura* designs recall features of different flora in the same inlay specimen. Also, it is difficult to relate the floral patterns to a living specimen, as the objective of the *pietra dura* work was not to educate, but rather playfully enact naturalistic compositions in colourful stones like lapis lazuli, jasper and so on. In general, however, it would be safe to say that

Previous page left (Fig. 25): *Water poured from the slit in the sill forms a sheet over the* chini khanas*; inlay of the iris and lotus flowers influenced by the Taj Mahal*

Previous page right (Fig. 26): *The transitional vestibule from the outer corner blocks to the raised pavilion is marked by a vaulted ceiling, carved niches and* pietra dura *on the dado*

Facing page (Fig. 28): *The most recurring patterns in the* pietra dura *work on the walls of the Suraj Bhawan are that of roses, poppy, tulip, iris with some buds predominantly in red jasper and blue lapis lazuli*

Below (Fig. 27): *Wall panels are decorated with fine* pietra dura *patterns running all along the dado and the corridor*

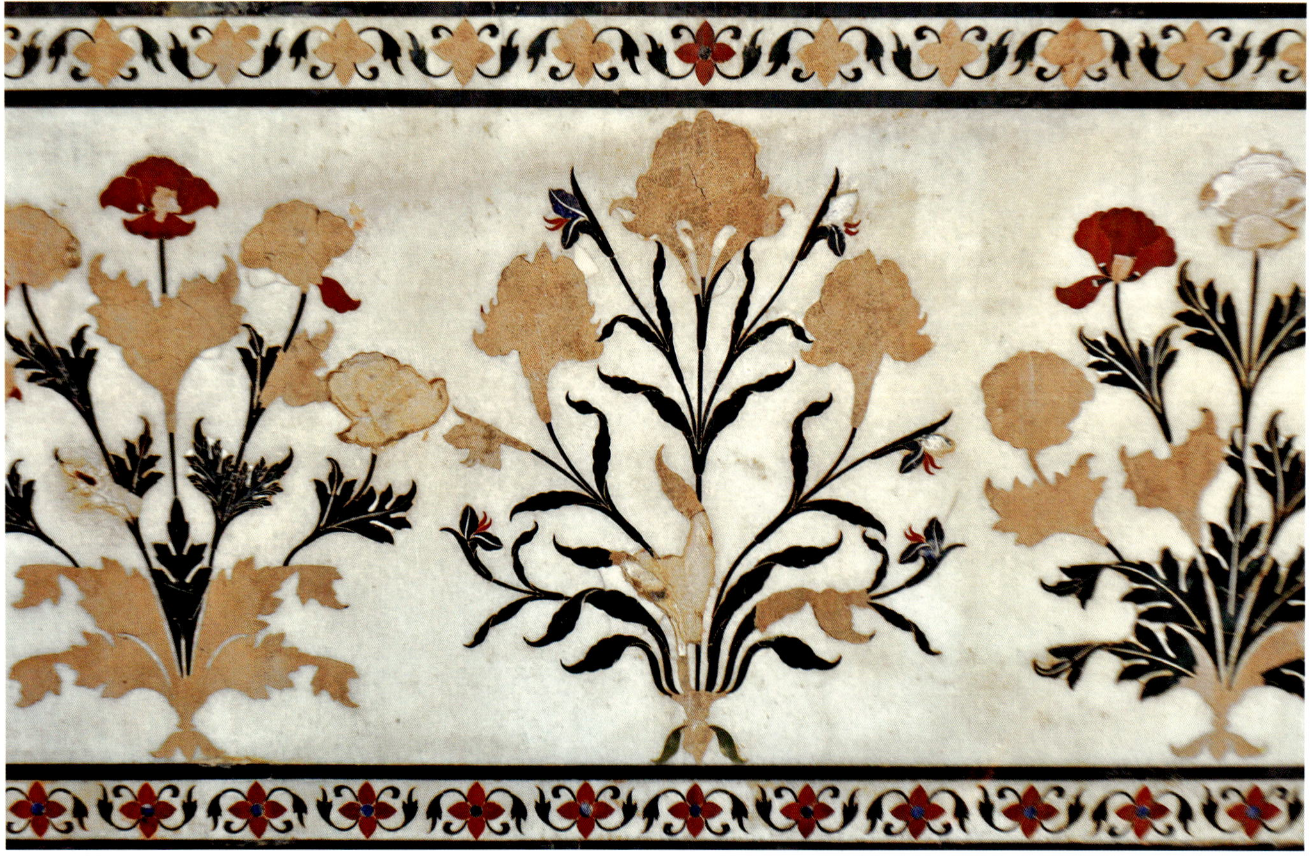

the playful compositions in stone were not intended to be botanical studies, but rather an expression of artistic freedom. The most recurring patterns in the *pietra dura* work on the walls of the Suraj Bhawan are that of roses, poppy, tulip, iris with some buds predominantly in red jasper and blue lapis lazuli to indicate a vibrant Hindu influence. (Fig. 28)

Though all four sides of the 3 feet and 6 inches high plinth are greatly decorated with inlay panels, fountain features and carved domes, the level of decoration differs on all the sides which perhaps were done according to the importance of the linking area. All the elevation columns are made of marble, except the ones occurring on the Suraj Pol side that are made of sandstone plastered with limestone, resembling marble. They follow the same rhythm and pattern as the rest of the columns in the Deeg Palace. The side facing the Hardev Bhawan is the most decorated, detailed and preserved. The side facing the Gopal Bhawan also has similar panels though only about four in number. These floral wall panels inlaid with semi-precious stones like lapis lazuli, bloodstone and red jasper also have occasional butterflies and birds which are rare in Mughal buildings. This points to the fact that though the work is inspired from the Mughals, it was done in Deeg only. The other two sides have panels with plain straight line borders inlaid in black stone.

This square building with perfect Hindu symmetry, Mughal-Rajput ornamentation and an Islamic mausoleum ambience reinforces the conclusion that the

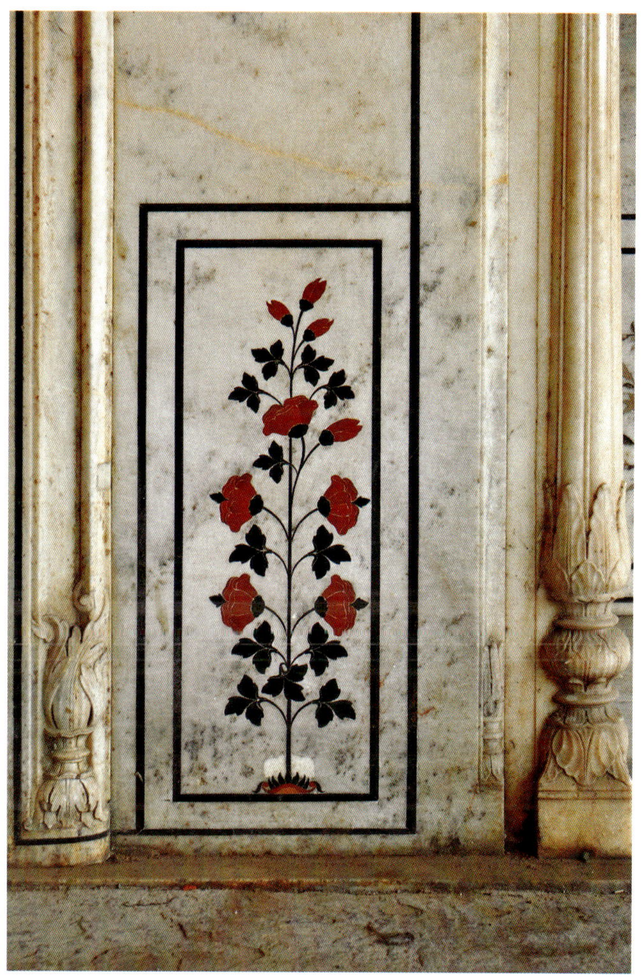

Deeg complex was intended to be a symbol of universal fraternity—a fact that assumes a greater significance as the symbol had risen amongst the tillers of the soil.

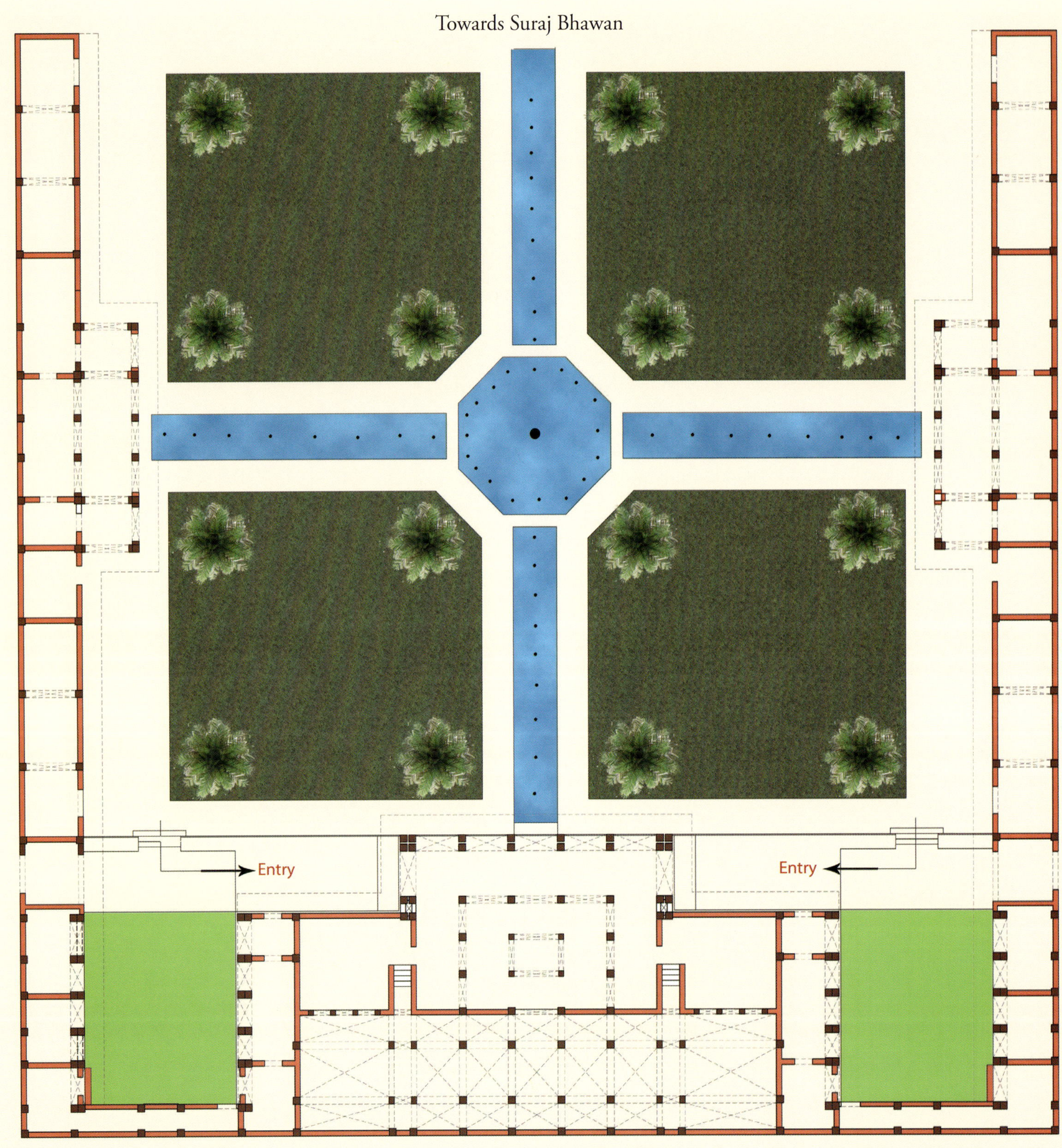
Towards Suraj Bhawan
Entry
Entry

ZENANAS
HARDEV BHAWAN

Immediately at the back of the Suraj Bhawan lies this secluded palace forming a charming quadrangle around an attached inner Charbagh. This three-sided development around a garden resembles a typical royal setting of Indian private courts of the Mughal times. This older complex is known as the Hardev Bhawan and was probably one of the earliest buildings of the Deeg Palace complex. (Fig. 2)

The principal block on the south stands in an impressive position overlooking the accessory garden. The central block consists of a five-arched projecting central hall faced with arches springing from a row of double pillars. This is flanked by double-storeyed palaces on either side. The extended balconies with a double roof, a typical feature of all the bhawans in the Deeg complex, are present on this structure as well. In the front of this block is a small typical Charbagh divided by a shallow water channel with broad walkways. The four channels meet to form an octagonal pool in the centre. The pool and all the water channels have short lotus-bud shaped fountain spouts arranged at regular intervals, though the older photographs show these spouts as much taller, similar to the rest of the complex, minus the octagonal base. The water in these channels enters from the north and south ends of the Hardev Bhawan and the Suraj Bhawan terrace. Two tall and elaborate *chini khanas* are built on the raised plinth of the bhawan to take advantage of the difference in height. Water is fed through carved decorative apertures above the respective *chini khanas* designed to form a sheet over the channels. On the eastern and western facade the palace quadrangle is completed by building symmetrical palaces. (Fig. 3) These are at the same level as the garden walkways. The parterres in the middle

Facing page (Fig. 1): *The Hardev Bhawan is distinguished by an assemblage of multiple chambers around a central Charbagh approximately 42 metres square*

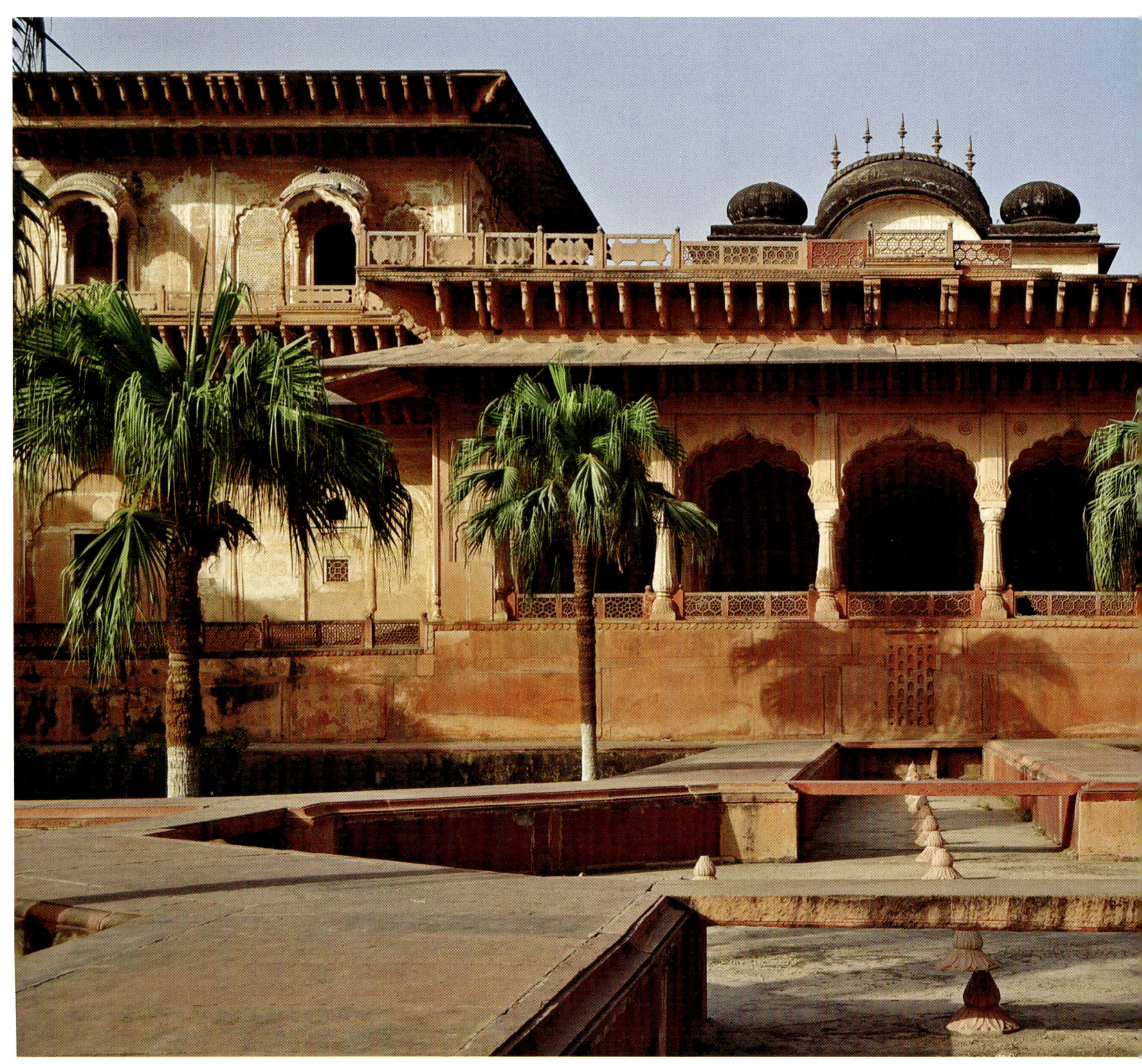

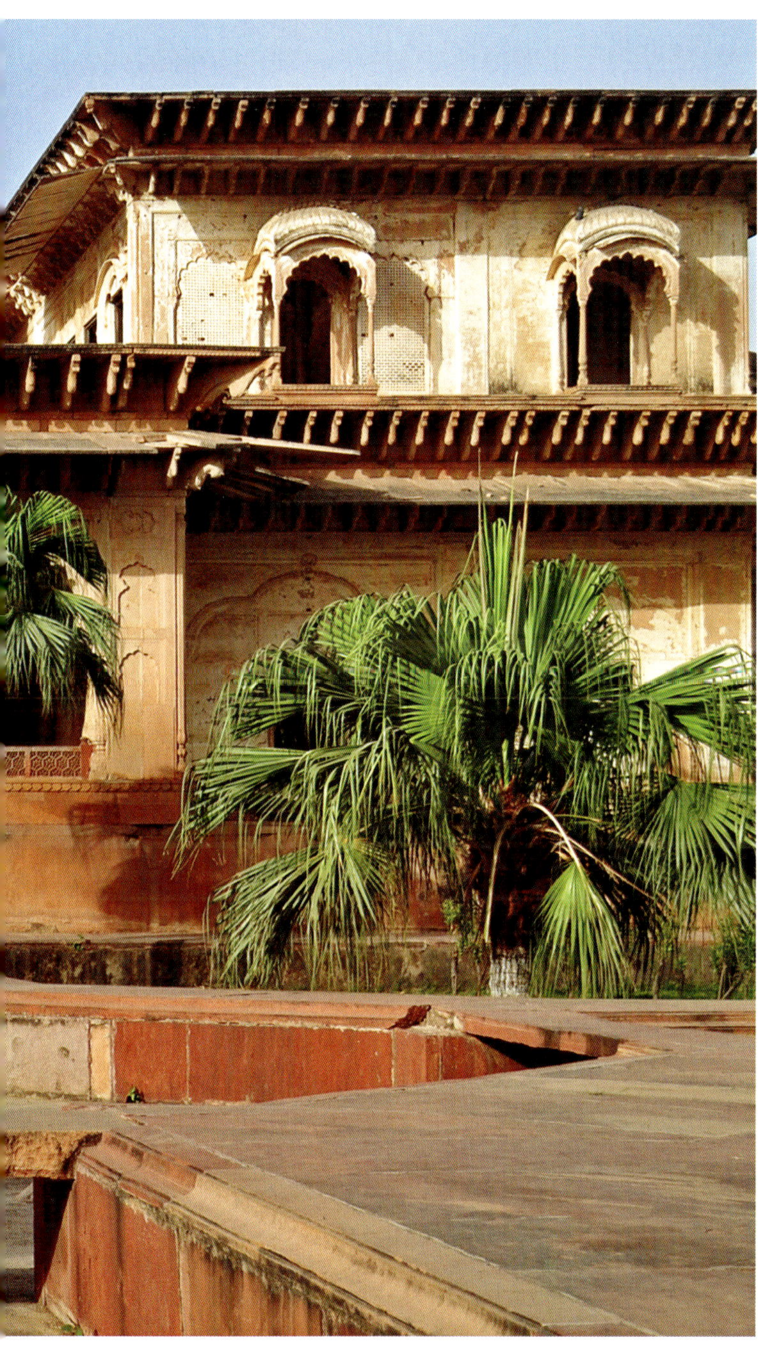

are substantially sunken with respect to the walkways suggesting thicker vegetation.

On careful analysis one could see the hidden blueprint of the Gopal Bhawan elevation within this whole complex. It is perhaps the miniature version of the Gopal Bhawan and its gardens. A similar five-arched projecting colonnade resting on double columns together with the double-storeyed palaces has been refined to create the eastern facade of the Gopal Bhawan. The small Charbagh in the front is proportionately amplified to emerge as the central Charbagh of the Deeg Palace. On the same lines, the four shallow water channels have become deeper and wider plus the central octagonal pool larger to house thirty-two spouts. The larger quadrangle is completed with three more bhawans namely the Nand Bhawan, the Keshav Bhawan and the Kishan Bhawan on the remaining three sides.

In the main building, behind the front arches is an arcaded colonnade running along the three sides of the inner group of four pillars (Fig. 4) roughly analogous to those available within the side wings of the Gopal Bhawan under the main bedrooms. At the back of the hall is an oblong corridor with a raised floor and domed

Left **(Fig. 2):** *The Hardev Bhawan, one of the earliest buildings of the Deeg Palace complex, is a three-sided development around a garden resembling a typical royal setting of private courts of the Mughal times*

Following page above **(Fig. 3):** *On the eastern and western facade the palace quadrangle is completed by building symmetrical palaces*

Following page below **(Fig. 4):** *An arcaded colonnade running along the three sides of the inner group of four pillars*

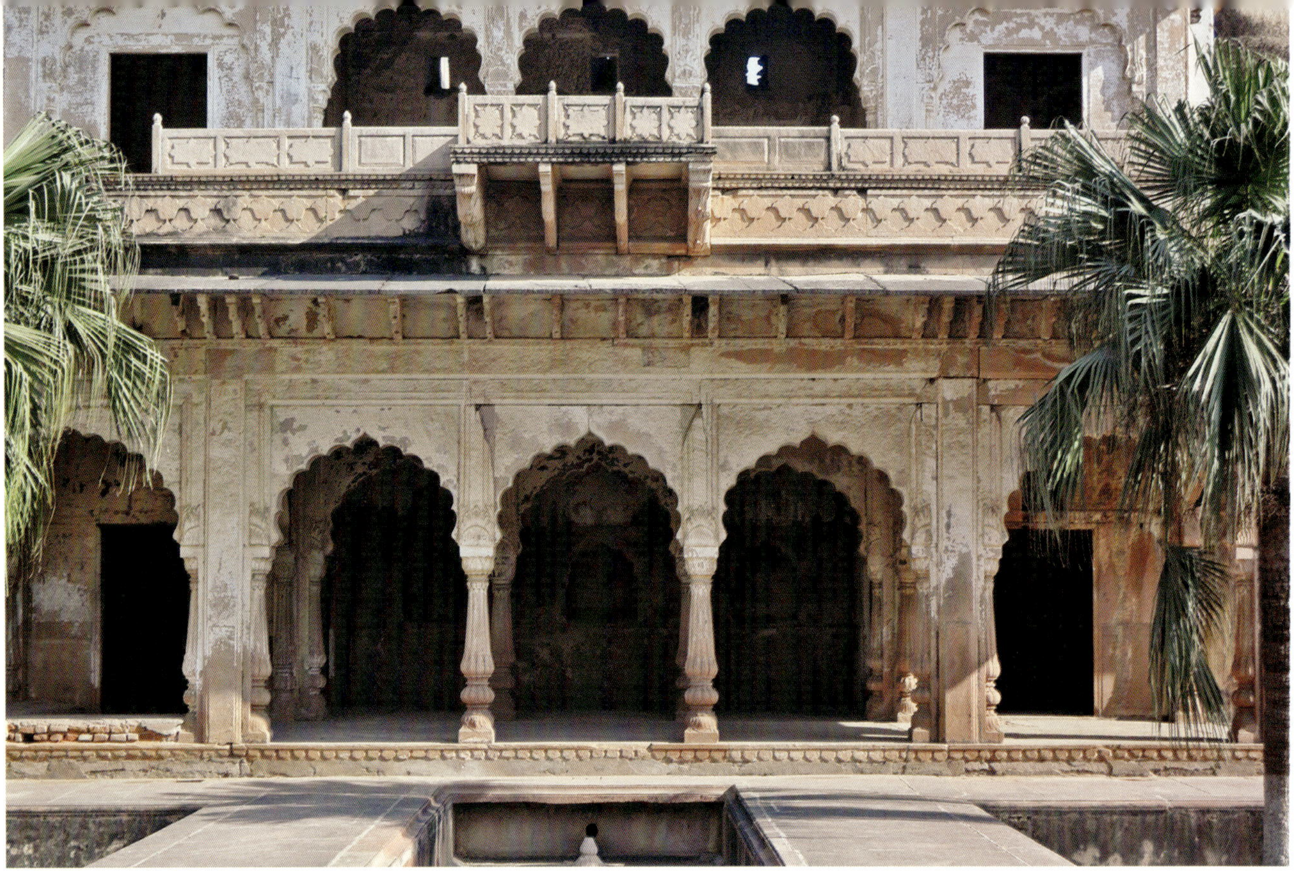

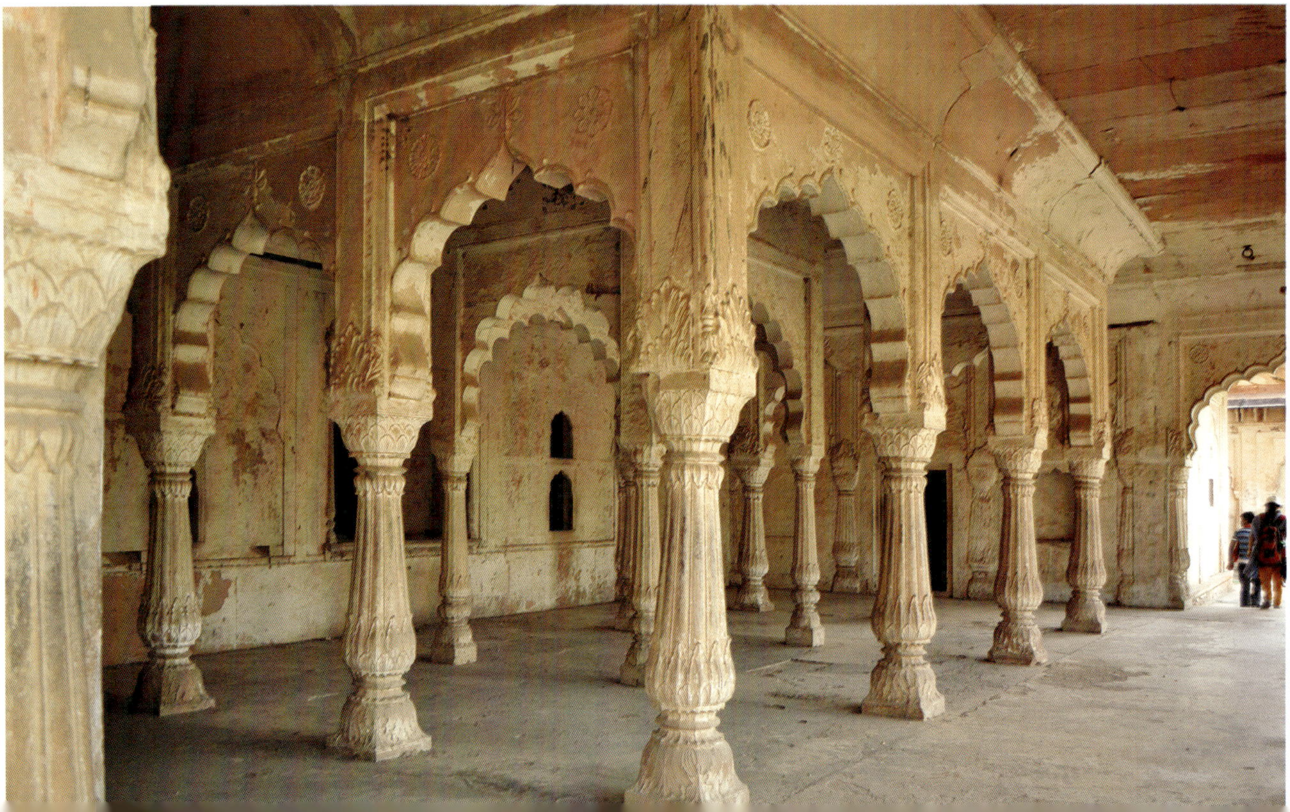

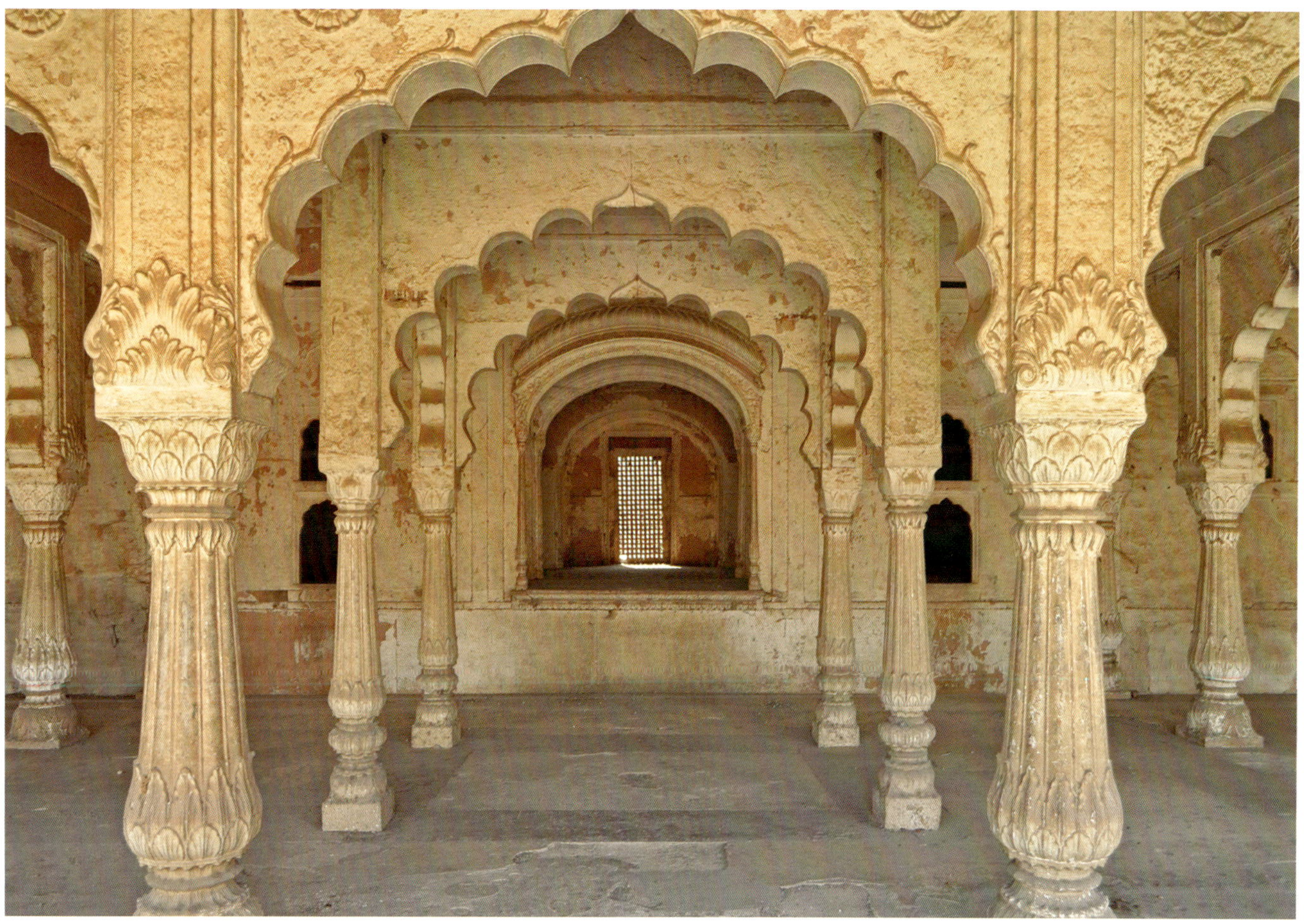

Above (Fig. 5): *At the back of the hall this oblong corridor is on a raised floor which appears like a small courtroom with an antechamber at the back*

cells at each end, a feature also common to the Suraj Bhawan, but much simpler otherwise. It appears like a small courtroom with an antechamber at the back. (Fig. 5) The striking feature is a stone latticework (*jali*) carved in louvre design, obliquely cut, very typical to this palace which becomes the focus of the back wall. (Fig. 6) The functional design of the *jalis* obstructs the vision of the outsiders while giving the correct angle to the eye of the insider.

A rectangular chamber with a veranda flanked by cells has been built on either side of the hall. On the east a comfortable ramp provides access to the upper storey which has a raised central terrace and two pillared *dalans* to its right and left. The hind part of the terrace is occupied by a crowning *bangladar chhatri* bearing a spiked, curved roof attended by

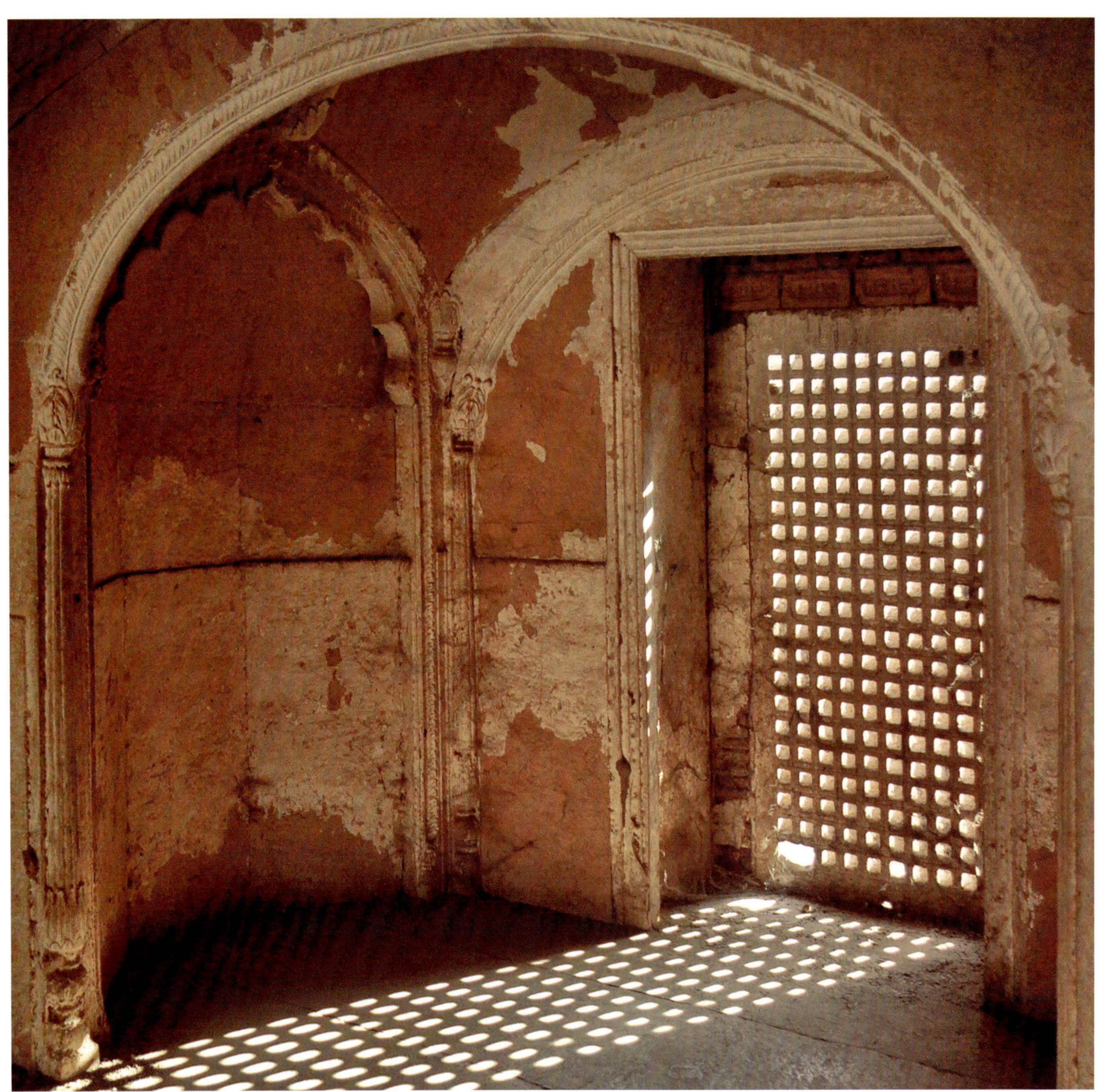

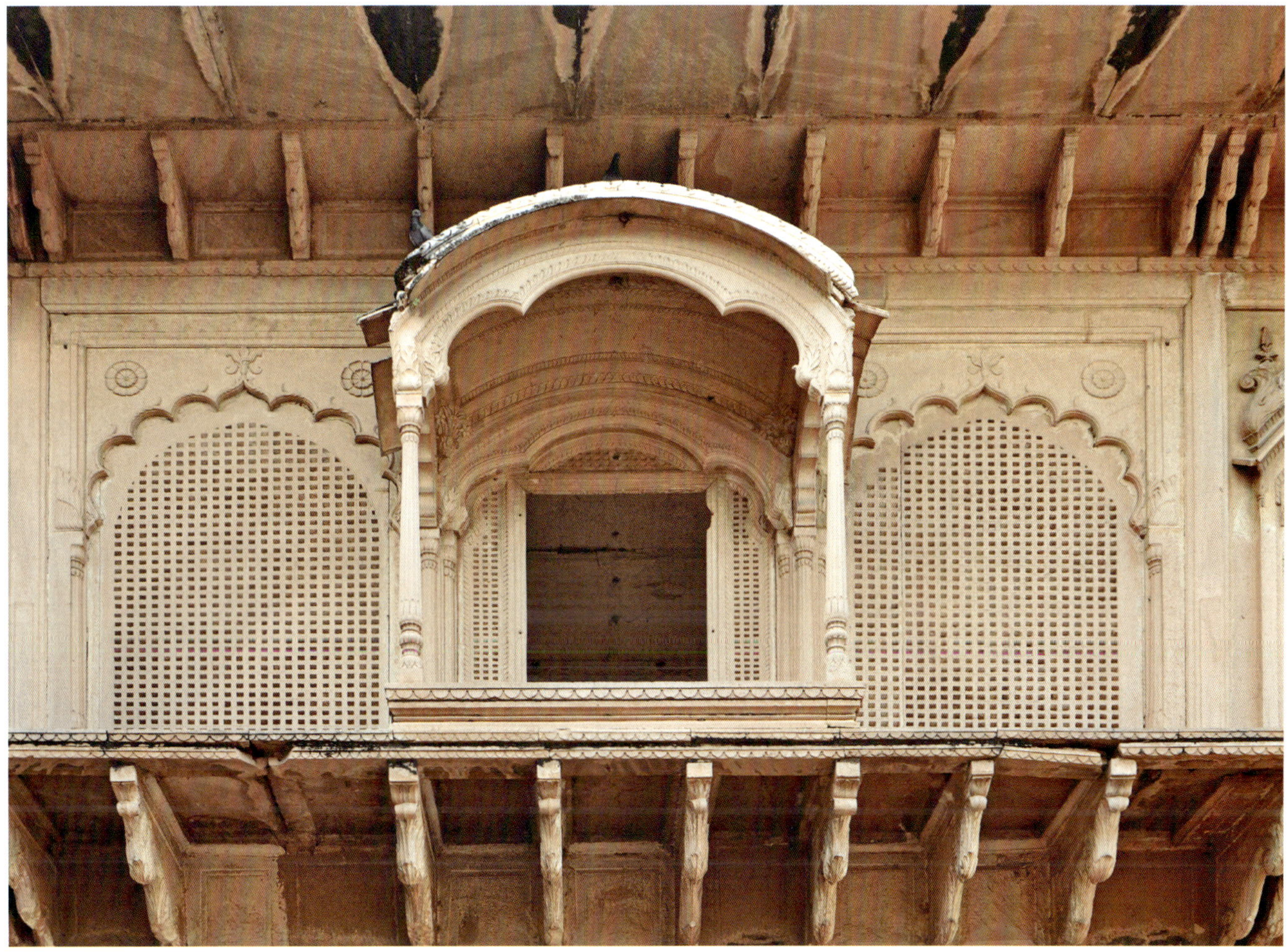

Above (Fig. 7): *A crowning* bangladar chhatri *bearing a spiked, curved roof is flanked by screens of fine latticework*

Facing page (Fig. 6): *The stone latticework carved in louvre design, obliquely cut, obstructs the vision of only the outsiders*

miniature side domes. This kind of grouping makes the building an effective composition. (Fig. 7) A narrow gallery screened with obliquely cut *jalis* runs at the back of the upper floor. The reclusive position of this complex suggests that it was solely meant for the royal ladies.

The other two sides of the quadrangle have ordinary rooms flanking a central veranda which is in two floors on the east. The typical feature of these extensions is the captivating projection of decorative balconies into the gardens.

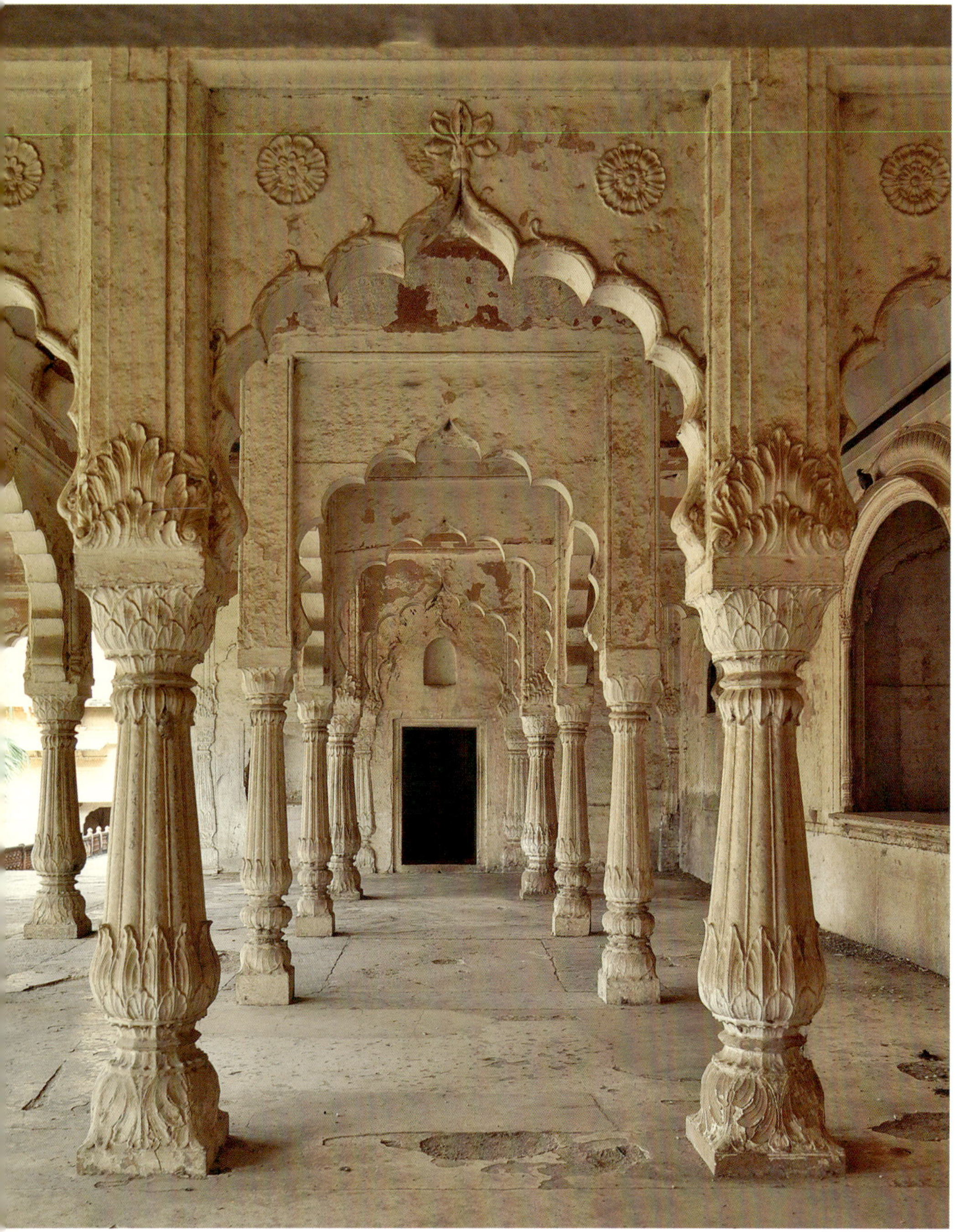

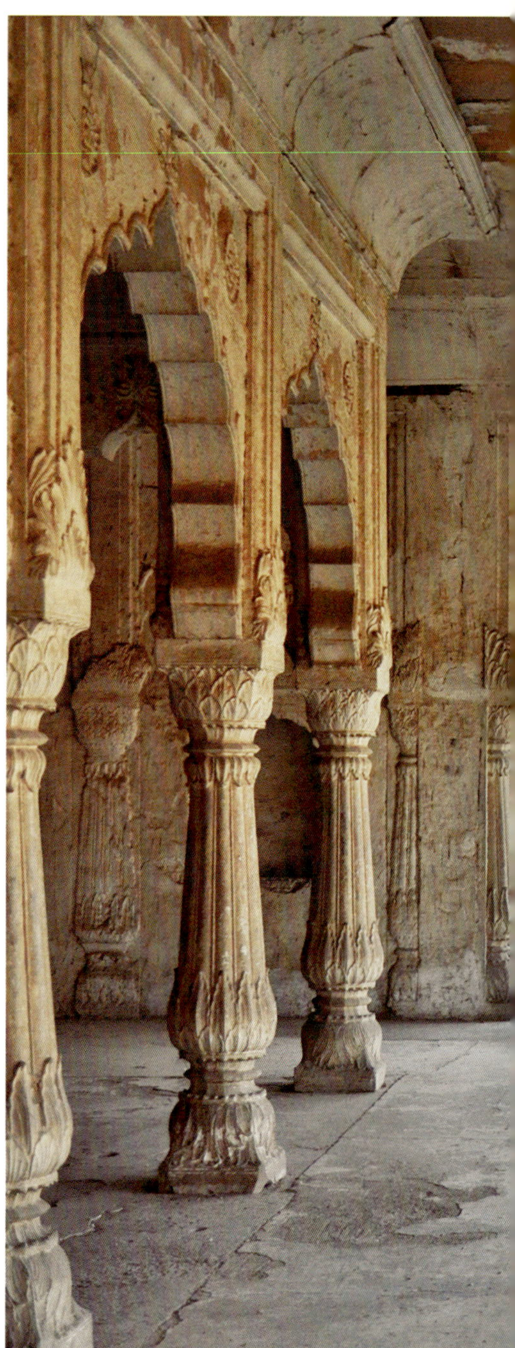

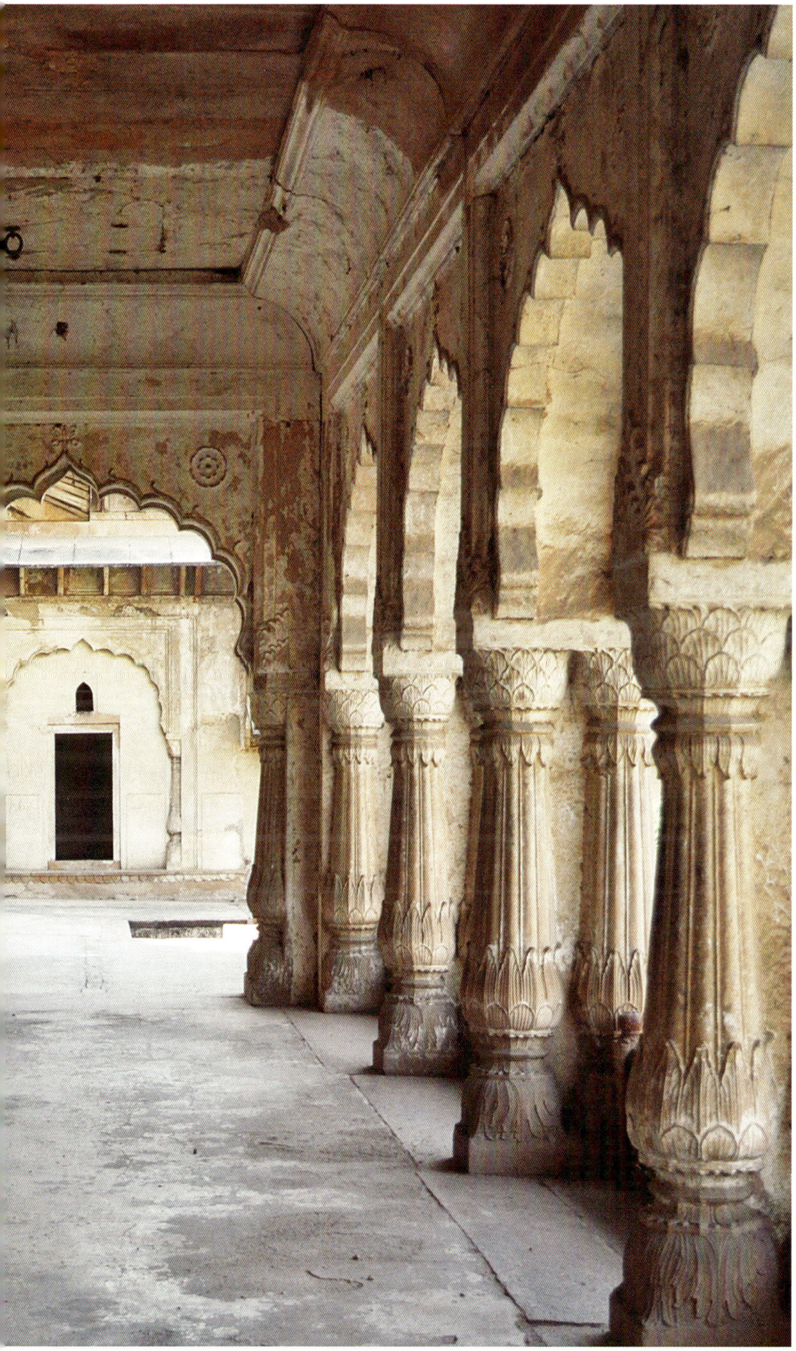

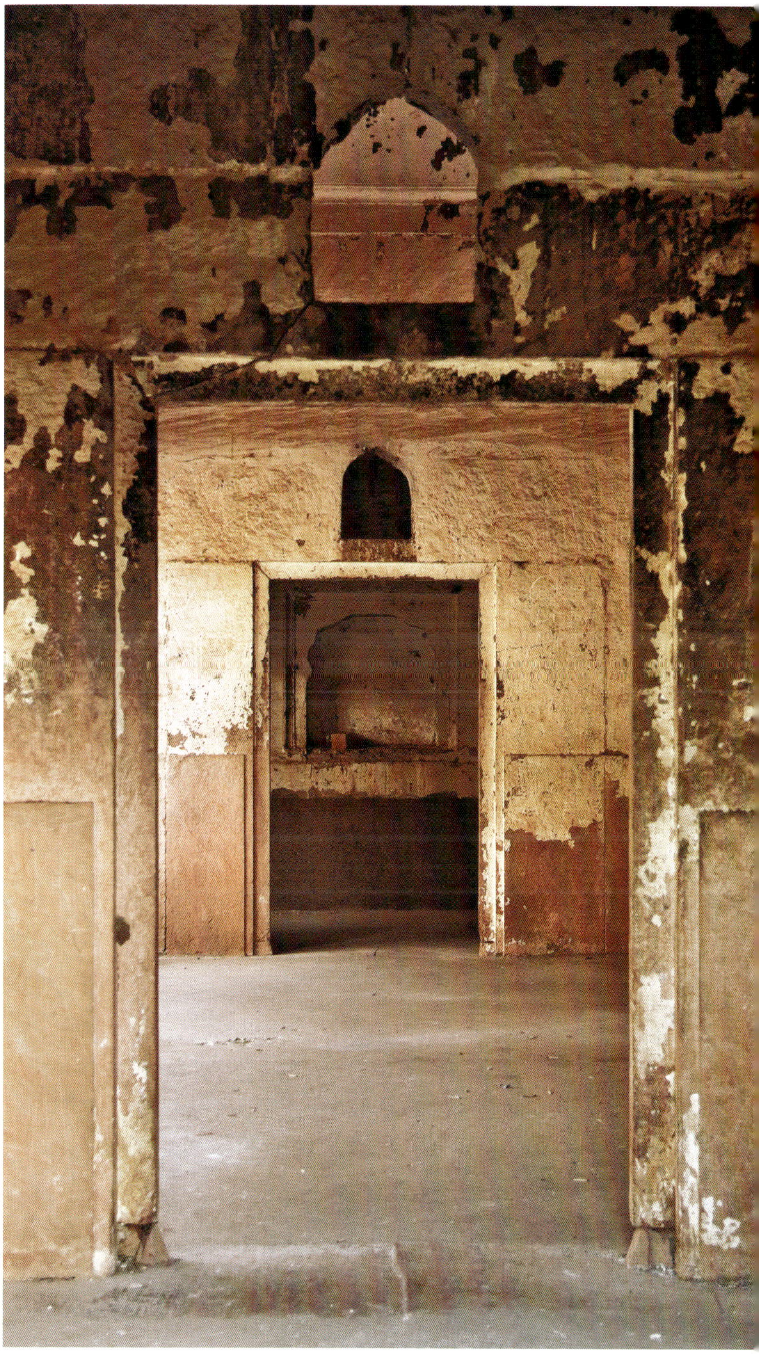

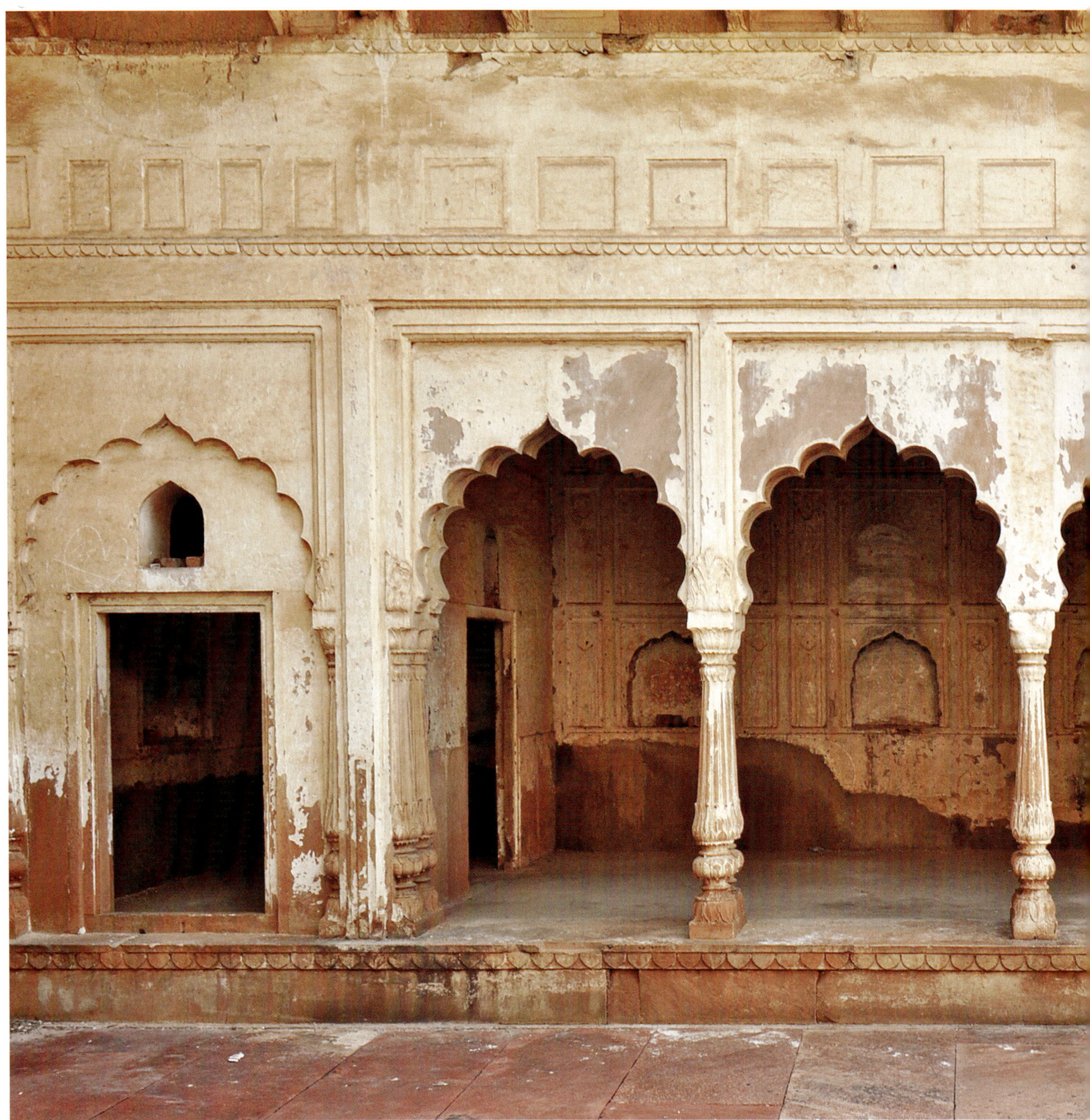

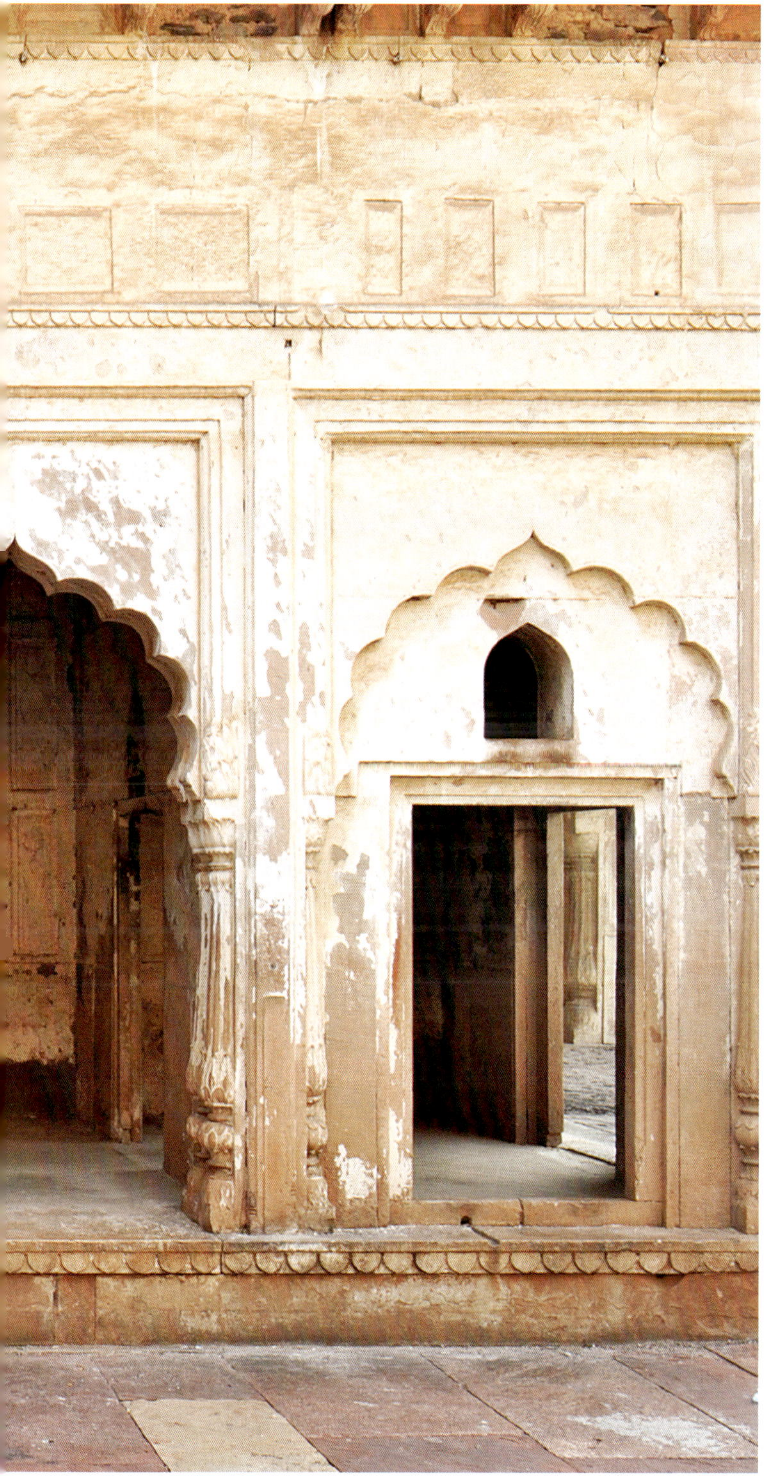

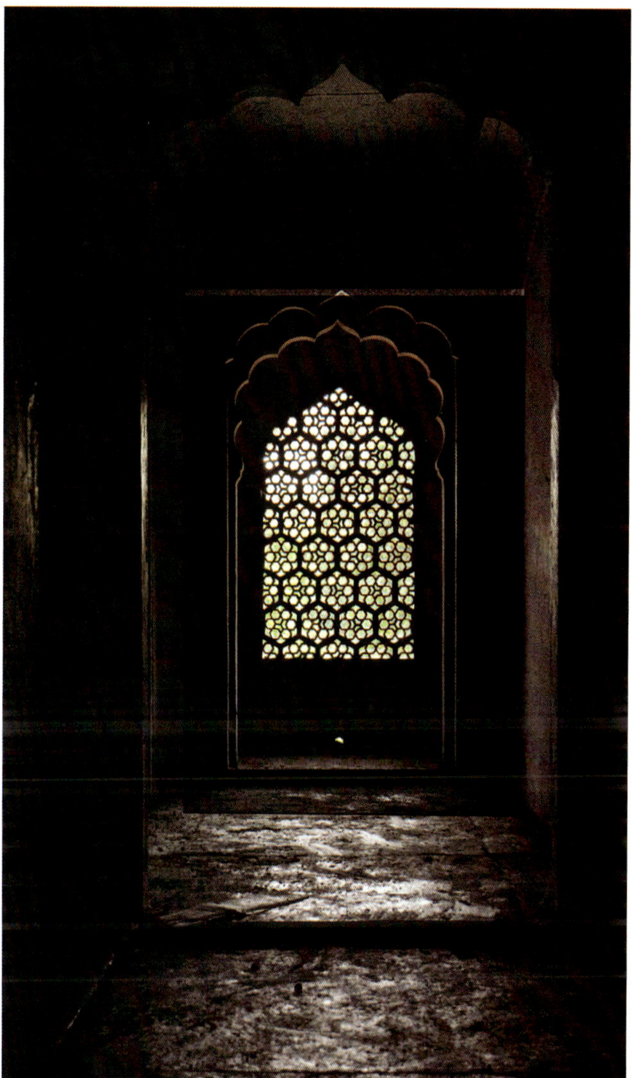

Above (Fig. 11): *Intricate* jalis *mark the southern facade to provide shade from the sun*

Left (Fig. 12): *The outer recreation chambers*

Previous page left (Fig. 8): *Embodiment of columns around the central courtroom*

Previous page centre (Fig. 9): *Patio-like colonnaded gallery in the front of the main palace overlooking the Charbagh*

Previous page right (Fig. 10): *Inner private chambers continue with the canonical symmetry*

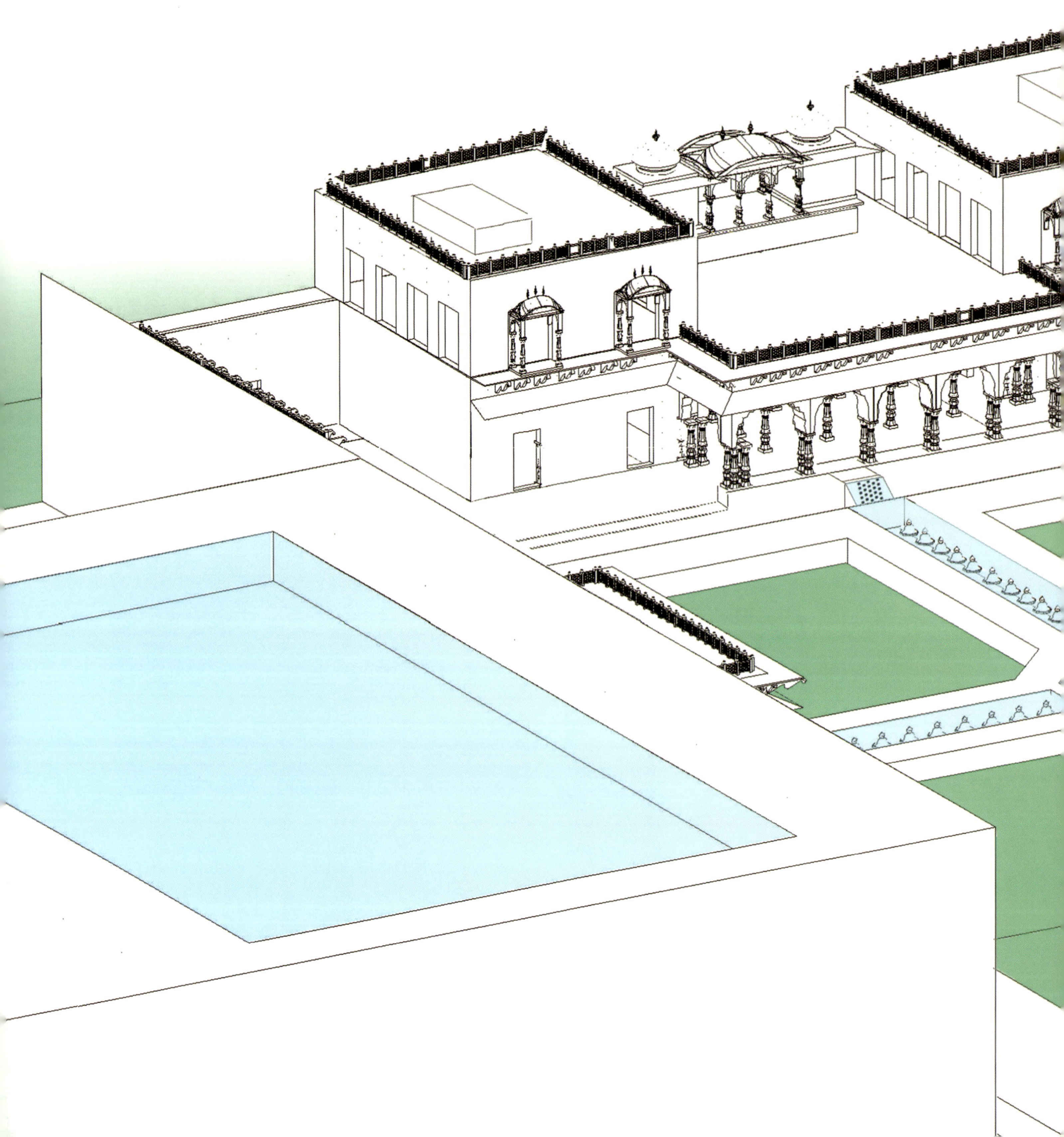

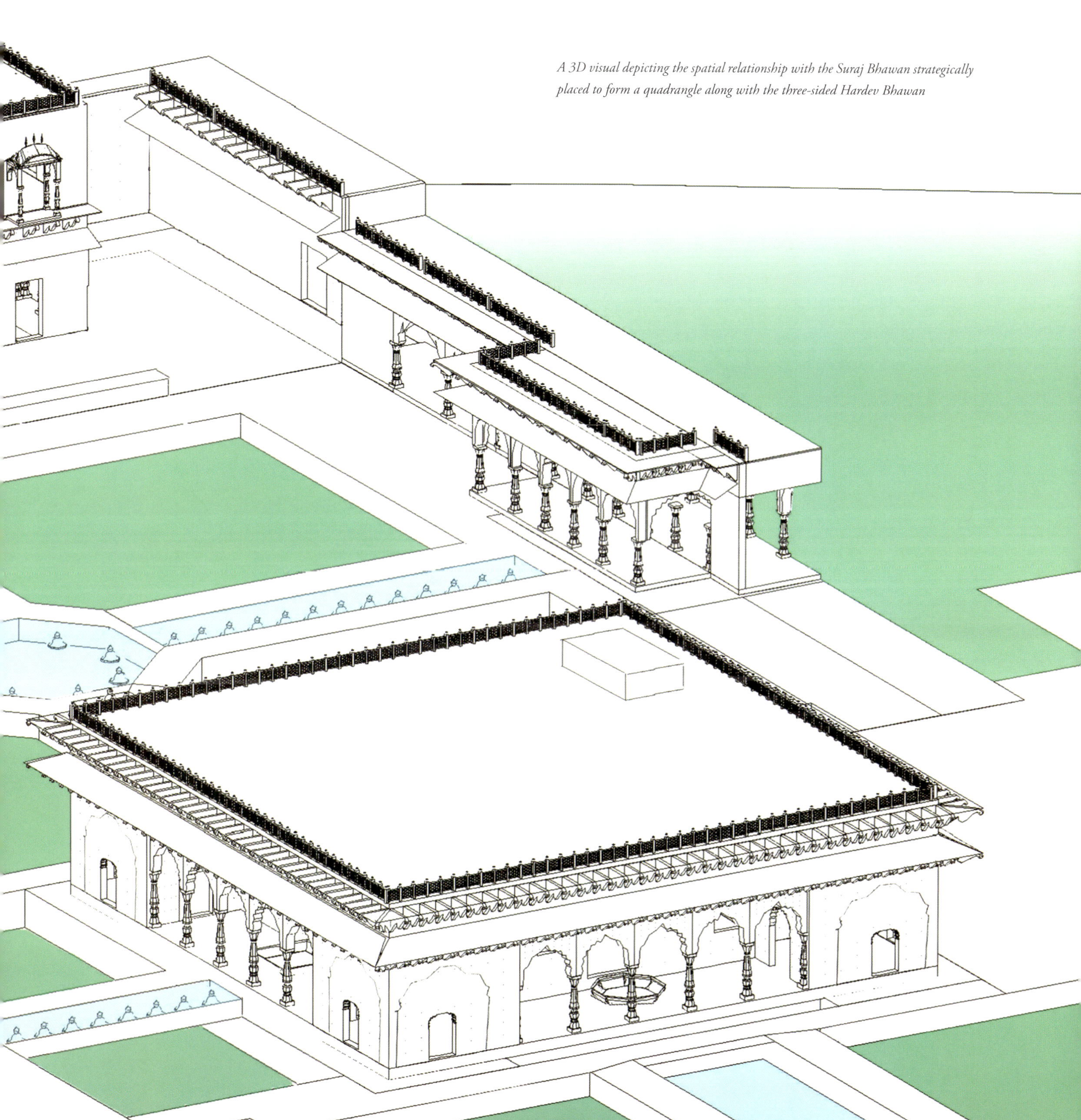

A 3D visual depicting the spatial relationship with the Suraj Bhawan strategically placed to form a quadrangle along with the three-sided Hardev Bhawan

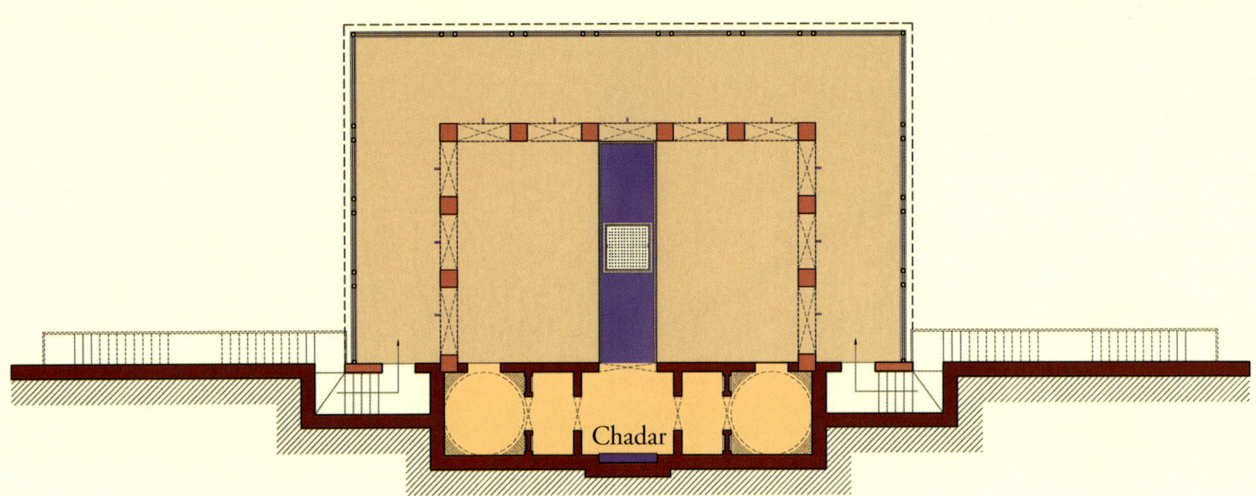

Lower Level Plan

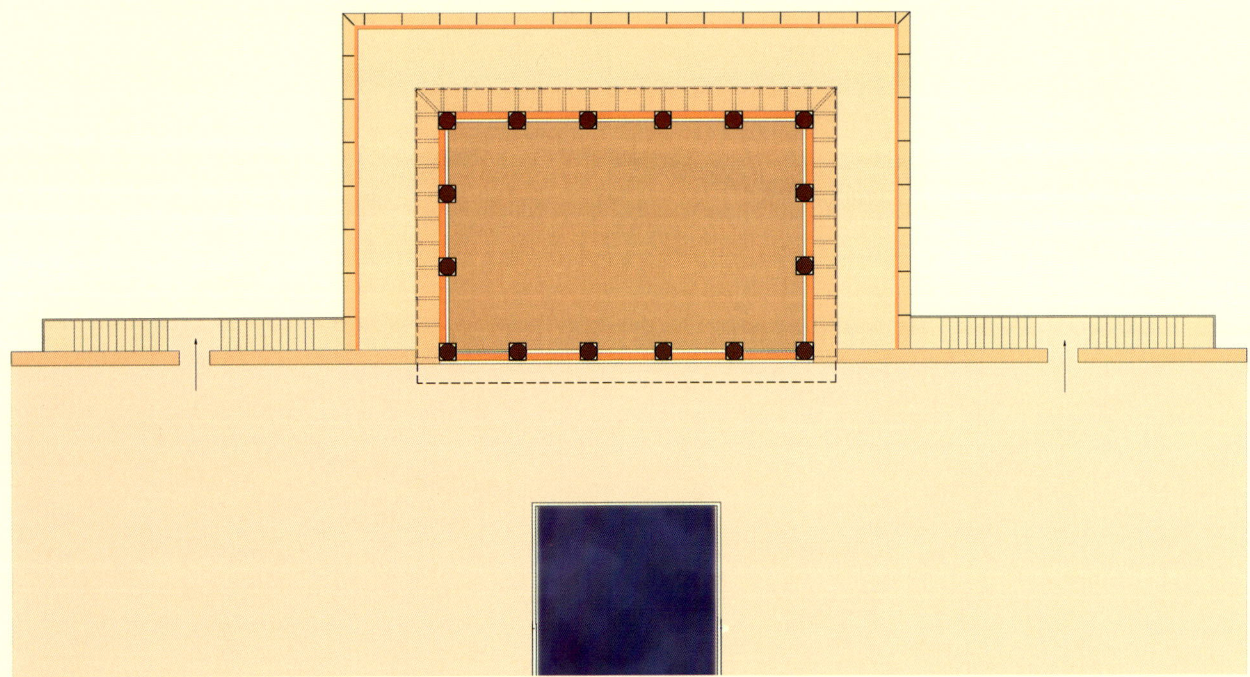

Terrace level Plan

AN OPERA OF RAINS

SAWAN AND BHADON PAVILIONS

Zi har favvaraash abi bar aflak
Ravan hamchun du'a az sina-i-pak.
Gar avval amadi baran zi gardun
Zamin bar asman mibarad aknun
Zi bas tardasti u san atnumai
Zi ab andakhta tir-I havai

From every one of its jets water runs up to the heavens
like a prayer from a pure breast.
If formerly rain came from the heavens,
now the earth rains upon the skies.
There is such cunning and artifice
that airy arrows are shot from the water.
–Kalim Qasaid[1]

1 W.M. Thackston, 'Mughal Gardens in Persian Poetry' in Mughal Gardens: Sources, Places, Representations, and Prospects, eds James L. Wescoat, Jr. and Joachim Wolschke-Bulmahn (Washington DC: Dumbarton Oaks Research Library and Collection, 1996), p. 244.

These lines suitably describe the two pavilions Sawan and Bhadon, named after the months of monsoon namely July-August and August-September respectively. The names are synonymous with twin pavilions in several of the Mughal gardens of that period, whether it be the Hayat Bakhsh in Delhi's Shahjahanabad, the Shalimar Gardens in Lahore or the Saheliyon ki Bari in Udaipur, Rajasthan.

India has always been fascinated by rains which is the lifeline for millions of people. From the epics like *Ramayana* to the romantic tales of Krishna or Kalidasa's poetry, many stories have been woven around rains. Perhaps to realise this fantasy as a perpetual affair, the twin pavilions of Sawan and Bhadon were created in order to symbolically depict artificial creation of rains in the style of *'Bin Badal Barsaat'*.

Facing page (Fig. 1): *Layout plan of the Sawan and Bhadon pavilions*

The subconscious aspect of the concept of Sawan and Bhadon can be seen in the tantric philosophy of the Vedanta and Upanishads. A dynamisation, transformation or sublimation of the physical, mental and spiritual state is only possible with the arousal of Shakti (kundalini awakening) and her uniting with Shiva, resulting in the flooding of the whole being with indescribable bliss. The two universal truths have to exist simultaneously and neither can sustain without the other. The universe cannot breed; neither can there be any creation without the union of Brahman (male) and Maya (female), *Purusha* and *Prakriti* or *sat* and *asat*. Thus creation of these two pavilions together symbolically satisfies a deep-rooted concept of creation in Hindu philosophy. Adam and Eve, Aadam and Havah or Yin and Yang is yet another parameter of the same coin, not far from the same thought. The Deeg Palace complex was not complete without a Sawan and a Bhadon pavilion, which were like twins, identical to each other and made as mirror copies of each other.

These pavilions can also be seen as a culmination of both the Bhakti and Sufi traditions that flowed from the 12th century onwards in the subcontinent. The objective of both the movements was to direct the amorous love of a young one towards an eventual unification with the Krishna spirit (in the Bhakti movement) or Ishq-e-haqiqi (in the Sufi movement). This was supposed to be nothing but a reunification with the universal spirit from where the being had sprung. While the artificial monsoon showers created in the Sawan and Bhadon pavilions with their artificial rain curtains recall a setting from the *Gita Govinda*; the *chadar* and the rivers of paradise symbolise the Sufi traditions. In effect, we see a physical representation of one philosophy which two distinct landscape elements brought together—striving to achieve the lofty ideal of universal love.

The simple and classical waterfalls over the *chini khanas* seen in the Sawan-Bhadon of the Shalimar

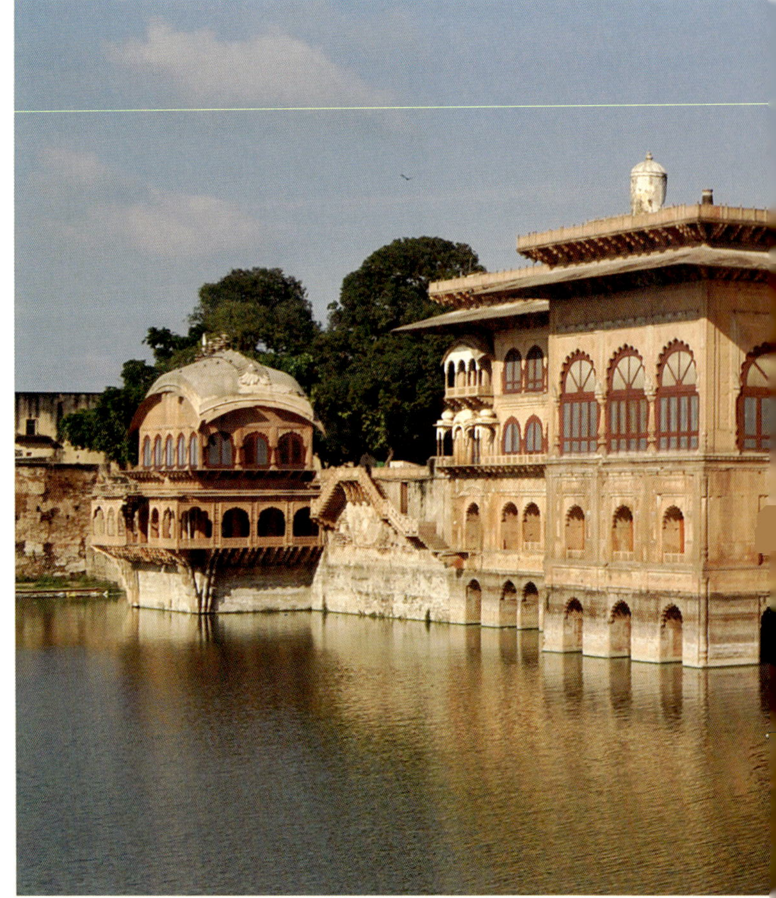

Gardens, Lahore and Red Fort, Delhi paved the way for the creation of the most intriguing Sawan and Bhadon pavilions of its time in Deeg. The elaborate water system of the complex has astonished and fascinated many minds. This ostentatious, complex and extensive water system revolves around several underground and hidden aqueducts, set for the desired effect of indigenous waterfalls and water curtains. The schematic blueprint that was meticulously executed must have undergone a tremendous amount of forethought.

These Sawan and Bhadon pavilions flank the Gopal Bhawan on the north and south side and beautifully frame it on the western face. (Fig. 2) They are projections from the western face of the terrace in the Gopal Sagar. When viewed from across the Gopal Sagar and the

Below (Fig. 2): *The Sawan and Bhadon pavilions flank the Gopal Bhawan and beautifully frame it on the western face*

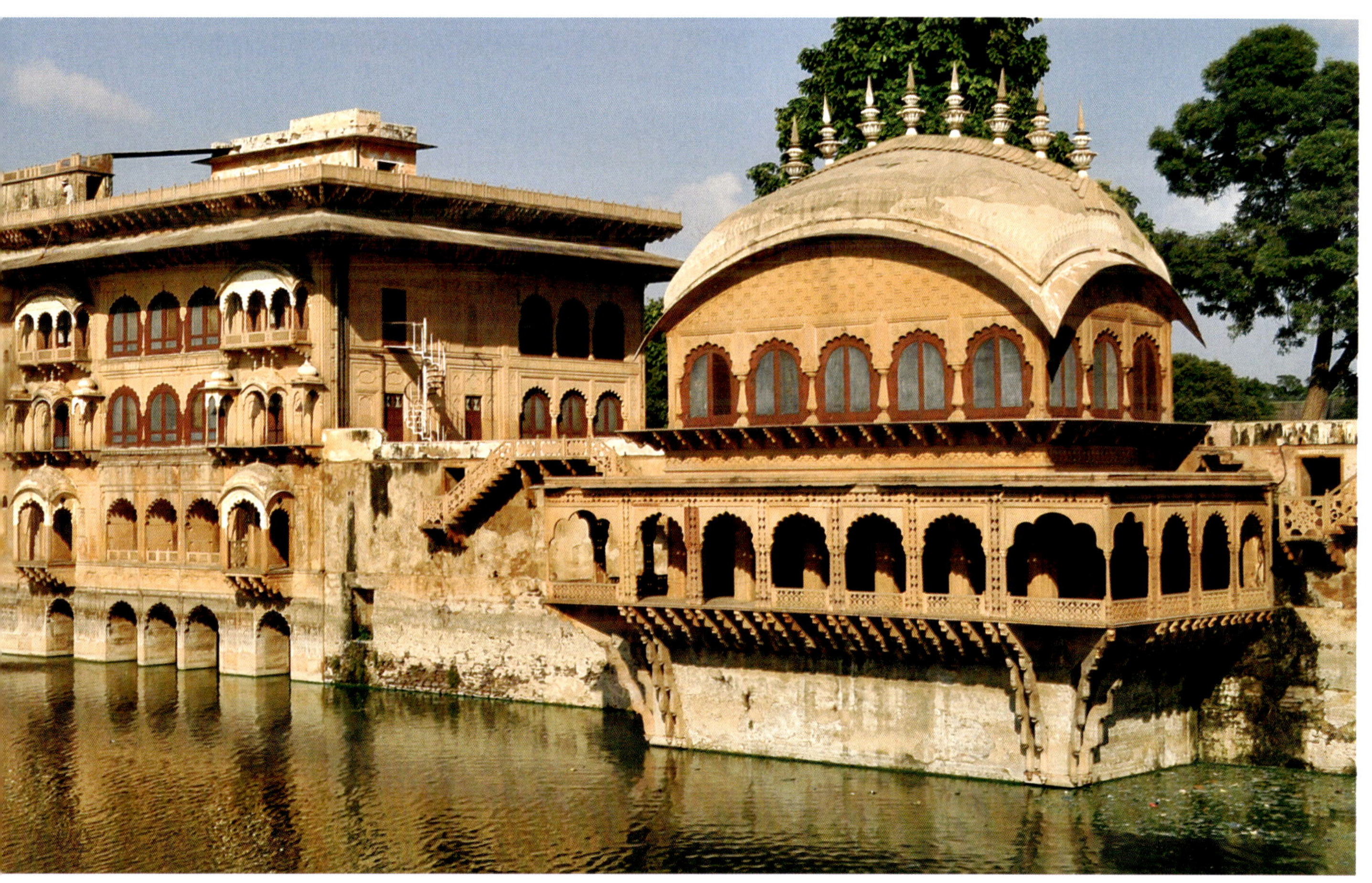

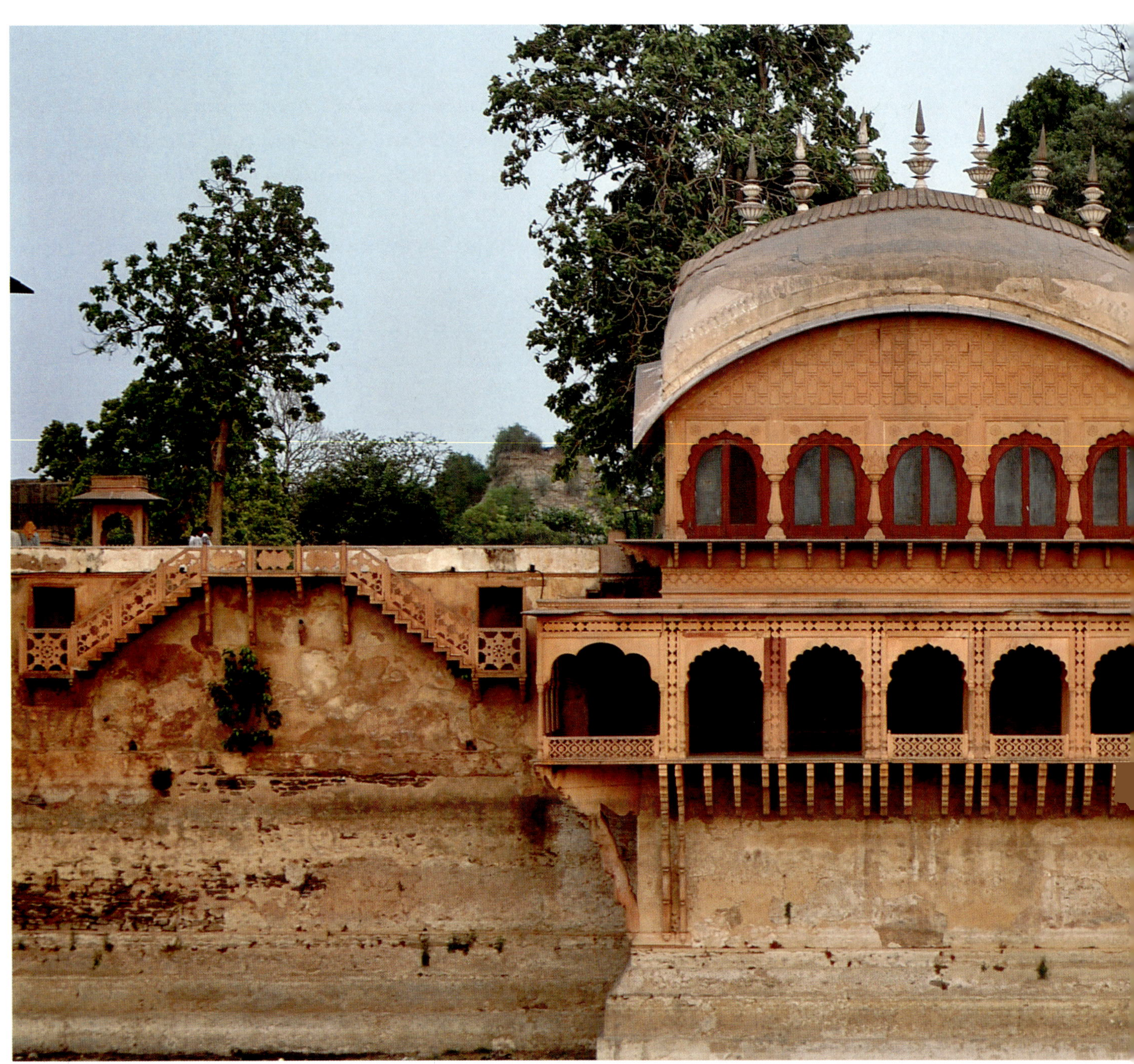

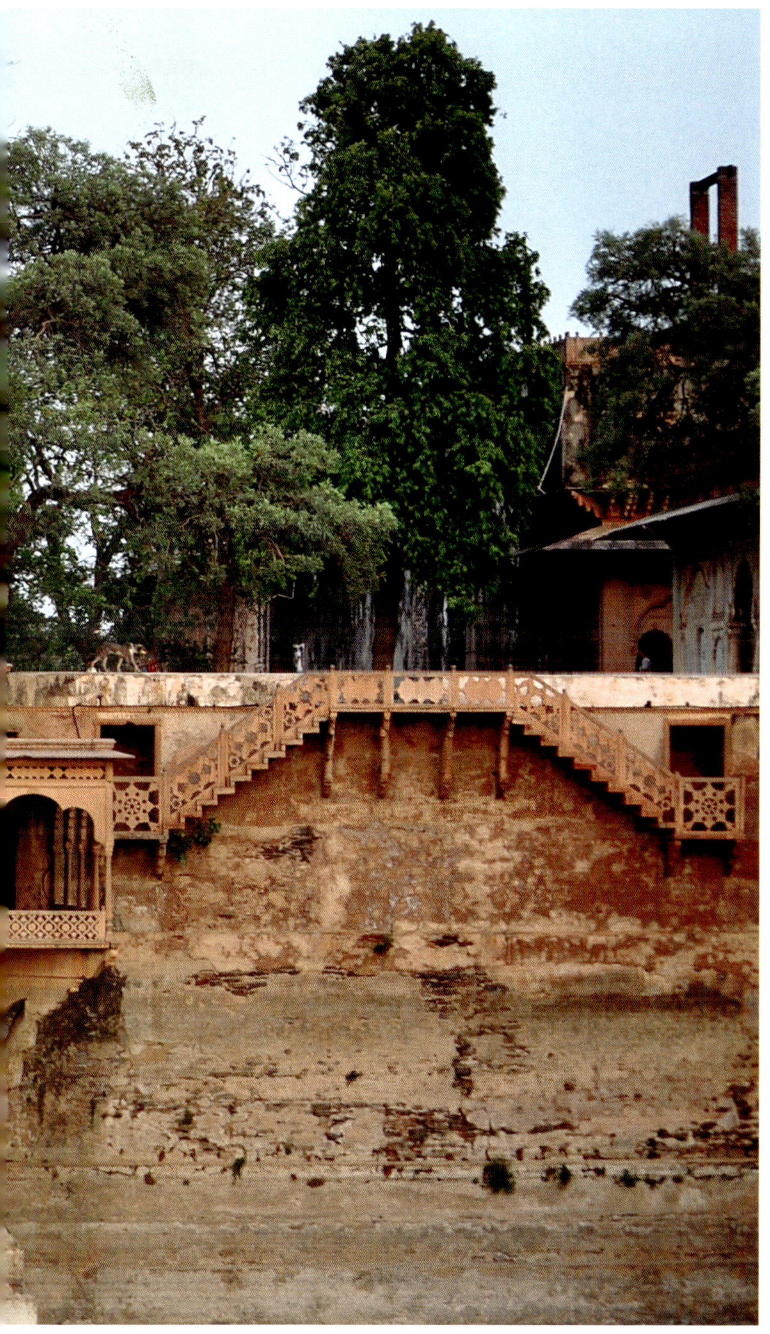

Rani Bagh it gives the appearance of two small ships floating on either side of the complex. The elevation seems to be inspired from the Khas Mahal elevation of the Red Fort at Agra from the Yamuna side, where two *bangladar* pavilions (namely Bangla-i-Darshan on the left and Bangla-i-Jahanara on the right when seen from west) frame the central sleeping pavilion (Khwabgah) in a similar way.

The pavilions are connected to the main garden terrace only via a cantilever staircase projecting into the Gopal Sagar. (Fig. 3) The approach to the cantilevered staircase that leads to the Sawan as well as the one that leads to the Bhadon pavilion is quite unobtrusive. It is just a gap in the boundary wall that overlooks the Gopal Sagar. The stone handrail that runs along the edge of the cantilevered staircase has stone *jali* work below it which resembles the cartouche panel designs of the Singh Pol. The only difference being that here the stone *jali* is not a relief panel, but rather a pattern of opaque and voids. (Fig. 4)

The pattern of the parapet *jalis* at the landings of the cantilevered staircase is a visually interesting sight, with a mixture of floral and 'chakra' pattern set within a square. (Fig. 5) The staircase itself is cantilevered over water, though the landings are supported by ornate stone brackets projecting from the wall. The treads and risers are made of 3-inch thick solid sandstone sections projecting from the wall of the reservoir. These stairs

Left (Fig. 3): *The pavilions are connected to the main garden terrace only via a cantilever staircase projecting into the Gopal Sagar*

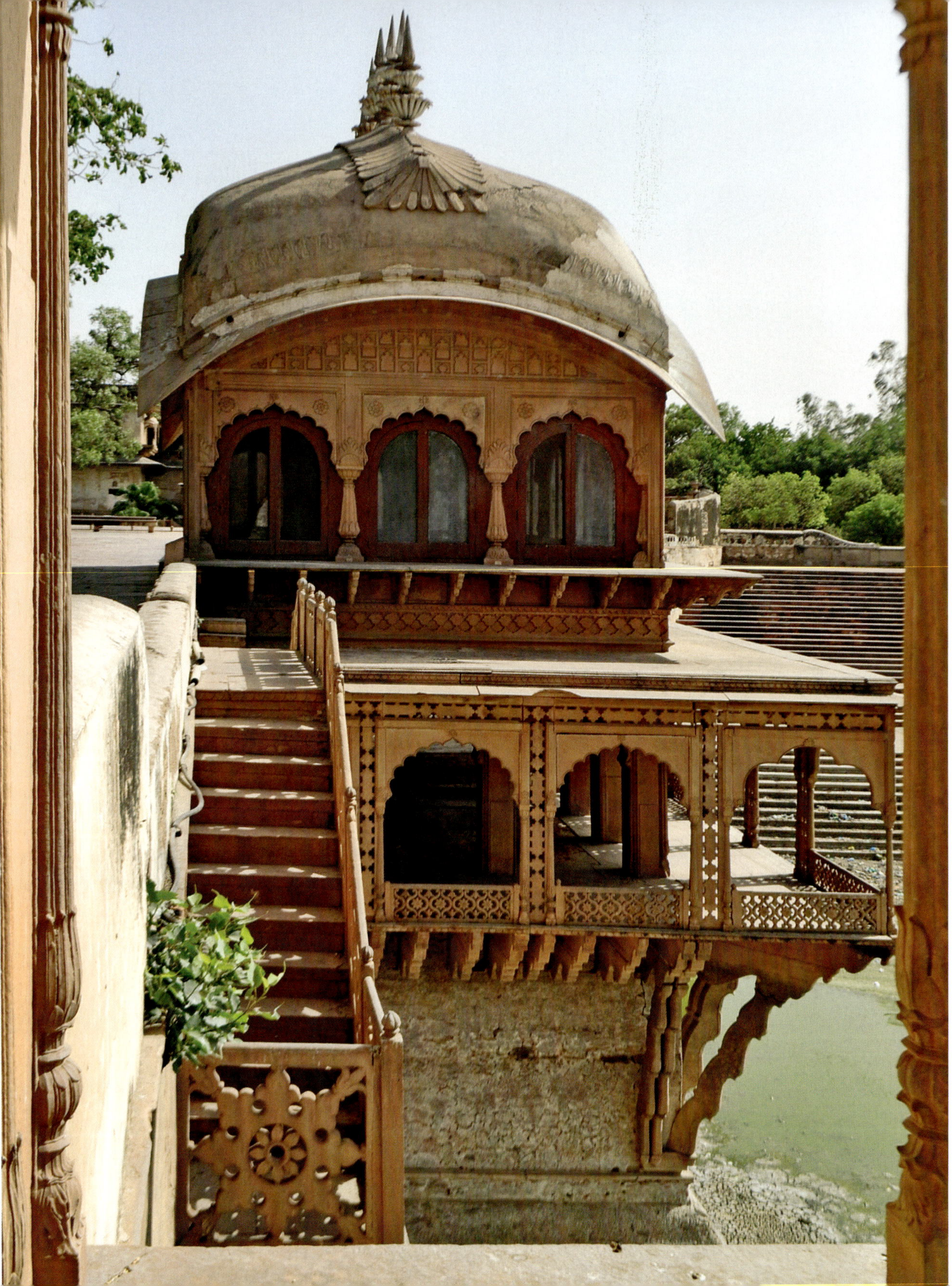

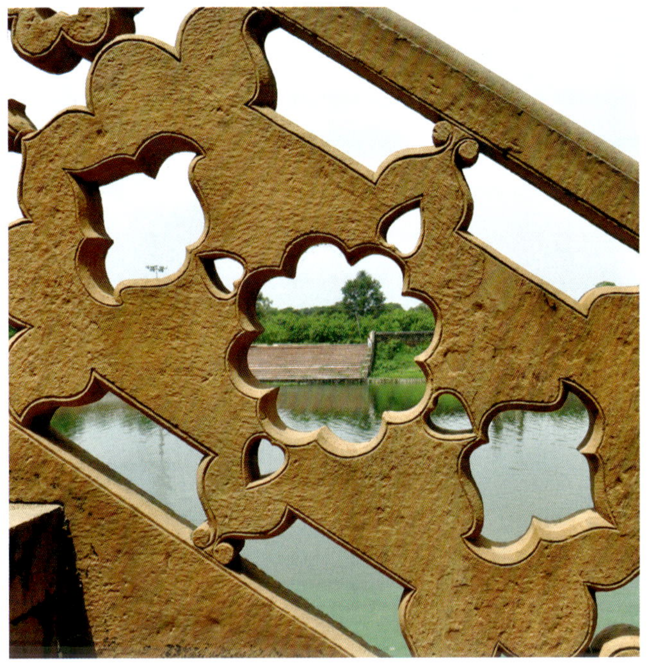

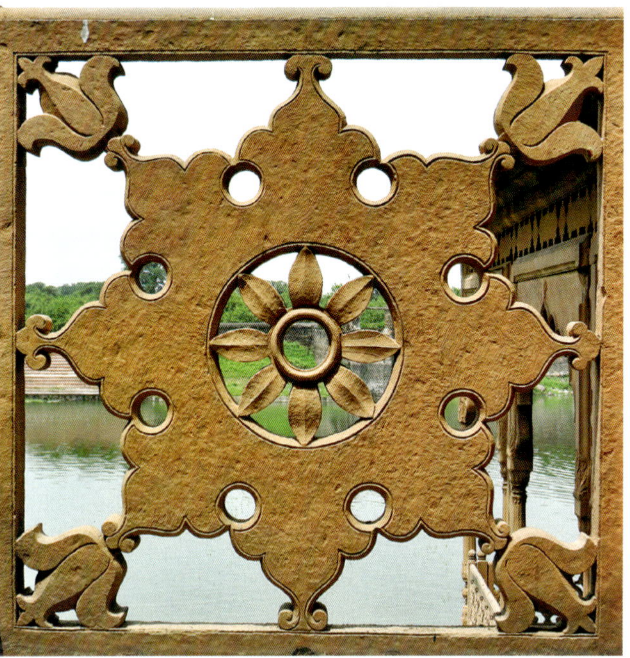

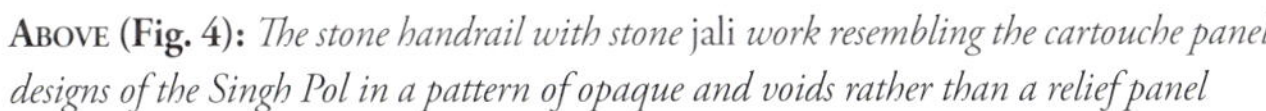

Above (Fig. 4): *The stone handrail with stone* jali *work resembling the cartouche panel designs of the Singh Pol in a pattern of opaque and voids rather than a relief panel*

Above right (Fig. 5): *A mixture of floral and 'chakra' pattern set within a square of the parapet* jalis *at the landings*

Facing page (Fig. 6): *The skilful placement of the stairs leads one to walk over the reservoir before going inside the wall and then unexpectedly into the hitherto invisible pavilion*

connect the lower stories of both the pavilions with the Gopal Bhawan.

The skilful placement of the stairs is done in such a way that they are not visible from the front or the main garden. This gives the staircase a beautiful articulation from the garden edge. One seems to walk over the reservoir and the staircase takes you inside the wall and then, surprisingly, opens into the hitherto invisible pavilion. (Fig. 6)

The pavilion consists of a central hall with a passage on three sides, which is also projecting into the reservoir. On its back there is a gallery which has a wide, carved water chute, locally known as the *chadar*. (Fig. 7) This *chadar* is carved with scalloped fish-scale patterns and a carved chevron border. This would give a shimmering effect to water which flows over it through a hidden drain. (Fig. 8) The water again disappears into the floor to reappear in a shallow oblong cistern in the hall. This channel has a flat 48-inch square basin, raised 6 inches in the centre with 169 fine needle-holes for water spray jets and two slits on either side to let the water fall back into the channel. (Fig. 9) This 63-inch wide and 20-foot long channel ends at the periphery of the room, going

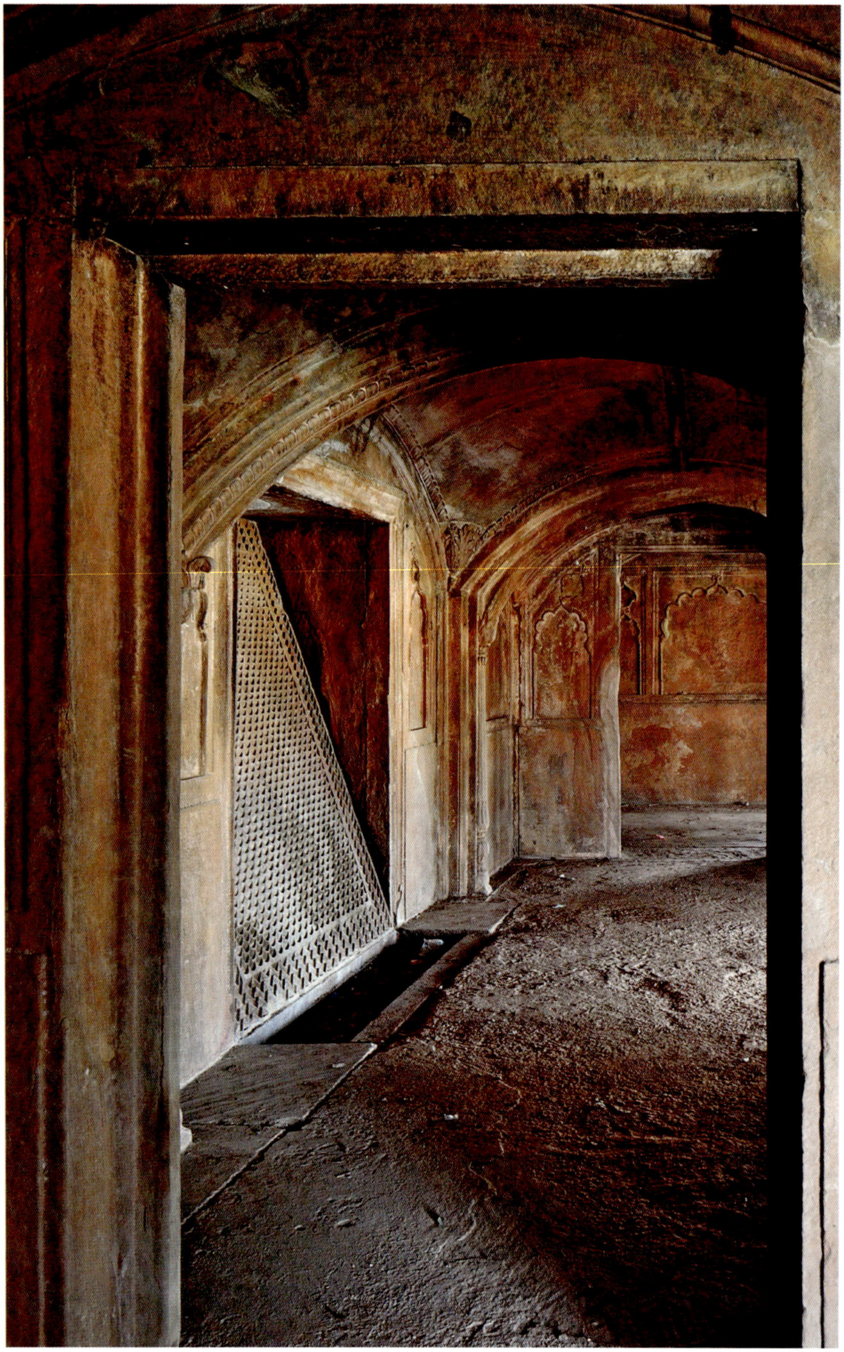

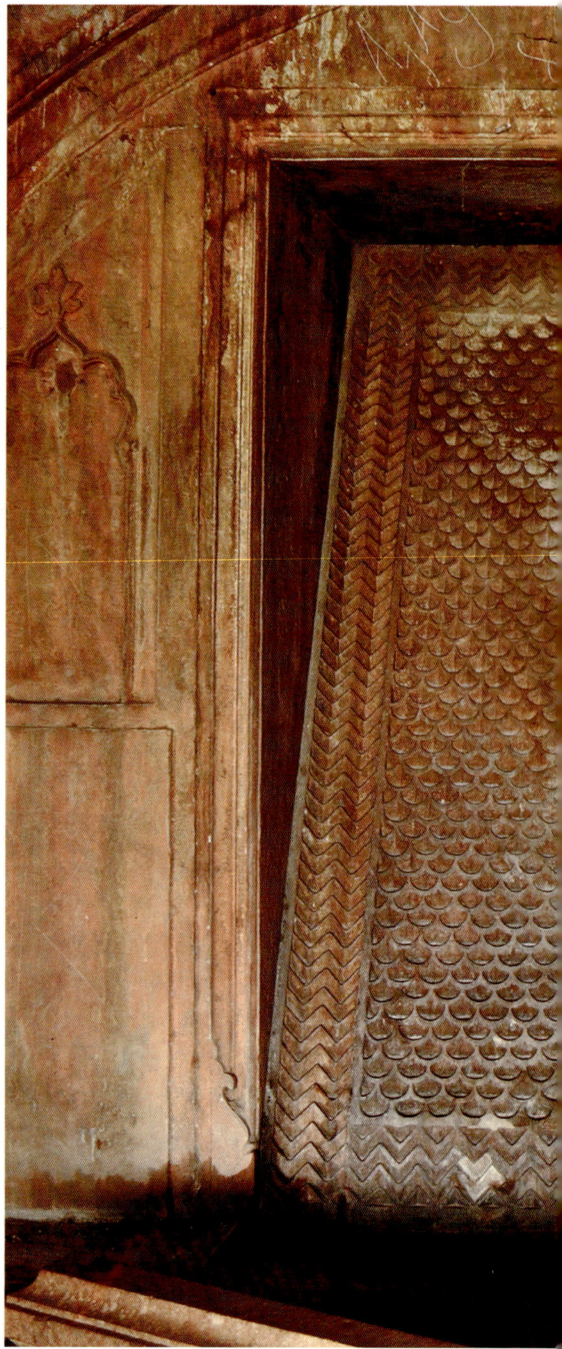

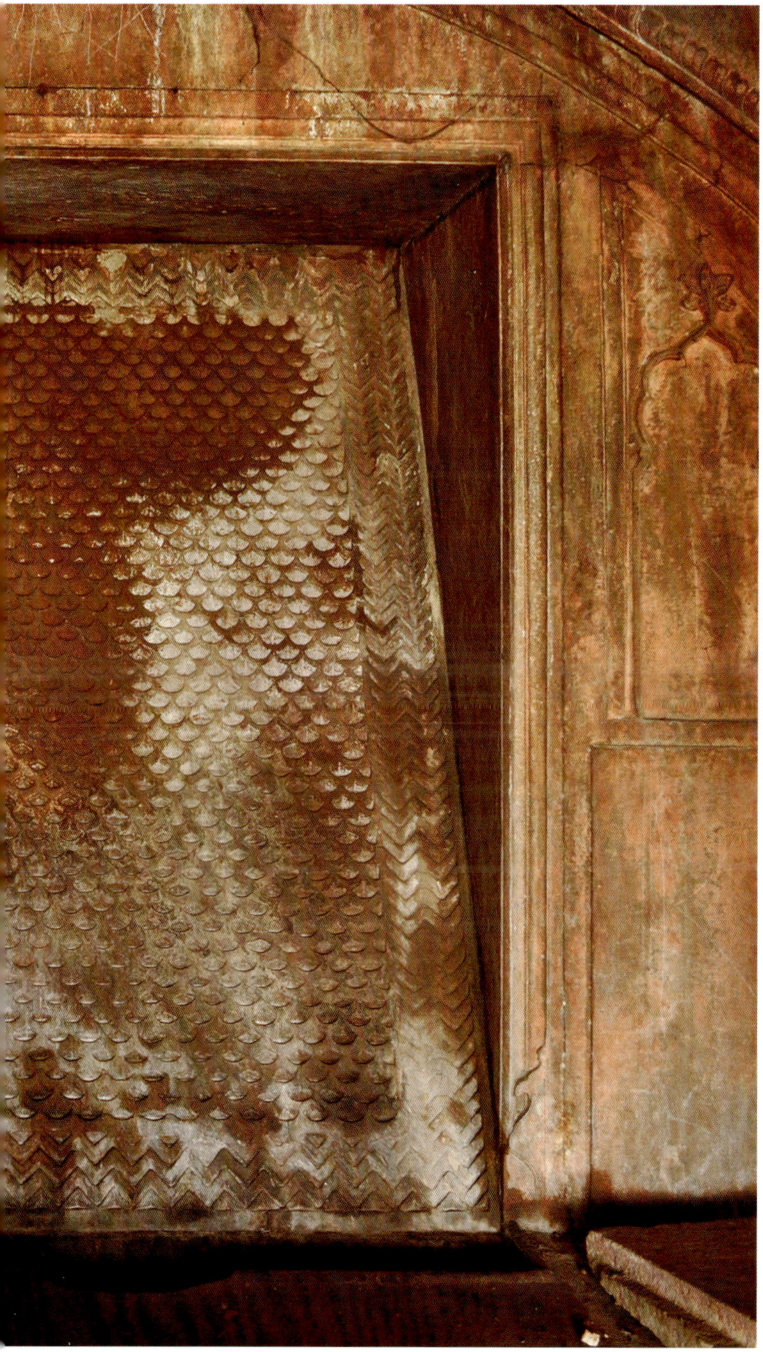

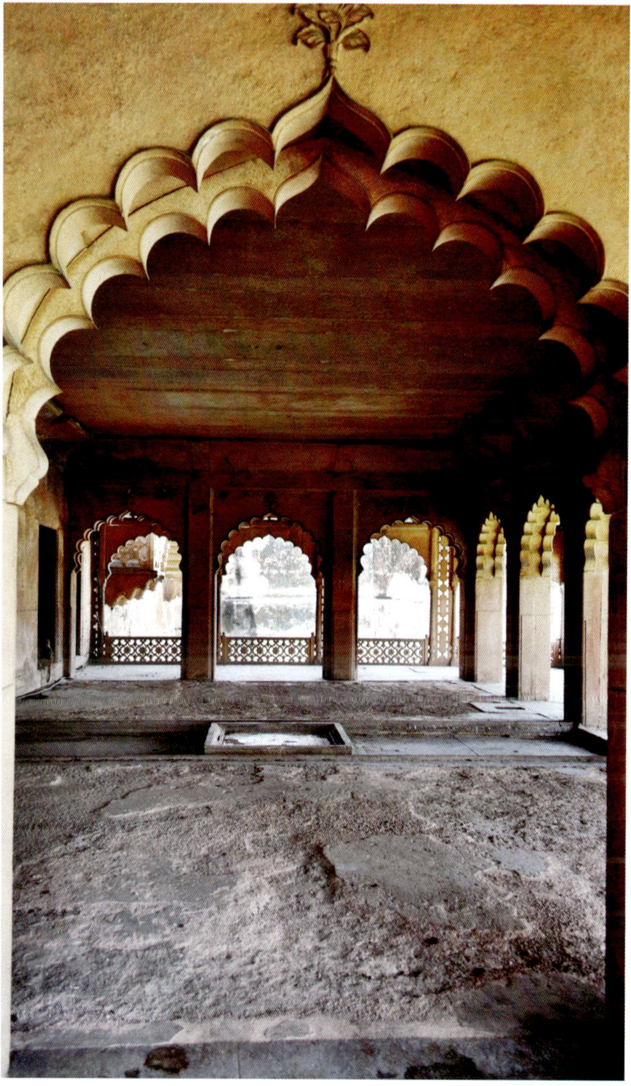

Above (Fig. 11): *Cross view of the hallway through the side vestibule*

Left (Fig. 8): *Carved* chadar *with scalloped fish-scale patterns and a carved chevron border, giving a shimmering effect to water flowing over it through a hidden drain*

Facing page left (Fig. 7): *The central room of the pavilion with a gallery at the back has a wide carved water chute, locally known as the* chadar

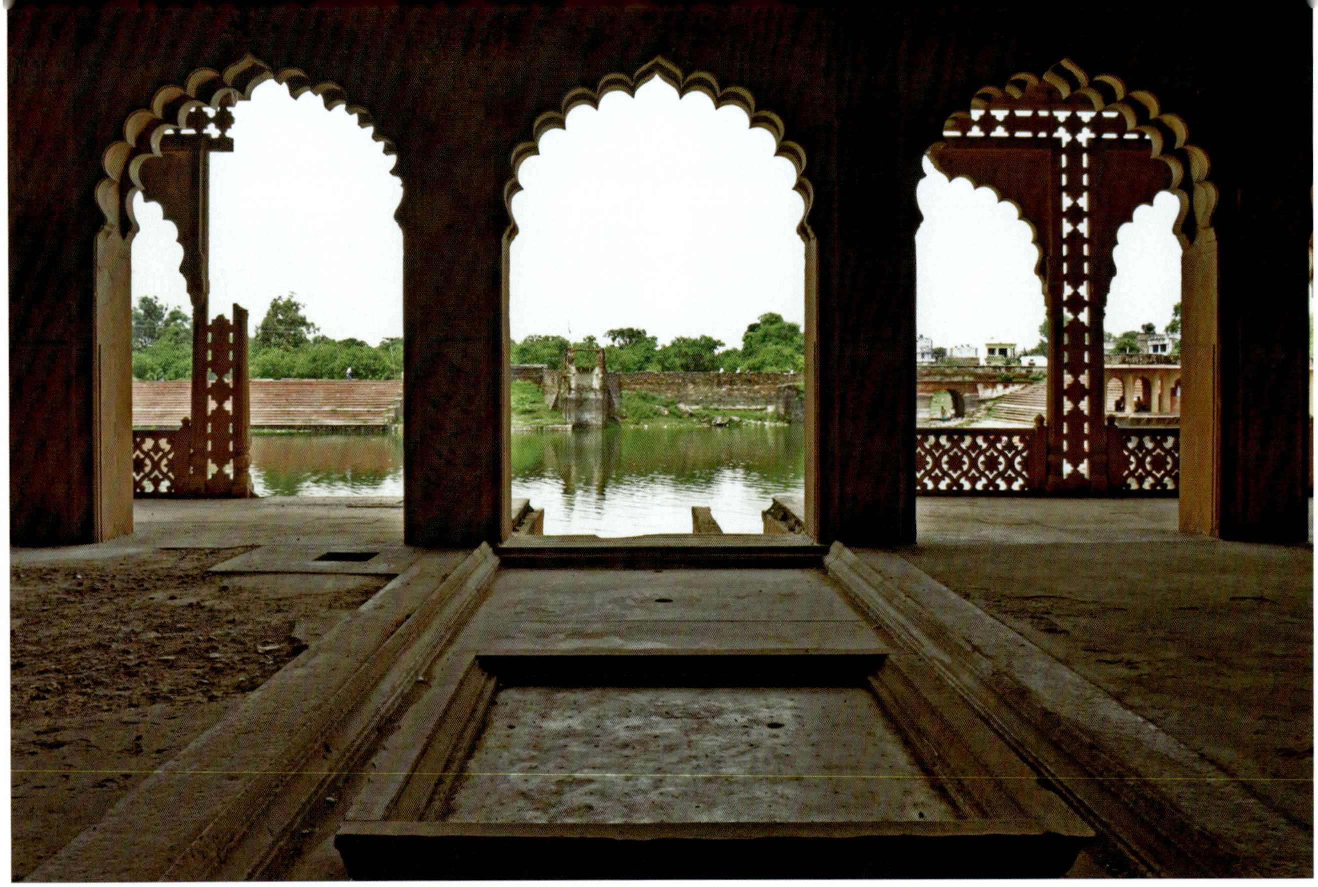

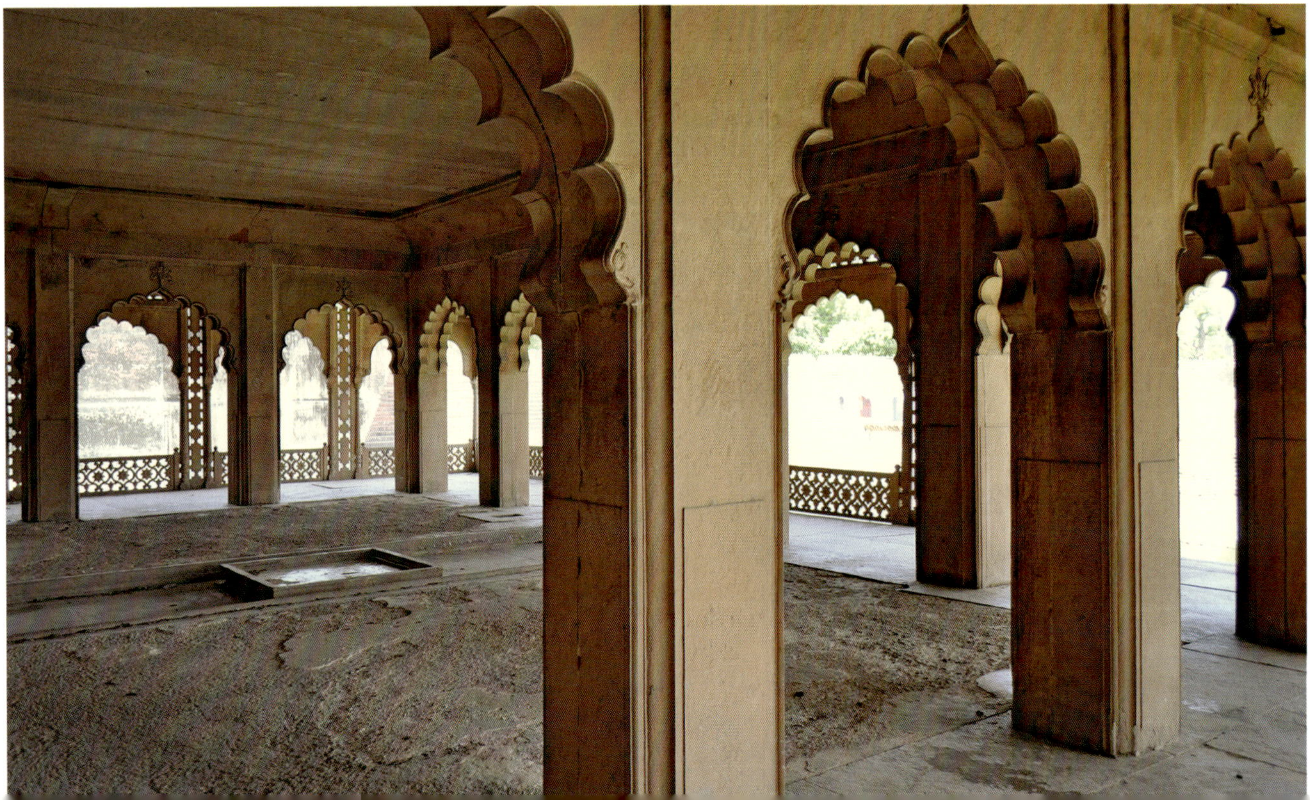

under the floor to fall back as a sheet of water in the Gopal Sagar.

This hall is separated by piers and simple cusped arches from the covered veranda on three sides. (Fig. 10) (Fig. 11) The spandrels of these arches facing the outside have copper pipes through which the water gushed out and splashed against the facade of the embellished veranda. It apparently would strike the intricately carved, pierced screen panels and scintillate down the outer elevation of the veranda. (Fig. 12) The right thickness of pillars and patterns forms a frangible

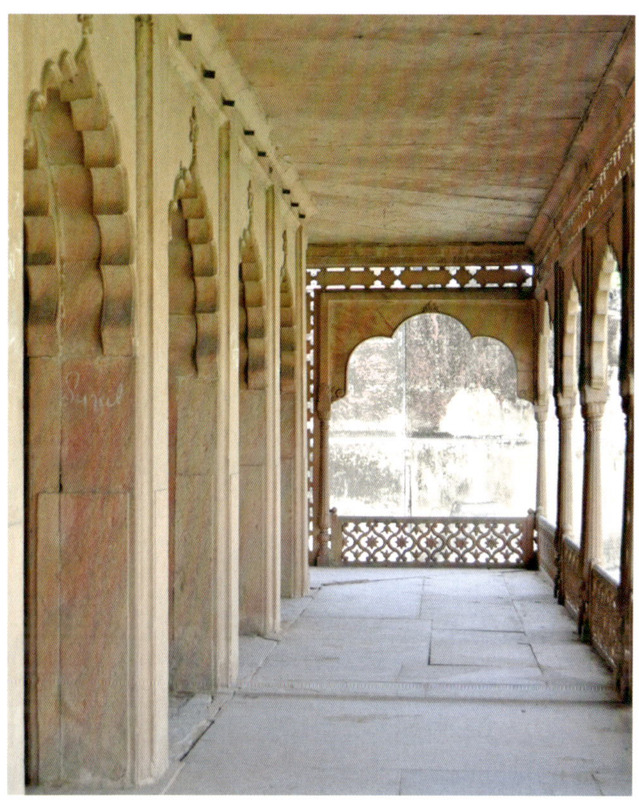

Right (Fig. 12): *The copper pipes seen above the spandrels through which the water gushed out and splashed against the facade of the embellished veranda*

Below (Fig. 15): *The classical 'badron'* jali *of the Mughals reinterpreted and expressed as vines holding an eight-petalled lotus on a larger scale.*

Facing page below (Fig. 10): *The hall is separated by piers and simple cusped arches forming a covered veranda on three sides*

Facing page above (Fig. 9): *Water channel with a flat square basin consisting of 169 fine needle-holes for water spray jets*

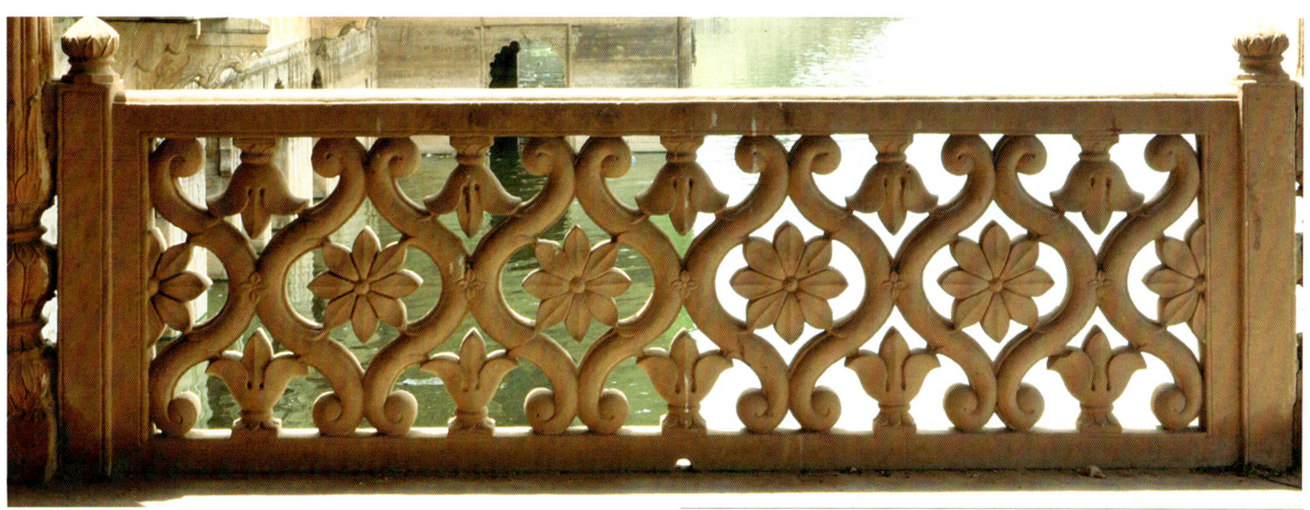

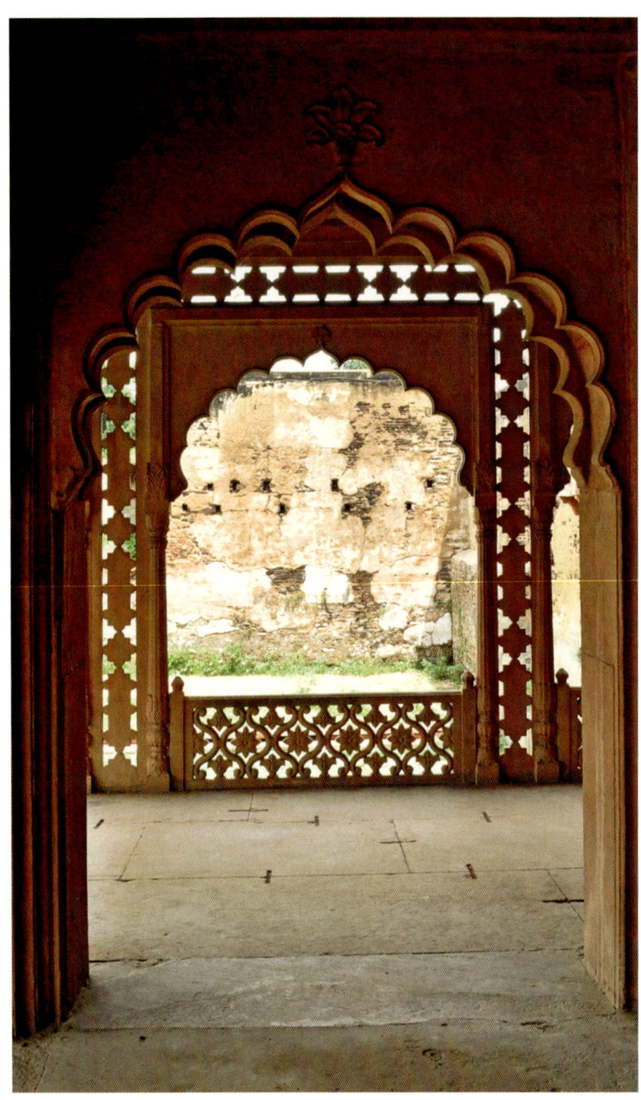

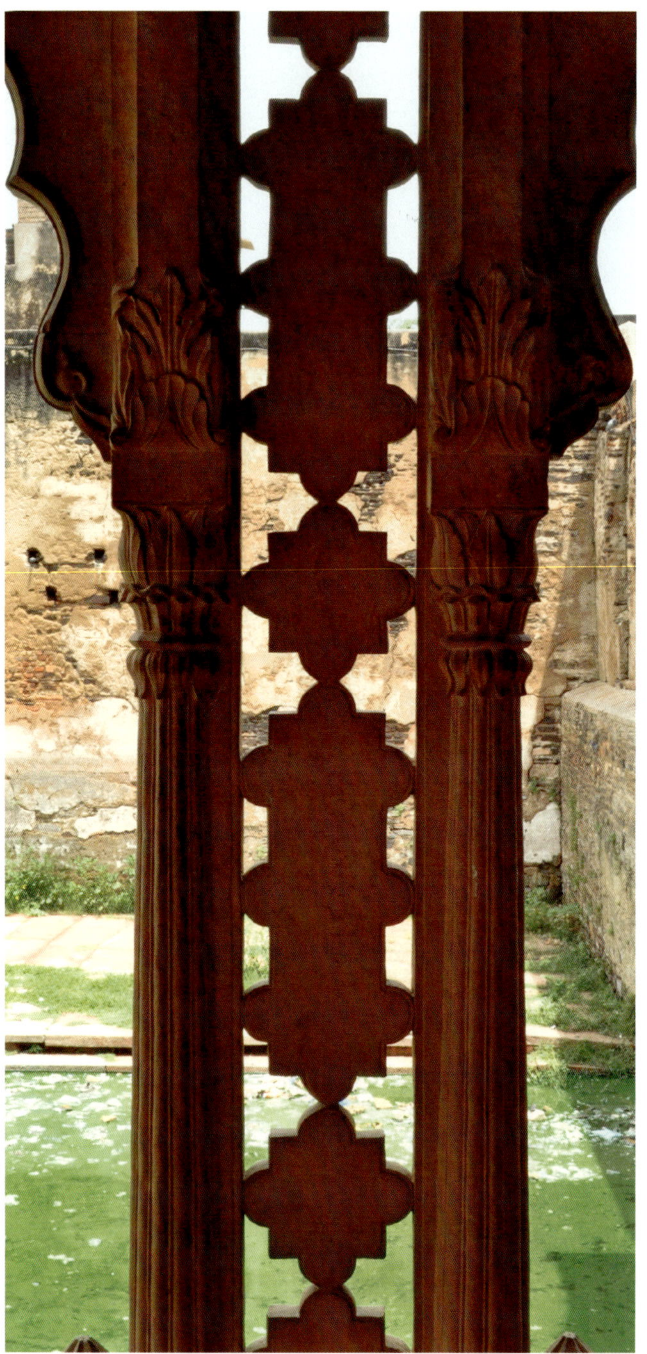

ABOVE (Fig. 13): *A beautifully carved screen of fine* jalis *through which the effect of light-created tiny rainbows to complete the monsoon scene*

RIGHT (Fig. 14): *A screen formed by panels of arches joined together with cartouche-like vertical panels, all in sandstone*

FACING PAGE (Fig. 16): *The base of the Sawan and Bhadon pavilions is elaborately designed to give an impression of a boat floating on water*

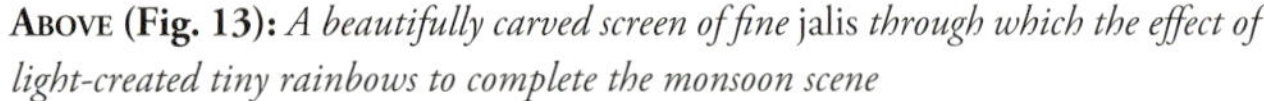

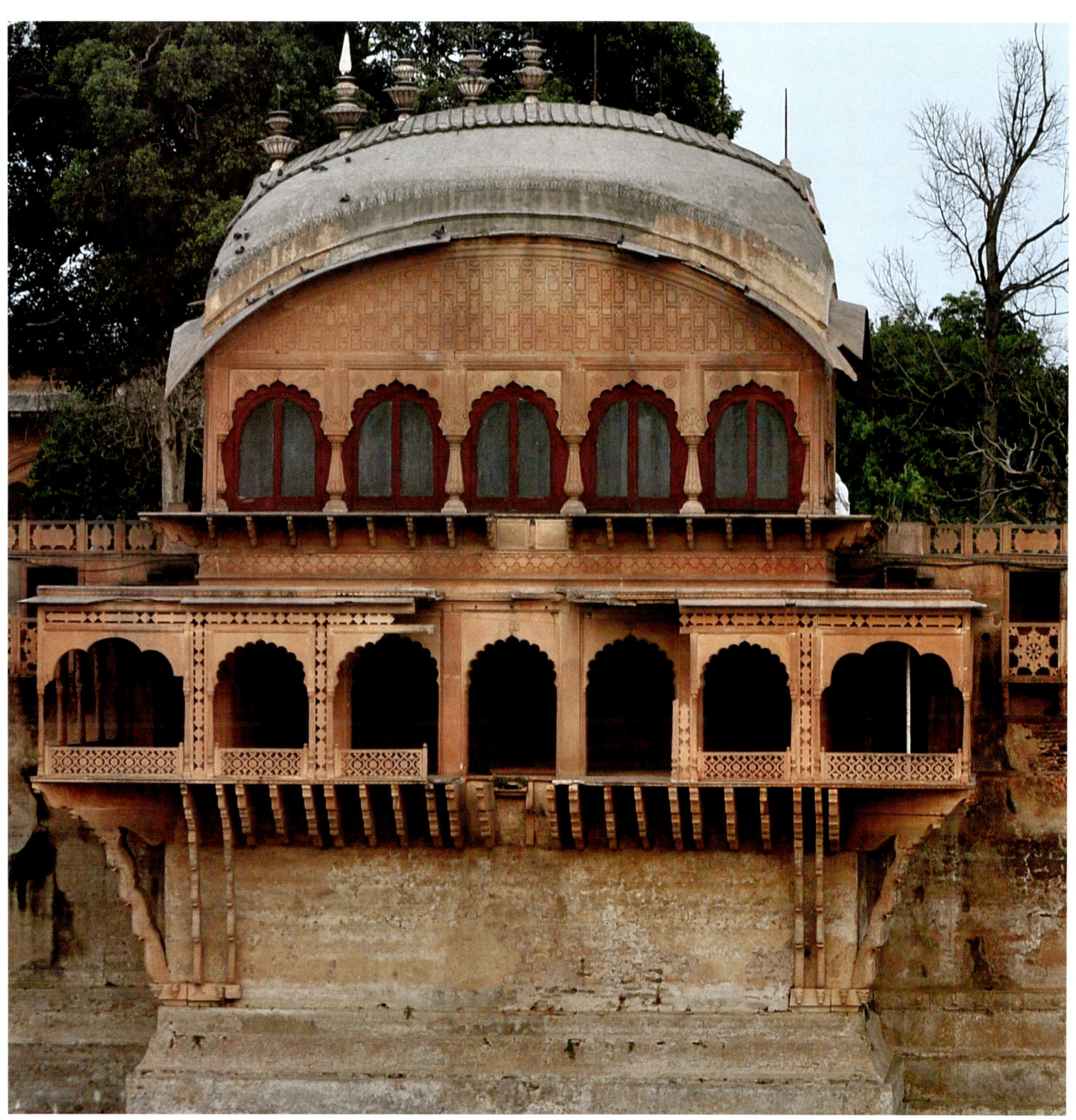

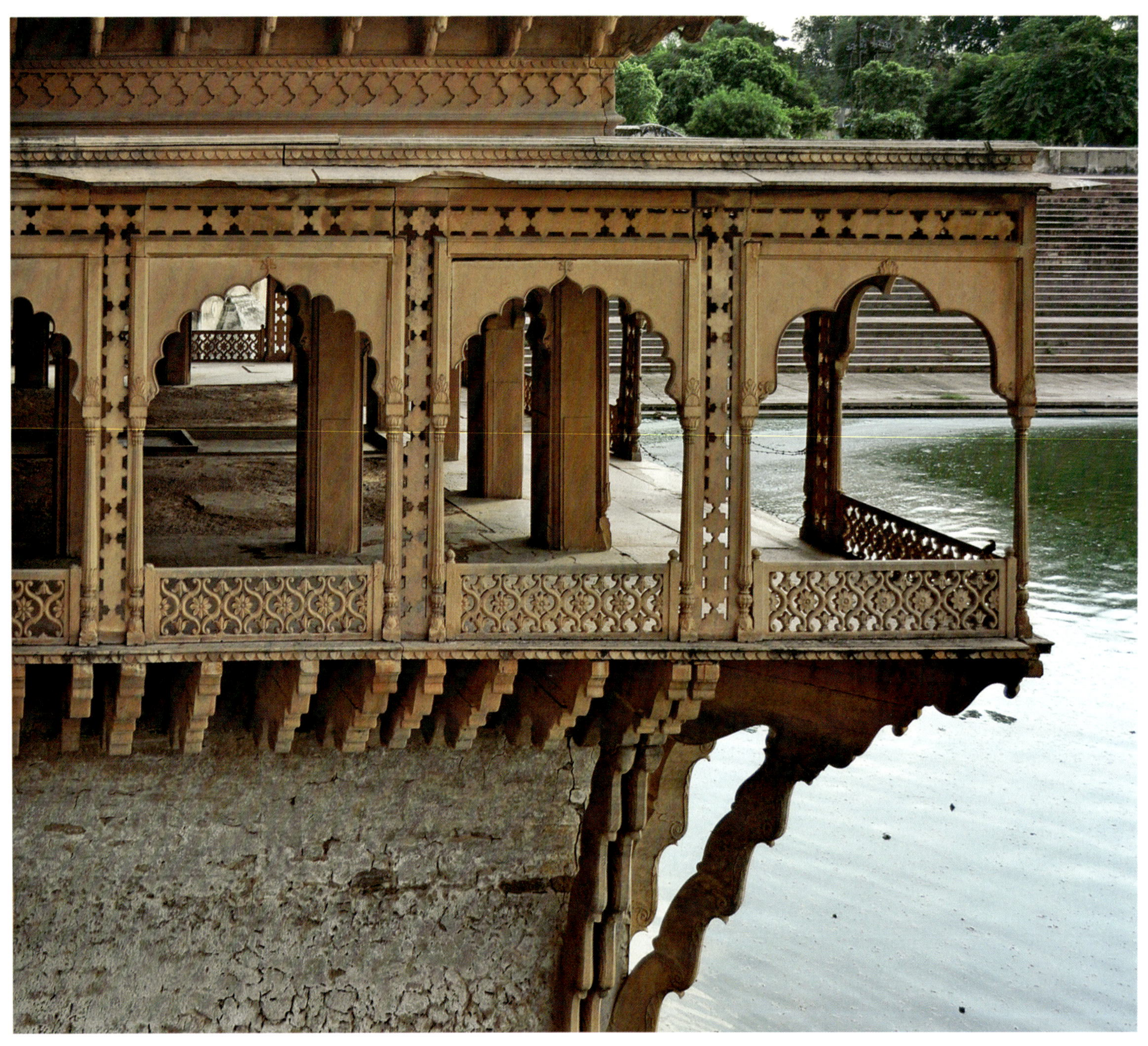

curtain wall with adorable handsomeness. This creates the impression of the rains as seen through the arches which would infuse life in anyone, especially the one who has experienced a harsh Indian summer. The screen of arches in the veranda is beautifully carved and has finely carved *jalis* through which the effect of light-created tiny rainbows complete the monsoon scene. (Fig. 13) The screen is actually formed by panels of arches and joined together with cartouche like vertical panels, all in sandstone. (Fig. 14) In the parapet, the classical 'badron' *jali* of the Mughals has been reinterpreted and expressed as vines holding an eight-petalled lotus on a larger scale. (Fig. 15)

The base of the Sawan and Bhadon pavilions is also elaborately designed to give an impression of a boat floating on water. (Fig. 16) There are intricately carved and designed brackets which support the veranda. The four brackets at both the corners are long and carved in the shape of a keel to give the appearance of a floating boat. (Fig. 17)

However, all this is not visible if one sees the pavilions from the garden side. Only a single storey oblong room with a *bangladar chhatri* is seen, crowned by a row of elegant spikes. The *chhatris* above the Sawan-Bhadon pavilions are of course, the traditional Bengali *chhatris* that were an integral part of the Rajput tradition of building. (Fig. 18) According to Prof. Satish Grover the origin of the *chhatris* can be traced to the traditional Bengali thatched hut. The curvilinear form of the roof with drooping eaves is now synonymous with the traditional stone buildings of the Mughals, the Sikhs and the Rajputs. Ebba Koch points out the influence of these roofs from European arches and tents.

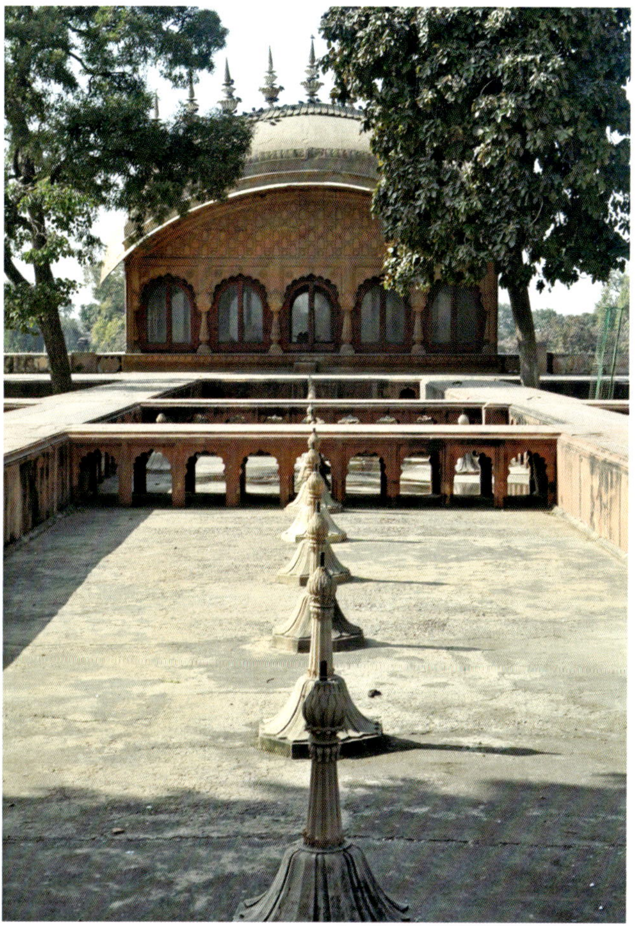

Above (Fig. 18): *A water channel starting from these* bangladar *pavilions, perpendicular to the channels along Gopal Bhawan, forms a cross to culminate at massive and impressive kamal burjis from where water fall into the central Charbagh*

Facing page (Fig. 17): *Intricately carved and designed brackets which support the veranda. The four brackets at the corners are long and carved in the shape of a keel to give the appearance of a floating boat*

The oblong room is in fact a rectangular pavilion enclosed by five-arched openings on the longer side and three on the shorter side. The engrailed arches rest on traditional Mughal-Rajput acanthus columns. The spandrels have carved lotuses with acanthus scroll framing.

The fascia above the arches and below the soffit of the *bangladar* roof of both these pavilions is carved in low relief with an array of multiple cartouche arches. All the panels displaying stone arches that occur in the Sawan-Bhadon pavilions are cusped arches carved in counter relief. The entire pediment is filled with repeated carved panels whose beauty is the cleverly worked out designs of the corner areas, which not only decorate the facade but adjust to the available shape.

A separate water channel starts from these pavilions, perpendicular to the channels along Gopal Bhawan, forming a cross to culminate at massive and impressive *kamal burjis* from where the water falls into the central Charbagh. (Refer to Fig. 18) Colossal fluting and petals on the *kamal burjis*, carved in the shape of a two-headed drum (*damaru*) forms an innovative waterfall with the recessed centre giving a shimmering backdrop.

A view of the *kamal burjis* from the Charbagh with the Sawan or Bhadon pavilions in the backdrop is exhilarating and quenches one's desire for beauty.

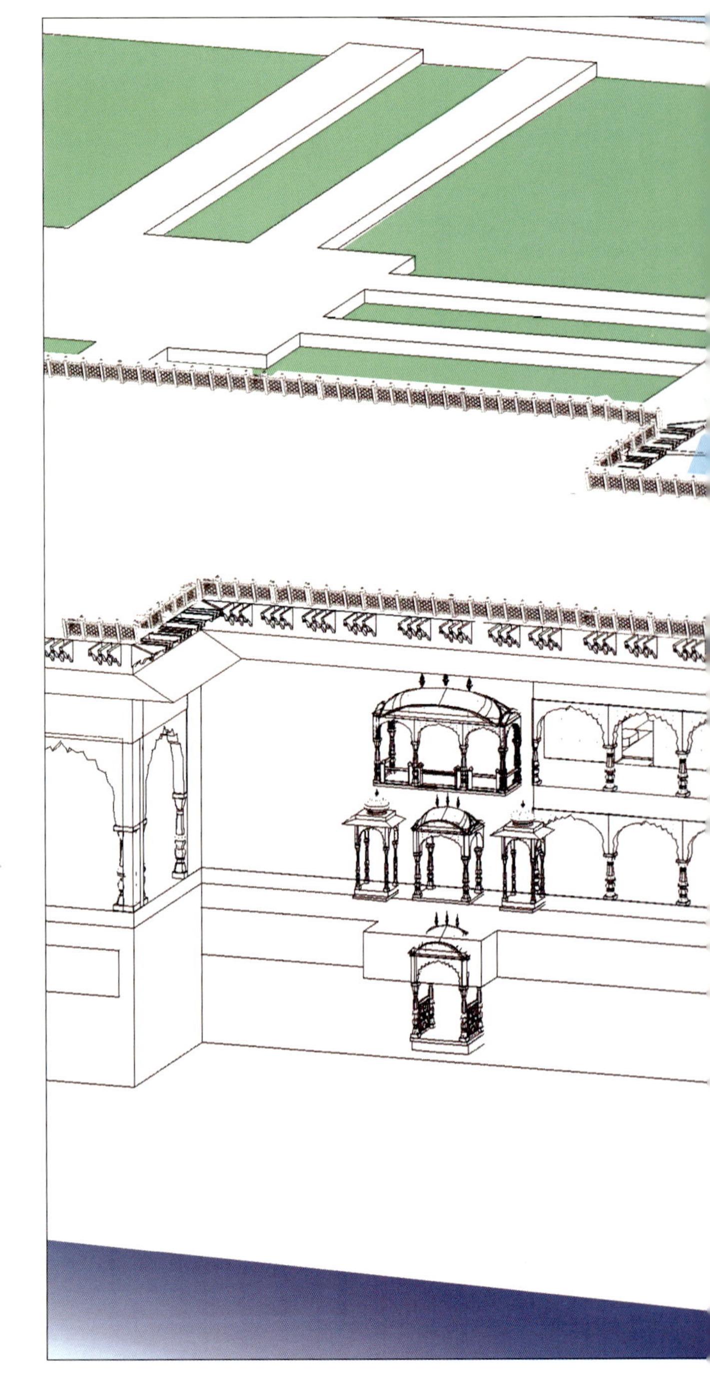

Right (Fig. 19): *A 3D depiction of the visual alignment of the Bhadon pavilion with respect to Gopal Bhawan and the Charbagh in the backdrop*

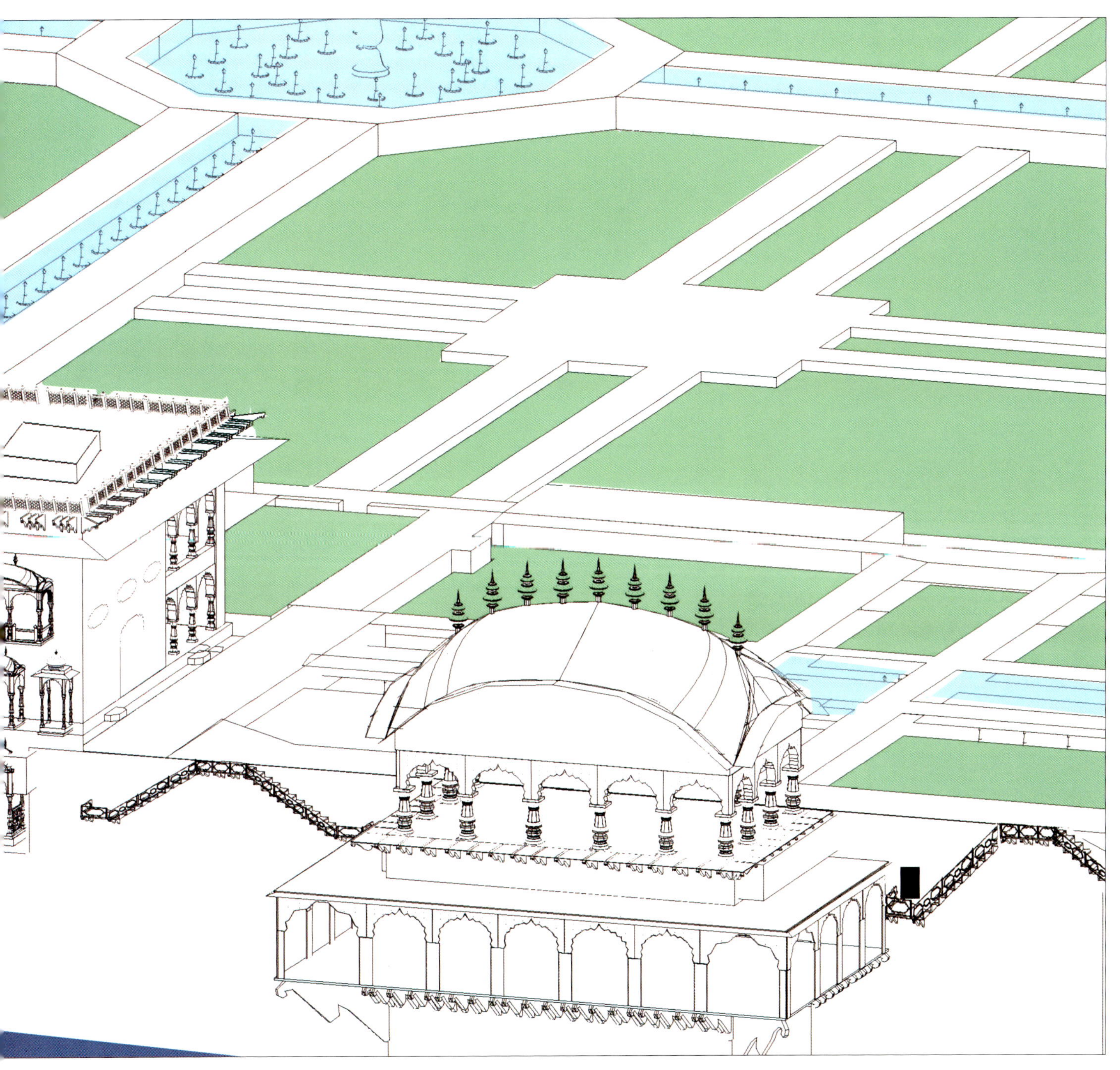

Towards Charbagh

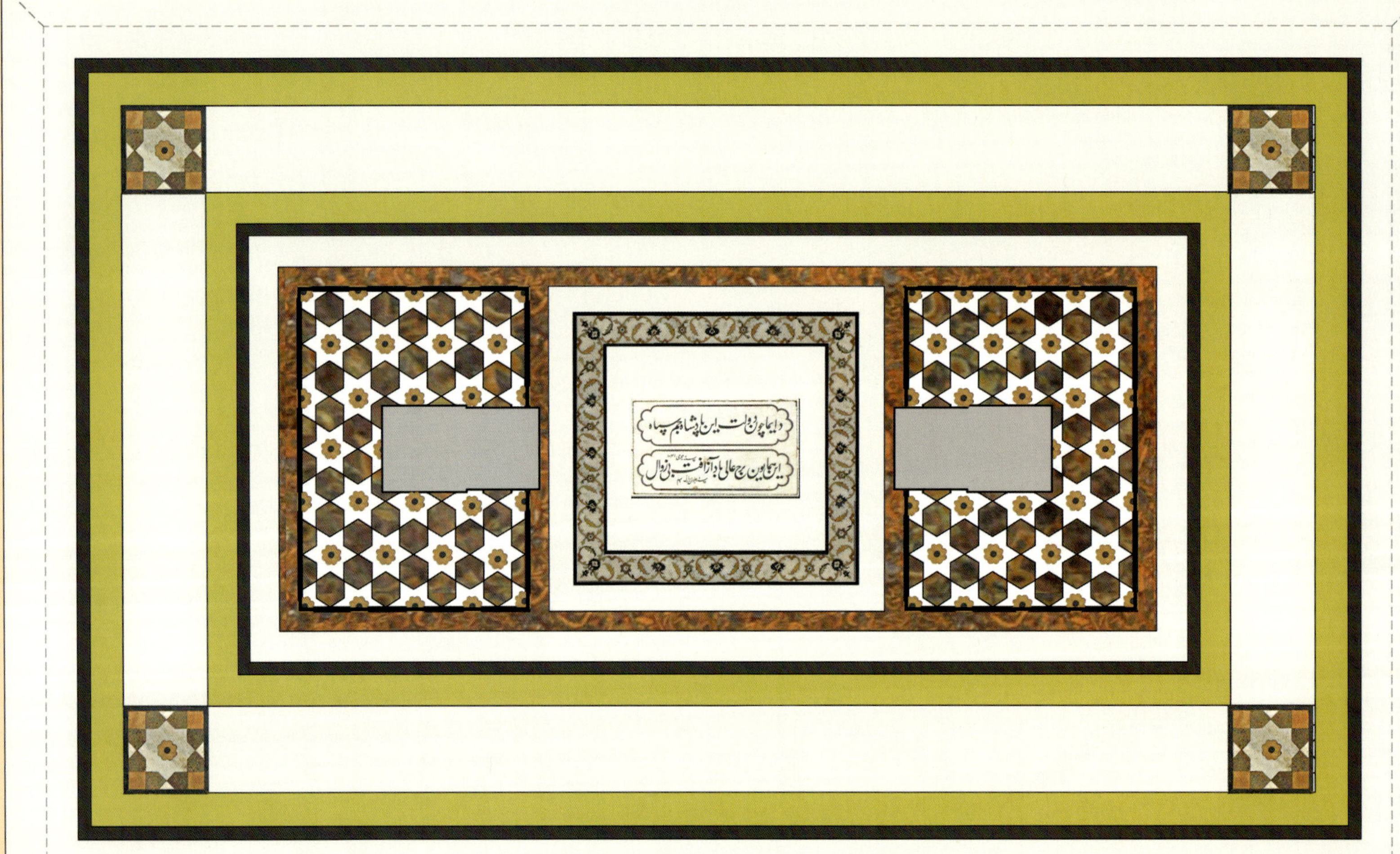

Towards Gopal Bhawan

THE SOLITAIRE HINDOLA

Indians have a natural love for swings. Swings and their use is a significant aspect of many Indian festivals. In north India, Teej, also known as the 'Festival of Swings', marks the advent of the monsoon season. It is a festival which is especially deep-rooted in the culture of Rajasthan and Braj. The festival invokes the image of swings as people hang beautiful swings in their gardens and outside their houses. Teej swings are decorated with colourful and fragrant flowers or even *lehariya* print fabric. In other parts of India too, similar festivals are celebrated during the summer or monsoon months. In Orissa, during Raja Sankranti festival in June, swings are tied under the branches of large trees and unmarried women and young girls enjoy swinging while the male members in the family take care of the household chores. During Onam in Kerala, swings are tied to the branches of trees and beautifully decorated with flowers. In northern Karnataka, it is during the month of *Sravana* that Naga Panchami is celebrated by tying swings.

Perhaps this innate love for swings led to the placement of a free-standing white marble arch at the vantage point of the whole Deeg complex. It has suspended iron hooks which gives this frame the appearance of a swing. On introspection, this is probably the only example of an individual standing marble swing of such a scale present anywhere in India.

An imposing and beautiful structure, also called the *hindola* or 'a free-standing arch', it occupies the prime position on the eastern side of the Gopal Bhawan. This is the major structure which catches the eye apart from the bhawans from all around the Deeg Palace complex. Its central position on the terrace in front of the principal pavilion Gopal Bhawan, along with its

Facing page (Fig. 1): *Layout plan of the* hindola *terrace showing the positioning of the marble arch on a decorative platform*

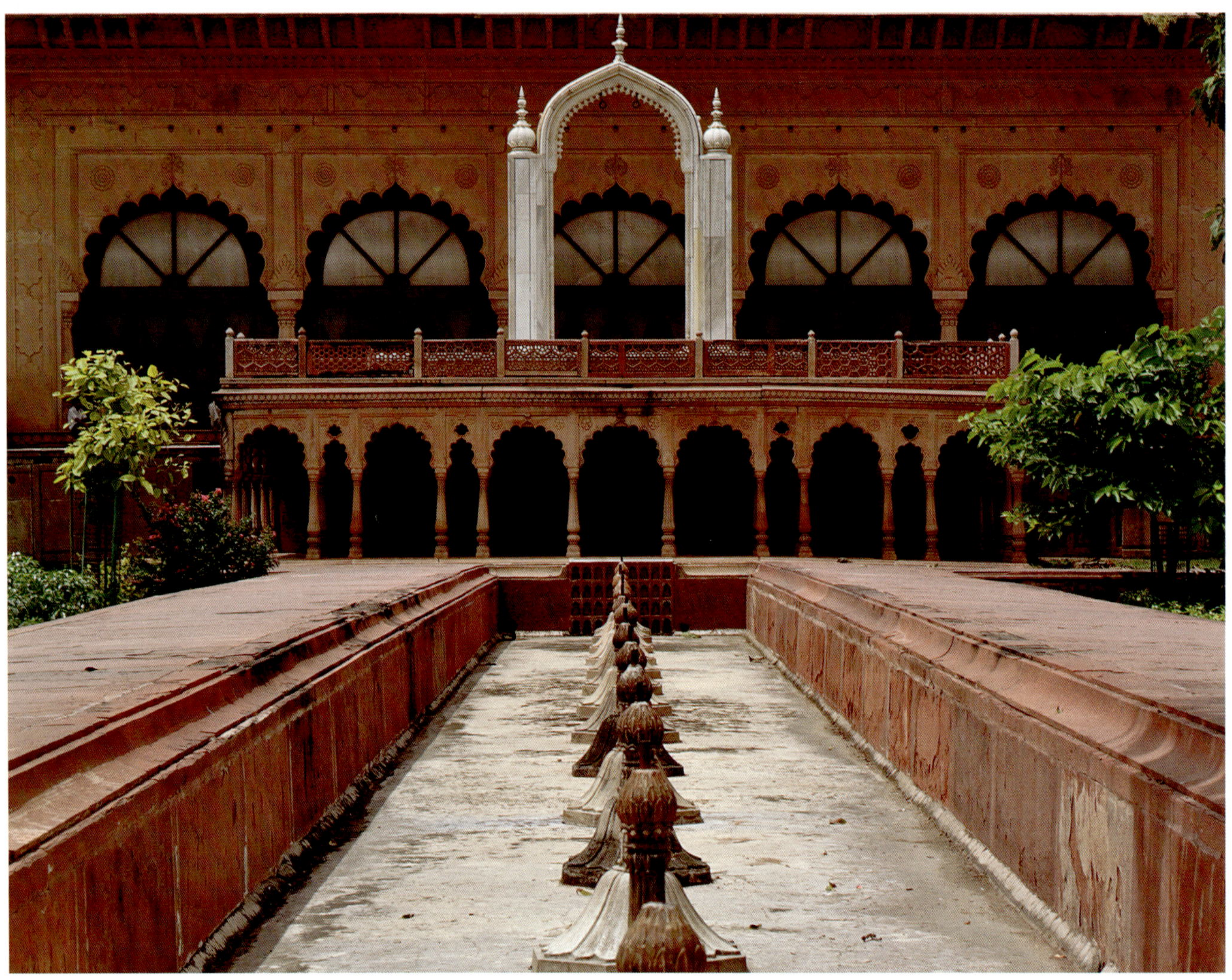

contrasting white colour among pink shades adds to the charm of the swing. The placement is right on the axis which divides the Deeg garden into two parts and connects the Gopal Bhawan to the Keshav Bhawan. The arch has a very commanding appearance, dominating the gardens. The view of the gardens is framed through this arch giving it an impression of a garland on the gardens of Deeg. (Fig. 2)

The *hindola* is positioned on a raised platform in front of the terrace of the Gopal Bhawan which is actually the roof of a small *baradari* built at the Charbagh level. This entire structure is made up of pink sandstone. A similar structure can be seen in front of the northern gardens of the Nand Bhawan. This low-height *baradari* had a dual purpose. First, its roof formed a low-rise platform protruding from the terrace of the Gopal Bhawan into the gardens to offer a dramatic view of the gardens below. Secondly, the *baradari* also served as a recreation pavilion, gracing the starting point of a waterfall over the *chini khanas* for the water channels. The pavilion with its own water spout could have been designed for sitting in the cool shade beside the gardens. (Fig. 3)

The eastern elevation of this beautiful colonnaded *baradari* facing the front garden has a central portion of three-arched openings with two sets of smaller and bigger arches alternating each other on either side, making a total of eleven arches. On the shorter sides of the *baradari* there are five equal arched openings.

Facing page (Fig. 2): *The imposing and beautiful* hindola *or 'a free-standing arch', occupying the prime position on the eastern side of the Gopal Bhawan*

Below (Fig. 3): *The raised platform in front of the terrace of the Gopal Bhawan was actually the roof of a small* baradari *built at the Charbagh level.*

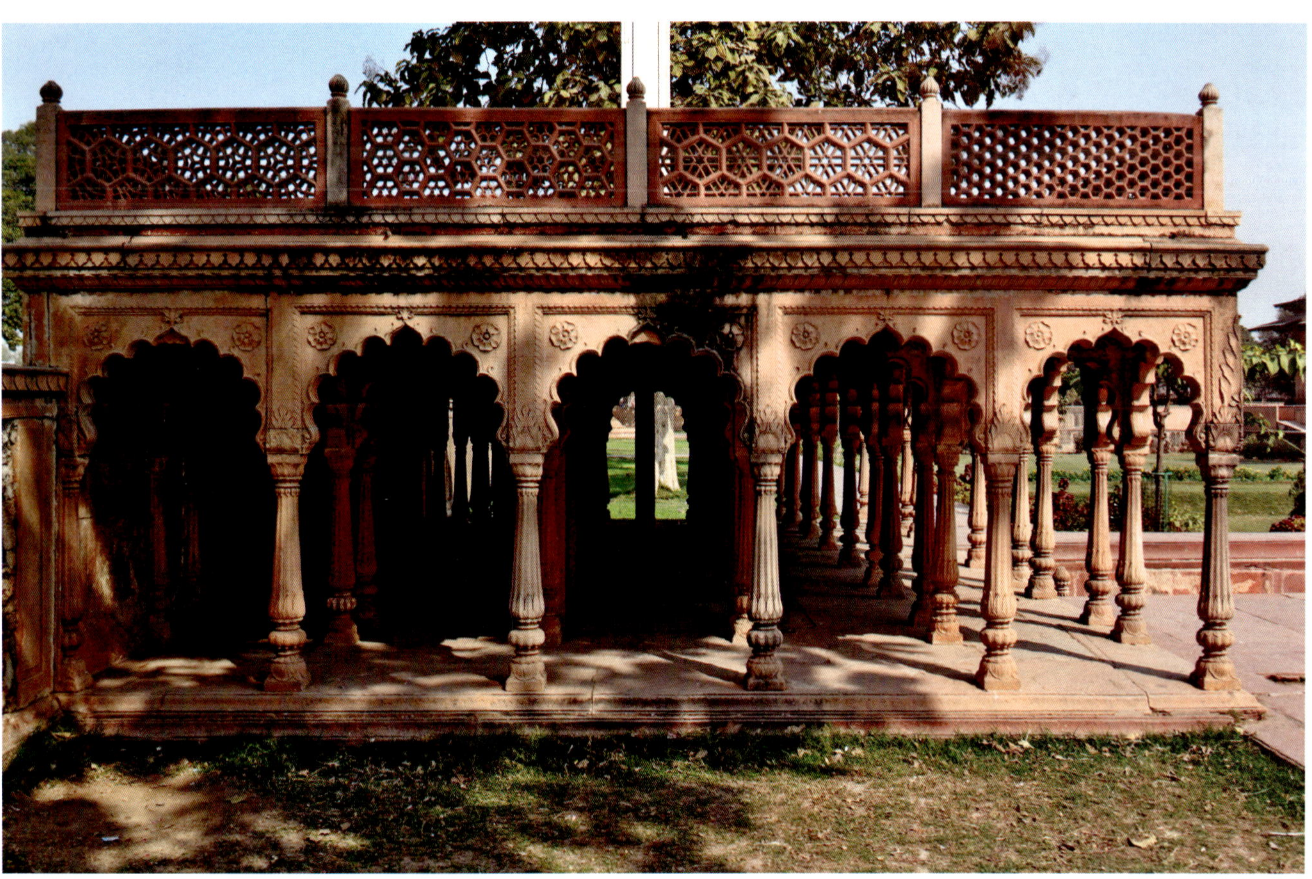

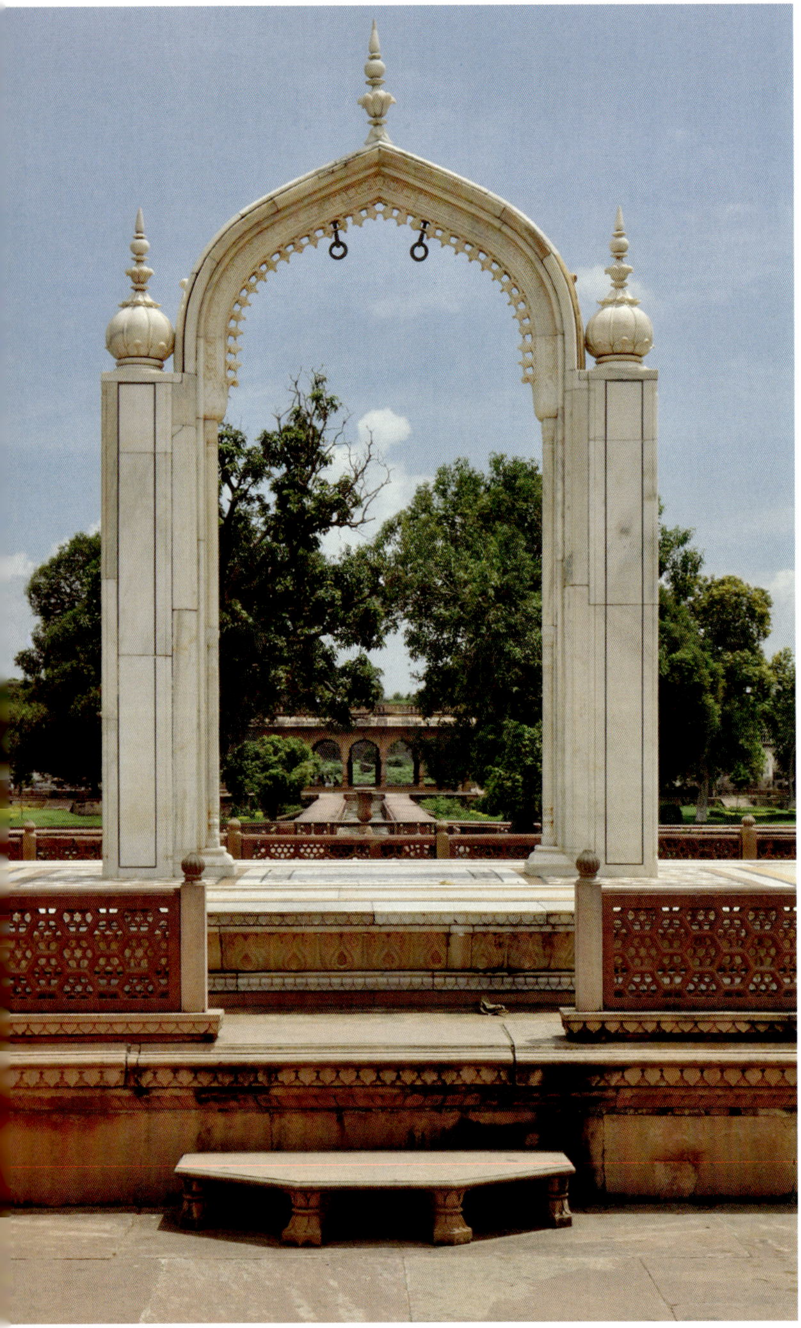

All along these arches run arrayed columns to the alternating arches as shown in the plan. These arched openings comprise of the similar five-cusped arch carved with single lotus medallions on both sides of its spandrels. The arches rest on fluted baluster columns. The centre of this *baradari* was initially empty and might have been used for a fountain, the water from which flowed down the *chini khanas* into the main water channel. Alternatively, it could have been used as a sitting area built with the intention to watch the

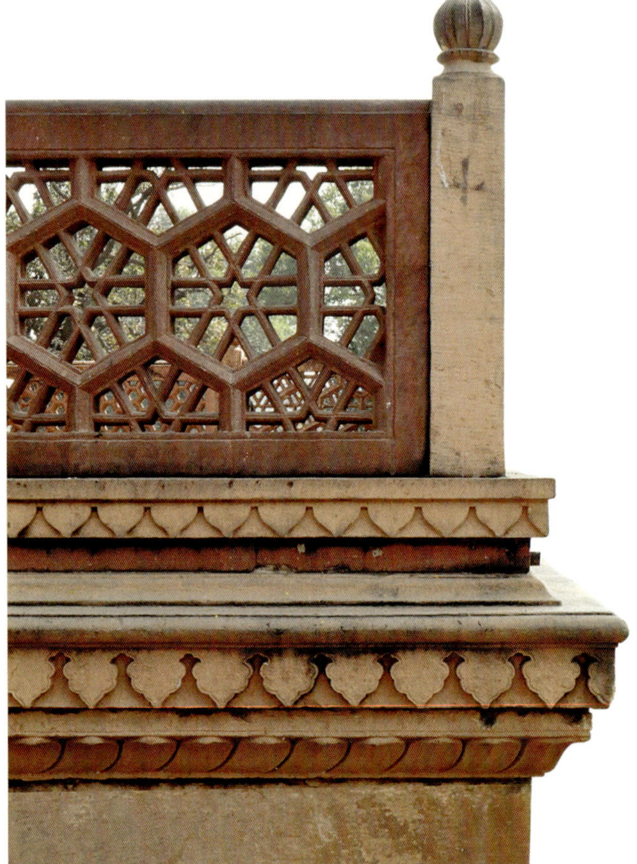

central water channels and fountains. The same centre has now been reinforced with additional plain slabs supported by piers following the geometry of existing arches and columns. This must have been done to bear the added load when the *hindola* was installed over the platform. On analysing the plan one can easily differentiate between the original columns and the new columns added to take the weight of the swing and its platform.

The terrace of the *baradari* is enclosed with parapet *jalis* all around with a single opening to enter the *hindola* terrace. (Fig. 4) All these *jalis* have different patterns and do not follow a fixed symmetry. These red sandstone *jalis* in an otherwise pink monument are in fact a later addition to the whole structure. (Fig. 5) Interestingly, as seen from old photographs of 1900s, these *jalis* were not present. Instead, all along the terrace there can be seen cemented balusters which are absent today.

Inside this enclosure on the terrace of the *baradari*, there is a 17-inch high raised marble podium. The centrally placed podium is shaped in a *cyma recta* profile. (Fig. 6) The platform or podium is made from white

Facing page left (Fig. 4): *The terrace of the* baradari *is enclosed with parapet* jalis *all round with a single opening to enter the* hindola *terrace*

Facing page right (Fig. 5): *The red sandstone* jalis *in an otherwise pink monument*

Below (Fig. 6): *The centrally placed podium is shaped in a* cyma recta *profile and formed the base for the* hindola

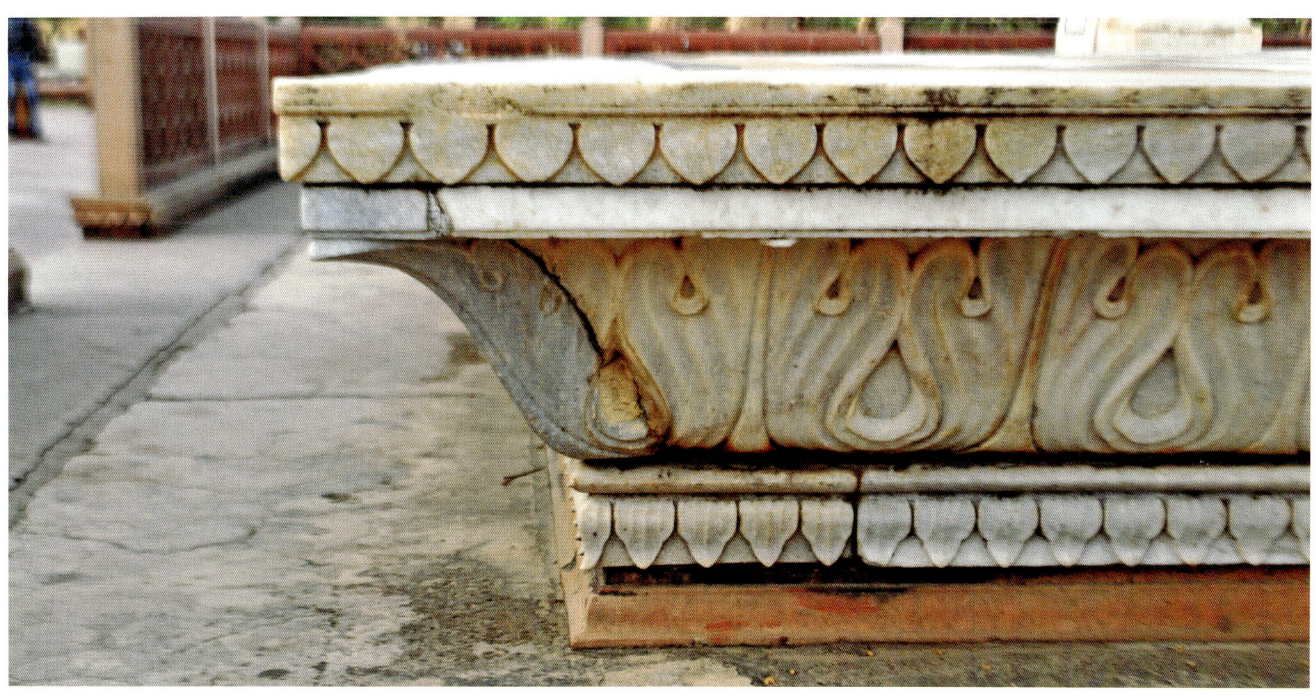

marble with a 240in × 151in rectangular top stone. The ledge of the top plinth and the base stone are carved with inverted pointed leaves. While the leaves on the top are flat carved, the lower leaves are more fragile with ribs. The broad central portion is decorated with tall, carved acanthus leaves. The transaction is achieved with layers of decorative mouldings. The platform becomes 226in × 137in at the base, leaving approximately 63 inches at the top and 70 inches of walkway at the bottom, around the podium.

The top white marble of the podium is finely inlaid with *ajuba*, *abri*, black Belgian and Jaisalmer stones. The geometric pattern and style of these designs resembles closely the ornamentation of Itmad-ud-Daulah's tomb at Agra. Similar designs can also be found on the floor and inside wall panels in the Suraj Bhawan. (Fig. 7)

In the centre of this platform is a plaque which attributes its origin to Shah Jahan. (Fig. 8) It says:

Dayma chun daulat-i ein Badshah-i-Jam Sipah
In Humayun burj-i 'ali bad az afat be-zawal.

Its English translation is:
May the empire of this gem like king remain forever,
And this high, holy burj should not fall prey to any calamity or downfall.

Two years—Sanh Hijri 1041 and Sanh Julus Mubarak 4—are also inscribed. Hijri 1041 is equivalent to AD

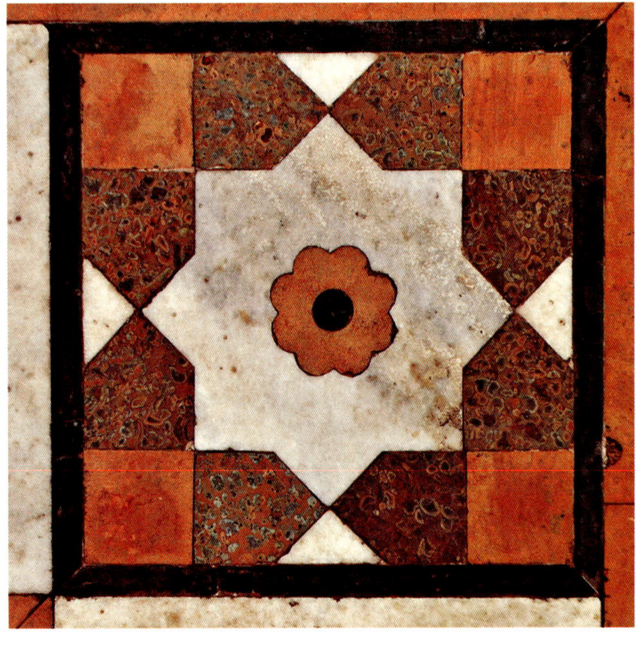

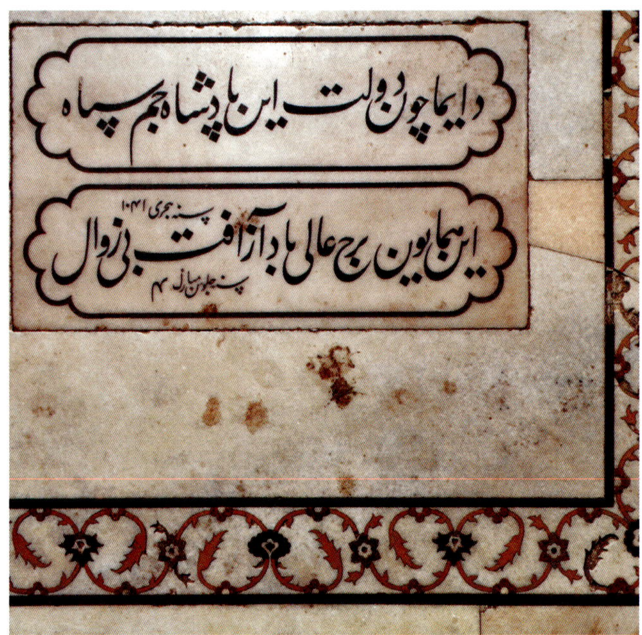

1631 and the second date means the fourth year of crowning. Shah Jahan ascended the throne in AD 1627 and hence the inscription might refer to him.

This articulation and placement shows that the patterns on the top were contrived to hold the white marble floriated pedestals of the *hindola* over the two-line Persian epigraph with its stylised inlaid border set in between. The podium has been designed and planned just to place the arch in a majestic and royal way, like displaying an *objet d'art* in this palace complex.

The *hindola* is an ideally proportioned arch built from lustrous white marble blocks. (Fig. 9) It is an accurate frame from which two iron rings are suspended which held a ceremonial seat. One of the last seats supposedly used by Mrs Indira Gandhi now lies in the Gopal Bhawan Museum. (Fig. 10)

The arch is an elegant Islamic pointed arch standing tall like a *torana* (gateway) for a temple. The arch measures 13.5in × 12.25in at the base which recedes rhythmically with a series of mouldings towards the inner three sides to give rise to a decorative pair of engaged columns on either of the insides. These engaged octagonal delicate pillars are exquisitely carved with chevron pattern at the shaft, bracketed by lotus leaves at the base and capital. (Fig. 11) The double collinear shafts stand tall for the entire

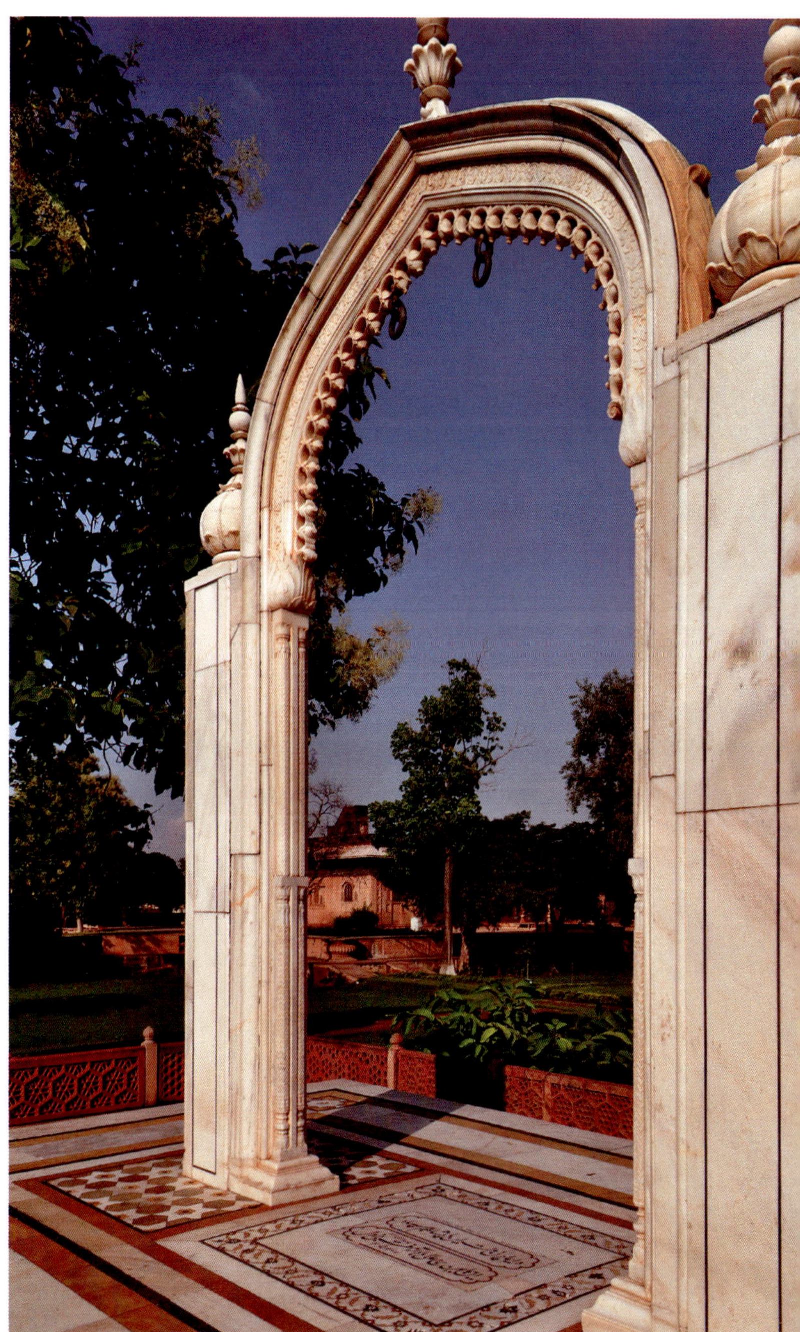

Right (Fig. 9): *The ideally proportioned arch or* hindola *built from lustrous white marble*

Facing page left (Fig. 7): *The top white marble of the podium is finely inlaid with a geometric pattern and style using* ajuba, abri, *black Belgian and Jaisalmer stones*

Facing page right (Fig. 8): *The plaque with the two-line Persian epigraph along with its stylised inlaid border set in between*

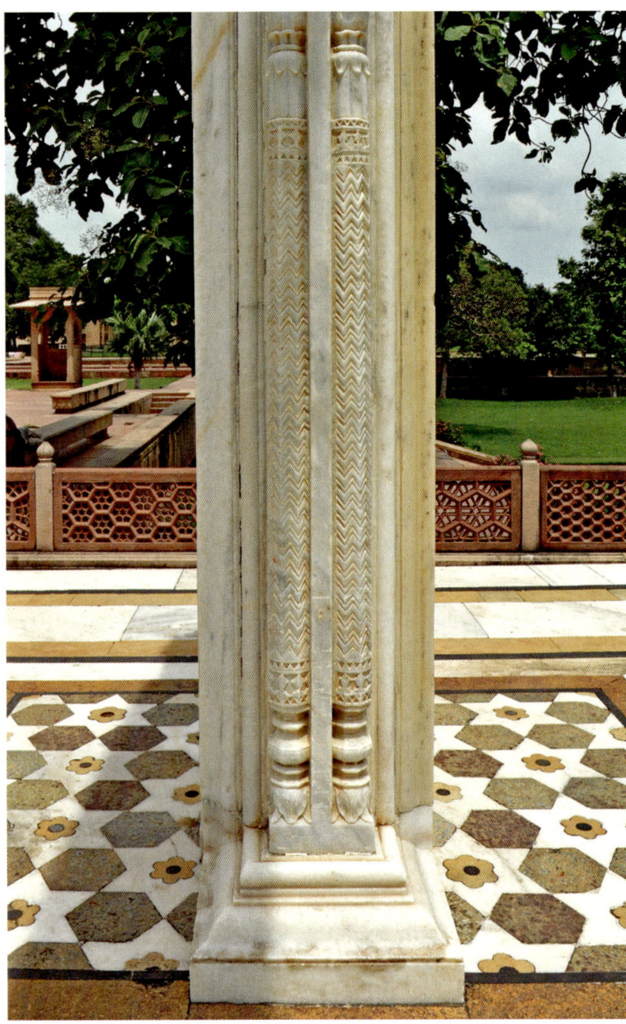

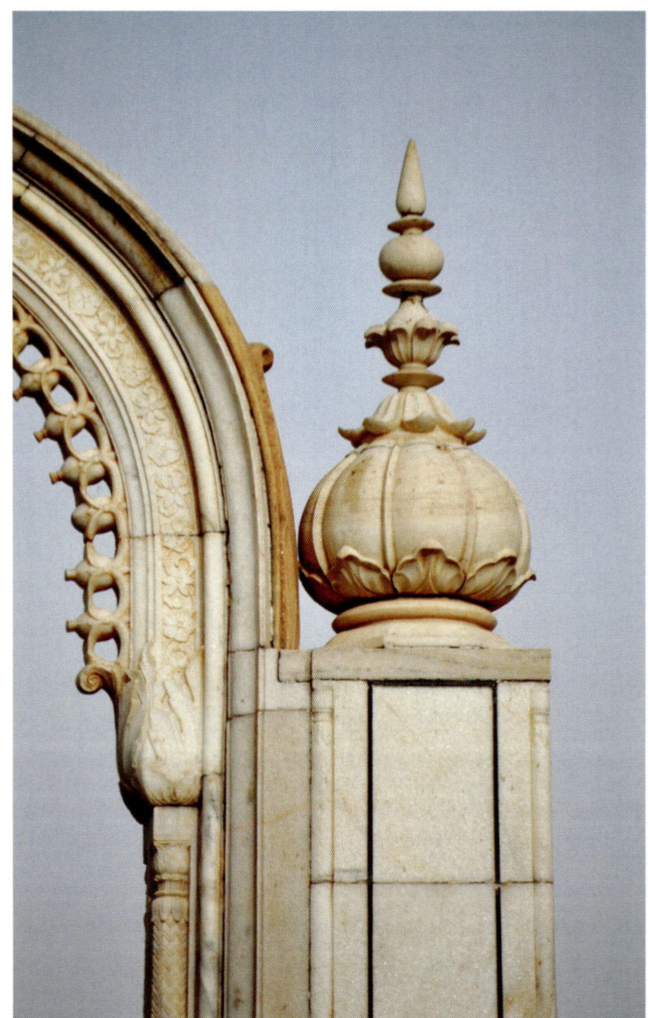

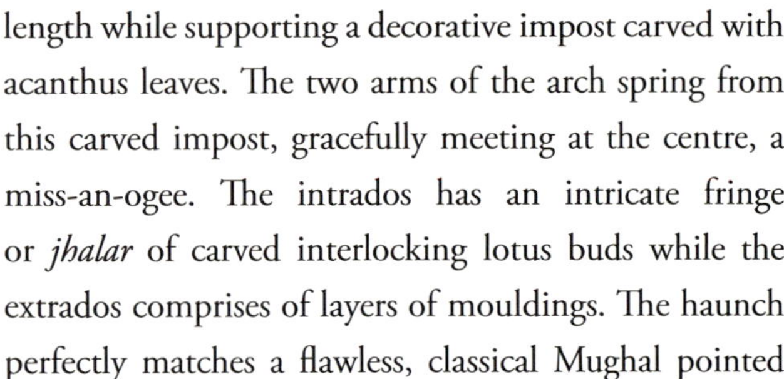

length while supporting a decorative impost carved with acanthus leaves. The two arms of the arch spring from this carved impost, gracefully meeting at the centre, a miss-an-ogee. The intrados has an intricate fringe or *jhalar* of carved interlocking lotus buds while the extrados comprises of layers of mouldings. The haunch perfectly matches a flawless, classical Mughal pointed arch curve. The voussoir facing the Gopal Mahal is carved with fine *chikankari* floral pattern of low relief similar to the one at Itmad-ud-Daulah's tomb. (Fig. 12) The opposite face has a disparate Ottoman geometric scroll. (Fig. 13)

The arch is buttressed on either side by strong and consolidated 14in × 14in marble piers sporting

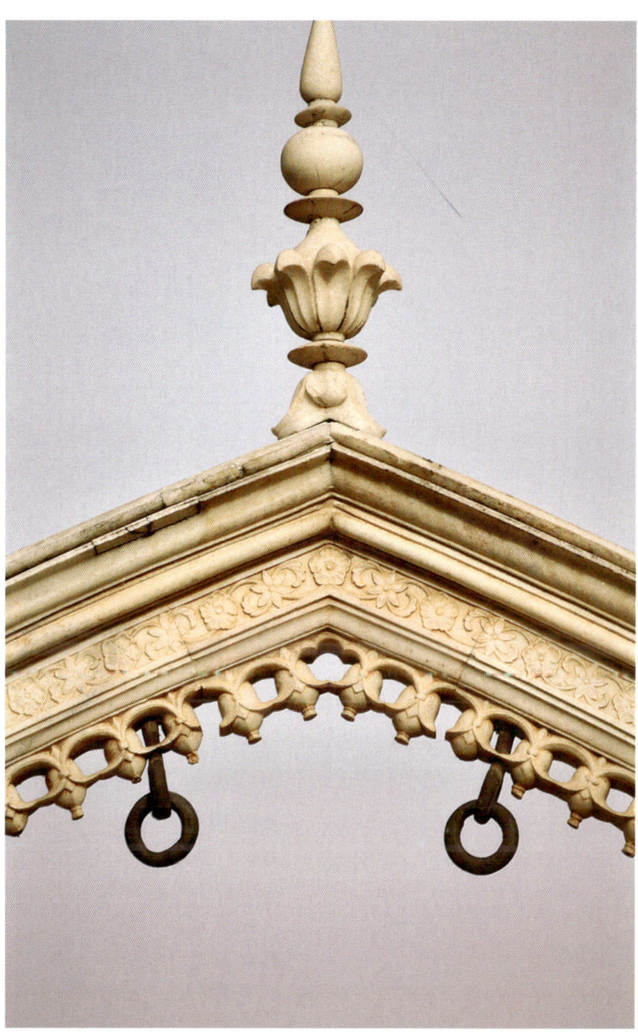

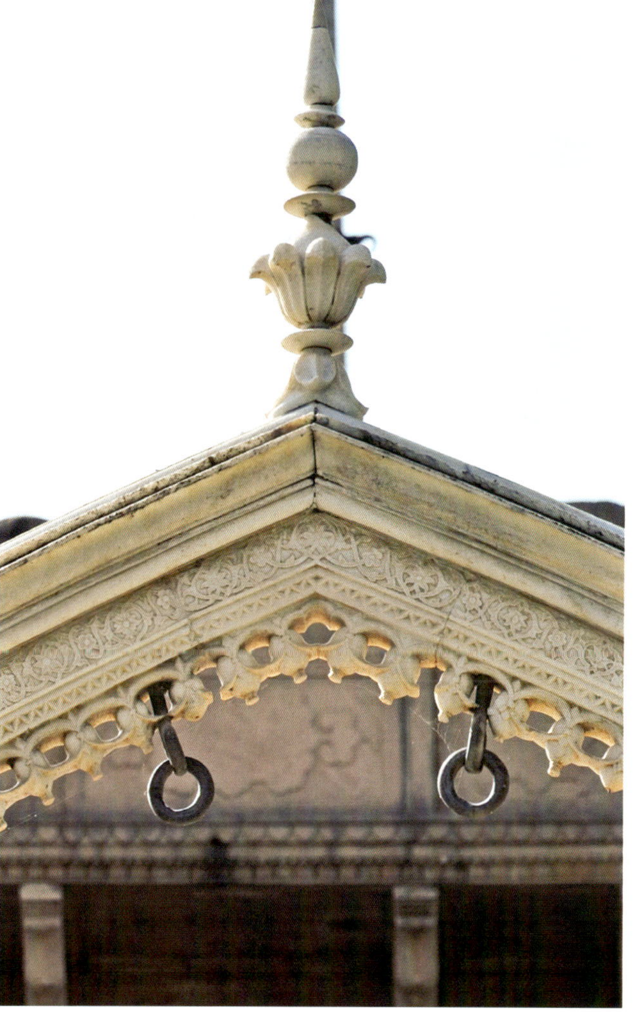

Above (Fig. 13): *The Ottoman geometric scroll carving on the other side of the arch*

Above left (Fig. 12): Chikankari *floral pattern of low relief similar to the one at Itmad-ud-Daulah's tomb*

Facing page right (Fig. 14): *The arch of the* hindola *buttressed on either side by marble piers sporting melon-shaped finials*

Facing page left (Fig. 11): *The engaged octagonal delicate pillars exquisitely carved with chevron pattern at the shaft, bracketed by lotus leaves at the base and capital*

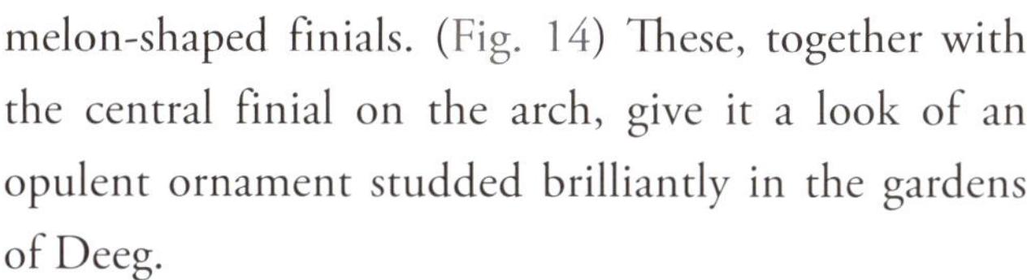

melon-shaped finials. (Fig. 14) These, together with the central finial on the arch, give it a look of an opulent ornament studded brilliantly in the gardens of Deeg.

This impeccable placement of the marble archway together with an Islamic inlay on the marble podium and its bona fide Persian inscription demonstrates

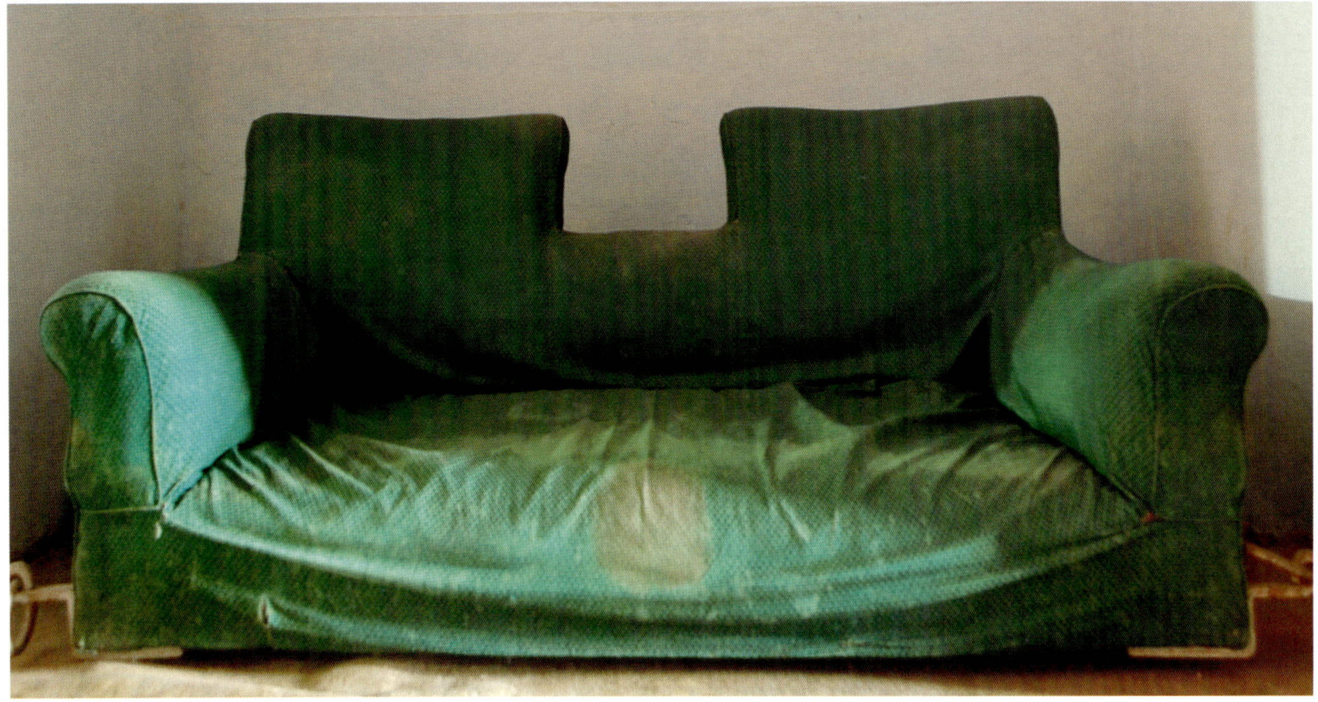

Above (Fig. 10): *One of the last seats supposedly used by Mrs Indira Gandhi now lies in the Gopal Bhawan Museum*

Facing page left (Fig. 15): *A view of the Charbagh from the small* baradari *built in front of the Gopal Bhawan*

Facing page right (Fig. 16): *A view of the* hindola *from the Charbagh with the Gopal Bhawan in the backdrop*

the straightforward attitude of the Jat rulers who very staunchly appreciated the *hindola* without laying any false claims and credits.

Historians differ as regards the original location of the arch. According to M.C. Joshi, the swing was removed from the Phulbari Palace at Weir near Bayana and set up in the present position sometime during the third quarter of the 19th century. But there is also a view among many historians who consider this to be the *jharokha darshan* of Shah Jahan as the Persian date AH 1041 (AD 1631) mentioned on the plaque corresponds to the fourth year of Shah Jahan's rule. This might be true to some extent since there is record of the Jats plundering the Agra and Delhi forts.

One viewpoint can be that this independent arch was probably a gateway and may have been converted into a swing by the Jats. It was rarely used as a swing though, as even the old photographs show the structure without any seat. We do not see any reference in history or in essays describing the use of the arch as a swing. It might have been used only for ceremonial purposes or that the arch was converted to a swing in the name of the deity Krishna. The entire region revolves around

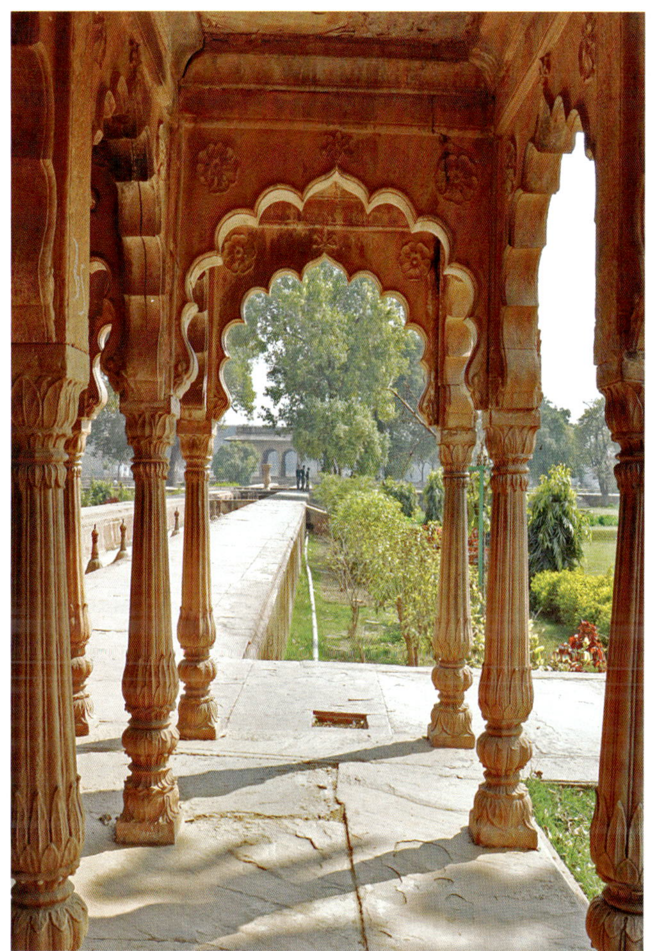

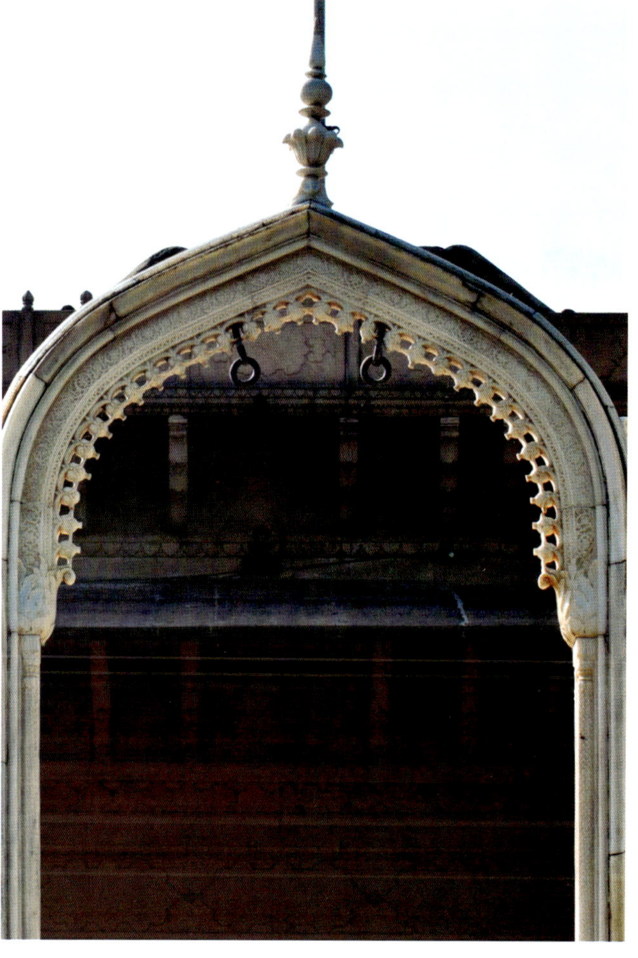

the Krishna legacy and practically every royal Rajput household had an elaborate swing (wooden) to celebrate Krishna Janmashtami, when the statue of baby Krishna is put in a swing and made to swing. It is possible that it was used for presiding deities till maybe the customs were changed after wars, with the swing not being used or just used for rare occasions.

Whatever be the origin of the swing, it is clear that the Jat builders provided the ideal setting for this 'jewel' by providing the 'crown' in the form of such a beautiful setting, at such an eminent point.

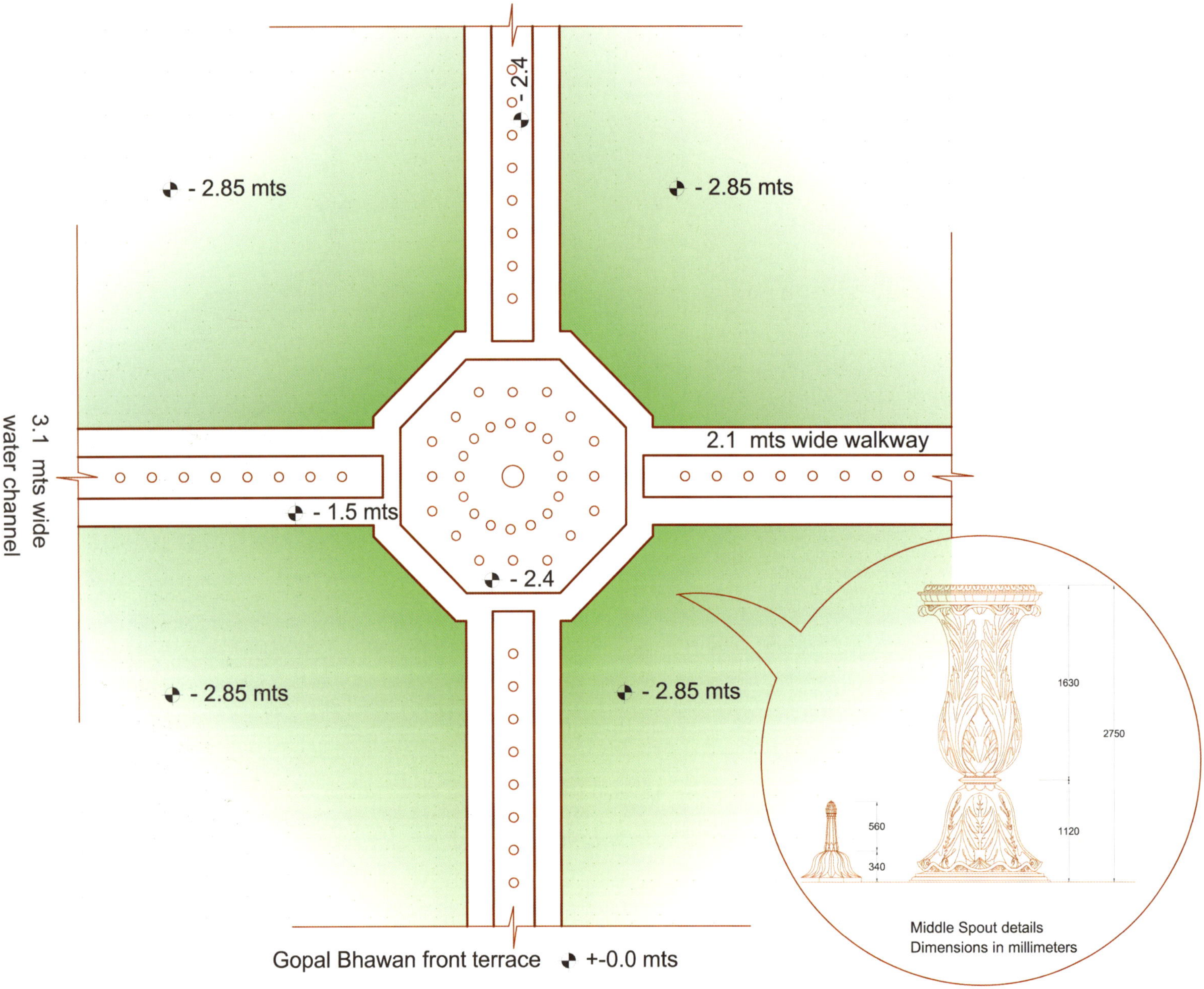

- 2.4

- 2.85 mts

- 2.85 mts

3.1 mts wide water channel

2.1 mts wide walkway

- 1.5 mts

- 2.4

- 2.85 mts

- 2.85 mts

1630

2750

560

1120

340

Middle Spout details
Dimensions in millimeters

Gopal Bhawan front terrace +-0.0 mts

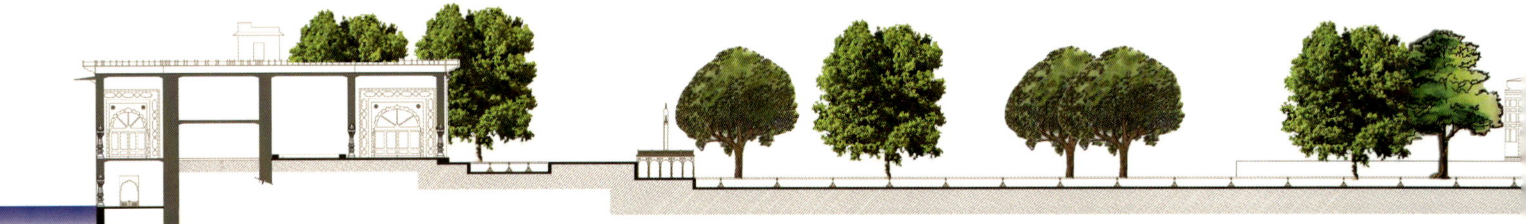

THE ALLURING BAGHS

WATER GARDENS AND THEIR FEATURES

The journey through the architecture of the Deeg Palace cannot be complete without experiencing the gardens and its landscape, which weave the concept of love in the months of monsoon all over the complex. Dazzling fountains, over 900 in number, which played with Holi inspired colours; huge channels which were like swimming pools; thunder palaces; the whole complex was a dream palace which could make anyone's fantasy come true. It was a lovely retreat where the king could spend time with his concubines playing Holi almost every day.

The layout of the Deeg gardens is based on the strict formality of the Mughal horticultural plan known as the Charbagh. (Fig. 2) Series of Charbaghs have been created all along the complex, connecting various axes and buildings with one principal, central, sunken garden. The formality, geometry and similarity were extended all around to form the basis of the layout of each and every landscape element including fountains, cascades and water channels. Its large pavilions and gardens are laid out, as Fergusson remarks, 'With a regularity which would satisfy the most fastidious renaissance architect.' Beyond doubt, this lovely garden palace is Suraj Mal's fairy creation at its best.

The primary terraces all along the Deeg complex are paved with the same pink Bansi Paharpur sandstone as used in the elevation of the buildings. All of these are almost at the same level throughout the complex and carry the major palaces or bhawans. The gardens in turn are sunken with raised walkways. Some of the

Facing page (Fig. 1a): *Layout plan of the Charbagh gardens*

Below (Fig. 1b): *Section view of the Charbagh gardens with the Gopal Bhawan on the left, the Keshav Bhawan on the right and the Nand Bhawan in between*

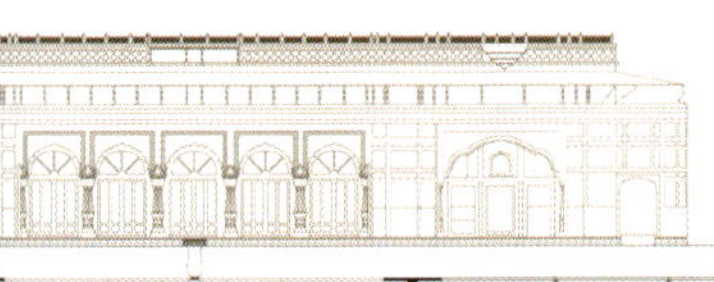
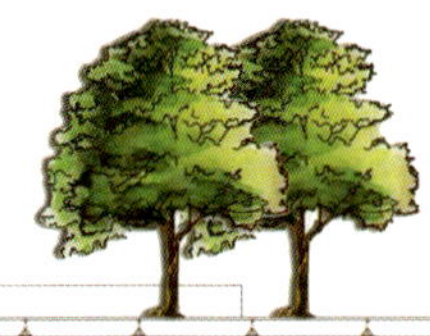
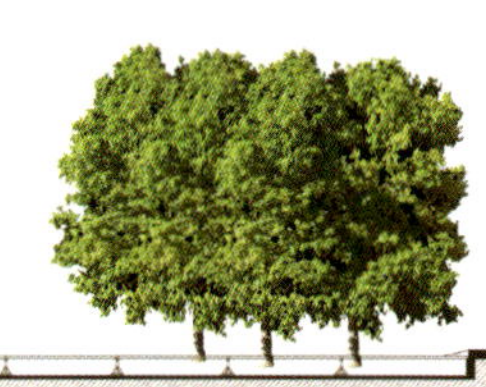
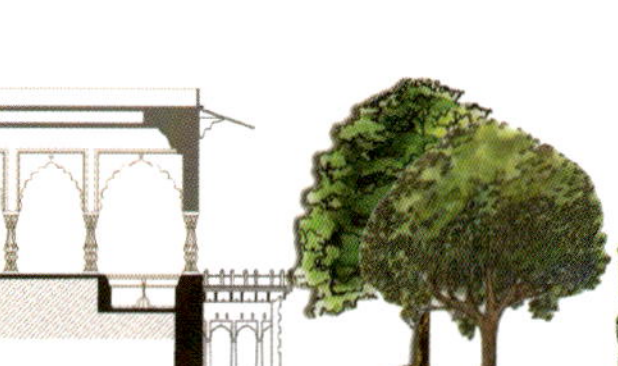

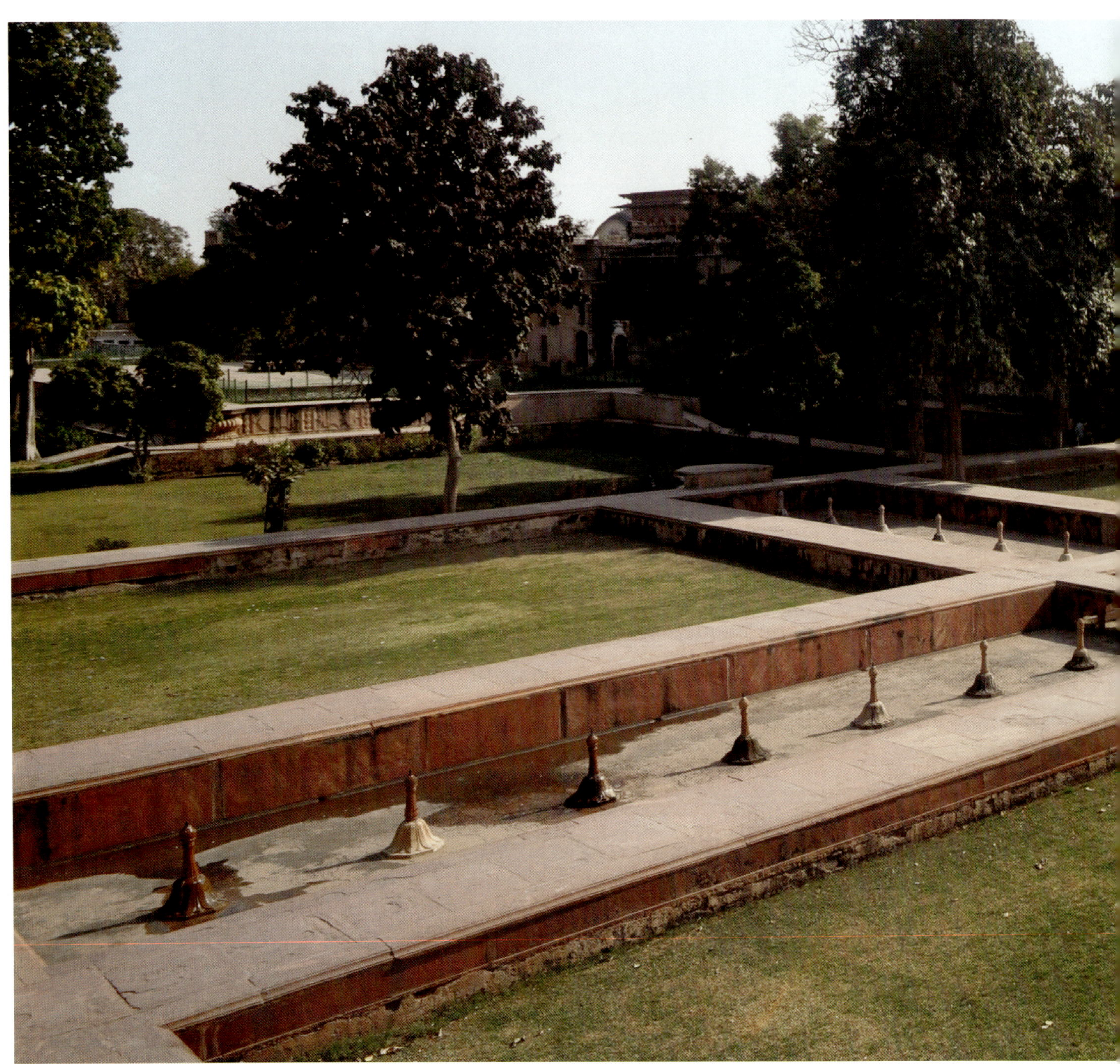

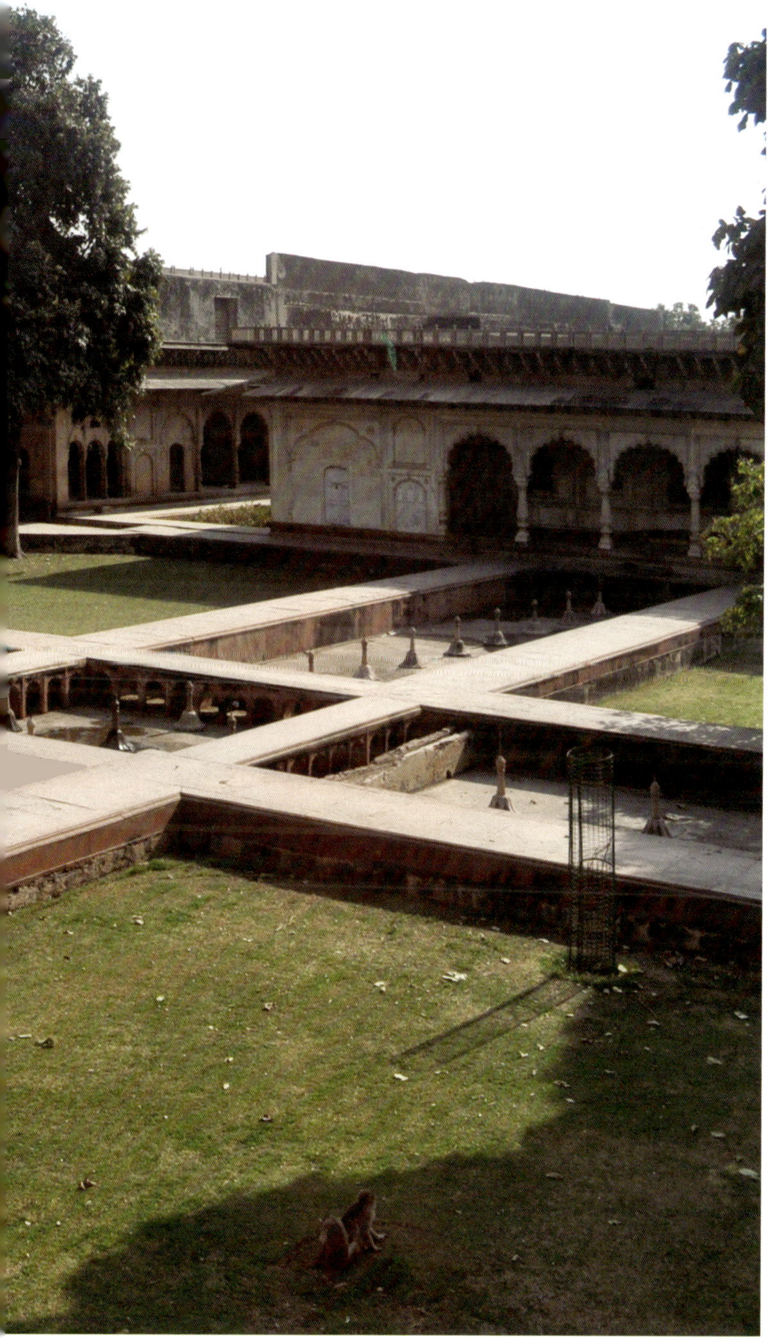

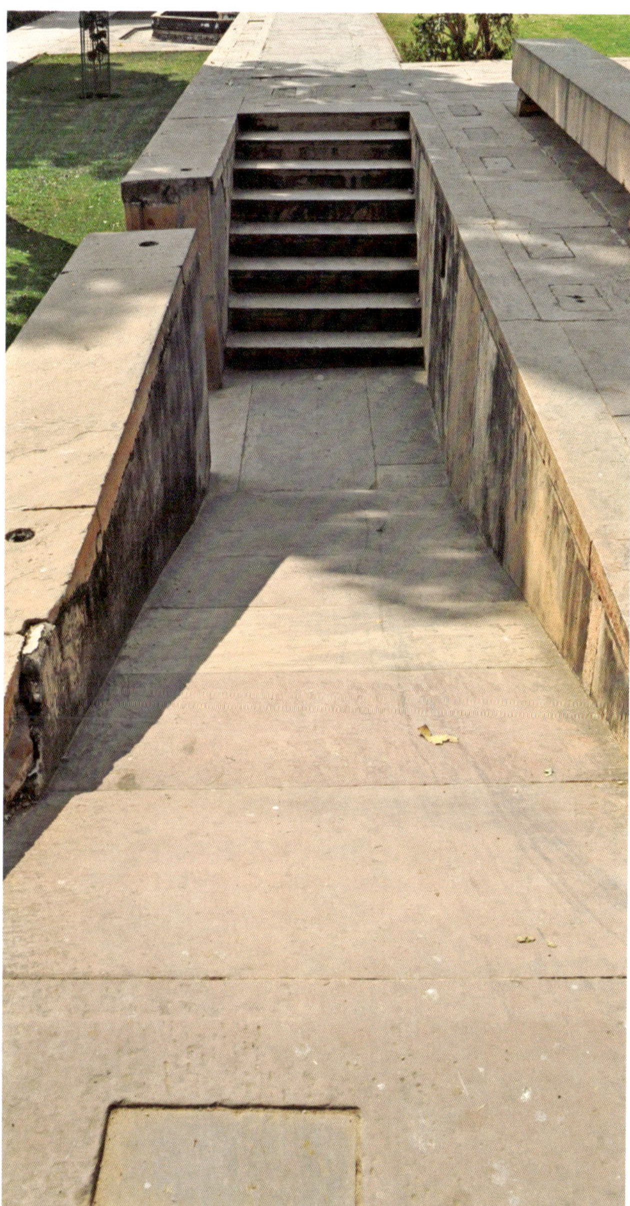

Above (Fig. 4): *On one side of the cloaked entrance is a ramp facing the staircase*

Left (Fig. 2): *A canonical Charbagh formed by wide water channels with arcades supporting the small crossover bridges*

walkways are on either side forming a water channel in between. The floor of the water channel is at the same level as the garden, perhaps to use the drained water for irrigation. The access to the central gardens from the terraces is via well-expressed and cloaked two-sided staircases, in front of each bhawan, within the plinth. (Fig. 3) Foresightedly, instead of building a staircase on opposite sides as in case of the Mughals, a ramp was built on one side, possibly to show consideration for challenged people and for carts or animals. (Fig. 4) One can also see here the use of iron clamps and hooks to bind the retaining stone walls of the stairs. (Fig. 5)

As rightly pointed out by M.C. Joshi, all the flower parterres are deep-set, giving the garden a sunken appearance because of the fact that the vegetation proposed was much thicker as opposed to the Mughal plantations. The Jats probably preferred a vegetation style more like a forest with thick trees rather than a planned shrubbery. Perhaps the entire landscape was envisaged on the lines of an Indian moonlit forest.

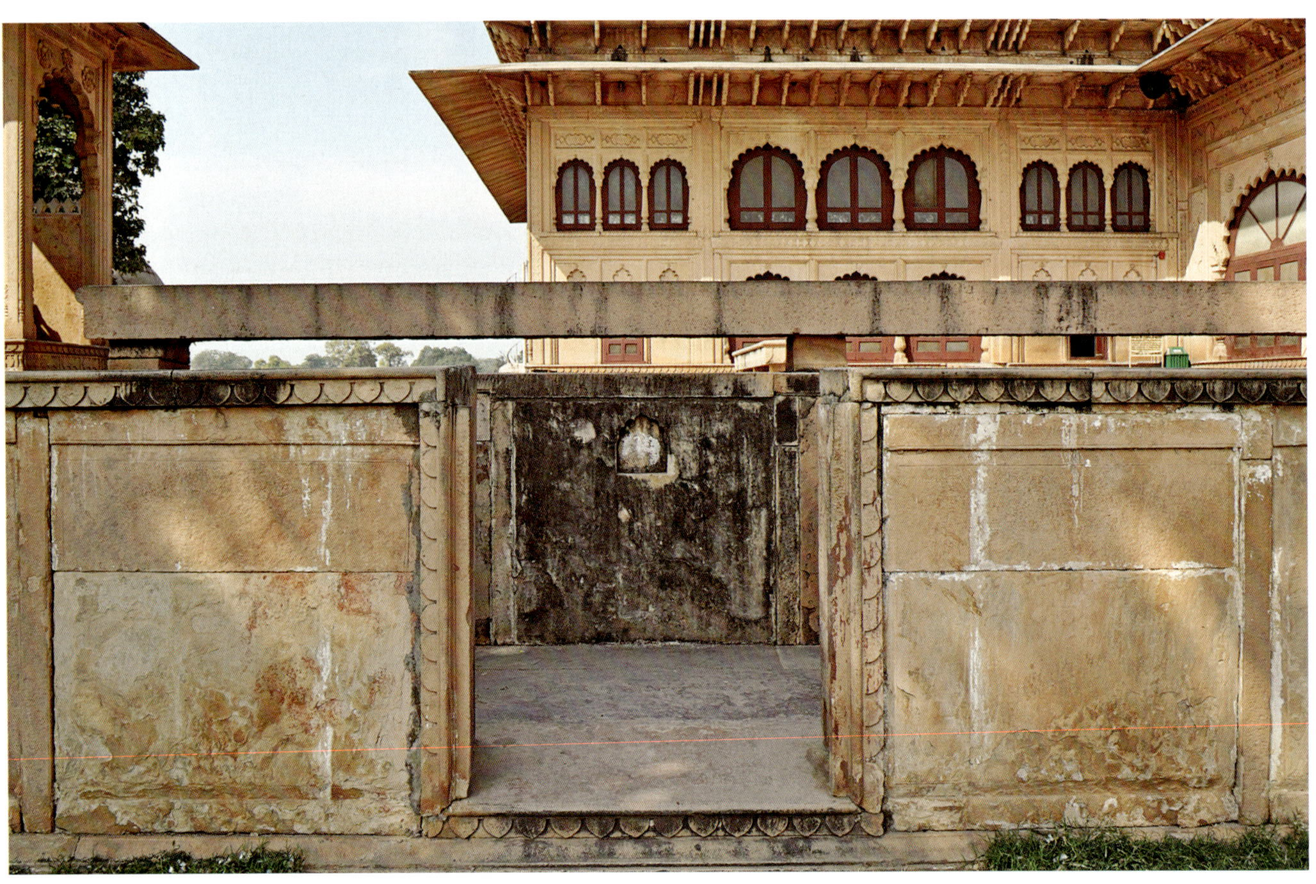

Some old photographs from the British Library also seem to suggest a thick and rough plantation. The stone-edged flower beds with ornate carvings on the sides, very common and illustrative of Mughal gardens, are conspicuous by their absence in Deeg. These geometric flower beds were used to skirt the green parterres in most of the later Mughal gardens.

The Deeg gardens have a large number of water devices and elements to bring Suraj Mal's stupendous delusions into veracity. All through the garden are strewn an assortment of fountain spouts, water channels, *chini khanas*, mazes, waterfalls, cascades and carved elements acting as sculpture fountains. Yet, all of these are bound together in a cohesive setup producing the overall effect of an extraordinary hydrodynamic reverie.

Some of the water channels in Deeg are as deep as 3 feet and as wide as 10 feet, which is a first in the history of gardens. The first aqueducts created by Babur at Dholpur were just 5-6 inches wide and 2-3 inches deep. This leads us to conclude that the channels could also have been used for swimming or as splash pools. It also shows that the obsession of the Jat rulers with water was manyfold than that of Babur.

In fact, each palace is characterised by a trough built in front of its approach or forecourt to give a sense of an entranceway. It also served well during the summers by cooling the breeze blowing into the palace. Also, visually these pools were valuable as the reflection of the bhawan in their waters gave an illusion of height to these otherwise low-height pavilions (Fig. 6). These

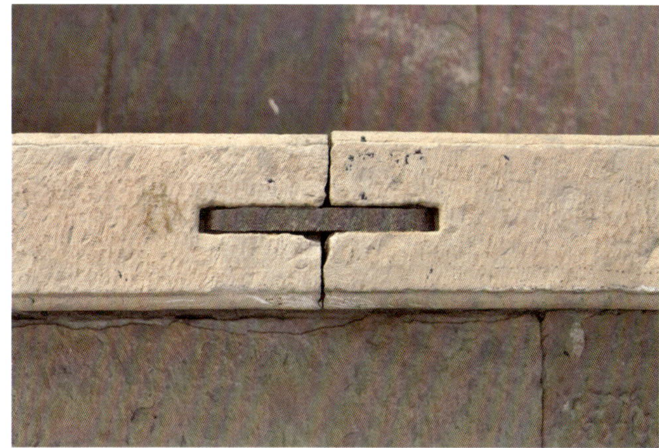

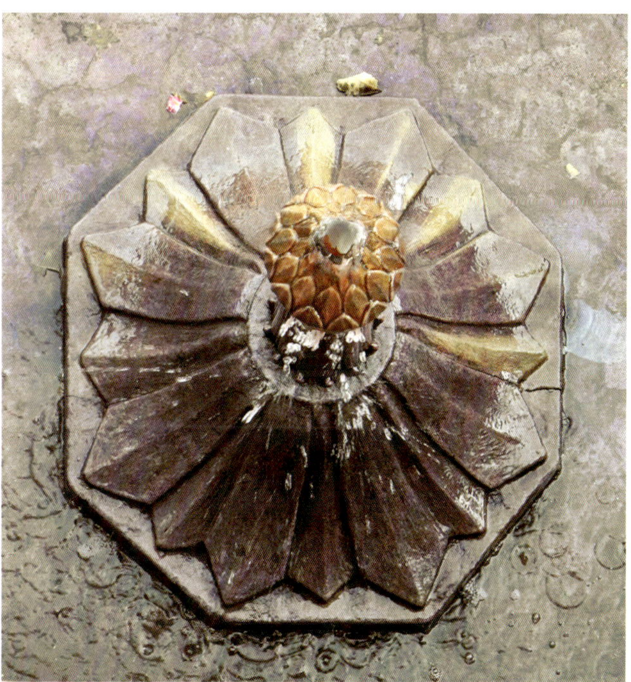

Above (Fig. 8): *Paradigmatic pattern of a carved floricomous fountain spout with a lotus bud and octagonal base (top view)*

Top (Fig. 5): *Iron clamping of parapets and stairs are a prevalent phenomenon in the architecture at Deeg Palace*

Facing page (Fig. 3): *Cloaked two-sided entrance to the plinth from the gardens*

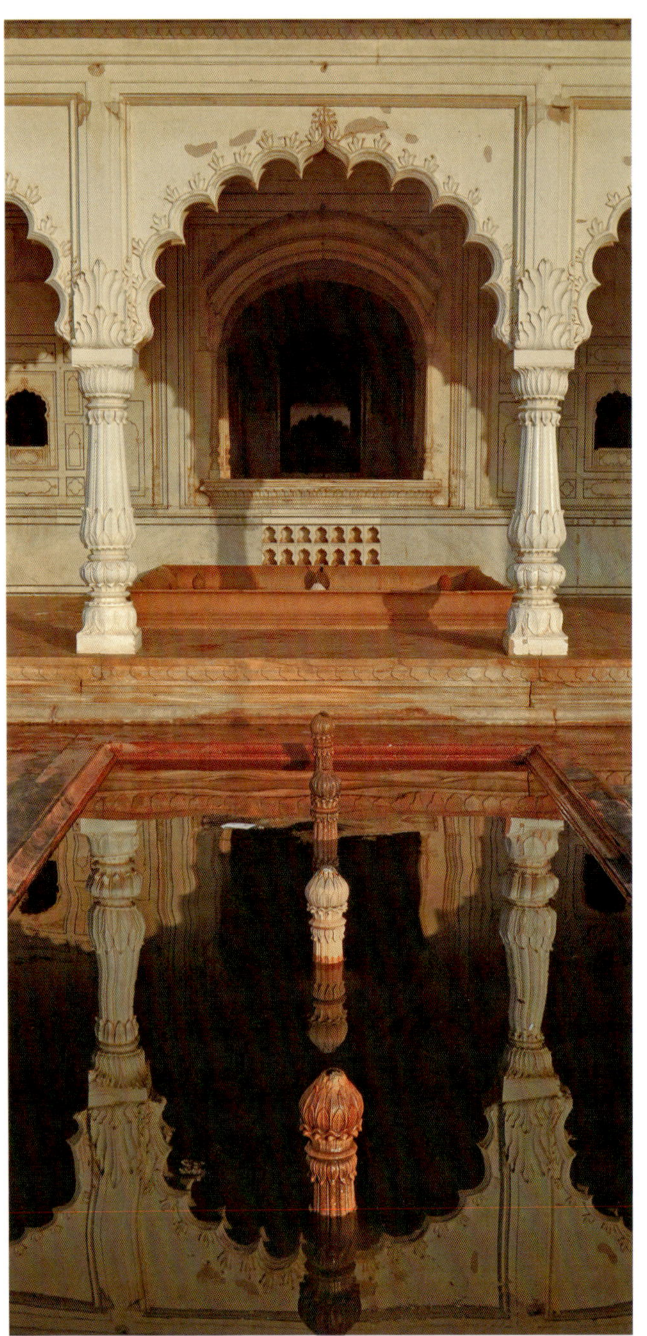

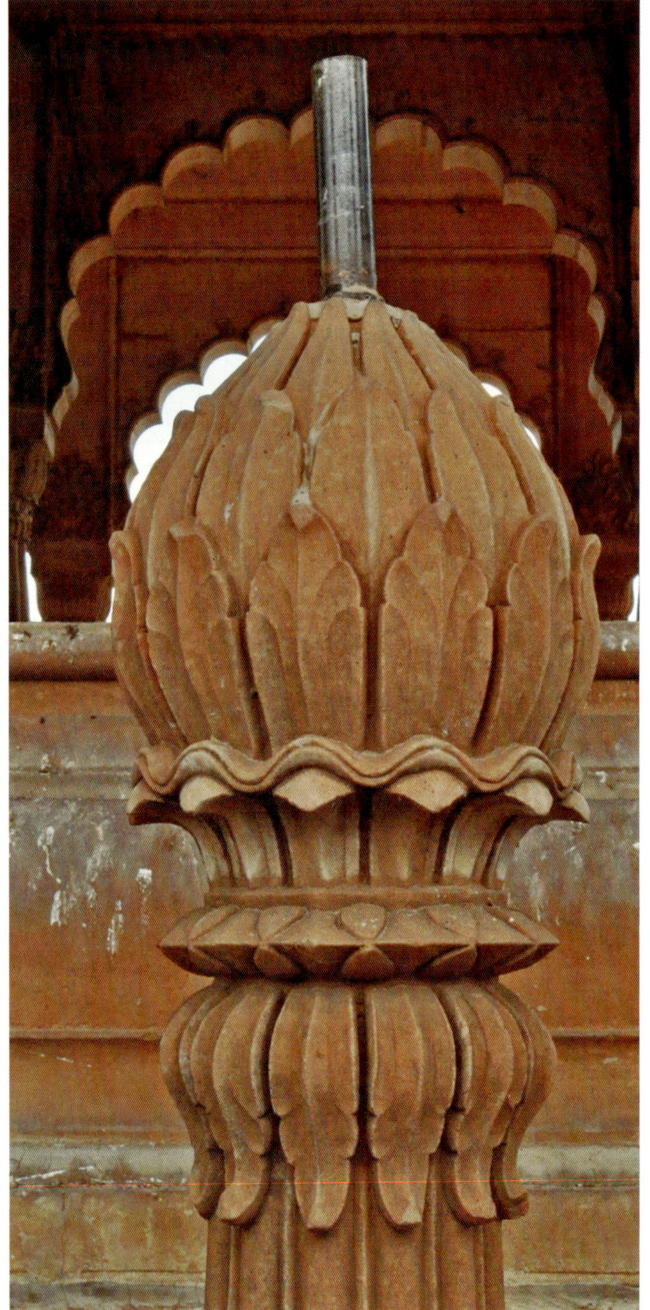

tanks were also studded with spouts in a geometric layout. Especially mentionable is the tank in front of the Nand Bhawan that resembles a modern-day swimming pool with varying depth, the steps of which remind us of the lotus edgings devised by Babur in Dholpur and used extensively by the Mughals throughout.

The fountain spouts in the different channels are all similar in design and are very typical of the Deeg Palace. (Fig. 7) Most of them have sculptured 'floricomous' elongated bodies similar in pattern to the pillars of many of the bhawans. The designs are based on the patterns of leaves for the base and flower buds for the floret spout head. The foundation of these fountain spouts comprises of an octagonal platform with a bell-shaped flaring base of carved petals from which props a fluted stone shaft. This upright statuesque shaft holds a delicately carved lotus bud spout. (Fig. 8)

The main Charbagh is the central sunken garden. This stellar Charbagh has four main plots divided by as many water canals running along cardinal axes, linking the Gopal Bhawan to the Keshav Bhawan and the Nand Bhawan to the Kishan Bhawan. The canals have raised walkways on either of their sides. (Fig. 9) These four plots were further divided into four each, making a total of sixteen parterres by means of walkways, marked by a central tree at their intersection which is apparent

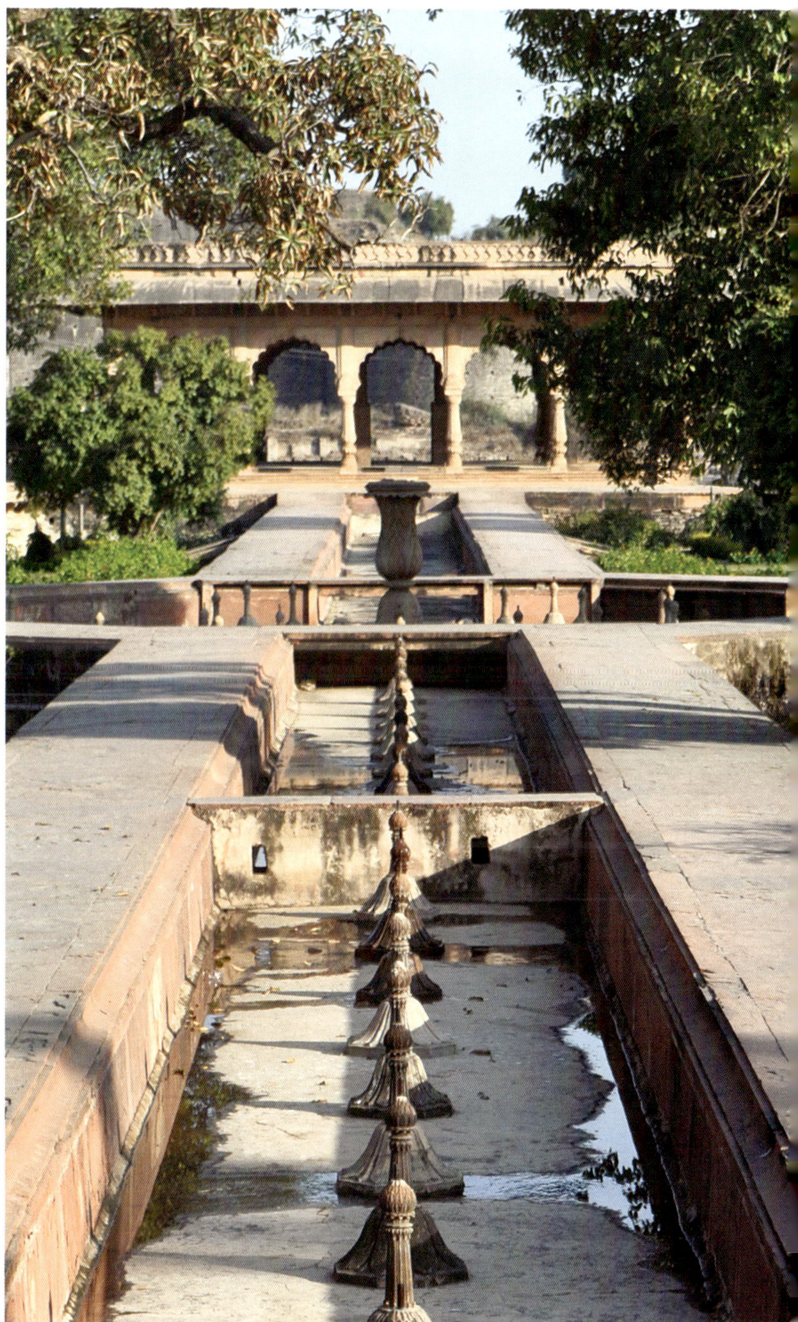

Right (Fig. 9): *Main central axis highlighted by a wide water channel leading from the* hindola *towards the Keshav Bhawan with walkways on either side*

Facing page left (Fig. 6): *Recurring reflections of built forms in the pool creates visual delights*

Facing page right (Fig. 7): *Detail of a water spout*

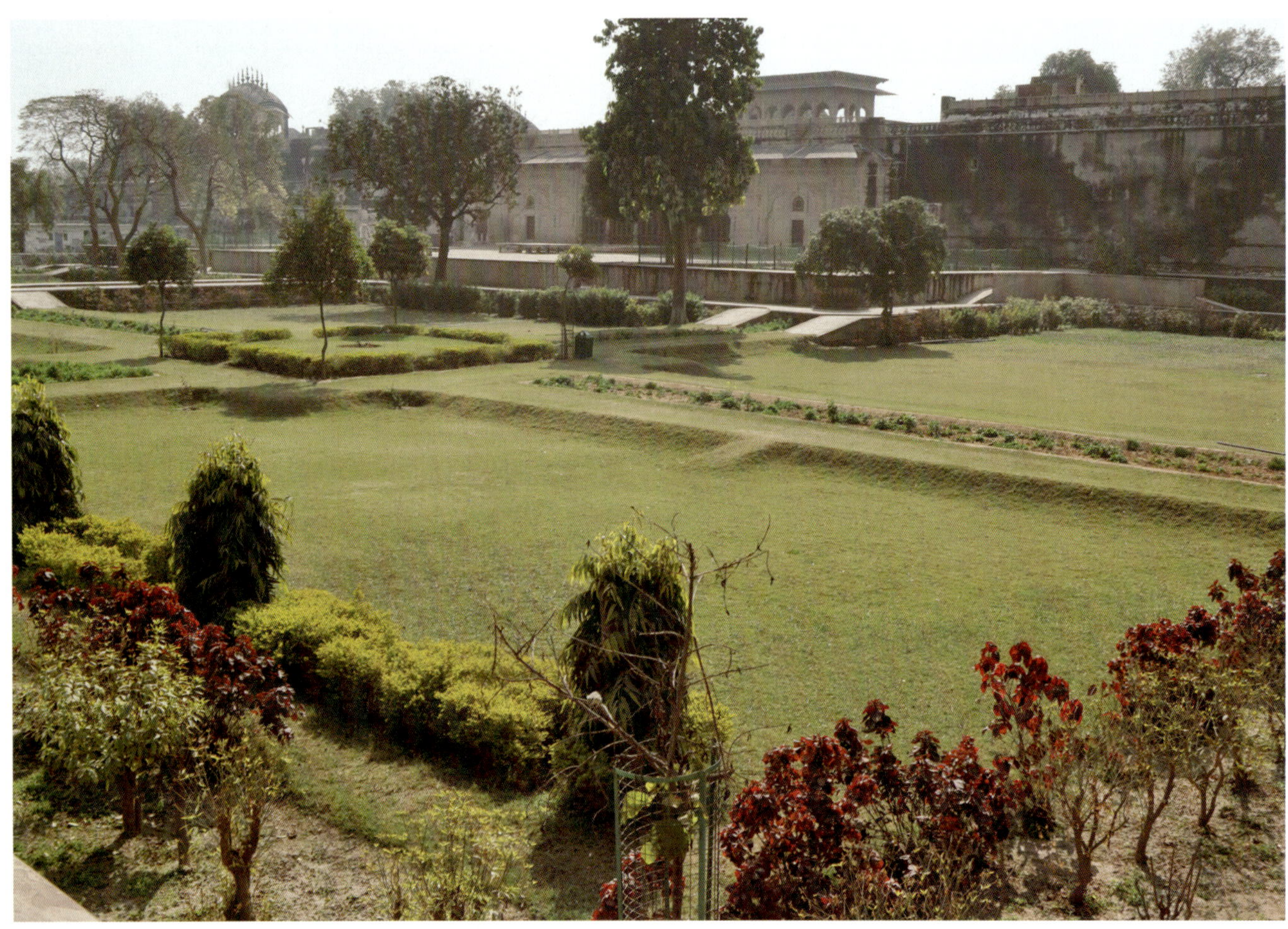

in old pictures. Remnants of these old walkways can still be seen. (Fig. 10)

The four water channels starting from the four cardinal directions culminate into a central octagonal pool. This is a huge trough and is marked by a double-headed elongated drum (*damaru*) shaped carved bud, the petals of which are confined within a wavy zigzag moulding running above and below, which is also very typical of Deeg's carving style (Fig. 11). It perhaps is just an ornamental feature and did not work as a fountain during the play of water features. A similar element can be seen in one of the old photographs as a feature in the fountain next to the Gopal Bhawan. These fountains do not exist today at those positions. Thirty-two water spouts are arranged in this trough around this central feature in a geometric pattern.

The origin of the four channels from the plinths of their respective bhawans, namely the Gopal, Kishan,

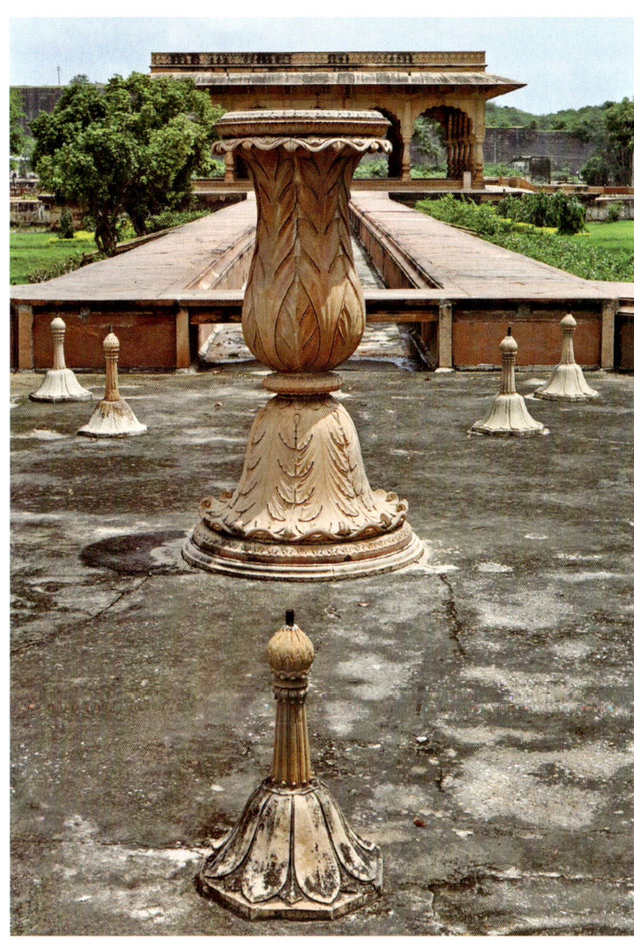

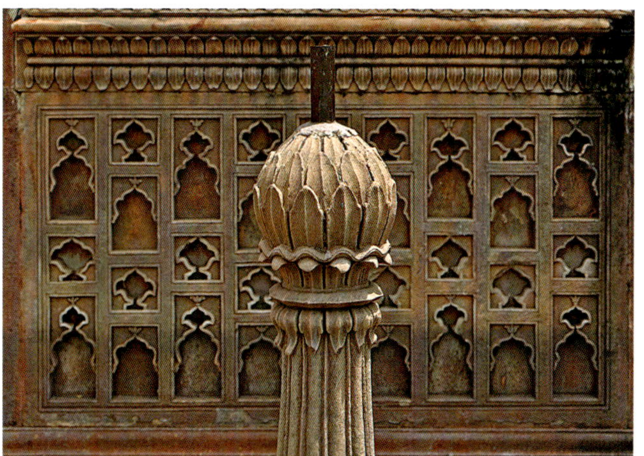

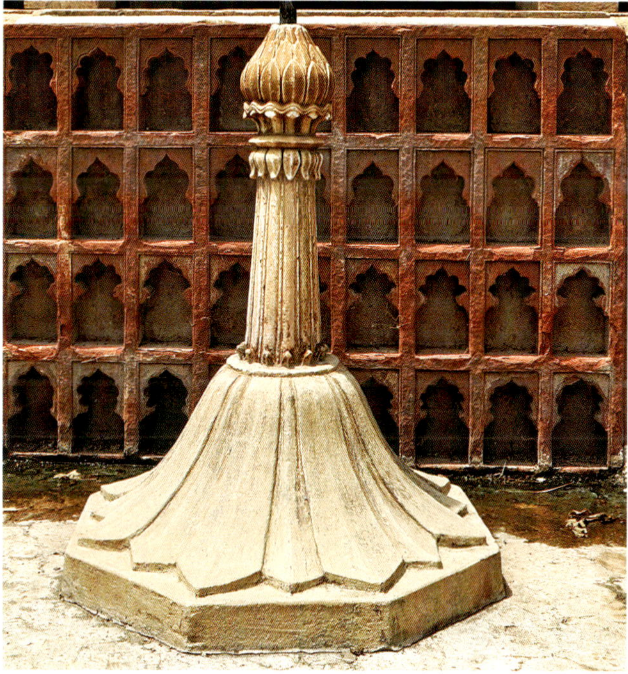

Keshav and Nand are defined by a cascade and a sheet of water flowing over the *chini khanas*. The *chini khanas* of the four bhawans have different designs. (Fig. 12) The *chini khanas* towards the Keshav Bhawan are the most carved amongst these with four rows of niches of finely carved arches in a staggered design and a moulding on top. The *chini khanas* of the Kishan Bhawan now have only a single row of niches. The Gopal Bhawan side has *chini khanas* with four rows of carved niches. There are

Above both (Fig. 12): *Array of carved niches or* chini khanas *around the Deeg Palace complex*

Above left (Fig. 11): *The emblematic central fountain in the shape of a two-sided Indian drum acts as the* axis mundi *of the Deeg Palace and its gardens*

Facing page right (Fig. 10): *Remnants of the pathways and secondary divisions are still seen in the main central sunken gardens*

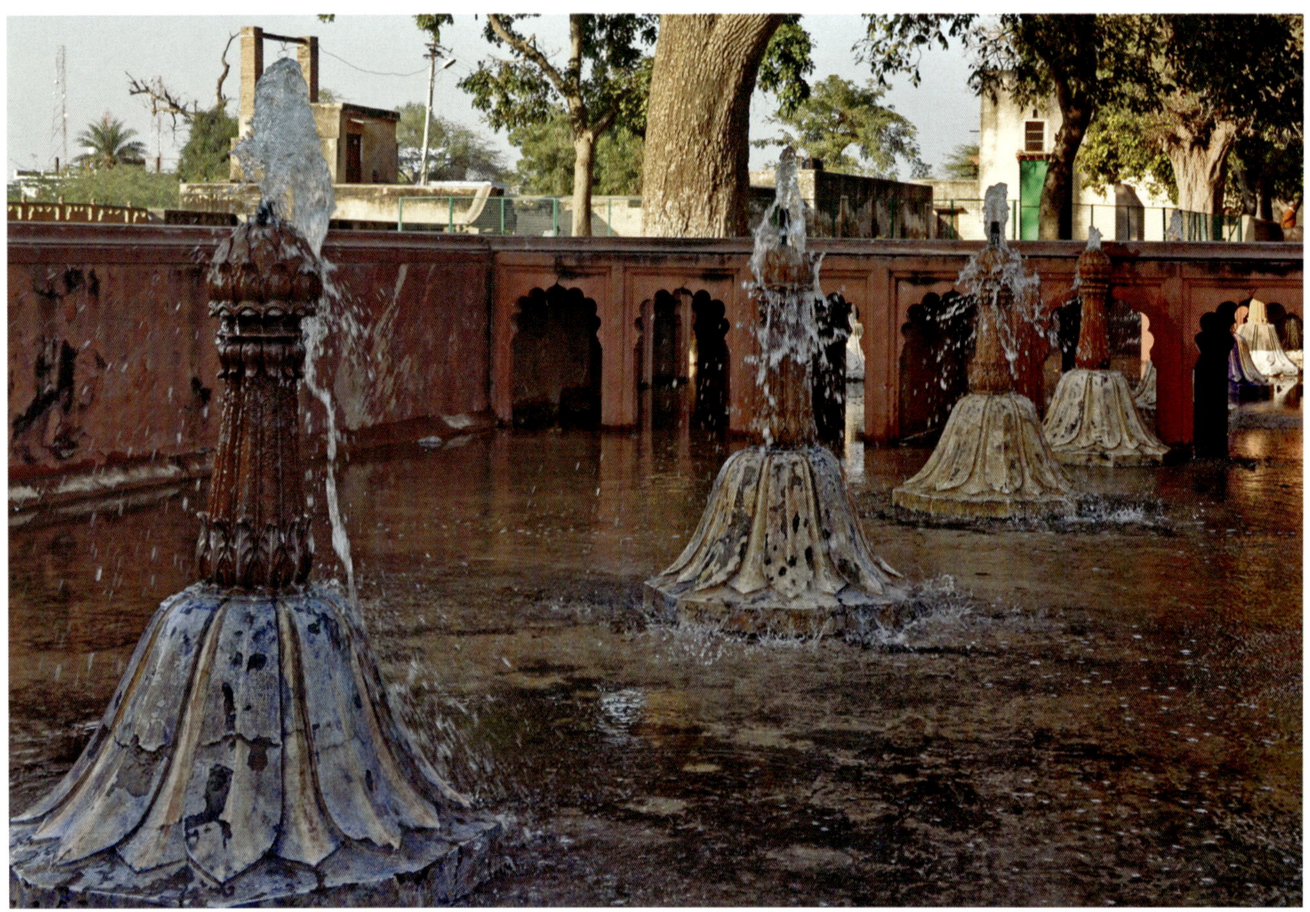

water spouts of the usual kind in all the channels with twenty-two towards the Keshav Bhawan, nineteen each on the Kishan and Nand Bhawan side and twenty-six towards the *hindola* or the Gopal Bhawan.

A parallel can be drawn between the Taj Mahal along with its gardens and the Gopal Bhawan in the Deeg Palace gardens. The alignment of the Gopal Bhawan with its own water channels, the Charbagh gardens in the forecourt on one side and the Gopal Sagar substituting for the river Yamuna on the other to see its reflection adds beauty of another dimension. Unlike the Taj Mahal though, this bhawan is not superior in standing to the other bhawans of the complex.

On both the north and south sides of the Gopal Bhawan, in front of the Sawan and Bhadon pavilions are two prominent Charbaghs, which are mirror images of each other. These Charbaghs are separated by the water channels. The two channels on the axis parallel to the Gopal Sagar are joined together by another channel curving around the silhouette of the Gopal Bhawan. The channels on the perpendicular axes connect the Sawan and Bhadon to their respective *kamal burjis*. Where the channels cross each other, the walkways on either side of them continue as bridges over an arcade of small and elegant arches through which the channels communicate with each other. (Fig. 13) The centre of this crossing takes the shape of a square tank.

A third Charbagh is formed between the Suraj Bhawan and the Hardev Bhawan complexes. The water channels start from the *chini khanas* on both sides and culminate in the central octagonal pool. The *chini khanas* which start from the Suraj Mahal have carved wine bottle shapes along with the usual niches. (Fig. 14) The spouts now are all small buds, but earlier photos show them to be the same as that of rest of Deeg. One of the corner squares between the Kishan and Suraj Bhawan gardens had a geometric subdivision with stone edging conceptually similar to Anguri Bagh, but bolder and more colonial.

Other than the Charbaghs there are more green parcels, plots and gardens around the major buildings. On both sides of the Kishan Bhawan are rectangular green areas. The corner plot between the Kishan Bhawan and the Suraj Bhawan was also subdivided into flower beds with stone edging. This may have been repeated in the other parterres but there is no remnant to prove that. There were other smaller gardens on the side terraces of the Nand Bhawan and the Kishan

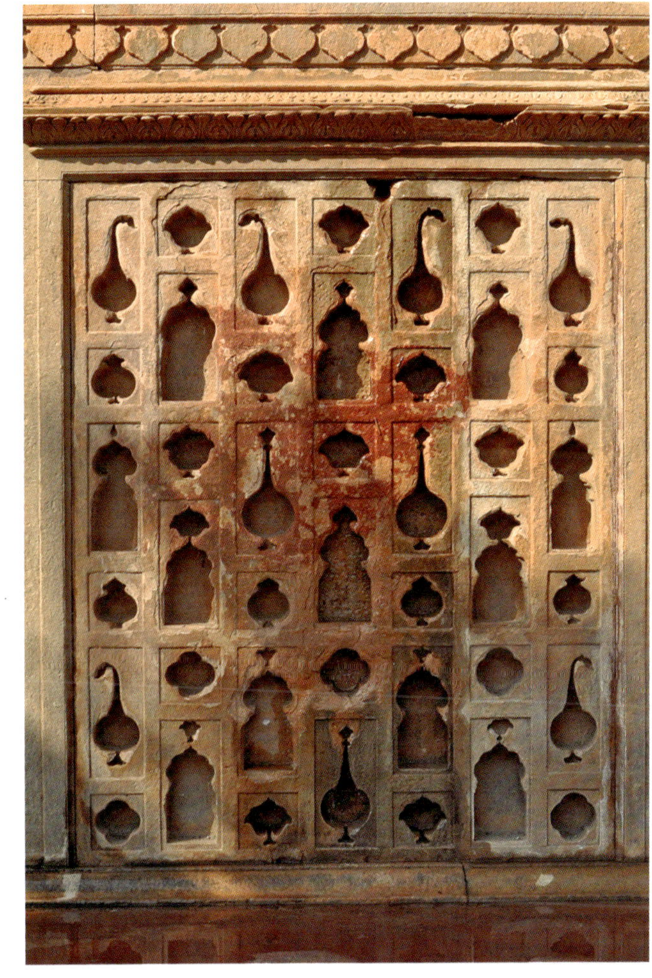

Above (Fig. 14): *The* chini khanas *which start from the Suraj Mahal have carved wine bottle shapes along with the usual niches*

Facing page (Fig. 13): *Lines of floricomous spouts and arcaded bridges enrich the voluminous water channels*

Bhawan as marked in the plan. Also, behind the Kishan Bhawan, where there is a nursery now, existed a garden. This large space must have been a personal zenana garden as it falls in between the Suraj Bhawan, the Hardev Bhawan and the Kishan Bhawan. It could also have been used as a service yard with tents for the servants to live in since it is adjacent to the enclosure where bulls were made to run to draw water from the well for the tank.

One major green stretch is to the north of the Nand Bhawan on the other side of the Charbagh. (Fig. 15) This has a small pavilion with a raised terrace, stepped-up from the Nand Bhawan terrace and conceptually very similar to the pavilion underneath the *hindola* in front of the Gopal Bhawan, giving credence to the fact that there was a plan to expand the complex on that side. The separate garden between the Singh Pol and the Nand Bhawan has a massive platform too which was used for official engagements and ceremonies.

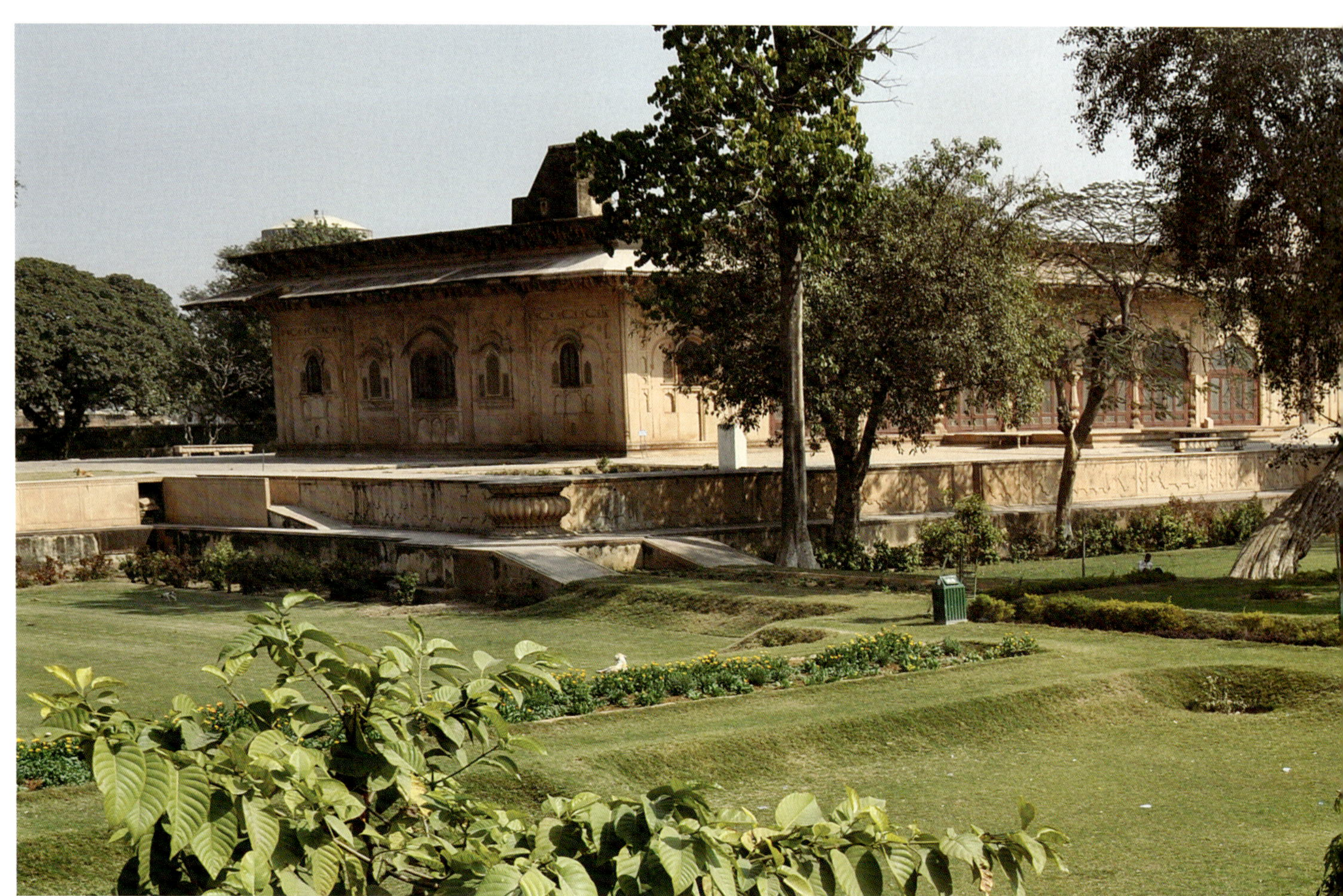

A conglomeration of diverse water features adorn the gardens such as:

Kamal Burjis: The axis and the water channels emanating from the Sawan and Bhadon pavilions culminate at two dominant elements, both in terms of size and use, known as the *kamal burjis*. These *kamal burjis* are semicircular projections in the central gardens, shaped as *damarus* (Indian two-sided drums) with truncated tops. Their fascias, deeply scalloped with lotus and acanthus petal carvings, also sport a slit for a waterfall in the coping stone. The shimmering sheet of water falling about this carved edifice must have created a fascinating *chef-d'œuvre*. The water fell into a trough specially created by a kerb stone pool around the *burjis* to prevent splashing and to redirect the water into further channels. The walls of the pool as well as the plinths of the *kamal burjis* have two layers of different leafy scrolls. (Fig. 16) The charisma of these structures is

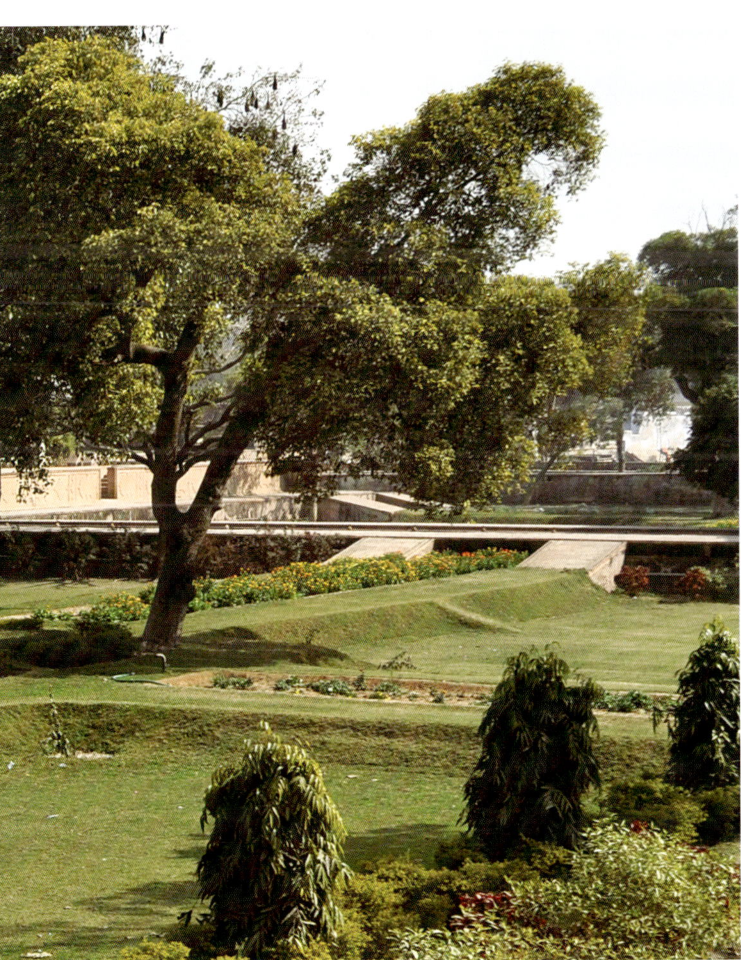

Left (Fig. 15): *An expansive view of the Nand Bhawan front gardens from the sunken Charbagh*

Below (Fig. 16): Kamal Burjis–*The dominant lotus carved water cascades in the shape of a two-sided drum with a kerb surround*

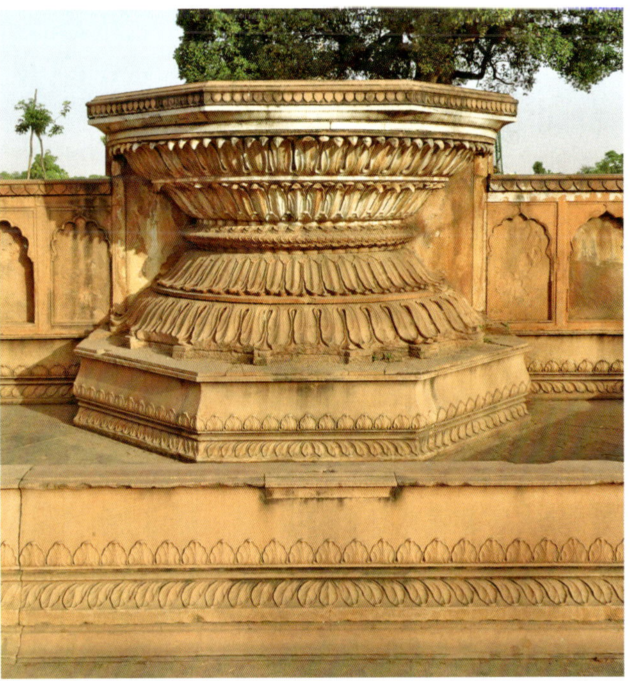

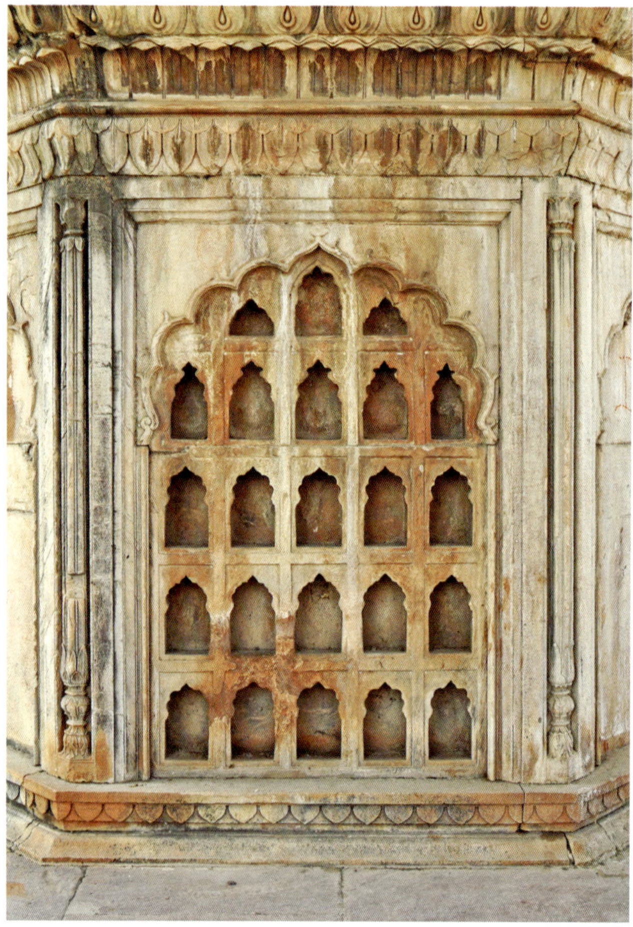

Above (Fig. 17): *One face of the entire turret is a* chini khana
Facing page (Fig. 18): *Carved and recessed floor fountain*

lost when viewed from the Gopal Bhawan terrace as the *burjis* appear as just raised parapets on the garden walls.

Chini Khanas: A surprise element is the sandstone geometric maze next to the Kishan Bhawan. It is situated in an obscure corner along with the ornate turret-like structure which is decorated with carvings of *chini khanas* on its projecting facades. Five sides of this octagonal pillar have projections with four as niches and one with elaborate *chini khanas* (Fig. 17). One should notice a carved face mask, now broken, with spouts mounted on the lower side wall intuitively to water the maze. Here also one can notice a crevice for a waterfall over the *chini khanas*. At most places where the water channels meet the bhawans there are *chini khanas* to provide a difference of level and a sense of drama. Disparately styled niches of the *chini khanas* could be a result of explorations by some ingenious mind or could also be an assemblage of so-called architectural war trophies brought back by the rulers. Experimentation can be seen with various shapes, sizes and depths of the *chini khanas*. The subtle ones at the sources of the four main water channels are classically Mughal. The ones in front of the Hardev Bhawan are carved in the shape of wine bottles. The craftsmanship of the deep *chini khanas* of the Suraj Bhawan is comparable to the work of the best Mughal artisans.

Budbudas: In some cases there are arrangements for diverting the current of water into several smaller ones (*budbudas*) by means of a basin with a perforated bottom attached to a cistern, thus producing quite a fanciful fountain inside a building. Square and shallow flat basins with needle-hole jets for upward spraying fountains are placed in the channels of the Sawan-Bhadon pavilions to create this effect. The excess water falls back into the channel via two overflow slits on either side.

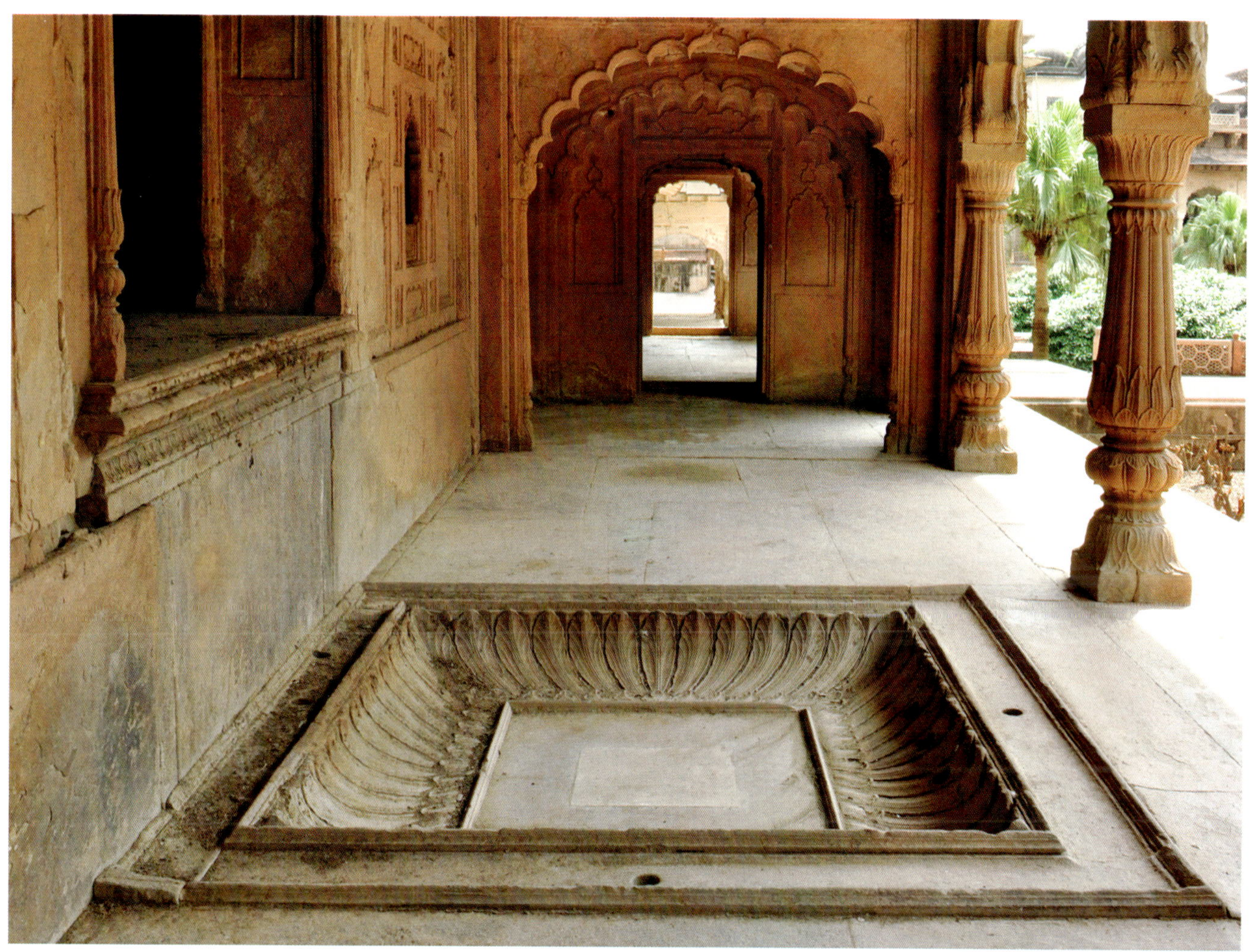

Chadars: Though not used a lot, are very boldly depicted in the Sawan-Bhadon pavilions and are carved in a fish scallop design with a chevron pattern border. These marble or stone chutes were carved in a variety of patterns, cut ingeniously at an angle so that the water flowing over them was thrown up and broken into ripples and splashes. Shell and wave designs were the favourites and their name was as prettily fashioned as their carving. They were called *chadars*, meaning white shawls of water. These water chutes are a characteristic feature of the Mughal gardens and were used with much effect where the terrain allowed the garden to be laid out in a series of high terraces. But in small gardens or in the plains, even the slightest slope was made use of. Only a foot or two of difference in level sufficed to create one of these charming little waterfalls, inspiration for which was directly drawn from the memories of dancing sprays and the white foam of mountain rivulets in the builders' northern home.

Floor basins: Carved floor fountains in the Khas Mahal at Agra seem to be the antecedent to the various versions and interpretations of the array of sunken fountains spread around the Deeg Palace complex. These manifest every now and then both in the exterior and interior of the palace. (Fig. 18) Brilliantly curved and carved basins suggest the extent of the deep-seated influence that the opulent lifestyle of the Mughals must have had on the Jat rulers. There is a mixture in the shapes of these basins, such as squares and rectangles, which are elegantly curved but left uncarved. In the next phase of evolution, the entire fountain springs out from the ground, as in the dining room of the Gopal Bhawan, to reveal the outer crescent arch of the basin. The profile of this fascia is analogous to the inside *cyma recta* and tapers at the top to complete the curvature. This hand-carved flawless profile of curves can even put the modern-day CNC (Computer Numerical Control) machines to test.

Below (Fig. 19): *A panoramic view of the overhead water reservoir with a* solahdari *in the backdrop*

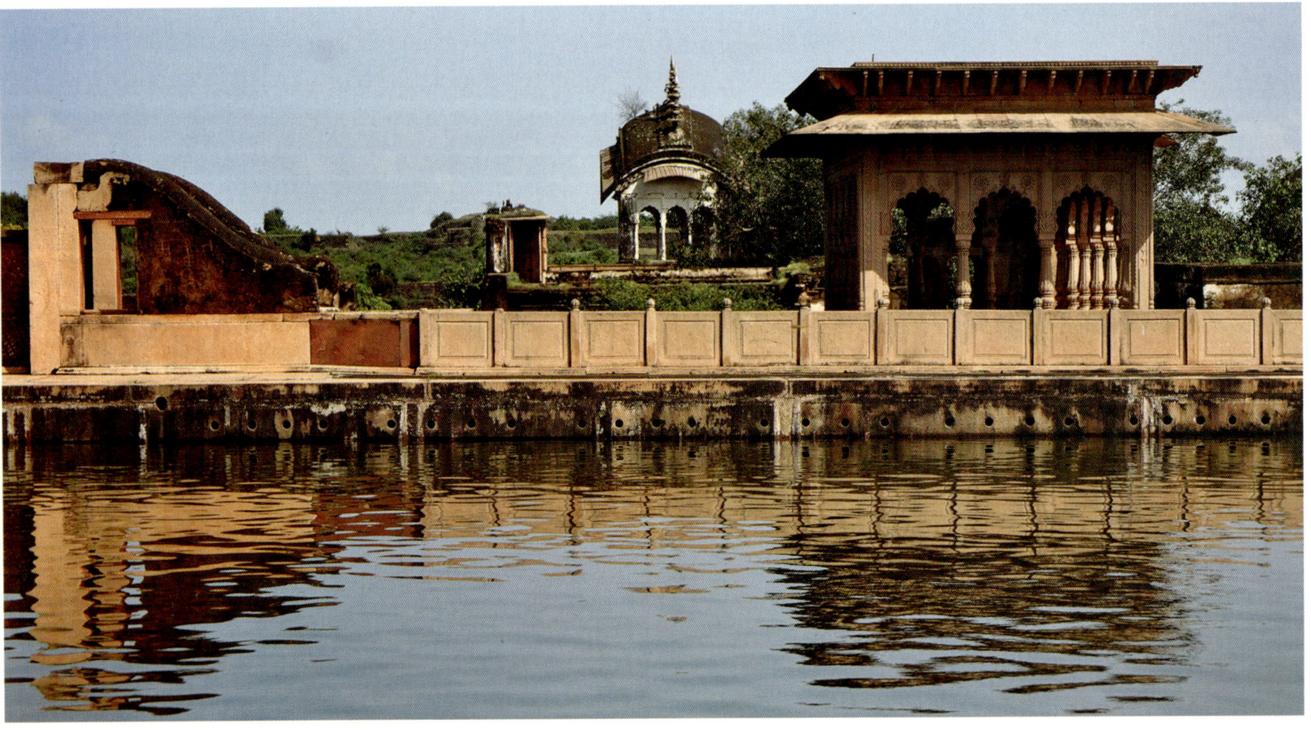

Accomplishing this impeccable profile, made with manual tools, probably required the grinding of stone with hand emeries for weeks all together. The profile of the transverse edge has to be chamfered at a specific angle when it meets its corresponding member to complete its square or octagon, so that a perfect sharp ridge is formed on the outside. This can be termed as a major accomplishment of the Jats which even the Mughals did not attempt. The resulting raised edge formed a lotus-shaped curved brim all around the fountains which is unique to Deeg. Although fragile, they have withstood hundreds of years of battering. Even today it is difficult to carve this stone profile with modern hand grinders. Similar profiles are echoed at almost all the tanks and troughs.

The most intriguing aspect of this garden is that the water system is still functioning. The entire waterworks of the Deeg complex seems to be designed around an overhead tank for the smooth functioning of the gravity-fed system, where different water pressures are required for different levels. (Fig. 19) It suggests that the designers were aware of water circulation and the water cycle. This extensive water garden is supplied by four Persian wheels which raise the water to a massive tank at the level of the palace roof. The purpose of erecting the tank at such a height was only to operate the fountains, chutes and cascades. Each of the water sources has its own network, from origin to destination, going through buildings, gardens and culminating in the two *sagars* (large lakes).

On the west side of the Kishan Bhawan, at the level of its roof, is the massive water reservoir resting on imposing arches which are covered by a high enclosure wall on the north. The tank measures about 42m × 31m and is 2 metres deep, thus having a vast capacity. For filling it up four wells were built in its vicinity and the water from them was raised by means of leather buckets drawn by bullocks. (Fig. 20) The capacity of the tank can be gauged by the fact that when full, its weight would equal to about 600 elephants. The capacity of the tank is (42 × 31 × 2 = 2604 kg/m^3 = 26,04,000 litres) 2,604 tons (where 1 kg/m^3 of water = 1,000 litres) and the average weight of one elephant is 4 tons. Building such a massive overhead tank was a major feat of the Jats which even the Mughals did not try.

The tank in olden days used to take about a week's time to be filled but with the use of modern pumps it takes a day or two. This huge amount of water ran out in a few hours when all the fountains were operated at once. This was done only twice a year during celebrations. It is possible that only a series of fountains were run at a time in everyday use to achieve a longer duration rather than operating all of them at once. Rain water was also collected in the water tank.

There are numerous holes arranged on the walls of the tank which form the mouths of various pipelines connected with different groups of fountains. There are hundreds of pipes connected to the tank to control certain areas and fountains in the buildings and the garden in the best possible way. Each set of pipes is duly

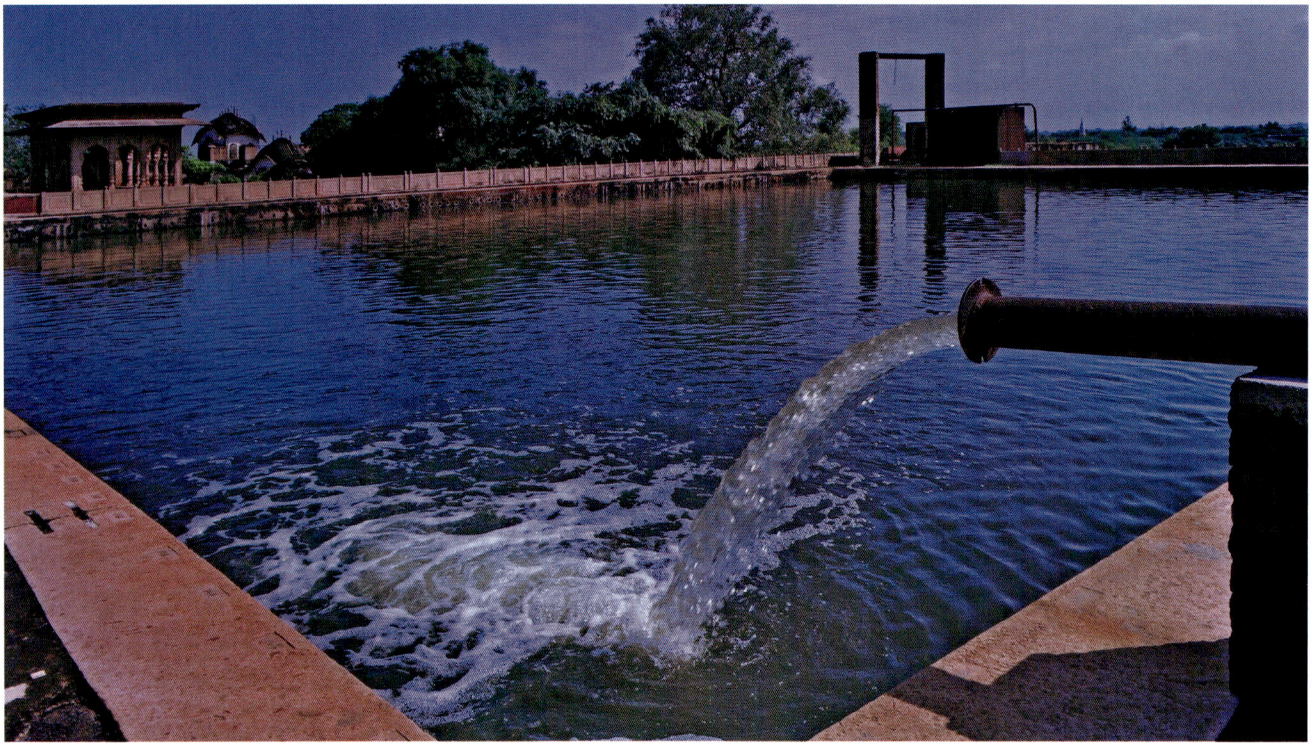

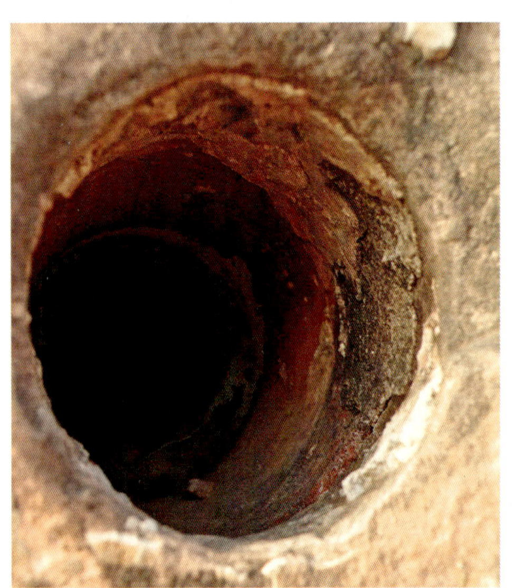

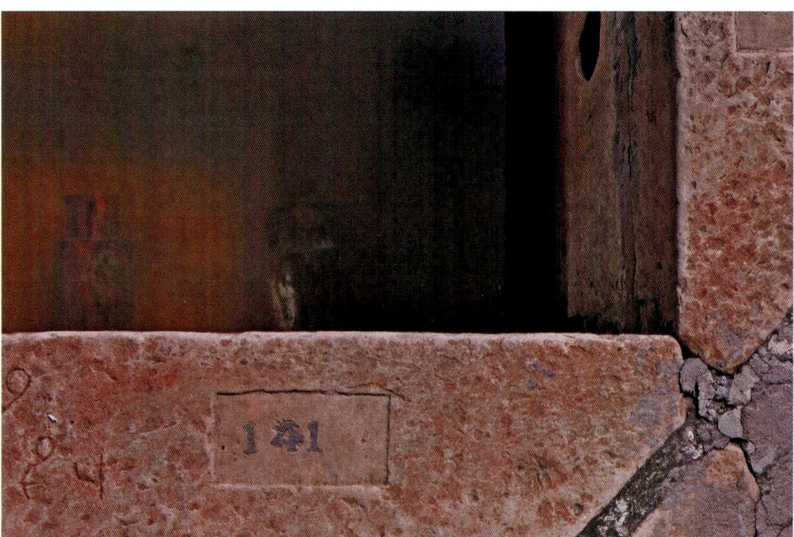
141

numbered on the ledge. Wooden plugs in the tank walls control the flow of water into the gravity-fed system. (Fig. 21) Boys swim in the tank for the purpose of pulling the plugs which open the pipelines to the fountains and water devices. Various small, coloured bags or pouches are placed in these holes so that the water coming out of the fountains gives the sensation of the festival of Holi. (Fig. 22) Each hole supplies water to about three to four fountain spouts. Unfortunately, no diagram or plan is available as to which number corresponds to which fountain. Even the ASI (Archaeological Survey of India) has made no effort to do the same, though they still fill the tank and run the fountains twice a year.

A play of levels has been maintained for the smooth flowing of the gravity-fed system. Water to some of the fountains was perhaps also supplied manually. Tapered clay pipes, made using small, well-burnt sections, have been used. (Fig. 23) This method did not allow for right-angle bends, necessitating large diameter turns where the direction of the pipe was to be changed. Obviously, some calculation of gradients and symphonic and hydraulic pressures were used for distances, play and spray of fountains. Another feat the designers have managed to accomplish is the interconnection of the two *sagars*, Gopal and Rup, by means of a drain running through the entire length of the complex. There is also a theory that a canal was dug from Gurgaon to get water from the Yamuna at the time of Suraj Mal, when he ruled up to Gurgaon, to supply the Gopal Sagar and from there to the Rup Sagar. The gardens have undergone several generations of ownerships before being taken over by the ASI, thus transformations cannot be ruled out. An example of this are the fountain spouts present in the water channel of the Charbagh of the Hardev Bhawan, which are shown to be similar to the ones in the rest of the complex in old photographs but now exist only in the shape of lotus buds. Another missing feature is a thick stone or concrete baluster cum trellis, very colonial in design and appearance, around the terrace of the Gopal Bhawan during the 1900s.

Facing page above (Fig. 20): *Four wells on each corner were used to fill the humongous water reservoir*

Facing page below left (Fig. 22): *Close-up of a clay pipe outlet of the overhead water reservoir. A fragment of the metal screen is still visible. The colour pouch was also placed against this mesh*

Facing page below right (Fig. 21): *Each set of pipes is duly numbered on the ledge. Wooden pegs are used to control the flow of water into the gravity-fed system*

Below (Fig. 23): *An archetype to demonstrate clay pipe constructions at Deeg Palace and garden*

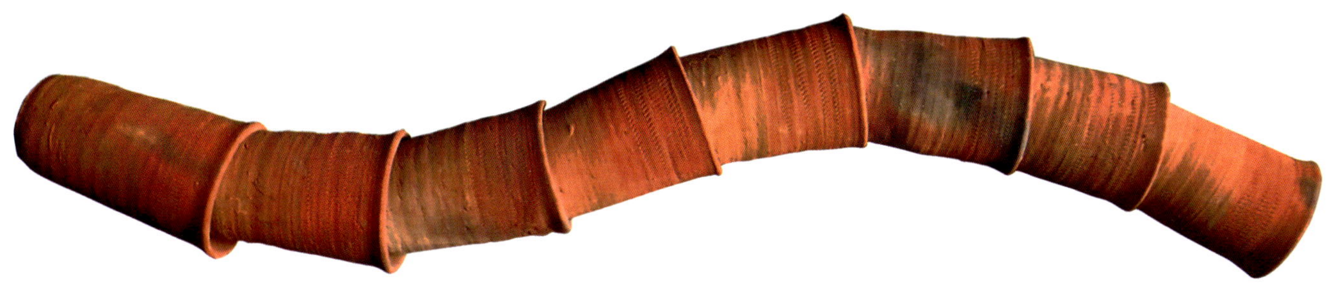

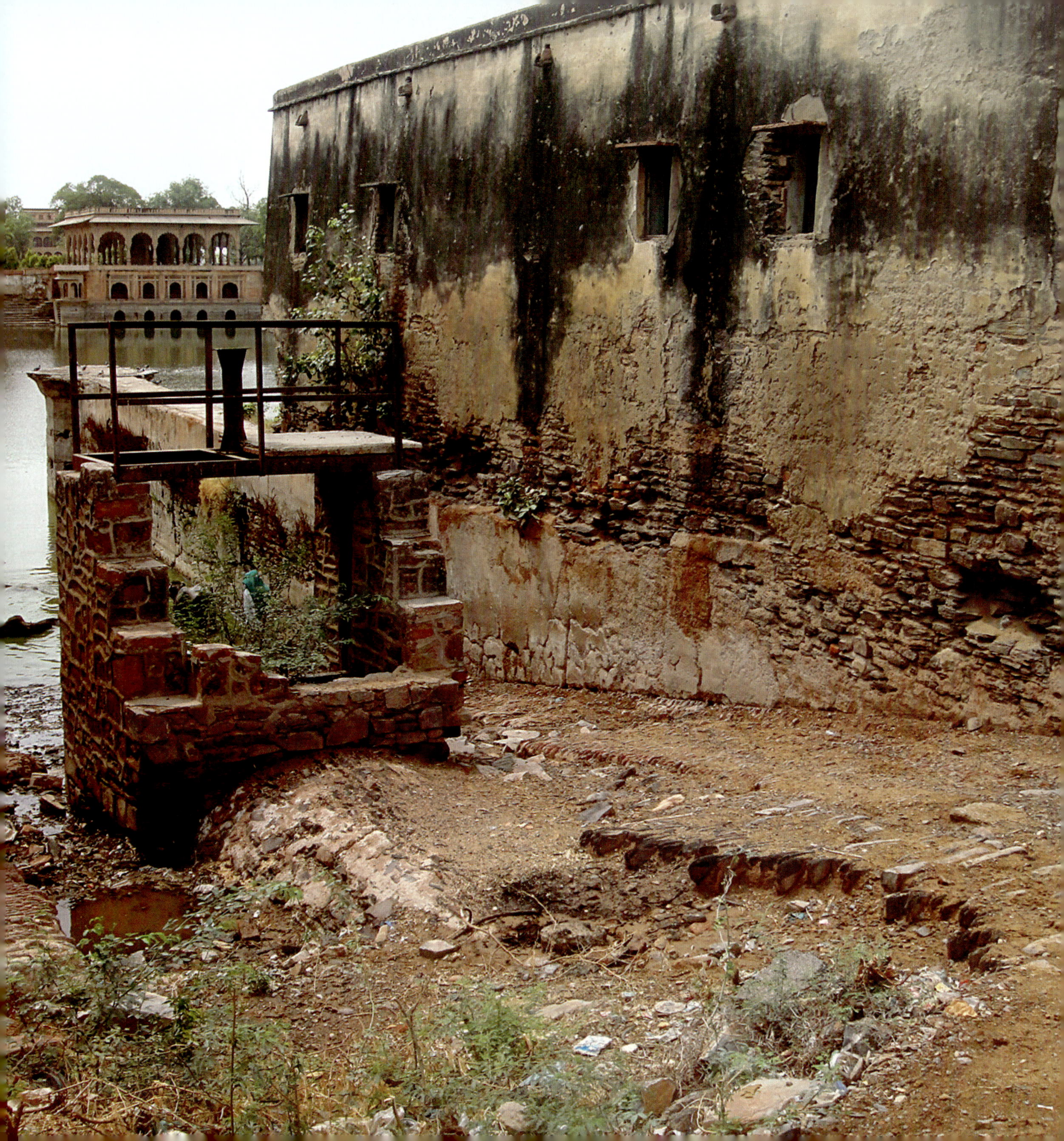

ARCHITECTURAL CONSERVATION OF THE DEEG PALACE COMPLEX

The Deeg Palace and complex with many of its associated buildings has shown remarkable strength over its 300-year history. However, at present they show signs of decay, have erosions and vegetation growth at places and so if it is not preserved, it may lead to serious damages and major loss of this heritage resource. Most of the structures are structurally sound, except the Nand Bhawan and the Keshav Bhawan.

The problem with these palace structures is because of the inherent design flaws made by the original designers. Though the Jat rulers of Deeg were inspired by Mughal architecture and even used a number of original Mughal architectural fragments acquired as war trophies from Mughal buildings, they aspired for even grander and more elaborate buildings than that of the Mughals. Some of the buildings designed at Deeg were with larger spans and at times went beyond the spanning limitation of the local construction techniques used at that time. These created problems of roof settlement and masonry displacement as is evident from the historic props in the Nand Bhawan.

The main types of defects noticed in the buildings of the Deeg Palace are cracks and dampness.

The cracks may be attributed to the unequal settlement of foundations, inherent construction flaws, deterioration or erosion of connecting iron dowels. Apart from the major structural cracks, there are a number of superficial or minor cracks in the palace buildings. One can also find multiple cracks in the roofs, resulting in the seepage below in the buildings.

Most of the palace buildings suffer from some sort of moisture ingress. It is evident from the condition of many walls on the lower ground floor, which are affected with visible eroded patches. It can be observed mainly

Facing page: *Significant problems confronting the palace surroundings with a sluice gate from the moat of the fort*

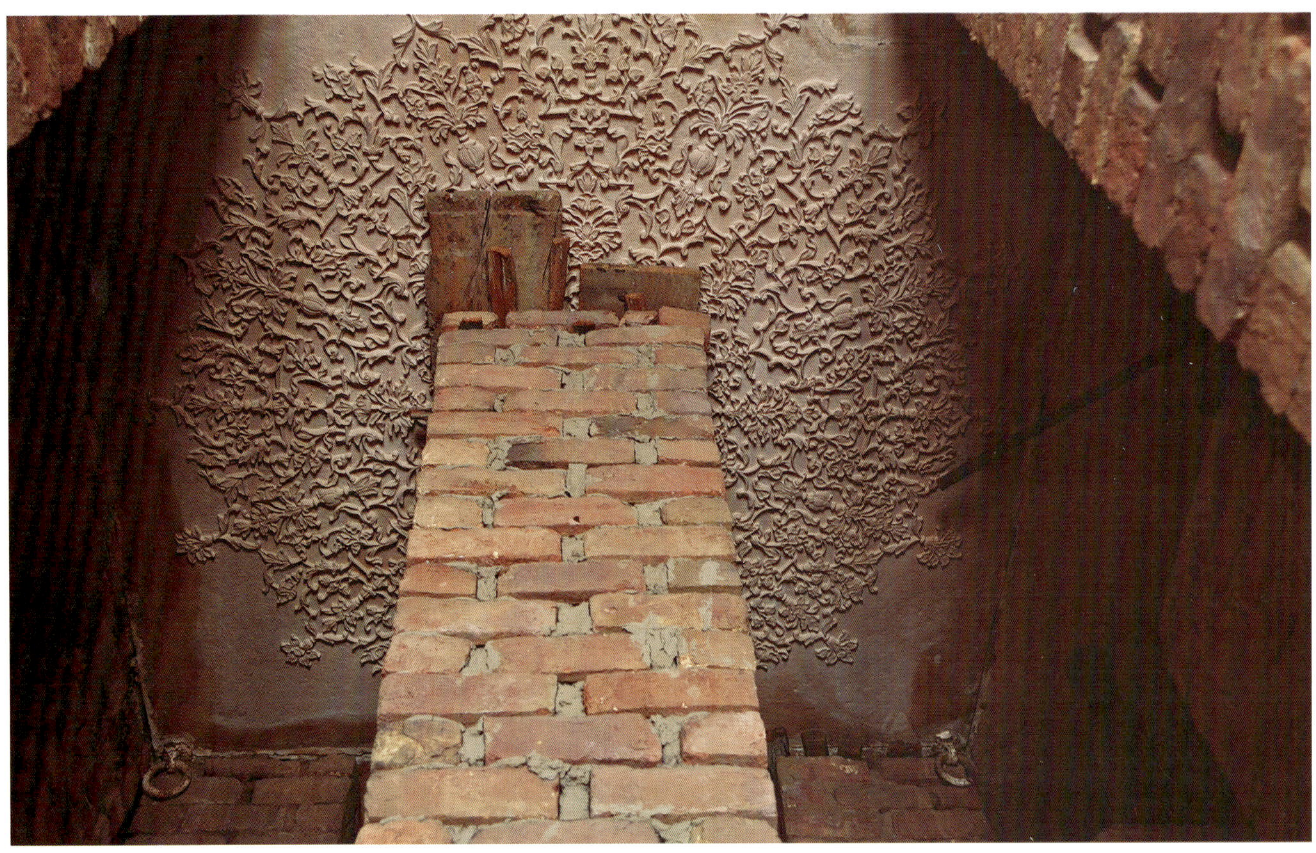

Above: *Propping with brick piers on Gopal Bhawan's north wing ceiling*

rising up from the ground and could be attributed to the lack of a damp-proof course (DPC) and their positioning next to a large water tank. Moisture ingress has also led to efflorescence in some rooms in the lower ground floor like the Sawan-Bhadon pavilions and the Keshav Bhawan. Even the walls are severely affected and the plaster is crumbling at this level. The walls, over the years, seem to have retained the moisture and are not drying up. This may also be due to the fact that the buildings are surrounded by water tanks with polluted water, which is a constant source of water ingress.

Some of the ceilings also show visible patches of dampness. This defect is due to waterlogging at the terrace level because of improper slopes, inadequate waterproofing and weak joints (roof and parapet wall) causing water to penetrate the terrace. It was also observed that the terrace flooring was uneven and some layers were missing with cracks in the buildings.

Dampness, vandalism and bird droppings have resulted in the disfigurement of the decorative stonework.

These need to be addressed and the stonework needs to be cleaned and restored to get back their original surface. The wall paintings which have either been damaged or lost from most of the areas require restoration by appropriate research on the original pattern. Only traces of them have survived at few places like the external facade of the Gopal Bhawan and the pillars of the Nand Bhawan.

The other concerns can be listed as follows:

1. Missing architectural features like brackets, *chhajjas*, finials, *kangoras*, etc.
2. Structural movements and structural deformity
3. Masonry displacement and dislocation of stone joints
4. Natural ageing, wearing and weathering
5. Misuse, alterations and additions
6. Neglect and lack of maintenance
7. Peeling of plaster

Though, there may be the same defect at different parts of the structure they may occur because of different causes. For ascertaining the condition and conservation state of the building, detailed condition mapping needs to be undertaken. However long-term monitoring is also required for establishing any significant structural damages to the building especially to ascertain active cracks for its proper remedial.

The conservation and management issues at the Deeg Palace can be divided into 3 zones namely:

- Issues related to the entire site
- Issues related to individual buildings
- Additional issues

SITE LEVEL

The site of the palace retains a part of its authenticity in its setting, its immediate environs also form an integral part of the same, which need to be conserved and enhanced. The main issue however is related to the site drainage. Though the site has a proper planned drainage system, the ground level has undergone changes over the years. The moat of the adjoining fort is on a higher level and connected with the Rup Sagar through a sluice gate. Most of the city's sewage is dumped into the moat making it a cesspool. The natural drainage and water flow of the moat is choked resulting in water stagnation and eventually flooding of the Rup Sagar. This not only creates unhygienic conditions, but the acidic nature of the resulting water has also been eroding the historic walls from its base thereby creating structural instability in many places. This is most prominently seen in the Keshav Bhawan.

Within the complex, a large area is under landscaping and formal gardening. Although some historic trees and plants are seen, most of the plantation does not seem authentic.

The most significant aspect of the Deeg Palace is its waterworks and fountains which are still working. However its actual scheme and functioning is still a mystery and needs better understanding through research for its proper revival and restoration. It would be worth reviving the entire waterworks and making all the fountains functional to experience the palace in its full original glory.

INDIVIDUAL BUILDINGS LEVEL

Singh Pol: It is the main entrance to the entire complex and most of it is presently used as a ticket counter, staff parking and offices of the Archaeological Survey of India (ASI). The building is believed to have never been completed as seen from the missing roof in its middle section. Though structurally the building is in good condition, delamination and cracks in the joinings of the stone veneers are prominently seen which may be attributed to rusting of the iron dowels.

Many other minor problems like broken railings, missing architectural elements, dampness and so on are also seen, though they do not distract as much as the modern interventions made to utilise the building as an office space.

The Gopal Bhawan: This is now being used as a museum. However parts of it, especially the basement and northern wing, are in a neglected and dilapidated state. The main reason for this can be attributed to the damaged roof drainage, inappropriate use, as well as rising dampness from the water tank. The building also has extensive basements, some of which could not be accessed and thus its state was not fully ascertained.

The north wing where propping has been done with brick piers may damage the carved ceiling above and better modern structural techniques like steel struts should be employed in such cases. The external facade also has evidence of fresco paintings which are presently in a vulnerable state. Inside the building 'araish' work has been painted over with enamel paint. The western facade overlooking the Gopal Sagar has damages to its external plaster, domes and *chhatris*.

The Sawan-Bhadon Pavilions: Flanking the Gopal Bhawan were two open pavilions which have now been enclosed with timber doors. This is distractive to its original intent and appreciation. The lower floors have major problems in the form of dampness and efflorescence, which may be attributed to the blocked channels behind the carved stone *chadar*. These lower areas are also less frequented by the visitors and are thus susceptible to misuse and neglect. A projected balcony facing the Gopal Sagar in the Bhadon pavilion has also partially collapsed. The *bangladar* roofs of both the pavilions show some minor damages and the finials are missing in the Bhadon pavilion.

Hindola: The *hindola,* as generally believed, is a trophy from the Agra Fort and has been placed over the roof of an existing sandstone pavilion as evident from the strengthening measures taken. However the base pavilions show substantial ground movement and sinking towards the corners because of which the safety of the *hindola* above is compromised. The main problem seen in the marble of the *hindola* is its staining and yellowing due to ageing and erosion. The joints in the marble also show openings which again may be attributed to rusting of the clamps embedded in the *hindola*. The *pietra dura* floors are suffering due to excessive tourist activity.

The Keshav Bhawan: It is among the most affected buildings and due to its weak structural condition, its roof has been supported with large brick piers. The 'araish' floors are highly damaged and need to be restored. The under-structure levels, some of which are walled up are also highly damaged with openings in the

Below: *The lowest level of the Keshav Bhawan, which is mainly under water, is highly damaged and the stone walls are corroded due to the acidic nature of the polluted water*

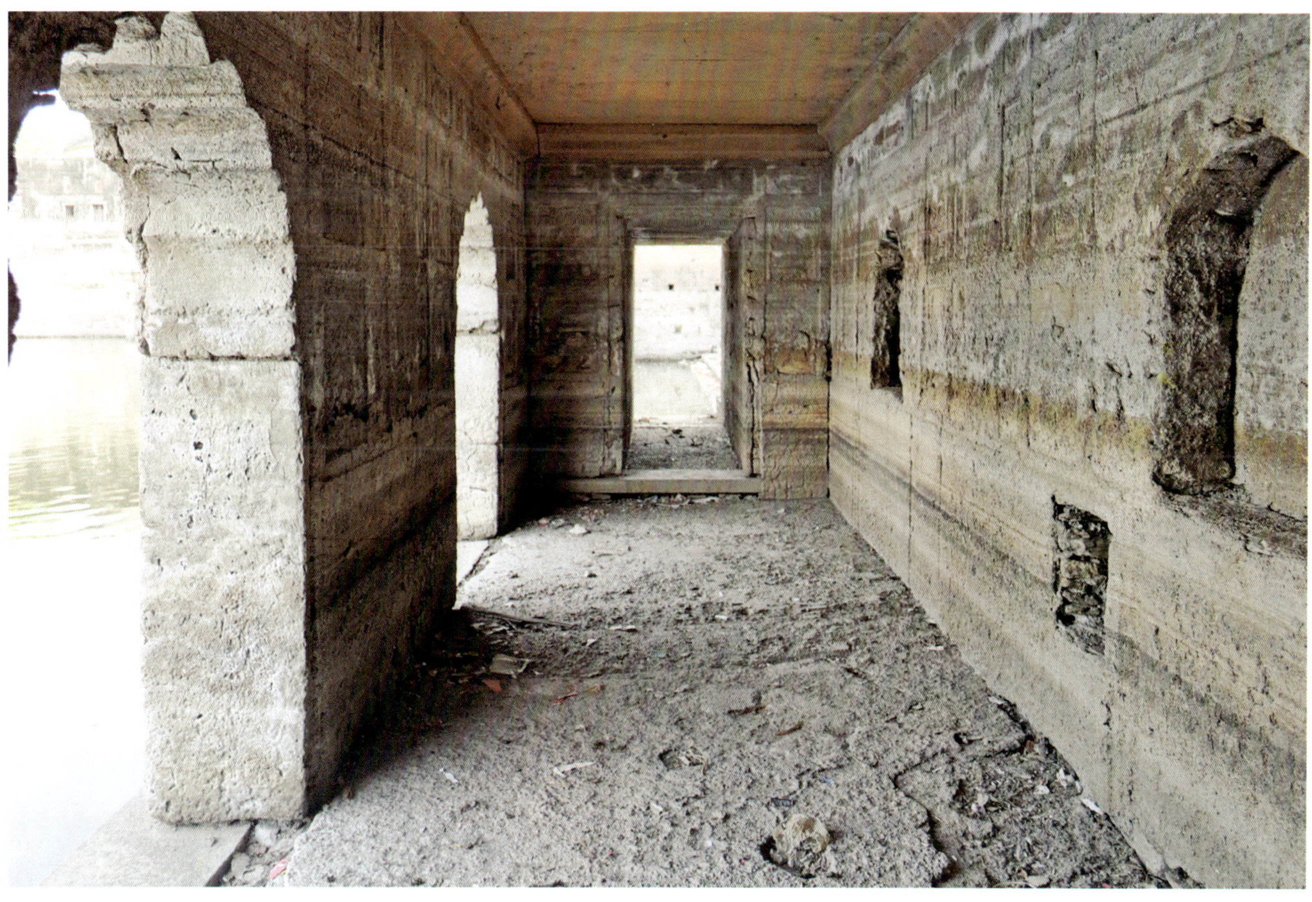

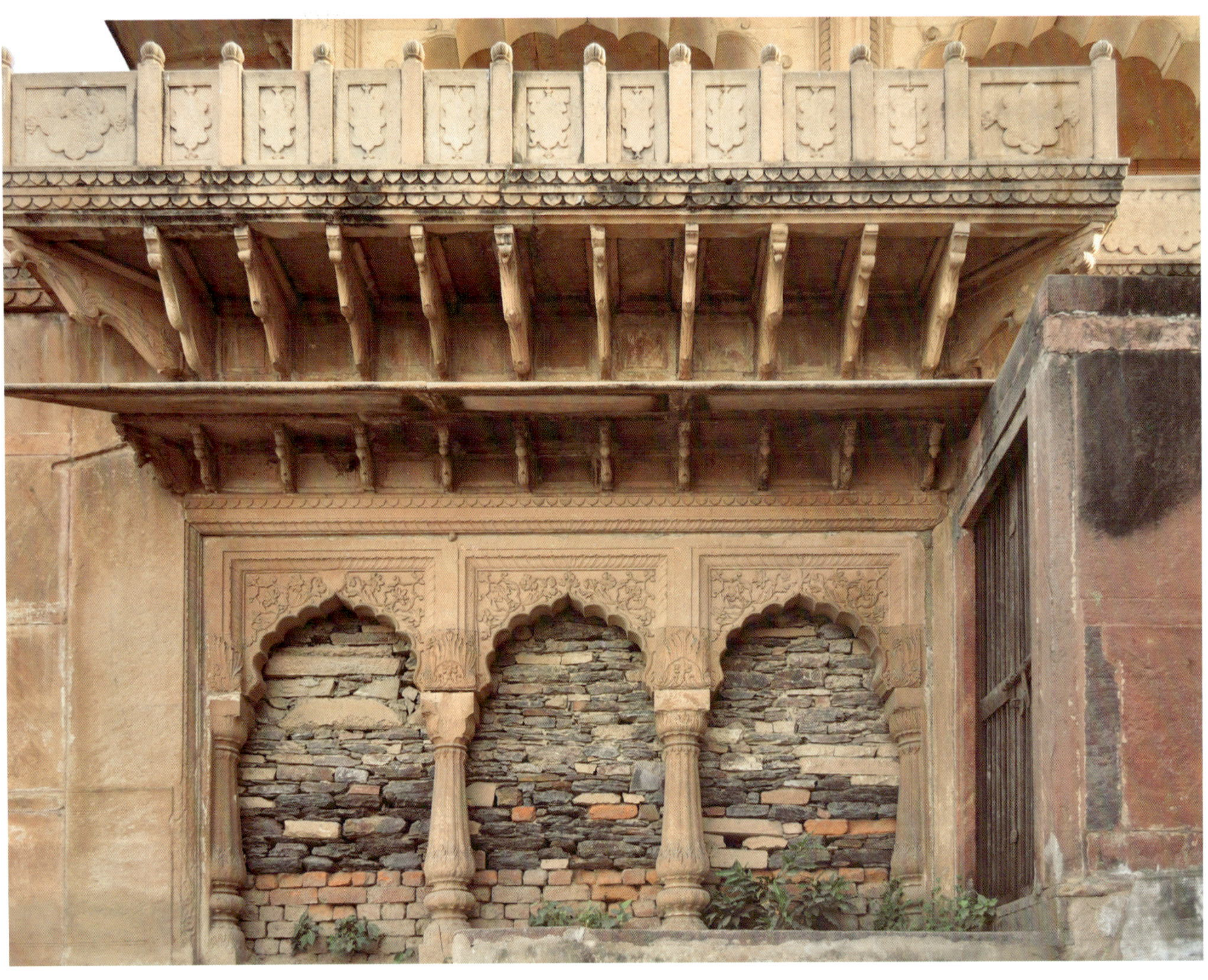

Above: *Some of the under-structure levels of the Keshav Bhawan have been walled up at present*

stone joinery and drooping of arch stones. The lowest level, which is mostly under water, is highly damaged and the stone walls are corroded mainly due to the acidic nature of the polluted water.

The Suraj Mahal: It has one of the most beautiful inlay works and is also believed to be a war trophy from Agra Fort. The main problem with the building is vandalism and erosion of its inlay, 'araish' and mosaic works due to excessive footfall of visitors. The unrestricted access of this building needs to be controlled so that its architectural features can be preserved.

The Kishan Bhawan: This building is also being used as a museum. Though from the front facade no major problems are seen, its rear facade is highly damaged as well as overgrown with vegetation due to which its plaster is peeling and its dampness is rising. The rooftop pavilion also called the *solahdari* has its parapet missing. The stone *takht* placed in front of the building, one of the largest *takhts* seen, is misused by the visitors for exercising and many of its decorative elements have been demolished.

The Nand Bhawan: This bhawan is presently inaccessible due to its highly deteriorated and unsafe condition. Even historically, structural problems with the Nand Bhawan's roof were there as is evident in the form of additional painted piers used to prop the sinking roof. The problem can be attributed to the very heavy load of the roof as well as inherent design flaws related to its overambitious span.

The Hardev Bhawan: These set of buildings are considered ancillary and somehow relegated in a corner due to which they are in a neglected condition. They show many problems like wrecked flooring, dampness, peeling plaster as well as broken elements. Though it is among the only plastered building using lime punning, its historic plasters are in a deteriorating condition. The rear parts of the buildings are also overgrown and neglected contributing to the dampness in the front parts. Due to neglect the building is also infested with bats causing staining of its *jalis* and decorative features by bird droppings. This building has the potential for a period museum that will enhance its tourist value as well as ensure better maintenance.

Miscellaneous Issues:

Besides the problems related to age, lack of maintenance and its inherent concerns, there are other issues mainly linked to their reuse, circulation and interpretation.

The main entry into the building at the moment lacks any sense of discovery as the main gate is being used as offices and parking instead of being a welcome and information centre. Many of the original arches and windows have been closed to create additional space for offices and museums. These are not only creating a conservation problem in terms of effective ventilation, but are also affecting the spatial relation of the rooms and their relationships to the exterior views. This impacts the heritage character of the buildings in the Deeg Palace complex.

The site's interpretation and promotion are also lacking. There is also a need for proper signage and other interpreters to help us get a clearer understanding of the building and its significance within the Deeg Palace complex for both its staff and the visitors. Though some of the buildings function as museums or display areas, a proper interpretation about the sites' significance and special features is lacking. Also there is need for the users and visitors to understand the conservation requirement of the site and its sensitivity to damage due to inappropriate use, weather conditions and other external forces.

Another important issue is related to the lack of proper public amenities within the site. Though there are a large numbers of visitors using the site on daily basis there are no proper toilets and other facilities with the building. Due to this some parts of the building are misused. Thus there is a need to provide proper amenities for the users, especially if the building is to attract more number of visitors in the future.

NEED FOR CONSERVATION AND SPECIALISED RESTORATION

Over the decades, the magnificent palaces of Deeg have deteriorated with partial collapses, the peeling of plaster, erosion of its walls and fading of its wall paintings and some alterations and additions that detract from its aesthetic integrity. Parts of the palace are also in a state of neglect and inappropriate use for many years, which brings with it a host of issues impacting the structural and aesthetic integrity and concerns regarding the continued preservation of this edifice. Though the palaces have exhibited remarkable structural strength over the years, a range of issues such as structural cracks, erosion, collapses, overgrown vegetation, water seepage, additions, as well as deterioration of its external masonry and renders has confronted the sites. Though the ASI as its custodian has done a commendable job and has been over the years maintaining and undertaking periodic repairs and restoration works, a comprehensive conservation plan needs to be drawn for the integrated restoration and management of the site in a phased manner to highlight its significance as a masterpiece.

Purana Mahal, Fort, Rani Bagh and Ram Bagh—though a part of the original layout of the palace—now lie outside the purview of the ASI. They have a great potential to be integrated into a larger fabric of the cultural heritage site. The entire site should be developed by integrating the conservation requirement, proper adaptive reuse and management, to serve as a landmark conservation project in this region.

The preparation of this book is thus a small step towards establishing the significance and unique quality of this cultural heritage site in its entirety and we also hope that it will be helpful to preserve the special qualities of these buildings for the future generations. An appropriate framework for a coordinated conservation, management and development of the Deeg Palace as an important heritage site should thus be established at the earliest.

Divay Gupta
Principal Director
Architectural Heritage Division, INTACH

INDEX

T

U

V

W